W9-BRJ-048

CHILTON BOOK COMPANY

REPAIR & TUNE-UP GUIDE

FORD AEROSTAR 1986-87

All U.S. and Canadian models of Ford Aerostar

Vice President and General Manager JOHN P. KUSHNERICK
Editor-in-Chief KERRY A. FREEMAN, S.A.E.
Managing Editor DEAN F. MORGANTINI, S.A.E.
Senior Editor RICHARD J. RIVELE, S.A.E.
Senior Editor W. CALVIN SETTLE, JR., S.A.E.
Editor MARTIN J. GUNTHER
Editor TONY MOLLA, S.A.E.

CHILTON BOOK COMPANY
Radnor, Pennsylvania
19089

SAFETY NOTICE

Proper service and repair procedures are vital to the safe, reliable operation of all motor vehicles, as well as the personal safety of those performing repairs. This book outlines procedures for servicing and repairing vehicles using safe, effective methods. The procedures contain many NOTES, CAUTIONS and WARNINGS which should be followed along with standard safety procedures to eliminate the possibility of personal injury or improper service which could damage the vehicle or compromise its safety.

It is important to note that repair procedures and techniques, tools and parts for servicing motor vehicles, as well as the skill and experience of the individual performing the work vary widely. It is not possible to anticipate all of the conceivable ways or conditions under which vehicles may be serviced, or to provide cautions as to all of the possible hazards that may result. Standard and accepted safety precautions and equipment should be used during cutting, grinding, chiseling, prying, or any other process that can cause material removal or projectiles.

Some procedures require the use of tools specially designed for a specific purpose. Before substituting another tool or procedure, you must be completely satisfied that neither your personal safety, nor the performance of the vehicle will be endangered.

Although the information in this guide is based on industry sources and is as complete as possible at the time of publication, the possibility exists that the manufacturer made later changes which could not be included here. While striving for total accuracy, Chilton Book Company cannot assume responsibility for any errors, changes, or omissions that may occur in the compilation of this data.

PART NUMBERS

Part numbers listed in this reference are not recommendations by Chilton for any product by brand name. They are references that can be used with interchange manuals and aftermarket supplier catalogs to locate each brand supplier's discrete part number.

SPECIAL TOOLS

Special tools are recommended by the vehicle manufacturer to perform their specific job. Use has been kept to a minimum, but where absolutely necessary, they are referred to in the text by the part number of the tool manufacturer. These tools can be purchased, under the appropriate part number, from Owatonna Tool Company, Owatonna, MN 55060 or an equivalent tool can be purchased locally from a tool supplier or parts outlet. Before substituting any tool for the one recommended, read the SAFETY NOTICE at the top of this page.

ACKNOWLEDGMENTS

The Chilton Book Company expresses its appreciation to the Ford Motor Company, Dearborn, Michigan for their generous assistance.

Chilton's Repair & Tune-Up Guide: Ford Aerostar 1986—87
ISBN: 0-8019-7747-9 pbk.
Library of Congress Catalog Card No. 86-47769

CONTENTS

Quick Reference Specifications For Your Vehicle

Fill in this chart with the most commonly used specifications for your vehicle. Specifications can be found in Chapters 1 through 3 or on the tune-up decal under the hood of the vehicle.

 Tune-Up

Firing Order_____

Spark Plugs:

    Type_____

    Gap (in.)_____

Torque (ft. lbs.)_____

Idle Speed (rpm)_____

Ignition Timing (°)_____

    Vacuum or Electronic Advance (Connected/Disconnected)_____

Valve Clearance (in.)

    Intake_____   Exhaust_____

Capacities

Engine Oil Type (API Rating)_____

    With Filter Change (qts)_____

    Without Filter Change (qts)_____

Cooling System (qts)_____

Manual Transmission (pts)_____

    Type_____

Automatic Transmission (pts)_____

    Type_____

Front Differential (pts)_____

    Type_____

Rear Differential (pts)_____

    Type_____

Transfer Case (pts)_____

    Type_____

FREQUENTLY REPLACED PARTS

Use these spaces to record the part numbers of frequently replaced parts.

PCV VALVE	**OIL FILTER**	**AIR FILTER**	**FUEL FILTER**
Type_____	Type_____	Type_____	Type_____
Part No._____	Part No._____	Part No._____	Part No._____

General Information and Maintenance

1

HOW TO USE THIS BOOK

This book covers all Ford Aerostar models from 1985 through 1987.

The first two chapters will be the most used, since they contain maintenance and tune-up information and procedures. Studies have shown that a properly tuned and maintained engine can get at least 10% better gas mileage (which translates into lower operating costs) and periodic maintenance will catch minor problems before they turn into major repair bills. The other chapters deal with the more complex systems of your Aerostar. Operating systems from engine through brakes are covered to the extent that the average do-it-yourselfer becomes mechanically involved. This book will not explain such things as rebuilding the differential for the simple reason that the expertise required and the investment in special tools make this task uneconomical. It will give you the detailed instructions to help you change your own brake pads and shoes, tune-up the engine, replace spark plugs and filters, and do many more jobs that will save you money, give you personal satisfaction and help you avoid expensive problems.

A secondary purpose of this book is a reference guide for owners who want to understand their Aerostar and/or their mechanics better. In this case, no tools at all are required. Knowing just what a particular repair job requires in parts and labor time will allow you to evaluate whether or not you're getting a fair price quote and help decipher itemized bills from a repair shop.

Before attempting any repairs or service on your Aerostar, read through the entire procedure outlined in the appropriate chapter. This will give you the overall view of what tools and supplies will be required. There is nothing more frustrating than having to walk to the bus stop on Monday morning because you were short one gasket on Sunday afternoon. So read ahead and plan ahead. Each operation should be approached logically and all procedures thoroughly understood before attempting any work. Some special tools that may be required can often be rented from local automotive jobbers or places specializing in renting tools and equipment. Check the yellow pages of your phone book.

All chapters contain adjustments, maintenance, removal and installation procedures and overhaul procedures. When overhaul is not considered practical, we tell you how to remove the failed part and then how to install the new or rebuilt replacement. In this way, you at least save the labor costs. Backyard overhaul of some components (such as the alternator or water pump) is just not practical, but the removal and installation procedure is often simple and well within the capabilities of the average Aerostar owner.

Two basic mechanic's rules should be mentioned here. First, whenever the LEFT side of the van or engine is referred to, it is meant to specify the DRIVER'S side. Conversely, the RIGHT side of the van means the PASSENGER'S side. Second, all screws and bolts are removed by turning counterclockwise, and tightened by turning clockwise.

Safety is always the most important rule. Constantly be aware of the dangers involved in working on or around any vehicle and take proper precautions to avoid the risk of personal injury or damage to the vehicle. See the section in this chapter, Servicing Your Vehicle Safely, and the SAFETY NOTICE on the acknowledgment page before attempting any service procedures and pay attention to the instructions provided. There are three common mistakes in mechanical work:

1. Incorrect order of assembly, disassembly or adjustment. When taking something apart or putting it together, doing things in the

wrong order usually just costs you extra time, however it CAN break something. Read the entire procedure before beginning disassembly. Do everything in the order in which the instructions say you should do it, even if you can't immediately see a reason for it. When you're taking apart something that is very intricate (for example a carburetor), you might want to draw a picture of how it looks when assembled at one point in order to make sure you get everything back in its proper position. We will supply exploded views whenever possible, but sometimes the job requires more attention to detail than an illustration provides. When making adjustments (especially tune-up adjustments), do them in order. One adjustment often affects another and you cannot expect satisfactory results unless each adjustment is made only when it cannot be changed by any other.

2. Overtorquing (or undertorquing) nuts and bolts. While it is more common for overtorquing to cause damage, undertorquing can cause a fastener to vibrate loose and cause serious damage, especially when dealing with aluminum parts. Pay attention to torque specifications and utilize a torque wrench in assembly. If a torque figure is not available remember that, if you are using the right tool to do the job, you will probably not have to strain yourself to get a fastener tight enough. The pitch of most threads is so slight that the tension you put on the wrench will be multiplied many times in actual force on what you are tightening. A good example of how critical torque is can be seen in the case of spark plug installation, especially where you are putting the plug into an aluminum cylinder head. Too little torque can fail to crush the gasket, causing leakage of combustion gases and consequent overheating of the plug and engine parts. Too much torque can damage the threads or distort the plug, which changes the spark gap at the electrode. Since more and more manufacturers are using aluminum in their engine and chassis parts to save weight, a torque wrench should be in any serious do-it-yourselfer's tool box.

There are many commercial chemical products available for ensuring that fasteners won't come loose, even if they are not torqued just right (a very common brand is Loctite®). If you're worried about getting something together tight enough to hold, but loose enough to avoid mechanical damage during assembly, one of these products might offer substantial insurance. Read the label on the package and make sure the product is compatible with the materials, fluids, etc. involved before choosing one.

3. Crossthreading. This occurs when a part such as a bolt is screwed into a nut or casting at the wrong angle and forced, causing the threads to become damaged. Crossthreading is more likely to occur if access is difficult. It helps to clean and lubricate fasteners, and to start threading with the part to be installed going straight in, using your fingers. If you encounter resistance, unscrew the part and start over again at a different angle until it can be inserted and turned several times without much effort. Keep in mind that many parts, especially spark plugs, use tapered threads so that gentle turning will automatically bring the part you're threading to the proper angle if you don't force it or resist a change in angle. Don't put a wrench on the part until it's been turned in a couple of times by hand. If you suddenly encounter resistance and the part has not seated fully, don't force it. Pull it back out and make sure it's clean and threading properly.

Always take your time and be patient. Once you have some experience, working on your Aerostar will become an enjoyable hobby.

TOOLS AND EQUIPMENT

Naturally, without the proper tools and equipment it is impossible to properly service your vehicle. It would be impossible to catalog each tool that you would need to perform each or every operation in this book. It would also be unwise for the amateur to rush out and buy an expensive set of tools an the theory that he may need one or more of them at sometime.

The best approach is to proceed slowly, gathering together a good quality set of those tools that are used most frequently. Don't be misled by the low cost of bargain tools. It is far better to spend a little more for better quality. Forged wrenches, 10 or 12 point sockets and fine tooth ratchets are by far preferable to their less expensive counterparts. As any good mechanic can tell you, there are few worse experiences than trying to work on any vehicle with bad tools. Your monetary savings will be far outweighed by frustration and mangled knuckles.

Certain tools, plus a basic ability to handle them, are required to get started. A basic mechanics tool set, a torque wrench and a Torx® bits set. Torx® bits are hexlobular drivers which fit both inside and outside on special Torx® head fasteners used in various places on modern vehicles. Begin accumulating those tools that are used most frequently; those associated with routine maintenance and tune-up.

In addition to the normal assortment of screwdrivers and pliers you should have the

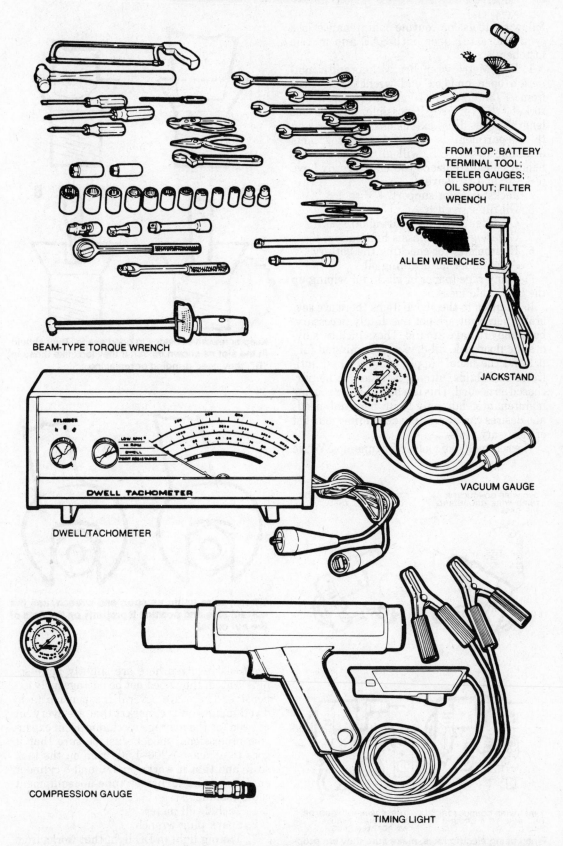

FROM TOP: BATTERY TERMINAL TOOL; FEELER GAUGES; OIL SPOUT; FILTER WRENCH

ALLEN WRENCHES

BEAM-TYPE TORQUE WRENCH

JACKSTAND

DWELL TACHOMETER

DWELL/TACHOMETER

VACUUM GAUGE

COMPRESSION GAUGE

TIMING LIGHT

You need only a basic assortment of hand tools and test instruments for most maintenance and repair jobs

following tools for routine maintenance jobs (your Aerostar uses both SAE and metric fasteners):

1. SAE/Metric wrenches, sockets and combination open end/box end wrenches in sizes from ⅛″ (3mm) to ¾″ (19mm) and a spark plug socket ($^{13}/_{16}$″ or ⅝″). If possible, buy various length socket drive extensions. One break in this department is that the metric sockets available in the U.S. will all fit the ratchet handles and extensions you may already have (¼″, ⅜″, and ½″ drive).

2. Jackstands for support.
3. Oil filter wrench.
4. Oil filter spout for pouring oil.
5. Grease gun for chassis lubrication.
6. Hydrometer for checking the battery.
7. A container for draining oil.
8. Many rags (paper or cloth) for wiping up the inevitable mess.

In addition to the above items there are several others that are not absolutely necessary, but handy to have around. These include a hydraulic floor jack, oil-dry, a transmission funnel and the usual supply of lubricants, antifreeze and fluids, although these can be purchased as needed. This is a basic list for routine maintenance, but only your personal needs and desires can accurately determine your list of necessary tools.

The second list of tools is for tune-ups. While

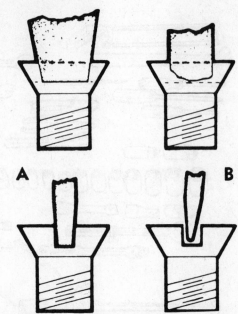

Keep screwdriver blades in good shape. They should fit the slot as shown in "A". If they look like those in "B", they need grinding or replacing

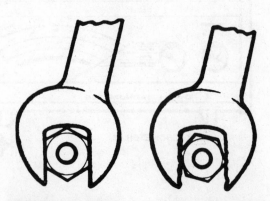

When you're using an open end wrench, use the correct size and position it properly on the flats of the nut or bolt

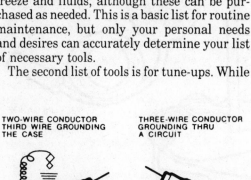

TWO-WIRE CONDUCTOR THIRD WIRE GROUNDING THE CASE

THREE-WIRE CONDUCTOR GROUNDING THRU A CIRCUIT

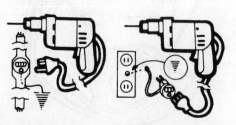

THREE-WIRE CONDUCTOR ONE WIRE TO A GROUND

THREE-WIRE CONDUCTOR GROUNDING THRU AN ADAPTER PLUG

When using electric tools, make sure they are properly grounded

the tools involved here are slightly more sophisticated, they need not be outrageously expensive. There are several inexpensive tach/dwell meters on the market that are every bit as good for the average mechanic as an expensive professional model. Just be sure that it goes to at least 1,200–1,500 rpm on the tach scale and that it works on 4, 6 and 8-cylinder engines. A basic list of tune-up equipment could include:

1. Tach/dwell meter.
2. Spark plug wrench.
3. Timing light (a DC light that works from the Aerostar's battery is best, although an AC

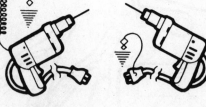

light that plugs into 110V house current will suffice at some sacrifice in brightness).

4. Wire spark plug gauge/adjusting tools.

Here again, be guided by your own needs. While not absolutely necessary, an ohmmeter can be useful in determining whether or not a spark plug wire is any good by measuring its resistance. In addition to these basic tools, there are several other tools and gauges you may find useful. These include:

1. A compression gauge. The screw-in type is slower to use, but eliminates the possibility of a faulty reading due to escaping pressure.

2. A manifold vacuum gauge.

3. A test light.

4. An induction meter. This is used for determining whether or not there is current in a wire. These are handy for use if a wire is broken somewhere in a wiring harness.

As a final note, you will probably find a torque wrench necessary for all but the most basic work. The beam type models are perfectly adequate, although the newer click (breakaway) type are more precise, and you don't have to crane your neck to see a torque reading in awkward situations. The breakaway torque wrenches are more expensive and should be recalibrated periodically.

Torque specification for each fastener will be given in the procedure in any case that a specific torque value is required. If no torque specifications are given, use the following values as a guide, based upon fastener size:

Bolts marked 6T

6mm bolt/nut – 5–7 ft.lb.
8mm bolt/nut – 12–17 ft.lb.
10mm bolt/nut – 23–34 ft.lb.
12mm bolt/nut – 41–59 ft.lb.
14mm bolt/nut – 56–76 ft.lb.

Bolts marked 8T

6mm bolt/nut – 6–9 ft.lb.
8mm bolt/nut – 13–20 ft.lb.
10mm bolt/nut – 27–40 ft.lb.
12mm bolt/nut – 46–69 ft.lb.
14mm bolt/nut – 75–101 ft.lb.

Special Tools

Normally, the use of special factory tools is avoided for repair procedures, since these are not readily available for the do-it-yourself mechanic. When it is possible to perform the job with more commonly available tools, it will be pointed out, but occasionally a special tool was designed to perform a specific function and should be used. Before substituting another tool, you should be convinced that neither your safety nor the performance of the vehicle will be compromised. Where possible, an illustration of the special tool will be provided so that an equivalent tool may be used.

Some special tools are available commercially from Owatonna Tool Co., Owatonna, MN 55060. Others can be purchased through your Ford dealer or local parts supplier.

SERVICING YOUR VEHICLE SAFELY

It is virtually impossible to anticipate all of the hazards involved with automotive maintenance and service, but care and common sense will prevent most accidents.

The rules of safety for mechanics range from "don't smoke around gasoline," to "use the proper tool for the job." The trick to avoiding injuries is to develop safe work habits and take every possible precaution.

Dos

• Do keep a fire extinguisher and first aid kit within easy reach.

• Do wear safety glasses or goggles when cutting, drilling or prying, even if you have 20–20 vision. If you wear glasses for the sake of vision, they should be made of hardened glass that can also serve as safety glasses, or wear safety goggles over your regular glasses.

• Do shield your eyes whenever you work around the battery. Batteries contain sulphuric acid. In case of contact with the eyes or skin, flush the area with water or a mixture of water and baking soda and get medical attention immediately.

• Do use safety stands for any under-van service. Jacks are for raising vehicles; safety stands are for making sure the vehicle stays raised until you want it to come down. Whenever the vehicle is raised, block the wheels remaining on the ground and set the parking brake.

• Do use adequate ventilation when working with any chemicals. Like carbon monoxide, the asbestos dust resulting from brake lining wear can be poisonous in sufficient quantities.

• Do disconnect the negative battery cable when working on the electrical system. The primary ignition system can contain up to 40,000 volts.

• Do follow manufacturer's directions whenever working with potentially hazardous materials. Both brake fluid and antifreeze are poisonous if taken internally.

• Do properly maintain your tools. Loose hammerheads, mushroomed punches and chisels, frayed or poorly grounded electrical cords, excessively worn screwdrivers, spread wrenches (open end), cracked sockets, slipping ratchets, or faulty droplight sockets can cause accidents.

• Do use the proper size and type of tool for the job being done.

• Do when possible, pull on a wrench handle rather than push on it, and adjust your stance to prevent a fall.

• Do be sure that adjustable wrenches are tightly adjusted on the nut or bolt and pulled so that the face is on the side of the fixed jaw.

• Do select a wrench or socket that fits the nut or bolt. The wrench or socket should sit straight, not cocked.

• Do strike squarely with a hammer—avoid glancing blows.

• Do set the parking brake and block the drive wheels if the work requires that the engine be running.

Don'ts

• Don't run an engine in a garage or anywhere else without proper ventilation—EVER! Carbon monoxide is poisonous. It takes a long time to leave the human body and you can build up a deadly supply of it in your system by simply breathing in a little every day. You may not realize you are slowly poisoning yourself. Always use power vents, windows, fans or open the garage doors.

• Don't work around moving parts while wearing a necktie or other loose clothing. Short sleeves are much safer than long, loose sleeves and hard-toed shoes with neoprene soles protect your toes and give a better grip on slippery surfaces. Jewelry such as watches, fancy belt buckles, beads or body adornment of any kind is not safe working around any vehicle. Long hair should be hidden under a hat or cap.

• Don't use pockets for toolboxes. A fall or bump can drive a screwdriver deep into your body. Even a wiping cloth hanging from the back pocket can wrap around a spinning shaft or fan.

• Don't smoke when working around gasoline, cleaning solvent or other flammable material.

• Don't smoke when working around the battery. When the battery is being charged, it gives off explosive hydrogen gas.

• Don't use gasoline to wash your hands; there are excellent soaps available. Gasoline may contain lead, and lead can enter the body through a cut, accumulating in the body until you are very ill. Gasoline also removes all the natural oils from the skin so that bone dry hands will suck up oil and grease.

• Don't service the air conditioning system unless you are equipped with the necessary tools and training. The refrigerant, R-12, is extremely cold and when exposed to the air, will instantly freeze any surface it comes in contact with, including your eyes. Although the refrigerant is normally non-toxic, R-12 becomes a deadly poisonous gas in the presence of an open flame. One good whiff of the vapors from burning refrigerant can be fatal.

SERIAL NUMBER IDENTIFICATION

Vehicle Identification (VIN) Number

A seventeen digit combination of numbers and letters forms the vehicle identification number (VIN). The VIN is stamped on a metal tab that is riveted to the instrument panel close to the windshield. The VIN plate is visible by looking through the windshield on the driver's side. The VIN number is also found on the Safety Compliance Certification Label.

By looking at the seventeen digit VIN num-

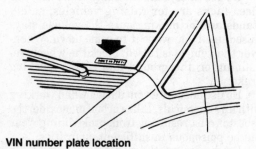

VIN number plate location

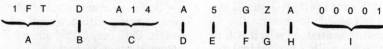

A. Position 1, 2, and 3—Manufacturer, Make and Type
    (World Manufacturer Identifier)
B. Position 4—Brake System/GVWR
C. Position 5, 6, and 7—Model or Line, Series, Chassis, Cab Type
D. Position 8—Engine Type
E. Position 9—Check Digit
F. Position 10—Model Year
G. Position 11—Assembly Plant
H. Position 12—Constant "A" until sequence number of 99,999 is reached, then changes to a constant "B" and so on
I. Position 13 through 17—Sequence number—begins at 00001

Sample VIN number

World Manufacturer Identifier (VIN Positions 1, 2, and 3)

$$\boxed{\text{1FT}} \quad \text{DA14A 5G ZA00001}$$

VIN Code	Manufacturer	Make	Type
1 F M	Ford Motor Company, USA	Ford	Multi-Purpose Vehicle (MPV)
1 F T	Ford Motor Company, USA	Ford	Truck (Complete Vehicle)
1 F D	Ford Motor Company, USA	Ford	Incomplete Vehicle (IV)
1 F C	Ford Motor Company, USA	Ford	Basic (Stripped) Chassis
2 F M	Ford Motor Company of Canada, Ltd.	Ford	MPV
2 F T	Ford Motor Company of Canada, Ltd.	Ford	Truck (Complete Vehicle)
2 F D	Ford Motor Company of Canada, Ltd.	Ford	Incomplete Vehicle
2 F C	Ford Motor Company of Canada, Ltd.	Ford	Basic (Stripped) Chassis

Brake System and GVWR Class for Trucks and MPV's—Brake System (only) for Incomplete Vehicles (VIN Position 4)

$$\text{1F T} \quad \boxed{\text{D}} \quad \text{A14A 5 GZ A00001}$$

Brake System	GVWR Class	GVWR Range	VIN Code
Hydraulic	Class A:	Not greater than 3,000 pounds	A
Hydraulic	Class B:	3,001-4,000 pounds	B
Hydraulic	Class C:	4,001-5,000 pounds	C
Hydraulic	Class D:	5,001-6,000 pounds	D
Hydraulic	Class E:	6,001-7,000 pounds	E
Hydraulic	Class F:	7,001-8,000 pounds	F
Hydraulic	Class G:	8,001-8,500 pounds 8,501-9,000 pounds	G H
Hydraulic	Class H:	9,001-10,000 pounds	J

Vehicle Identification (VIN) codes

ber, a variety of information about the vehicle can be determined. The first three digits identify the manufacturer and the vehicle make and type. The fourth digit determines the gross vehicle weight rating (GVWR Class) and brake system. For incomplete vehicles, the fourth digit determines the brake system only. Digits five, six and seven identify the model or line, series, class and body type. The eighth digit points out the particular engine found in the vehicle. Digit nine is a check digit and the tenth determines the model year. The eleventh digit determines the assembly plant, while digits twelve through seventeen make up the sequential serial and warranty number. Digit twelve uses the letter A until the production or sequence of 99,999 units (digits thirteen through seventeen) is reached. Letter A then becomes B for the next production sequence of vehicles.

Build Date Stamp Location

The vehicle build date is stamped on the front surface of the radiator support on the passenger side of the vehicle. Yellow ink is used for the date stamp. When the marking surface is painted the body color, the date stamp will be marked in red ink. Units from the Ontario truck plant (code C) will be marked with silver ink.

Vehicle Data

The vehicle data appears on the Safety Compliance Certification Label on the second and third lines following the identification number. The code set (two numbers or a number and letter) above COLOR identify the exterior paint color, with two sets of codes designating two tone paint. The three digits under W.N. designate the wheelbase in inches. The letter

Model or Line, Series, Chassis, Cab Type
(VIN Positions 5, 6 and 7)

1 F T D [A14] A 5 G Z A 0 0 0 0 1

VIN Code	Line	Series	Chassis Type	Cab or Body Type	Vehicle Type
A11	Aerostar	Base	4x2	Window Wagon	MPV
A14	Aerostar	Base	4x2	Cargo Van	Truck or IV
A15	Aerostar	Base	4x2	Window Van	Truck or IV

NOTE:
One of the following optional exterior nameplates (indicating higher trim levels) may also be affixed to the vehicle in addition to the Aerostar nameplate:
- XL
- XLT (Excluding Vans)

Engine Type, Displacement, Cylinders, Fuel Type, and Manufacturer
(VIN Position 8)

1 F T D A 1 4 [A] 5 G Z A 0 0 0 0 1

VIN Code	Displacement		Cylinders	Fuel	Manufacturer
	Liter	CID			
A	2.3 (EFI)	140	I-4	Gasoline	Ford
S	2.8	171	V-6	Gasoline	Ford
U	3.0	183	V-6	Gasoline	Ford

Check Digit for All Vehicles
(VIN Position 9)

1FTDA14A [5] GZA00001

Vehicle Model Year for All Vehicles
(VIN Position 10)

1FTDA14A 5 [G] ZA00001

VIN Code	Year
F	1985
G	1986
H	1987
J	1988
K	1989
L	1990
M	1991
N	1992
P	1993
R	1994
S	1995

Assembly Plant
(VIN Position 11)

1FTDA14 A 5 G [Z] A 0 0 0 0 1

VIN Code	Vehicle Assembly Plant Name: Location
Z	St. Louis: Hazelwood, Missouri

Production Sequence Number
(VIN Positions 12 through 17)

1FTDA14 A 5 GZ [A 0 0 0 0 1]

SEQUENCE NUMBER
A 00001 — A 99,999
B 00001 — B 99,999
and so on.

Safety Compliance Certification Labels
COMPLETE VEHICLES

(UNITED STATES)

```
MFD. BY FORD MOTOR. CO. IN U.S.A.
DATE:  2/85                    GVWR:        3740 LBS/1696 KG
FRONT GAWR:  1910 LBS          REAR GAWR:   2012 LBS
    866 KG                WITH     912 KG            WITH
    P195/75R14SL          TIRES    P195/75RSL        TIRES
    14x5.0JJ              RIMS     14x5.0JJ          RIMS
AT 35 PSI COLD                 AT 35 PSI COLD

THIS VEHICLE CONFORMS TO ALL APPLICABLE FEDERAL MOTOR VEHICLE SAFETY
   STANDARDS IN EFFECT ON THE DATE OF MANUFACTURE SHOWN ABOVE

VEHICLE IDENTIFICATION NO.
1FTCR10A5FUA00001
                                              F0083
TYPE TRUCK                                    T0112
   4J    9W                             48
EXTERIOR PAINT COLORS                         DSO
 WB  | TYPE GVW | BODY | TRANS | AXLE | TAPE | SPRING
 108 |   R11L   | CH2  |       | 822  |  B   | C22D
```

(QUEBEC)

```
FABR. AUX É-U PAR LA FORD MOTOR CO.
DATE:                 PNBV:
PNBE AV:                               PNBE AR:
                        AVEC
                       ◄PNEUS►
                       ◄JANTES►
A    LB/PO² À FROID          À      LB/PO² À FROID
CE VÉHICULE EST CONFORME À TOUTES LES NORMES FEDERALES DE SÉCURITÉ
     DES V.A. EN VIGUEUR À LA DATE DE FABR. INIQUÉE CI-DESSUS.
N° D'IDENT. DU VÉH

TYPE
COULEUR                                    N COMM SPEC
 EMPATT. | TYPE-PBV | CARR | TRANSM | PONT | BANDE | RESSORT

                                         E4TA-1020472-AA
```

FOR VEHICLES MFD IN U.S.A. FOR QUEBEC, CANADA

DECAL APPLIED TO ALL
CANADIAN BUILT UNITS AND
ALL U.S.A. BUILT UNITS SOLD
IN CANADA

INCOMPLETE VEHICLES

THE INCOMPLETE VEHICLE RATING DECAL IS INSTALLED ON THE DRIVER'S DOOR
LATCH EDGE IN PLACE OF THE SAFETY STANDARD CERTIFICATION LABEL.

VEHICLE RATING DECAL

```
INCOMPLETE VEHICLE MANUFACTURED BY

GVWR: 4220 LBS/1914 KG
VEHICLE IDENTIFICATION NUMBER      1FTCR10A5FUA00001

EXTERIOR PAINT COLORS     4J    9W                48  DSO
  WB  | TYPE-GVW | BODY | TRANS | AXLE | TAPE | SPRING

 108  |  R11L    | CH2  |   T   |  822  |  B    C22D
```

and three digits under TYPE/G.V.W. designate the truck model within a series and the gross vehicle weight rating. The letters and/or numbers under BODY designate the interior trim, seat and body type. The transmission installed in the vehicle is identified under TRANS by an alphabetical code.

A letter and a number or two numbers under AXLE identify the rear axle ratio and, when required, a letter or number is also stamped after the rear axle code to identify the front axle. The letters and/or numerals under TAPE designate the external body side tape stripe code. The spring usage codes for the vehicle are identified under SPRING.

A two digit number is stamped above D.S.O. to identify the district which originally ordered the vehicle. If the vehicle is built to special order (Domestic Special Order, Foreign Special Order, Limited Production Option or other special order), the complete order number will also appear above D.S.O.

ROUTINE MAINTENANCE

Air Cleaner Element

All engines are equipped with a dry type, replaceable air filter element. The element should be replaced at the recommended intervals shown on the maintenance chart in this chapter. If your vehicle is operated under severely dusty conditions or regularly in stop-and-go traffic, more frequent changes are necessary. Inspect the element at least twice a year; early spring and fall are good times of the year for inspection. Remove the element and check for holes in the filter, then check the element housing for signs of dirt or dust that has leaked through the filter element. Place a light

Body Tape Codes—Aerostar

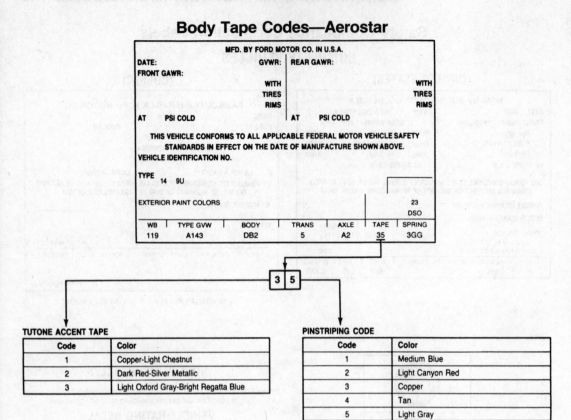

MFD. BY FORD MOTOR CO. IN U.S.A.

DATE: GVWR: REAR GAWR:
FRONT GAWR:

	WITH		WITH
	TIRES		TIRES
	RIMS		RIMS
AT   PSI COLD | AT   PSI COLD |

THIS VEHICLE CONFORMS TO ALL APPLICABLE FEDERAL MOTOR VEHICLE SAFETY
STANDARDS IN EFFECT ON THE DATE OF MANUFACTURE SHOWN ABOVE.
VEHICLE IDENTIFICATION NO.

TYPE   14 9U

EXTERIOR PAINT COLORS   23
                                                         DSO

WB	TYPE GVW	BODY	TRANS	AXLE	TAPE	SPRING
119	A143	DB2	5	A2	35	3GG

3 5

TUTONE ACCENT TAPE

Code	Color
1	Copper-Light Chestnut
2	Dark Red-Silver Metallic
3	Light Oxford Gray-Bright Regatta Blue

PINSTRIPING CODE

Code	Color
1	Medium Blue
2	Light Canyon Red
3	Copper
4	Tan
5	Light Gray

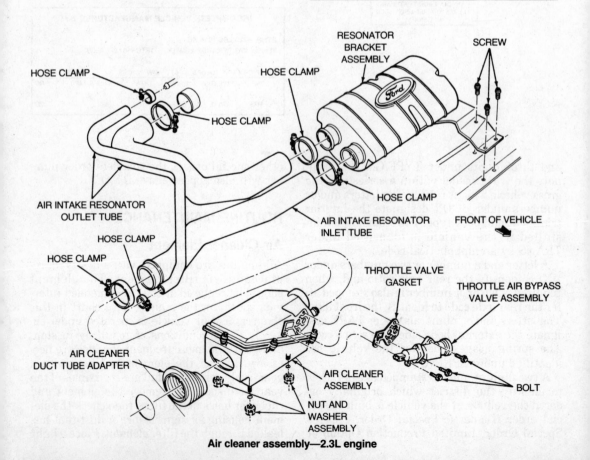

Air cleaner assembly—2.3L engine

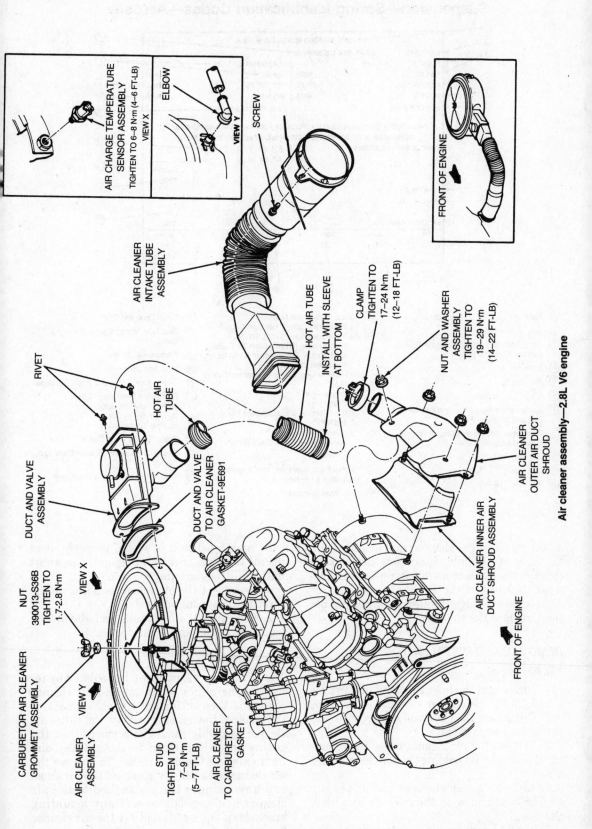

AIR CHARGE TEMPERATURE SENSOR ASSEMBLY
TIGHTEN TO 6–8 N·m (4–6 FT-LB)
VIEW X

ELBOW

VIEW Y

SCREW

FRONT OF ENGINE

AIR CLEANER INTAKE TUBE ASSEMBLY

HOT AIR TUBE

INSTALL WITH SLEEVE AT BOTTOM

CLAMP
TIGHTEN TO 17–24 N·m (12–18 FT-LB)

NUT AND WASHER ASSEMBLY
TIGHTEN TO 19–29 N·m (14–22 FT-LB)

RIVET

HOT AIR TUBE

DUCT AND VALVE ASSEMBLY

DUCT AND VALVE TO AIR CLEANER GASKET-9E691

AIR CLEANER OUTER AIR DUCT SHROUD

AIR CLEANER INNER AIR DUCT SHROUD ASSEMBLY

FRONT OF ENGINE

NUT
390013-S36B
TIGHTEN TO 1.7–2.8 N·m

VIEW X

CARBURETOR AIR CLEANER GROMMET ASSEMBLY

VIEW Y

AIR CLEANER ASSEMBLY

STUD
TIGHTEN TO 7–9 N·m (5–7 FT-LB)

AIR CLEANER TO CARBURETOR GASKET

Air cleaner assembly—2.8L V6 engine

Suspension—Spring Identification Codes—Aerostar

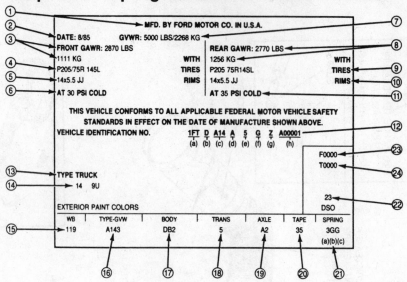

① Name and Location of Manufacturer

② Date of Manufacture

③ Front Gross Axle Weight Ratings in Pounds (LB) and Kilograms (KG)

④ Front Tire Size

⑤ Rim Size

⑥ Front Tire Cold PSI

⑦ Gross Vehicle Weight Rating in Pounds (LB) and Kilograms (KG)

⑧ Rear Gross Axle Weight Rating in Pounds (LB) and Kilograms (KG)

⑨ Rear Tire Size

⑩ Rim Size

⑪ Rear Tire Cold PSI

⑫ Vehicle Identification Number
(a) World Manufacturer Identifier
(b) Brake System and Gross Vehicle Weight Rating (GVWR) Class for Trucks and MPV's — Brake System (Only) for Incomplete Vehicles.
(c) Model or Line, Series, Chassis and Cab Type
(d) Engine Type
(e) Check Digit
(f) Model Year — (Ford-Complete Trucks and MPV's)
(g) Assembly Plant Code
(h) Sequential Serial and Model Year

⑬ Type Vehicle

⑭ Exterior Paint Codes (two sets of figures designates a two-tone)

⑮ Wheelbase in Inches

⑯ Model Code and GVW

⑰ Seat Type, Interior Color and Seating Codes

⑱ Transmission Code

⑲ Rear Axle Code

⑳ Tutone Accent Tape and Pinstriping Codes

㉑ Suspension Identification Codes
(a) Aux/Opt Front Spring Code
(b) Front Spring Code
(c) Rear Spring Code

㉒ District/Special Order Codes

㉓ Front Axle Accessory Reserve Capacity in Pounds

㉔ Total Accessory Reserve Capacity in Pounds

---

on the inside of the element and look through the filter at the light. If no glow can be seen through the element material, replace the element. If holes in the filter are apparent or signs of dirt leakage through the filter are noticed, replace the element.

REMOVAL AND INSTALLATION

2.3L EFI Engine

1. Disconnect the inlet tube and idle bypass tube from the air cleaner cover.

2. Disconnect the electrical connector to the throttle air bypass valve.

3. Remove the air cleaner cover by loosening the knurl nuts holding the air cleaner case together.

4. Lift the paper element out of the air cleaner case and wipe the case clean with a clean rag.

5. Install a new air cleaner element into the case, making sure it is seated properly, then install the case cover and tighten the knurl nuts until they are finger tight.

6. Reconnect the electrical connector to the throttle air bypass valve.

7. Reconnect the inlet tube and idle air bypass tube to the air cleaner cover.

2.8L V6 Engine

The air cleaner element can be replaced by removing the center wing nut and air cleaner cover and then lifting out the old element. If the inside of the housing is dirty, the entire air cleaner assembly should be removed from the engine and wiped clean to prevent any dirt from entering the carburetor. To remove the air cleaner assembly, disconnect the air ducts and any vacuum lines attached to the air cleaner housing. Disconnect any mounting brackets (if equipped) and lift the air cleaner housing off of the engine. Replace the cleaner

Safety Compliance Certification Label Vehicle Data Codes

Exterior Paint Color Codes—Aerostar

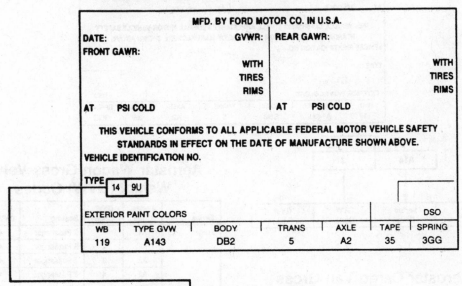

Exterior Paint Color Codes

NOTE — Two sets of codes indicates two-tone paint.

Code	Color
14①	Silver Metallic
23①	Dark Canyon Red
3U	Dark Regatta Blue
34	Light Regatta Blue
5Z①	Light Chestnut Metallic
51	Medium Dark Fire Red
5Z①	Light Chestnut Metallic
53	Medium Desert Tan
7J①	Medium Regatta Blue
8E①	Bright Copper Metallic
9M	White
9R①	Deep Silver Smoke Grey
9U①	Dark Walnut Metallic

NOTE:
①Indicates Clear Coat Hi-Solid Color

mounting gasket if it is worn or broken. When installing, reconnect all brackets, ducts and vacuum hoses and tighten the wing nut finger tight.

Fuel Filter

The fuel filters for mechanical fuel pumps are located on the carburetor where the fuel inlet

Type—Gross Vehicle Weight (GVW) Codes—Aerostar

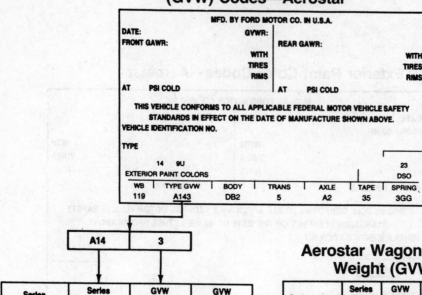

Aerostar Cargo Van Gross Vehicle Weight (GVW) Codes

Series	Series Code	GVW Code	Payload Package (Lbs.)	GVW (Lbs.)
Cargo Van	A14	1	1200	4060
	A14	2	1200	4180
	A14	3	1600	4500
	A14	4	2000	5060

Aerostar Window Van Gross Vehicle Weight (GVW) Codes

Series	Series Code	GVW Code	Payload Package (Lbs.)	GVW (Lbs.)
Window Van	A15	1	1200	4060
	A15	2	1200	4180
	A15	3	1600	4500
	A15	4	2000	5060

Aerostar Wagon Gross Vehicle Weight (GVW) Codes

Series	Series Code	GVW Code	Seating	GVW (Lbs.)
Wagon	All	1	5 Passenger	4460
	All	2	5 Passenger	4620
	All	3	7 Passenger	4740
	All	4	7 Passenger	4820
	All	5	7 Passenger	4880
	All	6	7 Passenger	4940
	All	7	7 Passenger	5000
	All	8	7 Passenger	5040

line is attached. Fuel injected engines with electric fuel pumps have three filters: one inside the inline reservoir, one at the electric fuel pump mounted on the chassis and a third on the low pressure electric fuel pump mounted inside the fuel tank itself. Normally, only the filters at the chassis mounted pump and fuel reservoir are replaced as part of normal maintenance. A high speed surge problem is indicative of a clogged fuel filter.

CAUTION: *On fuel injected engines, the fuel system is under constant pressure, even when the engine is turned off. Follow the instructions for relieving fuel system pressure before attempting any service to the fuel system. Whenever working on or around any open*

Body Codes

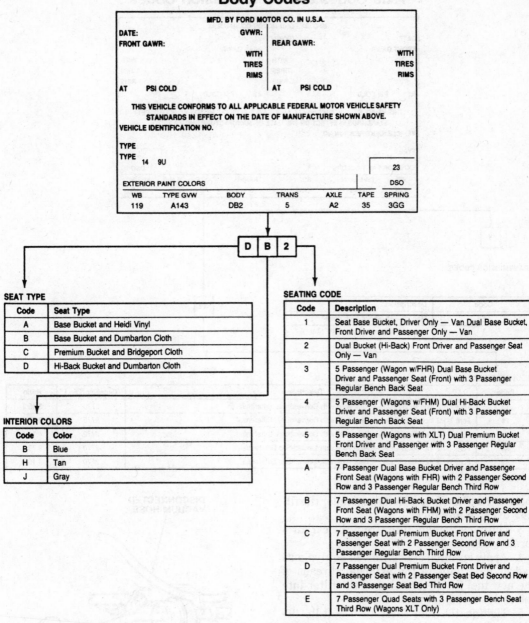

MFD. BY FORD MOTOR CO. IN U.S.A.

DATE: GVWR:
FRONT GAWR: REAR GAWR:
                        WITH   WITH
                        TIRES   TIRES
                        RIMS   RIMS
AT   PSI COLD   AT   PSI COLD

THIS VEHICLE CONFORMS TO ALL APPLICABLE FEDERAL MOTOR VEHICLE SAFETY
STANDARDS IN EFFECT ON THE DATE OF MANUFACTURE SHOWN ABOVE.
VEHICLE IDENTIFICATION NO.

TYPE
TYPE   14   9U   23
                                                        DSO
EXTERIOR PAINT COLORS

WB	TYPE GVW	BODY	TRANS	AXLE	TAPE	SPRING
119	A143	DB2	5	A2	35	3GG

D B 2

SEAT TYPE

Code	Seat Type
A	Base Bucket and Heidi Vinyl
B	Base Bucket and Dumbarton Cloth
C	Premium Bucket and Bridgeport Cloth
D	Hi-Back Bucket and Dumbarton Cloth

SEATING CODE

Code	Description
1	Seat Base Bucket, Driver Only — Van Dual Base Bucket, Front Driver and Passenger Only — Van
2	Dual Bucket (Hi-Back) Front Driver and Passenger Seat Only — Van
3	5 Passenger (Wagon w/FHR) Dual Base Bucket Driver and Passenger Seat (Front) with 3 Passenger Regular Bench Back Seat
4	5 Passenger (Wagons w/FHM) Dual Hi-Back Bucket Driver and Passenger Seat (Front) with 3 Passenger Regular Bench Back Seat
5	5 Passenger (Wagons with XLT) Dual Premium Bucket Front Driver and Passenger with 3 Passenger Regular Bench Back Seat
A	7 Passenger Dual Base Bucket Driver and Passenger Front Seat (Wagons with FHR) with 2 Passenger Second Row and 3 Passenger Regular Bench Third Row
B	7 Passenger Dual Hi-Back Bucket Driver and Passenger Front Seat (Wagons with FHM) with 2 Passenger Second Row and 3 Passenger Regular Bench Third Row
C	7 Passenger Dual Premium Bucket Front Driver and Passenger Seat with 2 Passenger Second Row and 3 Passenger Regular Bench Third Row
D	7 Passenger Dual Premium Bucket Front Driver and Passenger Seat with 2 Passenger Seat Bed Second Row and 3 Passenger Seat Bed Third Row
E	7 Passenger Quad Seats with 3 Passenger Bench Seat Third Row (Wagons XLT Only)

INTERIOR COLORS

Code	Color
B	Blue
H	Tan
J	Gray

fuel system, take precautions to avoid the risk of fire and use clean rags to catch any fuel spray while disconnecting fuel lines.

REMOVAL AND INSTALLATION

Carbureted Engine

1. Remove the air cleaner assembly.
2. Using two wrenches, one on the fuel line and one holding the filter, loosen and disconnect the fuel inlet line from the carburetor fuel

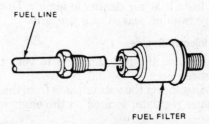

FUEL LINE

FUEL FILTER

Fuel filter used on carbureted engines

Axle Codes and Transmission Codes

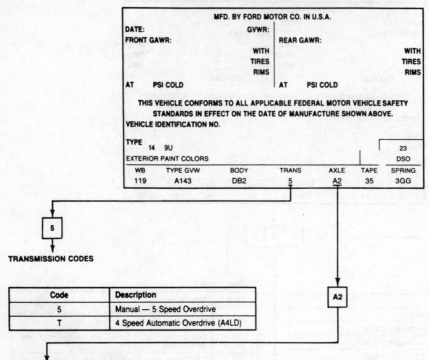

```
MFD. BY FORD MOTOR CO. IN U.S.A.
DATE:                          GVWR:
FRONT GAWR:                    REAR GAWR:
                    WITH                              WITH
                    TIRES                             TIRES
                    RIMS                              RIMS
AT    PSI COLD                 AT    PSI COLD

    THIS VEHICLE CONFORMS TO ALL APPLICABLE FEDERAL MOTOR VEHICLE SAFETY
    STANDARDS IN EFFECT ON THE DATE OF MANUFACTURE SHOWN ABOVE.
VEHICLE IDENTIFICATION NO.

TYPE   14  9U                                          23
EXTERIOR PAINT COLORS                                  DSO
    WB     TYPE GVW    BODY     TRANS    AXLE   TAPE   SPRING
    119    A143        DB2      5        A2     35     3GG
```

TRANSMISSION CODES

Code	Description
5	Manual — 5 Speed Overdrive
T	4 Speed Automatic Overdrive (A4LD)

REAR AXLE CODES

Code	Description	Capacity (Lbs.)	Ratio
13	Ford 7-1/2 Inch Ring Gear — Rear Axle with Conventional Differential	2770	3.45:1
14	Ford 7-1/2 Inch Ring Gear — Rear Axle with Conventional Differential	2770	3.73:1
12	Ford 7-1/2 Inch Ring Gear — Rear Axle with Conventional Differential	2770	4.10:1
A4	Ford 7-1/2 Inch Ring Gear — Rear Axle with Limited-Slip Differential	2770	3.73:1
A2	Ford 7-1/2 Inch Ring Gear — Rear Axle with Limited-Slip Differential	2770	4.10:1

inlet at the filter. Use a clean rag under the fitting to catch any fuel.

3. Unscrew the fuel filter from the carburetor fuel inlet.

4. Apply one drop of Loctite® (or equivalent) hydraulic sealant to the external threads of the new fuel filter, then thread the filter into the carburetor inlet port.

5. Tighten the fuel filter to 6–8 ft.lb. (9–11Nm). Do not overtighten.

6. Thread the fuel supply line into the filter and, using two wrenches as before, tighten the fuel supply line nut to 15–18 ft.lb. (20–24Nm).

7. Start the engine and check for fuel leaks.

8. Install the air cleaner assembly. Dispose of any gasoline soaked rags properly.

Fuel Injected Engine

1. Remove the fuel tank cap to vent tank pressure.

2. Disconnect the vacuum hose from the fuel pressure regulator located on the engine fuel rail.

3. Connect a hand vacuum pump to the fuel

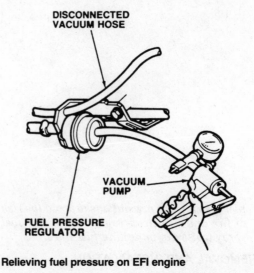

Relieving fuel pressure on EFI engine

pressure regulator and apply 25 in.Hg for ten seconds. This will release the fuel pressure into the fuel tank through the fuel return line.

4. Raise the vehicle and support it safely.

Suspension—Spring Identification Code

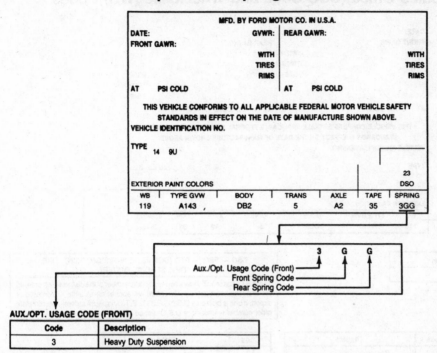

DATE:
FRONT GAWR: GVWR: REAR GAWR:

WITH   WITH
TIRES   TIRES
RIMS   RIMS

AT   PSI COLD   AT   PSI COLD

THIS VEHICLE CONFORMS TO ALL APPLICABLE FEDERAL MOTOR VEHICLE SAFETY
STANDARDS IN EFFECT ON THE DATE OF MANUFACTURE SHOWN ABOVE.
VEHICLE IDENTIFICATION NO.

TYPE   14 9U

23
DSO

EXTERIOR PAINT COLORS

WB	TYPE GVW	BODY	TRANS	AXLE	TAPE	SPRING
119	A143	DB2	5	A2	35	3GG

3   G   G

Aux./Opt. Usage Code (Front)
Front Spring Code
Rear Spring Code

AUX./OPT. USAGE CODE (FRONT)

Code	Description
3	Heavy Duty Suspension

FRONT SPRING CODE

Code	Part Number
G	E59A-5310-GB
H	E59A-5310-HB
J	E59A-5310-JB
K	E59A-5310-KB
L	E59A-5310-LB

REAR SPRING CODE

Code	Part Number
G	E59A-5534-GB
H	E59A-5534-HB
J	E59A-5534-JB
K	E59A-5534-KB
L	E59A-5534-LA

5. Locate the fuel filter which is mounted on the underbody, forward of the right rear wheel well, on the same bracket as the electric fuel pump.

6. Clean all dirt and/or grease from the fuel filter fittings. "Quick Connect" fittings are used on all models equipped with a pressurized fuel system. These fittings must be disconnected using the proper procedure or the fittings may be damaged. The fuel filter uses a "hairpin" clip retainer.

7. Spread the two hairpin clip legs about ⅛" (3mm) each to disengage it from the fitting, then pull the clip outward. Use finger pressure

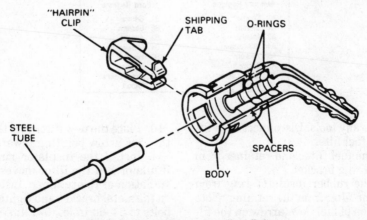

"HAIRPIN" CLIP   SHIPPING TAB   O-RINGS

STEEL TUBE

SPACERS

BODY

Typical 5/16 in. quick connect fuel fitting

District Sales Office (DSO Code and Wheelbase (WB) Codes

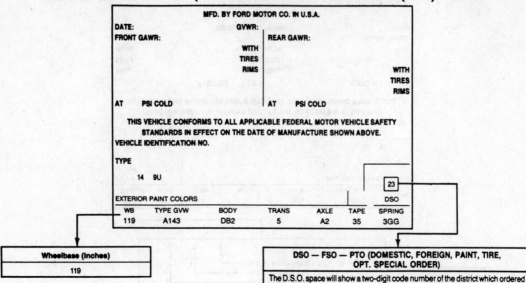

Code	District		Code	District
11	Boston		52	Dallas
12	Buffalo		53	Kansas City
14	Pittsburgh		54	Omaha
15	New York		55	St. Louis
16	Philadelphia		57	Houston
17	Washington		58	Twin Cities
21	Atlanta		71	Los Angeles
22	Charlotte		72	San Jose
23	Memphis		73	Salt Lake City
24	Jacksonville		74	Seattle
25	Richmond		75	Phoenix
26	New Orleans		76	Denver
28	Louisville			
			83	Government
41	Chicago		84	Home Office Reserve
42	Cleveland		85	American Red Cross
43	Milwaukee		86	Recreation Vehicles
46	Indianapolis		87	Body Company
47	Cincinnati		89	Transportation Services
48	Detroit		90's	Export
			00	Special

Ford Of Canada

Mercury Regions		Ford Regions	
A1	Central	B1	Central
A2	Eastern	B2	Eastern
A3	Atlantic	B3	Atlantic
A4	Midwestern	B4	Midwestern
A6	Western	B6	Western
A7	Pacific	B7	Pacific
A8	Great Lakes	B8	Great Lakes
I1	Export	I1	Export

only; do not use any tools. Disconnect both fittings from the fuel filter.

8. Remove the fuel filter and retainer from the metal mounting bracket.

9. Remove the rubber insulator ring from the filter and the filter from the retainer. Note that the direction of fuel flow (arrow on the filter) points to the open end of the retainer.

10. Place the new filter into the retainer with the flow arrow pointing toward the open end.

11. Install the insulator ring. Replace the insulator(s) if the filter moves freely after installation of the retainer. Install the retainer on the metal bracket and tighten the mounting bolts to 51–60 in.lb. (5–7Nm).

12. Push the quick connect fittings onto the

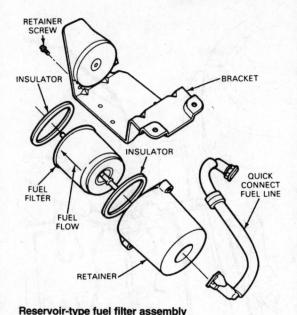

Reservoir-type fuel filter assembly

PCV Valve

All models use a closed crankcase ventilation system with a sealed breather cap connected to the air cleaner by a rubber hose. The PCV valve is usually mounted in the valve cover and connected to the intake manifold by a rubber hose. The system is used to regulate the amount of crankcase (blow-by) gases which are recycled into the combustion chambers for burning with the normal fuel charge.

The only maintenance required on the PCV system is to replace the PCV valve and/or air filter element in the air cleaner at the intervals specified in the maintenance chart. Replacement involves removing the valve from the grommet in the valve cover and installing a new valve. No attempt should be made to clean an old PCV valve; it should be replaced.

Evaporative Emissions Canister

The canister functions to cycle the fuel vapor from the fuel tank and carburetor float chamber into the intake manifold and eventually into the cylinders for combustion with the normal fuel charge. The activated charcoal within the canister acts as a storage device for the fuel vapor at times when the engine is not operating or when the engine operating condition will not permit fuel vapor to burn efficiently.

The only required service for for the evaporative canister is inspection at the interval

filter ends. Ford recommends that the retaining clips be replaced whenever removed. A click will be heard when the hairpin clip snaps into its proper position. Pull on the lines to insure proper connection.

13. Start the engine and check for fuel leaks.
14. Lower the vehicle.

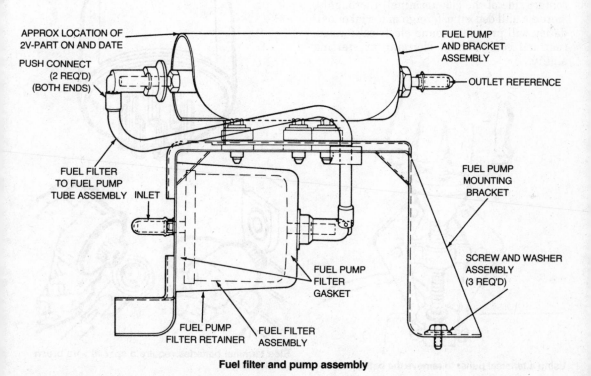

Fuel filter and pump assembly

specified in the maintenance chart. If the charcoal element is saturated with fuel, the entire canister should be replaced. Disconnect the canister purge hose(s), loosen the canister retaining bracket and lift out the canister. Installation is the reverse of removal.

Battery

All Aerostars use a maintenance free battery as standard equipment, eliminating the need for periodic fluid level checks and the possibility of specific gravity tests. Nevertheless, the battery does require some attention. An indicator is built into the top of the maintenance free battery to show the condition and state of charge. If the indicator is dark, the battery can be assumed to be OK. If the indicator is light, the specific gravity is low and the battery should either be recharged or replaced.

NOTE: *Never disconnect the battery with the ignition ON or the engine running or serious on-board computer damage could occur.*

Once a year, the battery terminals and cable clamps should be cleaned. Loosen the terminal mounting bolt (if equipped) and remove the cable and clamp with a suitable terminal removal tool. Clean the cable clamps and terminal posts with a suitable wire brush until all corrosion is removed and the clamps and posts are shiny. Special wire brush terminal cleaning tools are available from aftermarket sources to make this job quick and easy. It is especially important to clean the inside of the clamp (or contact side of the side terminal) thoroughly, since a small deposit of foreign material or oxidation will prevent a sound electrical connection and could inhibit charging or starting ability.

Clean battery cable clamps with a wire brush

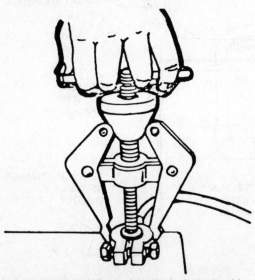

Using a terminal puller to remove the battery cable

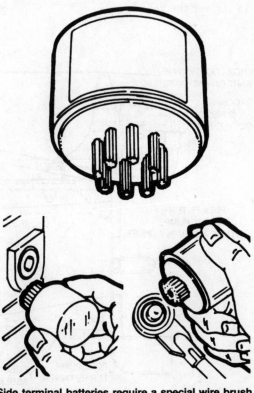

Side terminal batteries require a special wire brush for cleaning

Before installing the cables, loosen the battery holddown clamp, lift out the battery and check the battery tray. Clear any debris such as leaves or dirt and check the tray for soundness. Rust and corrosion should be wire brushed away and the metal coated with anti-rust paint. Reinstall the battery and tighten the holddown clamp securely, but be careful not to overtighten and crack the battery case.

After the clamps and terminals are clean, install the terminals (positive cable first), then apply a thin external coat of grease to retard corrosion. Check the cables while cleaning the clamps, looking for frayed or broken insulation. If the cable has frayed ends or excessive corrosion is present, the cable should be replaced with a new cable of the same length and gauge.

CAUTION: *Keep flame or sparks away from the battery as it gives off explosive hydrogen gas. Battery electrolyte contains sulfuric acid. If you should get any on your skin or in your eyes, flush the affected area with plenty of clear water immediately. In the case of eye contact, seek medical help immediately. It's also a good idea to wear some sort of filter when wire brushing excessive corrosion to avoid inhaling dust particles.*

Belts
INSPECTION

The belts which drive the engine accessories such as the alternator or generator, the air pump, power steering pump, air conditioning compressor and water pump are of either the V-belt design or flat, serpentine design. Older belts show wear and damage readily, since their basic design was a belt with a rubber casing. As the casing wore, cracks and fibers were readily apparent. Newer design, caseless belts do not show wear as readily, and many untrained people cannot distinguish between a good, serviceable belt and one that is worn to the point of failure. It is a good idea, therefore, to visually inspect the belts regularly and replace them, routinely, every two to three years.

ADJUSTING

Belts are normally adjusted by loosening the bolts of the accessory being driven and moving that accessory on its pivot points until the proper tension is applied to the belt. The accessory is held in this position while the bolts are tightened. To determine proper belt tension, you can purchase a belt tension gauge or simply use the deflection method. To determine deflection, press inward on the belt at the midpoint of its longest straight run. The belt

should deflect (move inward) 3/8–1/2" (10–13mm). Some long V-belts and most serpentine belts have idler pulleys which are used for adjusting purposes. Just loosen the idler pulley and move it to take up tension on the belt.

REMOVAL AND INSTALLATION

To remove a drive belt, simply loosen the accessory being driven and move it on its pivot point to free the belt. Then, remove the belt. If an idler pulley is used, it is often necessary, only, to loosen the idler pulley to provide enough slack the remove the belt.

It is important to note, however, that on engines with many driven accessories, several or all of the belts may have to be removed to get at the one to be replaced.

Hoses
REMOVAL AND INSTALLATION

Radiator hoses are generally of two constructions, the preformed (molded) type, which is custom made for a particular application, and the spring loaded type, which is made to fit several different applications. Heater hoses are all of the same general construction.

Hoses are retained by clamps. To replace a hose, loosen the clamp and slide it down the hose, away from the attaching point. Twist the hose from side to side until it is free, then pull it off. Before installing the new hose, make sure that the outlet fitting is as clean as possible. Coat the fitting with non-hardening sealer and slip the hose into place. Install the clamp and tighten it.

Air Conditioning System

NOTE: *This book contains simple testing and charging procedures for your car's air conditioning system. More comprehensive testing, diagnosis and service procedures may be found in CHILTON'S GUIDE TO AIR CONDITIONING SERVICE AND REPAIR, book part number 7580, available at your local retailer.*

PRECAUTIONS

There are two particular hazards associated with air conditioning systems and they both relate to the refrigerant gas. First, the refrigerant gas is an extremely cold substance. When exposed to the air it will instantly freeze any surface it comes in contact with, including skin and eyes. Always wear safety goggles when performing any service on the air conditioning system. The other hazard relates to fire. Although normally non-toxic, R-12 or Freon refrigerant gas becomes highly poisonous in

HOW TO SPOT WORN V-BELTS

V-Belts are vital to efficient engine operation—they drive the fan, water pump and other accessories. They require little maintenance (occasional tightening) but they will not last forever. Slipping or failure of the V-belt will lead to overheating. If your V-belt looks like any of these, it should be replaced.

Cracking or weathering

This belt has deep cracks, which cause it to flex. Too much flexing leads to heat build-up and premature failure. These cracks can be caused by using the belt on a pulley that is too small. Notched belts are available for small diameter pulleys.

Softening (grease and oil)

Oil and grease on a belt can cause the belt's rubber compounds to soften and separate from the reinforcing cords that hold the belt together. The belt will first slip, then finally fail altogether.

Glazing

Glazing is caused by a belt that is slipping. A slipping belt can cause a run-down battery, erratic power steering, overheating or poor accessory performance. The more the belt slips, the more glazing will be built up on the surface of the belt. The more the belt is glazed, the more it will slip. If the glazing is light, tighten the belt.

Worn cover

The cover of this belt is worn off and is peeling away. The reinforcing cords will begin to wear and the belt will shortly break. When the belt cover wears in spots or has a rough jagged appearance, check the pulley grooves for roughness.

Separation

This belt is on the verge of breaking and leaving you stranded. The layers of the belt are separating and the reinforcing cords are exposed. It's just a matter of time before it breaks completely.

HOW TO SPOT BAD HOSES

Both the upper and lower radiator hoses are called upon to perform difficult jobs in an inhospitable environment. They are subject to nearly 18 psi at under hood temperatures often over 280°F., and must circulate nearly 7500 gallons of coolant an hour—3 good reasons to have good hoses.

A good test for any hose is to feel it for soft or spongy spots. Frequently these will appear as swollen areas of the hose. The most likely cause is oil soaking. This hose could burst at any time, when hot or under pressure.

Swollen hose

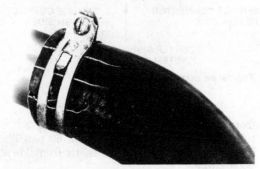

Cracked hoses can usually be seen but feel the hoses to be sure they have not hardened; a prime cause of cracking. This hose has cracked down to the reinforcing cords and could split at any of the cracks.

Cracked hose

Weakened clamps frequently are the cause of hose and cooling system failure. The connection between the pipe and hose has deteriorated enough to allow coolant to escape when the engine is hot.

Frayed hose end (due to weak clamp)

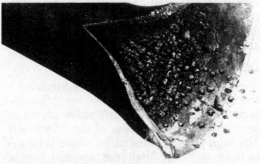

Debris, rust and scale in the cooling system can cause the inside of a hose to weaken. This can usually be felt on the outside of the hose as soft or thinner areas.

Debris in cooling system

the presence of an open flame. One good whiff of the vapor formed by burning refrigerant can be fatal. Keep all forms of fire (including cigarettes) well clear of the air conditioning system.

SYSTEM INSPECTION

Refrigerant leaks show up as oily areas on the various components because the compressor oil is transported around the entire system along with the refrigerant. Look for oily spots on all the hoses and lines, especially on the hose and tubing connections. If there are oily deposits visible, the system may have a leak. The oily residue soon picks up dust or dirt particles from the surrounding air and appears greasy, eventually building up into a heavy, dirt impregnated grease.

NOTE: *A small area of oil on the front of the compressor is normal and no cause for alarm.*

Another type of leak may appear at the internal Schraeder type A/C charging valve core in the service access gauge port valve fittings. If tightening the valve core does not stop the leak, it should be replaced. Missing service access gauge port valve caps can also cause a refrigerant leak by allowing dirt to contaminate the valve during charging.

Periodically inspect the front of the condenser for bent fins or foreign material (dirt, bugs, leaves, etc.), and clean the condenser thoroughly. Straighten any bent fins carefully with needlenosed pliers. Debris may be removed with a stiff bristle brush or water pressure from a garden hose.

A lot of air conditioner problems can be avoided by simply running the system at least once a week, regardless of the season. Let the A/C run for at least five minutes (even in the winter) and you'll keep the internal parts lubricated and prevent the hoses from hardening.

REFRIGERANT LEVEL CHECK

The only way to check the refrigerant level on the Aerostar is to measure the system evaporator pressures with a manifold gauge set, although rapid on/off cycling of the compressor clutch indicates that the A/C system is low on refrigerant. The normal refrigerant capacity is 3½ lbs.

TEST GAUGES

Most of the service work performed in air conditioning requires the use of a set of two gauges, one for the high (head) pressure side of the system, the other for the low (suction) side.

The low side gauge records both pressure and vacuum. Vacuum readings are calibrated

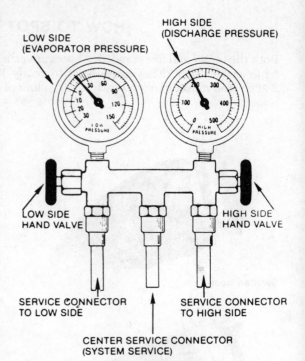

Typical air conditioning gauge set

from 0 to 30 inches and the pressure graduations read from 0 to no less than 60 psi. The high side gauge measures pressure from 0 to at least 600 psi.

Both gauges are threaded into a manifold that contains two hand shut-off valves. Proper manipulation of these valves and the use of the attached test hoses allow the user to perform the following services:

1. Test high and low side pressures.
2. Remove air, moisture, and contaminated refrigerant.
3. Purge the system (of refrigerant).
4. Charge the system (with refrigerant).

The manifold valves are designed so that they have no direct effect on gauge readings, but serve only to provide for, or cut off, flow of refrigerant through the manifold. During all testing and hook-up operations, the valves are kept in a close position to avoid disturbing the refrigeration system. The valves are opened only to purge the system or refrigerant or to charge it.

DISCHARGING THE SYSTEM

Service access gauge port valves are used in the refrigerant system. These are Schraeder type valves, similar to a tire valve with a depressing pin in the center of the valve body. The high pressure (discharge) valve is located in the compressor discharge manifold, just before the accumulator/drier. This valve requires

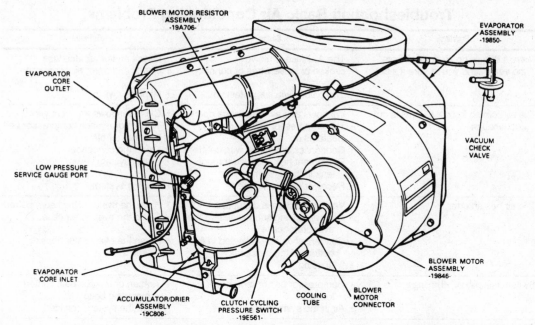

Evaporator case assembly. Note the location of the low pressure service gauge port

an adapter (YT-354 or 355) to connect a manifold gauge set to it. The other service access port valve is located on the side of the accumulator and is the low pressure (suction) connection. It is extremely important that these two valves not be confused, since connecting a can of Freon to the high pressure side of the A/C system will cause the can to explode.

To connect a manifold gauge set to the service gauge port valves, proceed as follows:

1. Turn both manifold gauge set valves fully clockwise to close the high and low pressure hoses.

2. Remove the caps from the high and low pressure service gauge port valves.

3. If the manifold gauge set hoses do not have the valve depressing pins in them, install fitting adapters (T71P-19703-S and R) containing the pins on the manifold gauge hoses. Remember that an adapter is necessary to connect the manifold gauge hose to the high pressure fitting.

4. Connect the high and low pressure refrigerant hoses to their respective service ports, making sure they are hooked up correctly and fully seated. Tighten the fittings by hand and make sure they are not cross-threaded.

5. Place the open end of the center hose on the manifold gauge set away from your body, then slowly open the LOW pressure valve on the manifold set a slight amount to allow the refrigerant to flow out the center hose and slowly depressurize the A/C system.

6. After the system is nearly discharged,

open the high pressure valve very slowly to avoid losing any refrigerant oil and allow any remaining Freon in the compressor and high pressure line to discharge.

CAUTION: *Do not attempt this procedure in a closed garage. The refrigerant will displace the oxygen in the air and could result in suffocation in a very short time. Allowing the refrigerant to vent quickly will carry away the refrigerant oil; open the valves slowly and only slightly. Remember that escaping refrigerant will freeze any surface it touches, including skin and eyes. Wear safety glasses at all times.*

CHARGING THE SYSTEM

If the system has been completely purged of refrigerant, it must be evacuated before charging. A vacuum pump should be connected to the center hose of the manifold gauge set, both valves should be opened, and the vacuum pump operated until the low pressure gauge reads as close to 30 in.Hg as possible. If a part in the system has been replaced or excessive moisture is suspected, continue the vacuum pump operation for about 30 minutes.

Close the manifold gauge valves to the center hose, then disconnect the vacuum pump and connect the center hose to a charging cylinder, refrigerant drum or a small can refrigerant dispensing valve. Disconnect the wire harness from the clutch cycling pressure switch and install a jumper wire across the two terminals of the connector. Open the manifold gauge

Troubleshooting Basic Air Conditioning Problems

Problem	Cause	Solution
There's little or no air coming from the vents (and you're sure it's on)	• The A/C fuse is blown • Broken or loose wires or connections • The on/off switch is defective	• Check and/or replace fuse • Check and/or repair connections • Replace switch
The air coming from the vents is not cool enough	• Windows and air vent wings open • The compressor belt is slipping • Heater is on • Condenser is clogged with debris • Refrigerant has escaped through a leak in the system • Receiver/drier is plugged	• Close windows and vent wings • Tighten or replace compressor belt • Shut heater off • Clean the condenser • Check system • Service system
The air has an odor	• Vacuum system is disrupted • Odor producing substances on the evaporator case • Condensation has collected in the bottom of the evaporator housing	• Have the system checked/repaired • Clean the evaporator case • Clean the evaporator housing drains
System is noisy or vibrating	• Compressor belt or mountings loose • Air in the system	• Tighten or replace belt; tighten mounting bolts • Have the system serviced

Sight glass condition
    Constant bubbles, foam or oil streaks
    Clear sight glass, but no cold air
    Clear sight glass, but air is cold
    Clouded with milky fluid
	
	• Undercharged system
	
	• No refrigerant at all
	• System is OK
	• Receiver drier is leaking dessicant
		
		• Charge the system
		
		• Check and charge the system
		
		• Have system checked

Large difference in temperature of lines	• System undercharged	• Charge and leak test the system
Compressor noise	• Broken valves • Overcharged • Incorrect oil level • Piston slap • Broken rings • Drive belt pulley bolts are loose	• Replace the valve plate • Discharge, evacuate and install the correct charge • Isolate the compressor and check the oil level. Correct as necessary. • Replace the compressor • Replace the compressor • Tighten with the correct torque specification
Excessive vibration	• Incorrect belt tension • Clutch loose • Overcharged • Pulley is misaligned	• Adjust the belt tension • Tighten the clutch • Discharge, evacuate and install the correct charge • Align the pulley
Condensation dripping in the passenger compartment	• Drain hose plugged or improperly positioned • Insulation removed or improperly installed	• Clean the drain hose and check for proper installation • Replace the insulation on the expansion valve and hoses
Frozen evaporator coil	• Faulty thermostat • Thermostat capillary tube improperly installed • Thermostat not adjusted properly	• Replace the thermostat • Install the capillary tube correctly • Adjust the thermostat
Low side low—high side low	• System refrigerant is low • Expansion valve is restricted	• Evacuate, leak test and charge the system • Replace the expansion valve
Low side high—high side low	• Internal leak in the compressor—worn	• Remove the compressor cylinder head and inspect the compressor. Replace the valve plate assembly if necessary. If the compressor pistons, rings or

Troubleshooting Basic Air Conditioning Problems (cont.)

Problem	Cause	Solution
Low side high—high side low (cont.)		cylinders are excessively worn or scored replace the compressor
	· Cylinder head gasket is leaking	· Install a replacement cylinder head gasket
	· Expansion valve is defective	· Replace the expansion valve
	·· Drive belt slipping	· Adjust the belt tension
Low side high—high side high	· Condenser fins obstructed	· Clean the condenser fins
	· Air in the system	· Evacuate, leak test and charge the system
	· Expansion valve is defective	· Replace the expansion valve
	· Loose or worn fan belts	· Adjust or replace the belts as necessary
Low side low—high side high	· Expansion valve is defective	· Replace the expansion valve
	· Restriction in the refrigerant hose	· Check the hose for kinks—replace if necessary
	· Restriction in the receiver/drier	· Replace the receiver/drier
	· Restriction in the condenser	· Replace the condenser
Low side and high side normal (inadequate cooling)	· Air in the system	· Evacuate, leak test and charge the system
	· Moisture in the system	· Evacuate, leak test and charge the system

LOW side valve to allow refrigerant to enter the system, keeping the can(s) in an upright position to prevent liquid from entering the system.

When no more refrigerant is being drawn into the system, start the engine and move the function selector lever to the NORM A/C position and the blower switch to HI to draw the remaining refrigerant in. Continue to add refrigerant until the specified 3½ lbs. is reached. Close the manifold gauge low pressure valve and the refrigerant supply valve. Remove the jumper wire from the clutch cycling pressure switch connector and reconnect the pressure switch. Disconnect the manifold gauge set and install the service port caps.

Charging From Small Containers

When using a single can A/C charging kit, such as is available at local retailers, make the connection at the low pressure service port, located on the accumulator/drier. This is very important as connecting the small can to the high pressure port will cause the can to explode. Once the can is connected, charge the system as described above. If a manifold gauge set is being used, the low pressure valve must be closed whenever another can is being connected to the center hose. Hold the cans upright to prevent liquid refrigerant from entering the system and possibly damaging the compressor.

Windshield Wipers

For maximum effectiveness and longest element life, the windshield and wiper blades should be kept clean. Dirt, tree sap, road tar and so on will cause streaking, smearing and blade deterioration if left on the windshield. It is advisable to wash the windshield carefully with a commercial glass cleaner at least once a month. Wipe off the rubber blades with a wet rag afterwards. Do not attempt to move the wipers back and forth by hand; damage to the motor and drive mechanism will result.

If the blades are found to be cracked, broken or torn they should be replaced immediately. Replacement intervals will vary with usage, although ozone deterioration usually limits blade lift to about one year. If the wiper pattern is smeared or streaked, or if the blade chatters across the glass, the blades should be replaced. It is easiest and most sensible to replace them in pairs.

There are basically three different types of wiper blade refills, which differ in their method of replacement. One type has two release buttons, approximately ⅓ of the way up from the ends of the blade frame. Pushing the buttons down releases a lock and allows the rubber blade to be removed from the frame. The new blade slides back into the frame and locks in place.

The second type of refill has two metal tabs which are unlocked by squeezing them togeth-

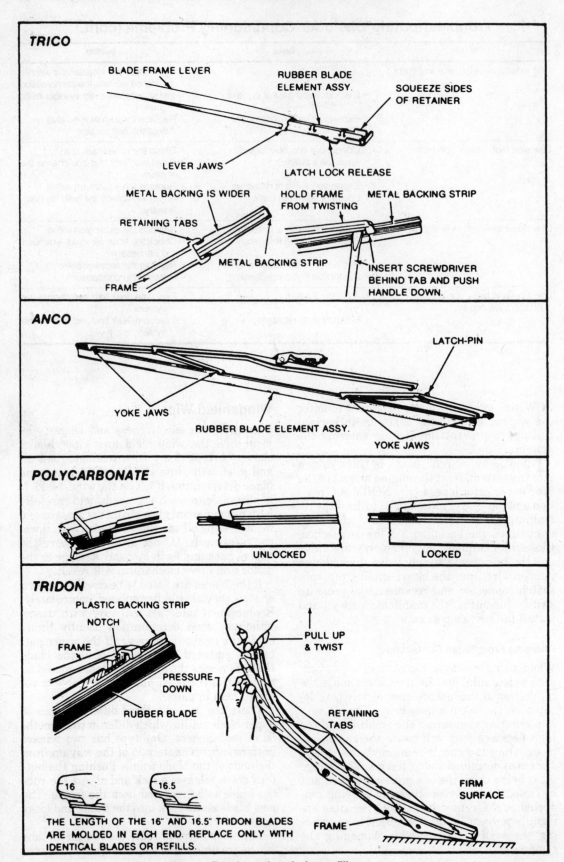

TRICO

BLADE FRAME LEVER

RUBBER BLADE ELEMENT ASSY.

SQUEEZE SIDES OF RETAINER

LEVER JAWS

LATCH LOCK RELEASE

METAL BACKING IS WIDER

HOLD FRAME FROM TWISTING

METAL BACKING STRIP

RETAINING TABS

METAL BACKING STRIP

FRAME

INSERT SCREWDRIVER BEHIND TAB AND PUSH HANDLE DOWN.

ANCO

LATCH-PIN

YOKE JAWS

RUBBER BLADE ELEMENT ASSY.

YOKE JAWS

POLYCARBONATE

UNLOCKED

LOCKED

TRIDON

PLASTIC BACKING STRIP

NOTCH

FRAME

PULL UP & TWIST

PRESSURE DOWN

RUBBER BLADE

RETAINING TABS

16   16.5

THE LENGTH OF THE 16" AND 16.5" TRIDON BLADES ARE MOLDED IN EACH END. REPLACE ONLY WITH IDENTICAL BLADES OR REFILLS.

FIRM SURFACE

FRAME

Popular styles of wiper refills

er. The rubber blade can then be withdrawn from the frame jaws. A new one is installed by inserting it into the front frame jaws and sliding it rearward to engage the remaining frame jaws. There are usually four jaws; be certain when installing that the refill is engaged in all of them. At the end of its travel, the tabs will lock into place on the front jaws of the wiper blade frame.

The third type is a refill made from polycarbonate. The refill has a simple locking device at one end which flexes downward out of the groove into which the jaws of the holder fit, allowing easy release. By sliding the new refill through all the jaws and pushing through the slight resistance when it reaches the end of its travel, the refill will lock into position.

Regardless of the type of refill used, make sure that all of the frame jaws are engaged as the refill is pushed into place and locked. The metal blade holder and frame will scratch the glass if allowed to touch it.

Tires and Wheels

Inspect the tire treads for cuts, bruises and other damage. Check the air valves to be sure that they are tight. Replace any missing valve caps. The tires should be checked frequently for proper air pressure. A chart in the glove compartment or on the driver's door pillar gives the recommended inflation pressure. Pressures can increase as much as 6 psi due to heat buildup. It is a good idea to have your own accurate gauge, and to check pressures weekly. Not all gauges on service station air pumps can be trusted.

Inspect tires for uneven wear that might indicate the need for front end alignment or tire rotation. Tires should be replaced when a tread wear indicator appears as a solid band across the tread. When buying new tires, give some thought to the following points, especially if you are switching to larger tires or a different profile series (50, 60, 70, 78):

1. All four tires should be of the same construction type. Radial, bias, or bias/belted tires should not be mixed.

2. The wheels must be the correct width for the tire. Tire dealers have charts of tire and rim compatibility. A mismatch can cause sloppy handling and rapid tire wear. The tread width should match the rim width (inside bead to inside bead) within an inch. For radial tires, the rim width should be 80% or less of the tire (not tread) width.

3. The height (mounted diameter) of the new tires can greatly change speedometer accuracy, engine speed at a given road speed, fuel mileage, acceleration, and ground clearance. Tire manufacturers furnish full measurement specifications.

NOTE: *Dimensions of tires marked the same size may vary significantly, even among tires from the same manufacturer.*

4. The spare tire should be usable, at least for low speed operation, with the new tires.

Troubleshooting Basic Wheel Problems

Problem	Cause	Solution
The car's front end vibrates at high speed	• The wheels are out of balance • Wheels are out of alignment	• Have wheels balanced • Have wheel alignment checked/adjusted
Car pulls to either side	• Wheels are out of alignment • Unequal tire pressure • Different size tires or wheels	• Have wheel alignment checked/adjusted • Check/adjust tire pressure • Change tires or wheels to same size
The car's wheel(s) wobbles	• Loose wheel lug nuts • Wheels out of balance • Damaged wheel • Wheels are out of alignment • Worn or damaged ball joint • Excessive play in the steering linkage (usually due to worn parts) • Defective shock absorber	• Tighten wheel lug nuts • Have tires balanced • Raise car and spin the wheel. If the wheel is bent, it should be replaced • Have wheel alignment checked/adjusted • Check ball joints • Check steering linkage • Check shock absorbers
Tires wear unevenly or prematurely	• Incorrect wheel size • Wheels are out of balance • Wheels are out of alignment	• Check if wheel and tire size are compatible • Have wheels balanced • Have wheel alignment checked/adjusted

Troubleshooting Basic Tire Problems

Problem	Cause	Solution
The car's front end vibrates at high speeds and the steering wheel shakes	• Wheels out of balance • Front end needs aligning	• Have wheels balanced • Have front end alignment checked
The car pulls to one side while cruising	• Unequal tire pressure (car will usually pull to the low side) • Mismatched tires • Front end needs aligning	• Check/adjust tire pressure • Be sure tires are of the same type and size • Have front end alignment checked
Abnormal, excessive or uneven tire wear See "How to Read Tire Wear"	• Infrequent tire rotation • Improper tire pressure • Sudden stops/starts or high speed on curves	• Rotate tires more frequently to equalize wear • Check/adjust pressure • Correct driving habits
Tire squeals	• Improper tire pressure • Front end needs aligning	• Check/adjust tire pressure • Have front end alignment checked

Tire Size Comparison Chart

"Letter" sizes			Inch Sizes	Metric-inch Sizes		
"60 Series"	"70 Series"	"78 Series"	1965–77	"60 Series"	"70 Series"	"80 Series"
			5.50-12, 5.60-12	165/60-12	165/70-12	155-12
		Y78-12	6.00-12			
		W78-13	5.20-13	165/60-13	145/70-13	135-13
		Y78-13	5.60-13	175/60-13	155/70-13	145-13
			6.15-13	185/60-13	165/70-13	155-13, P155/80-13
A60-13	A70-13	A78-13	6.40-13	195/60-13	175/70-13	165-13
B60-13	B70-13	B78-13	6.70-13	205/60-13	185/70-13	175-13
			6.90-13			
C60-13	C70-13	C78-13	7.00-13	215/60-13	195/70-13	185-13
D60-13	D70-13	D78-13	7.25-13			
E60-13	E70-13	E78-13	7.75-13			195-13
			5.20-14	165/60-14	145/70-14	135-14
			5.60-14	175/60-14	155/70-14	145-14
			5.90-14			
A60-14	A70-14	A78-14	6.15-14	185/60-14	165/70-14	155-14
	B70-14	B78-14	6.45-14	195/60-14	175/70-14	165-14
	C70-14	C78-14	6.95-14	205/60-14	185/70-14	175-14
D60-14	D70-14	D78-14				
E60-14	E70-14	E78-14	7.35-14	215/60-14	195/70-14	185-14
F60-14	F70-14	F78-14, F83-14	7.75-14	225/60-14	200/70-14	195-14
G60-14	G70-14	G77-14, G78-14	8.25-14	235/60-14	205/70-14	205-14
H60-14	H70-14	H78-14	8.55-14	245/60-14	215/70-14	215-14
J60-14	J70-14	J78-14	8.85-14	255/60-14	225/70-14	225-14
L60-14	L70-14		9.15-14	265/60-14	235/70-14	
	A70-15	A78-15	5.60-15	185/60-15	165/70-15	155-15
B60-15	B70-15	B78-15	6.35-15	195/60-15	175/70-15	165-15
C60-15	C70-15	C78-15	6.85-15	205/60-15	185/70-15	175-15
	D70-15	D78-15				
E60-15	E70-15	E78-15	7.35-15	215/60-15	195/70-15	185-15
F60-15	F70-15	F78-15	7.75-15	225/60-15	205/70-15	195-15
G60-15	G70-15	G78-15	8.15-15/8.25-15	235/60-15	215/70-15	205-15
H60-15	H70-15	H78-15	8.45-15/8.55-15	245/60-15	225/70-15	215-15
J60-15	J70-15	J78-15	8.85-15/8.90-15	255/60-15	235/70-15	225-15
	K70-15		9.00-15	265/60-15	245/70-15	230-15
L60-15	L70-15	L78-15, L84-15	9.15-15			235-15
	M70-15	M78-15				255-15
		N78-15				

Note: Every size tire is not listed and many size comparisons are approximate, based on load ratings. Wider tires than those supplied new with the vehicle, should always be checked for clearance.

5. There shouldn't be any body interference when loaded, on bumps, or in turning.

TIRE ROTATION

Tire rotation is recommended every 6,000 miles or so, to obtain maximum tire wear. The pattern you use depends on whether or not you have a usable spare. Radial tires should not be cross-switched (from one side of the van to the other); they last longer if their direction of rotation is not changed. They will wear very rapidly if their direction of rotation is reversed.

NOTE: *Mark the wheel position or direction of rotation on radial tires or studded snow tires before removing them.*

CAUTION: *Avoid overtightening the lug nuts to prevent damage to the brake disc or drum. Alloy wheels can also be cracked by overtightening. Use of a torque wrench is highly recommended. Lug nuts should be tightened in sequence to 85–115 ft.lb.*

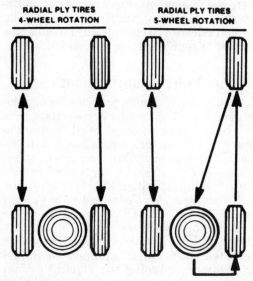

Tire rotation patterns

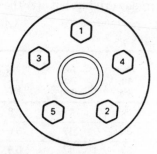

Lug nut tightening sequence

TEMPORARY SPARE TIRE

The temporary spare tire is lighter in weight and easier to handle than a conventional tire, but it is limited to emergency use only. The

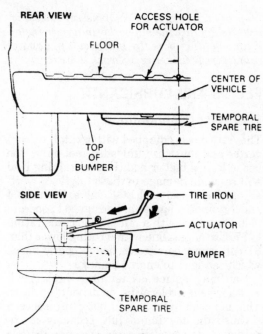

Lowering temporary spare tire

temporary spare tire pressure should be checked periodically and inflated to the pressure marked on the sidewall. When the temporary spare tire is in use, vehicle speed should be kept below 50 mph and the flat conventional tire should be repaired or replaced as soon as possible. The temporary spare is stored underneath the cargo bed in the rear of the vehicle. To remove the temporary spare from storage:

1. Insert the lugwrench into the actuator hole at the rear of the van and rotate it counterclockwise.

2. Slide the spare rearward and separate it from the retainer.

3. To stow the cable/retainer without the temporary spare, insert the cable fitting into the tire carrier rear wall slot. Position the wheel retainer against the carrier and rotate the lugwrench clockwise until all slack is removed. Do not overtighten.

4. To install the temporary spare tire into its holder, first insert the lugwrench into the actuator and rotate it counterclockwise while pulling on the cable until adequate cable is available.

5. Install the retainer through the wheel center with the valve stem facing downward and rearward to allow the tire pressure to be checked.

6. Rotate the lugwrench clockwise until the tire is secured; the raising mechanism will slip. Check for proper seating against the underbody brackets and retighten if necessary.

CAUTION: *Do not overtighten the retaining bolt with the lugwrench as damage to the* spare may occur by compressing the sidewalls against the supports. Improper installation of the spare tire may result in damage to the rear axle, tire or brake lines.

FLUIDS AND LUBRICANTS

Fuel Recommendations

The Aerostar is equipped with a catalytic converter and must use unleaded fuel only. The use of leaded fuel or additives containing lead will result in damage to the catalytic converter, oxygen sensor and EGR valve. Both the 4 and 6 cylinder engines are designed to operate using gasoline with a minimum octane rating of 87. Use of gasoline with a rating lower than 87 can cause persistent, heavy spark knock which can lead to engine damage.

You may notice occasional, light spark knock when accelerating or driving up hills. This is normal and should not cause concern because the maximum fuel economy is obtained under conditions of occasional light spark knock. Gasoline with an octane rating higher than 87 may be used, but it is not necessary for proper operation.

Gasohol, a mixture of gasoline and ethanol (grain alcohol) is available in some areas. Your Aerostar should operate satisfactorily on gasohol blends containing no more than 10% ethanol by volume and having an octane rating of 87 or higher. In some cases, methanol (wood alcohol) or other alcohols may be added to gasoline. Again, your Aerostar should operate satisfactorily on blends containing up to 5% methanol by volume when cosolvents and other necessary additives are used. If not properly formulated with appropriate cosolvents and corrosion inhibitors, such blends may cause driveability problems or damage emission and fuel system materials. If you are uncertain as to the presence of alcohols in the gasoline you are purchasing, check the label on the pump or ask the attendant.

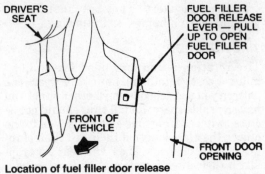

Location of fuel filler door release

NOTE: *Discontinue use of any gasohol or alcohol/gasoline blend if driveability or fuel system problems occur. Do not use such fuels unless they are unleaded.*

Some models are equipped with a remote fuel filler door release, located between the driver seat and the door. If the filler door cannot be opened by pulling the release lever, there is a manual override cord located on the left side of the jack stowage compartment. The manual release is a cord attached to a handle marked "Fuel Filler Door Manual Release."

Engine Oil Recommendations

To insure proper engine performance and durability, the proper quality engine oil is essential. Using the proper grade of oil for your engine will not only prolong its life, it will improve fuel economy. Ford recommends that you use Motorcraft® oil or an equivalent that meets Ford Specification ESE-M2C153-C and API (American Petroleum Institute) Categories SF, SF/CC or SF/CD.

Engine oils with improved fuel economy properties are currently available. They offer the potential for small improvements in fuel economy by reducing the amount of fuel burned by the engine to overcome friction. These improvements are often difficult to measure in everyday driving, but over the course of

Capacities Chart

Years	Engine cu. in. (liter)	Crankcase Includes Filter (qt)	Transmission (pts)		Drive Axle (pts)	Fuel Tank (gal)	Cooling System (qt)	
			5-spd	Auto			MT	AT
1986–87	140 (2.3)	5.0	3.6 ①	19	3.5	17	6.8	7.6
	171 (2.8)	5.0	3.6 ①	19	3.5	17	6.8	7.6
	182 (3.0)	4.5	3.6 ①	19	3.5	17	6.8	7.6

Note: Automatic transmission capacity includes torque converter. When changing pan contents, add 2 qts, run engine and check with dipstick at idle. Add fluid as necessary. Add ½ qt to crankcase if equipped with oil cooler.
MT Manual Transmission
AT Automatic Transmission
① Mitsubishi 5 spd—4.8 pts

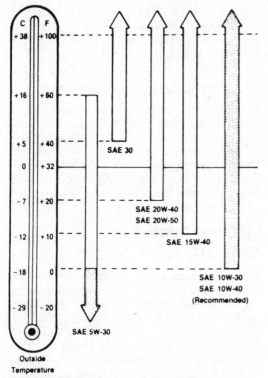

Oil viscosity recommendations for 2.3L and 2.8L engines

a year can offer significant savings. These oils are recommended to be used in conjunction with the recommended API Category.

A symbol has been developed by the API to help consumers select the proper grade of engine oil. It should be printed on top of the oil container to show oil performance by the API designation. This symbol should match the manufacturer recommendation. The center section will show the SAE (Society of Automotive Engineers) rating, while the top outer ring contains the API rating. The bottom outer ring will have the words "Energy Conserving" only if the oil has proven fuel saving capabilities.

CHECKING ENGINE OIL LEVEL

It is normal to add some oil between oil changes. The engine oil level should be checked every 500 miles.

1. Park the van on a level surface and turn the engine off. Open the hood.

2. Wait a few minutes to allow the oil to drain back into the crankcase.

3. While protecting yourself from engine heat, pull the dipstick out and wipe it clean with a suitable paper towel or clean rag.

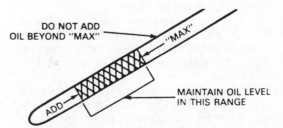

Reading the engine oil dipstick

4. Reinsert the dipstick and make sure it is pushed all the way down and seated on the tube, then remove the dipstick again and look at the oil level scale on the end of the dipstick. The oil level should fall within the safe range on the dipstick scale.

5. If necessary, add oil to the engine to bring the level up. Be careful not to overfill the crankcase and wipe the dipstick off before checking the oil level again.

OIL AND FILTER CHANGE

The engine oil and filter should be changed at the recommended intervals on the maintenance schedule chart. The oil filter protects the engine by removing harmful, abrasive or sludgy particles from the system without blocking the flow of oil to vital engine parts. It is recommended that the filter be changed along with the oil at the specified intervals.

NOTE: *Changing the oil requires the use of*

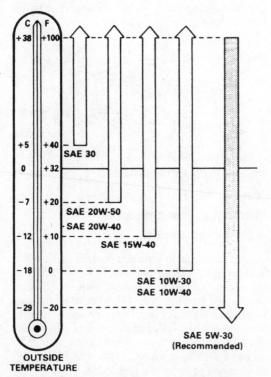

Oil viscosity recommendations for 3.0L engine

2.3L AND 2.8L ENGINES

3.0L ENGINE

Recommended oil viscosity for Aerostar

an oil filter wrench to remove the filter. It's also a good idea to have some oil dry (or kitty litter) handy to absorb any oil that misses the drain pan.

1. Start the engine and allow it to reach normal operating temperature. Park the truck on a level surface and shut the engine off.

2. Set the parking brake firmly and block the drive wheels.

3. Place a drip pan of at least 5 quart capacity beneath the oil pan.

4. Loosen the oil pan drain plug with a suitable wrench, then finish threading it out by hand while pressing in slightly until it is free. Be careful, the oil will be hot.

5. Allow the oil to drain completely before replacing the drain plug. Tighten the plug securely, but do not overtighten.

6. Position the drain pan under the oil filter, then use an oil filter band wrench to loosen the filter. Once the filter is loose, finish removing it by hand. Again, be careful, the oil and filter will be hot.

7. Clean the filter mounting base on the engine block and lightly coat the gasket of the new filter with a thin film of oil. Install the new filter by hand and tighten it another ½–¾ turn after the gasket contacts the filter base. Tighten the filter by hand, do not use the filter wrench.

8. Fill the crankcase with the recommended oil and start the engine to check for leaks. It is normal for the oil warning light to remain on for a few seconds after startup until the oil filter fills up. Once the oil light goes out, check for leaks from the filter mounting and drain plug. If no leaks are noticed, stop the engine and check the oil level on the dipstick. Top up if necessary.

Manual Transmission
FLUID LEVEL CHECK

The 5-speed manual transmission uses standard transmission lubricant, Ford part number D8DZ-19C547-A or equivalent. The fluid level is checked by removing the filler plug on the side of the transmission case. Clean the plug and remove it. The fluid should be up to the bottom of the filler plug hole.

If additional fluid is required, add it through the filler plug hole to bring the level up. Use only fluid meeting Ford specification ESP-M2C83-C. Install the filler plug when the fluid level is correct, making sure it is fully seated.

DRAINING MANUAL TRANSMISSION

The fluid can be drained from the manual transmission simply by removing the drain plug on the transmission bottom pan. Use a suitable container to catch the old fluid, then replace the plug and remove the filler plug on the side of the transmission to add new fluid. Add fluid until the level is at the base of the filler plug hole.

Hydraulic Clutch
FLUID LEVEL CHECK

The clutch system in the Aerostar does not have free play. It is automatically self-adjusting and should not require any routine service throughout the life of the vehicle. The fluid level in the clutch reservoir will slowly increase as the clutch wears. As long as the fluid is visible at or above the step in the translucent reservoir body, top-off is not recommended and should be avoided. This will help prevent overflow and possible contamination of the fluid while the diaphragm and cap are removed. If it becomes necessary to remove the reservoir cap, thoroughly clean the reservoir cap before removing it to prevent dirt or water from entering the reservoir.

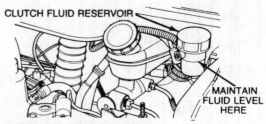

CLUTCH FLUID RESERVOIR

MAINTAIN FLUID LEVEL HERE

Checking hydraulic clutch fluid

Automatic Transmission
FLUID LEVEL CHECK

Correct automatic transmission fluid level is important for proper operation. Low fluid level causes transmission slippage, while overfilling can cause foaming, loss of fluid or malfunction. Since transmission fluid expands as temperature rises, it is advisable to check the fluid level at operating temperature (after about 20 miles of driving), however, the fluid level can be checked at room temperature.

To check the fluid level, park the vehicle on

a level surface and apply the parking brake. Start the engine and hold the foot brake while moving the transmission shift lever through all the gear positions, allowing sufficient time for each gear to engage. Return the shifter to the PARK position and leave the engine running.

Secure all loose clothing and remove any jewelry, then open the hood. While protecting

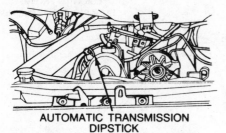

AUTOMATIC TRANSMISSION
DIPSTICK
Location of automatic transmission dipstick

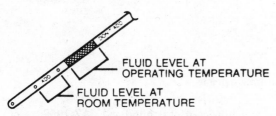

FLUID LEVEL AT
OPERATING TEMPERATURE

FLUID LEVEL AT
ROOM TEMPERATURE

Checking automatic transmission fluid level

yourself against engine heat, wipe the dipstick cap clean, then remove the dipstick. Wipe the dipstick clean then reinsert it into the tube, making sure it is fully seated. Remove the dipstick again and read the fluid level on the dipstick scale. At normal operating temperature, the level on the dipstick should be within the crosshatched area or between the arrows. At room temperature, the level should be between the middle and top hole on the dipstick.

If fluid has to be added, use a small necked funnel to add the necessary amount of Dexron®II through the dipstick tube to bring the level up to normal. Do not bring the level above the crosshatched area on the dipstick. If overfilled, the excess transmission fluid must be removed. Once the fluid level is correct, reinsert the dipstick and make sure it is fully seated.

PAN AND FILTER SCREEN SERVICE

Normal maintenance and lubrication requirements do not include periodic automatic transmission fluid changes. However, if the transmission is used under continuous or severe conditions, the transmission and torque converter should be drained and refilled with Dexron®II. The following procedure is for a partial draining of the transmission, in order to remove the pan to replace the pan gasket or clean the filter screen.

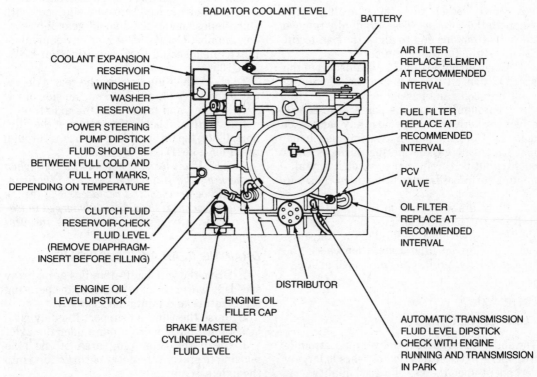

RADIATOR COOLANT LEVEL

BATTERY

COOLANT EXPANSION
RESERVOIR

WINDSHIELD
WASHER
RESERVOIR

POWER STEERING
PUMP DIPSTICK
FLUID SHOULD BE
BETWEEN FULL COLD AND
FULL HOT MARKS,
DEPENDING ON TEMPERATURE

CLUTCH FLUID
RESERVOIR-CHECK
FLUID LEVEL
(REMOVE DIAPHRAGM-
INSERT BEFORE FILLING)

ENGINE OIL
LEVEL DIPSTICK

BRAKE MASTER
CYLINDER-CHECK
FLUID LEVEL

ENGINE OIL
FILLER CAP

DISTRIBUTOR

AIR FILTER
REPLACE ELEMENT
AT RECOMMENDED
INTERVAL

FUEL FILTER
REPLACE AT
RECOMMENDED
INTERVAL

PCV
VALVE

OIL FILTER
REPLACE AT
RECOMMENDED
INTERVAL

AUTOMATIC TRANSMISSION
FLUID LEVEL DIPSTICK
CHECK WITH ENGINE
RUNNING AND TRANSMISSION
IN PARK

2.8L V6 lubrication points

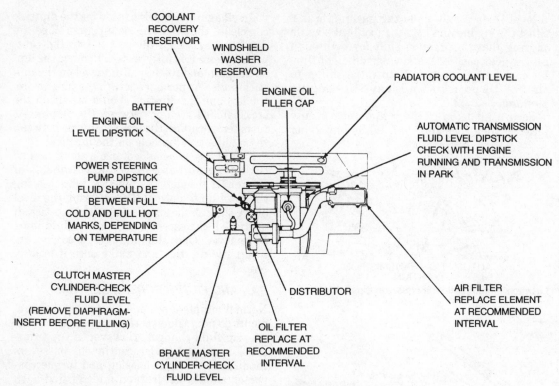

COOLANT RECOVERY RESERVOIR

WINDSHIELD WASHER RESERVOIR

ENGINE OIL FILLER CAP

RADIATOR COOLANT LEVEL

BATTERY

ENGINE OIL LEVEL DIPSTICK

AUTOMATIC TRANSMISSION FLUID LEVEL DIPSTICK CHECK WITH ENGINE RUNNING AND TRANSMISSION IN PARK

POWER STEERING PUMP DIPSTICK FLUID SHOULD BE BETWEEN FULL COLD AND FULL HOT MARKS, DEPENDING ON TEMPERATURE

CLUTCH MASTER CYLINDER-CHECK FLUID LEVEL (REMOVE DIAPHRAGM- INSERT BEFORE FILLLING)

DISTRIBUTOR

AIR FILTER REPLACE ELEMENT AT RECOMMENDED INTERVAL

OIL FILTER REPLACE AT RECOMMENDED INTERVAL

BRAKE MASTER CYLINDER-CHECK FLUID LEVEL

2.3L 4 cylinder lubrication points

1. Park the van on a level surface and place a drip pan under the transmission to catch the fluid.

2. Slowly loosen the pan attaching bolts. When all the bolts are loose, gradually remove the bolts from one end to allow the pan to tilt down and the fluid to drain out.

3. When all of the fluid has drained from the transmission oil pan, remove the remaining mounting bolts and lower the pan.

4. Thoroughly clean the pan and screen in solvent or kerosene and remove any old gasket material from the pan or transmission housing. Clean all gasket mating surfaces thoroughly, but be careful not to scratch any aluminum surfaces. Do not attempt to reuse an old pan gasket.

5. Place a new gasket on the pan, then install the pan on the transmission.

6. Add three quarts of fluid to the transmission through the filler tube, then check the transmission fluid level as described above.

Drive Axle

FLUID LEVEL CHECK

The ability of any axle to deliver quiet, trouble free operation over a period of years is largely dependent upon the use of a good quality gear lubricant. Ford recommends the use of hypoid

gear lubricant part number E0AZ-19580-A or any equivalent lubricant meeting Ford specification ESP-M2C154-A in their conventional or Traction-Lok® axles. Aerostars equipped with Dana axles should use hypoid gear lubricant part number C6AZ-19580-E or any equivalent lubricant meeting Ford specification ESW-M2C105-A.

To check the fluid level in the rear axle, remove the filler plug located on the side of the axle housing and make sure the axle fluid is within ¼" (6mm) below the bottom of the filler hole. If not, top up by adding lubricant through the filler hole. Do not overfill.

NOTE: *If any water is noted in the axle when checking the fluid level, the axle lubricant should be drained and replaced. Change the axle lubricant if the axle is submerged in water, especially if the water covers the vent hole.*

DRAINING REAR AXLE LUBRICANT

1. Drive the van for 10–15 miles at highway speeds to warm the axle lubricant to operating temperature and minimum viscosity.

2. Raise the van and support it safely with jackstands. Place a drain pan under the axle.

3. Clean the filler plug area of the axle housing to prevent the entry of rust or dirt into the axle assembly.

4. Remove the filler plug and use a suitable

suction type utility pump (manual or powered) to drain the axle lubricant by inserting the pump suction hose through the axle filler hole down into the lowest portion of the axle carrier housing. Make sure all the lubricant is removed.

5. Fill the axle housing with 3.5 pints of the specified hypoid gear lubricant (3.6 pints on Dana axles), then check the fluid level as described above. Top off if necessary, but do not overfill.

6. Install the filler plug and torque it to 15–30 ft.lb. (20–40 Nm).

Cooling System

The Aerostar is equipped with a coolant recovery system with a one piece, molded reservoir. Coolant in the system expands with heat and overflows into the coolant expansion reservoir. When the system cools down, coolant is drawn back into the radiator. Be careful not to confuse the windshield washer reservoir with the coolant recovery reservoir.

The coolant level should be checked in both the radiator and recovery reservoir at least once a month and then only when the engine is cool. Never, under any circumstances, attempt to check the coolant level in the radiator when the engine is hot or operating. On a full system, it is normal to have coolant in the expansion reservoir when the engine is hot.

Whenever coolant level checks of the radiator are made, check the condition of the radiator cap rubber seal. Make sure it is clean and free of any dirt particles. Rinse with water, if necessary, and make sure the radiator filler neck seat is clean. Check that the overflow hose is not kinked and is attached to the reservoir. If you have to add coolant more than once a month, or if you have to add more than one quart at a time, check the cooling system for leaks.

COOLANT CHECK AND CHANGE

CAUTION: *Never attempt to check the radiator coolant level while the engine is hot. Use extreme care when removing the radiator cap. Wrap a thick towel around the cap and turn it slowly to the first stop. Step back while the pressure is released from the cooling system. When all pressure has vented, press down on the cap (still wrapped in the towel) and remove it. Failure to follow this procedure may result in serious personal injury from hot coolant or steam blowout and/or damage to the cooling system.*

On systems with a coolant recovery tank, maintain the coolant level at the level marks on the recovery bottle. The coolant should be at

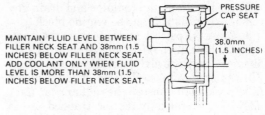

MAINTAIN FLUID LEVEL BETWEEN FILLER NECK SEAT AND 38mm (1.5 INCHES) BELOW FILLER NECK SEAT. ADD COOLANT ONLY WHEN FLUID LEVEL IS MORE THAN 38mm (1.5 INCHES) BELOW FILLER NECK SEAT.

PRESSURE CAP SEAT

38.0mm (1.5 INCHES)

Checking radiator coolant level

the base of the filler neck in the radiator. The Aerostar uses an aluminum radiator and requires coolant with corrosion inhibitors to prevent radiator damage. Use only a permanent type coolant that meets Ford specification ESE-M97B44-A. Do not use alcohol or methanol antifreeze.

For best protection against freezing and overheating, maintain an approximate 50% water and 50% ethylene glycol antifreeze mixture in the cooling system. Do not mix different brands of antifreeze to avoid possible chemical damage to the cooling system. Avoid using water that is known to have a high alkaline content or is very hard, except in emergency situations. Drain and flush the cooling system as soon as possible after using such water.

NOTE: *Never add cold water to an overheated engine while the engine is not running.*

After filling the radiator, run the engine until it reaches normal operating temperature, to make sure that the thermostat has opened and all the air is bled from the system.

DRAINING, FLUSHING AND REFILLING

To drain the cooling system, allow the engine to cool down **BEFORE ATTEMPTING TO REMOVE THE RADIATOR CAP**. Then turn the cap until it hisses. Wait until all pressure is off the cap before removing it completely. To avoid burns and scalding, always handle a warm radiator cap with a heavy rag.

CAUTION: *When draining the coolant, keep in mind that cats and dogs are attracted by the ethylene glycol antifreeze, and are quite likely to drink any that is left in an uncovered container or in puddles on the ground. This will prove fatal in sufficient quantity. Always drain the coolant into a sealable container. Coolant should be reused unless it is contaminated or several years old.*

1. At the dash, set the heater TEMP control lever to the fully HOT position.

2. With the radiator cap removed, drain the radiator by loosening the petcock at the bottom of the radiator. Flush the radiator with water until the fluid runs clear. Disconnect the lower

radiator hose from the radiator and drain any remaining coolant from the engine block.

3. Close the petcock and reconnect the lower radiator hose, then refill the system with a 50/50 mix of ethylene glycol antifreeze and water. Fill the system to the bottom of the radiator filler neck, then reinstall the radiator cap after allowing several minutes for trapped air to bubble out. Back the radiator cap off to the first stop (pressure relief position).

NOTE: *Fill the fluid reservoir tank up to the MAX COLD level.*

4. Operate the engine at 2,000 rpm for a few minutes with the heater control lever in the MAX HEAT position.

5. Turn the engine off, then wrap a rag around the radiator cap and remove it. Be careful, the coolant will be hot. Top off the radiator coolant level, if necessary, then reinstall the radiator cap to its down and locked position.

6. Start the engine and allow it to reach normal operating temperature, then check the system for leaks.

RADIATOR CAP INSPECTION

Allow the engine to cool sufficiently before attempting to remove the radiator cap. Use a rag to cover the cap, then remove by pressing down and turning counterclockwise to the first stop. If any hissing is noted (indicating the release of pressure), wait until the hissing stops completely, then press down again and turn counterclockwise until the cap can be removed.

CAUTION: *DO NOT attempt to remove the radiator cap while the engine is hot. Severe personal injury from steam burns can result.*
Check the condition of the radiator cap gasket and seal inside of the cap. The radiator cap is designed to seal the cooling system under normal operating conditions which allows the build up of a certain amount of pressure (this pressure rating is stamped or printed on the cap). The pressure in the system raises the

boiling point of the coolant to help prevent overheating. If the radiator cap does not seal, the boiling point of the coolant is lowered and overheating will occur. If the cap must be replaced, purchase the new cap according to the pressure rating which is specified for your vehicle.

Prior to installing the radiator cap, inspect and clean the filler neck. If you are reusing the old cap, clean it thoroughly with clear water. After turning the cap on, make sure the arrows align with the overflow hose.

Brake Master Cylinder

To check the brake fluid level, visually inspect the translucent master cylinder reservoir. The fluid level should be at the maximum level line of the reservoir. If the level is low, top it off using DOT 3 brake fluid meeting Ford specification ESA-M6C25-A. It is normal for the brake fluid level to decrease as the brake linings wear. If the level is excessively low, inspect the brake linings for wear and/or the brake system for leaks.

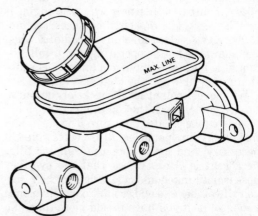

Brake fluid should reach the MAX line on the master cylinder reservoir

Power Steering Pump

Before attempting to check the fluid level, first clean all dirt from the outside of the power steering pump reservoir before removing the cap. Start the engine and allow it to reach normal operating temperature, then turn the steering wheel from lock-to-lock several times to bleed any air out of the system. Turn the engine off and check the fluid level on the power steering pump dipstick. The level should be within the FULL HOT scale on the dipstick. If necessary, top the reservoir up with fluid that meets Ford specification ESW-M2C33-F, such as Motorcraft Automatic Transmission and Power Steering Fluid Type F. Do not overfill.

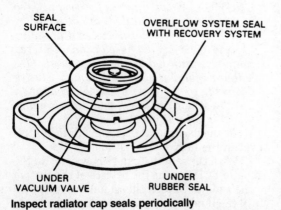

SEAL SURFACE

OVERFLOW SYSTEM SEAL WITH RECOVERY SYSTEM

UNDER VACUUM VALVE

UNDER RUBBER SEAL

Inspect radiator cap seals periodically

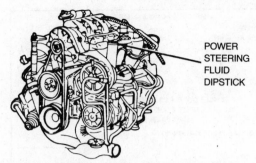

Location of power steering dipstick on 3.0L engine

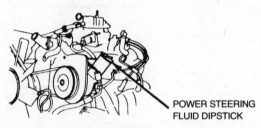

Location of power steering dipstick on 2.8L engine

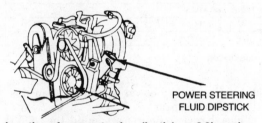

Location of power steering dipstick on 2.3L engine

Chassis Greasing

The front ball joints should be lubricated at 30,000 mile intervals. Locate the ball joint grease fittings, wipe them clean, then use a suitable grease gun to lubricate the ball joints. Inspect the ball joints for any obvious wear or damage and replace parts as necessary. Although there are no lubrication requirements, all suspension bushings should be inspected at this time for wear or damage and replaced as required. If equipped with grease fittings, the universal joints should be greased at this time also. U-joints without grease fittings require no lubrication.

WHEEL BEARINGS

The front wheel bearings should be inspected and repacked with grease every 30,000 miles. A good quality, high temperature wheel bearing grease should be used. The procedure involves removing the front brake rotors. Refer to Chapter 8 for removal and repacking information.

THROTTLE AND TRANSMISSION LINKAGE

Inspect the transmission linkage for signs of wear or damage and service as required. Lubricate the shift linkage at the points illustrated with multi-purpose lubricant such as Ford part number C1AZ-19590-B or equivalent.

Disconnect the throttle cable from the ball stud on the throttle lever and lubricate the stud with multi-purpose lubricant, then reconnect the ball stud and cable.

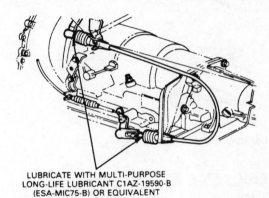

LUBRICATE WITH MULTI-PURPOSE LONG-LIFE LUBRICANT C1AZ-19590-B (ESA-MIC75-B) OR EQUIVALENT

Automatic transmission linkage

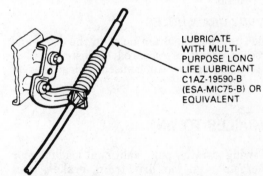

LUBRICATE WITH MULTI-PURPOSE LONG LIFE LUBRICANT C1AZ-19590-B (ESA-MIC75-B) OR EQUIVALENT

Automatic transmission kickdown cable

PARKING BRAKE LINKAGE

Once a year, or whenever binding is noticed in the parking brake mechanism, lubricate the cable guides, levers and linkages with multi-purpose grease.

LOCK CYLINDERS AND LATCH ASSEMBLIES

Apply graphite lubricant sparingly thought the key slot. Insert the key and operate the lock several times to be sure that the lubricant is worked into the lock cylinder.

Lubricate the hood, rear liftgate and door latches with polyethylene grease, then operate the mechanism several times to be sure the lubricant is worked into the latch assembly.

DOOR HINGES AND HINGE CHECKS

Spray a silicone lubricant on the hinge pivot points to eliminate any binding conditions. Open and close the door several times to be sure that the lubricant is evenly and thoroughly distributed.

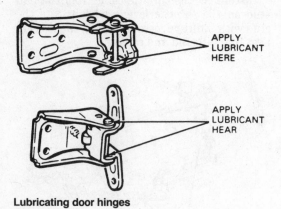

Lubricating door hinges

REAR LIFTGATE

Spray a silicone lubricant on all of the pivot and friction surfaces to eliminate any squeaks or binds. Work the tailgate to distribute the lubricant.

BODY DRAIN HOLES

Be sure that the drain holes in the doors and rocker panels are cleared of obstruction. A small screwdriver can be used to clear them of any debris.

TRAILER TOWING

Towing a trailer puts additional load on your Aerostar's engine, drivetrain, brakes, tires and suspension. For your safety and the care of your van, make sure the trailer towing equipment is properly matched to the trailer. All towing equipment should be safely attached to the vehicle and of the proper weight class.

The maximum trailer weight that your Aerostar is rated to tow can be calculated after determining two numbers:

1. The Loaded Vehicle Weight, which is the weight of the van as loaded for towing including trailer hitch, passengers and gear. Scales to weigh your vehicle are available at trucking companies, usually listed in the yellow pages.

2. The Maximum Gross Combined Weight Rating, which is the maximum combined weight of the loaded vehicle plus trailer that will meet acceptance tests with your engine, transmission and axle combination (powertrain). The GCWR can be found in the

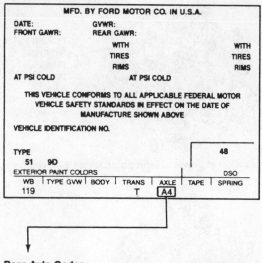

Rear Axle Codes

Code	Description	Capacity (lbs.)	Ratio	Brake Size
12	Ford	2,790	4.10	10"
13	Ford	2,790	3.45	9"
14	Ford	2,790	3.73	9"
13	Ford	2,790	3.45	10"
14	Ford	2,790	3.73	10"
LIMITED SLIP AXLES				
A2	Ford	2,790	4.10	10"
A4	Ford	2,790	3.73	10"

Axle codes

charts that follow based on engine, transmission and axle ratio.

Once these two figures are found, the GCWR minus the Loaded Vehicle Weight determines the maximum trailer weight for your particular Aerostar. The axle ratio can be determined from the axle code on the Safety Standard Certification Label attached to the door pillar.

NOTE: *A heavy duty cooling system is re-*

Maximum Gross Combined Weight Rating (GCWR)				
Engine	Rear Axle Ratio	Max. GCWR lb (Kg)	Trailer Weight lb (Kg)	Max. Frontal Area Sq. Ft.
2.3L EFI	3.45	4,800 (2 177)	0-2,000 (0-907)	①
	3.73	4,800 (2 177)	0-2,000 (0-907)	①
	4.10	4,800 (2 177)	0-2,000 (0-907)	①
2.8L	3.45	5,000 (2 268)	0-2,000 (0-907)	①
	3.73	5,000 (2 268)	0-2,000 (0-907)	50
3.0L EFI	3.45	5,000 (2 268)	0-2,000 (0-907)	①
	3.73	5,000 (2 268)	0-2,000 (0-907)	50

①Trailer frontal area is not to exceed base vehicle frontal area.
NOTE — For altitude operation, reduce GCW by 2% per 1,000 ft. elevation.

Manual transmissions

Maximum Gross Combined Weight Rating (GCWR)				
Engine	Rear Axle Ratio	Max. GCWR lb (Kg)	Trailer Weight lb (Kg)	Max. Frontal Area Sq. Ft.
2.3L EFI	3.73	4,800 (2 177)	0-2,000 (0-907)	①
		6,000 (2 722)	2,000-3,000 (907-1 361)	①
	4.10	4,800 (2 177)	0-2,000 (0-907)	①
		6,500 (2 948)	2,000-3,500 (907-1 587)	①
2.8L	3.45	5,500 (2 495)	0-2,000 (0-907)	①
		7,500 (3 402)	2,000-4,500 (907-2 041)	50
	3.73	5,500 (2 495)	0-2,000 (0-907)	①
		8,000 (3 629)	2,000-4,500 (907-2 041)	50
	4.10	5,500 (2 495)	0-2,000 (0-907)	①
		8,500 (3 856)	2,000-5,000 (907-2 268)	50
3.0L EFI	3.45	5,500 (2 495)	0-2,000 (0-907)	①
		7,500 (3 402)	2,000-4,500 (907-2 041)	50
	3.73	5,500 (2 495)	0-2,000 (0-907)	①
		8,000 (3 629)	2,000-4,500 (907-2 041)	50
	4.10	5,500 (2 495)	(0-2000) (0-907)	①
		8,500 (3 856)	2,000-5,000 (907-2 268)	50

①Trailer frontal area is not to exceed base vehicle frontal area.
NOTE — For altitude operation, reduce GCW by 2% per 1,000 ft. elevation.

Automatic transmissions

quired with the 2.3L engine, automatic transmission and a trailer over 2,000 lb. A trailer tow package is required with the 2.8L or 3.0L engine, automatic transmission and trailer over 2,000 lb.

Vehicles equipped with a 5 speed overdrive manual transmission should not use the overdrive gear for trailer towing. Shift as though you were driving a 4 speed transmission. Vehicles equipped with an A4LD automatic overdrive transmission should drive with the transmission selector in D (direct drive) when towing a trailer or driving a heavily loaded vehicle in very hilly terrain. When descending a steep grade, place the automatic transmission selector in 2 (manual second) to shift the transmission into second gear and provide engine braking. The same downshifting procedure can be used to maintain speed (not to exceed 40 mph) when traveling on a long upgrade.

Trailer Hitches

Choose a proper hitch and ball and make sure its location is compatible with that of the trailer. Use a good weight carrying hitch that uniformly distributes the trailer tongue loads through the underbody structure for towing trailers up to 2,000 lb. For trailers over this weight, use a frame mounted, weight distributing hitch.

CAUTION: *Under no circumstances should a single or multi-clamp type hitch be installed on your Aerostar, which is equipped with a non-metallic thermoplastic bumper. Nor should any hitch which attaches to the axle be used. Underbody mounted hitches are acceptable if installed properly. Never attach safety chains to the bumper.*

Always use safety chains between the vehicle and trailer to avoid any danger to other vehicles should the hitch fail. Cross the chains under the trailer tongue and allow enough slack for turning corners. Connect the safety chains to the frame or hook retainers, avoiding contact with the bumper.

Separate trailer brakes are recommended and required on most trailers weighing over 1,500 lb. Make sure your trailer brakes conform to local and Federal regulations. Vehicles with trailers should not be parked on a grade, but if you must, the trailer wheels should be chocked. Trailer lights should be connected to the vehicle lighting systems (taillights and brake lights) per the manufacturers instructions included with the trailer harness adapter kit. Vehicles equipped with a factory trailer towing package should have the van connections already installed.

TRAILER TOWING TIPS

Before starting on a trip, practice turning, stopping and backing up in an area away from other traffic (such as a deserted shopping center parking lot) to gain experience in handling the extra weight and length of the trailer. Take enough time to get the feel of the vehicle/ trailer combination under a variety of situations.

Skillful backing requires practice; back up slowly with an assistant acting as a guide and watching for obstructions. Use both rear view mirrors. Place your hand at the bottom of the steering wheel and move it in the direction you want the rear of the trailer to swing. Make small corrections, instead of exaggerated ones, as a slight movement of the steering wheel will result in a much larger movement of the rear of the trailer.

Allow considerable more room for stopping when a trailer is attached to the vehicle. If you have a manual brake controller, lead with the trailer brakes when approaching a stop. Trailer brakes are also handy for correcting side sway; just touch them for a moment without using your vehicle brakes and the trailer should settle down and track straight again.

To assist in obtaining good handling with the truck/trailer combination, it is important that the trailer tongue load be maintained at approximately 10–15% of the loaded trailer weight.

Check everything before starting out on the road, then stop after you've traveled about 50 miles and double check the trailer hitch and electrical connections to make sure everything is still OK. Listen for sounds like chains dragging on the ground (indicating that a safety chain has come loose) and check your rear view mirrors frequently to make sure the trailer is still there and tracking properly. Check the trailer wheel lug nuts to make sure they're tight and never attempt to tow the trailer with a space saver spare installed on the van.

Remember that a van/trailer combination is more sensitive to cross winds and slow down when crossing bridges or wide open expanses in gusty wind conditions. Exceeding the speed limit while towing a trailer is not only illegal, it is foolhardy and invites disaster. A strong gust of wind can send a speeding van/trailer combination out of control.

Because the trailer wheels are closer than the towing vehicle wheels to the inside of a turn, drive slightly beyond the normal turning point when negotiating a sharp turn at a corner. Allow extra distance for passing other vehicles and downshift if necessary for better acceleration. Allow at least the equivalent of one vehicle and trailer length combined for each 10 mph of road speed.

Finally, remember to check the height of the loaded van/trailer, allowing for luggage racks, antenna, etc. mounted on the roof and take note of low bridges or parking garage clearances.

PUSHING AND TOWING

Vehicles with catalytic converters should never be push started due to the possibility of serious converter damage. If the vehicle won't start, follow the instructions for the use of jumper cables.

Improper towing of the Aerostar could result in transmission damage. Always unload the vehicle before towing it. Tow chain attachments must be make to the structural members of the vehicle, with the chains routed under a 4" x 4" x 48" wood crossbeam placed under the bottom edge of the front bumper against the air spoiler or under the metal rear bumper supports against the wrecker towing tabs, in

FRONT WHEELS OFF GROUND		
Manual or Automatic Transmission		
1. Transmission in neutral. 2. Max speed 35 mph (56 km/h). 3. Max distance 50 miles (80 km). NOTE — If a distance of 50 miles (80 km) or speed of 35 mph (56 km/h) must be exceeded, disconnect driveshaft.		
REAR WHEELS OFF GROUND		
Manual or Automatic Transmission		
1. Lock steering wheel straight ahead.		
ALL FOUR WHEELS ON GROUND		
Manual or Automatic Transmission		
1. Transmission in neutral. 2. Max speed 35 mph (56 km). 3. Max distance 50 miles (80 km). NOTE — If a distance of 50 miles (80 km) or speed of 35 mph (56 km/h) must be exceeded, disconnect driveshaft.		

Towing 2-wheel drive vehicles

such a manner that they do not come into contact with suspension, steering, brake, cooling system, exhaust system, bumper or air spoiler components. Make sure the parking brake is released and the transmission gearshift lever is in Neutral. To move a vehicle with an inoperative rear axle, the rear wheels must be raised. If the transmission is inoperative, the rear wheels must be raised or the driveshaft disconnected.

CAUTION: *Never tow your Aerostar by using a tow bar that attaches to the bumper only. This will damage the bumper and result in property damage or personal injury. Do not attempt to use the steering column lock to hold the front wheels in a straight ahead position when towing from the rear.*

JACKING AND HOISTING

Scissors jacks or hydraulic jacks are recommended for all vehicles. To change a front tire, place the jack in position from the side of the vehicle under the horizontal portion of the underbody member behind the wheel. To change a rear tire, place the jack in position from the side of the vehicle under the horizontal portion of the underbody member ahead of the wheel.

Make sure that you are on level ground, that the transmission is in Reverse or, with automatic transmissions, Park. The parking brake is set, and the tire diagonally opposite to the one to be changed is blocked so that it will not roll. Loosen the lug nuts before you jack the wheel to be changed completely free of the ground.

CAUTION: *Never crawl under any vehicle when it is supported only by a jack. The jack is meant to raise the vehicle only. If any ser-*

JUMP STARTING A DEAD BATTERY

The chemical reaction in a battery produces explosive hydrogen gas. This is the safe way to jump start a dead battery, reducing the chances of an accidental spark that could cause an explosion.

Jump Starting Precautions

1. Be sure both batteries are of the same voltage.
2. Be sure both batteries are of the same polarity (have the same grounded terminal).
3. Be sure the vehicles are not touching.
4. Be sure the vent cap holes are not obstructed.
5. Do not smoke or allow sparks around the battery.
6. In cold weather, check for frozen electrolyte in the battery. Do not jump start a frozen battery.
7. Do not allow electrolyte on your skin or clothing.
8. Be sure the electrolyte is not frozen.
CAUTION: *Make certain that the ignition key, in the vehicle with the dead battery, is in the OFF position. Connecting cables to vehicles with on-board computers will result in computer destruction if the key is not in the OFF position.*

Jump Starting Procedure

1. Determine voltages of the two batteries; they must be the same.
2. Bring the starting vehicle close (they must not touch) so that the batteries can be reached easily.
3. Turn off all accessories and both engines. Put both cars in Neutral or Park and set the handbrake.
4. Cover the cell caps with a rag—do not cover terminals.
5. If the terminals on the run-down battery are heavily corroded, clean them.
6. Identify the positive and negative posts on both batteries and connect the cables in the order shown.
7. Start the engine of the starting vehicle and run it at fast idle. Try to start the car with the dead battery. Crank it for no more than 10 seconds at a time and let it cool off for 20 seconds in between tries.
8. If it doesn't start in 3 tries, there is something else wrong.
9. Disconnect the cables in the reverse order.
10. Replace the cell covers and dispose of the rags.

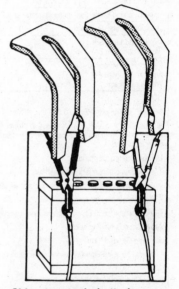

Side terminal batteries occasionally pose a problem when connecting jumper cables. There frequently isn't enough room to clamp the cables without touching sheet metal. Side terminal adaptors are available to alleviate this problem and should be removed after use.

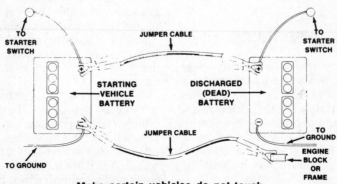

Make certain vehicles do not touch

This hook-up for negative ground cars only

Maintenance Schedule B—2.3L EFI 4 Cylinder and 2.8L 6 Cylinder Engines

	NORMAL DRIVING SERVICE INTERVALS Perform at the months or distances shown, whichever comes first.								
Maintenance Operation	Miles (Thousands)	7.5	15	22.5	30	37.5	45	52.5	60
	Kilometers (Thousands)	12	24	36	48	60	72	84	96
Check Wheel Lug Nut Torque ▲		B	B	B	B	B	B	B	B
Check Brake Master Cylinder Fluid Level					B				B
Check Clutch Reservoir Fluid Level					B				B
Inspect Automatic Transmission Shift Linkage (Shift Cable)		B	B	B	B	B	B	B	B
Inspect and Lubricate Front Wheel Bearings					B				B
Inspect Disc Brake System and Lubricate Caliper Slide Rails					B				B
Inspect Drum Brake Linings, Lines and Hoses					B				B
Inspect Exhaust System for Leaks, Damage or Loose Parts					B				B
Lubricate Driveshaft U-Joint if Equipped with Grease Fitting		B	B	B	B	B	B	B	B
Inspect Parking Brake System for Damage and Operation					B				B
Lubricate Throttle Ball Stud					B				B
Inspect and Lubricate Front Suspension Ball Joints					B				B
Inspect Suspension Bushings, Arms and Springs For Wear or Damage					B				B

NOTE:

Beyond 96 000 kilometers (60,000 miles) continue recommended maintenance operations at intervals for 0-96 000 kilometers (60,000 miles).

▲ Wheel lug nuts must be retightened to proper torque specification at 800 km (500 miles) of new vehicle operation. Refer to the appropriate portion of this section. Also retighten to proper torque specification at 800 km (500 miles) after (1) any wheel change or (2) any other time the wheel lug nuts have been loosened.

Unique Driving Conditions

The automatic transmission fluid should be changed every 48 000 km (30,000 miles) if your vehicle(s) operate under any of the following conditions:

— Sustained high-speed driving during hot weather (+90°F, +32°C).

— Towing a trailer for long distances.

— Accumulating 8000 km (5,000 miles) or more per month.

— Continuous running service.

Extreme Service Items

If the vehicle is off-highway, perform the following every 1609 km (1,000 miles). If the vehicle is operated in mud and/or water, perform the following items daily.

● Inspect disc brake system

● Inspect front wheel bearings and lubrication

● Inspect exhaust system for leaks, damage or loose parts

Non-emission system scheduled maintenance chart

vice is to be performed under the van, use jackstands to support the weight and make sure they are secure before placing any portion of your body under the truck. Never start the engine while the van is supported only by a jack.

HOW TO BUY A USED TRUCK

Many people believe that a two or three year old, or older, truck is a better buy than a new one. This may be true. The new truck suffers the heaviest depreciation in the first few years, but is not old enough to present a lot of costly repairs. Whatever the age of the used truck you want to buy, this section and a little patience will help you select one that should be safe and dependable.

Shopping Tips

1. First, decide what model you want and how much you want to spend.

2. Check the used car lots and your local newspaper ads. Privately owned trucks are usually less expensive, however, you will not get a warranty that, in most cases, comes with a used truck purchased from a dealer.

3. Never shop at night. The glare of the lights makes it easy to miss defects in the paint and faults in the body caused by accident or rust repair.

4. Once you've found a truck that you're interested in, try to get the name and phone number of the previous owner. Contact that person for details about the truck. If he or she refuses information about the truck, shop elsewhere. A private seller can tell you about the truck and its maintenance history, but there

are few laws requiring honesty from private citizens who are selling used vehicles. There are laws forbidding the tampering with or turning back a vehicle's odometer mileage reading. These laws apply to both a private seller as well commercial dealers. The law also requires that the seller, or anyone transferring ownership of a vehicle, must provide the buyer with a signed statement indicating the mileage on the odometer at the time of transfer.

5. Write down the year, model and serial number of the truck before you buy it. Then, dial 1-800-424-9393, the toll-free number of the National Highway Traffic Safety Administration, and ask if the truck has ever been included on any manufacturer's recall list. If so, make sure the necessary repairs were made.

6. Use the Used Car Checklist in this section, and check all the items on the used truck that you are considering. Some items are more important than others. You've already determined how much money you can afford for repairs, and, depending on the price of the truck, you should consider doing some of the needed repairs yourself. Beware, however, of trouble in areas involving operation, safety or emissions. Problems in the Used Car Checklist are arranged as follows:

1–8: Two or more problems in this segment indicate a lack of maintenance. You should reconsider your selection.

9–13: Indicates a lack of proper care, however, these can usually be corrected with a tune-up or relatively simple parts replacement.

14–17: Problems in the engine or transmission can be very expensive. Walk away from any truck with problems in these areas.

7. If you are satisfied with the apparent condition of the truck, take it to an independent diagnostic center or mechanic for a complete checkout. If your state has a state inspection program, have it inspected immediately before purchase, or specify on the invoice that purchase is conditional on the truck's passing a state inspection.

8. Road test the truck. Refer to the Road Test Checklist in this section. If your original evaluation, and the road test agree, the rest is up to you.

Used Vehicle Checklist

NOTE: *The numbers on the illustration correspond to the numbers in this checklist.*

1. *Mileage:* Average mileage is about 12,000 miles per year. More than average may indicate hard usage. Catalytic converter equipped models may need converter service beyond the 50,000 mile mark.

2. *Paint:* Check around the tailpipe, molding and windows for overspray, indicating that the truck has been repainted.

3. *Rust:* Check fenders, doors, rocker panels, window moldings, wheelwells, flooring and in the bed, for signs of rust. Any rust at all will be a problem. There is no way to stop the spread of rust, except to replace the part or panel.

4. *Body Appearance:* Check the moldings, bumpers, grille, vinyl roof, glass, doors, tail gate and body panels for overall condition. Check for misalignment, loose holddown clips, ripples, scratches in the glass, rips or patches in the top. Mismatched paint, welding in the bed, severe misalignment of body panels or ripples may indicate crash work.

5. *Leaks:* Get down under the truck and take a good look. There are no "normal" leaks, other than water from the air conditioning condenser drain tube.

6. *Tires:* Check the tire air pressure. A common trick is to pump the tires up hard to make the truck roll more easily. Check the tread wear and the spare tire condition. Uneven wear is a sign that the front end is, or was, out of alignment. See the Troubleshooting Chapter for indications of treadwear.

7. *Shock Absorbers:* Check the shocks by forcing downward sharply on each corner of the truck. Good shocks will not allow the truck to rebound more than twice after you let go.

8. *Interior:* Check the entire interior. You're looking for an interior condition that agrees with the overall condition of the truck. Reasonable wear can be expected, but be suspicious of new seatcovers on sagging seats, new pedal pads, and worn armrests. These indicate an attempt to cover up hard usage. Pull back the carpets and/or mats and look for signs of water leaks or flooding. Look for missing hardware, door handles, control knobs, etc. Check lights and signal operations. Make sure that all accessories, such as air conditioner, heater, radio, etc., work. Air conditioning, especially automatic temperature control units, can be very expensive to repair. Check the operation of the windshield wipers.

9. *Belts and Hoses:* Open the hood and check all belts and hoses for wear, cracks, or weak spots. Check around hose connections for stains, indicating leaks.

10. *Battery:* Low electrolyte level, corroded terminals and/or a cracked battery case, indicate a lack of maintenance.

11. *Radiator:* Look for corrosion or rust in the coolant, indicating a lack of maintenance.

12. *Air Filter:* A dirty air filter element indicates a lack of maintenance.

13. *Spark Plug Wires:* Check the wires for

cracks, burned spots or wear. Worn wires will have to be replaced.

14. *Oil Level:* If the level is low, chances are that the engine either uses an excessive amount of oil, or leaks. If the oil on the dipstick appears foamy or tan in color, a leakage of coolant into the oil is indicated. Stop here, and go elsewhere for your truck. If the oil appears thin or has the smell of gasoline, stop here and go elsewhere for your truck.

15. *Automatic Transmission:* Pull the transmission dipstick out when the engine is running in PARK. If the fluid is hot, the dipstick should read FULL. If the fluid is cold, the level will show about one pint low. The fluid itself should be bright red and translucent, with no burned odor. Fluid that is brown or black and has a burned odor is a sign that the transmission needs major repairs.

16. *Exhaust:* Check the color of the exhaust smoke. Blue smoke indicates excessive oil usage, usually due to major internal engine problems. Black smoke can indicate burned valves or carburetor problems. Check the exhaust system for leaks. A leaky system is dangerous and expensive to replace.

17. *Spark Plugs:* Remove one of the spark plugs. An engine in good condition will have spark plugs with a light tan or gray deposit on the electrodes. See the color Tune-Up section for a complete analysis of spark plug condition.

Road Test Check List

1. *Engine Performance:* The truck should have good accelerator response, whether cold or warm, with adequate power and smooth acceleration through the gears.

2. *Brakes:* Brakes should provide quick, firm stops, with no squealing, pulling or fade.

3. *Steering:* Sure control with no binding, harshness or looseness, and no shimmy in the wheel should be encountered. Noise or vibration from the steering wheel means trouble.

4. *Clutch:* Clutch action should be quick and smooth with easy engagement of the transmission.

5. *Manual Transmission:* The transmission should shift smoothly and crisply with easy change of gears. No clashing and grinding should be evident. The transmission should not stick in gear, nor should there be any gear whine evident at road speed.

6. *Automatic Transmission:* The transmission should shift rapidly and smoothly, with no noise, hesitation or slipping. The transmission should not shift back and forth, but should stay in gear until an upshift or downshift is needed.

7. *Differential:* No noise or thumps should be present. No external leakage should be present.

8. *Driveshaft, Universal Joints:* Vibration and noise could mean driveshaft problems. Clicking at low speed or coast conditions means worn U-joints.

9. *Suspension:* Try hitting bumps at different speeds. A truck that bounces has weak shock absorbers. Clunks mean worn bushings or ball joints.

10. *Frame:* Wet the tires and drive in a straight line. Tracks should show two straight lines, not four. Four tire tracks indicates a frame bent by collision damage. If the tires can't be wet for this purpose, have a friend drive along behind you and see if the truck appears to be traveling in a straight line.

Tune-Up and Performance Maintenance

2

TUNE-UP PROCEDURES

The engine tune-up is a routine service designed to restore the maximum capability of power, performance, reliability and economy to the engine. It is essential for efficient and economical operation and becomes increasingly more important each year to insure that pollutant levels are in compliance with federal emission standards.

The interval between tune-ups is a variable factor which depends on the year and engine in your van and the way it is driven in average use. The extent of the tune-up is usually determined by the length of time since the previous service. It is advisable to follow a definite and thorough tune-up procedure consisting of three steps: Analysis, the process of determining whether normal wear is responsible for performance loss and the inspection of various parts such as spark plugs; Parts Replacement or Service; and Adjustment, where engine adjustments are returned to the original factory specifications.

The replaceable parts normally involved in a major tune-up include the spark plugs, air filter, fuel filter, distributor cap, rotor and spark plug wires. In addition to these parts and the adjustments involved in properly adapting them to your engine, the normal tune-up should include a check of the ignition timing and idle speed, although with modern electronic engine controls, these items are usually not adjustable. Refer to the underhood emission control sticker for specific instructions on checking the timing, as well as specifications for spark plug gap and idle speed. In addition to the above, the valve adjustment should be checked with the engine cold. The 2.3L 4-cylinder and the 3.0L V6 engines have hydraulic lash adjusters that do not require periodic service, however, the 2.8L V6 valves are adjustable and clearances should be checked and adjusted, if necessary, at every tune-up.

CAUTION: *When working on or around a running engine, make sure there is adequate ventilation. Make sure the transmission is in Neutral or Park with the parking brake firmly applied and always keep hands, clothing and tools well clear of the hot exhaust manifold(s) and radiator. Remove any jewelry, do not wear loose clothing and tuck long hair up*

Tune-Up Specifications

| Years | Engine cu. in. (liter) | Spark Plugs | | Ignition Timing (deg.) | | Idle Speed | | Valve Clearance | |
		Type	Gap (in.)	Man. Trans.	Auto. Trans.	Man. Trans.	Auto. Trans.	In.	Exh.
1986–87	140 (2.3)	AWSF-44C	.042–.046	10B	10B	725– 875	625– 775	Hyd	Hyd
	171 (2.8)	AWSF-42C	.042–.046	10B	10B	800– 900	700– 800	0.014	0.016
	182 (3.0)	AWSF-32C	.042–.046	10B	10B	Not Adjustable		Hyd	Hyd

Note: Idle speed specifications are for reference only. Idle speed and mixture is computer-controlled on all models.
Hyd—Hydraulic lash adjusters
B—Before Top Dead Center

under a cap. Use EXTREME caution when working around spinning fan blades or belts. When the engine is running, do not grasp the ignition wires, distributor cap or coil wire, as the high energy ignition system can deliver a potentially fatal shock of 20,000 volts. Whenever working around the distributor, even if the engine is not running, make sure the ignition is switched OFF.

This chapter gives specific procedures on how to tune-up your van and is intended to be as complete and basic as possible. It is advisable to read the entire chapter before beginning a tune-up.

Spark Plugs

The function of a spark plug is to ignite the air/fuel mixture in the cylinder as the piston reaches the top of its compression stroke. The expansion of the ignited mixture forces the piston down, which turns the crankshaft and supplies power to the drivetrain.

A typical spark plug consists of a metal shell surrounded by a ceramic insulator. A metal electrode extends downward through the center of the insulator and protrudes a small distance. Located at the end of the plug and attached to the side of the outer metal shell is the side electrode. The side electrode bends in at a 90° angle so that its tip is even with, and parallel to, the tip of the center electrode. The distance between these two electrodes (measured in thousandths of an inch) is called the spark plug gap.

The spark plug in no way produces a spark, but merely provides a gap across which the current from the ignition coil can arc. The ignition coil produces from 20,000 to 40,000 volts which travels to the distributor where it is distributed through the spark plug wires to the spark plugs. This current passes along the center electrode and jumps the gap to the side electrode and, in doing so, ignites the air/fuel mixture.

The average life of a spark plug is about 25,000 miles, depending on the type of driving and vehicle use. If the van is driven at high speeds more often, the plugs will probably not need as much attention as those used for constant stop-and-go driving. The electrode end of the spark plug is a good indicator of the internal condition of your engine. If a spark plug is fouled and causing the engine to misfire, the problem will have to be found and corrected. Spark plug conditions and probable causes are shown in the color insert section of this chapter. It is a good idea to remove the plugs once in a while to check their condition and see just how the engine is performing. A small amount of light tan colored deposits on the electrode end of the spark plug is normal and the plugs do not require replacement unless extremely worn.

SPARK PLUG HEAT RANGE

Spark plug heat range is the ability of the plug to dissipate heat. The longer the insulator (or the farther it extends into the engine), the hotter the plug will operate. Conversely, the shorter the insulator, the cooler the plug will operate. A plug that absorbs little heat and remains too cool will quickly accumulate deposits of oil and carbon since it is not hot enough to burn them off. This can lead to plug fouling and misfiring. A plug that absorbs too much heat will have no deposits but, due to the excess heat, the electrodes will burn away quickly and in some instances preignition may result. Preignition takes place when the plug tips get so hot that they glow sufficiently to ig-

PORCELAIN INSULATOR

INSULATOR CRACKS OFTEN OCCUR HERE

SHELL

ADJUST FOR PROPER GAP

SIDE ELECTRODE (BEND TO ADJUST GAP)

CENTER ELECTRODE; FILE FLAT WHEN ADJUSTING GAP; DO NOT BEND!

Cross section of a spark plug

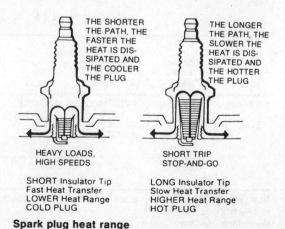

THE SHORTER THE PATH, THE FASTER THE HEAT IS DISSIPATED AND THE COOLER THE PLUG

THE LONGER THE PATH, THE SLOWER THE HEAT IS DISSIPATED AND THE HOTTER THE PLUG

HEAVY LOADS, HIGH SPEEDS

SHORT TRIP STOP-AND-GO

SHORT Insulator Tip
Fast Heat Transfer
LOWER Heat Range
COLD PLUG

LONG Insulator Tip
Slow Heat Transfer
HIGHER Heat Range
HOT PLUG

Spark plug heat range

nite the fuel/air mixture before the actual spark occurs. This condition is usually described as a spark knock or "ping" during low speeds and under heavy load.

The general rule of thumb for choosing the correct heat range when picking a spark plug is to use a colder plug for long distance, high speed operation and a hotter plug for stop-and-go, heavy traffic operation. Original equipment plugs are usually a compromise, but most owners never have occasion to change from the factory recommended heat range.

REPLACING SPARK PLUGS

A set of spark plugs usually requires replacement after about 20,000 to 30,000 miles on engines with electronic ignition, depending on your style of driving. In normal operation, the spark plug gap will increase about 0.001" for every 1,000–2,500 miles. As the gap increases, the plug's voltage requirement also increases. It requires a greater voltage to jump the wider gap and about two to three times as much voltage to fire a plug at high speeds than at idle.

When removing the spark plugs, you should work on one at a time. Don't start by removing all the plug wires at once or they may become mixed up. Take a minute and number all the plug wires with tape before removing them from the plugs. The best location for numbering is near where the plug wires come out of the cap.

1. Twist the spark plug boot and remove the boot and wire from the plug. Do not pull on the wire itself or you will ruin it.

2. If possible, use a brush or rag to clean the area around the spark plug. Make sure that all the dirt is removed so that none will enter the cylinder after the plug is removed.

3. Remove the spark plug from the cylinder head using the proper size socket (⅝" for AWSF and ASF plugs) and ratchet. A universal joint and short extension may make this job easier. Turn the socket counterclockwise to remove the plug, but make sure the socket is firmly seated and straight on the plug or you will crack the insulator or round off the hex.

4. Once the plug is removed, check its condition against the plugs shown in the color insert to determine engine condition. This is crucial since plugs readings are vital signs of engine operating condition.

5. Use a round wire feeler gauge to check the plug gap. The correct size gauge should pass through the electrode gap with a slight drag. If in doubt, try one size smaller and one size larger. The smaller should pass through easily, while the larger shouldn't go through at

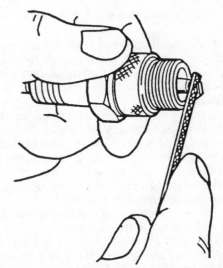

Plugs that are in good condition can be filed and reused

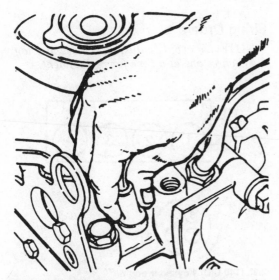

Twist and pull on the rubber boot to remove the spark plug wires; never pull on the wire itself

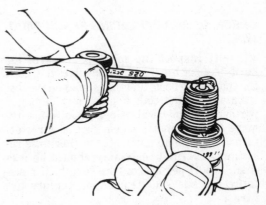

Checking the spark plug gap with a gap gauge

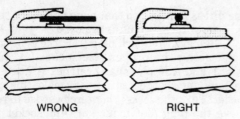

WRONG   RIGHT

Gapping spark plugs

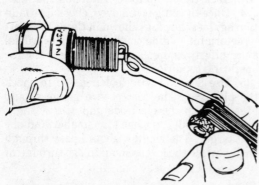

Adjusting the spark plug gap with a gapping tool

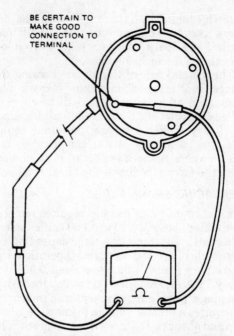

BE CERTAIN TO
MAKE GOOD
CONNECTION TO
TERMINAL

Testing spark plug wire resistance with an ohmmeter

all. If the gap is incorrect, use the electrode bending tool on the end of the gauge to adjust the gap. When adjusting the gap, always bend the side electrode; the center electrode is non-adjustable.

6. Squirt a drop of penetrating oil on the threads of the spark plug and install it. Don't oil the plug too heavily. Turn the plug in clockwise by hand until it is snug. Be careful not to cross-thread the plug when installing.

7. When the plug is finger tight, tighten it with a torque wrench to 10–15 ft.lb.

8. Install the spark plug boot firmly over the plug and proceed to the next one.

NOTE: *Coat the inside of each spark plug boot with silicone grease (Motorcraft WA-10-D7AZ-19A331A, Dow Corning No. 111 or General Electric G627 are acceptable). Failure to do so could result in a misfired plug.*

CHECKING AND REPLACING SPARK PLUG WIRES

Visually inspect the spark plug wires for burns, cuts or breaks in the insulation. Check the spark plug boots and the nipples on the distributor cap and coil. Replace any damaged wiring. If no physical damage is obvious, remove the distributor cap with the wires attached and use an ohmmeter to check the resistance. Normal resistance should be less than 7,000Ω per foot of wire length. If resistance exceeds 7,000Ω per foot, replace the wire.

CAUTION: *Do not, under any circum-*

stances, puncture a spark plug wire with a sharp probe when checking resistance. Check the resistance only as illustrated.

When installing a new set of spark plug wires, replace them one at a time so there is no mixup. Start by replacing the longest wire first and make sure the boot is installed firmly over the spark plug and distributor cap tower. Route the wire exactly the same way as the original and make sure the wire loom clips are fastened securely when done.

Firing Orders

NOTE: *To avoid confusion, remove and tag the wires one at a time for replacement.*

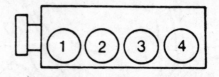

2.3L (140 CID) 4 cylinder engine
Firing order: 1-3-4-2
Distributor rotation: clockwise

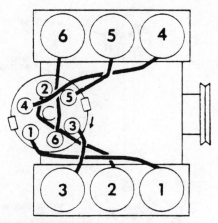

2.8L (171 CID) V6 engine
Firing order: 1-4-2-5-3-6
Distributor rotation: clockwise

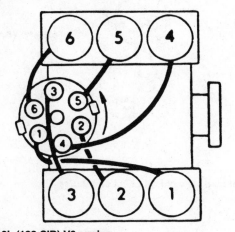

3.0L (182 CID) V6 engine
Firing order: 1-4-2-5-3-6
Distributor rotation: counterclockwise

VALVE ADJUSTMENT

2.8L V6 Engine

This procedure applies to the 2.8L V6 engine only. The engine should be cold for valve adjustment.

1. Remove the air cleaner assembly, then remove the rocker arm covers. This may involve removing some thermactor components to gain working clearance.

2. Place a finger on the adjusting screw of the intake valve rocker arm for cylinder No. 5 to detect the slightest motion.

3. Using a remote starter button, or an assistant turning the ignition key on and off, "bump" the engine over in small increments until the intake valve for No. 5 cylinder just begining to open. This will place the camshaft in the correct position to adjust the valves on No. 1 cylinder.

4. Adjust the No. 1 intake valve so that a

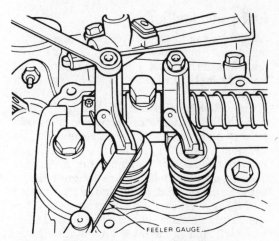

Adjusting the valve lash on the 2.8L V6 engine

0.014" (0.35mm) feeler gauge has a light to moderate drag and a 0.015" (0.36mm) feeler gauge is very tight. Turn the adjusting screw clockwise to decrease lash and counterclockwise to increase lash. The adjusting screws are self-locking and will stay in a set position.

NOTE: *Do not use a step-type go/no-go feeler gauge. Use a blade-type set. When checking lash, insert the feeler between the rocker arm and valve tip at the front (or rear) edge of the valve tip and move toward the opposite edge with a rearward (or forward) motion that is parallel to the centerline of the crankshaft. Do not insert the feeler at the outboard edge and move inward toward the carburetor perpendicular to the crankshaft centerline or this will result in an erroneous "feel" that will lead to excessively tight valves.*

5. Using the same method, adjust the No. 1 exhaust valve lash so that a 0.016" (0.40mm) feeler gauge has a slight to moderate drag and a 0.017" (0.41mm) is very tight.

6. Adjust the remaining valves in firing order 1-4-2-5-3-6 by positioning the camshaft according to the following chart:

To adjust both valves for cylinder number	1	4	2	5	3	6
The intake valve must be opening for cylinder number	5	3	6	1	4	2

Valve adjustment chart for the 2.8L V6 engine

7. Clean the rocker arm gasket mounting surfaces. Using new gaskets or a suitable RTV sealant, install the rocker arm covers. Install any thermactor components that were removed.

8. Reinstall the air cleaner assembly. Start the engine and check for oil and vacuum leaks.

Electronic Ignition

All engines used in the Aerostar have a universal distributor design which is gear driven and has a die cast metal base that incorporates an integrally mounted TFI-IV ignition module.

The distributor uses a "Hall Effect" stator assembly and eliminates the conventional centrifugal and vacuum advance mechanisms. No distributor calibration is required and it is not normally necessary to adjust initial timing. The cap, adapter and rotor are designed for use with the universal distributor and the ignition module is a Thick Film Integrated (TFI) design. The module is contained in molded thermoplastic and is mounted on the distributor base. The distributor assembly can be identified by the part number information printed on a decal attached to the side of the distributor base.

The operation of the universal distributor is accomplished through the Hall Effect vane switch assembly, causing the ignition coil to be switched on and off by the EEC-IV and TFI-IV modules. The vane switch is an encapsulated package consisting of a Hall sensor on one side and a permanent magnet on the other side. A rotary vane cup, made of ferrous (magnetic) metal is used to trigger the Hall Effect switch.

When the window of the vane cup is between the magnet and Hall Effect device, a magnetic flux field is completed from the magnet

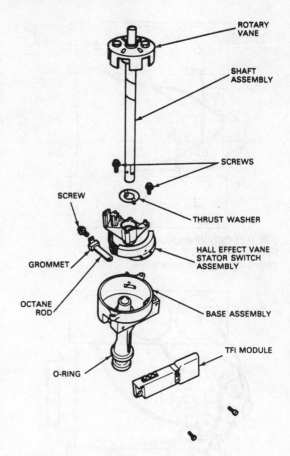

Exploded view of Hall Effect distributor

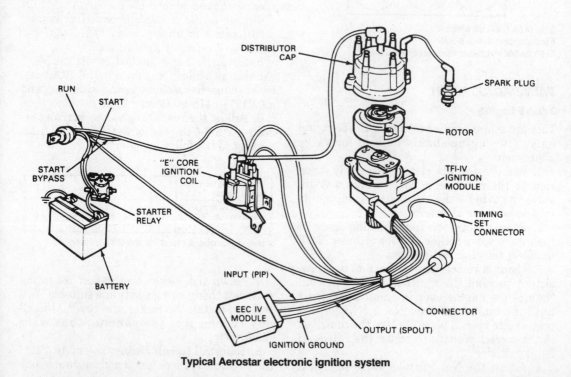

Typical Aerostar electronic ignition system

through the Hall Effect device and back to the magnet. As the vane passes through this opening, the flux lines are shunted through the vane and back to the magnet. As the vane passes through this opening, the flux lines are shunted through the vane and back to the magnet. A voltage is produced while the vane passes through the opening. When the vane clears the opening, the window causes the signal to go to zero volts. The signal is then used by the EEC-IV system for crankshaft position sensing and the computation of the desired spark advance based on engine demand and calibration. The conditioned spark advance and voltage distribution is accomplished through a conventional rotor, cap and ignition wires.

NOTE: *The ignition timing is preset at the factory and computer controlled. No attempt should be made to alter the ignition timing from the factory specifications.*

Initial Timing

ADJUSTMENT

1. Place transmission in Park (automatic) or Neutral (manual), with the A/C and heater off.

2. Connect an inductive timing light (Rotunda 059-00006 or equivalent) according to the manufacturer's instructions.

3. Disconnect the single wire inline spout connector near the distributor.

4. Start the engine and allow it to reach normal operating temperature.

5. With the engine at the timing rpm specified, check and/or adjust the initial timing to the specification listed on the underhood emission control label by loosening the distributor holddown bolt and rotating the distributor

slightly. A Torx® bit may be necessary to loosen the security type distributor holddown, if equipped.

6. Reconnect the single wire inline spout connector and check the timing advance to verify the distributor is advancing beyond the initial setting.

7. Once the timing is set, shut off the engine and disconnect the timing light.

Idle Speed

ADJUSTMENT

2.3L Engine

NOTE: *This procedure us to be performed only if the curb idle is not within the 700 drive (AT), 650 (MT) ± 75 rpm specification. Curb idle speed is controlled by the EEC-IV processor and the idle speed control air bypass valve assembly.*

1. Place the transmission in Neutral and make sure the A/C-Heat selector is off.

2. Start the engine and allow it to reach normal operating temperature, then turn the ignition off.

3. Disconnect the idle speed control air bypass valve power lead.

4. Start the engine and operate it at 1,500 rpm for 20 seconds.

5. Allow the engine to idle and check that the base idle speed is 550–600 rpm. The engine may stall when the ISC is disconnected. This is acceptable as long as the throttle plate is not stuck in the bore.

6. If the idle speed requires adjustment, disconnect the throttle cable and adjust the engine rpm by turning the throttle plate stop screw. Reconnect the throttle cable and recheck the idle speed.

7. Once the idle speed is set, turn the engine

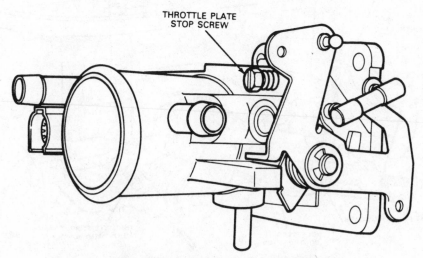

Adjusting the idle speed on the 2.3L engine

off and reconnect the power lead to the idle speed control air bypass valve.

8. Verify that the throttle plate is not stuck in the bore by moving the throttle plate linkage.

2.8L Engine

1. Place the transmission in Park (automatic) or Neutral (manual), then start the engine and allow it to reach normal operating temperature. Turn the engine off, block the drive wheels and set the parking brake firmly. Turn all accessories off.

2. Remove the air charge temperature (ACT) sensor and adapter from the air cleaner tray by disengaging the retainer clip; leave the wiring harness connected. Remove the air cleaner, disconnect and plug the vacuum line at the cold weather duct and valve motor.

3. Start the engine, then turn it off and verify that the idle speed control (ISC) plunger moves out to its maximum extension within 10 seconds of key off.

4. Disconnect the idle speed control. Disconnect and plug the EGR vacuum hose.

5. Start the engine and manually open the throttle, then set the fast idle adjusting screw on the high step of the fast idle cam.

6. Adjust the fast idle speed to specifications listed on the underhood sticker.

7. Open the throttle manually to release the fast idle cam, allowing the throttle lever to rest on the ISC plunger.

8. Loosen the ISC bracket lock screw. Adjust the ISC bracket screw to 2,000 rpm, then retighten the bracket lock screw.

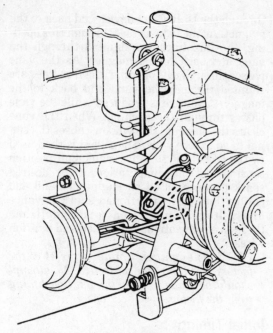

FAST IDLE RPM ADJUSTING SCREW
(SHOWN ON HIGH CAM/FAST IDLE STEP)

Fast idle rpm adjustment on 2.8L engine

9. Reconnect the ISC connector. The engine rpm should automatically be adjusted to curb idle.

10. Simultaneously:

a. Manually hold the throttle above 1,000 rpm

b. Push the ISC plunger until it retracts fully

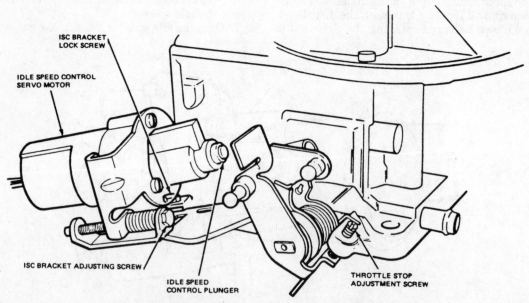

ISC BRACKET LOCK SCREW

IDLE SPEED CONTROL SERVO MOTOR

ISC BRACKET ADJUSTING SCREW

IDLE SPEED CONTROL PLUNGER

THROTTLE STOP ADJUSTMENT SCREW

Idle speed control adjustment on 2.8L engine

c. After the plunger retracts, release the throttle and quickly unplug the connection.

11. Adjust the anti-dieseling speed throttle stop screw to 750 rpm. The anti-dieseling speed is NOT the curb idle speed.

12. Reconnect the ISC and EGR vacuum hose.

13. Stop the engine, then restart it to verify that curb idle speed is within specifications.

3.0L Engine

Curb idle speed is controlled by the EEC-IV processor and the idle speed control air bypass valve assembly. The throttle plate stop screw is factory set and does not directly control idle speed. Adjustments to this setting should be performed only as part of a full EEC-IV diagnosis of irregular idle conditions or idle speed. Failure to accurately set the throttle plate stop position to the procedure below could result in erroneous idle speed control.

1. Place the transmission in Neutral (MT) or Park (AT), turn the A/C-Heat selector off, apply the parking brake firmly and block the drive wheels.

2. Bring the engine to normal operating temperature and check for vacuum leaks downstream of the throttle plates.

3. Unplug the single wire, inline spout connector near the distributor and verify ignition timing is 8–12° BTDC. If not, reset the ignition timing as described above.

4. Turn off the engine and disconnect the air bypass valve assembly connector.

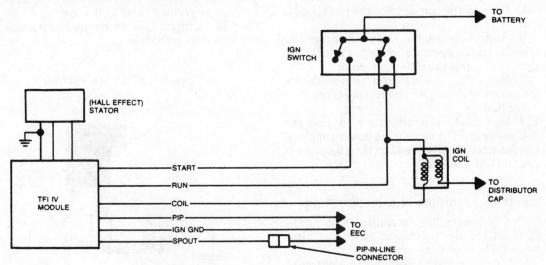

TFI-IV system electrical schematic typical of all vehicles

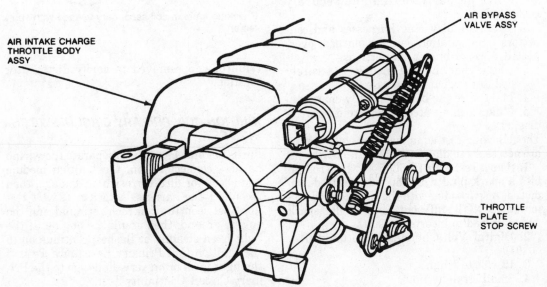

Idle speed adjustment on 3.0L engine

5. Remove the PCV entry line at the PCV valve.

6. Install Orifice Tool T86P-9600-A (0.200" orifice diameter) in the PCV entry line.

7. Start the engine. The vehicle should be idling in Drive with automatic transmission or in Neutral with manual transmission. Make sure the drive wheels are blocked and the parking brake is firmly set.

NOTE: *If the electric cooling fan comes on during idle set, unplug the fan motor power leads or wait until the fan switches off.*

8. Check the idle speed. It should be 820–870 rpm on models with an automatic transmission or 1,015–1,065 rpm on models with manual transmission. If the idle speed is not as stated, adjust by turning the throttle plate stop screw.

9. Turn off the engine after the idle speed is set.

10. Restart the engine and confirm the idle speed is within specifications after 3 to 5 minutes. If not, repeat setting procedure.

11. If the idle speed is correct, turn off the engine, remove the orifice and reconnect the PCV entry line.

12. Reconnect the distributor spout line, the ISC motor and the cooling fan power supply, if disconnected. Verify that the throttle plate is not stuck in the bore.

Electronic Ignition Troubleshooting

Before beginning any organized test procedures on the electronic ignition system, first perform these simple checks:

1. Visually inspect the engine compartment to make sure all vacuum hoses and spark plug wires are properly routed and securely connected.

2. Examine all wiring harnesses and connectors for insulation damage, burned, overheated, loose or broken connections.

3. Check that the TFI module is securely fastened to the distributor base.

4. Make sure the battery is fully charged.

5. Make sure all accessories are off during diagnosis.

The following test equipment, or equivalents, are necessary to diagnose the ignition system:

1. Spark Tester D81P-6666-A, which resembles a spark plug with the side electrode removed. A spark plug with the side electrode removed IS NOT sufficient to check for spark and may lead to incorrect results.

2. Digital Volt/Ohmmeter (Rotunda 014-00407).

3. 12 volt test light.

4. Small straight pin.

When instructed to inspect a wiring harness, both a visual inspection and a continuity test should be performed. When making measurements on a wiring harness or connector, it is good practice to wiggle the wires while measuring. The following tests are designed to be performed in order to gradually narrow down the cause of a problem in the ignition system.

IGNITION COIL SECONDARY VOLTAGE TEST

Connect the spark tester (D81P-6666-A or equivalent) between the ignition coil wire and engine ground, then crank the engine. If spark is present, the secondary voltage is OK. If there is no spark, measure the resistance of the ignition coil wire and replace the wire if the resistance is greater than 7,000Ω per foot. Inspect the ignition coil for damage or carbon tracking and crank the engine with the dis-

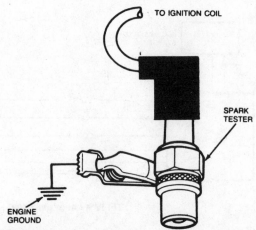

Checking ignition coil secondary voltage with spark tester

tributor cap removed to verify distributor rotation.

IGNITION COIL PRIMARY CIRCUIT SWITCHING TEST

Push the connector tabs to separate the wiring harness connector from the ignition module and check for dirt, corrosion or damage, then reconnect the harness. Attach a 12 volt test light between the coil tach terminal and the engine ground, then crank the engine. If the light is on steadily or flashes, continue on to the Ignition Coil Primary Resistance Test. If the light is off or on very dimly, go to the Primary Circuit Continuity Test.

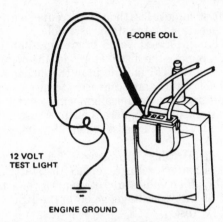

Ignition coil primary circuit switching test

IGNITION COIL PRIMARY RESISTANCE TEST

Turn the ignition switch off, then disconnect the ignition coil connector. Check for dirt, corrosion or damage. Use an ohmmeter to measure the resistance from the positive (+) to negative (–) terminals of the ignition coil. If the reading is between 0.3–1.0Ω the ignition coil is OK; continue on to the Ignition Coil Secondary Resistance Test. If the reading is less than 0.3Ω or greater than 1.0Ω, replace the ignition coil.

IGNITION COIL SECONDARY RESISTANCE TEST

Use an ohmmeter to measure the resistance between the negative (–) terminal to the high voltage terminal of the ignition coil. If the reading is between 6,500–11,500Ω, the ignition coil is OK; go on to the Wiring Harness Test. If the reading is less than 6,500Ω or more than 11,500Ω, replace the ignition coil.

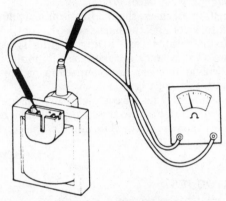

Ignition coil secondary resistance test

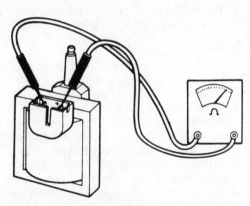

Ignition coil primary resistance test

WIRING HARNESS TEST

1. Separate the wiring harness connector from the ignition module and check for dirt, corrosion and damage. Push the connector tabs to separate the connector.

2. Disconnect the wire at the **S** terminal of the starter relay.

3. Attach the negative (–) lead from a volt/ohmmeter to the distributor base.

4. Measure battery voltage.

5. Following the table below, measure the connector terminal voltage by attaching the positive volt/ohmmeter lead to a small straight

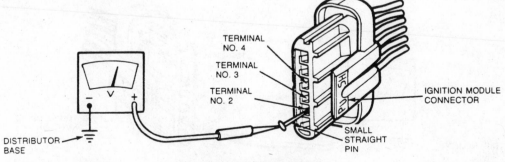

Wiring harness connector test

pin inserted into the connector terminal and turning the ignition switch to the position shown.

CONNECTOR TERMINAL	WIRE/CIRCUIT	IGNITION SWITCH TEST POSITION
#2	TO IGNITION COIL (−) TERMINAL	RUN
#3	RUN CIRCUIT	RUN AND START
#4	START CIRCUIT	START

CAUTION: *Do not allow the straight pin to touch any electrical ground*

6. If, in all cases, the reading is at least 90% of battery voltage, the harness is OK; continue on to the Stator Test. If any reading is less than 90% of battery voltage, check for faults in the wiring harness and connectors or for a damaged or worn ignition switch.

7. After all tests are complete, turn the ignition switch off. Remove the straight pin and reconnect the wire to the **S** terminal of the starter relay.

STATOR TEST

1. Turn the ignition switch off.
2. Remove the coil wire and ground it.
3. Attach the negative (−) lead from a volt/ohmmeter to the distributor base.
4. Disconnect the pin-in-line connector near the distributor and attach the positive (+) volt/ohmmeter lead to the TFI module side of the connector.
5. Turn the ignition switch on.
6. Bump the starter and measure the voltage levels with the engine not moving. Allow sufficient time for the digital voltage reading to stabilize before taking the measurement. Record all values for possible use in additional tests.
7. If the highest reading is greater than 90 percent of battery voltage, go to Step 8. If the

highest value is less than 90 percent of battery voltage, replace the stator assembly.

8. If the lowest value is greater than 0.5 volts, remove the distributor from the engine. Remove the TFI module from the distributor and check the stator connector terminals and TFI terminals for misalignment; service as necessary. If OK, replace the stator assembly. If the lowest value is less than 0.5 volts, go to Step 9.

9. If all values are between 0.5 volts and 90% of battery voltage, replace the stator assembly. If no values are between 0.5 volts and 90% of battery voltage, go on to the EEC-IV/TFI-IV Test.

EEC-IV/TFI-IV TEST

Connect a spark tester between the ignition coil wire and engine ground. Crank the engine and check for spark. If no spark is present, replace the TFI-IV module. If spark is present, check the PIP (Profile Ignition Pickup) and ground wires for continuity and repair as necessary. If OK, the EEC-IV system will have to be diagnosed. See Chapter 4 for details.

PRIMARY CIRCUIT CONTINUITY TEST

1. Push the connector tabs and separate the wiring harness connector from the ignition module. Check for dirt, corrosion and damage and repair as necessary.

2. Attach the negative (−) lead from a volt/ohmmeter to the distributor base.

3. Measure battery voltage.

4. Attach the positive (+) lead of the volt/ohmmeter to a small straight pin inserted into connector terminal No. 2. Be careful not to let the pin touch any electrical ground.

5. Turn the ignition switch to the RUN position and measure the voltage at terminal No. 2. If the reading is at least 90% of battery voltage, go back to the Wiring Harness Test. If the reading is less than 90% of battery voltage,

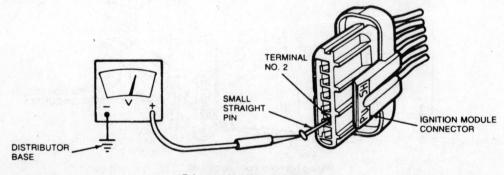

Primary circuit continuity test

continue on to the Ignition Coil Primary Voltage Test.

IGNITION COIL PRIMARY VOLTAGE TEST

1. Attach the negative (–) lead of the volt/ohmmeter to the distributor base.
2. Measure the battery voltage.
3. Turn the ignition switch to the RUN position and measure the voltage at the negative (–) terminal of the ignition coil.
4. If the reading is at least 90% of battery voltage, check the wiring harness between the ignition module and coil negative terminal. If the reading is less than 90% of battery voltage, check the wiring harness between the ignition module and coil negative terminal, then go on to the next test.

IGNITION COIL SUPPLY VOLTAGE TEST

1. Remove the coil connector.
2. Attach the negative (–) lead from a volt/ohmmeter to the distributor base.
3. Measure the battery voltage.
4. Turn the ignition switch to the RUN position.
5. Measure the voltage at the positive (+) terminal of the ignition coil. If the reading is at least 90% of battery voltage, check the ignition coil connector for dirt, corrosion and damage. Check the ignition coil terminals for dirt, corrosion and damage; if no problem is found, replace the ignition coil. If the reading is less than 90% of battery voltage, check the wiring between the ignition coil and ignition switch, or for a worn or damaged ignition switch.

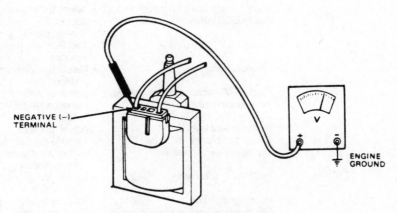

NEGATIVE (–) TERMINAL

V

ENGINE GROUND

Ignition coil primary voltage test

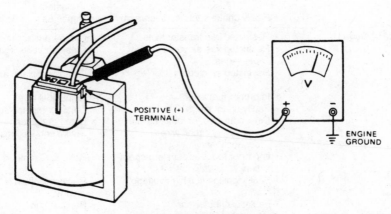

POSITIVE (+) TERMINAL

V

ENGINE GROUND

Ignition coil supply voltage test

Troubleshooting Engine Performance

Problem	Cause	Solution
Hard starting (engine cranks normally)	• Binding linkage, choke valve or choke piston	• Repair as necessary
	• Restricted choke vacuum diaphragm	• Clean passages
	• Improper fuel level	• Adjust float level
	• Dirty, worn or faulty needle valve and seat	• Repair as necessary
	• Float sticking	• Repair as necessary
	• Faulty fuel pump	• Replace fuel pump
	• Incorrect choke cover adjustment	• Adjust choke cover
	• Inadequate choke unloader adjustment	• Adjust choke unloader
	• Faulty ignition coil	• Test and replace as necessary
	• Improper spark plug gap	• Adjust gap
	• Incorrect ignition timing	• Adjust timing
	• Incorrect valve timing	• Check valve timing; repair as necessary
Rough idle or stalling	• Incorrect curb or fast idle speed	• Adjust curb or fast idle speed
	• Incorrect ignition timing	• Adjust timing to specification
	• Improper feedback system operation	• Refer to Chapter 4
	• Improper fast idle cam adjustment	• Adjust fast idle cam
	• Faulty EGR valve operation	• Test EGR system and replace as necessary
	• Faulty PCV valve air flow	• Test PCV valve and replace as necessary
	• Choke binding	• Locate and eliminate binding condition
	• Faulty TAC vacuum motor or valve	• Repair as necessary
	• Air leak into manifold vacuum	• Inspect manifold vacuum connections and repair as necessary
	• Improper fuel level	• Adjust fuel level
	• Faulty distributor rotor or cap	• Replace rotor or cap
	• Improperly seated valves	• Test cylinder compression, repair as necessary
	• Incorrect ignition wiring	• Inspect wiring and correct as necessary
	• Faulty ignition coil	• Test coil and replace as necessary
	• Restricted air vent or idle passages	• Clean passages
	• Restricted air cleaner	• Clean or replace air cleaner filler element
	• Faulty choke vacuum diaphragm	• Repair as necessary
Faulty low-speed operation	• Restricted idle transfer slots	• Clean transfer slots
	• Restricted idle air vents and passages	• Clean air vents and passages
	• Restricted air cleaner	• Clean or replace air cleaner filter element
	• Improper fuel level	• Adjust fuel level
	• Faulty spark plugs	• Clean or replace spark plugs
	• Dirty, corroded, or loose ignition secondary circuit wire connections	• Clean or tighten secondary circuit wire connections
	• Improper feedback system operation	• Refer to Chapter 4
	• Faulty ignition coil high voltage wire	• Replace ignition coil high voltage wire
	• Faulty distributor cap	• Replace cap
Faulty acceleration	• Improper accelerator pump stroke	• Adjust accelerator pump stroke
	• Incorrect ignition timing	• Adjust timing
	• Inoperative pump discharge check ball or needle	• Clean or replace as necessary
	• Worn or damaged pump diaphragm or piston	• Replace diaphragm or piston

Troubleshooting Engine Performance (cont.)

Problem	Cause	Solution
Faulty acceleration (cont.)	• Leaking carburetor main body cover gasket	• Replace gasket
	• Engine cold and choke set too lean	• Adjust choke cover
	• Improper metering rod adjustment (BBD Model carburetor)	• Adjust metering rod
	• Faulty spark plug(s)	• Clean or replace spark plug(s)
	• Improperly seated valves	• Test cylinder compression, repair as necessary
	• Faulty ignition coil	• Test coil and replace as necessary
	• Improper feedback system operation	• Refer to Chapter 4
Faulty high speed operation	• Incorrect ignition timing	• Adjust timing
	• Faulty distributor centrifugal advance mechanism	• Check centrifugal advance mechanism and repair as necessary
	• Faulty distributor vacuum advance mechanism	• Check vacuum advance mechanism and repair as necessary
	• Low fuel pump volume	• Replace fuel pump
	• Wrong spark plug air gap or wrong plug	• Adjust air gap or install correct plug
	• Faulty choke operation	• Adjust choke cover
	• Partially restricted exhaust manifold, exhaust pipe, catalytic converter, muffler, or tailpipe	• Eliminate restriction
	• Restricted vacuum passages	• Clean passages
	• Improper size or restricted main jet	• Clean or replace as necessary
	• Restricted air cleaner	• Clean or replace filter element as necessary
	• Faulty distributor rotor or cap	• Replace rotor or cap
	• Faulty ignition coil	• Test coil and replace as necessary
	• Improperly seated valve(s)	• Test cylinder compression, repair as necessary
	• Faulty valve spring(s)	• Inspect and test valve spring tension, replace as necessary
	• Incorrect valve timing	• Check valve timing and repair as necessary
	• Intake manifold restricted	• Remove restriction or replace manifold
	• Worn distributor shaft	• Replace shaft
	• Improper feedback system operation	• Refer to Chapter 4
Misfire at all speeds	• Faulty spark plug(s)	• Clean or replace spark plug(s)
	• Faulty spark plug wire(s)	• Replace as necessary
	• Faulty distributor cap or rotor	• Replace cap or rotor
	• Faulty ignition coil	• Test coil and replace as necessary
	• Primary ignition circuit shorted or open intermittently	• Troubleshoot primary circuit and repair as necessary
	• Improperly seated valve(s)	• Test cylinder compression, repair as necessary
	• Faulty hydraulic tappet(s)	• Clean or replace tappet(s)
	• Improper feedback system operation	• Refer to Chapter 4
	• Faulty valve spring(s)	• Inspect and test valve spring tension, repair as necessary
	• Worn camshaft lobes	• Replace camshaft
	• Air leak into manifold	• Check manifold vacuum and repair as necessary
	• Improper carburetor adjustment	• Adjust carburetor
	• Fuel pump volume or pressure low	• Replace fuel pump
	• Blown cylinder head gasket	• Replace gasket
	• Intake or exhaust manifold passage(s) restricted	• Pass chain through passage(s) and repair as necessary
	• Incorrect trigger wheel installed in distributor	• Install correct trigger wheel

Troubleshooting Engine Performance (cont.)

Problem	Cause	Solution
Power not up to normal	• Incorrect ignition timing	• Adjust timing
	• Faulty distributor rotor	• Replace rotor
	• Trigger wheel loose on shaft	• Reposition or replace trigger wheel
	• Incorrect spark plug gap	• Adjust gap
	• Faulty fuel pump	• Replace fuel pump
	• Incorrect valve timing	• Check valve timing and repair as necessary
	• Faulty ignition coil	• Test coil and replace as necessary
	• Faulty ignition wires	• Test wires and replace as necessary
	• Improperly seated valves	• Test cylinder compression and repair as necessary
	• Blown cylinder head gasket	• Replace gasket
	• Leaking piston rings	• Test compression and repair as necessary
	• Worn distributor shaft	• Replace shaft
	• Improper feedback system operation	• Refer to Chapter 4
Intake backfire	• Improper ignition timing	• Adjust timing
	• Faulty accelerator pump discharge	• Repair as necessary
	• Defective EGR CTO valve	• Replace EGR CTO valve
	• Defective TAC vacuum motor or valve	• Repair as necessary
	• Lean air/fuel mixture	• Check float level or manifold vacuum for air leak. Remove sediment from bowl
Exhaust backfire	• Air leak into manifold vacuum	• Check manifold vacuum and repair as necessary
	• Faulty air injection diverter valve	• Test diverter valve and replace as necessary
	• Exhaust leak	• Locate and eliminate leak
Ping or spark knock	• Incorrect ignition timing	• Adjust timing
	• Distributor centrifugal or vacuum advance malfunction	• Inspect advance mechanism and repair as necessary
	• Excessive combustion chamber deposits	• Remove with combustion chamber cleaner
	• Air leak into manifold vacuum	• Check manifold vacuum and repair as necessary
	• Excessively high compression	• Test compression and repair as necessary
	• Fuel octane rating excessively low	• Try alternate fuel source
	• Sharp edges in combustion chamber	• Grind smooth
	• EGR valve not functioning properly	• Test EGR system and replace as necessary
Surging (at cruising to top speeds)	• Low carburetor fuel level	• Adjust fuel level
	• Low fuel pump pressure or volume	• Replace fuel pump
	• Metering rod(s) not adjusted properly (BBD Model Carburetor)	• Adjust metering rod
	• Improper PCV valve air flow	• Test PCV valve and replace as necessary
	• Air leak into manifold vacuum	• Check manifold vacuum and repair as necessary
	• Incorrect spark advance	• Test and replace as necessary
	• Restricted main jet(s)	• Clean main jet(s)
	• Undersize main jet(s)	• Replace main jet(s)
	• Restricted air vents	• Clean air vents
	• Restricted fuel filter	• Replace fuel filter
	• Restricted air cleaner	• Clean or replace air cleaner filter element
	• EGR valve not functioning properly	• Test EGR system and replace as necessary
	• Improper feedback system operation	• Refer to Chapter 4

TROUBLESHOOTING BASIC POINT-TYPE IGNITION SYSTEM PROBLEMS

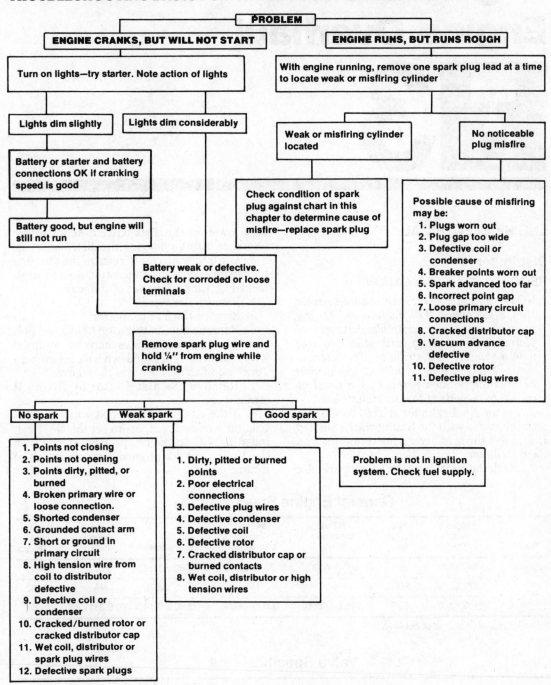

PROBLEM

ENGINE CRANKS, BUT WILL NOT START

ENGINE RUNS, BUT RUNS ROUGH

Turn on lights—try starter. Note action of lights

With engine running, remove one spark plug lead at a time to locate weak or misfiring cylinder

Lights dim slightly

Lights dim considerably

Weak or misfiring cylinder located

No noticeable plug misfire

Battery or starter and battery connections OK if cranking speed is good

Check condition of spark plug against chart in this chapter to determine cause of misfire—replace spark plug

Possible cause of misfiring may be:
1. Plugs worn out
2. Plug gap too wide
3. Defective coil or condenser
4. Breaker points worn out
5. Spark advanced too far
6. Incorrect point gap
7. Loose primary circuit connections
8. Cracked distributor cap
9. Vacuum advance defective
10. Defective rotor
11. Defective plug wires

Battery good, but engine will still not run

Battery weak or defective. Check for corroded or loose terminals

Remove spark plug wire and hold ¼" from engine while cranking

No spark

Weak spark

Good spark

1. Points not closing
2. Points not opening
3. Points dirty, pitted, or burned
4. Broken primary wire or loose connection.
5. Shorted condenser
6. Grounded contact arm
7. Short or ground in primary circuit
8. High tension wire from coil to distributor defective
9. Defective coil or condenser
10. Cracked/burned rotor or cracked distributor cap
11. Wet coil, distributor or spark plug wires
12. Defective spark plugs

1. Dirty, pitted or burned points
2. Poor electrical connections
3. Defective plug wires
4. Defective condenser
5. Defective coil
6. Defective rotor
7. Cracked distributor cap or burned contacts
8. Wet coil, distributor or high tension wires

Problem is not in ignition system. Check fuel supply.

Engine and Engine Overhaul

3

ENGINE ELECTRICAL

Distributor

REMOVAL AND INSTALLATION

NOTE: *Except for the cap, adapter, rotor, Hall Effect stator, TFI module and O-ring, no other distributor assembly parts are replaceable. There is no calibration required with the universal distributor. The distributor assembly can be identified by the part number information printed on a decal attached to the side of the distributor base.*

1. Set the No. 1 cylinder at TDC on the compression stroke with the timing marks aligned. Disconnect the primary wiring connector from the distributor.

2. Mark the position of the No. 1 spark plug wire tower on the distributor base for future reference before removing the distributor cap.

3. Use a screwdriver to remove the distributor cap and adapter and position it and the attached ignition wires out of the way.

4. Remove the rotor.

5. Remove the TFI connector.

6. Remove the distributor holddown bolt and clamp. Some engines may be equipped with a security type holddown bolt, requiring a Torx® bit of the proper size to remove it.

7. Remove the distributor by lifting it straight up.

8. If the engine was rotated while the distributor was removed, again set the No. 1 cylinder at TDC on the compression stroke with the timing marks aligned for correct initial timing.

General Engine Specifications

Years	Engine cu. in. (liter)	Fuel System Type	SAE net Horsepower @ rpm	SAE net Torque ft. lb. @ rpm	Bore x Stroke	Comp. Ratio	Oil Press. (psi.) @ 2000 rpm
1986–87	140 (2.3)	EFI	88 @ 4000	132 @ 2200	3.780 x 3.126	9.5:1	40–60
	171 (2.8)	FBC	NA	NA	3.65 x 2.70	NA	40–60
	182 (3.0)	EFI	145 @ 4800	165 @ 3600	3.50 x 3.14	9.3:1	40–60

NA—Not available at time of publication

Valve Specifications

Year	Engine cu. in. (liter)	Seat Angle (deg)	Face Angle (deg)	Spring Test Pressure (lbs. @ in.)	Spring Installed Height (in.)	Stem to Guide Clearance (in.) Intake	Stem to Guide Clearance (in.) Exhaust	Stem Diameter (in.) Intake	Stem Diameter (in.) Exhaust
1986–87	140 (2.3)	45	44	142 @ 1.12	1.49–1.55	.0010–.0027	.0015–.0032	.3416–.3423	.3411–.3418
	171 (2.8)	45	44	138 @ 1.22	1.58–1.61	.0008–.0025	.0018–.0035	.3159–.3167	.3149–.3156
	182 (3.0)	45	44	185 @ 1.11	1.85	.0010–.0027	.0015–.0032	.3134–.3126	.3129–.3121

Torque Specifications
All specifications in foot pounds

Years	Engine cu. in. (liter)	Cyl. Head	Conn. Rod	Main Bearing	Crankshaft Damper	Flywheel	Manifold	
							Intake	Exhaust
1986–87	140 (2.3)	80–90 ①	30–36 ②	80–90 ①	100–120	56–64	13–18	16–23 ③
	171 (2.8)	70–85 ④	19–24	65–75	85–96	47–52	15–18 ⑤	20–30
	182 (3.0)	63–80 ⑥	20–25 ⑦	65–81	141–169	54–64	24	15–22 ⑧

① Torque in two steps:
   Step 1: 50–60
   Step 2: 80–90
② Torque in two steps:
   Step 1: 25–30
   Step 2: 30–36
③ Torque in two steps:
   Step 1: 5–7
   Step 2: 16–23
④ Torque in three steps:
   Step 1: 29–40
   Step 2: 40–51
   Step 3: 70–85
⑤ Torque in four steps:
   Step 1: 3–6
   Step 2: 6–11
   Step 3: 11–15
   Step 4: 15–18
⑥ Torque in two steps:
   Step 1: 48–54
   Step 2: 63–80
⑦ Torque in three steps:
   Step 1: 20–28
   Step 2: Back off 2 turns
   Step 3: 20–25
⑧ Torque in three steps:
   Step 1: 11
   Step 2: 18
   Step 3: 24

Crankshaft and Connecting Rod Specifications
All specifications in inches

Years	Engine cu. in. (liter)	Crankshaft				Connecting Rod		
		Main Bearing Journal Dia.	Main Bearing Oil Clearance	Shaft End Play	Thrust on No.	Journal Dia.	Oil Clearance	Side Clearance
1986–87	140 (2.3)	2.399–2.398	.0008–.0015	.0004–.0008 ①	3	2.0462–2.0472	.0008–.0015	.004–.011 ②
	171 (2.8)	2.2433–2.2441	.0008–.0015	.0004–.0008 ①	3	2.1252–2.1260	.0006–.0016	.004–.011 ②
	182 (3.0)	2.5190–2.5198	.0010–.0014	.0004–.0008	3	2.1253–2.1261	.0010–.0014	.006–.014 ②

① .012 max
② .014 max

Piston and Ring Specifications
All specifications in inches

Years	Engine cu. in. (liter)	Ring Gap			Ring Side Clearance			
		#1 Compr.	#2 Compr.	Oil Control	#1 Compr.	#2 Compr.	Oil Control	Piston Clearance
1986–87	140 (2.3)	0.010–0.020	0.010–0.020	0.015–0.055	.0020–.0040	.0020–.0040	Snug fit	.0014–.0022
	171 (2.8)	0.015–0.023	0.015–0.023	0.015–0.055	.0020–.0033	.0020–.0033	Snug fit	.0011–.0019
	182 (3.0)	0.010–0.020	0.010–0.020	0.010–0.049	.0016–.0037	.0016–.0037	Snug fit	.0012–.0023

Camshaft Specifications

All specifications in inches

Years	Engine cu. in. (liter)	Journal Diameter				Bearing Clearance	Elevation		End Play
		1	2	3	4		Int.	Exh.	
1986–87	140 (2.3)	— All 1.7713–1.7720 —				0.001–0.003 ①	0.390	0.390	0.001–0.007
	171 (2.8)	1.7285–1.7293	1.7135–1.7143	1.6985–1.6992	1.6835–1.6842	0.001–0.0026 ①	0.3730	0.3730	0.0008–0.0040
	182 (3.0)	— All 2.0074–2.0084 —				0.001–0.003	0.419	0.419	②

① 0.006 max
② No end play. Camshaft is restrained by spring

Starter Specifications

Years	Engine cu. in. (liter)	Current Draw Under Normal Load (amps)	Normal Cranking Speed (rpm)	No-Load Current Draw (amps)	Starter Brushes		
					Brush Length (in.)	Wear Limit (in.)	Spring Tension (oz)
1986–87	All	150–200	180–250	80	0.50	0.25	80

Note: Maximum starting circuit voltage drop (battery positive terminal to starter terminal) at normal engine temperature is 0.5 volt

9. Rotate the distributor shaft so that the rotor tip is pointing toward the mark previously made on the distributor base (No. 1 spark plug tower). Continue rotating slightly so that the leading edge of the vane is centered in the vane switch stator assembly.

10. Rotate the distributor in the engine block to align the leading edge of the vane and the vane switch and verify that the rotor is pointing at No. 1 cap terminal.

NOTE: *If the vane and vane switch stator cannot be aligned by rotating the distributor in the engine block, pull the distributor out of the block enough to disengage the distributor and rotate the distributor to engage a different distributor gear tooth. Repeat Steps 9 and 10 if necessary.*

11. Install the distributor holddown bolt and clamp, but do not tighten yet.

12. Connect the distributor TFI and primary wiring harnesses.

13. Install the distributor rotor and tighten the attaching screws to 24–36 in.lb. (3–4 Nm).

14. Install the distributor cap and tighten the attaching screws to 18–23 in.lb. (2–3 Nm). Check that the ignition wires are securely attached to the cap towers.

15. Install the ignition wires to the spark plugs, making sure they are in the correct firing order and tight on the spark plugs.

16. Check and adjust the initial timing to specifications with a timing light. Refer to the tune-up chart or the underhood emission control sticker for initial timing specifications. The ignition timing procedure is outlined in Chapter 2. No attempt should be made to alter the timing from factory specifications.

17. Once the initial timing is set, tighten the distributor holddown bolt to 17–25 ft.lb. (23–34 Nm). Recheck the timing, then remove the timing light.

Distributor Cap, Adapter and Rotor
REMOVAL AND INSTALLATION

1. Tag all spark plug wires with a piece of tape according to cylinder number for reference when installing the wires, then remove them from the distributor cap. Note the position of No. 1 spark plug tower.

2. Unclip the distributor cap and lift it straight up and off the distributor.

3. Using a screwdriver, loosen the adapter attaching screws and remove the adapter.

4. Loosen the screws attaching the rotor to the distributor and remove the rotor.

5. Wipe the distributor cap and rotor with a clean, damp cloth. Inspect the cap for cracks, broken carbon button, carbon tracks, dirt or corrosion on the terminals and replace the cap if questionable. Replace the rotor if cracks, carbon tracks, burns, damaged blade or a damaged spring is noted.

6. Position the distributor rotor with the

square and round locator pins matched to the rotor mounting plate. Tighten the screws to 24–36 in.lb. (2–4 Nm).

7. Install the adapter and tighten the attaching screws to 18–23 in.lb. (2–3 Nm).

8. Install the cap, noting the square alignment locator, then tighten the holddown screws to 18–23 in.lb. (2–3 Nm).

9. Install the spark plug wires in firing order, starting from No. 1 tower and working in sequence around the cap. Refer to the firing order illustrations in Chapter 2, if necessary. Make sure the ignition wires are installed correctly and are firmly seated in the distributor cap towers.

TFI Ignition Module

REMOVAL AND INSTALLATION

1. Remove the distributor cap with the ignition wires attached and position it out of the way. Remove the adapter.

2. Disconnect the TFI harness connector.

3. Remove the distributor from the engine as previously described.

4. Place the distributor on a clean workbench and remove the two TFI module attaching screws.

5. Pull the right side of the module down toward the distributor mounting flange and then back up to disengage the module terminals from the connector in the distributor base. The module may then be pulled toward the flange and away from the distributor.

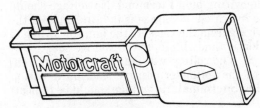

Typical TFI ignition module

CAUTION: *Do not attempt to lift the module from its mounting surface prior to moving the entire TFI module toward the distributor flange or you will break the pins at the distributor/module connector.*

6. Coat the metal base of the new TFI module with a $\frac{1}{32}''$ (0.8mm) thick film of Silicone Dielectric Compound D7AZ-19A331-A or equivalent. This is extermely important to help dissipate the heat when the module is operating.

7. Place the TFI module on the distributor base mounting flange.

8. Carefully position the TFI module assembly toward the distributor bowl and engage the three distributor connector pins securely. Be careful when performing this step. It is very easy to bend one of the connector pins when installing.

9. Install the two TFI mounting screws and tighten them to 15–35 in.lb. (1–4 Nm).

10. Install the distributor on the engine as previously described.

11. Install the distributor cap and tighten the mounting screws to 18–23 in.lb. (2–3 Nm).

12. Reconnect the TFI wiring harness connector.

13. Attach a timing light according to the manufacturer's instructions and set the initial timing. See Chapter 2 for details.

Octane Rod

REMOVAL AND INSTALLATION

1. Remove the distributor cap, adapter and rotor as previously described.

2. Remove the octane rod 4mm retaining screw carefully. Don't drop it.

3. Slide the octane rod grommet out to a point where the rod can be disengaged from the stator retaining post and remove the octane rod. Retain the grommet for use with the new octane rod.

4. Install the grommet on the new octane rod.

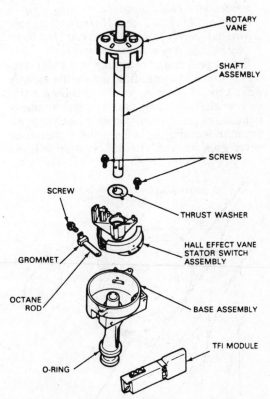

Exploded view of universal distributor assembly

5. Install the octane rod into the distributor, making sure it engages the stator retaining post.

6. Install the retaining screw and tighten it to 15–35 in.lb. (2–4 Nm).

7. Install the rotor, adapter and cap as described above.

Alternator

The alternator charging system is a negative ground system, consisting of an alternator, regulator, charge indicator, storage battery, fusible link and associated wiring. The integral alternator/regulator is belt driven from the engine.

The fusible link is a short length of insulated wire located between the starter relay and the alternator that is designed to burn out, thus protecting the alternator and wiring when heavy reverse current flows, such as when a booster battery is connected incorrectly or a short to ground occurs in the wiring harness. If an alternator or charging system problem is being diagnosed, always check the condition of the fusible link first.

NOTE: *The alternator warning light on the Aerostar can have a different meaning than with other systems. The light may indicate a high or low voltage condition. Extended vehicle idling with high electrical loads (all accessories on) could cause the warning lamp to come on. This is not meant to indicate a problem, but merely to warn the driver that there may be a battery discharge condition.*

Before performing charging or starting system tests on the van, first determine exactly what type of problem you are dealing with, such as slow cranking, battery dead, ammeter light shows charge at all times or no charge, alternator warning light does not come on or never goes out, etc. This information will aid in isolating the part of the system causing the problem. Next, the system should be visually inspected as follows:

1. Check the fusible link located between the starter solenoid and the alternator. Replace the fusible link if burned.

2. Check the battery posts and cable terminals for clean and tight connections.

3. Check for clean and tight wiring connections at the alternator, regulator and engine.

4. Check the alternator belt tension using belt tension gauge T63L-8620-A, or equivalent and adjust the belt tension if necessary.

Alternator Testing

A voltmeter, ohmmeter, jumper wire and a 12 volt test lamp are the only tools necessary to perform an accurate check of the complete charging system. Perform the visual checks described above before attempting these diagnosis procedures.

FIELD CIRCUIT DRAIN TEST

NOTE: *Connect the voltmeter negative lead to the alternator rear housing for all of the following voltage readings.*

1. With the ignition switch turned off, contact the voltmeter positive lead to the regulator **F** terminal screw. The meter should indicate battery voltage (12 volts) if the system is operating properly. If less than battery voltage is indicated, proceed to the next step.

2. Disconnect the wiring plug from the regulator and contact the voltmeter positive lead to the wiring plug **I** terminal. No voltage should be indicated. If voltage is indicated, check the wiring from the **I** lead to the ignition switch to identify and eliminate the voltage source.

3. If no voltage was indicated in Step 2, contact the voltmeter positive lead to the wiring plug **S** terminal. No voltage should be indicat-

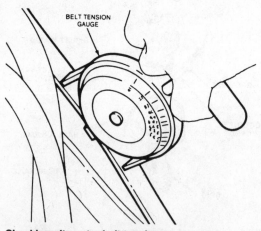

Checking alternator belt tension

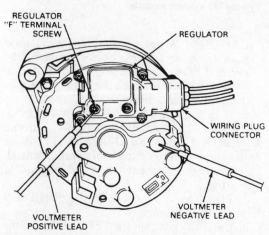

Field circuit drain test alternator connections

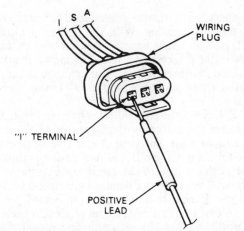

Field circuit drain test regulator harness connections

ed. If no voltage is indicated, replace the regulator.

4. If voltage was indicated in Step 3, disconnect the wiring plug from the alternator. Again, connect the voltmeter positive lead to the regulator wiring plug **S** terminal. If voltage is still indicated, service the **S** lead to the alternator plug to eliminate the voltage source. If no voltage is indicated, replace the alternator.

BASE VOLTAGE TEST

With the ignition off and no electrical load on, connect the negative lead of a voltmeter to the negative battery cable clamp. Connect the positive lead of the voltmeter to the positive battery cable clamp. Record the voltage shown on the voltmeter scale; this is called the base voltage and should be 12 volts. Leave the voltmeter connected for the following tests.

NO LOAD TEST

Connect a tachometer to the engine. Start the engine and increase the speed to about 1,500 rpm. With no other electrical load (foot off the brake pedal and all doors closed), the voltmeter should show an increase of not more than 2 volts above base voltage recorded above. The reading should be taken when the voltmeter indicates peak voltage (stops rising), which may take a few minutes. If the voltage increases to the proper level, continue on to the Load Test. If the voltmeter reading continues to rise, perform the Over Voltage Test. If the voltmeter reading fails to increase, perform the Under Voltage Test.

LOAD TEST

With the engine running, turn the heater or A/C blower motor on high speed and the headlamps on high beam. Increase the engine speed

to about 2,000 rpm. The voltmeter should indicate a minimum of 0.5 volt above base voltage. If not, perform the Under Voltage Test.

NOTE: *If the above tests indicate proper voltage readings, the charging system is operating normally. Proceed to the tests below if one or more of the readings is different than shown above and use a test lamp to check for battery drain.*

OVER VOLTAGE TEST

1. With the ignition on and engine off, connect the voltmeter positive lead first to the alternator output connection at the starter solenoid and then to the regulator **A** screw head. If the voltage difference between the two locations is greater than 0.5 volt, service the **A** wiring circuit to eliminate the high resistance condition indicated by the excessive voltage drop.

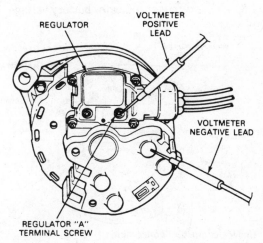

Over voltage test

2. If the over voltage condition still exists, check for loose regulator to alternator grounding screws. Tighten loose regulator grounding screws to 15–26 in.lb. (1–3 Nm).

3. If the over voltage condition still exists, connect the voltmeter negative lead to the alternator rear housing. With the ignition off, contact the voltmeter positive lead first to the regulator **A** screw head and then to the regulator **F** screw head. Different voltage readings at the two screw heads indicates a defective regulator, grounded brush lead or a grounded rotor coil.

4. If the same voltage reading (battery voltage) is obtained at both screw heads in Step 3 and there is no high resistance in the ground or A+ circuits, then the regulator calibration is high. Replace the regulator.

UNDER VOLTAGE TEST

1. If the voltage does not indicate more than 0.5 volt above base voltage, disconnect the wiring plug from the regulator and connect an ohmmeter between the regulator **A** and **F** terminal screws. The ohmmeter should indicate more than 2.4Ω. If less than 2.4Ω is indicated, replace the alternator and repeat the Load Test.

2. If the ohmmeter reading is greater than 2.4Ω, reconnect the regulator wiring plug and connect the voltmeter ground lead to the alternator rear housing. Contact the voltmeter positive lead to the regulator **A** terminal screw. The voltmeter should indicate battery voltage. If there is no voltage, check the **A** circuit, then repeat the Load Test.

NOTE: *A shorted rotor coil or field circuit will damage the regulator. If the regulator is replaced before the rotor coil or field circuit is repaired, the new regulator will be damaged.*

3. If the voltmeter indicates battery voltage, connect the voltmeter ground lead to the alternator rear housing. With the ignition switch off, contact the voltmeter positive lead to the regulator **F** terminal screw. The meter should indicate battery voltage. If no voltage is indicated, there is an open field circuit in the alternator. Replace the alternator.

4. If the voltmeter indicates battery voltage, connect the voltmeter negative lead to the alternator rear housing. Turn the ignition switch on (engine off) and contact the voltmeter positive lead to the regulator **F** terminal screw. The voltmeter should indicate 1.5 volts or less. If more than 1.5 volts is indicated, perform the **I** circuit test. If the **I** circuit checks normal, replace the regulator and repeat the Load Test.

5. If 1.5 volts or less is indicated, disconnect the alternator wiring plug and connect a set of 12 gauge jumper wires between the alternator B+ terminal blades and the mating wiring connector terminals. Perform the Load Test, but connect the voltmeter positive lead to one

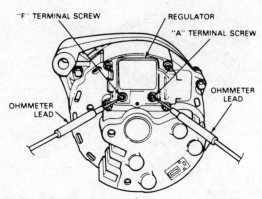

Under voltage test connections

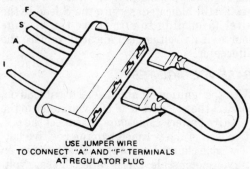

USE JUMPER WIRE
TO CONNECT "A" AND "F" TERMINALS
AT REGULATOR PLUG

Under voltage test jumper wire connection at regulator plug

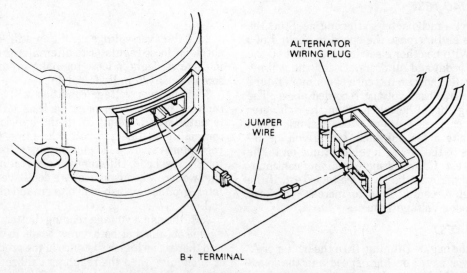

Under voltage test jumper wire connection at alternator

of the B+ jumper wire terminals. If the voltage rises more than 0.5 volt above base voltage, service the alternator-to-starter relay wiring. Repeat the load test measuring the voltage at the battery cable clamps after servicing.

6. If the voltage does not rise more than 0.5 volt above base voltage, connect a jumper wire from the alternator rear housing to the regulator **F** terminal. Repeat the Load Test with the voltmeter positive lead connected to one of the B+ jumper wire terminals. If the voltage rises more than 0.5 volt, replace the regulator. If the voltage does not rise more than 0.5 volt, replace the alternator.

REGULATOR S AND/OR I CIRCUIT TEST

1. Disconnect the wiring plug from the regultor. Connect a jumper wire from the regulator **A** terminal to the wiring plug **A** lead. Add a jumper wire from the regulator **F** screw to the alternator rear housing.

2. With the engine idling and the voltmeter negative lead connected to the battery ground terminal, connect the voltmeter positive lead to the **S** terminal and then to the **I** terminal of the regulator wiring plug. The voltage at the **S** circuit should read approximately one-half that of the **I** circuit. If the voltage readings are normal, remove the jumper wires. Replace the regulator and connect the wiring plug to it, then repeat the Load Test.

3. If no voltage is present, remove the jumper wires and service the faulty wiring circuit or alternator.

tion and the engine not running, check the indicator bulb for continuity and replace the bulb if it is burned out. If the bulb checks good, perform the regulator **I** circuit test.

2. If the indicator lamp does not light, remove the jumper wire and reconnect the wiring plug to the regulator. Connect the voltmeter negative lead to the battery negative post cable clamp and contact the voltmeter positive lead to the regulator **A** terminal screw. Battery voltage should be indicated. If battery voltage is not indicated, check the **A** circuit wiring.

3. If battery voltage is indicated, clean and tighten the ground connections to the engine, alternator and regulator. Tighten loose regulator mounting screws to 15–26 in.lb. (1–3 Nm).

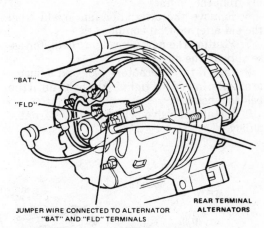

Alternator indicator lamp system test

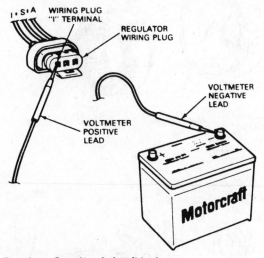

Regulator S and/ or I circuit test

ALTERNATOR INDICATOR LAMP SYSTEM TEST

1. If the charge indicator lamp does not come on with the ignition switch in the on posi-

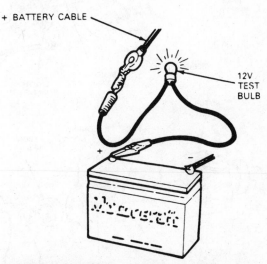

Testing for constant current drain with a test light. If the bulb glows, check the individual circuits to locate and eliminate the cause of the current drain on the battery. Underhood lamp, glove box lamp, reading or vanity lamps are prime suspects

4. Turn the ignition on with the engine off. If the indicator lamp still does not light, replace the regulator.

ALTERNATOR REMOVAL AND INSTALLATION

1. Disconnect the negative (–) battery cable.

2. Disconnect the wiring harness attachments to the integral alternator/regulator assembly. Pull the two connectors straight out.

3. Loosen the alternator pivot bolt and remove the adjustment arm bolt from the alternator.

4. Disengage the alternator drive belt from the alternator pulley.

5. Remove the alternator pivot bolt and carefully lift the alternator/regulator assembly from the engine.

6. Remove the alternator fan shield from the old alternator, if equipped.

7. Position the new alternator/regulator assembly on the engine.

8. Install the alternator pivot and adjuster arm bolts, but do not tighten the bolts until the belt is tensioned.

9. Install the drive belt over the alternator pulley.

10. Adjust the belt tension, then tighten the adjuster and pivot bolts.

NOTE: *Apply pressure to alternator front housing only when when adjusting belt tension*

11. Connect the wiring harness to the alternator/regulator assembly. Push the two connectors straight in.

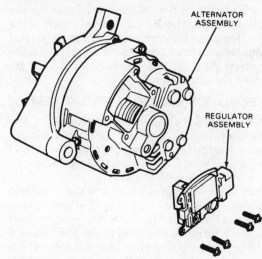

Removing the voltage regulator from the alternator

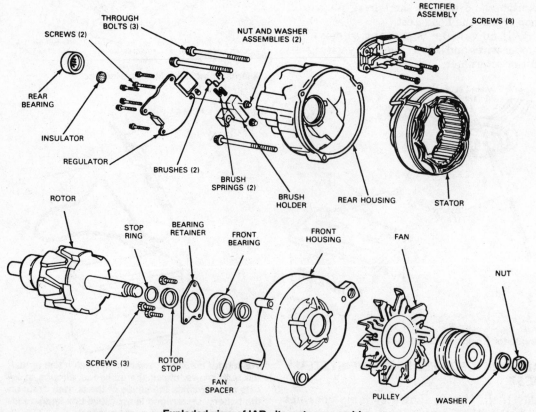

Exploded view of IAR alternator assembly

12. Attach the alternator fan shield to the alternator, if equipped.

13. Reconnect the ground cable to the battery.

REGULATOR REMOVAL AND INSTALLATION

The regulator is attached to the back of the alternator by four Torx® screws. Disonnect the wiring connector and remove the mounting screws to replace the regulator. Remove the regulator with the brush holder attached and transfer components to the replacement regulator as necessary. Make sure all wiring connectors are clean and tight.

Starter

REMOVAL AND INSTALLATION

1. Disconnect the negative battery cable.

2. Raise the vehicle and support it safely on jackstands.

3. Disconnect the relay-to-starter cable at the starter terminal.

4. Remove the starter mounting bolts and lower the starter from the engine.

5. Position the new starter assembly to the flywheel housing and start the mounting bolts in by hand.

6. Snug all bolts while holding the starter squarely against its mounting surface and fully inserted into the pilot hole. Tighten the mounting bolts to 15–20 ft.lb. (21–27 Nm).

7. Reconnect the relay-to-starter cable assembly to the starter motor. Tighten the screw and washer assemblies to 70–130 in.lb. (8–15 Nm).

8. Lower the vehicle, then connect the negative battery cable.

STARTER DRIVE REPLACEMENT

1. Remove the starter as described above.

2. Remove the starter drive plunger cover.

3. Remove the pivot pin retaining the starter drive plunger lever.

4. Loosen the through bolts enough to allow removal of the drive end housing, starter drive plunger lever and return spring.

5. Remove the drive gear stop ring retainer and stop ring from the end of the armature shaft and remove the drive gear assembly.

6. Apply a thin coating of Lubriplate® 777 or equivalent on the armature shaft splines.

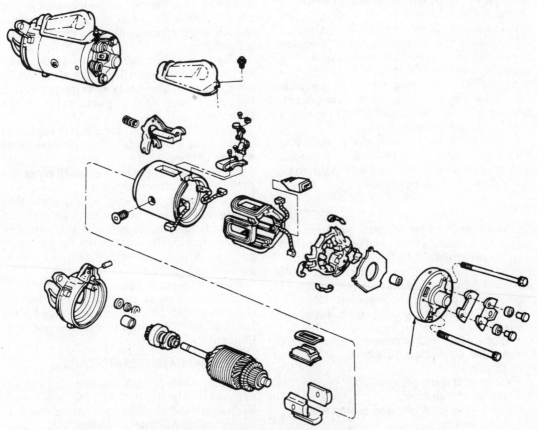

Exploded view of the starter assembly

Install the drive gear assembly on the armature shaft and install a new stop ring.

7. Position the starter gear plunger lever on the starter frame. Make sure the plunger lever properly engages the starter drive assembly.

8. Install a new stop ring retainer. Partially fill the drive end housing bearing bore with grease (approximately ¼ full), then position the starter drive plunger lever return spring and drive end housing to the starter frame. Tighten the through bolts to 55–75 in.lb. (6–8 Nm).

9. Position the starter drive plunger lever cover, with its gasket, on the starter and tighten the attaching screw.

10. Install the starter to the engine as previously described.

ENGINE MECHANICAL

Engine Overhaul

Most engine overhaul procedures are fairly standard. In addition to specific parts replacement procedures and complete specifications for each individual engine, this chapter is also a guide to acceptable rebuilding procedures. Examples of standard rebuilding practice are shown and should be used along with specific details concerning your particular engine.

Competent and accurate machine shop services will insure maximum performance, reliability and engine life. In most instances, it is more profitable for the do-it-yourself mechanic to remove, clean and inspect the component, buy the necessary parts and deliver these to a shop for actual machine work.

On the other hand, much of the rebuilding work (crankshaft, block, bearings, piston rods, and other components) is well within the scope of the do-it-yourself mechanic.

TOOLS

The tools required for an engine overhaul or parts replacement will depend on the depth of your involvement. With few exceptions, they will be the tools found in any mechanic's tool kit (see Chapter 1). More in-depth work will require some or all of the following:
• a dial indicator (reading in thousandths) mounted on a universal base
  • micrometers and telescope gauges
  • jaw and screw-type pullers
  • scraper
  • valve spring compressor
  • ring groove cleaner
  • piston ring expander and compressor
  • ridge reamer
  • cylinder hone or glaze breaker

• Plastigage®
• engine stand

The use of most of these tools is illustrated in this chapter. Many can be rented for a one-time use from a local parts jobber or tool supply house specializing in automotive work. Occasionally, the use of special tools is called for. See the information on Special Tools and Safety Notice in the front of this book before substituting another tool.

INSPECTION TECHNIQUES

Procedures and specifications are given in this chapter for inspecting, cleaning and assessing the wear limits of most major components. Other procedures such as Magnaflux® and Zyglo® can be used to locate material flaws and stress cracks. Magnaflux® is a magnetic process applicable only to ferrous materials. The Zyglo® process coats the material with a flourescent dye penetrant and can be used on any material Check for suspected surface cracks can be more readily made using spot check dye. The dye is sprayed onto the suspected area, wiped off and the area sprayed with a developer. Cracks will show up brightly.

OVERHAUL NOTES

Aluminum has become extremely popular for use in engines, due to its low weight. Observe the following precautions when handling aluminum parts:
• Never hot tank aluminum parts; the caustic hot-tank solution will eat the aluminum.
• Remove all aluminum parts (identification tag, etc.) from engine parts prior to the tanking.
• Always coat threads lightly with engine oil or anti-seize compounds before installation, to prevent seizure.
• Never over-torque bolts or spark plugs, especially in aluminum threads.

When assembling the engine, any parts that will be in frictional contact must be prelubed to provide lubrication at initial start-up. Any product specifically formulated for this purpose can be used, but engine oil is not recommended as a prelube.

When semi-permanent (locked, but removable) installation of bolts or nuts is desired, threads should be cleaned and coated with Loctite® or other similar, commercial non-hardening sealant.

REPAIRING DAMAGED THREADS

Several methods of repairing damaged threads are available. Heli-Coil® (shown here), Keenserts® and Microdot® are among the most widely used. All involve basically the same principle (drilling out stripped threads, tap-

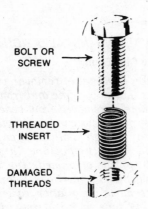

Damaged bolt holes can be repaired with thread repair inserts

Standard thread repair insert (left) and spark plug thread insert (right)

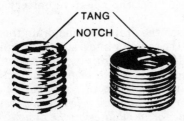

Drill out the damaged threads with specified drill. Drill completely through the hole or to the bottom of a blind hole

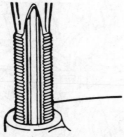

With the tap supplied, tap the hole to receive the thread insert. Keep the tap well oiled and back it out frequently to avoid clogging the threads

ping the hole and installing a prewound insert), making welding, plugging and oversize fasteners unnecessary.

Two types of thread repair inserts are usual-

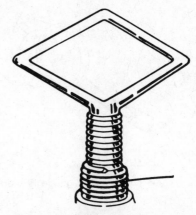

Screw the threaded insert onto the installation tool until the tang engages the slot. Screw the insert into the tapped hole until it is ¼–½ turn below the top surface. After installation break off the tang with a hammer and punch

ly supplied; a standard type for most Inch Coarse, Inch Fine, Metric Course and Metric Fine thread sizes and a spark lug type to fit most spark plug port sizes. Consult the individual manufacturer's catalog to determine exact applications. Typical thread repair kits will contain a selection of prewound threaded inserts, a tap (corresponding to the outside diameter threads of the insert) and an installation tool. Spark plug inserts usually differ because they require a tap equipped with pilot threads and a combined reamer/tap section. Most manufacturers also supply blister-packed thread repair inserts separately in addition to a master kit containing a variety of taps and inserts plus installation tools.

Before effecting a repair to a threaded hole, remove any snapped, broken or damaged bolts or studs. Penetrating oil can be used to free frozen threads; the offending item can be removed with locking pliers or with a screw or stud extractor. After the hole is clear, the thread can be repaired.

CHECKING ENGINE COMPRESSION

A noticeable lack of engine power, excessive oil consumption and/or poor fuel mileage measured over an extended period are all indicators of internal engine war. Worn piston rings, scored or worn cylinder bores, blown head gaskets, sticking or burnt valves and worn valve seats are all possible culprits here. A check of each cylinder's compression will help you locate the problems.

As mentioned in the Tools and Equipment section of Chapter 1, a screw-in type compression gauge is more accurate that the type you simply hold against the spark plug hole, although it takes slightly longer to use. It's

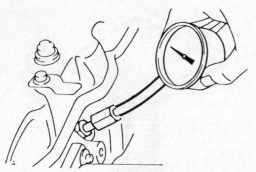

The screw-in type compression gauge is more accurate

worth it to obtain a more accurate reading. Follow the procedures below.

1. Warm up the engine to normal operating temperature.

2. Remove all spark plugs.

3. Disconnect the high tension lead from the ignition coil.

4. Disconnect all fuel injector electrical connections.

5. Screw the compression gauge into the No. 1 spark plug hole until the fitting is snug.

NOTE: *Be careful not to crossthread the plug hole. On aluminum cylinder heads use extra care, as the threads in these heads are easily ruined.*

6. Have an assistant depress the accelerator pedal fully. Then, while you read the compression gauge, ask the assistant to crank the engine two or three times in short bursts using the ignition switch.

7. Read the compression gauge at the end of each series of cranks, and record the highest of these readings. Repeat this procedure for each of the engine's cylinders. Maximum compression should be 175–185 psi. A cylinder's compression pressure is usually acceptable if it is not less than 80% of maximum. The difference between each cylinder should be no more than 12–14 psi.

8. If a cylinder is unusually low, pour a tablespoon of clean engine oil into the cylinder through the spark plug hole and repeat the compression test. If the compression comes up after adding the oil, it appears that the cylinder's piston rings or bore are damaged or worn. If the pressure remains low, the valves may not be seating properly (a valve job is needed), or the head gasket may be blown near that cylinder. If compression in any two adjacent cylinders is low, and if the addition of oil doesn't help the compression, there is leakage past the head gasket. Oil and coolant water in the combustion chamber can result from this problem. There may be evidence of water droplets on the engine dipstick when a head gasket has blown.

Engine
REMOVAL AND INSTALLATION
2.3L (140 CID) Engine

NOTE: *The engine removal procedure requires that the engine and front suspension subframe be removed from beneath the van. Unless provisions can be made to safely raise the body enough to allow the engine to be removed from the bottom, this procedure should not be attempted. Tag all electrical and vacuum connections before disconnection to make installation easier. A piece of masking tape on each connector end with matching numbers is the easiest way to do this.*

1. Disconnect the negative battery cable terminal.

2. Loosen the draincock and drain the coolant from the radiator into a suitable container.

CAUTION: *When draining the coolant, keep in mind that cats and dogs are attracted by the ethylene glycol antifreeze, and are quite likely to drink any that is left in an uncovered container or in puddles on the ground. This will prove fatal in sufficient quantity. Always drain the coolant into a sealable container. Coolant should be reused unless it is contaminated or several years old.*

3. Disconnect the air cleaner outlet tube at the throttle body and the idle speed control hose.

4. Remove the upper and lower hoses from the radiator and engine. Disconnect the lower

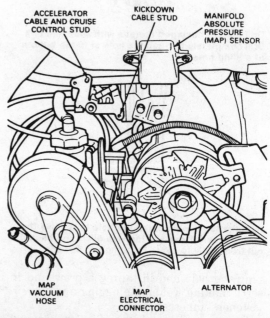

Component and linkage locations

Standard Torque Specifications and Fastener Markings

In the absence of specific torques, the following chart can be used as a guide to the maximum safe torque of a particular size/grade of fastener.
- There is no torque difference for fine or coarse threads.
- Torque values are based on clean, dry threads. Reduce the value by 10% if threads are oiled prior to assembly.
- The torque required for aluminum components or fasteners is considerably less.

U.S. Bolts

SAE Grade Number	1 or 2			5			6 or 7		
Number of lines always 2 less than the grade number.									
Bolt Size (Inches)—(Thread)	**Maximum Torque**			**Maximum Torque**			**Maximum Torque**		
	Ft./Lbs.	Kgm	Nm	Ft./Lbs.	Kgm	Nm	Ft./Lbs.	Kgm	Nm
¼ — 20	5	0.7	6.8	8	1.1	10.8	10	1.4	13.5
— 28	6	0.8	8.1	10	1.4	13.6			
⁵⁄₁₆ — 18	11	1.5	14.9	17	2.3	23.0	19	2.6	25.8
— 24	13	1.8	17.6	19	2.6	25.7			
³⁄₈ — 16	18	2.5	24.4	31	4.3	42.0	34	4.7	46.0
— 24	20	2.75	27.1	35	4.8	47.5			
⁷⁄₁₆ — 14	28	3.8	37.0	49	6.8	66.4	55	7.6	74.5
— 20	30	4.2	40.7	55	7.6	74.5			
½ — 13	39	5.4	52.8	75	10.4	101.7	85	11.75	115.2
— 20	41	5.7	55.6	85	11.7	115.2			
⁹⁄₁₆ — 12	51	7.0	69.2	110	15.2	149.1	120	16.6	162.7
— 18	55	7.6	74.5	120	16.6	162.7			
⅝ — 11	83	11.5	112.5	150	20.7	203.3	167	23.0	226.5
— 18	95	13.1	128.8	170	23.5	230.5			
¾ — 10	105	14.5	142.3	270	37.3	366.0	280	38.7	379.6
— 16	115	15.9	155.9	295	40.8	400.0			
⅞ — 9	160	22.1	216.9	395	54.6	535.5	440	60.9	596.5
— 14	175	24.2	237.2	435	60.1	589.7			
1 — 8	236	32.5	318.6	590	81.6	799.9	660	91.3	894.8
— 14	250	34.6	338.9	660	91.3	849.8			

Metric Bolts

Relative Strength Marking	4.6, 4.8			8.8		
Bolt Markings						
Bolt Size Thread Size x Pitch (mm)	**Maximum Torque**			**Maximum Torque**		
	Ft./Lbs.	Kgm	Nm	Ft./Lbs.	Kgm	Nm
6 x 1.0	2–3	.2–.4	3–4	3–6	.4–.8	5–8
8 x 1.25	6–8	.8–1	8–12	9–14	1.2–1.9	13–19
10 x 1.25	12–17	1.5–2.3	16–23	20–29	2.7–4.0	27–39
12 x 1.25	21–32	2.9–4.4	29–43	35–53	4.8–7.3	47–72
14 x 1.5	35–52	4.8–7.1	48–70	57–85	7.8–11.7	77–110
16 x 1.5	51–77	7.0–10.6	67–100	90–120	12.4–16.5	130–160
18 x 1.5	74–110	10.2–15.1	100–150	130–170	17.9–23.4	180–230
20 x 1.5	110–140	15.1–19.3	150–190	190–240	26.2–46.9	160–320
22 x 1.5	150–190	22.0–26.2	200–260	250–320	34.5–44.1	340–430
24 x 1.5	190–240	26.2–46.9	260–320	310–410	42.7–56.5	420–550

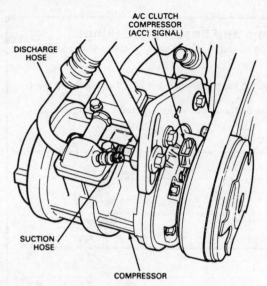

Discharge the A/C system before attempting to disconnect any refrigerant lines

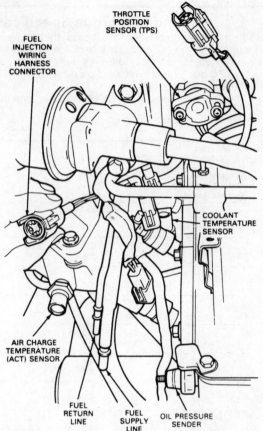

Fuel line and electrical component connector locations

intake manifold hose from the tee fitting in the heater hose.

5. Remove the bolts retaining the fan shroud to the radiator, then remove the fan shroud.

6. Disconnect the electrical connectors to the alternator.

7. Remove the throttle linkage shield and disconnect the accelerator cable and cruise control (if equipped) from the throttle body. Unbolt the cables from the bracket and position them out of the way.

8. If equipped with air conditioning, discharge the system as described in Chapter 1. After discharging, disconnect the suction and discharge hoses from the compressor. Disconnect the A/C compressor clutch electrical connector from the compressor.

9. From the lower left front of the engine, disconnect the electrical connector for the coil.

10. From beneath the lower intake manifold, disconnect the electrical connector for the TFI module on the distributor.

11. Disconnect the electrical connector from the knock sensor on the side of the upper intake manifold.

12. Tag and disconnect all hoses to the vacuum tree at the top of the upper intake manifold.

13. Disconnect the electrical connector and vacuum hose from the exhaust gas recirculation (EGR) valve at the rear of the upper intake manifold.

14. Remove the engine cover from inside the cab.

15. Disconnect the electrical connector for

the throttle position sensor (TPS) at the rear of the throttle body.

16. Disconnect the electrical elbow connector for the oil pressure sender at the left rear of the engine.

17. Depressurize the fuel system as described in Chapter 1, then disconnect the fuel return and supply lines.

18. Disconnect the electrical connector for the fuel injection wiring harness.

19. Disconnect the electrical connector for the air charge temperature (ACT) sensor at the rear side of the lower intake manifold.

20. Disconnect the electrical connector for the coolant temperature sensor at the center of the lower intake manifold.

21. Remove the nut and disconnect the ground strap from the right rear side of the engine below the lifting eye.

22. If equipped with manual transmission, place the shift lever in Neutral and remove the bolts retaining the shift lever to the floor. Remove the bolts retaining the shift lever assembly to the transmission and remove the lever assembly.

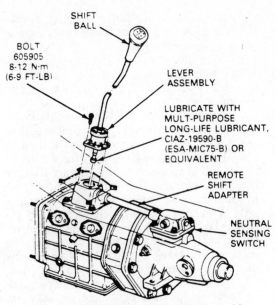

Removing manual transmission shifter assembly

23. Raise the van and support it safely with jackstands.

24. If equipped with automatic transmission, disconnect the fluid lines at the radiator.

25. If equipped with power steering, disconnect the electrical connector for the power steering pressure switch from the gear.

26. Remove the bolt retaining the intermediate steering column shaft to the steering gear and disconnect the shaft from the gear. The

steering wheel and tires should be straight ahead (centered) prior to removal.

27. Remove the bolts and disconnect the starter cable and ground cable from the starter. Route the ground and starter cables out from the crossmember.

28. On vehicles equipped with manual transmission, remove the lockpin retaining the hydraulic hose to the clutch slave cylinder in the clutch housing. Remove and plug the hose.

29. Disconnect the electrical connector for the exhaust gas oxygen sensor at the exhaust manifold.

30. Loosen and remove the exhaust manifold stud nuts. Remove the bolts and nuts retaining the catalytic converter pipe to the muffler and outlet pipe. Disconnect and remove the exhaust pipe and catalytic converter. Remove all traces of gasket material from the mounting surfaces.

31. Disconnect the speedometer and/or tachometer cable from the transmission. Disconnect the electrical connector from the backup lamp switch.

32. On manual transmissions, disconnect the electrical connector for the shift indicator sender.

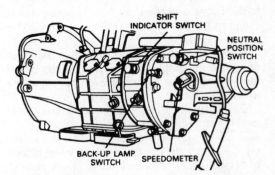

Component locations on manual transmission

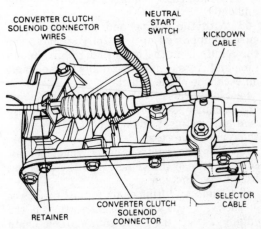

Component locations on automatic transmission

SQUARE SHOULDER ON BOLT MUST BE SEATED WITH SQUARE HOLE ON THE INTERMEDIATE SHAFT

STEERING COLUMN INTERMEDIATE SHAFT

NUT 41-56 N·m (30-42 FT-LB)

STEERING GEAR

STEERING COLUMN LOWER SHAFT

BOLT-801614 41-56 N·m (30-42 FT-LB)

Disconnecting the steering column linkage

33. On automatic transmissions, disconnect the electrical connector for the neutral start switch. Disconnect the throttle and kickdown cable from the transmission lever. Route the kickdown cable out of the engine compartment and remove the cable.

34. Remove the nuts and U-bolts retaining the driveshaft to the rear axle yoke and remove the driveshaft. Insert a plug in the extension housing to prevent fluid leakage.

35. Remove the lug nuts and remove both front wheel and tire assemblies.

36. Remove the bar nuts and disconnect the stabilizer bar from the lower control arms. Discard the bar nuts.

37. Disconnect the brake lines at the bracket on the frame behind the spindles.

38. Position a jack under the lower control arm and raise the arm until tension is applied to the coil spring. Remove the bolt and nut retaining the spindle to the upper control arm ball joint. Slowly lower the jack under the lower control arm to disconnect the spindle from the ball joint. Place safety chains around the lower arms and spring upper seat.

39. Position a jack under the transmission and slightly raise the transmission. Remove the nuts and bolts retaining the crossmember to the frame and the nuts retaining the transmission to the crossmember. Remove the crossmember.

40. If required, remove the transmission as described in Chapter 6. The engine may be removed with the transmission removed or attached.

41. Position a suitable dolly under the crossmember and engine assembly.

42. Slowly lower the vehicle until the crossmember rests on the dolly. Place wood blocks under the front crossmember and the rear of the engine block (or transmission, if installed) to keep the engine and crossmember assembly level. Install safety chains around the engine and dolly.

43. With the engine and crossmember securely supported on the dolly, remove the three nuts from the bolts that retain the engine and crossmember assembly to the frame on each side of the vehicle.

44. Slowly raise the body off the engine and crossmember assembly on the dolly. Make sure that any wiring or hoses do not interfere with the removal process.

45. With the engine and crossmember assembly clear of the vehicle, roll the dolly out from under the van.

46. Connect a lifting chain to the lifting eyes on the right rear and front left portions of the engine. Attach the chain to a suitable chain hoist or shop crane.

47. If equipped with power steering, disconnect the hoses from the pump and plug them to prevent the entry of dirt.

48. With lifting tension applied, remove the nuts retaining the engine to the crossmember assembly, then lift the engine off the crossmember.

49. Remove the required components to attach the engine assembly to a suitable engine stand and continue disassembly as desired.

50. To install the engine, first attach a lifting chain and shop crane to the engine. Remove the bolts retaining the engine to the engine stand and lift the engine with the shop crane.

51. With the front crossmember securely positioned on a dolly, slowly lower the engine until the motor mount studs are piloted in the crossmember holes. Install the remaining nuts and tighten them to 45–65 ft.lb. (61–81 Nm).

52. Install wood blocks under the oil pan and/or transmission and crossmember, then remove the lifting chain and shop crane.

53. If equipped with power steering, connect the hoses to the power steering pump.

54. Roll the support dolly under the vehicle. Make sure the van body is securely supported. Align the dolly so that the engine/subframe assembly is correctly lined up with the three mounting bolts on each side of the frame. The bolts should align with the holes in the corssmember.

55. Slowly lower the body so the bolts are piloted in the corssmember holes. Continue lowering until the crossmember is against the frame. Install the nuts retaining the crossmember to the frame and tighten them to 187–260 ft.lb. (254–352 Nm).

56. Raise the vehicle and remove the support dolly.

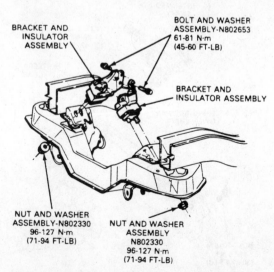

Engine and transmission mounts on 2.3L engine

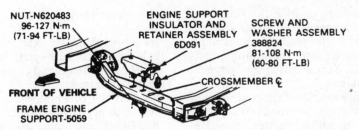

NUT-N620483
96-127 N·m
(71-94 FT-LB)

ENGINE SUPPORT
INSULATOR AND
RETAINER ASSEMBLY
6D091

SCREW AND
WASHER ASSEMBLY
388824
81-108 N·m
(60-80 FT-LB)

CROSSMEMBER C̶L

FRONT OF VEHICLE

FRAME ENGINE
SUPPORT-5059

Installation of rear transmission support on 2.3L engine with 5 spd manual transmission

57. If removed, install the transmission as described in Chapter 6.

58. Position a transmission jack under the transmission and slightly raise the transmission to place the crossmember in position on the frame and transmission. Install the retaining nuts and bolts to the crossmember, then install the nut retaining the transmission mount and insulator to the crossmember and tighten to 71–94 ft.lb. (97–127 Nm).

59. Remove the safety chains from around the lower control arm and upper spring seat.

60. Install a floor jack under the lower control arms. Slowly raise the control arm until the coil spring is under tension. Continue to raise the arm until the spindle upper arm can be connected to the upper control arm ball joint. Install a new nut and bolt and tighten to 80–120 ft.lb. (108–163 Nm).

61. Connect the stabilizer bar to the lower control arms. Install new bar nuts.

62. Connect the front brake lines to the caliper hoses at the frame brackets.

63. Install the front wheels and tighten the lug nuts to 85–115 ft.lb. (115–155 Nm).

64. Connect the driveshaft to the transmission and rear axle yoke. Install the nuts and U-bolts retaining the driveshaft to the rear axle yoke.

65. On vehicles with automatic transmission, connect the throttle and kickdown cables to the transmission lever. Connect the electrical connector to the neutral start switch and route the kickdown cable into the engine compartment.

66. On manual transmissions, connect the electrical connector for the shift indicator sender.

67. Connect the speedometer and/or tachometer to the transmission, then connect the electrical connector for the backup lamp switch.

68. Install new non-asbestos gaskets on the exhaust manifold and catalytic converter. Place the assembly in position on the exhaust manifold, muffler and outlet pipe. Install the two nuts and bolts retaining the converter to the muffler and outlet pipe and tighten to 18–26 ft.lb. (25–35 Nm). Install the nuts retaining the pipe to the exhaust manifold and tighten alternately to 18–26 ft.lb. (34–46 Nm).

69. Connect the electrical connector for the exhaust gas oxygen sensor on the exhaust manifold.

70. On manual transmissions, attach the hydraulic hose to the slave cylinder in the clutch housing. Install the lockpin retaining the hose to the cylinder.

71. Position the ground cable on the starter and install and tighten the mounting bolt to 15–20 ft.lb. (21–27 Nm). Connect the starter cable to the motor and install the screw and washer. Tighten to 70–100 in.lb. (9–12 Nm). Route the starter and ground cables over the crossmember and into position in the engine compartment.

72. With the front wheels and steering wheel centered (straight ahead), connect the steering column lower shaft to the steering gear. Install the bolt and tighten it to 31–42 ft.lb. (41–56 Nm).

73. If equipped with power steering, connect the power steering pressure switch at the gear.

74. If equipped with automatic transmission, connect the fluid lines at the radiator.

75. Lower the vehicle.

76. From inside the cab, if equipped with

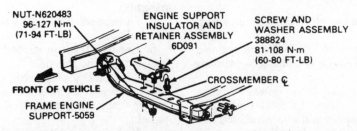

NUT-N620483
96-127 N·m
(71-94 FT-LB)

ENGINE SUPPORT
INSULATOR AND
RETAINER ASSEMBLY
6D091

SCREW AND
WASHER ASSEMBLY
388824
81-108 N·m
(60-80 FT-LB)

CROSSMEMBER C̶L

FRONT OF VEHICLE

FRAME ENGINE
SUPPORT-5059

Installation of rear transmission support on 2.3L engine with automatic transmission

manual transmission, position the shift lever assembly on the transmission. Make sure the transmission and shifter are in the Neutral position. Install and tighten the retaining bolts to 6–9 ft.lb. (8–12 Nm). Position the boot over the lever assembly.

77. On the right rear side of the engine below the lifting eye, position the ground strap on the lifting eye, then install and tighten the retaining nut.

78. In the center of the lower intake manifold, connect the electrical connector for the coolant temperature sensor.

79. Connect the electrical connector for the air charge temperature (ACT) sensor at the rear side fo the lower intake manifold.

80. Connect the electrical connector for the fuel injection wiring harness.

81. Connect the hoses to the fuel return and fuel supply lines.

82. Connect the electrical connector for the oil pressure sender at the left rear side of the engine.

83. Connect the electrical connector for the throttle position sensor (TPS) at the rear of the throttle body.

84. Install the engine cover inside the cab.

85. Connect the electrical connector and vacuum hose for the EGR valve at the rear of the upper intake manifold.

86. Connect all vacuum hoses in their proper positions on the vacuum tree at the top of the upper intake manifold.

87. Connect the electrical connector for the knock sensor at the side of the upper intake manifold.

88. Connect the electrical connector for the thick film ignition (TFI) module on the distributor, underneath the lower intake manifold.

89. Connect the electrical connector for the coil at the lower left front side of the engine.

90. If equipped with air conditioning, connect the A/C clutch compressor connector to the compressor. Connect the suction and discharge hoses to the compressor and recharge the A/C system as described in Chapter 1.

91. Connect the accelerator cable and cruise control cable (if equipped) to the throttle body. Install the cables in the retaining bracket and install and tighten the bolt. Install the throttle linkage shield.

92. Connect the two electrical connections to the alternator.

93. Connect the electrical connector and vacuum hose to the manifold absolute pressure (MAP) sensor.

94. Position the fan shroud on the radiator, then install and tighten the retaining bolts.

95. Install the upper and lower radiator hoses and the heater hoses. Install the lower intake manifold hose to the tee in the heater hose.

96. Connect the air cleaner tube at the throttle body and the idle speed control hose.

97. Install the ground cable on the negative battery terminal.

98. Fill the cooling system to the specified level with approved coolant.

99. Check and adjust all fluid levels as described in Chapter 1.

100. Bleed the brake system as described in Chapter 8.

101. Start the engine and check for leaks. Correct as required. The front end alignment should be checked and, if necessary, adjusted as soon as possible.

2.8L (171 CID) and 3.0L (182 CID) V6 Engines

NOTE: *The engine removal procedures for the 2.8L and 3.0L are basically identical with the exception of the fuel system. The 2.8L engine uses a carburetor, while the 3.0L engine is equipped with port fuel injection. In addition, certain components may be used on carbureted engines that are not on fuel injection models and vice versa. In both cases, the engine is removed from the bottom along with the subframe and front suspension. Unless provisions can be made to safely raise the body enough to allow the engine to be removed from the bottom, this procedure should not be attempted. Tag all electrical and vacuum connections before disconnection to make installation easier; a piece of masking tape on each connector with matching numbers is the easiest way.*

1. Disconnect the negative battery cable.

2. Loosen the draincock and drain the coolant from the radiator into a suitable clean container.

CAUTION: *When draining the coolant, keep in mind that cats and dogs are attracted by the ethylene glycol antifreeze, and are quite likely to drink any that is left in an uncovered container or in puddles on the ground. This will prove fatal in sufficient quantity. Always drain the coolant into a sealable container. Coolant should be reused unless it is contaminated or several years old.*

3. Remove the air cleaner and intake duct assembly.

4. Disconnect the upper and lower hoses at the radiator.

5. Remove the fan shroud retaining bolts and remove the shroud.

6. On 2.8L engines, disconnect the manifold absolute pressure (MAP) sensor electrical connector from the sensor, located on the dash panel.

7. If equipped with air conditioning, discon-

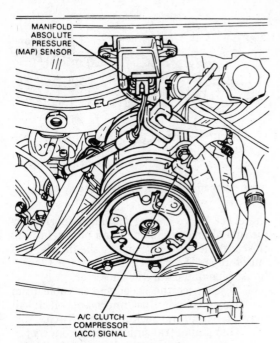

MAP sensor location on 2.8L engine

nect the A/C clutch electrical connector from the compressor. On the 2.8L engine, loosen the idler pulley adjustment bolt to slacken drive belt tension and remove the belt from the compressor clutch pulley, then remove the compressor mounting bolts and position the compressor out of the way. On the 3.0L engine, discharge the A/C system as described in Chapter 1 and disconnect the compressor discharge and suction hoses from the compressor.

8. Disconnect the accelerator able and the transmission kickdown cable at the throttle lever ball stud or throttle body.

9. Disconnect the electrical connector for

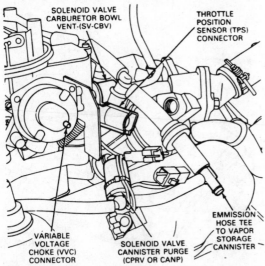

Electrical component locations on 2.8L engine

the idle speed control (ISC) motor (2.8L) or the idle air control (IAC) valve (3.0L).

10. Disconnect the electrical connectors for the engine coolant temperature sensor and the water temperature sender switch, located in the thermostat housing.

11. Disconnect the vacuum hose from the exhaust gas recirculation (EGR) valve and the electrical connector from the EGR valve position sensor.

12. Disconenct the electrical connectors from the alternator.

13. On the 2.8L, tag and disconnect the electrical connectors for the throttle position sensor on the carburetor choke shield, canister purge valve solenoid and the solenoid valve carburetor bowl vent. Disconnect the electrical connector to the variable voltage choke cap. Disconnect the evaporative emission hose from the solenoid valve carburetor bowl vent to the vapor storage canister. Route the wiring harness out of the engine compartment.

14. Remove the engine cover from inside the cab.

15. On the 3.0L, tag and disconnect the evaporative emission line, fuel injector wiring harness (including 6 injectors), air charge temperature sensor, throttle position sensor and the radio frequency supressor, if equipped.

16. Remove the retaining bolt, then remove the bracket and accelerator cable and transmission kickdown linkage.

17. If equipped with cruise control, disconnect the cruise control cable from the throttle linkage.

18. Disconnect the electrical connector and supressor wire from the ignition coil.

19. On the 2.8L, disconnect the hose from the air control valve to the catalytic converter.

20. Disconnect the electrical connector for the thick film ignition (TFI) module at the distributor. Disconnect the electrical connector for the knock sensor on the 3.0L.

21. On the 2.8L, disconnect the electrical connector for the feedback control solenoid at the rear of the carburetor.

22. Tag and disconnect all the hoses from the vacuum manifold fitting.

23. Disconnect the brake booster vacuum hose from the clip.

24. If equipped with manual transmission, place the shift lever in Neutral and remove the bolts retaining the shift lever to the floor. Remove the bolts retaining the shift lever assembly to the transmission and remove the lever assembly.

25. Raise the vehicle and support it safely on jackstands.

26. If equipped with automatic transmission, disconnect the fluid lines at the radiator.

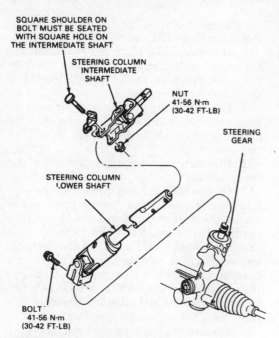

SQUARE SHOULDER ON
BOLT MUST BE SEATED
WITH SQUARE HOLE ON
THE INTERMEDIATE SHAFT

STEERING COLUMN
INTERMEDIATE
SHAFT

NUT
41-56 N·m
(30-42 FT-LB)

STEERING
GEAR

STEERING COLUMN
LOWER SHAFT

BOLT
41-56 N·m
(30-42 FT-LB)

Disconnecting the steering gear

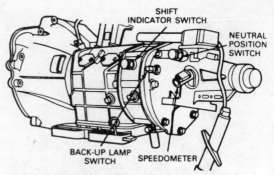

SHIFT
INDICATOR SWITCH

NEUTRAL
POSITION
SWITCH

BACK-UP LAMP
SWITCH

SPEEDOMETER

Manual transmission electrical connections

27. Remove the heater hoses from the bracket underneath the engine at the front of the crossmember.

28. Make sure the steering wheel and front wheels are straight ahead (centered), then remove the bolt retaining the intermediate steering column shaft to the steering gear and disconnect the shaft from the gear.

29. Disconnect the elbow connector from the oil pressure sender beneath the fuel pump (2.8L), or the oil pressure sending switch connector (3.0L).

30. On the 2.8L, disconnect and plug the inlet hose on the fuel pump from the lines on the frame. On the 3.0L, depressurize the fuel system as described in Chapter 1 and disconnect the fuel delivery and return lines.

31. Remove the bolt retaining the ground strap to the engine and remove the strap.

32. Remove the bolts and disconnect the starter cable and ground cable from the starter. Route the ground and starter cables out from the crossmember.

33. On vehicles with manual transmission, remove the lockpin retaining the hydraulic hose to the slave cylinder in the clutch housing. Remove and plug the hose.

34. Disconnect the electrical connector for the exhaust gas oxygen sensor from the left exhaust manifold. Disconnect the electrical connector for the knock sensor from the engine block above the starter.

35. Loosen and remove the exhaust manifold stud nuts. On the 2.8L, disconnect the tube to the check valve on the managed thermactor air tube. Remove the bolts and nuts retaining the catalytic converter pipe to the muffler and outlet pipe. Disconnect and remove the exhaust pipe and catalytic converter.

36. Disconnect the speedometer cable from the transmission. Disconnect the electrical connector from the backup lamp switch.

37. On manual transmissions, disconnect the electrical connector for the shift indicator sender.

38. On automatic transmissions, disconnect the electrical connector for the neutral start switch. Disconnect the throttle and kickdown cable from the transmission lever. Route the kickdown cable out of the engine compartment and remove the cable.

39. Remove the nuts and U-bolts retaining the driveshaft to the rear axle and remove the driveshaft. Insert a plug in the extension housing to prevent fluid leakage.

40. Remove the front tires.

41. Remove the bar nuts and disconnect the stabilizer bar from the lower control arms. Discard the bar nuts.

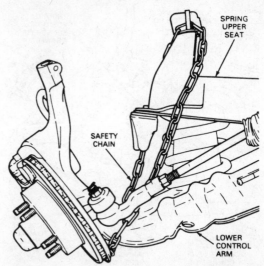

SPRING
UPPER
SEAT

SAFETY
CHAIN

LOWER
CONTROL
ARM

Safety chain installation on lower control arm

42. Disconnect and plug the brake lines at the bracket on the frame behind the spindles.

43. Position a jack under the lower control arm and raise the arm until tension is applied to the coil spring. Remove the bolt and nut retaining the spindle to the upper control arm ball joint. Slowly lower the jack under the lower control arm to disconnect the spindle from the ball joint.

CAUTION: *Place safety chains around the lower control arms and spring upper seat.*

44. Position a transmission jack under the transmission and slightly raise the transmission. Remove the nuts and bolts retaining the crossmember to the frame and the nuts retaining the transmission to the crossmember. Remove the crossmember.

45. If required, remove the transmission as described in Chapter 6.

46. Position a wheeled dolly under the crossmember and engine assembly.

47. Slowly lower the vehicle until the crossmember rests on the dolly. Place wood blocks under the front crossmember and the rear of the engine block (or transmission, if installed), to keep the engine and crossmember assembly level. Install safety chains around the crossmember and dolly.

48. With the engine and crossmember securely supported on the dolly, remove the three nuts from the bolts that retain the engine and crossmember assembly to the frame on each side of the vehicle.

49. Slowly raise the body off the engine and crossmember assembly on the dolly. Make sure that any wiring or hoses do not snag or interfere with the removal process.

50. When the engine and crossmember assembly are clear of the van body, roll the dolly out from under the vehicle.

51. Install lifting eyes (Ford No. D81L-6001-D) on each side of the exhaust manifold, then connect a suitable chain to the lifting eyes and attach a shop crane or chain hoist.

52. If equipped with power steering, disconnect the power steering hoses from the pump to the gear and plug the hose ends.

53. With lifting tension applied, loosen the nuts retaining the motor mounts to the crossmember and lift the engine off the crossmember.

54. Remove the necessary components to attach the engine to a suitable engine stand. Make sure the engine is securely bolted to the stand before releasing tension on the hoist. Continue disassembly as desired.

55. To install the engine, again attach a suitable shop crane or chain hoist and remove the engine from the work stand.

56. With the front crossmember securely at-

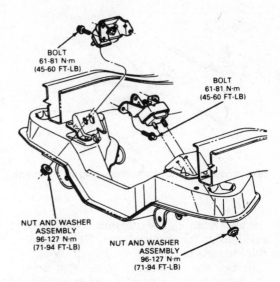

V6 engine mounts

tached to a wheeled dolly, slowly lower the engine until the motor mount studs are piloted in the crossmember holes. Install the retaining nuts and tighten them to 71–94 ft.lb. (96–127 Nm). Install wood blocks under the oil pan and crossmember to level the assembly, then detach the lifting chain and hoist. Remove the lifting eyes.

57. If equipped with power steering, attach the hoses to the pump and gear. Roll the dolly under the vehicle and make sure the three mounting bolts on each side of the frame are in alignment with the holes in the crossmember.

58. Slowly lower the body so the bolts are piloted in the crossmember holes. When the crossmember is against the frame, install the retaining nuts and tighten them to 187–260 ft.lb. (254–352 Nm). Raise the vehicle and remove the dolly.

59. If removed, install the transmission as described in Chapter 6.

60. Position a transmission jack under the transmission and slightly raise the transmission. Place the crossmember in position in the frame and on the transmission, then install

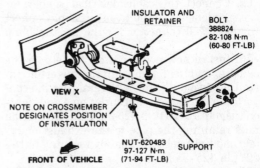

Rear transmission mount on V6 engine

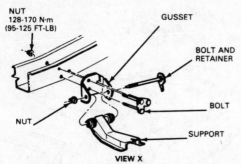

NUT
128-170 N·m
(95-125 FT-LB)

GUSSET

BOLT AND RETAINER

BOLT

NUT

SUPPORT

VIEW X

Rear crossmember-to-frame mounting on V6 engine

the nuts retaining the transmission mount and insulator to the crossmember. Tighten the retaining nuts to 71–94 ft.lb. (97–127 Nm).

61. Remove the safety chains from around the lower control arms and spring seat.

62. Install a jack under the lower control arms, then slowly raise the control arm until the coil spring is under tension. Continue to raise the arm until the spindle upper arm can be connected to the lower control arm ball joint. Install a new nut and tighten to 12–18 ft.lb. (37–50 Nm).

63. Connect the stabilizer bar to the lower control arms. Install new bar nuts and tighten them to 12–18 ft.lb. (16–24 Nm).

64. Connect the front brake lines to the caliper hoses at the frame brackets.

65. Install the front wheels and tighten the lug nuts to 85–115 ft.lb. (115–155 Nm).

66. Connect the driveshaft to the rear axle and transmission. Install the nuts and bolts retaining the driveshaft to the rear axle end yoke.

67. If equipped with automatic transmission, connect the throttle and kickdown cables to the transmission lever. Connect the electrical connector for the neutral start switch and route the kickdown cable into the engine compartment.

68. On manual transmissions, connect the electrical connector for the shift indicator sender.

69. Connect the cable/electrical sender for the speedometer to the transmission. Connect the electrical connector for the backup lamp switch.

70. Install new non-asbestos gaskets on the exhaust manifold and catalytic converter. Install the two nuts and bolts retaining the converter to the muffler and outlet pipe and tighten them to 18–26 ft.lb. (25–35 Nm). Install the nuts retaining the pipe to the exhaust manifold and tighten by alternately torquing to 18–26 ft.lb. (25–35 Nm).

71. Connect the electrical connectors for the exhaust gas oxygen sensor and the knock sensor.

72. On manual transmissions, attach the hydraulic hose to the slave cylinder in the clutch housing. Install the lockpin retaining the hose to the cylinder. Bleed the clutch hydraulic system as described in Chapter 6.

73. Position the ground cable on the starter and tighten the mounting bolt 15–20 ft.lb. (21–27 Nm). Connect the starter cable to the motor and install the screw and washer and tighten to 70–100 in.lb. (9–12 Nm). Route the starter and ground cables over the crossmember and into position in the engine compartment.

74. Position the ground strap on the engine and install and tighten the bolt.

75. On the 2.8L, connect the fuel pump inlet hose to the line on the frame. On the 3.0L, reconnect the fuel return and delivery lines.

76. Connect the elbow connector to the oil pressure sender beneath the fuel pump.

77. With the front wheel and steering wheel straight ahead (centered), connect the steering column intermediate shaft to the steering gear. Install and tighten the bolt to 30–42 ft.lb. (41–56 Nm).

78. Install the heater hoses to the bracket underneath the engine at the front of the crossmember.

79. If equipped with automatic transmission, connect the fluid lines at the radiator.

80. Lower the vehicle.

81. From inside the cab, connect the brake vacuum booster hose to the vacuum manifold fitting on the rear of the engine. Connect the hose to the clip. If equipped with cruise control, connect the vacuum hose from the cruise control to the fitting. Make sure all hoses disconnected prior to engine removal are connected to their correct ports.

82. On the 2.8L, connect the electrical connector for the feedback control solenoid at the rear of the carburetor. On the 3.0L, connect the fuel injection wiring harness and all injectors.

83. Connect the electrical connector for the thick film ignition (TFI) module at the distributor. On the 2.8L, connect the hose for the air control valve to the catalytic converter. Connect the electrical connector and supressor wire to the coil.

84. Connect the cruise control cable to the carburetor or throttle body assembly. Position the accelerator and kickdown cables in the bracket and install the bolt.

85. If equipped with manual transmission, position the shift lever assembly on the transmission. Make sure the transmission and shifter assembly are in Neutral, then install and tighten the retaining bolts. Position the boot over the lever assembly.

86. Reconnect all remaining wiring connectors accessible from the top of the engine, then replace the engine cover in the cab.

87. Route the wiring into position in the engine compartment.

88. On the 2.8L, connect the electrical connectors for the throttle position sensor, canister purge valve solenoid and solenoid valve/carburetor bowl vent. Connect the elbow connector to the variable voltage choke cap, then connect the evaporative emission hose from the solenoid valve/carburetor bowl vent to the vapor storage canister.

89. Connect the electrical connectors to the alternator. Connect the vacuum hose to the exhaust gas recirculation (EGR) valve and the electrical connectors for the engine coolant temperature sender and the water temperature sensor.

90. On the 2.8L, connect the electrical connector foe the idle speed control (ISC) motor. Connect the accelerator and transmission kickdown cables to the throttle lever ball stud.

91. Position the A/C compressor in the engine brackets. Install the retaining bolts and tighten to 25–35 ft.lb. (34–47 Nm). On the 3.0L, connect the compressor suction and discharge hoses. Install the drive belt on the compressor clutch and idler pulley, if removed, and adjust the drive belt tension. Connect the A/C compressor clutch electrical connector.

92. Connect the manifold absolute pressure (MAP) sensor electrical connector to the sensor on the dash panel.

93. Install the shroud over the fan and in position on the radiator, then install and tighten the retaining bolts. Connect the upper and lower radiator hoses.

94. Connect the ground cable to the battery and install the air cleaner and air intake duct assembly.

95. Refill the cooling system and check all fluid levels. Bleed the brakes as described in Chapter 8 and recharge the air conditioning system as described in Chapter 1, if the compressor hoses were disconnected during service (3.0L engine only).

96. Start the engine and check for leaks. The front end alignment should be checked and adjusted as soon as possible.

Rocker Arm (Valve) Cover
REMOVAL AND INSTALLATION
2.3L (140 CID) Engine

1. Disconnect the negative battery cable.
2. Remove the engine cover inside the cab.
3. Remove the air cleaner and intake ducts from the throttle body assembly.

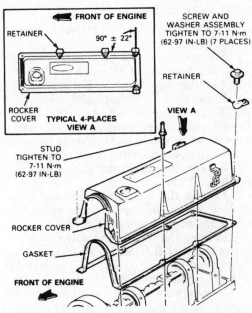

Rocker arm cover mounting on 2.3L (140 CID) engine

4. Remove the throttle linkage and throttle body as outlined in Chapter 4.

5. Disconnect the spark plug wires from the plugs and position the wires out of the way. Leave the spark plug wires in their looms to make installation easier.

6. Loosen and remove the seven screw and washer assemblies along the outside of the rocker cover and remove them along with their retainers. Loosen and remove the one stud on the right side of the rocker cover.

7. Tap the rocker cover lightly with a rubber mallet to break it loose, then lift the rocker arm cover straight up off the engine.

8. Remove and discard the rocker cover gasket.

9. Carefully clean all gasket mating surfaces, being careful not to scratch the rocker cover or cylinder head surfaces.

10. To install, set the new gasket in the rocker arm cover, then lower the cover straight down onto the cylinder head. Make sure the gasket is seated properly all the way around the cover.

11. Install the screw and washer assemblies with their retainers and tighten them to 62–97 in.lb. (7–11 Nm). The retainers should be gripping the edge of the rocker cover, 90° from the bolt holes. Install the stud and tighten to 62–97 in.lb. (7–11 Nm).

12. Install the ignition cables, throttle body and air cleaner assembly. Connect the negative battery cable, start the engine and check for leaks.

2.8L (171 CID) Engine

1. Remove the air cleaner and air duct assembly.

2. Remove the spark plug wires from the plugs, but leave them attached to their wire loom in order. Lay the wires out of the way.

3. Remove the PCV valve and hose.

4. Remove the two screws attaching the throttle position sensor connector to the carburetor choke air shield and route the connector forward to clear the valve cover area.

5. Remove the carburetor choke air deflector plate (shield).

6. Remove the A/C compressor and brackets, if equipped, and move it aside without disconnecting any refrigerant lines.

7. Remove the rocker arm cover attaching screws and load distribution washers. Lay the washers out in order so they may be installed in their original positions.

8. If equipped with automatic transmission, remove the transmission fluid level indicator tube and bracket, which is attached to the rocker cover.

9. Disconnect the kickdown linkage from the carburetor on automatic transmission models.

10. Position the thermactor air hose and wiring harness away from the right hand rocker cover.

11. Remove the engine oil filler tube and bracket assembly from the valve cover and exhaust manifold stud.

12. Disconnect the vacuum line at the canister purge solenoid and disconnect the line routed from the canister to purge solenoid. Disconnect the power brake booster hose, if equipped.

13. Tap the rocker arm cover lightly with a rubber mallet to break it loose. Remove the rocker arm cover by lifting it up and off the cylinder head.

14. Clean all gasket material from the rocker arm cover and cylinder head mating surfaces.

15. Install the rocker arm cover, using a new gasket, then install the attaching screws and rocker cover reinforcement pieces.

16. If equipped with an automatic transmission, install the transmission fluid level indictor tube and bracket to the rocker cover.

17. Connect the kickdown linkage (automatic transmission only).

18. Make sure all rocker cover load distribution washers are installed in their original positions, then tighten the rocker arm cover screws to 3–5 ft.lb. (4–7 Nm).

19. Install the spark plug wires, PCV valve and hose.

20. Install the carburetor choke air deflector plate (shield).

21. Install the two screws retaining the throttle position sensor connector to the choke air deflector shield.

22. Reposition the thermactor air hose and wiring harness in their original locations.

23. Install the engine oil filler tube an bracket to the valve cover and exhaust manifold studs.

24. Connect the vacuum line at the canister purge solenoid and connect the line routed from the the canister to the purge solenoid. Connect the power brake hose, if equipped.

25. Install the A/C compressor and brackets, if equipped.

26. Install the air cleaner assembly, start the engine and check for leaks.

3.0L (182 CID) Engine

1. Remove the engine cover in the cab. Disconnect the ignition wires from the spark plugs, but leave them attached to their wire looms.

2. Remove the ignition wire separators from the rocker arm cover attaching bolt studs with the wires attached, then lay the wires out of the way.

3. If the left hand cover is being removed, remove the oil filler cap and the PCV system hose. If the right hand cover is being removed, remove the PCV valve and disconnect the EGR tube and heater hoses.

4. Remove the rocker arm cover attaching screws and lift the cover off the engine. Tap the cover lightly with a rubber mallet to break it loose, if necessary.

5. Clean all gasket mating surfaces and re-

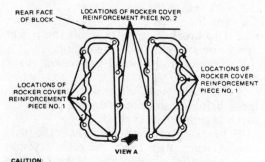

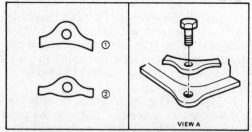

CAUTION:
IF ROCKER COVER IS TIGHTENED WITHOUT REINFORCEMENT PIECE, DEFORMATION OF THE ROCKER COVER WILL OCCUR. INSTALLING REINFORCEMENT PIECE AFTERWARD WILL NO LONGER PREVENT LEAKS.

Installing rocker cover on 2.8L (171 CID) engine

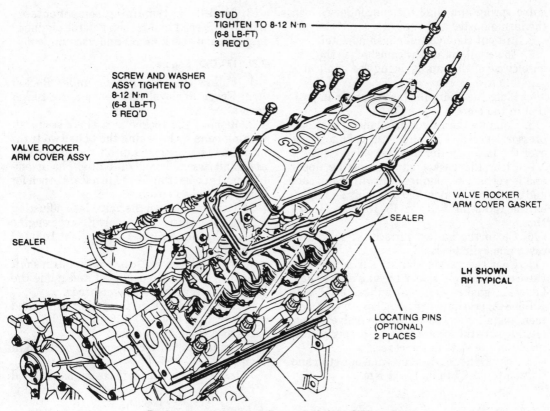

STUD
TIGHTEN TO 8-12 N·m
(6-8 LB-FT)
3 REQ'D

SCREW AND WASHER
ASSY TIGHTEN TO
8-12 N·m
(6-8 LB-FT)
5 REQ'D

VALVE ROCKER
ARM COVER ASSY

SEALER

VALVE ROCKER
ARM COVER GASKET

SEALER

LH SHOWN
RH TYPICAL

LOCATING PINS
(OPTIONAL)
2 PLACES

Rocker arm cover mounting on 3.0L (182 CID) engine

move any traces of the old gasket material and dirt.

6. To install, lightly oil all bolts and stud threads. Apply a bead of RTV sealant at the cylinder head to intake manifold rail step (two places per rail). Position a new cover gasket into place.

7. Place the rocker cover on the cylinder head and install five attaching bolts and three attaching studs. Note the location of the ignition wire separator clip stud bolts. Tighten the attaching bolts to 80–106 in.lb. (9–12 Nm).

8. Install the oil filler cap and PCV hose (left hand), or the PCV valve and EGR tube (right hand). Tighten the EGR tube to 25–36 ft.lb. (35–50 Nm).

9. Install the ignition wire separators.

10. Connect the ignition wires to the spark plugs and start the engine and check for leaks.

Rocker Arms/Shafts

REMOVAL AND INSTALLATION

2.3L (140 CID) Engine

1. Remove the upper intake manifold with throttle body attached and associated parts as required.

2. Remove the valve rocker arm cover and associated parts as required.

3. Rotate the camshaft so that the base circle of the cam is facing the applicable cam follower.

4. Using a valve spring compressor lever (T74P-6565-A or equivalent), collapse the

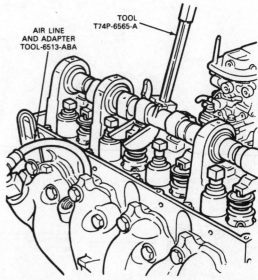

TOOL
T74P-6565-A

AIR LINE
AND ADAPTER
TOOL-6513-ABA

Collapsing the valve spring with compressor tool on 2.3L (140 CID) engine

valve spring and slide the cam follower over the lash adjuster and out.

5. Lift out the hydraulic lash adjuster.

6. To install, rotate the camshaft so that the base circle of the cam is facing the applicable cam follower.

7. Place the hydraulic lash adjuster in position in the bore.

8. Collapse the valve spring using the compressor lever and position the cam follower over the lash adjuster and the valve stem.

9. Clear the gasket surfaces of the upper and lower intake manifold. Install the gasket and upper intake manifold assembly and tighten the retaining bolts to 13–18 ft.lb. (18–24 Nm).

10. Clean the gasket surfaces of the valve cover and cylinder head.

11. Coat the gasket contact surfaces of the valve cover and UP side of the valve cover gasket with gasket and seal adhesive (D7AZ-19B508-A or equivalent). Allow to dry and then install the gasket in the valve cover, making sure the locator tabs are properly positioned in the slots in the cover.

12. Install the seven screws and one stud and tighten to 62–97 in.lb. (7–11 Nm).

13. Install the remaining components removed in Steps 1 and 2, then run the engine at fast idle and check for oil and vacuum leaks.

2.8L (171 CID) Engine

1. Follow the instructions under Rocker Arm Cover Removal and remove the rocker covers.

2. Remove the rocker arm shaft stand attaching bolts by loosening the bolts two turns at a time in sequence. Lift off the rocker arm and shaft assembly and oil baffle. The assembly may then be transferred to a workbench for disassembly as necessary.

3. To install, loosen the valve lash adjusting screws a few turns, then apply SF type engine oil to the assembly to provide initial lubrication.

4. Install the oil baffle and rocker arm shaft assembly to the cylinder head and guide the adjusting screws on to the pushrods.

5. Install and tighten the rocker arm stand attaching bolts to 43–50 ft.lb. (59–67 Nm), two turns at a time, in sequence.

6. Adjust the valve clearance as outlined in Chapter 2.

7. Install the rocker arm covers as outlined

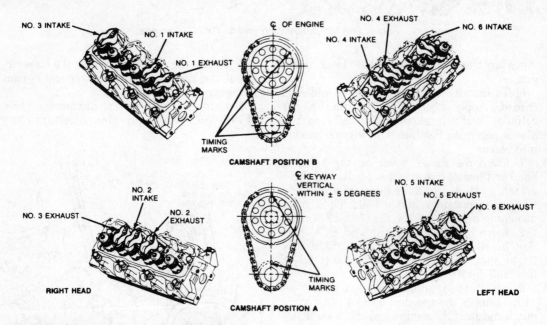

NOTE: CAMSHAFT POSITIONS "A" AND "B" ARE REQ'D TO PLACE TAPPET ASSY ON BASE CIRCLE OF CAMSHAFT LOBE TO CHECK COLLAPSED TAPPET GAP.

FULCRUM AND BOLT MUST BE FULLY SEATED AFTER FINAL TORQUE.

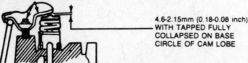

4.6-2.15mm (0.18-0.08 inch) WITH TAPPED FULLY COLLAPSED ON BASE CIRCLE OF CAM LOBE

CYL. NO.	CAMSHAFT POSITION	
	A	B
	SET GAP OF VALVES NOTED	
1	INT.	EXH.
2	EXH.	INT.
3	NONE	INT.-EXH.
4	INT.	EXH.
5	EXH.	INT.
6	NONE	INT.-EXH.

Initial valve adjustment and rocker arm assembly on 3.0L (182 CID) engine

under Rocker Arm Cover Installation, then start the engine and check for leaks.

3.0L (182 CID) Engine

The rocker arms can be removed by first removing the rocker arm covers as described earlier, then removing the single retaining bolt at each rocker arm. The rocker arm and pushrod may then be removed from the engine. Keep all rocker arms and pushrods in order so they may be installed in their original locations. Tighten the rocker arm fulcrum bolts in two stages, first to 5–11 ft.lb. (7–15 Nm), then to 18–26 ft.lb. (25–35 Nm). Refer to the illustration for initial valve adjustment.

Thermostat
REMOVAL AND INSTALLATION
2.3L (140 CID) Engine

CAUTION: *When draining the coolant, keep in mind that cats and dogs are attracted by the ethylene glycol antifreeze, and are quite likely to drink any that is left in an uncovered container or in puddles on the ground. This will prove fatal in sufficient quantity. Always drain the coolant into a sealable container. Coolant should be reused unless it is contaminated or several years old.*

The thermostat may be replaced by draining the cooling system (engine cold), then removing the retaining bolts for the thermostat housing. Lift the housing clear and remove the thermostat. It may be easier to clean the gasket mating surfaces with the heater and radiator hoses removed from the thermostat housing. Clean all gasket mating surfaces and make sure the thermostat is in the housing properly. Always use a new gasket. Tighten the thermostat housing retaining bolts to 14–21 ft.lb. (19–29 Nm). Refill the cooling system, start the engine and check for leaks.

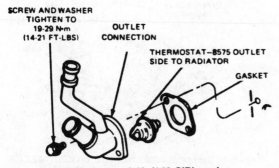

SCREW AND WASHER
TIGHTEN TO
19-29 N·m
(14-21 FT-LBS)

OUTLET
CONNECTION

THERMOSTAT—8575 OUTLET
SIDE TO RADIATOR

GASKET

Thermostat housing on 2.3L (140 CID) engine

2.8L (171 CID) and 3.0L (182 CID) V6 Engines

CAUTION: *When draining the coolant, keep in mind that cats and dogs are attracted by the ethylene glycol antifreeze, and are quite likely to drink any that is left in an uncovered container or in puddles on the ground. This will prove fatal in sufficient quantity. Always drain the coolant into a sealable container. Coolant should be reused unless it is contaminated or several years old.*

The thermostat housing is located at the front of the engine. Drain the cooling system (engine cold), then remove the retaining bolts from the thermostat housing. Move the housing out of the way, then lift out the thermostat. Clean all gasket mating surfaces and make sure the new thermostat is installed correctly in the housing. Always use a new gasket. Tighten the thermostat housing bolts to 12–15 ft.lb. (17–21 Nm). Refill the cooling system, start the engine and check for leaks.

Intake Manifold
REMOVAL AND INSTALLATION
2.3L (140 CID) Engine

The intake manifold is a two-piece (upper and lower) aluminum casting. Runner lengths are tuned to optimize engine torque and power output. The manifold provides mounting flanges for the air throttle body assembly, fuel supply manifold, accelerator control bracket and the EGR valve and supply tube. A vacuum fitting is installed to provide vacuum to various engine accessories. Pockets for the fuel injectors are machined to prevent both air and fuel leakage. The following procedure is for the removal of the intake manifold with the fuel charging assembly attached.

1. Make sure the ignition is off, then drain the coolant from the radiator (engine cold).

CAUTION: *When draining the coolant, keep in mind that cats and dogs are attracted by the ethylene glycol antifreeze, and are quite likely to drink any that is left in an uncovered container or in puddles on the ground. This will prove fatal in sufficient quantity. Always drain the coolant into a sealable container. Coolant should be reused unless it is contaminated or several years old.*

2. Disconnect the negative battery cable and secure it out of the way.

3. Remove the fuel filler cap to vent tank pressure. Release the pressure from the fuel system at the fuel pressure relief valve using EFI pressure gauge T80L-9974-A or equivalent. The fuel pressure relief valve is located on the fuel line in the upper right hand corner of the engine compartment. Remove the valve cap to gain access to the valve.

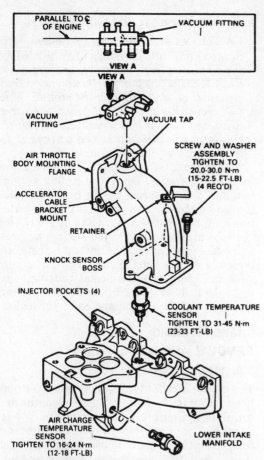

Upper and lower intake manifold assemblies on 2.3L (140 CID) engine

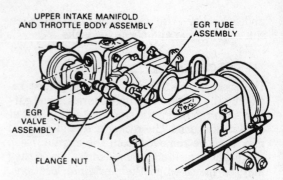

Disconnecting EGR valve on 2.3L (140 CID) engine

6. Remove the throttle linkage shield and disconnect the throttle linkage and speed control cable (if equipped). Unbolt the accelerator cable from the bracket and position the cable out of the way.

7. Disconnect the air intake hose, air bypass hose and crankcase vent hose.

8. Disconnect the PCV hose from the fitting on the underside of the upper intake manifold.

9. Loosen the clamp on the coolant bypass line at the lower intake manifold and disconnect the hose.

10. Disconnect the EGR tube from the EGR valve by removing the flange nut.

11. Remove the four upper intake manifold retaining nuts. Remove the upper intake manifold and air throttle body assembly.

12. Disconnect the push connect fitting at the fuel supply manifold and fuel return lines. Disconnect the fuel return line from the fuel supply manifold.

13. Remove the engine oil dipstick bracket retaining bolt.

14. Disconnect the electrical connectors from all four fuel injectors and move the harness aside.

4. Disconnect the electrical connectors at the throttle position sensor, knock sensor, injector wiring harness, air charge temperature sensor and engine coolant temperature sensor.

5. Tag and disconnect the vacuum lines at the upper intake manifold vacuum tree, at the EGR valve and at the fuel pressure regulator.

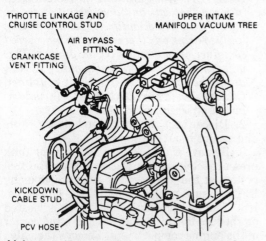

Linkage and hose locations on 2.3L (140 CID) engine

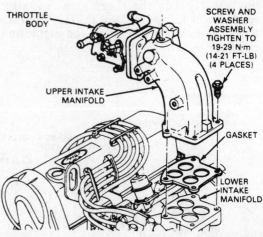

Removing the upper intake manifold on 2.3L (140 CID) engine

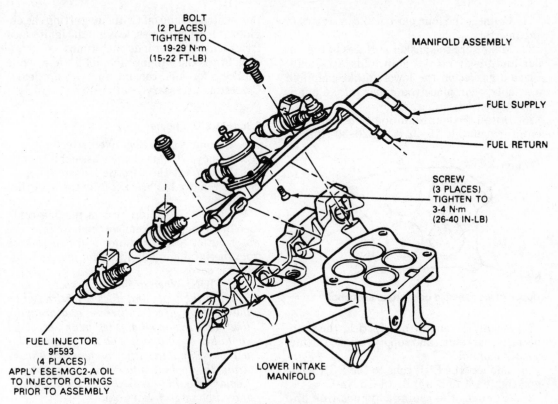

BOLT (2 PLACES) TIGHTEN TO 19-29 N·m (15-22 FT-LB)

MANIFOLD ASSEMBLY

FUEL SUPPLY

FUEL RETURN

SCREW (3 PLACES) TIGHTEN TO 3-4 N·m (26-40 IN-LB)

FUEL INJECTOR 9F593 (4 PLACES) APPLY ESE-MGC2-A OIL TO INJECTOR O-RINGS PRIOR TO ASSEMBLY

LOWER INTAKE MANIFOLD

Fuel supply manifold and injector mouting on 2.3L (140 CID) engine

15. Remove the two fuel supply manifold retaining bolts, then carefully remove the fuel supply manifold and injectors. Remove the injectors by exerting a slight twisting/pulling motion.

16. Remove the four bottom retaining bolts from the lower manifold. The front two bolts also secure an engine lifting bracket. Once the bolts are removed, remove the lower intake manifold.

17. Clean and inspect the mounting faces of the lower intake manifold and cylinder head. Both surfaces must be clean and flat.

NOTE: *If the intake manifold upper or lower section is being replaced, it will be necessary to transfer components from the old to the new part.*

18. To install, first clean and oil the manifold bolt threads. Install a new lower manifold gasket.

19. Position the lower manifold assembly to the head and install the engine lifting bracket. Install the four top manifold retaining bolts finger tight. Install the four remaining manifold bolts and tighten all bolts to 12–15 ft.lb. (16–20 Nm), following the sequence illustrated.

20. Install the fuel supply manifold and injectors with two retaining bolts. Tighten the retaining bolts to 12–15 ft.lb. (16–20 Nm).

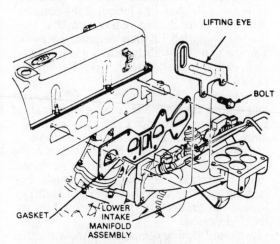

LIFTING EYE

BOLT

GASKET **LOWER INTAKE MANIFOLD ASSEMBLY**

Removing lower intake manifold on 2.3L (140 CID) engine

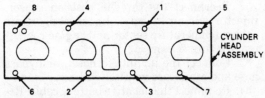

CYLINDER HEAD ASSEMBLY

Torque sequence for lower intake manifold attaching bolts

21. Connect the four electrical connectors to the injectors.

22. Make sure the gasket surfaces of the upper and lower intake manifolds are clean. Place a gasket on the lower intake manifold assembly, then place the upper intake manifold in position.

23. Install the four retaining bolts and tighten in sequence to 15–22 ft.lb. (20–30 Nm).

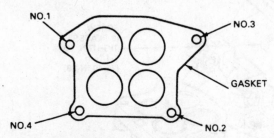

Upper intake manifold bolt torque sequence

24. Install the engine oil dipstick, then connect the fuel return and supply lines to the fuel supply manifold.

25. Connect the EGR tube to the EGR valve and tighten it to 6–9 ft.lb. (8–12 Nm).

26. Connect the coolant bypass line and tighten the clamp. Connect the PCV system hose to the fitting on the underside of the upper intake manifold.

27. If removed, install the vacuum tee on the upper intake manifold. Use Teflon® tape on the threads and tighten to 12–18 ft.lb. (16–24 Nm). Reconnect the vacuum lines to the tee, the EGR valve and the fuel pressure regulator.

28. Hold the accelerator cable bracket in position on the upper intake manifold and install the retaining bolt. Tighten the bolt to 10–15 ft.lb. (13–20 Nm).

29. Install the accelerator cable to the bracket.

30. Position a new gasket on the fuel charging assembly air throttle body mounting flange. Install the air throttle body to the fuel charging assembly. Install two retaining nuts and two bolts and tighten to 12–15 ft.lb. (16–20 Nm).

31. Connect the accelerator and speed control cable (if equipped), then install the throttle linkage shield.

32. Reconnect the throttle position sensor, injector wiring harness, knock sensor, air charge temperature sensor and engine coolant temperature sensor.

33. Connect the air intake hose, air bypass hose and crankcase ventilation hose.

34. Reconnect the negative battery cable. Refill the cooling system to specifications and pressurize the fuel system by turning the ignition switch on and off (without starting the engine) at least six times, leaving the ignition on for at least five seconds each time.

35. Start the engine and let it idle while checking for fuel, coolant and vacuum leaks. Correct as necessary.

2.8L (171 CID) Engine

1. Disconnect the negative battery cable.

2. Remove the air cleaner assembly.

3. Disconnect the throttle transmission cable and remove the bracket from the left cylinder head.

4. Drain the cooling system (engine cold), then disconnect and remove the hose from the water outlet to the radiator and bypass hose from the intake manifold to thermostat housing rear cover.

CAUTION: *When draining the coolant, keep in mind that cats and dogs are attracted by the ethylene glycol antifreeze, and are quite likely to drink any that is left in an uncovered container or in puddles on the ground. This will prove fatal in sufficient quantity. Always drain the coolant into a sealable container. Coolant should be reused unless it is contaminated or several years old.*

5. Remove the distributor cap and spark plug wires as an assembly. Disconnect the distributor wiring harness.

6. Observe and mark the location of the distributor rotor and housing so ignition timing can be maintained at reassembly. Remove the distributor hold down screw and clamp and lift out the distributor.

7. Remove the rocker arm covers as outlined previously.

8. Remove the fuel line from the fuel filter.

9. Remove the carburetor and EGR spacer.

10. Remove the intake manifold attaching bolts and nuts. Note the length of the manifold attaching bolts during removal so that they may be installed in their original positions. Tap the manifold lightly with a plastic mallet to break the gasket seal, then lift off the manifold.

11. Remove all traces of old gasket material and sealing compound from all gasket mating surfaces. Be careful not to scratch the intake manifold or cylinder head mating surfaces.

12. To install the intake manifold; first apply sealing compound to the joining surfaces. Place the intake manifold gasket in position, making sure that the tab on the right bank cylinder head gasket fits into the cutout on the manifold gasket.

13. Apply sealing compound to the attaching bolt bosses on the intake manifold and position the intake manifold on the engine. Follow the

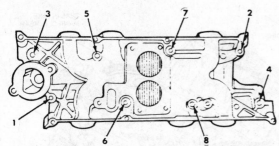

Intake manifold torque sequence on 2.8L (171 CID) engine

illustrated torque sequence and tighten the manifold mounting bolts in five steps:

    a. install bolts finger tight
    b. torque each to 3–6 ft.lb. (4–8 Nm)
    c. torque each to 6–11 ft.lb. (8–15 Nm)
    d. torque each to 11–15 ft.lb. (15–21 Nm)
    e. torque each to 15–18 ft.lb. (21–25 Nm)

14. Install the distributor so that the rotor and housing are in the same position marked at removal.

15. Install distributor clamp and attaching bolt and connect the distributor wire.

16. Install the EGR spacer and carburetor.

17. Install the fuel line.

18. Replace the rocker arm cover gaskets and install rocker arm valve covers.

19. Install the distributor cap. Coat the inside of each spark plug wire connector with silicone grease with a small screwdriver, then install the wires to the plugs. Connect the distributor wiring harness.

20. Install and adjust the throttle bracket and linkage.

21. Install the air cleaner and air cleaner tube at the carburetor.

22. Connect the negative battery cable.

23. Connect the hoses from the water outlet to the radiator and bypass hose from the thermostat housing rear cover to the intake manifold.

24. Refill and bleed the cooling system, check the ignition timing and idle speed and reset to specifications if necessary. Run the engine at fast idle and check for coolant or oil leaks.

3.0L (182 CID) Engine

1. Drain the cooling system (engine cold).
CAUTION: *When draining the coolant, keep in mind that cats and dogs are attracted by the ethylene glycol antifreeze, and are quite likely to drink any that is left in an uncovered container or in puddles on the ground. This will prove fatal in sufficient quantity. Always drain the coolant into a sealable container. Coolant should be reused unless it is contaminated or several years old.*

2. Disconnect the battery ground cable.

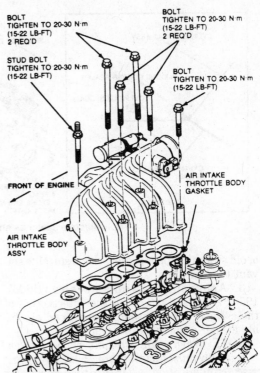

Removing the air intake throttle body on 3.0L (182 CID) engine

3. Depressurize the fuel system and remove the air intake throttle body as outlined in Chapter 4.

4. Disconnect the fuel return and supply lines.

5. Remove the fuel injector wiring harness from the engine.

6. Disconnect the upper radiator hose.

7. Disconnect the water outlet heater hose.

8. Disconnect the distributor cap with the spark plug wires attached. Matchmark and remove the distributor assembly.

9. Remove the intake manifold attaching bolts and studs.

10. Lift the intake manifold off the engine. Use a plastic mallet to tap lightly around the intake manifold to break it loose, if necessary. Do not pry between the manifold and cylinder head with any sharp instrument. The manifold can be removed with the fuel rails and injectors in place.

11. Remove the manifold side gaskets and end seals and discard. If the manifold is being replaced, transfer the fuel injector and fuel rail components to the new manifold on a clean workbench. Clean all gasket mating surfaces.

12. To install the intake manifold, first lightly oil all attaching bolts and stud threads. The intake manifold, cylinder head and cylinder block mating surfaces should be clean and free

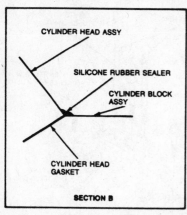

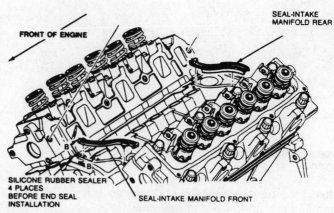

Apply silicone sealer as shown on 3.0L (182 CID) engine

of old silicone rubber sealer. Use a suitable solvent to clean these areas.

13. Apply silicone rubber sealer (D6AZ-19562-A or equivalent) to the intersection of the cylinder block assembly and head assembly at four corners as illustrated.

NOTE: *When using silicone rubber sealer, assembly must occur within 15 minutes after sealer application. After this time, the sealer may start to set-up and its sealing effectiveness may be reduced. In high temperature/ humidity conditions, the RTV will start to skin over in about 5 minutes.*

14. Install the front intake manifold seal and rear intake manifold seal and secure them with retaining features.

15. Position the intake manifold gaskets in place and insert the locking tabs over the tabs on the cylinder head gaskets.

16. Apply silicone rubber sealer over the gasket in the same places as in Step 13.

17. Carefully lower the intake manifold into position on the cylinder block and cylinder heads to prevent smearing the silicone sealer and causing gasketing voids.

18. Install the retaining bolts and tighten in two stages, in the sequence illustrated, first to 11 ft.lb. (15 Nm) and then to 18 ft.lb. (24 Nm).

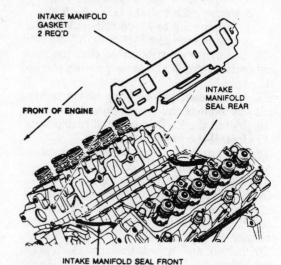

Installing intake manifold gaskets on 3.0L (182 CID) engine

19. Install the distributor assembly, using the matchmarks make earlier to insure correct alignment. Install the distributor cap and spark plug wires.

20. Install the injector wiring harness and reconnect the fuel lines.

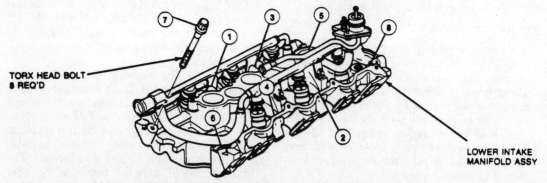

Intake manifold torque sequence on 3.0L (182 CID) engine

21. Install the air intake throttle body.

22. Reconnect the negative battery cable and refill the cooling system.

Exhaust Manifold

REMOVAL AND INSTALLATION

2.3L (140 CID) Engine

1. Remove the air cleaner ducts, if necessary to gain working clearance.

2. Disconnect the EGR line at the exhaust manifold and loosen it at the EGR tube.

3. Disconnect the oxygen sensor electrical connector.

4. Remove the screw attaching the heater hoses on the valve cover.

5. Remove the eight exhaust manifold mounting bolts, then move the exhaust manifold away from the cylinder head and remove the gasket.

6. Raise the van and support it safely.

7. Remove the two exhaust pipe bolts and separate the exhaust pipe from the exhaust manifold.

8. Carefully lower the exhaust manifold down and out of the engine compartment. Be careful not to damage the oxygen sensor during removal.

9. Clean all gasket mating surfaces. If the exhaust manifold is being replaced, the oxygen sensor will have to be transferred to the new manifold.

10. Place a new gasket on the exhaust mani-

fold, then position the manifold on the cylinder head.

11. Install the eight exhaust manifold bolts and tighten them in two stages, first to 5–7 ft.lb. (7–9 Nm) and then to 16–23 ft.lb. (22–31 Nm).

12. Install the two exhaust pipe bolts and tighten them to 25–34 ft.lb. (34–46 Nm).

13. Install the EGR line at the exhaust manifold and tighten the EGR tube.

14. Reconnect the oxygen sensor and install the air intake ducts, if removed.

2.8L (171 CID) Engine

1. Remove the carburetor air cleaner.

2. Remove the attaching nuts from the exhaust manifold shroud on the right side.

3. Raise the van and support it safely.

4. Working under the van, disconnect the attaching nuts from the Y-pipe. Remove the thermactor upstream crossover tube and other thermactor components as necessary to allow removal of exhaust manifold(s).

5. Disconnect the exhaust gas oxygen sensor connector on the left exhaust manifold.

6. Remove the manifold attaching nuts.

7. Lift the manifold from the cylinder head, then remove the manifold to head gaskets.

8. Clean all gasket mating surfaces. If the left exhaust manifold is being replaced, the oxygen sensor will have to be transferred to the new part.

9. Position the new gasket and the manifold on the studs and install and tighten the attaching bolts to 20–30 ft.lb. (27–37 Nm). Start at the center and work outward, alternating sides during the torque sequence.

10. Install a new inlet pipe gasket, then install and tighten the inlet pipe attaching bolts to 25–34 ft.lb. (34–36 Nm).

11. Position the exhaust manifold shroud on the manifold and install and tighten the attaching nuts.

12. Install the thermactor components that were removed to gain working clearance, then lower the van.

13. Install the carburetor air cleaner.

14. Connect the oxygen sensor wire on the left hand exhaust manifold.

3.0L (182 CID) Engine

1. Remove the air cleaner assembly, if necessary to gain working clearance.

2. Remove the oil level indicator tube support bracket. Remove the power steering pump pressure and return hoses if the left hand manifold is being removed. If the right hand manifold is being removed, disconnect the EGR tube from the exhaust manifold and the oxygen sensor connector.

Exhaust manifold mounting on 2.3L (140 CID) engine

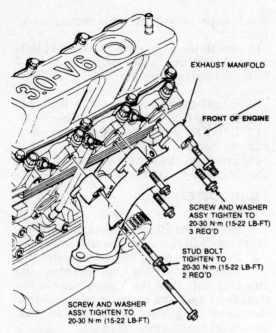

SCREW AND WASHER ASSY TIGHTEN TO 20-30 N·m (15-22 LB-FT) 3 REQ'D

STUD BOLT TIGHTEN TO 20-30 N·m (15-22 LB-FT) 2 REQ'D

SCREW AND WASHER ASSY TIGHTEN TO 20-30 N·m (15-22 LB-FT)

EXHAUST MANIFOLD

FRONT OF ENGINE

LH exhaust manifold on 3.0L (182 CID) engine

3. Raise the vehicle and support it safely.

4. Remove the manifold to exhaust pipe attaching nuts, then separate the exhaust pipe from the manifold.

5. Remove the exhaust manifold attaching bolts and the manifold.

6. Clean all gasket mating surfaces.

7. Lightly oil all bolt and stud threads before installation. If a new manifold is being installed, the oxygen sensor will have to be transferred to the new part.

8. Position the exhaust manifold on the cylinder head and install the manifold attaching bolts. Tighten them to 15–22 ft.lb. (20–30 Nm).

9. Connect the exhaust pipe to the manifold, then tighten the attaching nuts to 16–24 ft.lb. (21–32 Nm). Lower the vehicle.

10. Connect the power steering pump pressure and return hoses.

11. Install the oil level indicator tube support bracket.

Air Conditioning Compressor

REMOVAL AND INSTALLATION

Follow the procedures outlined in Chapter 1 to discharge the A/C system. Loosen the compres-

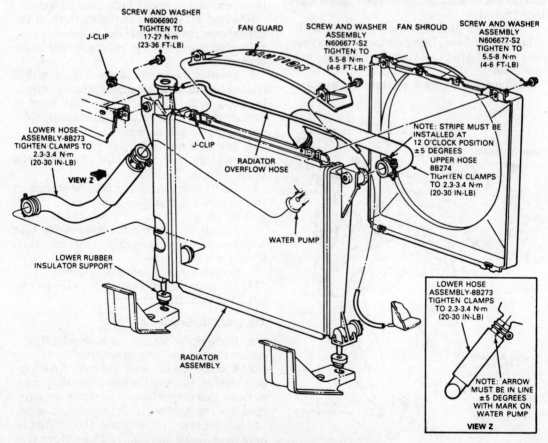

SCREW AND WASHER N6066902 TIGHTEN TO 17-27 N·m (23-36 FT-LB)

J-CLIP

FAN GUARD

SCREW AND WASHER ASSEMBLY N606677-S2 TIGHTEN TO 5.5-8 N·m (4-6 FT-LB)

FAN SHROUD

SCREW AND WASHER ASSEMBLY N606677-S2 TIGHTEN TO 5.5-8 N·m (4-6 FT-LB)

LOWER HOSE ASSEMBLY-8B273 TIGHTEN CLAMPS TO 2.3-3.4 N·m (20-30 IN-LB)

VIEW Z

J-CLIP

RADIATOR OVERFLOW HOSE

NOTE: STRIPE MUST BE INSTALLED AT 12 O'CLOCK POSITION ±5 DEGREES

UPPER HOSE 8B274 TIGHTEN CLAMPS TO 2.3-3.4 N·m (20-30 IN-LB)

WATER PUMP

LOWER RUBBER INSULATOR SUPPORT

RADIATOR ASSEMBLY

LOWER HOSE ASSEMBLY-8B273 TIGHTEN CLAMPS TO 2.3-3.4 N·m (20-30 IN-LB)

NOTE: ARROW MUST BE IN LINE ±5 DEGREES WITH MARK ON WATER PUMP

VIEW Z

Radiator installation on 2.3L (140 CID) engine

sor mounting bolts and remove the drive belt. Disconnect the refrigerant lines and cap them to prevent the entry of dirt or moisture into the system. Remove the mounting bolts and lift the compressor off the engine. Installation is the reverse of removal. Recharge the A/C system as outlined in Chapter 1 and adjust the drive belt tension.

Radiator

REMOVAL AND INSTALLATION

1. With the engine cold, drain the cooling system by removing the radiator cap and opening the draincock at the lower rear corner of the radiator tank.

CAUTION: *When draining the coolant, keep in mind that cats and dogs are attracted by the ethylene glycol antifreeze, and are quite likely to drink any that is left in an uncovered container or in puddles on the ground. This will prove fatal in sufficient quantity. Always drain the coolant into a sealable container. Coolant should be reused unless it is contaminated or several years old.*

2. Remove the rubber overflow tube from the radiator and store it up out of the way.

3. Remove the radiator fan shroud upper attaching screws, then lift the shroud out of the lower retaining clips and drape it on the fan.

4. Loosen the upper and lower hose clamps at the radiator and remove the hoses from the radiator connections.

5. If equipped with automatic transmission, disconnect the two transmission cooling lines from the radiator fittings. Disconnect the transmission cooler tube support bracket from the bottom flange of the radiator by removing the screw.

6. Remove the two radiator upper attaching screws.

7. Tilt the radiator back (rearward) about 1″ (25mm) and lift it directly upward, clear of the radiator support and the cooling fan.

8. If either hose is being replaced, loosen the clamp at the engine end and slip the hose off the connection with a twisting motion. Install the new hose(s) to the engine connections, making sure any bends are oriented exactly as the old hose for alignment purposes.

9. If the radiator is being replaced, transfer

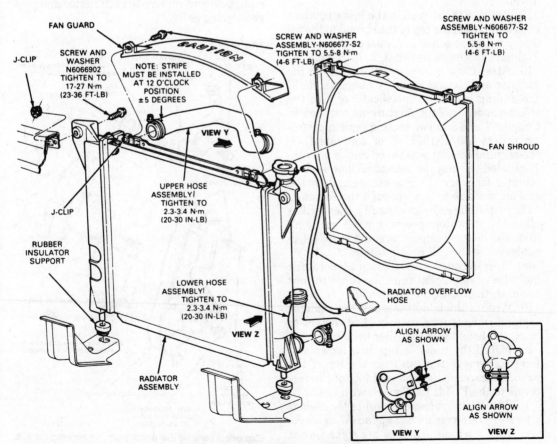

Typical radiator installation on V6 engines

the lower support rubber insulators to the new part. The radiator cooling fins should be cleaned of any dirt or debris and any bent fins should be carefully straightened.

10. Install the radiator into the engine compartment, making sure the lower rubber insulators are properly positioned in the radiator support. Be careful to clear the fan with the radiator to avoid damage to the cooling fins.

11. Connect the upper attaching bolts to the radiator support and tighten them to 12–20 ft.lb. (17–27 Nm).

12. If equipped with automatic transmission, loosely connect the two transmission cooling lines to the radiator fittings, then connect the transmission cooler tube support bracket to the bottom flange of the radiator with the attaching screw. Attach the cooler tubes to the plastic clip on the tube support bracket, then tighten the fittings at the radiator.

13. Attach the upper hose to the radiator, positioning the stripe on the hose at the 12 o'clock position. Tighten the hose clamp to 20–30 in.lb. (2–4 Nm).

14. Position the lower hose on the radiator with the hose stripe at the 6 o'clock position, then tighten the hose clamp to 20–30 in.lb. (2–4 Nm).

15. Position the shroud in the lower retainer clips and attach the top of the shroud to the radiator with two screw and washer assemblies. Tighten the screws to 4–6 ft.lb. (5–8 Nm).

16. Attach the rubber overflow tube to the radiator and coolant recovery reservoir. Refill the cooling system to specifications with the recommended coolant mixture as outlined in Chapter 1 and add two cooling system protector pellets (D9AZ-19558-A or equivalent). If the original coolant was saved and is not contaminated, it may be reused. Allow several minutes for trapped air to escape and for the coolant mixture to flow through the radiator.

17. Install the radiator cap fully, then back it off to the first stop (pressure relief position). Slide the heater temperature and mode selector levers to the full heat position.

18. Start the engine and allow it to operate at fast idle (about 2,000 rpm) for three to four minutes, then shut the engine off.

19. Wrap a thick cloth around the radiator cap and remove it cautiously. Add coolant to bring the level up to the filler neck seat.

20. Install the radiator cap fully (down and locked). Remove the cap from the top of the coolant recovery reservoir and top off the reservoir to the FULL HOT mark with coolant.

NOTE: *Be careful not to confuse the coolant recovery reservoir with the windshield washer fluid reservoir. The two are right next to one another.*

Water Pump

REMOVAL AND INSTALLATION

2.3L (140 CID) Engine

NOTE: *Provision for wrench clearance has been made in the timing belt inner cover, so only the outer cover must be removed in order to replace the water pump.*

1. Drain the cooling system (engine cold).

CAUTION: *When draining the coolant, keep in mind that cats and dogs are attracted by the ethylene glycol antifreeze, and are quite likely to drink any that is left in an uncovered container or in puddles on the ground. This will prove fatal in sufficient quantity. Always drain the coolant into a sealable container. Coolant should be reused unless it is contaminated or several years old.*

2. Remove the two bolts retaining the fan shroud and position the shroud over the fan.

3. Remove the four bolts retaining the fan assembly to the water pump shaft and remove the fan and shroud.

4. Loosen the A/C compressor adjusting idler pulley and remove the drive belt, if equipped.

5. Loosen the power steering bolts (if equipped) and remove the alternator and power steering belts.

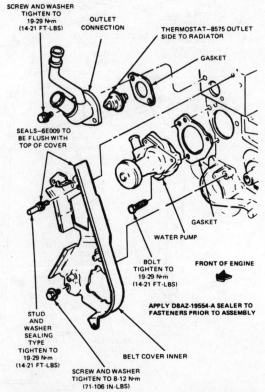

Exploded view of the water pump mounting on 2.3L (140 CID) engine

6. Remove the water pump pulley and the vent tube to the canister.

7. Remove the heater hose to the water pump.

8. Remove the cam belt cover.

9. Remove the lower radiator hose from the water pump.

10. Remove the water pump retaining bolts and remove the water pump from the engine.

11. Clean the water pump gasket surface at the engine block. Remove all traces of old gasket and/or sealer.

12. To install, use contact cement to position the new gasket to the water pump. Position the water pump to the engine block and install three retaining bolts. Apply sealer (D8AZ-19554-A or equivalent) to the water pump bolts prior to installation and tighten the bolts to 14–21 ft.lb. (19–29 Nm).

13. Install the lower radiator hose to the water pump.

14. Install the cam belt cover.

15. Position the water pump pulley to the water pump.

16. Install the power steering (if equipped) and alternator drive belts to the pulleys.

17. Install the A/C compressor belt (if equipped).

18. Install the shroud and fan assembly to the engine. Install the fan assembly with spacers to the water pump shaft.

19. Position the shroud to the radiator and install the retaining bolts.

20. Adjust the drive belts to specifications (see Chapter 1), refill the cooling system, then start the engine and check for leaks.

2.8L (171 CID) and 3.0L (182 CID) Engines

NOTE: *This procedure requires the use of special tools to remove the fan and clutch assembly.*

1. Drain the cooling system (engine cold) into a clean container and save the coolant for reuse.

CAUTION: *When draining the coolant, keep in mind that cats and dogs are attracted by the ethylene glycol antifreeze, and are quite likely to drink any that is left in an uncovered container or in puddles on the ground. This will prove fatal in sufficient quantity. Always drain the coolant into a sealable container. Coolant should be reused unless it is contaminated or several years old.*

2. Loosen the hose clamps and detach the lower radiator hose and heater return hose from the water inlet housing.

3. Remove the clutch and fan assembly using a fan clutch pulley holder (tool no. T83T-6312-A) and fan clutch nut wrench (tool no. T83T-6312-B).

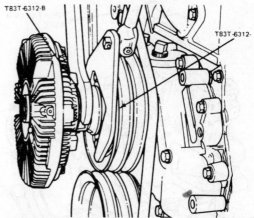

T83T-6312-B

T83T-6312-

Removing fan and clutch assembly with special tools on 2.8L (171 CID) engine

CAUTION: *The fan clutch nut is a left hand thread. Remove by turning the nut clockwise.*

4. Loosen the alternator mounting bolts and remove the belt. If equipped with A/C, remove the alternator and bracket.

5. Remove the water pump pulley.

6. Remove the water pump assembly attaching bolts, then remove the water pump assembly and water inlet housing from the front cover. Note the position of the different length bolts when removing them so they may be installed in their original locations.

7. Clean all gasket material and/or sealer from all gasket mating surfaces on the front cover and water pump assembly.

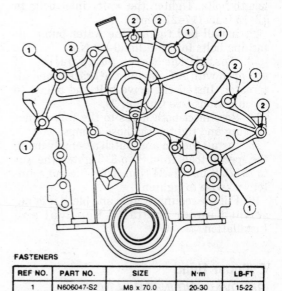

FASTENERS

REF NO.	PART NO.	SIZE	N·m	LB-FT
1	N606047-S2	M8 x 70.0	20-30	15-22
2	N605774-S2	M6 x 1.0 x 25.0	8-12	6-8

NOTE: APPLY PIPE SEALANT D8AZ-19558-A TO BOLT THREADS

Water pump torque specifications on 3.0L (182 CID) engine

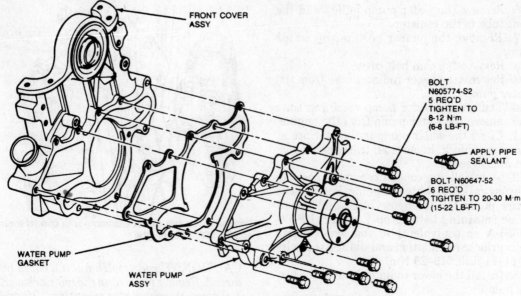

FRONT COVER
ASSY

BOLT
N605774-S2
5 REQ'D
TIGHTEN TO
8-12 N·m
(6-8 LB-FT)

APPLY PIPE
SEALANT

BOLT N60647-52
6 REQ'D
TIGHTEN TO 20-30 M·m
(15-22 LB-FT)

WATER PUMP
GASKET

WATER PUMP
ASSY

Water pump mounting on 3.0L (182 CID) engine

8. Apply sealer to both sides of the new gasket and place the gasket on the water pump.

9. Position the water pump assembly to the front cover and install two bolts finger tight to hold it in position.

10. Clean all gasket material and/or sealer from the mating surfaces of the water inlet housing. Apply sealer to both sides of a new gasket and place it on the water inlet housing.

11. Position the water inlet housing and install the attaching bolts. Note the different length bolts. Tighten the water inlet bolts to 12–15 ft.lb. (17–21 Nm).

12. Install and tighten the water pump attaching bolts to 7–9 ft.lb. (9–12 Nm).

13. Install the water pump pulley. If equipped with A/C, install the bracket and alternator. Install the drive belt and adjust to specifications (see Chapter 1).

14. Reconnect both hoses to the water inlet housing and tighten the hose clamps.

15. Install the fan and clutch assembly using the special tools from Step 3. Tighten the nut to 15–25 ft.lb. (21–34 Nm). Turn the nut counterclockwise to tighten.

16. Fill the cooling system and bleed it as described under Radiator Removal and Installation.

Cylinder Head

REMOVAL AND INSTALLATION

2.3L (140 CID) Engine

1. Drain the cooling system (engine cold) into a clean container and save the coolant for reuse.

CAUTION: *When draining the coolant, keep in mind that cats and dogs are attracted by the ethylene glycol antifreeze, and are quite likely to drink any that is left in an uncovered container or in puddles on the ground. This will prove fatal in sufficient quantity. Always drain the coolant into a sealable container. Coolant should be reused unless it is contaminated or several years old.*

2. Raise the vehicle and support it safely on jackstands.

3. Remove the resonator assembly.

4. Lower the vehicle.

5. Disconnect the distributor cap and spark plug wires from the plugs, then remove the cap and spark plug wires as an assembly.

6. Remove the spark plugs.

7. Tag and disconnect all vacuum hoses.

8. Remove the dipstick and tube from the engine.

9. Remove the rocker arm cover retaining bolts and lift off the cover.

10. Remove the intake manifold retaining bolts.

11. Loosen the alternator retaining bolts, remove the belt from the pulley and remove the mounting bracket retaining bolts from the head.

12. Disconnect the upper radiator hose at both ends and remove it from the engine compartment.

13. Remove the cam belt cover mounting bolts. If equipped with power steering, remove the power steering pump bracket.

14. Loosen the cam idler retaining bolts. Position the idler in the unloaded position and tighten the retaining bolts.

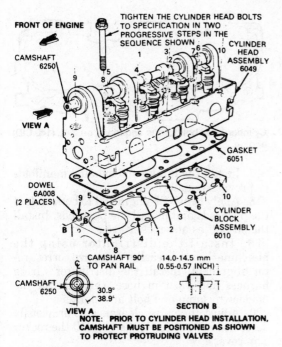

FRONT OF ENGINE

TIGHTEN THE CYLINDER HEAD BOLTS TO SPECIFICATION IN TWO PROGRESSIVE STEPS IN THE SEQUENCE SHOWN

CAMSHAFT 6250

VIEW A

CYLINDER HEAD ASSEMBLY 6049

GASKET 6051

DOWEL 6A008 (2 PLACES)

CYLINDER BLOCK ASSEMBLY 6010

CAMSHAFT 90° TO PAN RAIL

14.0-14.5 mm (0.55-0.57 INCH)

CAMSHAFT 6250

30.9°
38.9°

VIEW A

SECTION B

NOTE: PRIOR TO CYLINDER HEAD INSTALLATION, CAMSHAFT MUST BE POSITIONED AS SHOWN TO PROTECT PROTRUDING VALVES

Cylinder head installation on 2.3L (140 CID) engine

15. Remove the cam belt from the cam pulley and auxiliary pulley.

16. Remove the eight exhaust manifold retaining bolts.

17. Remove the cam belt idler and two bracket bolts.

18. Remove the cam belt idler spring stop from the cylinder head.

19. Disconnect the oil sending unit lead wire.

20. Remove the cylinder head retaining bolts in reverse of the tightening sequence.

21. Carefully lift the cylinder head off the engine. Refer to the following procedures for cylinder head component removal, valve replacement, resurfacing, etc.

22. Clean the cylinder head gasket surface at the block.

23. Clean the intake manifold gasket surface at the intake manifold and the exhaust manifold gasket surface at the exhaust manifold and cylinder head.

24. Clean the cylinder head gasket surface at the cylinder head and the intake manifold gasket surface at the cylinder head.

25. Blow oil out of the cylinder head bolt block holes with compressed air.

26. Clean the rocker cover gasket surface on the cylinder head and check the head for flatness.

27. To install the cylinder head, first position the head gasket on the block, then carefully lower the cylinder head down into place. See the illustration to make sure the camshaft is

positioned correctly to protect the valves when installing the cylinder head.

28. Install the cylinder head retaining bolts and tighten them in sequence first to 50–60 ft.lb. (68–81 Nm) and then to 80–90 ft.lb. (108–122 Nm).

29. Connect the oil sending unit lead wires.

30. Install the cam belt idler spring stop to the cylinder head.

31. Position the cam belt idler to the cylinder head and install the retaining bolts.

32. Install the eight exhaust manifold retaining bolts.

33. Align the distributor rotor with the No. 1 plug location in the distributor cap.

34. Align the camshaft gear with the pointer.

35. Align the crankshaft pulley TDC mark with the pointer on the cam belt cover.

36. Install the cam belt to the pulleys (cam and auxiliary).

37. Loosen the idler retaining bolts and allow it to tension the cam belt, then rotate the engine by hand and check the timing alignment.

38. Adjust the belt tensioner and tighten the retaining bolts. Install the cam belt cover and tighten the retaining bolts.

39. Connect the upper radiator hose to the engine and radiator and tighten the retaining clamps.

40. Position the alternator bracket to the cylinder head and install the retainers.

41. Install the drive belt to the pulleys and adjust the belt tension (see Chapter 1).

42. Install the intake manifold to the head and install the retaining bolts. Tighten them to 14–21 ft.lb. (19–28 Nm).

43. Install the rocker arm covers and retaining bolts, as previously described.

44. Install the spark plugs and torque to 5–10 ft.lb. (7–13 Nm).

45. Install the dipstick tube and dipstick.

46. Reconnect all disconnected vacuum hoses.

47. Install the distributor, spark plug wires and distributor cap. Reconnect the distributor wire harness.

48. Install the heater hose retainer to the valve cover.

49. Refill the cooling system as previously described.

50. Install the resonator assembly, then start the engine and check for leaks. Adjust the ignition timing and idle speed, if necessary.

2.8L (171 CID) Engine

1. Disconnect the battery ground cable.

2. Drain the cooling system (engine cold) into a clean container and save the coolant for reuse.

CAUTION: *When draining the coolant, keep*

in mind that cats and dogs are attracted by the ethylene glycol antifreeze, and are quite likely to drink any that is left in an uncovered container or in puddles on the ground. This will prove fatal in sufficient quantity. Always drain the coolant into a sealable container. Coolant should be reused unless it is contaminated or several years old.

3. Remove the air cleaner from the carburetor and disconnect the throttle linkage. Remove the linkage bracket.

4. Remove the distributor cap and wires as an assembly. Disconnect the distributor wiring harness.

5. Matchmark the location of the distributor rotor and housing so the ignition timing can be maintained at reassembly. Remove the distributor hold down screw and clamp, then lift out the distributor. Note the rotor movement as the distributor is installed so it may be positioned correctly on installation.

6. Remove the radiator and bypass hoses from the thermostat and intake manifold.

7. Remove the rocker arm covers and rocker arm shafts as previously described.

8. Disconnect the fuel line from the carburetor and remove the carburetor.

9. Remove the intake manifold as previously described.

10. Remove the pushrods, keeping them in order so they may be installed in their original locations.

11. Remove the exhaust manifold(s) as previously described.

12. Loosen the cylinder head attaching bolts in reverse of the torque sequence, the remove the bolts and lift off the cylinder head. Remove and discard the head gasket. Refer to the following procedures for cylinder head component removal, valve replacement, resurfacing, etc.

13. Clean the cylinder heads, intake manifold, valve rocker arm cover and cylinder block gasket surfaces of all traces of old gasket material and/or sealer.

14. Place the cylinder head gasket(s) in position on the cylinder block. Gaskets are marked with the words **Front** and **Top** for correct positioning. Left and right head gaskets are NOT interchangeable.

15. Install fabricated alignment dowels (head bolts with the heads cut off) in the cylinder block and install the cylinder head assembly.

16. Remove the alignment dowels and install the cylinder head attaching bolts. Tighten the bolts in sequence, in three stages:

    a. Step 1 to 29–40 ft.lb. (39–54 Nm)
    b. Step 2 to 40–51 ft.lb. (54–69 Nm)
    c. Step 3 to 70–85 ft.lb. (95–115 Nm)

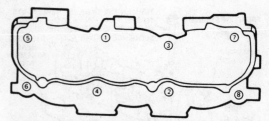

Cylinder head bolt torque sequence on 2.8L (140 CID) engine

17. Install the intake and exhaust manifolds as previously described.

18. Apply heavy SF engine oil to both ends of the pushrods and install the pushrods. Install the oil baffles and rocker arms.

19. Install the distributor using the matchmarks made earlier to insure correct rotor alignment. Install the distributor wiring harness and vacuum hose, then install the holddown clamp and bolt and tighten.

20. Adjust the valve clearance as previously described in Chapter 1, then install the rocker arm covers.

21. Install the carburetor and reconnect the fuel line.

22. Install the distributor cap and spark plug wires. Coat the inside of each plug wire with silicone lubricant before installing them on the spark plugs.

23. Install the throttle linkage, bracket and air cleaner.

24. Fill and bleed the cooling system as previously described.

25. Connect the battery ground cable, start the engine and check for leaks. Adjust the idle speed and ignition timing, if necessary.

3.0L (182 CID) Engine

1. Drain the cooling system (engine cold) into a clean container and save the coolant for reuse.

CAUTION: *When draining the coolant, keep in mind that cats and dogs are attracted by the ethylene glycol antifreeze, and are quite likely to drink any that is left in an uncovered container or in puddles on the ground. This will prove fatal in sufficient quantity. Always drain the coolant into a sealable container. Coolant should be reused unless it is contaminated or several years old.*

2. Disconnect the battery ground cable.

3. Remove the air cleaner and intake manifold as previously described.

4. Loosen the accessory drive belt idler and remove the belt.

5. If the left hand cylinder head is being removed, remove the alternator adjusting arm. If the right hand head is being removed, remove the accessory belt idler.

6. If equipped with power steering, remove the pump mounting bracket attaching bolts. Leaving the hoses connected, place the pump/bracket assembly aside in a position to prevent the fluid from leaking out. Secure the pump with wire or string during service.

7. If the left hand head is being removed, remove the coil bracket and dipstick tube. If the right hand cylinder head is being removed, remove the ground strap and throttle cable support bracket.

8. Remove the exhaust manifold(s), PCV valve and rocker arm covers as previously described.

9. Loosen the rocker arm fulcrum attaching bolts enough to allow the rocker arm to lifted off the pushrod and rotated to one side. Remove the pushrods, keeping them in order so they may be installed in their original locations.

10. Loosen the cylinder head attaching bolts in reverse of the torque sequence, then remove the bolts and lift off the cylinder head(s). Remove and discard the old cylinder head gasket(s).

11. Clean the cylinder heads, intake manifold, valve rocker arm cover and cylinder block gasket surfaces of all traces of old gasket material and/or sealer. Refer to the following overhaul procedures for cylinder head component removal, valve replacement, resurfacing, etc.

12. To install the cylinder head, first lightly oil all bolt and stud bolt threads except those specifying special sealant. Position the new head gasket(s) on the cylinder block, using the dowels for alignment. The dowels should be replaced if damaged.

13. Position the cylinder head(s) on the block and install the attaching bolts. Tighten the head bolts in sequence, in two stages; first to 48–54 ft.lb. (65–75 Nm) and then to 63–80 ft.lb. (85–110 Nm).

14. Dip each pushrod in heavy engine oil then install the pushrods in their original locations.

15. For each valve, rotate the crankshaft until the tappet rests on the heel (base circle) of the camshaft lobe before tightening the fulcrum attaching bolts. Position the rocker arms over the pushrods, install the fulcrums and then tighten the fulcrum attaching bolts to 19–29 ft.lb. (26–38 Nm).

CAUTION: *Fulcrums must be fully seated in the cylinder head and pushrods must be seated in the rocker arm sockets prior to final tightening.*

16. Lubricate all rocker arm assemblies with heavy engine oil. If the original valve train components are being installed, a valve clearance check is not required. If, however, a component has been replaced, the valve clearance should be checked.

17. Install the exhaust manifold(s) and the dipstick tube.

18. Install the intake manifold as previously described.

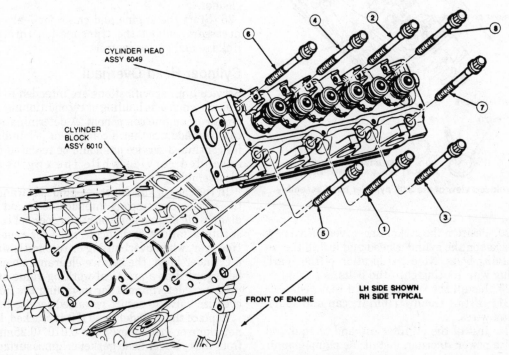

CYLINDER HEAD ASSY 6049

CLYINDER BLOCK ASSY 6010

FRONT OF ENGINE

LH SIDE SHOWN
RH SIDE TYPICAL

Cylinder head bolt torque sequence on 3.0L (182 CID) engine

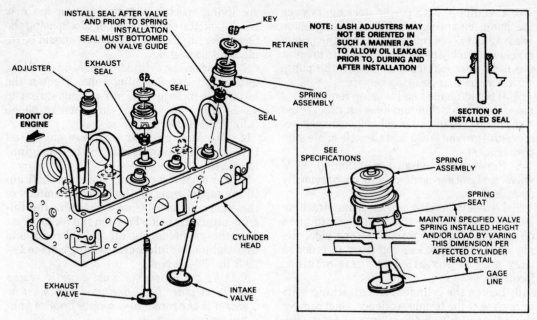

Exploded view of the 2.3L cylinder head assembly

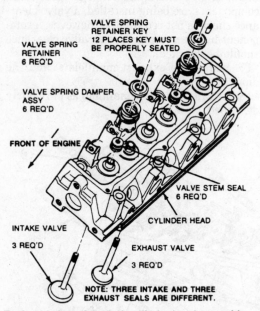

Exploded view of the 3.0L cylinder head assembly

19. Position the rocker arm cover with a new gasket on the cylinder head and install the retaining bolts. Note the location of the spark plug wire routing clip stud bolts.

20. Install the spark plugs, if removed.

21. Install the distributor, cap and spark plug wires.

22. Install the oil filler cap and, if equipped with power steering, install the pump mounting and support brackets.

23. Install the PCV valve and the throttle body.

24. Install the alternator bracket and tighten the attaching nuts to 30–40 ft.lb. (40–55 Nm).

25. Install the accessory drive belt and adjust it to specifications. Connect the battery cable and refill the cooling system. Install the air cleaner.

26. Start the engine and check for leaks. If necessary, adjust the transmission throttle linkage and cruise control.

Cylinder Head Overhaul

Service limit specifications are intended to be a guide when overhauling or reconditioning an engine or engine component. A determination can be made whether a component is suitable for continued service or should be replaced for extended service while the engine is disassembled.

In the case of valve stem-to-guide clearance, the service clearance is intended as an aid in diagnosing engine noise only and does not constitute a failure or indicate need for repair. However, when overhauling or reconditioning a cylinder head, the service clearance should be regarded as a practical working value and used as a determinant for installing the next oversize valve to assure extended service life.

Replace the cylinder head if it is cracked. Do not plane or grind more than 0.010″ (0.25mm) from the cylinder head gasket original surface. Burrs or scratches should be removed with an oil stone. The cylinder head should be disassembled on a clean workbench, with all parts kept in order so they may be installed in their original locations.

CLEANING

With the valves installed to protect the valve seats, remove carbon deposits from the combustion chambers and valve heads with a wire brush. Be careful not to damage the cylinder head gasket surface. After the valves are removed, clean the valve guide bores with a valve guide cleaning tool using solvent to remove dirt, grease and other deposits. Clean all bolt holes and make sure the oil transfer passage is clean. Remove all deposits from the valves with a fine wire brush or buffing wheel.

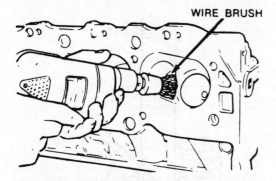

Remove the carbon from the cylinder head with a wire brush and electric drill

INSPECTION

Inspect the cylinder head for cracks or excessively burned areas in the exhaust outlet ports. Check the cylinder head for cracks and inspect the gasket surface for burrs and nicks. Replace the head if any cracks are found. Check the flatness of the cylinder head gasket surface using a feeler gauge and straight edge. Check the flatness at the three points illustrated. The cylinder head must be replaced if warpage exceeds 0.010″ (0.25mm).

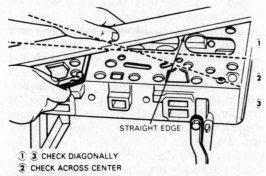

① ③ CHECK DIAGONALLY
② CHECK ACROSS CENTER

Checking the cylinder head for flatness

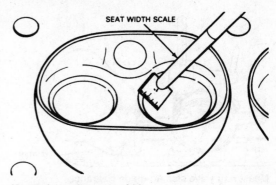

Measuring valve seat width

Measure the valve seat width and reface the valve seat if the width is not within 0.060–0.080″ (1.5–2.0mm) for intake and exhaust on V6 engines, or 0.060–0.080″ (1.5–2.0mm) for 4-cylinder intake and 0.070–0.090″ (1.8–2.3mm) for 4-cylinder exhaust.

Check the valve seat runout with a dial indicator. Follow the dial indicator manufacturer's instructions for installation on the cylinder head and measurement procedure. Seat runout should not exceed 0.0016″ (0.04mm) on 2.3L engines; 0.0015″ (0.038mm) on 2.8L engines; or 0.003″ (0.076mm) on 3.0L engines. If the runout exceeds the service limit, the valve seat will have to be refaced.

Check the valve stem-to-guide clearance of each valve in its respective guide with a dial indicator. Move the valve back and forth in its guide and take a measurement at two axis, 90° apart. If the readings exceed the values given in the Engine Specifications chart, the valve guide will have to be reamed to the next oversize valve stem size.

Inspect the valves for minor pits, grooves or scoring. Minor pitting may be removed with an oil stone. Check the valve stem diameter and

Measuring valve seat runout with dial indicator

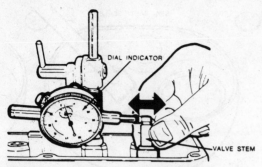

Measuring valve stem-to-guide clearance

face angle, as well as any bend in the stem itself. Discard any excessively worn or damaged valve train parts.

Check the valve spring pressure using a suitable tester. If the pressure of any valve spring is lower than the service limits given in the Valve Specifications Chart, replace the spring. Remove the damper by pulling it from the spring and check each spring for squareness using a steel square and a flat surface plate. Stand the spring and square on end on the surface plate, then slide the spring up to the square. Rotate the spring slowly and observe the space between the top coil of the spring and square. If the spring is out of square

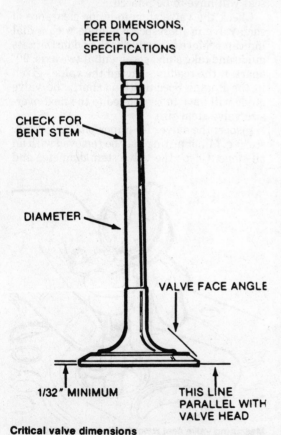

FOR DIMENSIONS, REFER TO SPECIFICATIONS

CHECK FOR BENT STEM

DIAMETER

VALVE FACE ANGLE

1/32" MINIMUM

THIS LINE PARALLEL WITH VALVE HEAD

Critical valve dimensions

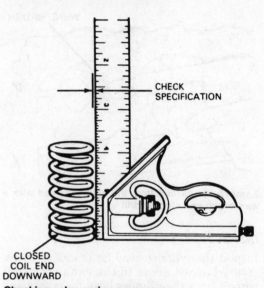

APPLY TORQUE UNTIL CLICK IS HEARD, READ TORQUE WRENCH AND MULTIPLY READING BY TWO

VALVE SPRING TESTER TOOL-6513-DD

VALVE SPRING

SET KNOB TO COMPRESSED LENGTH OF SPRING

Checking valve spring pressure

CHECK SPECIFICATION

CLOSED COIL END DOWNWARD

Checking valve spring squareness

by more than $5/64$" (1.984mm), replace the spring. Springs are color-coded for replacement purposes.

NOTE: *Make certain the springs are reassembled to their own original dampers by pushing the damper on the spring. Do not open the damper with any kind of tool in order to reassemble.*

Clean all parts of the valve rocker arm and/or shaft assembly thoroughly and make sure all oil passages are open. Inspect the shaft and the rocker arm bore for nicks, scratches, scores or scuffs. Replace any damaged components. Inspect the pad at the valve end of the rocker arm for indications of scuffing or abnormal wear. If the pad is grooved, replace the rocker arm. Do not attempt to true this surface by grinding. On pedestal mounted rocker arms, check the rocker arm pad, side rails and fulcrum seat for excessive wear, cracks, nicks or burrs. Check the rocker arm bolt for stripped or broken threads.

Clean the pushrods in suitable solvent and blow out the oil passage in the pushrods with compressed air. Check the ends of the pushrods for nicks, grooves, roughness or excessive wear. Replace any damaged pushrods. Check the pushrods for straightness by rolling them on a flat surface. If any bend is noted, replace the pushrod. Do not attempt to straighten any bent pushrod

RESURFACING

If the cylinder head gasket surface is warped beyond specifications, but not more than 0.010″ (0.25mm), it will be necessary to have it trued. All cylinder head grinding should be performed by a qualified machine shop, but in no case should any more than 0.010″ (0.25mm) be removed from the gasket surface.

If it becomes necessary to ream a valve guide to install a valve with an oversize stem, a reaming kit is available which contains the following reamer and pilot combinations: 0.015″ (0.38mm) OS reamer with 0.003″ (0.076mm) OS pilot and a 0.003″ (0.76mm) reamer with a 0.015″ (0.38mm) OS pilot. When replacing a standard size valve with an oversize valve, always use the reamer in sequence (smallest oversize first, then the next smallest, etc.) so as not to overload the reamers. Always reface the valve seat after the valve guide has been reamed and use a suitable scraper to break the sharp corner at the top ID of the valve guide. Oversize valves are available from the manufacturer.

Refacing of the valve seat should be closely coordinated with the refacing of the valve face so that the finished seat and valve face will be concentric and the specified interference angle will be maintained. This is important so that the valve and seat will have a compression-tight fit. Make sure the refacer grinding wheels are properly dressed. Grind the valve seats of all engines to a true 45° angle. Remove only enough stock to clean up pits and grooves or to correct the valve seat runout. After the seat has been refaced, use a seat width scale to measure the seat width. Narrow the seat, if necessary, to bring it within specifications.

On the valve seats of all engines, use a 60° angle grinding wheel to remove stock from the bottom of the seats to raise them, or a 30° angle grinding wheel to remove stock from the top of the seats to lower them. The finished valve seat should contact the approximate center of the valve face. It is good practice to determine where the valve seat contacts the face. To do this, coat the seat with Prussian Blue and set the valve in place. Rotate the valve lightly and

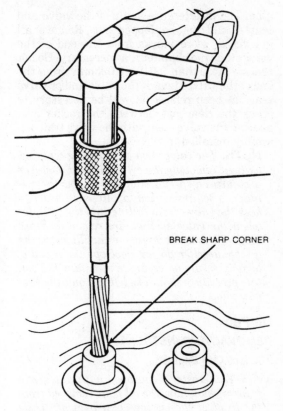

BREAK SHARP CORNER

Reaming the valve guide

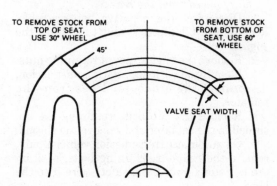

TO REMOVE STOCK FROM TOP OF SEAT, USE 30° WHEEL

45°

TO REMOVE STOCK FROM BOTTOM OF SEAT, USE 60° WHEEL

VALVE SEAT WIDTH

Refacing valve seats

remove it to see where the blue contacts the valve. If the blue is transferred to the center of the valve face, contact is satisfactory. If the blue is transferred to the top edge of the valve face, lower the seat. If the blue is transferred to the bottom edge of the valve face, raise the seat.

If the valve face runout is excessive and/or to remove pits and grooves, reface the valve to a true 44° angle. Remove only enough stock to correct the runout or to clean up the pits and grooves. If the edge of the valve head is less than $\frac{1}{32}$″ (0.79mm) thick after grinding, replace the valve as it will run too hot in the engine. The interference angle of the valve and seat should not be lapped out. Remove all grooves or score marks from the end of the valve stem and chamfer it as necessary. Do not remove more than 0.010″ (0.025mm) from the end of the valve stem. If the valve and/or valve seat has been refaced, it will be necessary to check the clearance between the rocker arm pad and the valve stem with the valve train assembly installed in the engine.

NOTE: *The valve stem seals can be replaced without removing the cylinder head, however it requires a special adapter to allow the cylinder to be pressurized to 140 psi in order to keep the valves from falling into the cylinder when the valve springs are removed. Since most of the air compressors available to the do-it-yourselfer do not develope the amount of air pressure necessary to maintain 140 psi, this procedure should be left to a qualified repair shop.*

Oil Pan

REMOVAL AND INSTALLATION

2.3L (140 CID) Engine

NOTE: *Aerostar's equipped with automatic transmission have the oil pans removed from the front of the engine compartment, while manual transmission vehicles have the oil pan removed from the rear.*

1. Disconnect the negative battery cable. Remove the oil dipstick and tube from the engine.
2. Remove the engine mount retaining nuts.
3. If equipped with automatic transmission, disconnect the oil cooler lines from the radiator.
4. Remove the two bolts retaining the fan shroud to the radiator and remove the shroud.
5. On automatic transmission vehicles only, remove the radiator retaining bolts, position the radiator upward and safety wire it to the hood.
6. Raise the van and support it safely on jackstands.
7. Drain the crankcase oil into a suitable container and dispose of it properly.
8. Disconnect the starter cable from the starter, then remove the starter from the engine.
9. Disconnect the exhaust manifold tube to the inlet pipe bracket at the thermactor check valve.
10. Remove the transmission mount retaining nuts from the crossmember.
11. On automatic transmission vehicles, remove the bellcrank from the converter housing. Disconnect the transmission oil cooler lines from the retainer at the block.

12. Remove the front crossmember (automatic only).
13. Disconnect the right front lower shock absorber mount (manual transmission only).
14. Position a hydraulic jack under the engine, then raise the engine and insert a wood block approximately 2½″ (63.5mm) high. Carefully lower the jack until the engine is resting securely on the wood block.
15. On automatic transmission vehicles, position the hydraulic jack under the transmission and raise it slightly.
16. Remove the oil pan retaining bolts and lower the pan to the chassis.
17. Remove the oil pump drive and pickup tube assembly.
18. Remove the oil pan from the front on automatics, or from the rear on manual transmissions.
19. Clean the oil pan and inspect it for damage. Remove the spacers, if any, attached to the oil pan transmission mounting pad.

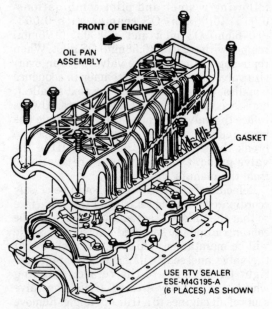

Oil pan mounting on 2.3L (140 CID) engine

20. Clean the oil pan gasket surface at the pan and engine block. Remove all traces of old gasket and/or sealer. Clean the oil pump exterior and oil pump pickup tube screen.
21. To install the pan, first position the one-piece oil pan gasket in the oil pan channel and press it into place.
22. Position the oil pan on the crossmember.
23. Install the oil pump and pickup tube assembly. Prime the oil pump with engine oil when making final installation.
24. Install the oil pan to the cylinder block

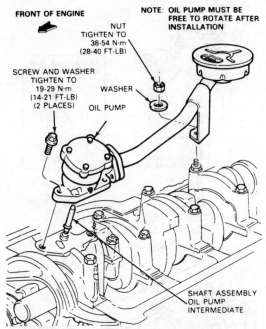

Oil pump mounting on 2.3L (140 CID) engine

with retaining bolts. Install the retaining bolts by hand, just enough to start the two oil pan-to-transmission bolts.

25. Tighten the two pan-to-transmission bolts to 29–40 ft.lb. (40–54 Nm) to align the pan with the rear face of the block, then loosen them ½ turn.

26. Tighten the oil pan-to-cylinder block bolts to 7–10 ft.lb. (10–14 Nm), then tighten the remaining two transmission bolts to 29–40 ft.lb. (40–54 Nm).

NOTE: *If the oil pan is being installed on the engine with the engine removed from the van, the transmission or a special fixture must be bolted to the block to insure the oil pan is installed flush with the rear face of the block.*

27. On automatic transmission models, lower the jack under the transmission. Position the jack under the engine, then raise the engine slightly and remove the wood block installed earlier.

28. Replace the oil filter.

29. Reconnect the exhaust manifold tube to the inlet pipe bracket at the thermactor check valve.

30. Install the transmission mount to the crossmember.

31. Install the oil cooler lines (automatic trans only) to the retainer at the block, then install the bellcrank to the converter housing.

32. Install the right front lower shock absorber mount (manual trans. only).

33. Install the front crossmember (automatic only).

34. Install the starter and connect the starter cable.

35. Lower the van.

36. Install the engine mount bolts.

37. Install the radiator and shroud. Reconnect the oil cooler lines (automatic only) to the radiator.

38. Install the oil dipstick and tube. Refill the crankcase with engine oil.

39. Start the engine and check for leaks.

2.8L (171 CID) and 3.0L (182 CID) Engines

1. Disconnect the negative battery cable.

2. Raise the van and support it safely on jackstands.

3. Remove the starter motor from the engine.

4. Remove the nuts attaching the engine front insulators to the crossmember.

5. Drain the engine oil from the crankcase into a suitable container and dispose of it properly.

6. Position a hydraulic jack under the engine and raise the engine enough to install wooden blocks between the front insulator mounts and No. 2 crossmember.

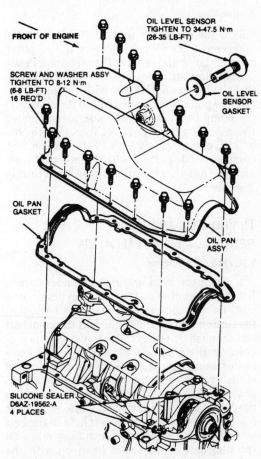

Oil pan mounting on 3.0L (182 CID) engine

7. Carefully lower the engine onto the blocks and remove the jack.

8. Remove the oil pan attaching bolts, then lower and remove the pan from the engine block.

9. Clean all gasket surfaces on the engine and oil pan. Remove all traces of old gasket and/or sealer.

10. To install the oil pan, first apply adhesive to the gasket mating surfaces and install oil pan gaskets. Install the oil pan to the engine block.

11. Position a hydraulic jack under the engine and raise the engine to remove the wooden blocks. Lower the engine and remove the jack.

12. Install the starter motor.

13. Lower the van.

14. Install the nuts attaching the engine front insulators to the crossmember and tighten them to specifications.

15. Connect the negative battery cable.

16. Start the engine and check for leaks.

Oil Pump

REMOVAL AND INSTALLATION

All Engines

Follow the procedure under Oil Pan Removal and remove the oil pan. Remove the oil pump retainer bolts and remove the oil pump. Prime the oil pump with clean engine oil by filling either the inlet or outlet port with engine oil. Rotate the pump shaft to distribute the oil within the pump body. Install the pump and tighten the mounting bolts to 14–21 ft.lb. (19–28 Nm) on 2.3L engines; 6–10 ft.lb. (9–13 Nm) on 2.8L engines; or 30–40 ft.lb. (40–55 Nm) on 3.0L engines. Install the oil pan as previously described.

Timing Belt and Cover

REMOVAL AND INSTALLATION

2.3L (140 CID) Engine

1. Open the hood and install fender covers. Rotate the engine so that No. 1 cylinder is at TDC on the compression stroke. Check that the timing marks are aligned on the camshaft and crankshaft pulleys. An access plug is provided in the cam belt cover so that the camshaft timing can be checked without removal of the cover or any other parts. Set the crankshaft to TDC by aligning the timing mark on the crank pulley with the TC mark on the belt cover. Look through the access hole in the belt cover to make sure that the timing mark on the cam drive sprocket is lined up with the pointer on the inner belt cover.

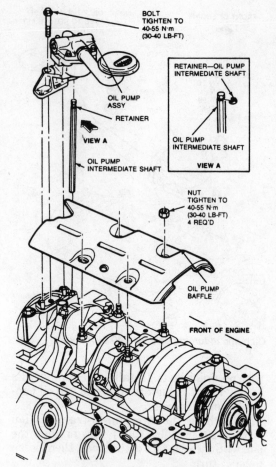

BOLT TIGHTEN TO 40-55 N·m (30-40 LB-FT)

RETAINER—OIL PUMP INTERMEDIATE SHAFT

OIL PUMP ASSY

RETAINER

VIEW A

OIL PUMP INTERMEDIATE SHAFT

OIL PUMP INTERMEDIATE SHAFT

VIEW A

NUT TIGHTEN TO 40-55 N·m (30-40 LB-FT) 4 REQ'D

OIL PUMP BAFFLE

FRONT OF ENGINE

Oil pump mounting on 3.0L (182 CID) engine

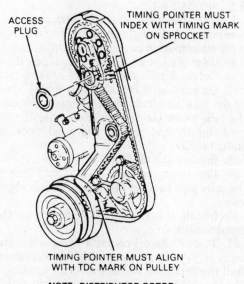

ACCESS PLUG

TIMING POINTER MUST INDEX WITH TIMING MARK ON SPROCKET

TIMING POINTER MUST ALIGN WITH TDC MARK ON PULLEY

NOTE: DISTRIBUTOR ROTOR MUST ALIGN WITH NO.1 FIRING POSITION

Timing mark alignment on 2.3L (140 CID) engine

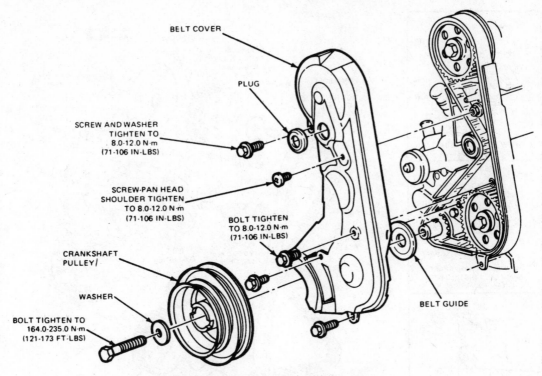

BELT COVER

PLUG

SCREW AND WASHER
TIGHTEN TO
8.0-12.0 N·m
(71-106 IN-LBS)

SCREW-PAN HEAD
SHOULDER TIGHTEN
TO 8.0-12.0 N·m
(71-106 IN-LBS)

BOLT TIGHTEN
TO 8.0-12.0 N·m
(71-106 IN-LBS)

CRANKSHAFT
PULLEY/

WASHER

BOLT TIGHTEN TO
164.0-235.0 N·m
(121-173 FT-LBS)

BELT GUIDE

Timing belt cover on 2.3L (140 CID) engine

NOTE: *Always turn the engine in the normal direction of rotation. Backward rotation may cause the timing belt to jump time, due to the arrangement of the belt tensioner.*

2. Remove the fan blade and water pump pulley bolts.

3. Loosen the alternator retaining bolts and remove the drive belt from the pulleys. Remove the water pump pulley.

4. Loosen and position the power steering pump mounting bracket and position it aside.

5. Remove the four timing belt outer cover retaining bolts and remove the cover. Remove the crankshaft pulley and belt guide.

6. Loosen the belt tensioner pulley assembly, then position a camshaft belt adjuster tool (T74P-6254-A or equivalent) on the tension spring rollpin and retract the belt tensioner away from the timing belt. Tighten the adjustment bolt to lock the tensioner in the retracted position.

7. Remove the timing belt.

8. Install the new belt over the crankshaft sprocket and then counterclockwise over the auxiliary and camshaft sprockets, making sure the lugs on the belt properly engage the sprocket teeth on the pulleys. Be careful not to rotate the pulleys when installing the belt.

9. Release the timing belt tensioner pulley, allowing the tensioner to take up the belt slack. If the spring does not have enough ten-

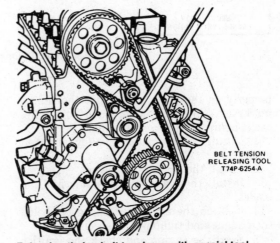

BELT TENSION
RELEASING TOOL
T74P-6254-A

Releasing timing belt tensioner with special tool

sion to move the roller against the belt (belt hangs loose), it might be necessary to manually push the roller against the belt and tighten the bolt.

NOTE: *The spring cannot be used to set belt tension; a wrench must be used on the tensioner assembly.*

10. Rotate the crankshaft two complete turns by hand (in the normal direction of rotation) to remove the slack from the belt, then tighten the tensioner adjustment and pivot bolts to specifications. Make sure the belt is seated

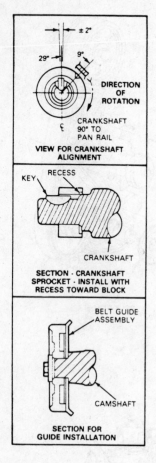

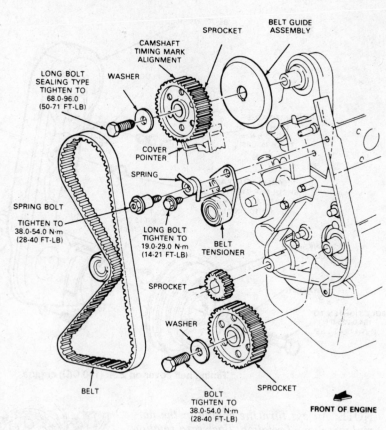

2.3L (140 CID) timing belt assembly

properly on the pulleys and that the timing marks are still in alignment when No. 1 cylinder is again at TDC/compression.

11. Install the crankshaft pulley and belt guide.

12. Install the timing belt cover.

13. Install the water pump pulley and fan blades.

14. Position the alternator and drive belts, then adjust and tighten it to specifications.

15. Start the engine and check the ignition timing. Adjust the timing, if necessary.

Timing Cover, Cover Seal and Gears
REMOVAL AND INSTALLATION
2.8L (171 CID) Engine

1. Remove the oil pan as previously described.

2. Drain the cooling system and remove the radiator as previously described.

CAUTION: *When draining the coolant, keep in mind that cats and dogs are attracted by the ethylene glycol antifreeze, and are quite likely to drink any that is left in an uncovered*

container or in puddles on the ground. This will prove fatal in sufficient quantity. Always drain the coolant into a sealable container. Coolant should be reused unless it is contaminated or several years old.

3. Remove the A/C compressor and power steering bracket, if equipped.

4. Remove the alternator, thermactor pump and drive belt(s).

5. Remove the fan.

6. Remove the water pump and heater and radiator hoses.

7. Remove the crankshaft pulley.

8. Remove the front cover retaining bolts. If necessary, tap the cover lightly with a plastic mallet to break the gasket seal, then remove the front cover. If the front cover plate gasket need replacement, remove the two screws and remove the plate. If necessary, remove the guide sleeves from the cylinder block.

9. If the timing gears are being removed, temporarily install the crankshaft pulley nut and rotate the engine by hand until the timing marks are in alignment as illustrated. Remove the timing gear bolts and slide the gears off the

crankshaft and camshaft using a suitable gear puller.

10. Clean the front cover mating surfaces of all gasket material and/or sealer. If the front cover seal is being replaced, support the cover to prevent damage and drive out the seal using tool T74P-6700-A or equivalent. Coat the new seal with heavy SF engine oil and install it in the cover, making sure it is not cocked. Install the timing gears, if removed, making sure the timing marks are correctly aligned. Tighten the camshaft gear bolt to 30–36 ft.lb. (41–49 Nm).

11. Apply sealing compound to the gasket surfaces on the cylinder block and back side of the front cover plate. Install the guide sleeves

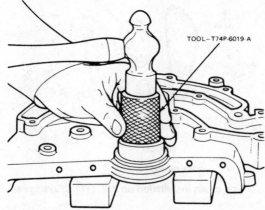

Installing oil seal in front cover on 2.8L (171 CID) engine

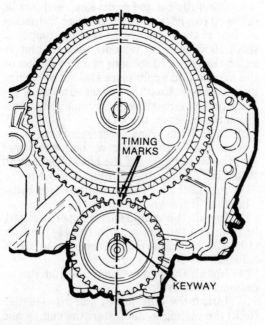

V6 timing gear alignment

with new seal rings lubricated with engine oil to prevent cutting the rings, with the chamfered end toward the front cover. Position the gasket and front cover plate on the cylinder block. Temporarily install four front cover screws to position the gasket and front cover plate in place. Install and tighten two cover plate attaching bolts, then remove the four screws that were temporarily installed.

12. Apply sealing compound to the front cover gasket surface, then place the gasket in position on the front cover.

13. Place the front cover on the engine and start all retaining screws two or three turns. Center the cover by inserting an alignment tool (T74P-6019-A or equivalent) in the oil seal.

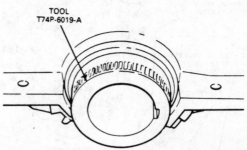

Front cover alignment tool used on 2.8L (171 CID) engine

14. Tighten the front cover attaching screws to 13–16 ft.lb. (17–21 Nm).

15. Install the crankshaft pulley and tighten the center bolt to 85–96 ft.lb. (115–130 Nm).

16. Install the oil pan as previously described.

17. Install the water pump, heater hose, A/C compressor, alternator, thermactor pump and drive belt(s). Adjust the belt tension.

18. Install the radiator. Fill and bleed the cooling system, then start and operate the engine at fast idle and check for leaks.

Timing Cover and Chain
REMOVAL AND INSTALLATION
3.0L (182 CID) Engine

1. Crank the engine until No. 1 cylinder is at TDC on the compression stroke with the timing marks aligned. Remove the idler pulley and bracket assembly.

2. Remove the drive and accessory belts.

3. Remove the radiator and water pump as previously described.

4. Remove the crankshaft pulley and damper.

5. Remove the lower radiator hose.

6. Remove the oil pan-to-timing cover bolts.

7. Remove the front cover bolts and the front cover. Tap the cover lightly with a plastic mallet, if necessary, to break it loose. Carefully clean all gasket mating surfaces on the cover and replace the crankshaft damper oil seal.

8. If the timing chain is being replaced, remove the camshaft sprocket attaching bolt and washer. Slide both sprockets and the timing chain forward and remove them as an assembly. Slide the new timing chain with sprockets on the shafts as an assembly with the timing marks aligned as illustrated. Install the camshaft bolt and washer and tighten it to 41–51

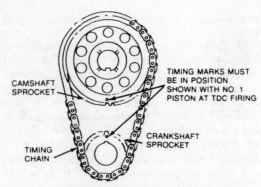

Timing mark alignment on 2.8L (171 CID) engine

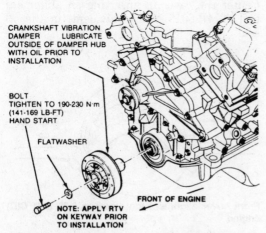

Removing crankshaft damper on 2.8L (171 CID) engine

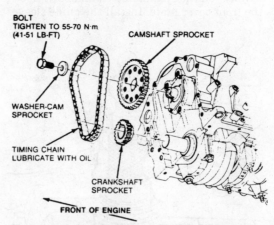

Timing chain installation on 2.8L (171 CID) engine

ft.lb. (55–70 Nm). Apply oil to the timing chain and sprockets after installation.

9. Carefully cut and remove exposed portion of the oil pan gasket. To install, coat the gasket surface of the oil pan with sealing compound (B5A-19554-A or equivalent), then cut and position the required sections of a new gasket on the oil pan and apply more sealing compound at the corners. Coat the gasket surfaces of the block and cover with sealing compound and position the cover on the block.

10. Install the front cover mounting bolts. Use sealant for the front cover bolt which goes into the water jacket of the block. Tighten all mounting bolts to 15–22 ft.lb. (20–30 Nm).

11. Install the oil pan-to-timing cover bolts.

12. Install the lower radiator hose.

13. Install the crankshaft damper and pulley. Tighten the damper bolt to 141–169 ft.lb. (190–230 Nm) and the pulley bolts to 19–26 ft.lb. (26–38 Nm).

14. Install the water pump and radiator as previously described.

15. Install the idler pulley and drive belt(s). Refill the cooling system, start the engine and check for leaks.

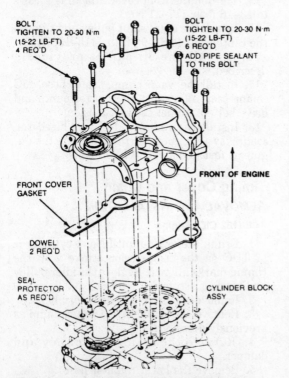

Timing cover installation on 2.8L (171 CID) engine

Camshaft and Auxiliary Shaft Sprockets and Seals

REMOVAL AND INSTALLATION

2.3L (140 CID) Engine

The cylinder front cover, camshaft and auxiliary shaft seals are replaced in the same manner with the same tools after the respective gear has been removed. Always use a new attaching bolt when replacing the camshaft sprocket or use new Teflon® sealing tape on the threads of the old bolt. To remove the sprockets, first remove the timing cover and belt, then use tool T74P-6256-B, or equivalent to pull the cam drive sprocket. The same tool is used in exactly the same manner to remove the auxiliary shaft sprocket, as well as to hold the sprockets while the attaching bolts are installed and tightened.

A front cover seal remover tool T74P-6700-B or equivalent is used to remove all the seals. When positioning this tool, make sure that the jaws are gripping the thin edge of the seal very tightly before operating the jack-screw portion of the tool.

To install the seals, a cam and auxiliary shaft seal replacer T74P-6150-A or equivalent with a stepped, threaded arbor is used. The tool acts as a press, using the internal threads of the various shafts as a pilot.

Camshaft

REMOVAL AND INSTALLATION

2.3L (140 CID) Engine

1. Drain the cooling system (engine cold).
CAUTION: *When draining the coolant, keep in mind that cats and dogs are attracted by the ethylene glycol antifreeze, and are quite likely to drink any that is left in an uncovered container or in puddles on the ground. This will prove fatal in sufficient quantity. Always drain the coolant into a sealable container. Coolant should be reused unless it is contaminated or several years old.*

2. Remove the air cleaner assembly.
3. Disconnect the spark plug wires at the plugs, then disconnect the harness at the rocker cover and position it aside.
4. Tag and disconnect the vacuum hoses as required.
5. Remove the rocker cover retaining bolts and remove the cover.

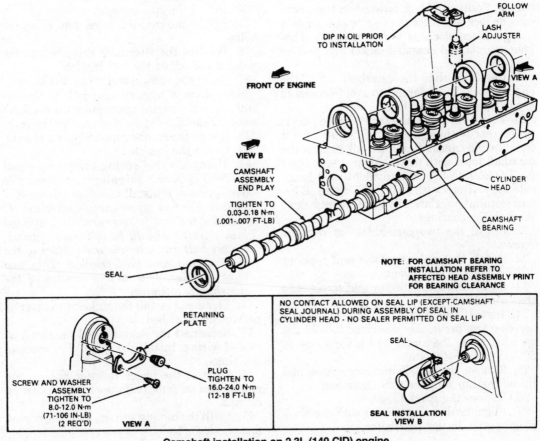

Camshaft installation on 2.3L (140 CID) engine

6. Loosen the alternator retaining bolts and remove the belt from the pulley.

7. Remove the alternator mounting bracket-to-head retaining bolts and position it aside.

8. Disconnect the upper radiator hose at both ends and remove it from the vehicle.

9. Remove the four cam belt cover bolts and remove the cover. If equipped with power steering, remove the power steering pump bracket.

10. Loosen the idler cam retaining bolts and position the idler in the unloaded position and tighten the retaining bolts.

11. Remove the cam belt from the cam pulley and auxiliary pulley.

12. Using valve spring compressor tool T74P-6565-A or equivalent, depress the valve springs and remove the camshaft followers.

13. Remove the camshaft gear using the sprocket remover tool described above.

14. Remove the seal using front cover seal remover tool described above.

15. Remove the two camshaft rear retainer bolts.

16. Raise the vehicle and support it safely.

17. Remove the right and left engine support bolts and nuts.

18. Position a transmission jack under the engine. Position a block of wood on the transmission jack and raise the engine as high as it will go. Place blocks of wood between the engine mounts and chassis bracket and remove the jack.

19. Carefully slide the camshaft out of the engine block, being careful to avoid damaging journals and camshaft lobes.

20. To install, make sure the threaded plug is in the rear of the camshaft. If not, remove it from the old camshaft and install it. Coat the camshaft lobes with polyethylene grease (part no. DOAZ-19584-A or equivalent) and lubricate the journals with heavy SF engine oil before installation. Carefully slide the camshaft through the bearings.

21. Install the two camshaft rear retainer screws.

22. Install the seal using the seal replacer T74P-6150-A or equivalent.

23. Install the belt deflector and sprocket to the camshaft.

24. Install the retaining bolt using the sprocket tool previously described to hold the sprocket while the center bolt is tightened to 50–71 ft.lb. (68–96 Nm).

25. Remove the distributor cap screws and lift off the cap with the wires attached.

26. Remove the spark plugs.

27. Align the distributor rotor with the No. 1 plug location in the distributor cap.

28. Align the cam gear with the pointer.

29. Align the crankshaft pulley timing mark with the pointer on the cam belt cover (TDC).

30. Install the cam belt over the crankshaft sprocket and then counterclockwise over the auxiliary and camshaft sprockets, making sure the lugs on the belt properly engage the sprocket teeth on the pulleys. Be careful not to rotate the pulleys when installing the belt.

31. Release the timing belt tensioner pulley, allowing the tensioner to take up the belt slack. If the spring does not have enough tension to move the roller against the belt (belt hangs loose), it might be necessary to manually push the roller against the belt and tighten the bolt.

NOTE: *The spring cannot be used to set belt tension; a wrench must be used on the tensioner assembly.*

32. Rotate the crankshaft two complete turns by hand (in the normal direction of rotation) to remove the slack from the belt, then tighten the tensioner adjustment and pivot bolts to specifications. Make sure the belt is seated properly on the pulleys and that the timing marks are still in alignment when No. 1 cylinder is again at TDC/compression.

33. Install the distributor cap.

34. Install the spark plugs.

35. Install the cam belt cover and retaining bolts.

36. Position the alternator drive belt to the pulleys and adjust the belt tension.

37. Raise the vehicle and support it safely.

38. Position a transmission jack to the engine, raise the engine and remove the blocks of wood. Lower the engine and remove the jack.

39. Install the engine support bolts and nuts.

40. Lower the vehicle.

41. Using a valve spring compressor tool (T74P-6565-A or equivalent), depress the valve spring and install camshaft followers.

NOTE: *For any repair that requires the removal of the cam follower arm, each affected lash adjuster should be collapsed approximately half way after the installation of the cam follower and then released. This step must be taken prior to any rotation of the camshaft is attempted.*

42. Clean and install the rocker arm cover as previously described.

43. Reconnect the disconnected vacuum hoses and wiring. Install the spark plug wires to the plugs.

44. Connect the upper radiator hose to the engine and radiator and tighten the retaining clamps.

45. Refill the cooling system, start the engine and check for leaks.

2.8L (171 CID) and 3.0L (182 CID) Engines

1. Disconnect the negative battery cable.
2. Drain the engine oil into a suitable container and dispose of it properly.
3. Remove the fan and spacer, drive belt and pulley and the radiator as previously described.
4. Disconnect the spark plug wires from the plugs.
5. Remove the distributor cap with the spark plug wires as an assembly.
6. Disconnect the distributor wiring harness and remove the distributor.
7. Remove the alternator.
8. Remove the thermactor pump.
9. On the 2.8L engine, remove the fuel lines, fuel filter and carburetor.
10. Remove the intake manifold as previously described.
11. Remove the rocker arm covers and rocker arm and shaft assemblies as previously described.
12. Remove the tappets from the engine block using a magnet or suitable tappet removal tool. Keep the tappets in order so they may be installed in their original locations.
13. Remove the oil pan as previously described.
14. Remove the crankshaft damper bolt and remove the damper with a suitable gear pulley.
15. Remove the engine front cover and water pump as an assembly.
16. On the 2.8L engine, remove the camshaft gear attaching bolt and washer, then slide the gear off the camshaft. On the 3.0L engine, remove the camshaft gear bolt and slide the cam and crankshaft gears off with the timing chain as an assembly.

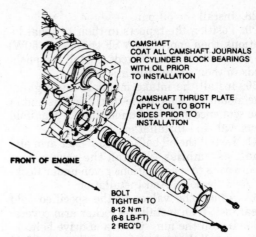

CAMSHAFT
COAT ALL CAMSHAFT JOURNALS
OR CYLINDER BLOCK BEARINGS
WITH OIL PRIOR
TO INSTALLATION

CAMSHAFT THRUST PLATE
APPLY OIL TO BOTH
SIDES PRIOR TO
INSTALLATION

FRONT OF ENGINE

BOLT
TIGHTEN TO
8-12 N·m
(6-8 LB-FT)
2 REQ'D

Camshaft installation on 3.0L engine

17. Remove the camshaft thrust plate.
18. Carefully slide the camshaft out of the engine block, using caution to avoid any damage to the camshaft bearings.
19. On the 2.8L engine, remove the camshaft drive gear and spacer ring.
20. To install the camshaft, first oil the camshaft journals and cam lobes with heavy SF engine oil (50W). Install the spacer ring with the chamfered side toward the camshaft, then insert the camshaft key.
21. Install the camshaft in the block, using caution to avoid any damage to the camshaft bearings.
22. Install the thrust plate so that it covers the main oil gallery. Tighten the attaching screws to 13–16 ft.lb. (17–21 Nm) on 2.8L engines, or to 6–8 ft.lb. (8–12 Nm) on 3.0L engines.
23. Rotate the camshaft and crankshaft as necessary to align the timing marks. On the 2.8L engine, install the camshaft gear and tighten the attaching bolt to 30–36 ft.lb. (41–49 Nm). On the 3.0L engine, slide the gears and timing chain onto the shafts with the marks aligned, the tighten the camshaft gear bolt to 40–51 ft.lb. (55–70 Nm).
24. Check the camshaft end play with a dial indicator. The spacer ring and/or thrust plate are available in two thicknesses to permit adjustment of the end play.
25. On the 2.8L engine, align the keyway in the crankshaft gear with the key in the crankshaft. Align the timing marks and install the gear.
26. Install the engine front cover and water pump assembly.
27. Install the crankshaft pulley and tighten the retaining bolt to 85–96 ft.lb. (115–130 Nm).

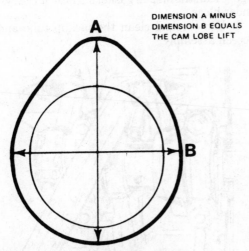

DIMENSION A MINUS
DIMENSION B EQUALS
THE CAM LOBE LIFT

Measuring camshaft lobe dimensions

28. Install the oil pan.

29. Position the tappets in their original locations, then apply heavy SF engine oil (50W) to both ends of the pushrods. Install the pushrods in their original locations.

30. Install the intake manifold and tighten the mounting bolts to the specifications and in the sequence described under Intake Manifold Removal And Installation.

31. Install the oil baffles and rocker arm and shaft assemblies. Tighten the rocker arm stand bolts to specifications given under Rocker Arm Removal And Installation.

32. Adjust the valves to the specified cold clearance, then install the rocker arm covers.

33. Install the fan, spacer and drive belt.

34. Install the carburetor, fuel filter and fuel line.

35. Install the thermactor pump.

36. Install the alternator.

37. Install the distributor, distributor wiring harness, distributor cap and spark plug wires. Reconnect the spark plug wires to the spark plugs.

NOTE: *Before installing the spark plug wires to the plugs, coat the inside of each boot with silicone lubricant using a small screwdriver.*

38. Install the radiator.

39. Refill the cooling system.

40. Replace the oil filter and refill the crankcase with the specified amount of engine oil.

41. Reconnect the battery ground cable.

42. Start the engine and check the ignition timing and idle speed. Adjust if necessary. Run the engine at fast idle and check for coolant, fuel, vacuum or oil leaks.

Auxiliary Shaft
REMOVAL AND INSTALLATION
2.3L (140 CID) Engine

The auxiliary shaft can be removed after first removing the timing belt and front cover as previously described. Remove the attaching screws for the auxiliary shaft retaining plate, then slide the auxiliary shaft carefully out of the engine. Do not allow the gear and fuel pump eccentric to touch the bearing surfaces during removal or installation. See the illustration for component location.

Pistons and Connecting Rods
REMOVAL AND INSTALLATION
2.3L (140 CID) Engine

NOTE: *The following procedure covers piston replacement with the engine installed in the vehicle, however if an engine requires pis-*

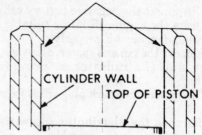

RIDGE CAUSED BY CYLINDER WEAR

CYLINDER WALL

TOP OF PISTON

Cylinder bore ridge

ton replacement, it is usually easier to remove the engine and complete the overhaul on an engine stand. Whether or not the engine is removed, the cylinder measuring and piston inspection, removal and installation procedures will be the same.

1. Remove the cylinder head as previously outlined. Use a ridge reamer to remove the ridge at the top of each cylinder before attempting to remove the piston assemblies.

2. Raise the vehicle and support it safely.

3. Remove the engine to insulator to chassis nuts.

4. Remove the starter lead wires and retaining bolts to the starter, then remove the starter.

5. Position a block of wood on a transmission jack, then position the jack under the engine and raise the engine as high as it will go. Place 2" x 4" (50 x 101mm) blocks of wood between the mounts and chassis brackets, then remove the jack.

6. Remove the rear engine support to crossmember nuts.

7. Remove the oil pan retaining bolts and remove the oil pan from the engine.

8. Clean the oil pan and inspect it for damage. Clean the oil pan gasket surface at the cylinder block.

9. Remove and clean the pickup tube and screen assembly.

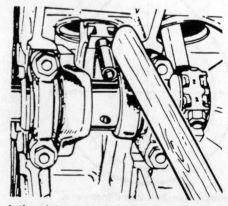

Push the piston out with a hammer handle

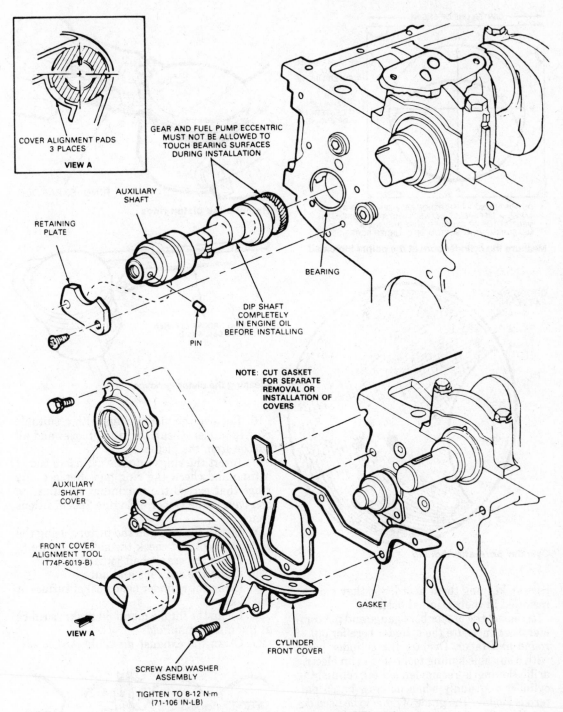

COVER ALIGNMENT PADS 3 PLACES

VIEW A

GEAR AND FUEL PUMP ECCENTRIC MUST NOT BE ALLOWED TO TOUCH BEARING SURFACES DURING INSTALLATION

AUXILIARY SHAFT

RETAINING PLATE

BEARING

DIP SHAFT COMPLETELY IN ENGINE OIL BEFORE INSTALLING

PIN

NOTE: CUT GASKET FOR SEPARATE REMOVAL OR INSTALLATION OF COVERS

AUXILIARY SHAFT COVER

FRONT COVER ALIGNMENT TOOL (T74P-6019-B)

VIEW A

GASKET

CYLINDER FRONT COVER

SCREW AND WASHER ASSEMBLY

TIGHTEN TO 8-12 N·m (71-106 IN-LB)

Auxiliary shaft removal on 2.3L (140 CID) engine

10. Position the oil pump pickup tube assembly to the oil pump and install two retaining bolts with a gasket.

11. Remove the connecting rod cap and bearing of each piston to be removed. Make sure the caps and bearings are kept in order for installation.

12. Using a wooden hammer handle and being careful not to let the rod bolts scratch the crankshaft bearing surfaces, push the piston **up into** the cylinder bore so that the top protrudes enough for removal from above.

13. Lower the vehicle.

14. Remove the pistons from the cylinder

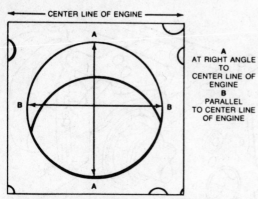

1. OUT-OF-ROUND = DIFFERENCE BETWEEN **A** AND **B**
2. TAPER = DIFFERENCE BETWEEN THE **A** MEASUREMENT AT TOP OF CYLINDER BORE AND THE **A** MEASUREMENT AT BOTTOM OF CYLINDER BORE.

Measure the cylinder bore at the points indicated

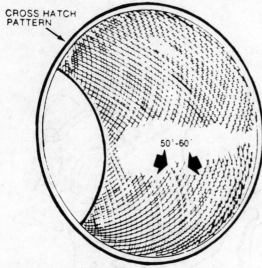

CROSS HATCH PATTERN

50°-60°

Cylinder bore after honing

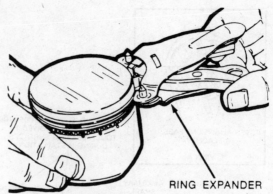

RING EXPANDER

Remove the piston rings

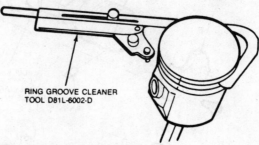

RING GROOVE CLEANER TOOL D81L-6002-D

Cleaning the piston grooves

16. Remove the piston rings with a suitable ring expander. Clean the ring grooves and all carbon from the piston.
17. Insert the rings into the cylinders one at a time and check the ring gap. Replace any rings that exceed the maximum specification as given in the General Engine Specifications chart.
18. Install the rings on the pistons using the expander tool and check the side clearance.
19. Clean the crankshaft journals.
20. Clean the rod caps and nuts.
21. Clean the cylinder head gasket surface at the block.
22. Clean the intake manifold gasket surface at the intake manifold.
23. Clean the exhaust manifold gasket sur-

bore(s), keeping them in order so they may be installed in their original positions.
15. Select the proper bore gauge and micrometer, then measure the cylinder bore for out of round and taper. Deglaze the cylinder bores with a suitable honing tool fitted to an electric drill. Honing is recommended for refinishing cylinder walls only when no cross-hatch pattern is visible. The grade of hone to be used depends on the amount of metal to be removed. Follow the instructions of the hone manufacturer.

NOTE: *Cylinder walls that are severely marred and/or worn beyond the specified limits should be refinished at a machine shop. All pistons are the same weight, both standard and oversize; therefore, various sizes of pistons may be used without upsetting engine balance.*

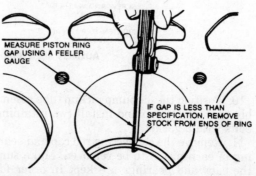

MEASURE PISTON RING GAP USING A FEELER GAUGE

IF GAP IS LESS THAN SPECIFICATION, REMOVE STOCK FROM ENDS OF RING

Measuring ring end gap

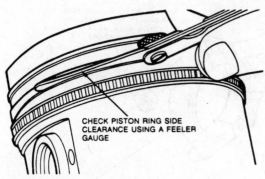

Measuring ring side clearance

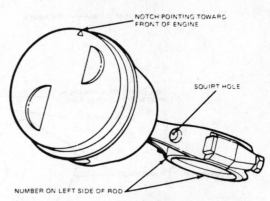

Correct piston alignment on 2.3L (140 CID) engine

face at the exhaust manifold and at the cylinder head.

24. Clean the cylinder head block bolt holes.

25. Clean the camshaft cover gasket surface on the head.

26. Clean the rocker arm cover.

27. Install the bearings in the rods and caps.

28. Install a ring compressor on each piston, then install the pistons in the block.

29. Raise the vehicle and support it safely.

30. Cut a piece of Plastigage® to size and position it in the rod cap. Install the rod caps and tighten them to 30–36 ft.lb. (41–49 Nm). Remove the rod cap and measure the Plastigage® with the scale provided with the kit. If the bearing clearance exceeds the maximum tolerance given in the Piston and Ring Specifications chart, oversize bearing shells will have to be installed on the rod and rod cap.

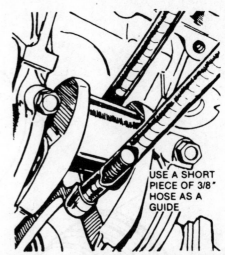

Use lengths of vacuum hose or rubber tubing to protect the crankshaft journals and cylinder walls during piston installation

31. Clean all Plastigage® material from the rod journals, bearings and oil bearings, then install the rod caps and tighten to 30–36 ft.lb. (41–49 Nm). Rotate the crankshaft.

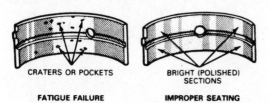

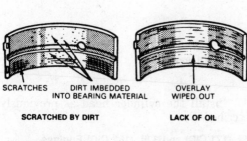

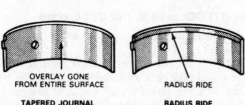

Inspecting the bearings for damage

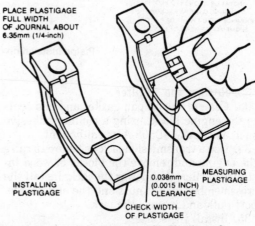

Measuring bearing clearance with Plastigage®

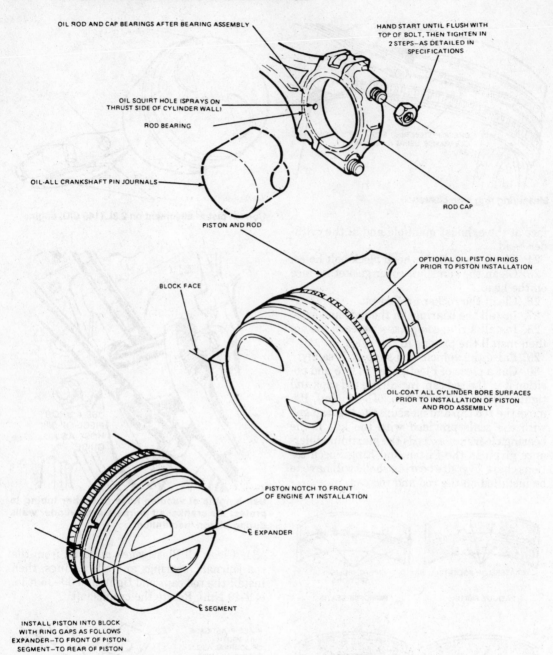

OIL ROD AND CAP BEARINGS AFTER BEARING ASSEMBLY

HAND START UNTIL FLUSH WITH
TOP OF BOLT, THEN TIGHTEN IN
2 STEPS—AS DETAILED IN
SPECIFICATIONS

OIL SQUIRT HOLE (SPRAYS ON
THRUST SIDE OF CYLINDER WALL)

ROD BEARING

OIL-ALL CRANKSHAFT PIN JOURNALS

ROD CAP

PISTON AND ROD

BLOCK FACE

OPTIONAL OIL PISTON RINGS
PRIOR TO PISTON INSTALLATION

OIL-COAT ALL CYLINDER BORE SURFACES
PRIOR TO INSTALLATION OF PISTON
AND ROD ASSEMBLY

PISTON NOTCH TO FRONT
OF ENGINE AT INSTALLATION

℄ EXPANDER

℄ SEGMENT

INSTALL PISTON INTO BLOCK
WITH RING GAPS AS FOLLOWS
EXPANDER—TO FRONT OF PISTON
SEGMENT—TO REAR OF PISTON

Piston installation on 2.3L (140 CID) engine

32. Replace the oil filter.

33. Cement the oil pan gasket and end seals to the engine block, using a contact adhesive such as D7AZ-19B508-A or equivalent.

34. Use a transmission jack as before to raise the engine and remove the blocks of wood installed earlier, then lower the jack, install the crossmember mount nuts and the engine support nuts and remove the jack.

35. Install the starter.

36. Lower the vehicle.

37. Install the cylinder head as previously described.

2.8L (171 CID) and 3.0L (182 CID) Engines

1. Drain the cooling system and crankcase oil.

CAUTION: *When draining the coolant, keep in mind that cats and dogs are attracted by the ethylene glycol antifreeze, and are quite likely to drink any that is left in an uncovered container or in puddles on the ground. This will prove fatal in sufficient quantity. Always drain the coolant into a sealable container. Coolant should be reused unless it is contaminated or several years old.*

2. Remove the intake manifold as previously described.

3. Remove the cylinder head(s).

4. Remove the oil pan, baffle (3.0L only) and oil pump.

5. Inspect the top of each cylinder bore for a ridge. If a ridge had formed, rotate the crankshaft until the piston to be removed is at the bottom of the cylinder bore. Place a clean shop towel over the piston to collect any shavings, then remove the ridge using a suitable ridge reamer (follow the manufacturer's instructions). Never cut more than $1/32$" (0.8mm) into the ring travel area when removing the ridge.

6. Make sure all connecting rods are marked so they may be installed in their original locations. The cylinder number is stamped on the top of the piston. Matched letters or numbers are stamped on the sides of corresponding rods and caps. Turn the crankshaft until the piston to be removed is at the high point of its travel.

7. Remove the connecting rod cap attaching nuts and cap.

8. Install short lengths of rubber hose over the connecting rod cap studs to avoid damage to the crankshaft journals during removal. Using a wooden hammer handle, push the piston up out of the bore.

9. Remove the piston from the engine.

10. Install the connecting rod caps and hold them in position with the nuts.

11. Inspect the cylinder bore. If new piston rings are to be installed on the pistons, a visible cross-hatch pattern should be obvious on the cylinder wall. If not, honing is required.

12. Remove the glaze from the cylinder wall using a spring-loaded hone. Follow the manufacturer's instructions. After honing, thoroughly clean the cylinder bore using a detergent and water solution.

13. Use a ring expander to remove the piston rings, then use a piston groove cleaner to remove carbon deposits from the ring grooves.

14. Insert the rings one at a time into the cylinder bore and check the ring end gap with the ring level. Replace any rings that exceed the maximum specification for ring end gap as given in the Piston and Ring Specifications Chart.

15. Install the rings to the piston with a suitable ring expander and check the ring side clearance in the ring groove. Arrange the ring end gaps as illustrated.

16. Oil the piston rings, pistons and cylinder walls with heavy SF engine oil, then install a ring compressor on each piston and tap it into

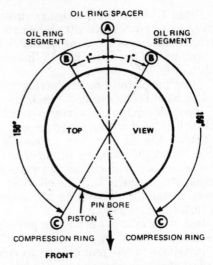

Ring gap placement on piston assembly

the bore with a wooden hammer handle. The notch on the piston should be toward the front of the engine. Be sure to install the pistons in the same cylinders that they were removed from and place short lengths of rubber hoses on the connecting rod studs to prevent damage to the crankshaft journals. Letters or numbers on the connecting rod and bearing cap must be on the same side when installing.

17. Cut a piece of Plastigage® to size and position it in the rod cap. Install the rod caps and tighten them to 19–24 ft.lb. (26–33 Nm) on 2.8L engines, or to 20–28 ft.lb. (26–38 Nm) on 3.0L engines. On 3.0L engines only, back the connecting rod nuts off a minimum of 2 revolutions, then retighten to 20–25 ft.lb. (26–34 Nm). Remove the rod cap and measure the Plastigage® with the scale provided with the kit. If the bearing clearance exceeds the maximum tolerance given in the Piston and Ring Specifications chart, oversize bearing shells will have to be installed on the rod and rod cap.

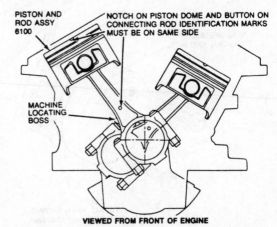

VIEWED FROM FRONT OF ENGINE
Correct piston installation on 3.0L (182 CID) engine

18. Clean all traces of Plastigage® from the bearing cap and crankshaft, lubricate the bearings with heavy SF engine oil, then install the caps and tighten as in Step 17. Rotate the crankshaft.

19. After the piston and connecting rod assemblies have been installed, check the side clearance between the connecting rods on each crankshaft journal with a feeler gauge.

20. Install the oil pump as previously described. Prime the pump by filling either the inlet or outlet port with engine oil and rotating the pump shaft to distribute the oil within the housing. Install the oil baffle on 3.0L engines.

21. Install the oil pan.

22. Install the cylinder head(s) as previously described.

23. Install the intake manifold as previously described.

24. Fill and bleed the cooling system.

25. Replace the oil filter, then refill the crankcase with the specified amount of engine oil.

26. Start then engine and check for oil, exhaust and coolant leaks. Check and adjust the ignition timing, if necessary. Adjust the transmission throttle linkage and speed control, if necessary. On carbureted engines, adjust the idle speed if necessary.

Rear Main Seal

REMOVAL AND INSTALLATION

2.3L (140 CID) and 3.0L (182 CID) Engines

1. Raise the van and support it safely.

2. Remove the transmission as described in Chapter 6.

3. If equipped with manual transmission, remove the bellhousing and clutch assembly.

4. Remove the flywheel.

5. Using a sharp awl, punch one hole into the seal metal surface between the seal lip and the engine block.

6. Screw in the threaded end of a slide hammer tool (T77L-9533-B or equivalent), then use the slide hammer to remove the seal. Use caution to avoid scratching or damaging the oil seal surface.

7. Lubricate the new seal with clean engine oil.

8. Position the oil seal on a rear seal installer tool (T82L-6701-A or equivalent), then position the tool and seal on the rear of the engine. Alternately tighten the bolts to properly seat the seal.

9. Install the flywheel and tighten the retaining bolts to 56–64 ft.lb. (73–87 Nm).

10. Install the clutch and bellhousing assemblies, if equipped with manual transmission.

11. Install the transmission as described in Chapter 6.

2.8L (171 CID) Engine

1. Raise the van and support it safely on jackstands.

2. Remove the transmission as described in Chapter 6.

3. If equipped with manual transmission, remove the bellhousing and clutch assembly.

4. Remove the flywheel and rear plate.

5. Use a sharp awl to punch two holes in the crankshaft rear oil seal on opposite sides of the crankshaft and just above the bearing cap to cylinder block split line.

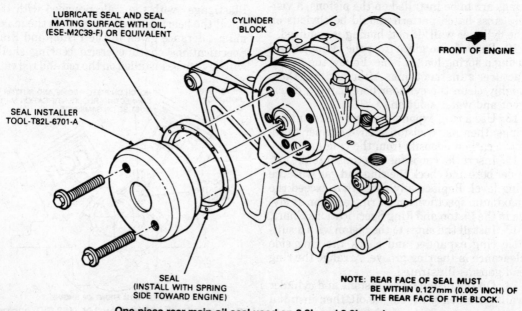

LUBRICATE SEAL AND SEAL MATING SURFACE WITH OIL, (ESE-M2C39-F) OR EQUIVALENT

CYLINDER BLOCK

FRONT OF ENGINE

SEAL INSTALLER TOOL-T82L-6701-A

SEAL (INSTALL WITH SPRING SIDE TOWARD ENGINE)

NOTE: REAR FACE OF SEAL MUST BE WITHIN 0.127mm (0.005 INCH) OF THE REAR FACE OF THE BLOCK.

One-piece rear main oil seal used on 2.3L and 3.0L engines

6. Install a sheet metal screw in each hole, then use two large screwdrivers or small pry bars to pry against both screws at the same time to remove the crankshaft rear oil seal. It may be necessary to place small blocks of wood against the cylinder block to provide a fulcrum point for the pry bars.

CAUTION: *Exercise care throughout this procedure to avoid scratching or otherwise damaging the crankshaft oil seal surface.*

7. Clean the oil seal recesses in the cylinder block and main bearing cap. Inspect and clean the oil seal contact surface on the crankshaft.

8. Coat the oil seal to cylinder block surface of the oil seal with oil. Coat the seal contact surface of the oil seal and crankshaft with heavy SF engine oil. Start the seal in the recess and install it with crankshaft rear seal installer tool T72C-6165-R or equivalent. Drive the seal into position until it is firmly seated.

9. Install the rear plate and flywheel. Tighten the flywheel bolts to 47–52 ft.lb. (64–70 Nm).

10. Install the clutch and bellhousing assembly on manual transmission models.

11. Install the transmission as described in Chapter 6.

Crankshaft and Main Bearings
REMOVAL AND INSTALLATION
All Engines

1. Remove the engine from the van as previously described, then place it on a work stand.

2. Remove the transmission (if attached), bell housing, flywheel or flex plate and rear plate.

3. Drain the crankcase and remove the oil pan with the engine in a normal upright position.

4. Remove the components from the front of the engine and the front cover.

5. Invert the engine and remove the oil pump, pickup tube and baffle, if equipped.

6. Make sure all main and connecting rod bearing caps are marked so they can be installed in their original locations.

7. Remove the connecting rod nuts and lift off the cap with its bearing insert. Install short pieces of rubber hose over the connecting rod studs to protect the crankshaft journals, then carefully push the piston and rod assemblies down into the cylinder bores.

8. Remove the main bearing caps with their bearing inserts. Inspect the crankshaft journals for nicks, burrs or bearing pickup that would cause premature bearing wear. When replacing standard bearings with new bearings, it is good practice to fit the bearing to minimum specified clearance. If the desired clearance cannot be obtained with a standard bearing, try one half of a 0.001″ (0.025mm) or 0.002″ (0.050mm) undersize in combination with a standard bearing to obtain the proper clearance.

9. Place a piece of Plastigage® on the bearing surface across the full width of the bearing cap, about ¼″ (6mm) off center. Install the cap

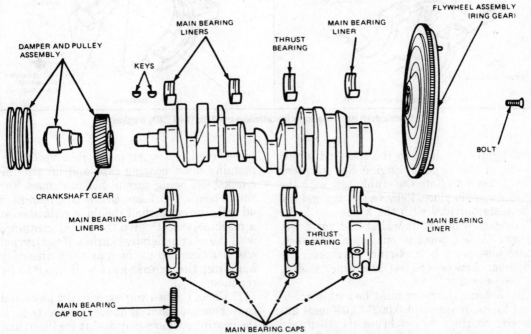

Crankshaft and bearing assembly on 2.8L (171 CID) engine

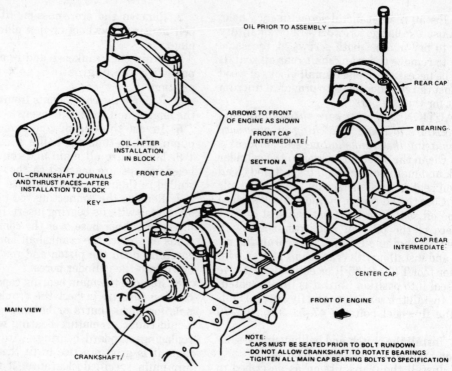

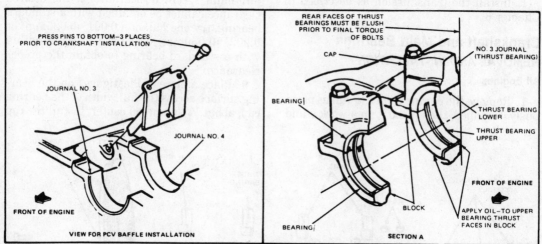

Crankshaft and bearings installation on 2.3L (140 CID) engine

and tighten the bolts to the specified torque given in the General Engine Specifications Chart. Do not rotate the crankshaft with the Plastigage® in place. Remove the cap and use the scale provided with the kit to check the Plastigage width at its widest and narrowest points. Widest point is minimum clearance, narrowest point is maximum clearance; the difference between the two is the taper reading of the journal.

10. Bearing clearance must be within specified limits. If standard 0.002″ (0.050mm) undersize bearings do not bring the clearance within desired limits, the crankshaft will have to be refinished or replaced. Remove the remaining main bearing caps and lift out the crankshaft, being careful not to damage the thrust bearing surfaces. Discard the rear main oil seal. The crankshaft should be refinished at a machine shop to give the proper clearance with the next undersize bearing. If the journal will not clean up to the maximum undersize bearing, the crankshaft will have to be replaced.

11. Clean the bearing bores in the block and caps. Foreign material under the inserts or on the bearing surfaces may distort the insert and cause bearing failure.

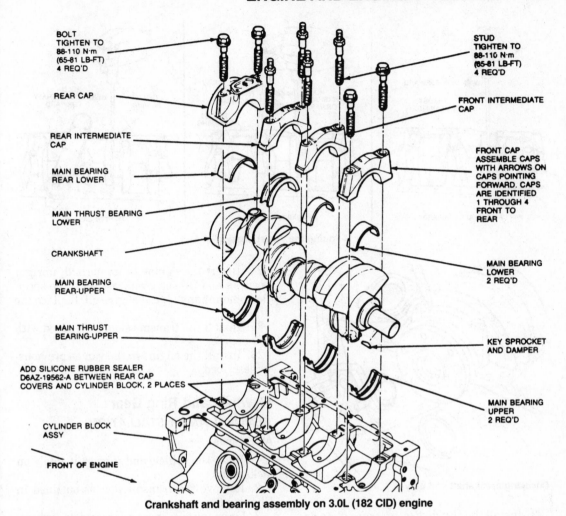

BOLT
TIGHTEN TO
88-110 N·m
(65-81 LB-FT)
4 REQ'D

STUD
TIGHTEN TO
88-110 N·m
(65-81 LB-FT)
4 REQ'D

REAR CAP

FRONT INTERMEDIATE
CAP

REAR INTERMEDIATE
CAP

MAIN BEARING
REAR LOWER

FRONT CAP
ASSEMBLE CAPS
WITH ARROWS ON
CAPS POINTING
FORWARD. CAPS
ARE IDENTIFIED
1 THROUGH 4
FRONT TO
REAR

MAIN THRUST BEARING
LOWER

CRANKSHAFT

MAIN BEARING
LOWER
2 REQ'D

MAIN BEARING
REAR-UPPER

MAIN THRUST
BEARING-UPPER

KEY SPROCKET
AND DAMPER

ADD SILICONE RUBBER SEALER
D6AZ-19562-A BETWEEN REAR CAP
COVERS AND CYLINDER BLOCK, 2 PLACES

MAIN BEARING
UPPER
2 REQ'D

CYLINDER BLOCK
ASSY

FRONT OF ENGINE

Crankshaft and bearing assembly on 3.0L (182 CID) engine

12. Assemble the main bearing inserts in their correct location in the bearing caps and cylinder block. Check the oil hole alignment between the bearing inserts and block. Apply a liberal coating of clean heavy SF engine oil to the bearing surfaces, then carefully lower the crankshaft into position.

13. Insert the remaining bearing shells into the main bearing caps and coat the bearings with clean heavy SF engine oil, then install the caps with the arrows pointing toward the front of the engine. Apply a thin even coating of sealing compound to the rear sealing surface of the rear main bearing cap before installing. Install and tighten all main bearing cap bolts finger tight after lightly oiling the threads.

14. Tighten all bearing cap bolts, except for the thrust bearing cap, to the specifications given in the Torque Specifications Chart.

15. Align the thrust bearing surfaces by forcing the crankshaft forward and the thrust bearing cap rearward. While holding in this position, tighten the thrust bearing cap to specifications.

16. Install a new rear main oil seal as previously described.

17. On the 2.8L (171 CID) engine, use a flat tool such as a large blunt end screwdriver to push the two wedge shaped seals between the cylinder block and rear main bearing cap. Position the seals with the round side facing the main bearing cap.

18. Pull the connecting rods up one at a time and install rod caps after applying a liberal coating of heavy SF engine oil to the bearings. Tighten all bearing caps to specifications. On V6 engines, check the connecting rod side clearance as previously described. Check the crankshaft end play with a dial indicator.

19. Install the oil pump, pickup tube and baffle, if equipped. Prime the oil pump before installation as described under Oil Pump Removal and Installation.

20. Install the front cover and timing chain, belt or gears. Replace the front cover oil seal.

21. Install the rear cover plate (if equipped) and the flywheel or flex plate. Tighten the mounting bolts to specifications.

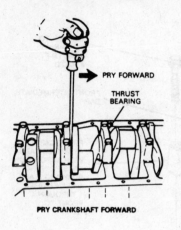

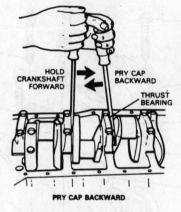

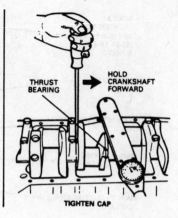

PRY CRANKSHAFT FORWARD

PRY CAP BACKWARD

TIGHTEN CAP

Aligning the thrust bearing

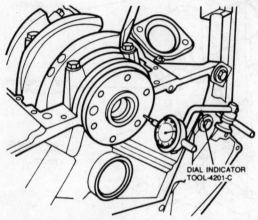

Checking crankshaft end play

22. Install the clutch disc, pressure plate and bell housing on manual transmission models.

23. Install the oil pan and tighten the bolts to specifications. See Oil Pan Removal and Installtion for gasket and sealer placement.

24. Invert the engine to its normal, upright position and fill the crankcase with the specified amount and type of engine oil. Replace the oil filter.

25. Install the transmission, if removed with the engine.

26. Install the engine in the van as previously described.

Flywheel and Ring Gear
REMOVAL AND INSTALLATION
All Engines

1. Raise the vehicle and support it safely on jackstands.

2. Remove the transmission as outlined in Chapter 6.

3. On manual transmission models, remove the bellhousing, clutch pressure plate and clutch disc.

4. On automatic transmission models, remove the torque converter.

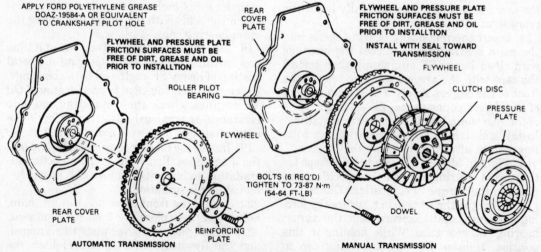

APPLY FORD POLYETHYLENE GREASE
DOAZ-19584-A OR EQUIVALENT
TO CRANKSHAFT PILOT HOLE

FLYWHEEL AND PRESSURE PLATE
FRICTION SURFACES MUST BE
FREE OF DIRT, GREASE AND OIL
PRIOR TO INSTALLTION

ROLLER PILOT
BEARING

REAR
COVER
PLATE

FLYWHEEL

REAR COVER
PLATE

REINFORCING
PLATE

BOLTS (6 REQ'D)
TIGHTEN TO 73-87 N·m
(54-64 FT-LB)

AUTOMATIC TRANSMISSION

FLYWHEEL AND PRESSURE PLATE
FRICTION SURFACES MUST BE
FREE OF DIRT, GREASE AND OIL
PRIOR TO INSTALLATION

INSTALL WITH SEAL TOWARD
TRANSMISSION

FLYWHEEL

CLUTCH DISC

PRESSURE
PLATE

DOWEL

MANUAL TRANSMISSION

Flywheel assembly on 2.3L (140 CID) engine

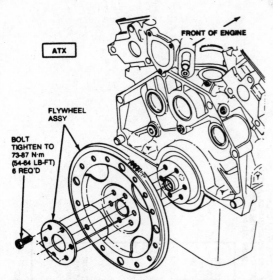

Flywheel installation on 3.0L (182 CID) engine-automatic transmission shown

5. Install a dial indicator so that the indicator rests against the face of the ring gear adjacent to the gear teeth (automatic), or against the flywheel face (manual). Hold the flywheel and crankshaft forward or backward as far as possible to prevent crankshaft end play from being indicated as flywheel runout. Zero the dial indicator, then turn the flywheel one complete revolution by hand while observing the total dial indicator reading. If the runout exceeds 0.001" (0.025mm) on 2.3L engines; 0.025" (0.635mm) for manual, or 0.060" (1.5mm) for automatic on 2.8L engines; or 0.070" (1.8mm) on 3.0L engines, the flywheel will have to be replaced. On manual transmissions, the flywheel clutch surface can be machined true if the runout is not excessive.

6. Remove the flywheel mounting bolts and remove the flywheel and ring gear assembly.

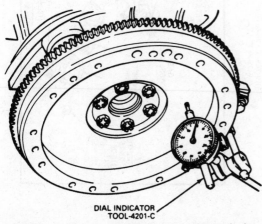

Checking flywheel runout on manual transmission models

7. On automatic transmission models, inspect the flywheel for cracks or other indications that would make it unfit for further use. Check the ring gear teeth for worn, chipped or cracked teeth and replace the flywheel and ring gear if any damage is found.

8. On manual transmission models, inspect the flywheel for cracks, heat damage or other problems that would make it unfit for further use. Machine the clutch friction surface if it is scored or worn. If it is necessary to remove more than 0.045" (1.14mm) of stock from the original thickness, replace the flywheel. Check the ring gear for worn, chipped or cracked teeth and replace the ring gear if any damage is found. To replace a damaged ring gear on a manual transmission flywheel, heat the ring gear with a blow torch on the engine side of the gear and knock it off the flywheel. Do not hit the flywheel when removing the gear. Heat the new ring gear evenly until the gear expands enough to slip onto the flywheel. Make sure the gear is seated properly against the shoulder. Do not heat any portion of the gear more than 500°F or the temper will be removed from the ring gear teeth.

NOTE: *All major rotating components including the flex plate/flywheel are individually balanced. Do not attempt to install balance weights on a new flywheel.*

9. Position the flywheel on the crankshaft flange and apply oil resistant sealer to the mounting bolts. Install and tighten the bolts in a criss-cross pattern to the specifications given in the Torque Specifications Chart.

10. On manual transmission models, install the clutch disc and pressure plate as outlined in Chapter 6. On automatic transmission models, install the torque converter.

11. Install the transmission as outlined in Chapter 6 and lower the vehicle.

EXHAUST SYSTEM

Inspect inlet pipes, outlet pipes and mufflers for cracked joints, broken welds and corrosion damage that would result in a leaking exhaust system. It is normal for a certain amount of moisture and staining to be present around the muffler seams. The presence of soot, light surface rust or moisture does not indicate a faulty muffler. Inspect the clamps, brackets and insulators for cracks and stripped or badly corroded bolt threads. When flat joints are loosened and/or disconnected to replace a shield pipe or muffler, replace the bolts and flange nuts if there is reasonable doubt that its service life is limited.

The exhaust system, including brush

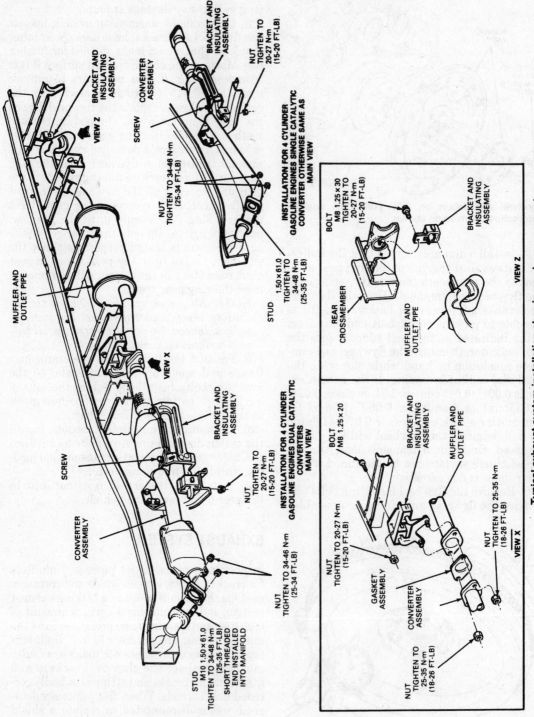

VIEW Z

BRACKET AND INSULATING ASSEMBLY

SCREW

CONVERTER ASSEMBLY

BRACKET AND INSULATING ASSEMBLY

NUT
TIGHTEN TO
20-27 N·m
(15-20 FT-LB)

SCREW

NUT
TIGHTEN TO 34-46 N·m
(25-34 FT-LB)

STUD
1.50 × 61.0
TIGHTEN TO
34-48 N·m
(25-35 FT-LB)

INSTALLATION FOR 4 CYLINDER
GASOLINE ENGINES SINGLE CATALYTIC
CONVERTER OTHERWISE SAME AS
MAIN VIEW

MUFFLER AND
OUTLET PIPE

VIEW X

BRACKET AND
INSULATING
ASSEMBLY

SCREW

NUT
TIGHTEN TO
20-27 N·m
(15-20 FT-LB)

CONVERTER
ASSEMBLY

NUT
TIGHTEN TO 34-46 N·m
(25-34 FT-LB)

INSTALLATION FOR 4 CYLINDER
GASOLINE ENGINES DUAL CATALYTIC
CONVERTERS
MAIN VIEW

STUD
M10 1.50 × 61.0
TIGHTEN TO 34-48 N·m
(25-35 FT-LB)
SHORT THREADED
END INSTALLED
INTO MANIFOLD

BOLT
M8 1.25 × 30
TIGHTEN TO
20-27 N·m
(15-20 FT-LB)

BRACKET AND
INSULATING
ASSEMBLY

REAR
CROSSMEMBER

MUFFLER AND
OUTLET PIPE

VIEW Z

BOLT
M8 1.25 × 20

BRACKET AND
INSULATING
ASSEMBLY

MUFFLER AND
OUTLET PIPE

NUT
TIGHTEN TO 20-27 N·m
(15-20 FT-LB)

GASKET ASSEMBLY

CONVERTER
ASSEMBLY

NUT
TIGHTEN TO 25-35 N·m
(18-26 FT-LB)

VIEW X

NUT
TIGHTEN TO
25-35 N·m
(18-26 FT-LB)

Typical exhaust system installation showing major components

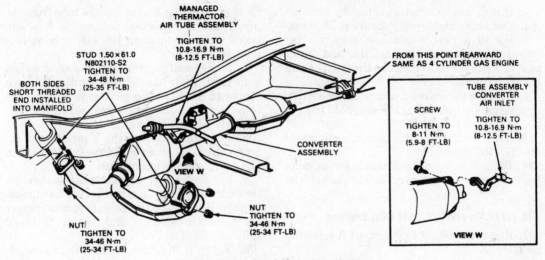

MANAGED
THERMACTOR
AIR TUBE ASSEMBLY
TIGHTEN TO
10.8-16.9 N·m
(8-12.5 FT-LB)

STUD 1.50 × 61.0
N802110-S2
TIGHTEN TO
34-48 N·m
(25-35 FT-LB)

BOTH SIDES
SHORT THREADED
END INSTALLED
INTO MANIFOLD

FROM THIS POINT REARWARD
SAME AS 4 CYLINDER GAS ENGINE

TUBE ASSEMBLY
CONVERTER
AIR INLET

SCREW
TIGHTEN TO
8-11 N·m
(5.9-8 FT-LB)

TIGHTEN TO
10.8-16.9 N·m
(8-12.5 FT-LB)

CONVERTER
ASSEMBLY

VIEW W

NUT
TIGHTEN TO
34-46 N·m
(25-34 FT-LB)

NUT
TIGHTEN TO
34-46 N·m
(25-34 FT-LB)

VIEW W

Typical V6 exhaust system installation

shields, must be free of leaks, binding, grounding and excessive vibrations. These conditions are usually caused by loose or broken flange bolts, shields, brackets or pipes. If any of these conditions exist, check the exhaust system components and alignment. Align or replace as necessary. Brush shields are positioned on the underside of the catalytic converter and should be free from bends which would bring any part of the shield in contact with the catalytic converter or muffler. The shield should also be clear of any combustible material such as dried grass or leaves.

Muffler and Outlet Pipe Assembly

REMOVAL AND INSTALLATION

1. Remove the two nuts at the muffler flange.
2. Apply a soap solution to the surface of the exhaust hanger slides at the support insulators.
3. Force the support slides out of the rubber insulators.
4. Remove the muffler and outlet pipe assembly by sliding forward, out over the axle housing.
5. To install, position the muffler and outlet pipe assembly to the converter and inlet pipe assembly by sliding it in over the axle housing.
6. Apply a soap solution to the metal support slides.
7. Force the metal support slides through the rubber insulators.
8. Install the two nuts to the muffler flange and tighten them to 18–26 ft.lb. (25–35 Nm).

Catalytic Converter and/or Pipe Assembly

REMOVAL AND INSTALLATION

2.3L (140 CID) Engine

1. Raise the vehicle and support it safely on jackstands.
2. Remove the two nuts attaching the converter pipe assembly to the muffler and outlet pipe.
3. Remove the two nuts attaching the converter pipe assembly to the exhaust manifold.
4. Apply a soap solution to the support slide of the converter support bracket at the support insulator.
5. Remove the converter pipe assembly from the van.
6. To install, apply a soap solution to the metal support slide of the converter support bracket.

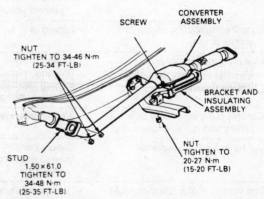

SCREW

CONVERTER
ASSEMBLY

NUT
TIGHTEN TO 34-46 N·m
(25-34 FT-LB)

BRACKET AND
INSULATING
ASSEMBLY

NUT
TIGHTEN TO
20-27 N·m
(15-20 FT-LB)

STUD
1.50 × 61.0
TIGHTEN TO
34-48 N·m
(25-35 FT-LB)

Single catalytic converter installation on 2.3L (140 CID) engine

7. Install the converter onto the exhaust manifold studs and loosely secure it in place.

8. Install a new, non-asbestos gasket between the converter pipe, muffler and outlet pipe assembly. Loosely secure the flanges and gasket with two nuts.

9. Tighten the exhaust manifold connection by alternately tightening the manifold bolts to 25–34 ft.lb. (34–46 Nm).

10. Tighten the converter to muffler flange to 18–26 ft.lb. (25–35 Nm).

11. Start the engine and check for exhaust leaks. Correct as necessary. Lower the vehicle.

2.8L (171 CID) and 3.0L (182 CID) Engines

1. Raise the vehicle and support it safely on jackstands.

2. Remove the two nuts attaching the converter pipe assembly to the muffler and outlet pipe.

3. On carbureted engines, remove the clamp securing the managed thermactor air tube to the catalytic converter. Remove the screw holding the tube bracket to the forward converter and separate the tube from the converter.

4. Disconnect the hose from the top of the managed thermactor air tube and check valve.

Heat may be required to pry the tube from the nipple on the converter. Remove the tube and check valve by rotating the assembly as it is lowered.

5. Loosen and remove the exhaust manifold stud nuts. Slide the muffler and outlet pipe rearward. Remove the gasket, then move the converter assembly rearward and rotate it to clear the studs for removal.

6. To install, position the Y-pipe on the exhaust manifold studs and loosely secure it in place with the retaining nuts.

7. Install a new, non-asbestos gasket between the converter and muffler/outlet pipe assembly. Secure the flange gasket and hanger bracket with two nuts and tighten to 18–26 ft.lb. (25–35 Nm).

8. Tighten the exhaust manifold connections by alternately tightening the manifold bolts to 25–34 ft.lb. (34–46 Nm).

9. Install the managed thermactor air tube and check valve. Tighten the tube to catalytic converter clamp to 8–12 ft.lb. (10–17 Nm).

10. Attach the tube bracket to the Y-pipe and tighten the fastener to 5–8 ft.lb. (8–11 Nm). Attach the rubber hose to the check valve and tighten the clamp.

11. Lower the vehicle, start the engine and check for exhaust leaks. Correct as necessary.

Troubleshooting Basic Charging System Problems

Problem	Cause	Solution
Noisy alternator	• Loose mountings • Loose drive pulley • Worn bearings • Brush noise • Internal circuits shorted (High pitched whine)	• Tighten mounting bolts • Tighten pulley • Replace alternator • Replace alternator • Replace alternator
Squeal when starting engine or accelerating	• Glazed or loose belt	• Replace or adjust belt
Indicator light remains on or ammeter indicates discharge (engine running)	• Broken fan belt • Broken or disconnected wires • Internal alternator problems • Defective voltage regulator	• Install belt • Repair or connect wiring • Replace alternator • Replace voltage regulator
Car light bulbs continually burn out— battery needs water continually	• Alternator/regulator overcharging	• Replace voltage regulator/alternator
Car lights flare on acceleration	• Battery low • Internal alternator/regulator problems	• Charge or replace battery • Replace alternator/regulator
Low voltage output (alternator light flickers continually or ammeter needle wanders)	• Loose or worn belt • Dirty or corroded connections • Internal alternator/regulator problems	• Replace or adjust belt • Clean or replace connections • Replace alternator or regulator

Troubleshooting Basic Starting System Problems

Problem	Cause	Solution
Starter motor rotates engine slowly	• Battery charge low or battery defective	• Charge or replace battery
	• Defective circuit between battery and starter motor	• Clean and tighten, or replace cables
	• Low load current	• Bench-test starter motor. Inspect for worn brushes and weak brush springs.
	• High load current	• Bench-test starter motor. Check engine for friction, drag or coolant in cylinders. Check ring gear-to-pinion gear clearance.
Starter motor will not rotate engine	• Battery charge low or battery defective	• Charge or replace battery
	• Faulty solenoid	• Check solenoid ground. Repair or replace as necessary.
	• Damage drive pinion gear or ring gear	• Replace damaged gear(s)
	• Starter motor engagement weak	• Bench-test starter motor
	• Starter motor rotates slowly with high load current	• Inspect drive yoke pull-down and point gap, check for worn end bushings, check ring gear clearance
	• Engine seized	• Repair engine
Starter motor drive will not engage (solenoid known to be good)	• Defective contact point assembly	• Repair or replace contact point assembly
	• Inadequate contact point assembly ground	• Repair connection at ground screw
	• Defective hold-in coil	• Replace field winding assembly
Starter motor drive will not disengage	• Starter motor loose on flywheel housing	• Tighten mounting bolts
	• Worn drive end busing	• Replace bushing
	• Damaged ring gear teeth	• Replace ring gear or driveplate
	• Drive yoke return spring broken or missing	• Replace spring
Starter motor drive disengages prematurely	• Weak drive assembly thrust spring	• Replace drive mechanism
	• Hold-in coil defective	• Replace field winding assembly
Low load current	• Worn brushes	• Replace brushes
	• Weak brush springs	• Replace springs

Troubleshooting Engine Mechanical Problems

Problem	Cause	Solution
External oil leaks	• Fuel pump gasket broken or improperly seated	• Replace gasket
	• Cylinder head cover RTV sealant broken or improperly seated	• Replace sealant; inspect cylinder head cover sealant flange and cylinder head sealant surface for distortion and cracks
	• Oil filler cap leaking or missing	• Replace cap
	• Oil filter gasket broken or improperly seated	• Replace oil filter
	• Oil pan side gasket broken, improperly seated or opening in RTV sealant	• Replace gasket or repair opening in sealant; inspect oil pan gasket flange for distortion
	• Oil pan front oil seal broken or improperly seated	• Replace seal; inspect timing case cover and oil pan seal flange for distortion

Troubleshooting Engine Mechanical Problems (cont.)

Problem	Cause	Solution
External oil leaks (cont.)	• Oil pan rear oil seal broken or improperly seated	• Replace seal; inspect oil pan rear oil seal flange; inspect rear main bearing cap for cracks, plugged oil return channels, or distortion in seal groove
	• Timing case cover oil seal broken or improperly seated	• Replace seal
	• Excess oil pressure because of restricted PCV valve	• Replace PCV valve
	• Oil pan drain plug loose or has stripped threads	• Repair as necessary and tighten
	• Rear oil gallery plug loose	• Use appropriate sealant on gallery plug and tighten
	• Rear camshaft plug loose or improperly seated	• Seat camshaft plug or replace and seal, as necessary
	• Distributor base gasket damaged	• Replace gasket
Excessive oil consumption	• Oil level too high	• Drain oil to specified level
	• Oil with wrong viscosity being used	• Replace with specified oil
	• PCV valve stuck closed	• Replace PCV valve
	• Valve stem oil deflectors (or seals) are damaged, missing, or incorrect type	• Replace valve stem oil deflectors
	• Valve stems or valve guides worn	• Measure stem-to-guide clearance and repair as necessary
	• Poorly fitted or missing valve cover baffles	• Replace valve cover
	• Piston rings broken or missing	• Replace broken or missing rings
	• Scuffed piston	• Replace piston
	• Incorrect piston ring gap	• Measure ring gap, repair as necessary
	• Piston rings sticking or excessively loose in grooves	• Measure ring side clearance, repair as necessary
	• Compression rings installed upside down	• Repair as necessary
	• Cylinder walls worn, scored, or glazed	• Repair as necessary
	• Piston ring gaps not properly staggered	• Repair as necessary
	• Excessive main or connecting rod bearing clearance	• Measure bearing clearance, repair as necessary
No oil pressure	• Low oil level	• Add oil to correct level
	• Oil pressure gauge, warning lamp or sending unit inaccurate	• Replace oil pressure gauge or warning lamp
	• Oil pump malfunction	• Replace oil pump
	• Oil pressure relief valve sticking	• Remove and inspect oil pressure relief valve assembly
	• Oil passages on pressure side of pump obstructed	• Inspect oil passages for obstruction
	• Oil pickup screen or tube obstructed	• Inspect oil pickup for obstruction
	• Loose oil inlet tube	• Tighten or seal inlet tube
Low oil pressure	• Low oil level	• Add oil to correct level
	• Inaccurate gauge, warning lamp or sending unit	• Replace oil pressure gauge or warning lamp
	• Oil excessively thin because of dilution, poor quality, or improper grade	• Drain and refill crankcase with recommended oil
	• Excessive oil temperature	• Correct cause of overheating engine
	• Oil pressure relief spring weak or sticking	• Remove and inspect oil pressure relief valve assembly
	• Oil inlet tube and screen assembly has restriction or air leak	• Remove and inspect oil inlet tube and screen assembly. (Fill inlet tube with lacquer thinner to locate leaks.)

Troubleshooting Engine Mechanical Problems (cont.)

Problem	Cause	Solution
Low oil pressure (cont.)	• Excessive oil pump clearance • Excessive main, rod, or camshaft bearing clearance	• Measure clearances • Measure bearing clearances, repair as necessary
High oil pressure	• Improper oil viscosity • Oil pressure gauge or sending unit inaccurate • Oil pressure relief valve sticking closed	• Drain and refill crankcase with correct viscosity oil • Replace oil pressure gauge • Remove and inspect oil pressure relief valve assembly
Main bearing noise	• Insufficient oil supply • Main bearing clearance excessive • Bearing insert missing • Crankshaft end play excessive • Improperly tightened main bearing cap bolts • Loose flywheel or drive plate • Loose or damaged vibration damper	• Inspect for low oil level and low oil pressure • Measure main bearing clearance, repair as necessary • Replace missing insert • Measure end play, repair as necessary • Tighten bolts with specified torque • Tighten flywheel or drive plate attaching bolts • Repair as necessary
Connecting rod bearing noise	• Insufficient oil supply • Carbon build-up on piston • Bearing clearance excessive or bearing missing • Crankshaft connecting rod journal out-of-round • Misaligned connecting rod or cap • Connecting rod bolts tightened improperly	• Inspect for low oil level and low oil pressure • Remove carbon from piston crown • Measure clearance, repair as necessary • Measure journal dimensions, repair or replace as necessary • Repair as necessary • Tighten bolts with specified torque
Piston noise	• Piston-to-cylinder wall clearance excessive (scuffed piston) • Cylinder walls excessively tapered or out-of-round • Piston ring broken • Loose or seized piston pin • Connecting rods misaligned • Piston ring side clearance excessively loose or tight • Carbon build-up on piston is excessive	• Measure clearance and examine piston • Measure cylinder wall dimensions, rebore cylinder • Replace all rings on piston • Measure piston-to-pin clearance, repair as necessary • Measure rod alignment, straighten or replace • Measure ring side clearance, repair as necessary • Remove carbon from piston
Valve actuating component noise	• Insufficient oil supply • Push rods worn or bent • Rocker arms or pivots worn • Foreign objects or chips in hydraulic tappets • Excessive tappet leak-down • Tappet face worn • Broken or cocked valve springs	• Check for: (a) Low oil level (b) Low oil pressure (c) Plugged push rods (d) Wrong hydraulic tappets (e) Restricted oil gallery (f) Excessive tappet to bore clearance • Replace worn or bent push rods • Replace worn rocker arms or pivots • Clean tappets • Replace valve tappet • Replace tappet; inspect corresponding cam lobe for wear • Properly seat cocked springs; replace broken springs

Troubleshooting Engine Mechanical Problems (cont.)

Problem	Cause	Solution
Valve actuating component noise (cont.)	• Stem-to-guide clearance excessive	• Measure stem-to-guide clearance, repair as required
	• Valve bent	• Replace valve
	• Loose rocker arms	• Tighten bolts with specified torque
	• Valve seat runout excessive	• Regrind valve seat/valves
	• Missing valve lock	• Install valve lock
	• Push rod rubbing or contacting cylinder head	• Remove cylinder head and remove obstruction in head
	• Excessive engine oil (four-cylinder engine)	• Correct oil level

Troubleshooting the Cooling System

Problem	Cause	Solution
High temperature gauge indication— overheating	• Coolant level low	• Replenish coolant
	• Fan belt loose	• Adjust fan belt tension
	• Radiator hose(s) collapsed	• Replace hose(s)
	• Radiator airflow blocked	• Remove restriction (bug screen, fog lamps, etc.)
	• Faulty radiator cap	• Replace radiator cap
	• Ignition timing incorrect	• Adjust ignition timing
	• Idle speed low	• Adjust idle speed
	• Air trapped in cooling system	• Purge air
	• Heavy traffic driving	• Operate at fast idle in neutral intermittently to cool engine
	• Incorrect cooling system component(s) installed	• Install proper component(s)
	• Faulty thermostat	• Replace thermostat
	• Water pump shaft broken or impeller loose	• Replace water pump
	• Radiator tubes clogged	• Flush radiator
	• Cooling system clogged	• Flush system
	• Casting flash in cooling passages	• Repair or replace as necessary. Flash may be visible by removing cooling system components or removing core plugs.
	• Brakes dragging	• Repair brakes
	• Excessive engine friction	• Repair engine
	• Antifreeze concentration over 68%	• Lower antifreeze concentration percentage
	• Missing air seals	• Replace air seals
	• Faulty gauge or sending unit	• Repair or replace faulty component
	• Loss of coolant flow caused by leakage or foaming	• Repair or replace leaking component, replace coolant
	• Viscous fan drive failed	• Replace unit
Low temperature indication— undercooling	• Thermostat stuck open	• Replace thermostat
	• Faulty gauge or sending unit	• Repair or replace faulty component
Coolant loss—boilover	• Overfilled cooling system	• Reduce coolant level to proper specification
	• Quick shutdown after hard (hot) run	• Allow engine to run at fast idle prior to shutdown
	• Air in system resulting in occasional "burping" of coolant	• Purge system
	• Insufficient antifreeze allowing coolant boiling point to be too low	• Add antifreeze to raise boiling point
	• Antifreeze deteriorated because of age or contamination	• Replace coolant

Troubleshooting the Cooling System (cont.)

Problem	Cause	Solution
Coolant loss—boilover (cont.)	• Leaks due to loose hose clamps, loose nuts, bolts, drain plugs, faulty hoses, or defective radiator	• Pressure test system to locate source of leak(s) then repair as necessary
	• Faulty head gasket	• Replace head gasket
	• Cracked head, manifold, or block	• Replace as necessary
	• Faulty radiator cap	• Replace cap
Coolant entry into crankcase or cylinder(s)	• Faulty head gasket	• Replace head gasket
	• Crack in head, manifold or block	• Replace as necessary
Coolant recovery system inoperative	• Coolant level low	• Replenish coolant to FULL mark
	• Leak in system	• Pressure test to isolate leak and repair as necessary
	• Pressure cap not tight or seal missing, or leaking	• Repair as necessary
	• Pressure cap defective	• Replace cap
	• Overflow tube clogged or leaking	• Repair as necessary
	• Recovery bottle vent restricted	• Remove restriction
Noise	• Fan contacting shroud	• Reposition shroud and inspect engine mounts
	• Loose water pump impeller	• Replace pump
	• Glazed fan belt	• Apply silicone or replace belt
	• Loose fan belt	• Adjust fan belt tension
	• Rough surface on drive pulley	• Replace pulley
	• Water pump bearing worn	• Remove belt to isolate. Replace pump.
	• Belt alignment	• Check pulley alignment. Repair as necessary.
No coolant flow through heater core	• Restricted return inlet in water pump	• Remove restriction
	• Heater hose collapsed or restricted	• Remove restriction or replace hose
	• Restricted heater core	• Remove restriction or replace core
	• Restricted outlet in thermostat housing	• Remove flash or restriction
	• Intake manifold bypass hole in cylinder head restricted	• Remove restriction
	• Faulty heater control valve	• Replace valve
	• Intake manifold coolant passage restricted	• Remove restriction or replace intake manifold

NOTE: *Immediately after shutdown, the engine enters a condition known as heat soak. This is caused by the cooling system being inoperative while engine temperature is still high. If coolant temperature rises above boiling point, expansion and pressure may push some coolant out of the radiator overflow tube. If this does not occur frequently it is considered normal.*

Troubleshooting the Serpentine Drive Belt

Problem	Cause	Solution
Tension sheeting fabric failure (woven fabric on outside circumference of belt has cracked or separated from body of belt)	• Grooved or backside idler pulley diameters are less than minimum recommended	• Replace pulley(s) not conforming to specification
	• Tension sheeting contacting (rubbing) stationary object	• Correct rubbing condition
	• Excessive heat causing woven fabric to age	• Replace belt
	• Tension sheeting splice has fractured	• Replace belt
Noise (objectional squeal, squeak, or rumble is heard or felt while drive belt is in operation)	• Belt slippage	• Adjust belt
	• Bearing noise	• Locate and repair
	• Belt misalignment	• Align belt/pulley(s)
	• Belt-to-pulley mismatch	• Install correct belt
	• Driven component inducing vibration	• Locate defective driven component and repair

Troubleshooting the Serpentine Drive Belt (cont.)

Problem	Cause	Solution
Noise (cont.)	• System resonant frequency inducing vibration	• Vary belt tension within specifications. Replace belt.
Rib chunking (one or more ribs has separated from belt body)	• Foreign objects imbedded in pulley grooves • Installation damage • Drive loads in excess of design specifications • Insufficient internal belt adhesion	• Remove foreign objects from pulley grooves • Replace belt • Adjust belt tension • Replace belt
Rib or belt wear (belt ribs contact bottom of pulley grooves)	• Pulley(s) misaligned • Mismatch of belt and pulley groove widths • Abrasive environment • Rusted pulley(s) • Sharp or jagged pulley groove tips • Rubber deteriorated	• Align pulley(s) • Replace belt • Replace belt • Clean rust from pulley(s) • Replace pulley • Replace belt
Longitudinal belt cracking (cracks between two ribs)	• Belt has mistracked from pulley groove • Pulley groove tip has worn away rubber-to-tensile member	• Replace belt • Replace belt
Belt slips	• Belt slipping because of insufficient tension • Belt or pulley subjected to substance (belt dressing, oil, ethylene glycol) that has reduced friction • Driven component bearing failure • Belt glazed and hardened from heat and excessive slippage	• Adjust tension • Replace belt and clean pulleys • Replace faulty component bearing • Replace belt
"Groove jumping" (belt does not maintain correct position on pulley, or turns over and/or runs off pulleys)	• Insufficient belt tension • Pulley(s) not within design tolerance • Foreign object(s) in grooves • Excessive belt speed • Pulley misalignment • Belt-to-pulley profile mismatched • Belt cordline is distorted	• Adjust belt tension • Replace pulley(s) • Remove foreign objects from grooves • Avoid excessive engine acceleration • Align pulley(s) • Install correct belt • Replace belt
Belt broken (Note: identify and correct problem before replacement belt is installed)	• Excessive tension • Tensile members damaged during belt installation • Belt turnover • Severe pulley misalignment • Bracket, pulley, or bearing failure	• Replace belt and adjust tension to specification • Replace belt • Replace belt • Align pulley(s) • Replace defective component and belt
Cord edge failure (tensile member exposed at edges of belt or separated from belt body)	• Excessive tension • Drive pulley misalignment • Belt contacting stationary object • Pulley irregularities • Improper pulley construction • Insufficient adhesion between tensile member and rubber matrix	• Adjust belt tension • Align pulley • Correct as necessary • Replace pulley • Replace pulley • Replace belt and adjust tension to specifications
Sporadic rib cracking (multiple cracks in belt ribs at random intervals)	• Ribbed pulley(s) diameter less than minimum specification • Backside bend flat pulley(s) diameter less than minimum • Excessive heat condition causing rubber to harden • Excessive belt thickness • Belt overcured • Excessive tension	• Replace pulley(s) • Replace pulley(s) • Correct heat condition as necessary • Replace belt • Replace belt • Adjust belt tension

Emission Controls and Fuel System

4

EMISSION CONTROLS

Positive Crankcase Ventilation (PCV) System

When the engine is running, a small portion of the gases which are formed in the combustion chamber leak by the piston rings and enter the crankcase, a process known as blow-by. Since these gases are under pressure, they tend to escape from the crankcase and enter the atmosphere. If these gases are allowed to remain in the crankcase for any period of time, they contaminate the engine oil and cause sludge build-up in the crankcase. If allowed to escape into the atmosphere, they pollute the air with unburned hydrocarbons. The job of the crankcase emission control system is to recycle these gases back into the engine combustion chambers where they are reburned with the normal fuel charge.

The crankcase (blow-by) gases are recycled in the following manner: as the engine is running, clean, filtered air is drawn through the air filter and into the crankcase. As the air passes through the crankcase, it picks up the combustion gases and carries them out of the crankcase, through an oil separator, through the PCV valve and then into the induction system.

The most critical component in the system is the PCV valve, which controls the amount of gases which are recycled into the combustion chambers. At low engine speeds, the valve is partially closed, limiting the flow of the gases into the intake manifold. As engine speed increases, the valve opens to admit greater quantities of the gases into the intake manifold. If the valve should become blocked or plugged, the gases will be prevented from escaping from the crankcase by the normal route. Since these gases are under pressure, they will find their own way out of the crankcase, usually through

a weak oil seal or gasket in the engine. As the gas escapes by the gasket, it also creates an oil leak. Besides causing oil leaks, a clogged PCV valve also allows these gases to remain in the crankcase for an extended period of time, promoting the formation of sludge in the engine.

PCV VALVE REPLACEMENT

The PCV valve in the rocker arm cover should be removed and checked periodically for clogging. Pull the valve from the grommet and shake it. If the valve rattles, it can be assumed good. If no rattling sound is heard, replace the PCV valve. Do not attempt to clean an old PCV valve using solvent or any other cleaning material. If the valve is suspect, it should be replaced.

Evaporative Emission Controls

When liquid gasoline is subjected to heat, it expands and vaporizes. If this expansion and vaporization takes place in a conventional fuel tank, the fuel vapor escapes and pollutes the atmosphere. To control this source of pollution, all models are equipped with an evaporative emission control system that collects gasoline vapors from the fuel tank and carburetor float bowl, if equipped.

The major components of this system are an expansion area in the fuel tank, an orifice valve which is mounted on the fuel tank, a carbon (charcoal) canister which stores the fuel vapors and the hoses which connect all this equipment together.

As the gasoline in the fuel tank of a parked vehicle begins to expand due to heat, the vapor that forms moves to the top of the tank. It leaves the fuel tank through the orifice valve, a liquid/vapor separator which permits fuel vapors to leave, but prevents liquid gasoline from escaping. The fuel vapor enters the vapor separator outlet hose and passes through the hose to the carbon canister, which is mounted in the

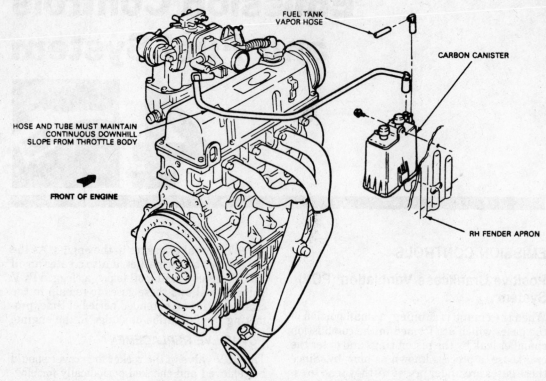

FUEL TANK
VAPOR HOSE

CARBON CANISTER

HOSE AND TUBE MUST MAINTAIN
CONTINUOUS DOWNHILL
SLOPE FROM THROTTLE BODY

FRONT OF ENGINE

RH FENDER APRON

Evaporative control system used with 2.3L (140 CID) engine

engine compartment. The vapor enters the canister, passes through a charcoal filter, then exits from the canister through its grated bottom. As the fuel vapor passes through the carbon, the hydrocarbons are removed so that the air that passes out of the canister is free of atmospheric pollutants.

When the engine is started, vacuum from the carburetor or throttle body draws fresh air into the carbon canister. Flow of these vapors

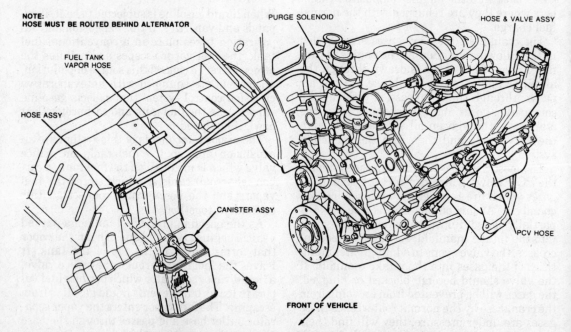

NOTE:
HOSE MUST BE ROUTED BEHIND ALTERNATOR

PURGE SOLENOID

HOSE & VALVE ASSY

FUEL TANK
VAPOR HOSE

HOSE ASSY

CANISTER ASSY

PCV HOSE

FRONT OF VEHICLE

Evaporative control system used with 3.0L (182 CID) engine

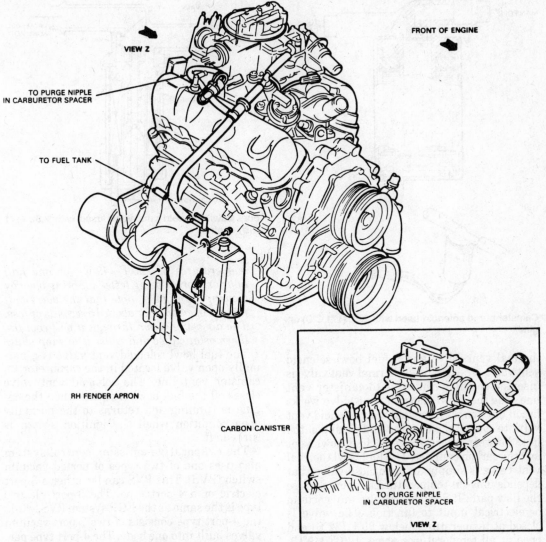

VIEW Z

FRONT OF ENGINE

TO PURGE NIPPLE
IN CARBURETOR SPACER

TO FUEL TANK

RH FENDER APRON

CARBON CANISTER

TO PURGE NIPPLE
IN CARBURETOR SPACER

VIEW Z

Evaporative control system used with 2.8L (171 CID) engine

from the carburetor bowl into the canister is controlled by the fuel bowl vent valve and thermal vent valve on the 2.8L engine. As the entering air passes through the carbon in the canister, it picks up the hydrocarbons that were deposited there and this gas mixture is then carried through a hose to the air cleaner or intake manifold, where it combines with the air/fuel mixture and is burned in the combustion chambers.

On the 2.8L engine only, a canister purge solenoid is installed. The canister purge solenoid is a normally closed valve that is connected inline between the carburetor spacer nipple and the carburetor bowl vent hose. The operation of the solenoid is controlled by the EEC-IV on-board computer. When the engine is off, the canister purge solenoid is not energized and is in a closed, non-flowing position. When the en-

gine is running, the EEC-IV computer reads engine rpm, engine load, engine temperature and other variables to decide the proper time for the engine to accept fuel vapors. When this occurs, the EEC-IV computer engergizes the canister purge solenoid to open, allowing flow from the carbon canister into the intake manifold through the carburetor spacer. This action purges the carbon canister of fuel vapors as fresh air is drawn into the carbon canister under the fresh air inlet cap of the canister.

NOTE: *Fuel injected engines do not use a canister purge solenoid. The carbon canister is connected directly to the throttle body, so purging of the canister is controlled directly by the throttle plate position, engine load and vacuum level.*

Two other valves are used in the evaporative control system of the 2.8L engine, a fuel bowl

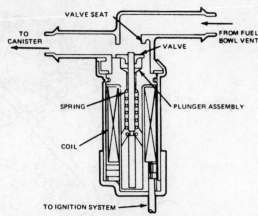

Fuel bowl solenoid vent valve used with 2.8L (171 CID) engine

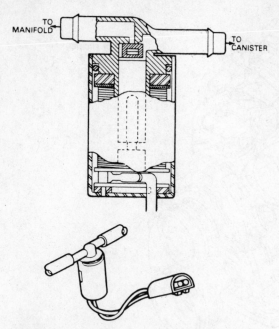

Canister purge solenoid used with 2.8L (171 CID) engine

thermal vent valve and a fuel bowl solenoid vent valve. The fuel bowl thermal vent valve is inserted in the carburetor-to-canister vent line. The fuel bowl thermal vent valve works in conjunction with the fuel bowl solenoid vent valve to control the opening and closing of the hose between the carburetor fuel bowl vent and the carbon canister. The fuel bowl thermal vent valve is simply an open/close valve that depends only on temperature to open or close the flow path. It does not require any vacuum or electrical input to function. The valve is closed at temperatures below 90°F (32°C) and open at all temperatures above 120°F (49°C). At temperatures between these limits, the valve may be open or closed because the valve operates by an internal disc of thermostatic material whose exact temperature switch point cannot be predicted.

NOTE: *If a valve that has been exposed to*

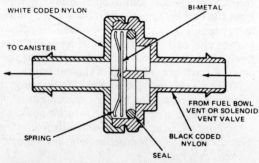

Fuel bowl thermal vent valve used with 2.8L (171 CID) engine

temperatures of 120°F (49°C) for one half hour or more is being tested for being open by blowing through it, note that the valve will remain open only for about 15 seconds or less. The air being blown through it will cool the thermostatic disc and cause it to snap shut.

The fuel bowl solenoid vent valve is a normally open valve located in the carburetor-to-canister vent line. The solenoid vent valve closes off the fuel bowl vent line when the engine is running and returns to the normally open condition when the ignition switch is turned off.

The evaporative emission control system also uses one of two types of ported vacuum switch (PVS). This PVS can be either a 3-port electric or a 4-port type. The 3-port electric type is the same as the EGR system PVS, while the 4-port type consists of two 2-port vacuum valves built into one body. The 4-port type performs the same function as two 2-port PVS valves. The PVS used in the evaporative emission control system turns the purge valve vacuum on as the engine warms up and allows the purge valve to close when the engine is turned off and vacuum is lost.

The final component of the evaporative emission control system is the fuel filler cap. This is a sealed cap with a built-in pressure/vacuum relief valve. Fuel system vacuum relief (necessary as the fuel is used by the engine) is provided after negative 0.50 psi and pressure relief is provided when the fuel tank pressure reaches 1.8 psi. Under normal operating conditions, the fill cap operates as a check valve, allowing air to enter the tank as gasoline is used, while preventing vapors from escaping the tank through the cap. The use of an aftermarket fuel filler cap other than the original factory equipment type could result in damage to the fuel system or improper system

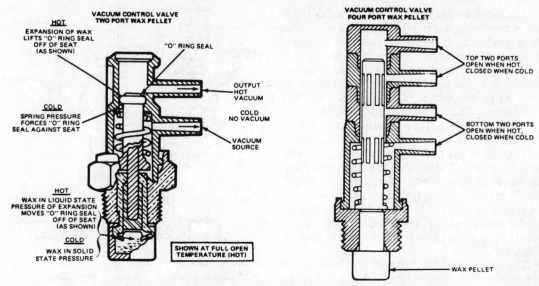

Two types of ported vacuum switch (PVS) used on evaporative systems

operation if not designed for pressure/vacuum relief as described.

EVAPORATIVE SYSTEM SERVICE

The only maintenance on the evaporative system is to periodically check all hoses and connections for leaks and deterioration. Replace any hoses which are found to be damaged in any way. Under normal circumstances, the charcoal canister is expected to last the life of the vehicle, but it should be periodically inspected for any damage or contamination by raw gasoline. Replace any gasoline soaked canister found. Refer to the illustrations for canister mounting and evaporative hose routing on the various engines. Filler cap damage or contamination that clogs the pressure/vacu-um valve may result in deformation of the fuel tank.

Catalytic Converter System

The engine exhaust consists mainly of Nitrogen, but it also contains Carbon Monoxide (CO), Carbon Dioxide (CO_2), Water Vapor (H_2O), Oxygen (O_2), Nitrogen Oxides (NOx) and Hydrogen (H), as well as various unburned Hydrocarbons (HC). Three of these exhaust gas components (CO, NOx and HC) are major air pollutants, so their emission to the atmosphere has to be controlled. The catalytic converter mounted in the exhaust system plays a major role in the emission control system.

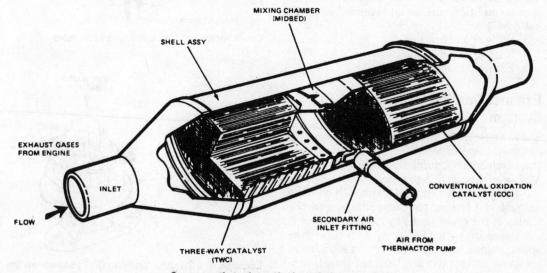

Cross section of a typical catalytic converter

The catalytic converter works as a gas reactor whose catalytic function is to speed up the heat producing chemical reaction between the exhaust gas components in order to reduce the air pollutants in the engine exhaust. In other words, it works kind of like an afterburner to convert pollutants into Carbon Dioxide (CO_2) and water. The catalyst material inside the converter is made of a ceramic substrate that is coated with a high surface area alumina and impregnated with catalytically active precious metals, usually Platinum, Palladuim and Rhodium. It is this surface of catalyst material that plays a major role in the heat producing chemical reaction. It is also this surface that is destroyed when contaminated by the use of leaded gasoline or fuel additive containing lead.

The catalytic converter assembly consists of a structured shell containing a ceramic, honeycomb construction called the substrate. In order to maintain the converter's feed gas (exhaust) oxygen content at a high level to obtain the maximum oxidation for producing the heated chemical reaction, the oxidation catalyst requires the use of a secondary air source. This secondary air source is provided by the pulse air or thermactor air injection system, covered later in this chapter. The catalytic converter system is protected by several devices that block out the secondary air supply from the thermactor air injection system when the engine is laboring under any abnormal hot or cold operating condition. Depending on the engine calibration, these block out devices are functional under the following conditions:

1. Cold engine operation with a rich choke mixture.

2. Abnormally high engine coolant temperatures above 225°F (107°C) which may result from a condition such as an extended idle on a hot day.

3. Wide open throttle.

4. Engine deceleration.

5. Extended idle operation.

Exhaust Gas Recirculation (EGR) System

The exhaust gas recirculation (EGR) system is designed to reintroduce inert exhaust gas into the combustion chamber, thereby lowering peak combustion temperatures and reducing the formation of Nitrous Oxide (NOx). The amount of exhaust gas recirculated and the timing of the cycle varies by calibration and is controlled by various factors, such as engine speed, engine vacuum, exhaust system backpressure, coolant temperature and throttle angle depending on the calibration. All EGR

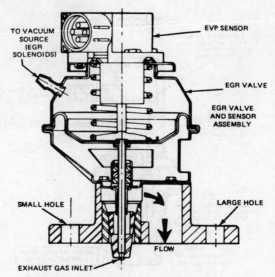

Cross section of base entry type EGR valve

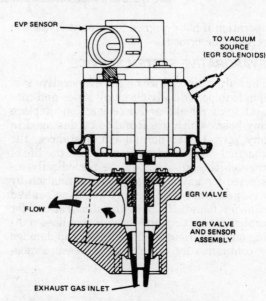

Cross section of side entry type EGR valve

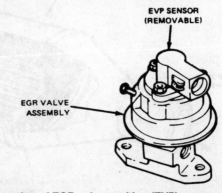

Location of EGR valve position (EVP) sensor on the EGR valve

valves are vacuum actuated, but controlled by the EEC-IV on-board computer. The electronic EGR valve is not serviceable, however the EGR valve position (EVP) sensor and EGR valve can be replaced as individual components.

EGR SYSTEM SERVICE

The EGR valve assembly (including the EVP sensor) should be replaced every 60,000 miles. Disconnect the vacuum hose, electrical connector and EGR line (if equipped), then remove the mounting bolts and lift off the EGR valve assembly. When replacing the EGR valve, the exhaust gas passages should be cleaned of carbon deposits. Excessive carbon deposits may require the removal of the mounting plate or intake manifold for cleaning. Excessive carbon deposits should not be pushed into the intake manifold where they can be drawn into the combustion chambers when the engine is started.

Thermactor (Air Pump) System

The thermactor air injection system reduces carbon monoxide and hydrocarbon content of exhaust gases by injecting fresh air into the exhaust gas stream as it leaves the combustion chambers. A belt driven air pump supplies air to the exhaust port near the exhaust valve, by either an external manifold or internal drilled passages. The oxygen in the fresh air plus the heat of the exhaust gases causes burning which converts exhaust gases to carbon dioxide and water vapor.

The air supply pump is a positive displacement, vane type that is available in 11 cu. in. and 19 cu. in. sizes, either of which may be driven with different pulley ratios for different applications. The 11 cu. in. pump receives its air through a remote filter attached to the air inlet nipple or through an impeller type centrifugal air filter fan. The 19 cu. in. pump uses an impeller type centrifugal air filter fan which separates dirt, dust and other contaminants from the intake air by centrifugal force. The air supply pump does not have a pressure

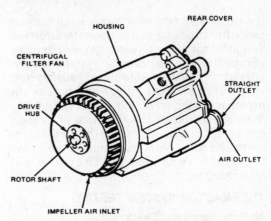

Typical 19 cu. in. thermactor air pump

relief valve, a function performed by the bypass valve. There are two general groups of air bypass valves, normally closed and normally open. Each group is available in remote (inline) versions or pump mounted versions. The bypass valves are part of the thermactor system.

Normally closed valves supply air to the exhaust system with medium and high applied vacuum signals during normal operating modes, short idles and some accelerations. With low or no vacuum applied, the pump air is dumped through the silencer ports of the valve. Normally open air bypass valves are available with or without vacuum vents and testing procedures are different for each type. Normally open valve with a vacuum vent provide a timed air dump during decelerations and also dump when a vacuum pressure difference is maintained between the signal port and the vent port. The signal port must have 3 in.Hg more vacuum than the vent port to hold the dump. This mode is used to protect the catalyst from overheating. Normally open valves without a vacuum vent provide a timed dump of air for 1–3 seconds when a sudden high vacuum of about 20 in.Hg is applied to the signal port to prevent backfire during deceleration.

In addition the the bypass valves, an air supply control valve is used to direct air pump output to the exhaust manifold or downstream to the catalyst system depending upon the engine control strategy. A combination air bypass/air control valve combines the functions of the air bypass valve and the air control valve into a single unit. There are two normally closed valves, the non-bleed type and the bleed type, all of which look alike. One distinguishing feature will be that the bleed type will have the percent of bleed molded into the plastic case.

Finally, the air check valve is a one-way valve that allows thermactor air to pass into

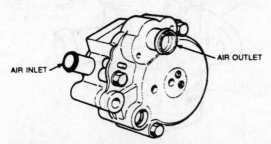

Typical 11 cu. in. thermactor air pump

the exhaust system while preventing exhaust gases from passing in the opposite direction. The pulse air valve replaces the air pump application in some thermactor systems. It permits air to be drawn into the exhaust system on vacuum exhaust pulses and blocks the backflow of high pressure exhaust pulses. The fresh air completes the oxidation of exhaust gas components. Although the two valves share the same basic part number and have the same appearance, they are not interchangeable.

THERMACTOR SYSTEM TESTING

Air Pump Functional Check

Check the air pump belt tension and adjust it, if necessary. Disconnect the air supply hose from the bypass control valve. The pump is operating properly if air flow is felt at the pump outlet and the flow increases as the engine speed is increased. Do not pry on the pump to adjust the belt as the aluminum housing is likely to collapse.

Normally Closed Bypass Valve Check

1. Disconnect the air supply hose at the valve outlet.
2. Remove the vacuum line to check to see that a vacuum signal is present at the vacuum nipple. Remove or bypass any restrictors or delay valves in the vacuum line. There must be a vacuum present at the nipple before proceeding.
3. With the engine at 1,500 rpm and the vacuum line connected to the vacuum nipple, air pump supply air should be heard and felt at the air bypass valve outlet.
4. With the engine at 1,500 rpm, disconnect the vacuum line. Air at the outlet should be significantly decreased or shut off. Air pump supply air should be heard or felt at the silencer ports.
5. If the normally closed air bypass valve

does not successfully complete the above tests, check the air pump. If the pump is operating properly, replace the air bypass valve.

Normally Open Bypass Valve Check

1. Disconnect the air pump supply line at the outlet.
2. Disconnect all vacuum lines from the vacuum nipple and the vacuum vent.
3. Start the engine and raise the engine speed to 1,500 rpm. The air pump supply air should be heard and felt at the outlet.
4. Using a length of vacuum hose with no restrictors or devices, connect the vacuum nipple to one of the manifold vacuum fittings on the intake manifold. With the vacuum vent open to the atmosphere and the engine at 1,500 rpm, virtually no air should be felt at the valve outlet and virtually all air should be bypassed through the silencer ports.
5. Using the same direct vacuum line to an intake manifold vacuum source, cap the vacuum vent. Accelerate the engine speed to 2,000 rpm and suddenly release the throttle. A momentary interruption of air pump supply air should be felt at the valve outlet.
6. Reconnect all vacuum and thermactor lines. If any of the above tests are not satisfactorily completed, check the air pump. If the air pump is operating properly, replace the bypass valve.

Normally Open Bypass Valve Without Vacuum Vent Check

1. Disconnect the air supply line at the valve outlet.
2. Disconnect the vacuum line at the vacuum nipple.
3. With the engine at 1,500 rpm, air should be heard and felt at the valve outlet.
4. Connect a direct vacuum line that is free from restrictions from any manifold vacuum source to the vacuum nipple on the air bypass

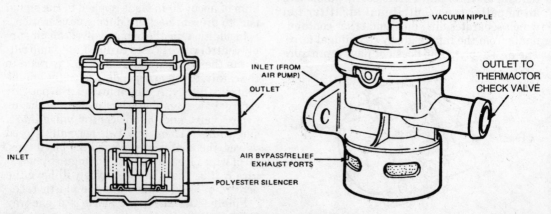

Normally closed air bypass valve

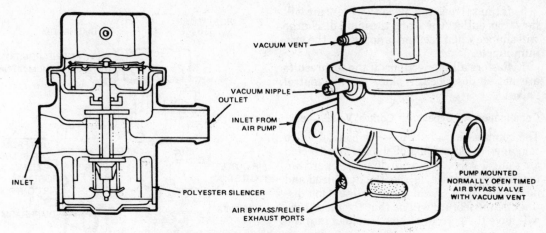

Normally open air bypass valve with vacuum vents

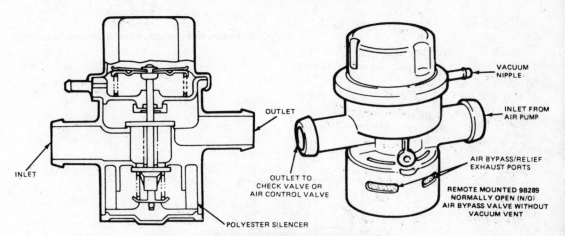

Normally open air bypass valve without vacuum vents

valve. Air at the outlet should be momentarily decreased or shut off.

5. Air pump supply air should be heard or felt at the silencer ports during the momentary dump. Restore all original connections. If any of the above tests are not as described, check the air pump. If the air pump is operating properly, replace the bypass valve.

Air Supply Control Valve Check

1. Verify that air flow is being supplied to the valve inlet by disconnecting the air supply hose at the inlet and verifying the presence of air flow with the engine at 1,500 rpm. Reconnect the air supply hose to the valve inlet.

2. Disconnect the air supply hoses at outlets A and B.

3. Remove the vacuum line at the vacuum nipple.

4. Accelerate the engine speed to 1,500 rpm. Air flow should be heard and felt at outlet B with little or no air flow at outlet A.

5. With the engine at 1,500 rpm, connect a

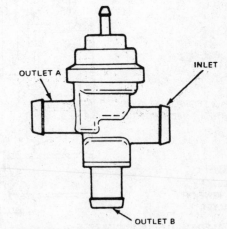

Air supply control valve

direct vacuum line from any manifold vacuum fitting to the air control valve vacuum nipple. Air flow should be heard and felt at outlet A with little or no air flow at outlet B.

6. If the valve is the bleed type, less air will flow from outlet A or B and the main discharge will change when vacuum is applied to the vacuum nipple.

7. Restore all connections. If the test results are not as described, replace the air control valve.

Combination Air Bypass/Air Control Valve Check

The combination air bypass/air control valve combines the functions of the air bypass and air control valve into a single unit. There are two normally closed valves; the non-bleed and bleed type, both of which look alike. One distinguishing feature will be that the bleed type will have the percent of bleed molded into the plastic case.

1. Disconnect the hoses from outlets A and B.

2. Disconnect and plug the vacuum line to port D.

3. With the engine operating at 1,500 rpm, air flow should be noted coming out of the bypass vents.

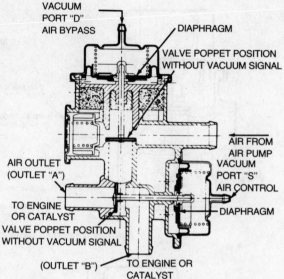

Combination air bypass/air control valve without bleed

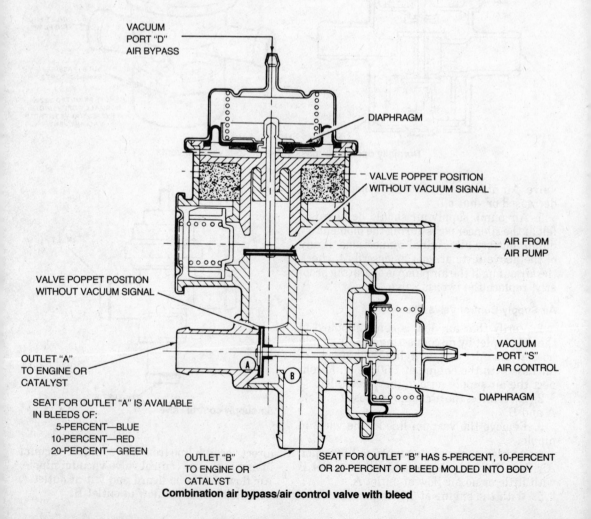

Combination air bypass/air control valve with bleed

4. Reconnect the vacuum line to port D and disconnect and plug the vacuum line to port S. Make sure vacuum is present in the line to vacuum port D.

5. With the engine operating at 1,500 rpm, air flow should be noted coming out of outlet B and no air flow should be coming from outlet A.

6. With the engine at 1,500 rpm, apply 8–10 in.Hg of vacuum to port S. Air should now flow from outlet A.

7. If the valve is the bleed type, some lesser amount of air will flow from outlet A or B and the main discharge will change when vacuum is applied to port S.

NOTE: *If there is a small air tap attached to the inlet tube from the air pump, air flow should be present during engine operation.*

Air Check Valve/Pulse Air Valve Test

1. Inspect all hoses, tubes and the air valve for leaks.

2. Disconnect the hose on the inlet side if the air valve and attempt to blow through the valve. Air should pass freely.

3. Repeat the test, only this time attempt to suck air through the valve. No air should pass.

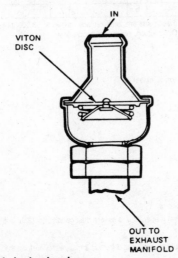

Typical air check valve

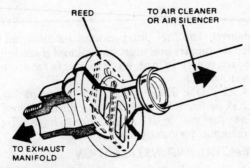

Typical pulse air valve

4. If any other results are obtained, replace the check valve.

Emission Maintenance Warning Light

The emission maintenance warning light system consists of an instrument panel mounted amber lens (with EGR or EMISS printed on it) that is electrically connected to a sensor module located under the instrument panel. The purpose of the system is to alert the driver that emission system maintenance is required. Specific maintenance requirements are listed in the Emission System Scheduled Maintenance Chart.

The system actually measures accumulated vehicle ignition key on-time and is designed to continuously close an electrical circuit to the amber lens after 2000 hours of vehicle operation. Assuming an average vehicle speed of 30 mph, the 2000 hours equates to approximately 60,000 miles of vehicle operation. Actual vehicle mileage intervals will vary considerably as individual driving habits vary.

Every time the ignition is switched on, the warning light will glow for 2–5 seconds as a bulb check and to verify that the system is operating properly. When approximately 60,000 miles is reached, the warning light will remain on continuously to indicate that service is required. After the required maintenance is performed, the sensor must be reset for another 60,000 mile period. The sensor is located under the dashboard, on a bracket below the EEC-IV computer.

EMISSION WARNING LIGHT RESET PROCEDURE

1. Make sure the ignition key is off.

2. Locate the sensor under the dashboard, on a bracket below the EEC-IV computer, and lightly push a phillips screwdriver through the 0.2" (5mm) diameter hole with the sticker labeled "RESET" and lightly press down and hold.

3. While lightly holding the screwdriver down, turn the ignition switch to the RUN position. The emission warning light will then light and should remain on for as long as the screwdriver is held down. Hold the screwdriver down for approximately five seconds.

4. Remove the screwdriver. The lamp should go out within 2–5 seconds, indicating that a reset has occurred. If the light remains on, begin again at Step 1. If the light goes out, turn the ignition off and go to the next step.

5. Turn the ignition to the RUN position. The warning light should illuminate for 2–5 seconds and then go out. This verifies that a

2.3L EFI, 3.0L EFI and 2.8L Engines Emission System Scheduled Maintenance

All items designated with a B code are required to be performed in all states and Canada. (B) coded items are required for Canada and all states except California, and recommended only for California: b coded items are required in all states except California, and recommended only for California and Canada vehicles: (B) coded items are recommended for all vehicles. However, Ford recommends that you perform maintenance on all designated items to achieve best vehicle operation.

NORMAL DRIVING SERVICE INTERVALS Perform at the months or distances shown, whichever comes first.																
MILES (Thousands)	7.5	15	22.5	30	37.5	45	52.5	60	67.5	75	82.5	90	97.5	105	112.5	120
MAINTENANCE OPERATION KILOMETERS (Thousands)	12	24	36	48	60	72	84	96	108	120	132	144	156	168	181	193
Emission Control Systems																
Change engine oil — every 12 months OR	B	B	B	B	B	B	b	b	b	b	b	b	b	b	b	b
Change engine oil filter — every 12 months OR	B	B	B	B	B	B	b	b	b	b	b	b	b	b	b	b
Replace spark plugs				B				b				b				b
Replace engine coolant — every 36 months OR				B				b				b				b
Check engine coolant condition & protection, hoses and clamps annually — prior to cold weather							ANNUALLY									
Inspect drive belt condition and tension				B				b				b				b
Replace air cleaner filter				B				b				b				b
Replace crankcase emission filter — if equipped				B				b				b				b
Inspect and clean injector tips — (2.3L EFI)								(b)								b
Replace PCV valves								b								b
Replace ignition wires								b								b
Check thermactor hoses and clamps								b								b
Clean choke linkages and external controls and inspect function of carburetor "hang on" devices — (2.8L only)				B				b				b				b
Replace EGR valve assembly (including EVP sensor on electronic EGR valve)*								b								b
Replace EGR vacuum solenoid(s) and filter (2.3L and 2.8L)								b								b
Replace EGO/HEGO sensor*								b								b
Check engine valve clearance (2.8L)	B			B				b				b				b

*This vehicle may be equipped with an Emissions Maintenance Warning Light. If so equipped, these parts are to be replaced either at 60,000 miles or when the Emissions Maintenance Warning Light remains on continuously with the key in the "On" position, whichever occurs first.

NOTES:
Unique Driving Conditions
If your driving habits **FREQUENTLY** include:
- Operating when outside temperatures remain **below freezing** and most trips are less than 8 km (5 miles).
- Operating during **HOT WEATHER** (above +90°F or +32°C) and
  — Driving continuously in excess of normal highway speeds;
  — Driving in stop-and-go "rush hour" traffic.
- Towing a trailer, using a camper or car-top carrier, or carrying maximum loads.
- Operating in severe dust conditions.
- Extensive idling, such as police, taxi or door-to-door delivery use.
- High speed operation with a fully loaded vehicle.

Change ENGINE OIL and OIL FILTER every 3 months or 4 800 km (3,000 miles) whichever occurs first.
Check/Regap SPARK PLUGS every 9 600 km (6,000 miles).
AIR CLEANER and CRANKCASE EMISSION AIR FILTERS — If operating in severe dust conditions.
Replace EGR SOLENOID FILTER(S) at 48 000 km (30,000 miles) and 144 000 km (90,000 miles) if operating in severe dust conditions. (2.3L and 2.8L)

Extreme Service Items
If vehicle is operated off-highway, perform the following items every 1 600 km (1,000 miles). If vehicle is operated in mud and/or water perform the following items daily:
- Inspect disc brake system.
- Inspect front wheel bearings and lubrication.
- Inspect exhaust system for leaks, damage or loose parts.

proper reset of the module has been accomplished. If the light remains on, repeat the reset procedure.

CARBURETED FUEL SYSTEM

Mechanical Fuel Pump

The fuel pump is bolted to the lower left side of the cylinder block. It is mechanically operated by an eccentric on the camshaft driving a pushrod. The fuel pump cannot be disassembled for repairs and must be replaced if testing indicates it is not within performance specifications.

CAUTION: *Take precautions to avoid the risk of fire whenever working on or around any fuel system. It's a good idea to have a fire extinguisher handy. Do not smoke.*

REMOVAL AND INSTALLATION

1. Loosen the fuel line nut at the pump outlet, using a clean rag to catch any fuel spray

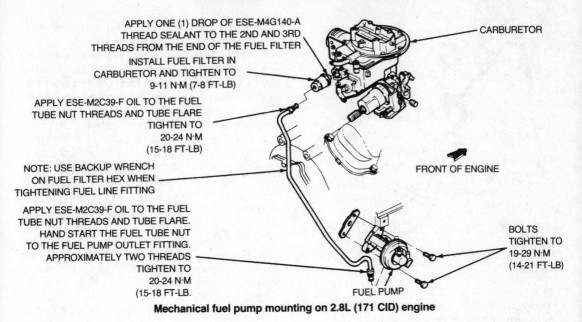

APPLY ONE (1) DROP OF ESE-M4G140-A
THREAD SEALANT TO THE 2ND AND 3RD
THREADS FROM THE END OF THE FUEL FILTER

INSTALL FUEL FILTER IN
CARBURETOR AND TIGHTEN TO
9-11 N·M (7-8 FT-LB)

APPLY ESE-M2C39-F OIL TO THE FUEL
TUBE NUT THREADS AND TUBE FLARE
TIGHTEN TO
20-24 N·M
(15-18 FT-LB)

NOTE: USE BACKUP WRENCH
ON FUEL FILTER HEX WHEN
TIGHTENING FUEL LINE FITTING

APPLY ESE-M2C39-F OIL TO THE FUEL
TUBE NUT THREADS AND TUBE FLARE.
HAND START THE FUEL TUBE NUT
TO THE FUEL PUMP OUTLET FITTING.
APPROXIMATELY TWO THREADS
TIGHTEN TO
20-24 N·M
(15-18 FT-LB.

CARBURETOR

FRONT OF ENGINE

BOLTS
TIGHTEN TO
19-29 N·M
(14-21 FT-LB)

FUEL PUMP

Mechanical fuel pump mounting on 2.8L (171 CID) engine

that will come out when the line is loosened.

2. Loosen the fuel pump mounting bolts approximately two turns. Apply force with your hand to loosen the fuel pump if the gasket is stuck. If excessive tension is on the pump, rotate the engine until the fuel pump cam lobe is near its low position.

3. Disconnect the fuel pump inlet and outlet lines.

4. Remove the fuel pump attaching bolts and remove the pump and gasket. Discard the old gasket.

5. Remove all fuel pump gasket material from the engine and fuel pump mating surfaces.

6. Install the attaching bolts into the fuel pump and install a new gasket on the bolts. Position the fuel pump to the pushrod and the mounting pad. Turn the attaching bolts alternately and evenly and tighten them to 14–21 ft.lb. (19–29 Nm).

7. Install the fuel outlet and inlet line and tighten the outlet fitting to specifications. If any rubber hoses are cracked, hardened or frayed, replace them with new fuel hose.

8. Start the engine and observe all connections for fuel leaks for two minutes. Stop the engine and check all fuel pump fuel line connections for fuel leaks by running a finger under the connections. Check for oil leaks at the fuel pump mounting pad.

DIAGNOSIS AND TESTING

If a problem exists with the fuel pump itself, it normally will deliver either no fuel at all, or not enough to sustain high engine speeds or loads. When an engine has a lean (fuel starva-

tion) condition, the fuel pump is often suspected as being the source of the problem, however similar symptoms will be present if the fuel filter is clogged or the fuel tank is plugged or restricted. It could also be a carburetor problem, kinked or plugged fuel line or a leaking fuel hose. If the fuel pump is noisy, check for:

1. Loose fuel pump mounting bolts. Tighten to specifications if loose and replace the gasket if damaged or worn.

2. Check for loose or missing fuel line attaching clips. This condition will result in the noise being more audible when sitting inside the vehicle than standing along side it. Tighten the fuel lines or clips, if necessary.

Before removing a suspect fuel pump:

1. Make sure there is fuel in the tank.

2. Replace the fuel filter to eliminate that possibility.

3. Check all rubber hoses from the fuel pump to the fuel tank for kinks or cracks. With the engine idling, inspect all fuel hoses and lines for leaks in the lines or connections. Tighten loose connections and replace kinked, cracked or leaking lines and/or hoses.

4. Check the fuel pump outlet connection for leaks and tighten to specification if required.

5. Inspect the fuel pump diaphragm crimp (the area where the stamped steel section is attached to the casting) and the breather hole(s) in the casting for evidence of fuel or oil leakage. Replace the fuel pump if leaking.

Capacity (Volume) Test

1. Remove the carburetor air cleaner.

2. Slowly disconnect the fuel line at the fuel filter, using a backup wrench on the filter hex

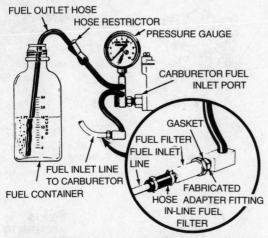

Fuel pump capacity (volume) test on 2.8L (171 CID) engine

to prevent damage. Use clean rags to catch any fuel spray. Exercise caution as the fuel line is pressurized and take precautions to avoid the risk of fire.

3. Place a suitable non-breakable container (1 pint minimum capacity) at the end of the disconnected fuel line. A small piece of hose may be necessary on the fuel line end.

4. With the high tension wire removed from the coil, crank the engine ten revolutions to fill the fuel lines, then crank the engine for 10 seconds and measure the fuel collected. The pump should deliver ⅓ pint (0.158 liters) of fuel, minimum.

5. If the fuel flow is within specifications, perform the Pressure Test.

6. If the fuel flow is low, repeat the test using a remote vented can of gasoline. Remove the fuel pump inlet hose, then connect a length of fuel hose to the pump inlet and insert the other end into the remote gasoline can. If the fuel flow is now within specifications, the problem is a plugged in-tank filter or a leaking, kinked or plugged fuel line or hose. Make sure the fuel pump pushrod length is 6.10–6.14 in. (155–156mm); if short, replace the pushrod and install the fuel pump. If the fuel flow is still low, replace the fuel pump.

Pressure Test

1. Connect a 0–15 psi fuel pump pressure tester (Rotunda No. 059-00008 or equivalent) to the carburetor end of the fuel line. No T-fitting is required.

2. Start the engine. It should be able to run for about 30 seconds on the fuel in the carburetor. Read the pressure on the gauge after about 10 seconds. It should be 4–6.5 psi (31–45 kPa).

3. If the pump pressure is too low or high, replace the fuel pump and retest.

4. Once all testing is complete, reconnect the fuel lines and remove the gauge.

Carburetor

The Motorcraft Model 2150A 2-bbl feedback carburetor is used on the 2.8L (171 CID) engine. The feedback carburetor system uses a

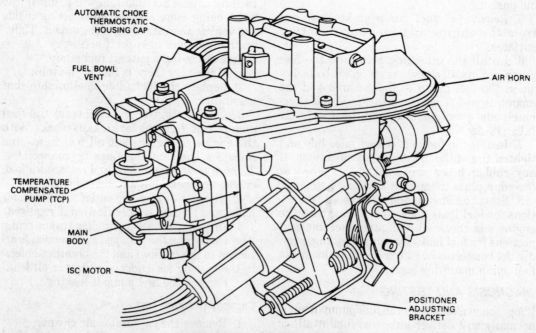

Left front view of 2150A carburetor

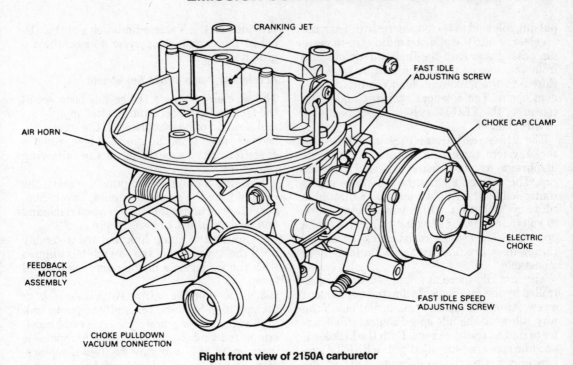

Right front view of 2150A carburetor

CRANKING JET

FAST IDLE
ADJUSTING SCREW

CHOKE CAP CLAMP

AIR HORN

ELECTRIC
CHOKE

FEEDBACK
MOTOR
ASSEMBLY

FAST IDLE SPEED
ADJUSTING SCREW

CHOKE PULLDOWN
VACUUM CONNECTION

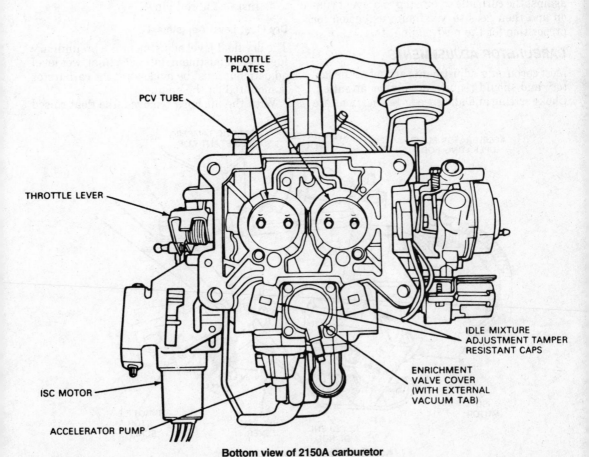

Bottom view of 2150A carburetor

THROTTLE
PLATES

PCV TUBE

THROTTLE LEVER

IDLE MIXTURE
ADJUSTMENT TAMPER
RESISTANT CAPS

ISC MOTOR

ENRICHMENT
VALVE COVER
(WITH EXTERNAL
VACUUM TAB)

ACCELERATOR PUMP

pulsing solenoid to introduce fresh air from the air cleaner into the idle and main system vacuum passages to lean the fuel and air mixture from the maximum rich condition (solenoid closed) to the maximum lean condition (solenoid open). The solenoid operates under the control of the EEC-IV system, described later in this chapter.

The 2150A carburetor uses an all electric choke system, consisting of the choke pulldown diaphragm, choke housing and electric choke cap. The voltage applied to the choke cap is controlled by the EEC-IV computer through a "duty cycle" output, which varies between 0% (0 volts) and 100% (12 volts) to control choke operation. The tamper resistant choke cap retainer uses breakaway screws and is non-adjustable.

The fast idle speed at engine startup is controlled by the mechanical cam and adjustment screw. After startup, the cam moves out of the way, allowing the idle speed control (ISC) motor to control the idle speed. Both the kickdown and idle rpm are controlled by the EEC-IV system, eliminating the need for idle and fast idle speed adjustments. When the ignition is turned off (warm engine), the throttle rests against the curb idle screw stop to prevent run-on and then goes to maximum extension for preposition for the next engine start.

CARBURETOR ADJUSTMENTS

Most carburetor adjustments are set at the factory and should require no further attention. Choke setting and idle speed specifications are provided on the Vehicle Emission Control Decal in the engine compartment or on the engine itself.

Accelerator Pump Stroke Adjustment

The accelerator pump stroke has been set at the factory for a particular engine application and should not be readjusted. If the stroke has been changed from the specified hole, reset to specifications by performing the following procedure:

1. Using a blunt tipped punch, remove the roll pin from the accelerator pump cover. Support the area under the roll pin when removing and be careful not to lose the pin.

2. Rotate the pump link and rod assembly until the keyed end of the assembly is aligned with the keyed hole in the pump over travel lever.

3. Reposition the rod and swivel assembly in the specified hole and reinstall the pump link in the accelerator pump cover. A service accelerator rod and swivel assembly is available (part no. 9F687) and must be used if replacement is necessary. Adjustment holes are not provided on the temperature compensated accelerator pump carburetor models.

4. Install the roll pin.

Dry Float Level Adjustment

The dry float level adjustment is a preliminary fuel level adjustment only. The final, wet level adjustment must be made after the carburetor is mounted on the engine.

With the air horn removed, the float raised

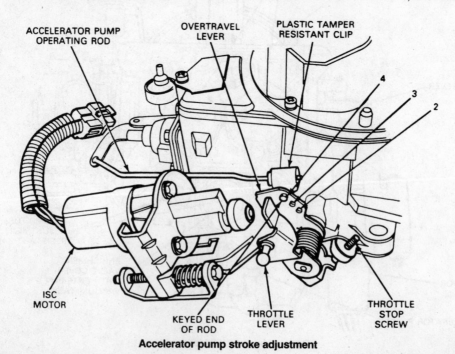

Accelerator pump stroke adjustment

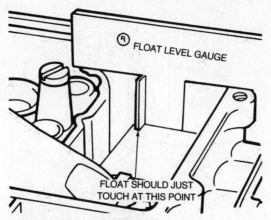

Dry float level adjustment

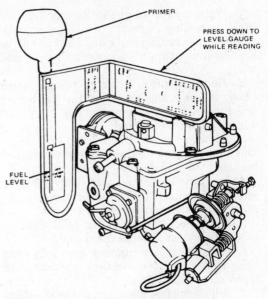

Wet fuel level adjustment gauge installed

and the fuel inlet needle seated, check the distance between the top surface of the main body (gasket removed) and the top surface of the float for conformance to specifications. Depress the float tab lightly to seat the fuel inlet needle.

CAUTION: *Excessive pressure can damage the viton tip on the needle.*

Take the measurement near the center of the float at a point ⅛″ (3.2mm) from the free end of the float. If a cardboard float gauge is used, place the gauge in the corner of the enlarged end section of the fuel bowl. The gauge should touch the float near the end, but not on the end radius. If necessary, bend the tab on the float to bring the setting within the specified limits. This should provide the proper preliminary fuel level setting.

Wet Float Level Adjustment

1. With the vehicle level, engine warm and running, remove the air cleaner.

2. Insert fuel float level gauge T83L-9550-A, or equivalent, with the pointed end into the fuel bowl vent stack and rest the level across the other vent.

3. Siphon fuel into the sight tube and allow the fuel to reach a steady level. Take precautions to avoid the risk of fire. Do not smoke during this procedure.

4. Press down to level the gauge and read the fuel level on the sight tube. If the level is in the specified band, adjustment is not necessary. If the level is not correct, note the level on the sight and proceed to the next step.

5. Stop the engine and remove the choke link, air horn attaching screws, the vent hose and the air horn assembly.

6. Measure the vertical distance from the top of the machined surface of the main body to the level of the fuel in the fuel bowl.

7. With this measurement as a reference,

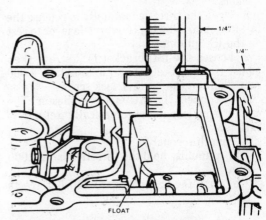

Measuring the fuel level in the fuel bowl

bend the float tab up to raise the level or down to lower the level. Adjust to bring the fuel level to specifications.

8. Recheck the fuel level on the sight gauge. If OK, install the remaining air horn screws. If not OK, repeat the adjustment procedure.

9. Install the choke link and check the choke plate to make sure its free.

10. Tighten the air horn screws. Install the carburetor vent (canister) hose, then check and adjust the curb idle speed. Install the air cleaner,

Idle Speed Adjustment

NOTE: *If the curb idle rpm is not within specifications after performing this procedure, it will be necessary to have the EEC-IV system diagnosed by a qualified service facility with the necessary electronic equipment.*

1. Warm up the engine in Park or Neutral until it reaches normal operating temperature. Set the parking brake and block the drive wheels. Make sure all accessories are turned off.

2. Remove the air charge temperature (ACT) sensor and adapter from the air cleaner tray by removing the retaining clip. Leave the wiring harness connected.

3. Remove the air cleaner and disconnect and plug the vacuum line at the cold weather duct and valve motor.

4. Turn the engine off and verify that the idle speed control (ISC) plunger moves to its maximum extension within 10 seconds.

5. Disconnect and plug the EGR vacuum hose. Disconnect the idle speed control.

6. With the engine running, manually open the throttle and set the fast idle adjusting screw on the high cam.

7. Adjust the fast idle speed to the specification given on the underhood emission control sticker.

8. Open the throttle manually to release the fast idle cam, allowing the throttle lever to rest on the ISC plunger.

9. Loosen the ISC bracket lock screw, then adjust the ISC bracket screw to obtain 2,000 rpm. Tighten the bracket lock screw.

10. Reconnect the ISC motor connector. The engine rpm should automatically return to curb idle.

11. Simultaneously:
    a. manually hold the throttle above 1,000 rpm
    b. push the ISC plunger until it retracts fully

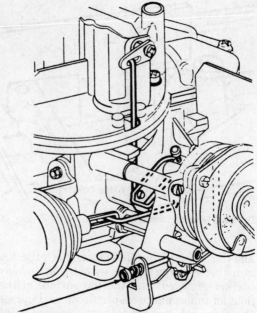

FAST IDLE RPM ADJUSTING SCREW
(SHOWN ON HIGH CAM/FAST IDLE STEP)

Fast idle adjustment on 2150A carburetor

    c. after plunger retracts, release the throttle and quickly unplug the connection.

12. Adjust the anti-dieseling speed throttle stop screw to 750 rpm with the transmission (automatic or manual) in Neutral. Be careful to adjust the anti-dieseling stop screw, NOT the curb idle stop screw.

13. Connect the ISC and EGR vacuum hoses.

14. Turn the engine off, then restart the engine and verify that curb idle speed is within specifications.

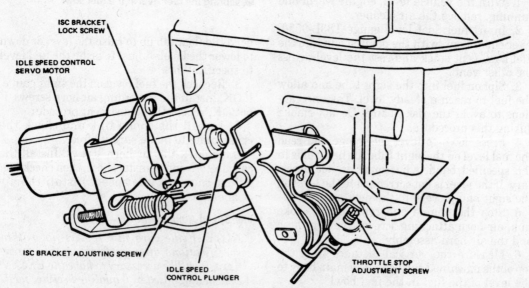

ISC BRACKET
LOCK SCREW

IDLE SPEED CONTROL
SERVO MOTOR

ISC BRACKET ADJUSTING SCREW

IDLE SPEED
CONTROL PLUNGER

THROTTLE STOP
ADJUSTMENT SCREW

Idle speed control adjustment on 2150A carburetor

Mixture Adjustment

The fuel mixture is preset at the factory and computer controlled thereafter. No adjustments are possible without the use of propane enrichment equipment that is not readily available to the do-it-yourself market. All mixture adjustments should be performed at a qualified service facility to insure compliance with Federal and/or State Emission Control Standards.

CARBURETOR REMOVAL AND INSTALLATION

1. Remove the air cleaner.
2. Remove the throttle cable from the throt-

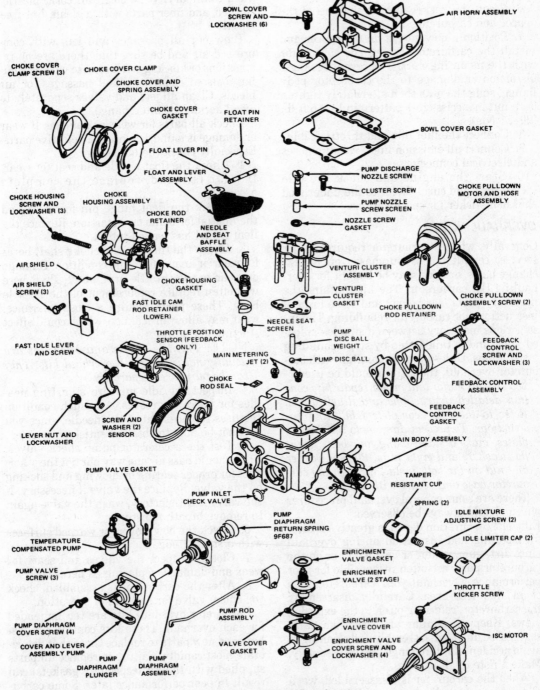

Exploded view of 2150A carburetor

tle lever. Tag and disconnect all vacuum lines, emission hoses and electrical connections.

3. Disconnect the fuel line at the carburetor. Use a clean rag to catch any fuel spray and use a backup wrench on the fuel filter hex to avoid twisting the line.

4. Remove the carburetor retaining nuts, then lift off the carburetor.

5. Remove the carburetor mounting gasket spacer, if equipped.

6. Clean the gasket mating surfaces of the spacer and carburetor.

7. Position a new gasket on the spacer and install the carburetor. Secure the carburetor with the mounting nuts. To prevent leakage, distortion or damage to the carburetor body flange, snug the nuts then alternately tighten each nut in a criss-cross pattern to 14–16 ft.lb. (20–21 Nm).

8. Connect the fuel line and throttle cable.

9. Connect all emission lines, vacuum hoses and electrical connectors.

10. Start the engine and check the idle speeds (fast and curb). Refer to the underhood emission sticker for specifications.

OVERHAUL NOTES

Generally, when a carburetor requires major service, rebuilt one is purchased on an exchange basis, or a kit may be bought for overhauling the carburetor. The kit contains the necessary parts (see below) and some form of instructions for carburetor rebuilding. The instructions may vary between a simple exploded view and detailed step-by-step rebuilding instructions. Unless you are familiar with carburetor overhaul, the latter should be used.

NOTE: *All major and minor repair kits contain detailed instructions and illustrations. Refer to them for complete rebuilding instructions. To prevent damage to the throttle plates, make a stand using four bolts, eight flat washers and eight nuts. Place a washer and nut on the bolt, install through the carburetor base and secure with a nut.*

There are some general overhaul procedures which should always be observed:

Efficient carburetion depends greatly on careful cleaning and inspection during overhaul since dirt, gum, water, or varnish in or on the carburetor parts are often responsible for poor performance. Overhaul your carburetor in a clean, dust-free area. Carefully disassembly the carburetor, referring often to the exploded views. Keep all similar and lookalike parts segregated during disassembly and cleaning to avoid accidental interchange during assembly. Make a note of all jet sizes.

When the carburetor is disassembled, wash all parts (except diaphragms, electric choke units. pump plunger, and any other plastic, leather, fiber, or rubber parts) in clean carburetor solvent. Do not leave parts in the solvent any longer than is necessary to sufficiently loosen the deposits. Excessive cleaning may remove the special finish from the float bowl and choke valve bodies, leaving these parts unfit for service. Rinse all parts in clean solvent and blow them dry with compressed air or allow them to air dry. Wipe clean all cork, plastic, leather, and fiber parts with a clean, lint free cloth.

Blow out all passages and jets with compressed air and be sure that there are no restrictions or blockages. Never use wire or similar tools to clean jets, fuel passages, or air bleeds. Clean all jets and valves separately to avoid accidental interchange.

Check all parts for wear or damage. If wear or damage is found, replace the defective parts. Especially check the following:

1. Check the float needle and seat for wear. If wear is found, replace the complete assembly.

2. Check the float hinge pin for wear and the float(s) for dents or distortion. Replace the float if fuel has leaked into it.

3. Check the throttle and choke shaft bores for wear or an out-of-round condition. Damage or wear to the throttle arm, shaft, shaft bore will often require replacement of the throttle body. These parts require a close tolerance; wear may allow air leakage, which could affect starting and idling.

NOTE: *Throttle shafts and bushings are usually not included in overhaul kits. They can be purchased separately.*

4. Inspect the idle mixture adjusting needles for burrs or grooves. Any such condition requires replacement of the needle, since you will not be able to obtain a satisfactory idle.

5. Test the accelerator pump check valves. They should pass air one way but not the other. Test for proper seating by blowing and sucking on the valve. Replace the valve if necessary. If the valve is satisfactory, wash the valve again to remove breath moisture.

6. Check the bowl cover for warped surfaces with a straightedge.

7. Closely inspect the valves and seats for wear and damage, replacing as necessary.

8. After the carburetor is assembled, check the choke valve for freedom of operation.

Carburetor overhaul kits are recommended for each overhaul. These kits contain all gaskets and new parts to replace those that deteriorate most rapidly. Failure to replace all parts supplied with the kit (especially gaskets) can result in poor performance later. Some carburetor manufacturers supply overhaul kits of three basic types: minor repair; major repair; and gasket kits. Basically, they contain the following:

Minor Repair Kits:
- All gaskets
- Float needle valve
- Volume control screw
- All diaphragms
- Spring for the pump diaphragm

Major Repair Kits:
- All jets and gaskets
- All diaphragms
- Float needle valve
- Volume control screw
- Pump ball valve
- Main jet carrier
- Float
- Other necessary items
- Some cover holddown screws and washers

Gasket Kits:
- All gaskets

After cleaning and checking all components, reassemble the carburetor, using new parts and referring to the exploded view. When reassembling, make sure that all screw and jets are tight in their seats, buy do not overtighten, as the tips will be distorted. Tighten all screws gradually, in rotation. Do not tighten needle valves into their seat; uneven jetting will result. Always use new gaskets. Be sure to adjust the float level when reassembling.

FUEL INJECTION SYSTEM

The electronic fuel injection (EFI) system used on the 2.3L and 3.0L engines is classified as a multi-point, pulse time, speed density fuel delivery system which meters fuel into the intake air stream in accordance with engine demand through four or six injectors mounted on a tuned intake manifold.

An on-board electronic engine control (EEC-IV) computer accepts inputs from various engine sensors to compute the required fuel flow rate necessary to maintain a prescribed air/fuel ratio throughout the entire engine operational range. The computer then outputs a command to the fuel injectors to meter the required quantity of fuel. The EEC-IV engine control system also determines and compensates for the age of the vehicle and its uniqueness. The system will automatically sense and compensate for changes in altitude, such as driving up and down a mountain road.

The fuel injection system uses a high pressure, chassis or tank mounted electric fuel pump to deliver fuel from the tank to the fuel charging manifold assembly. The fuel charging manifold assembly incorporates electrical-ly actuated fuel injectors directly above each of the engine's intake ports. The injectors, when energized, spray a metered quantity of fuel into the intake air stream. A constant pressure drop is maintained across the injector nozzles by a pressure regulator, connected in series with the fuel injectors and positioned downstream from them. Excess fuel supplied by the pump, but not required by the engine, passes through the regulator and returns to the fuel tank through a fuel return line.

On four cylinder engines, all injectors are energized simultaneously, once every crankshaft revolution. On V6 engines, the injectors are energized in two groups of three injectors, with each group activated once every other crankshaft revolution. The period of time that the injectors are energized (injector "on time" or "pulse width") is controlled by the EEC-IV computer. The input from various sensors is used to compute the required fuel flow rate necessary to maintain a prescribed air/fuel ratio.

NOTE: *This book contains simple testing and service procedures for the Aerostar fuel injection system. More comprehensive testing and diagnosis procedures may be found in CHILTON'S GUIDE TO FUEL INJECTION AND FEEDBACK CARBURETORS, book part number 7488, available at your local retailer.*

CAUTION: *Fuel supply lines on vehicles with fuel injection will remain pressurized for long periods of time after engine shutdown. This fuel pressure must be relieved before any service procedures are attempted on the fuel system.*

RELIEVING FUEL SYSTEM PRESSURE

All fuel injected engines are equipped with a pressure relief valve located on the fuel supply manifold. Remove the fuel tank cap and attach fuel pressure gauge T80L-9974-A, or equivalent, to the valve to release the fuel pressure. If a suitable pressure gauge is not available, disconnect the vacuum hose from the fuel pressure regulator and attach a hand vacuum pump. Apply about 25 in.Hg (84 kPa) of vacuum to the regulator to vent the fuel system pressure into the fuel tank through the fuel return hose. Note that this procedure will remove the fuel pressure from the lines, but not the fuel. Take precautions to avoid the risk of fire and use clean rags to soak up any spilled fuel when the lines are disconnected.

Quick Connect Fuel Line Fittings
REMOVAL AND INSTALLATION

NOTE: *Quick Connect (push) type fuel line fittings must be disconnected using proper* procedures or the fitting may be damaged. Two types of retainers are used on the push connect fittings. Line sizes of ⅜" and ⁵⁄₁₆" use a "hairpin" clip retainer. ¼" line connectors use a "duck bill" clip retainer. In addition, some engines use spring lock connections secured by a garter spring which requires a special tool (T81P-19623-G) for removal.

Hairpin Clip

1. Clean all dirt and/or grease from the fitting. Spread the two clip legs about ⅛" (3mm) each to disengage from the fitting and pull the clip outward from the fitting. Use finger pressure only, do not use any tools.

2. Grasp the fitting and hose assembly and pull away from the steel line. Twist the fitting and hose assembly slightly while pulling, if necessary, when a sticking condition exists.

3. Inspect the hairpin clip for damage, replace the clip if necessary. Reinstall the clip in position on the fitting.

4. Inspect the fitting and inside of the connector to insure freedom of dirt or obstruction. Install fitting into the connector and push to-gether. A click will be heard when the hairpin snaps into proper connection. Pull on the line to insure full engagement.

Duck Bill Clip

1. A special tool is available from Ford for removing the retaining clips (Ford Tool No. T82L-9500-AH). If the tool is not on hand see Step 2. Align the slot on the push connector disconnect tool with either tab on the retaining clip. Pull the line from the connector.

2. If the special clip tool is not available, use a pair of narrow 6" (152mm) channel lock pliers with a jaw width of 0.2 in. (5mm) or less. Align the jaws of the pliers with the openings of the fitting case and compress the part of the retaining clip that engages the case. Compressing the retaining clip will release the fitting which may be pulled from the connector. Both sides of the clip must be compressed at the same time to disengage.

3. Inspect the retaining clip, fitting end and connector. Replace the clip if any damage is apparent.

4. Push the line into the steel connector un-

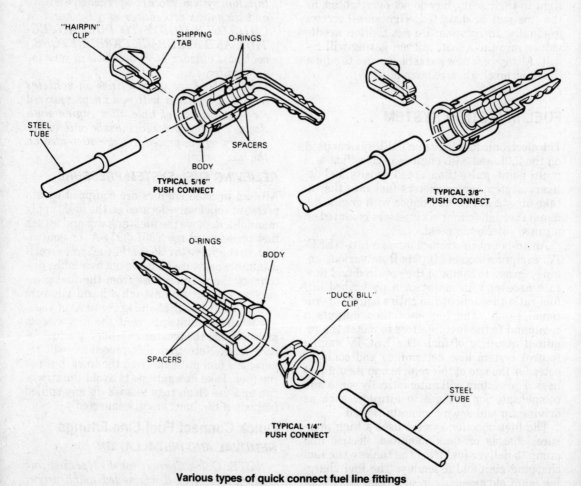

Various types of quick connect fuel line fittings

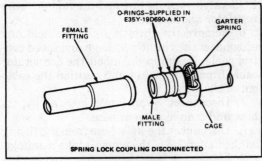

O-RINGS—SUPPLIED IN E35Y-19D690-A KIT

FEMALE FITTING

GARTER SPRING

MALE FITTING

CAGE

SPRING LOCK COUPLING DISCONNECTED

TO CONNECT COUPLING

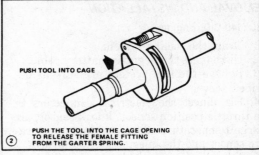

TO DISCONNECT COUPLING

CAUTION—DISCHARGE SYSTEM BEFORE DISCONNECTING COUPLING

NOTE:
EACH END OF TOOL T81P-19623-G IS A DIFFERENT SIZE TO FIT 3/8 AND 1/2 INCH COUPLINGS

TOOL
T81P-19623-G - 3/8 AND 1/2 INCH
T81P-19623-G1 - 3/8 INCH
T81P-19623-G2 - 1/2 INCH
T83P-19623-C - 5/8 INCH

CAGE

① FIT TOOL TO COUPLING SO THAT TOOL CAN ENTER CAGE TO RELEASE THE GARTER SPRING.

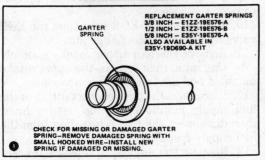

REPLACEMENT GARTER SPRINGS
3/8 INCH — E1ZZ-19E576-A
1/2 INCH — E1ZZ-19E576-B
5/8 INCH — E35Y-19E576-A
ALSO AVAILABLE IN
E35Y-19D690-A KIT

GARTER SPRING

① CHECK FOR MISSING OR DAMAGED GARTER SPRING—REMOVE DAMAGED SPRING WITH SMALL HOOKED WIRE—INSTALL NEW SPRING IF DAMAGED OR MISSING.

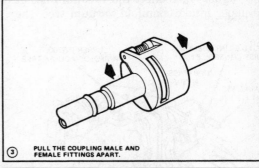

PUSH TOOL INTO CAGE

② PUSH THE TOOL INTO THE CAGE OPENING TO RELEASE THE FEMALE FITTING FROM THE GARTER SPRING.

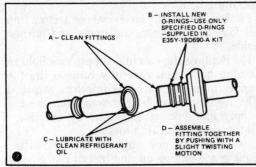

B – INSTALL NEW O-RINGS—USE ONLY SPECIFIED O-RINGS —SUPPLIED IN E35Y-19D690-A KIT

A – CLEAN FITTINGS

C – LUBRICATE WITH CLEAN REFRIGERANT OIL

D – ASSEMBLE FITTING TOGETHER BY PUSHING WITH A SLIGHT TWISTING MOTION

②

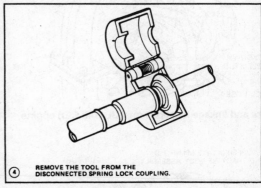

③ PULL THE COUPLING MALE AND FEMALE FITTINGS APART.

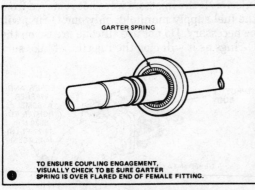

GARTER SPRING

③ TO ENSURE COUPLING ENGAGEMENT, VISUALLY CHECK TO BE SURE GARTER SPRING IS OVER FLARED END OF FEMALE FITTING.

④ REMOVE THE TOOL FROM THE DISCONNECTED SPRING LOCK COUPLING.

Spring lock coupling removal and installation procedure

til a click is heard, indicting the clip is in place. Pull on the line to check engagement.

Electric Fuel Pump
REMOVAL AND INSTALLATION

The electric fuel pump is either mounted on the chassis, in an assembly with the inline fuel filter, or at the base of the fuel tank sending unit in the fuel tank. For chassis mounted pumps, follow the procedures under "Fuel Filter Removal and Installation" in Chapter 1, then disconnect the electrical connector and remove the fuel pump and filter mounting bracket with the filter and pump attached. For tank mounted pumps, follow the procedures under "Fuel Tank Removal and Installation" at the end of this chapter and remove the sending unit and fuel pump from the top of the fuel tank once it is removed from the vehicle. In either case, the fuel pump is non-serviceable and must be replaced as a unit if defective. Do not attempt to apply battery voltage to the pump to check its operation while removed from the vehicle, as running the pump dry will destroy it. Depressurize the fuel system before attempting to remove any fuel lines.

Fuel Charging Assembly

REMOVAL AND INSTALLATION

2.3L (140 CID) Engine

1. Drain the cooling system.
2. Disconnect the negative battery cable.
3. Relieve the fuel system pressure as described above.
4. Disconnect the electrical connectors to the throttle position sensor, knock sensor, air charge temperature sensor, coolant temperature sensor and the injector wiring harness.
5. Tag and disconnect the vacuum lines at the upper intake manifold vacuum tree, the

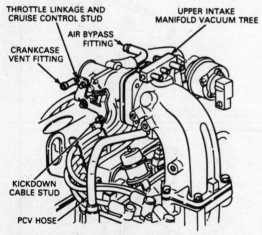

Hose and linkage locations on 2.3L (140 CID) engine

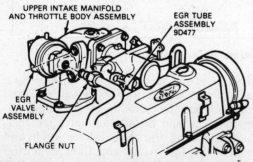

Disconnecting the EGR valve on 2.3L (140 CID) engine

EGR valve vacuum line and the fuel pressure regulator vacuum line.

6. Remove the throttle linkage shield and disconnect the throttle linkage and speed control cable, if equipped. Unbolt the accelerator cable from the bracket and position the cable out of the way.
7. Disconnect the air intake hose, air bypass hose and crankcase vent hose.
8. Disconnect the PCV hose from the fitting on the underside of the upper intake manifold.
9. Loosen the hose clamp on the coolant bypass line at the lower intake manifold and disconnect the hose.
10. Disconnect the EGR tube from the EGR valve by removing the flange nut.
11. Remove the four upper intake manifold retaining nuts, then remove the upper intake manifold and air throttle body assembly.
12. Disconnect the push connect fitting at the fuel supply manifold and fuel return lines, then disconnect the fuel return line from the fuel supply manifold.
13. Remove the engine oil dipstick bracket retaining bolt.
14. Disconnect the electrical connectors from all four fuel injectors and move the harness aside.
15. Remove the two fuel supply manifold retaining bolt, then carefully remove the fuel supply manifold with the injectors attached. The injectors may be removed from the fuel supply manifold at this time by exerting a slight twisting/pulling motion.
16. Lubricate new injector O-rings with a light grade engine oil and install two on each injector. If the injectors were not removed from the fuel supply manifold, only one O-ring will be necessary. Do not use silicone grease on the O-rings as it will clog the injectors. Make sure

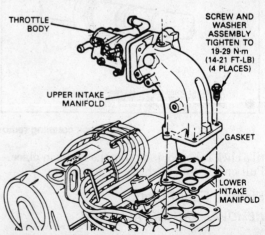

Removing upper intake manifold and throttle body on 2.3L (140 CID) engine

CHILTON'S
FUEL ECONOMY
& TUNE-UP TIPS

Tune-up • Spark Plug Diagnosis • Emission Controls

Fuel System • Cooling System • Tires and Wheels

General Maintenance

CHILTON'S FUEL ECONOMY & TUNE-UP TIPS

Fuel economy is important to everyone, no matter what kind of vehicle you drive. The maintenance-minded motorist can save both money and fuel using these tips and the periodic maintenance and tune-up procedures in this Repair and Tune-Up Guide.

There are more than 130,000,000 cars and trucks registered for private use in the United States. Each travels an average of 10-12,000 miles per year, and, and in total they consume close to 70 billion gallons of fuel each year. This represents nearly ⅔ of the oil imported by the United States each year. The Federal government's goal is to reduce consumption 10% by 1985. A variety of methods are either already in use or under serious consideration, and they all affect you driving and the cars you will drive. In addition to "down-sizing", the auto industry is using or investigating the use of electronic fuel delivery, electronic engine controls and alternative engines for use in smaller and lighter vehicles, among other alternatives to meet the federally mandated Corporate Average Fuel Economy (CAFE) of 27.5 mpg by 1985. The government, for its part, is considering rationing, mandatory driving curtailments and tax increases on motor vehicle fuel in an effort to reduce consumption. The government's goal of a 10% reduction could be realized — and further government regulation avoided — if every private vehicle could use just 1 less gallon of fuel per week.

How Much Can You Save?

Tests have proven that almost anyone can make at least a 10% reduction in fuel consumption through regular maintenance and tune-ups. When a major manufacturer of spark plugs sur-

TUNE-UP

1. Check the cylinder compression to be sure the engine will really benefit from a tune-up and that it is capable of producing good fuel economy. A tune-up will be wasted on an engine in poor mechanical condition.

2. Replace spark plugs regularly. New spark plugs alone can increase fuel economy 3%.

3. Be sure the spark plugs are the correct type (heat range) for your vehicle. See the Tune-Up Specifications.

Heat range refers to the spark plug's ability to conduct heat away from the firing end. It must conduct the heat away in an even pattern to avoid becoming a source of pre-ignition, yet it must also operate hot enough to burn off conductive deposits that could cause misfiring.

The heat range is usually indicated by a number on the spark plug, part of the manufacturer's designation for each individual spark plug. The numbers in bold-face indicate the heat range in each manufacturer's identification system.

Manufacturer	Typical Designation
AC	R **45** TS
Bosch (old)	WA **145** T30
Bosch (new)	HR **8** Y
Champion	RBL **15** Y
Fram/Autolite	4**15**
Mopar	P-**62** PR
Motorcraft	BRF-**42**
NGK	BP **5** ES-15
Nippondenso	W **16** EP
Prestolite	14GR **5** 2A

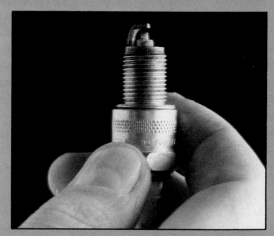

Periodically, check the spark plugs to be sure they are firing efficiently. They are excellent indicators of the internal condition of your engine.

On AC, Bosch (new), Champion, Fram/Autolite, Mopar, Motorcraft and Prestolite, a higher number indicates a hotter plug. On Bosch (old), NGK and Nippondenso, a higher number indicates a colder plug.

4. Make sure the spark plugs are properly gapped. See the Tune-Up Specifications in this book.

5. Be sure the spark plugs are firing efficiently. The illustrations on the next 2 pages show you how to "read" the firing end of the spark plug.

6. Check the ignition timing and set it to specifications. Tests show that almost all cars have incorrect ignition timing by more than 2°.

veyed over 6,000 cars nationwide, they found that a tune-up, on cars that needed one, increased fuel economy over 11%. Replacing worn plugs alone, accounted for a 3% increase. The same test also revealed that 8 out of every 10 vehicles will have some maintenance deficiency that will directly affect fuel economy, emissions or performance. Most of this mileage-robbing neglect could be prevented with regular maintenance.

Modern engines require that all of the functioning systems operate properly for maximum efficiency. A malfunction anywhere wastes fuel. You can keep your vehicle running as efficiently and economically as possible, by being aware of your vehicle's operating and performance characteristics. If your vehicle suddenly develops performance or fuel economy problems it could be due to one or more of the following:

PROBLEM	POSSIBLE CAUSE
Engine Idles Rough	Ignition timing, idle mixture, vacuum leak or something amiss in the emission control system.
Hesitates on Acceleration	Dirty carburetor or fuel filter, improper accelerator pump setting, ignition timing or fouled spark plugs.
Starts Hard or Fails to Start	Worn spark plugs, improperly set automatic choke, ice (or water) in fuel system.
Stalls Frequently	Automatic choke improperly adjusted and possible dirty air filter or fuel filter.
Performs Sluggishly	Worn spark plugs, dirty fuel or air filter, ignition timing or automatic choke out of adjustment.

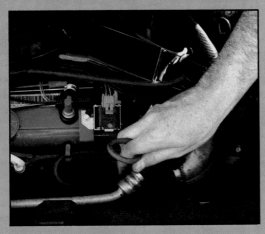

Check spark plug wires on conventional point type ignition for cracks by bending them in a loop around your finger.

Be sure that spark plug wires leading to adjacent cylinders do not run too close together. (Photo courtesy Champion Spark Plug Co.)

7. If your vehicle does not have electronic ignition, check the points, rotor and cap as specified.

8. Check the spark plug wires (used with conventional point-type ignitions) for cracks and burned or broken insulation by bending them in a loop around your finger. Cracked wires decrease fuel efficiency by failing to deliver full voltage to the spark plugs. One misfiring spark plug can cost you as much as 2 mpg.

9. Check the routing of the plug wires. Misfiring can be the result of spark plug leads to adjacent cylinders running parallel to each other and too close together. One wire tends to

pick up voltage from the other causing it to fire "out of time".

10. Check all electrical and ignition circuits for voltage drop and resistance.

11. Check the distributor mechanical and/or vacuum advance mechanisms for proper functioning. The vacuum advance can be checked by twisting the distributor plate in the opposite direction of rotation. It should spring back when released.

12. Check and adjust the valve clearance on engines with mechanical lifters. The clearance should be slightly loose rather than too tight.

SPARK PLUG DIAGNOSIS

Normal

APPEARANCE: This plug is typical of one operating normally. The insulator nose varies from a light tan to grayish color with slight electrode wear. The presence of slight deposits is normal on used plugs and will have no adverse effect on engine performance. The spark plug heat range is correct for the engine and the engine is running normally.

CAUSE: Properly running engine.

RECOMMENDATION: Before reinstalling this plug, the electrodes should be cleaned and filed square. Set the gap to specifications. If the plug has been in service for more than 10-12,000 miles, the entire set should probably be replaced with a fresh set of the same heat range.

Oil Deposits

APPEARANCE: The firing end of the plug is covered with a wet, oily coating.

CAUSE: The problem is poor oil control. On high mileage engines, oil is leaking past the rings or valve guides into the combustion chamber. A common cause is also a plugged PCV valve, and a ruptured fuel pump diaphragm can also cause this condition. Oil fouled plugs such as these are often found in new or recently overhauled engines, before normal oil control is achieved, and can be cleaned and reinstalled.

RECOMMENDATION: A hotter spark plug may temporarily relieve the problem, but the engine is probably in need of work.

Incorrect Heat Range

APPEARANCE: The effects of high temperature on a spark plug are indicated by clean white, often blistered insulator. This can also be accompanied by excessive wear of the electrode, and the absence of deposits.

CAUSE: Check for the correct spark plug heat range. A plug which is too hot for the engine can result in overheating. A car operated mostly at high speeds can require a colder plug. Also check ignition timing, cooling system level, fuel mixture and leaking intake manifold.

RECOMMENDATION: If all ignition and engine adjustments are known to be correct, and no other malfunction exists, install spark plugs one heat range colder.

Photos Courtesy Fram Corporation

Carbon Deposits

APPEARANCE: Carbon fouling is easily identified by the presence of dry, soft, black, sooty deposits.

CAUSE: Changing the heat range can often lead to carbon fouling, as can prolonged slow, stop-and-start driving. If the heat range is correct, carbon fouling can be attributed to a rich fuel mixture, sticking choke, clogged air cleaner, worn breaker points, retarded timing or low compression. If only one or two plugs are carbon fouled, check for corroded or cracked wires on the affected plugs. Also look for cracks in the distributor cap between the towers of affected cylinders.

RECOMMENDATION: After the problem is corrected, these plugs can be cleaned and reinstalled if not worn severely.

MMT Fouled

APPEARANCE: Spark plugs fouled by MMT (Methycyclopentadienyl Maganese Tricarbonyl) have reddish, rusty appearance on the insulator and side electrode.

CAUSE: MMT is an anti-knock additive in gasoline used to replace lead. During the combustion process, the MMT leaves a reddish deposit on the insulator and side electrode.

RECOMMENDATION: No engine malfunction is indicated and the deposits will not affect plug performance any more than lead deposits (see Ash Deposits). MMT fouled plugs can be cleaned, regapped and reinstalled.

High Speed Glazing

APPEARANCE: Glazing appears as shiny coating on the plug, either yellow or tan in color.

CAUSE: During hard, fast acceleration, plug temperatures rise suddenly. Deposits from normal combustion have no chance to fluff-off; instead, they melt on the insulator forming an electrically conductive coating which causes misfiring.

RECOMMENDATION: Glazed plugs are not easily cleaned. They should be replaced with a fresh set of plugs of the correct heat range. If the condition recurs, using plugs with a heat range one step colder may cure the problem.

Ash (Lead) Deposits

APPEARANCE: Ash deposits are characterized by light brown or white colored deposits crusted on the side or center electrodes. In some cases it may give the plug a rusty appearance.

CAUSE: Ash deposits are normally derived from oil or fuel additives burned during normal combustion. Normally they are harmless, though excessive amounts can cause misfiring. If deposits are excessive in short mileage, the valve guides may be worn.

RECOMMENDATION: Ash-fouled plugs can be cleaned, gapped and reinstalled.

Detonation

APPEARANCE: Detonation is usually characterized by a broken plug insulator.

CAUSE: A portion of the fuel charge will begin to burn spontaneously, from the increased heat following ignition. The explosion that results applies extreme pressure to engine components, frequently damaging spark plugs and pistons.

Detonation can result by over-advanced ignition timing, inferior gasoline (low octane) lean air/fuel mixture, poor carburetion, engine lugging or an increase in compression ratio due to combustion chamber deposits or engine modification.

RECOMMENDATION: Replace the plugs after correcting the problem.

Photos Courtesy Champion Spark Plug Co.

EMISSION CONTROLS

13. Be aware of the general condition of the emission control system. It contributes to reduced pollution and should be serviced regularly to maintain efficient engine operation.

14. Check all vacuum lines for dried, cracked or brittle conditions. Something as simple as a leaking vacuum hose can cause poor performance and loss of economy.

15. Avoid tampering with the emission control system. Attempting to improve fuel econ-

FUEL SYSTEM

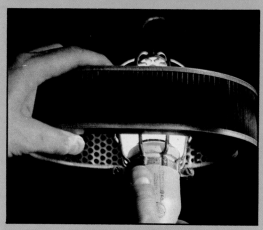

Check the air filter with a light behind it. If you can see light through the filter it can be reused.

Extremely clogged filters should be discarded and replaced with a new one.

18. Replace the air filter regularly. A dirty air filter richens the air/fuel mixture and can increase fuel consumption as much as 10%. Tests show that 1/3 of all vehicles have air filters in need of replacement.

19. Replace the fuel filter at least as often as recommended.

20. Set the idle speed and carburetor mixture to specifications.

21. Check the automatic choke. A sticking or malfunctioning choke wastes gas.

22. During the summer months, adjust the automatic choke for a leaner mixture which will produce faster engine warm-ups.

COOLING SYSTEM

29. Be sure all accessory drive belts are in good condition. Check for cracks or wear.

30. Adjust all accessory drive belts to proper tension.

31. Check all hoses for swollen areas, worn spots, or loose clamps.

32. Check coolant level in the radiator or expansion tank.

33. Be sure the thermostat is operating properly. A stuck thermostat delays engine warm-up and a cold engine uses nearly twice as much fuel as a warm engine.

34. Drain and replace the engine coolant at least as often as recommended. Rust and scale

TIRES & WHEELS

38. Check the tire pressure often with a pencil type gauge. Tests by a major tire manufacturer show that 90% of all vehicles have at least 1 tire improperly inflated. Better mileage can be achieved by over-inflating tires, but never exceed the maximum inflation pressure on the side of the tire.

39. If possible, install radial tires. Radial tires deliver as much as 1/2 mpg more than bias belted tires.

40. Avoid installing super-wide tires. They only create extra rolling resistance and decrease fuel mileage. Stick to the manufacturer's recommendations.

41. Have the wheels properly balanced.

omy by tampering with emission controls is more likely to worsen fuel economy than improve it. Emission control changes on modern engines are not readily reversible.

16. Clean (or replace) the EGR valve and lines as recommended.

17. Be sure that all vacuum lines and hoses are reconnected properly after working under the hood. An unconnected or misrouted vacuum line can wreak havoc with engine performance.

23. Check for fuel leaks at the carburetor, fuel pump, fuel lines and fuel tank. Be sure all lines and connections are tight.

24. Periodically check the tightness of the carburetor and intake manifold attaching nuts and bolts. These are a common place for vacuum leaks to occur.

25. Clean the carburetor periodically and lubricate the linkage.

26. The condition of the tailpipe can be an excellent indicator of proper engine combustion. After a long drive at highway speeds, the inside of the tailpipe should be a light grey in color. Black or soot on the insides indicates an overly rich mixture.

27. Check the fuel pump pressure. The fuel pump may be supplying more fuel than the engine needs.

28. Use the proper grade of gasoline for your engine. Don't try to compensate for knocking or "pinging" by advancing the ignition timing. This practice will only increase plug temperature and the chances of detonation or pre-ignition with relatively little performance gain.

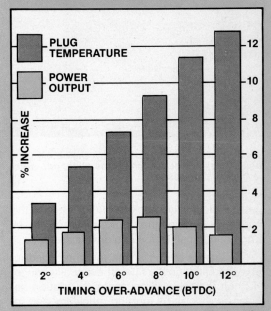

Increasing ignition timing past the specified setting results in a drastic increase in spark plug temperature with increased chance of detonation or preignition. Performance increase is considerably less. (Photo courtesy Champion Spark Plug Co.)

that form in the engine should be flushed out to allow the engine to operate at peak efficiency.

35. Clean the radiator of debris that can decrease cooling efficiency.

36. Install a flex-type or electric cooling fan, if you don't have a clutch type fan. Flex fans use curved plastic blades to push more air at low speeds when more cooling is needed; at high speeds the blades flatten out for less resistance. Electric fans only run when the engine temperature reaches a predetermined level.

37. Check the radiator cap for a worn or cracked gasket. If the cap does not seal properly, the cooling system will not function properly.

42. Be sure the front end is correctly aligned. A misaligned front end actually has wheels going in differed directions. The increased drag can reduce fuel economy by .3 mpg.

43. Correctly adjust the wheel bearings. Wheel bearings that are adjusted too tight increase rolling resistance.

Check tire pressures regularly with a reliable pocket type gauge. Be sure to check the pressure on a cold tire.

GENERAL MAINTENANCE

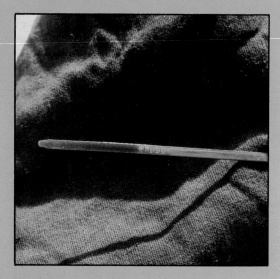

Check the fluid levels (particularly engine oil) on a regular basis. Be sure to check the oil for grit, water or other contamination.

A vacuum gauge is another excellent indicator of internal engine condition and can also be installed in the dash as a mileage indicator.

44. Periodically check the fluid levels in the engine, power steering pump, master cylinder, automatic transmission and drive axle.

45. Change the oil at the recommended interval and change the filter at every oil change. Dirty oil is thick and causes extra friction between moving parts, cutting efficiency and increasing wear. A worn engine requires more frequent tune-ups and gets progressively worse fuel economy. In general, use the lightest viscosity oil for the driving conditions you will encounter.

46. Use the recommended viscosity fluids in the transmission and axle.

47. Be sure the battery is fully charged for fast starts. A slow starting engine wastes fuel.

48. Be sure battery terminals are clean and tight.

49. Check the battery electrolyte level and add distilled water if necessary.

50. Check the exhaust system for crushed pipes, blockages and leaks.

51. Adjust the brakes. Dragging brakes or brakes that are not releasing create increased drag on the engine.

52. Install a vacuum gauge or miles-per-gallon gauge. These gauges visually indicate engine vacuum in the intake manifold. High vacuum = good mileage and low vacuum = poorer mileage. The gauge can also be an excellent indicator of internal engine conditions.

53. Be sure the clutch is properly adjusted. A slipping clutch wastes fuel.

54. Check and periodically lubricate the heat control valve in the exhaust manifold. A sticking or inoperative valve prevents engine warm-up and wastes gas.

55. Keep accurate records to check fuel economy over a period of time. A sudden drop in fuel economy may signal a need for tune-up or other maintenance.

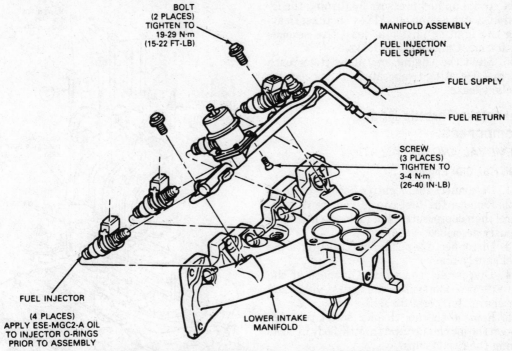

BOLT
(2 PLACES)
TIGHTEN TO
19-29 N·m
(15-22 FT-LB)

MANIFOLD ASSEMBLY

FUEL INJECTION
FUEL SUPPLY

FUEL SUPPLY

FUEL RETURN

SCREW
(3 PLACES)
TIGHTEN TO
3-4 N·m
(26-40 IN-LB)

FUEL INJECTOR

(4 PLACES)
APPLY ESE-MGC2-A OIL
TO INJECTOR O-RINGS
PRIOR TO ASSEMBLY

LOWER INTAKE
MANIFOLD

Location of fuel return and supply lines on 2.3L (140 CID) engine

the injector caps are clean and free of contamination.

17. Install the fuel injector supply manifold and injectors into the intake manifold, making sure the injectors are fully seated, then secure the fuel manifold assembly with the two retaining bolts. Tighten the retaining bolts to 15–22 ft.lb. (20–30 Nm).

18. Reconnect the four electrical connectors to the injectors.

19. Clean the gasket mating surfaces of the upper and lower intake manifold. Place a new gasket on the lower intake manifold, then place the upper intake manifold in position. Install the four retaining bolts and tighten them, in sequence, to 15–22 ft.lb. (20–30 Nm).

20. Install the engine oil dipstick.

21. Connect the fuel supply and return fuel lines to the fuel supply manifold.

22. Connect the EGR tube to the EGR valve

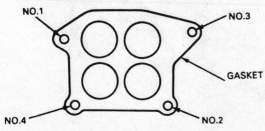

NO.1

NO.3

GASKET

NO.4

NO.2

Upper intake manifold torque sequence on 2.3L (140 CID) engine

and tighten the fitting to 6–8.5 ft.lb. (8–11.5 Nm).

23. Connect the coolant bypass line and tighten the clamp.

24. Connect the PCV system hose to the fitting on the underside of the upper intake manifold.

25. Reconnect the upper intake manifold vacuum lines, being careful to install them in their original locations. Reconnect the vacuum lines to the EGR valve and fuel pressure regulator.

26. Hold the accelerator cable bracket in position on the upper intake manifold and install the retaining bolt. Tighten the bolt to 10–15 ft.lb. (13–20 Nm).

27. Install the accelerator cable to the bracket.

28. If the air intake throttle body was removed from the upper intake manifold, position a new gasket on the mounting flange and install the throttle body.

29. Connect the accelerator cable and speed control cable. Install the throttle linkage shield.

30. Reconnect the electrical connectors to the throttle position sensor, knock sensor, air charge temperature sensor, coolant temperature sensor and injector wiring harness.

31. Connect the air intake hose, air bypass hose and crankcase vent hose.

32. Connect the negative battery cable.

33. Refill the cooling system.

34. Build up fuel pressure by turning the ignition switch on and off at least six times, leaving the ignition on for at least five seconds each time. Check for fuel leaks.

35. Start the engine and allow it to reach normal operating temperature, then check for coolant leaks.

Air Intake/Throttle Body Components

REMOVAL AND INSTALLATION

3.0L (182 CID) Engine

1. Disconnect the negative battery cable.
2. Remove the fuel cap to vent tank pressure, then depressurize the fuel system as previously described.
3. Disconnect the push connect fitting at the fuel supply line.
4. Disconnect the wiring harness at the throttle position sensor, air bypass valve and air charge temperature sensor.
5. Remove the air cleaner outlet tube between the air cleaner and throttle body by loosening the two clamps.
6. Remove the snow shield by removing the retaining nut on top of the shield and the two bolts on the side.
7. Tag and disconnect the vacuum hoses at the vacuum fittings on the intake manifold.
8. Disconnect and remove the accelerator and speed control cables (if equipped) from the accelerator mounting bracket and throttle lever.
9. Remove the transmission valve (TV)

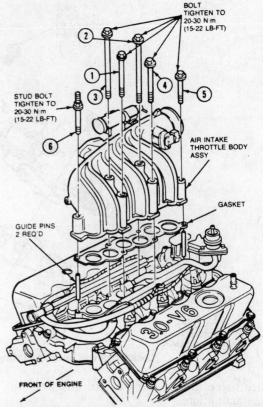

Removing air intake/throttle body assembly. Tighten the bolts in the numbered sequence when installing

linkage from the throttle lever on automatic transmission models.

10. Remove the six retaining bolts and lift

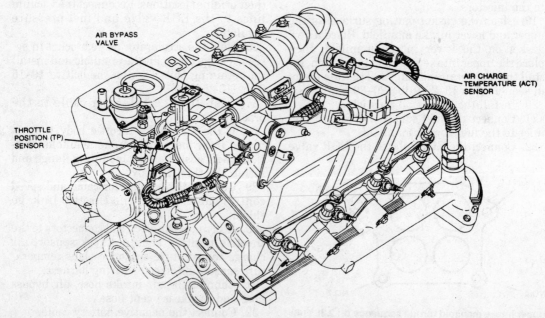

Wiring connections on 3.0L (182 CID) engine

the air intake/throttle body assembly off the guide pins on the lower intake manifold and remove the assembly from the engine.

11. Remove and discard the gasket from the lower intake manifold assembly.

12. Clean and inspect the mounting faces of the air intake/throttle body assembly and the lower intake manifold. Both surfaces must be clean and flat.

13. Clean and oil the manifold stud threads.

14. Install a new gasket on the lower intake manifold.

15. Using the guide pins as locators, install the air intake/throttle body assembly to the lower intake manifold.

16. Install the stud bolt and five retaining bolts as illustrated finger tight, then tighten them to 15–22 ft.lb (20–30 Nm) in the numbered sequence illustrated.

17. Connect the fuel supply and return lines to the fuel rail.

18. Connect the wiring harness to the throttle position sensor, air charge temperature sensor and air bypass valve.

19. Install the accelerator cable and speed control cable, if equipped.

20. Install the vacuum hoses to the vacuum fittings, making sure the hoses are installed in their original locations.

21. Install the throttle valve linkage to the throttle lever, if equipped with automatic transmission.

22. Reconnect the negative battery cable.

23. Install the fuel tank cap.

24. Install the snow shield and air cleaner outlet tube.

25. Build up fuel pressure by turning the ignition switch on and off at least six times, leaving the ignition on for at least five seconds each time. Check for fuel leaks.

26. Start the engine and adjust the idle speed, if necessary.

Air Bypass Valve
REMOVAL AND INSTALLATION
2.3L (140 CID) Engine

1. Disconnect the electrical connector at the air bypass valve.

2. Remove the air cleaner cover.

3. Separate the air bypass valve and gasket from the air cleaner by removing the three mounting bolts.

4. Install the air bypass valve and gasket to the air cleaner cover and tighten the retaining bolts to 6–8 ft.lb. (8–11 Nm).

5. Install the air cleaner cover.

6. Reconnect the air bypass valve electrical connector.

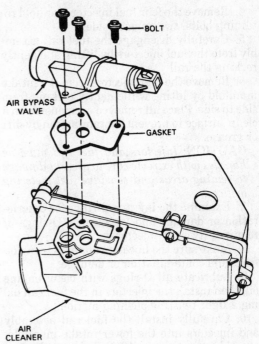

Air bypass valve mounting on 2.3L (140 CID) engine

3.0L (182 CID) Engine

1. Disconnect the air bypass valve connector.

2. Remove the air bypass valve retaining screws.

3. Remove the air bypass valve and gasket from the air intake/throttle body assembly. If scraping is necessary to remove old gasket material, be careful not to damage the air bypass valve or throttle body gasket mounting surfaces. Do not allow any foreign material to drop into the throttle body during service.

4. Installation is the reverse of removal. Tighten the mounting bolts to 6–8 ft.lb. (8–11 Nm).

Fuel Injector Manifold Assembly
REMOVAL AND INSTALLATION
2.3L (140 CID) Engine

For injector and fuel manifold removal, follow the procedures under "Fuel Charging Assembly Removal and Installation."

3.0L (182 CID) Engine

1. Remove the air intake/throttle body assembly as previously described. Be sue to depressurize the fuel system before disconnecting any fuel lines.

2. Carefully disconnect the wiring harness from the fuel injectors.

3. Disconnect the vacuum line from the fuel pressure regulator.

4. Remove the four fuel injector manifold retaining bolts, two on each side.

5. Carefully disengage the fuel rail assembly from the fuel injectors by lifting and gently rocking the rail.

6. Remove the fuel injectors from the intake manifold by lifting while gently rocking from side to side. Place all removed components on a clean surface to prevent contamination by dirt or grease.

CAUTION: *Injectors and fuel rail must be handles with extreme care to prevent damage to sealing areas and sensitive fuel metering orifices.*

7. Examine the injector O-rings for deterioration or damage and install new O-rings, if required (two per injector).

8. Make sure the injector caps are clean and free from contamination or damage.

9. Lubricate all O-rings with clean engine oil, then install the injectors in the fuel rail using a light twisting/pushing motion.

10. Carefully install the fuel rail assembly and injectors into the lower intake manifold, one side at a time, pushing down on the fuel rail to make sure the O-rings are seated.

11. Hold the fuel rail assembly in place and install the retaining bolts finger tight. Tighten the retaining bolts to 6–8 ft.lb. (8–12 Nm).

12. Connect the fuel supply and return lines.

13. Connect the fuel injector wiring harness at the injectors.

14. Connect the vacuum line to the fuel pressure regulator.

15. Install the air intake/throttle body as previously described.

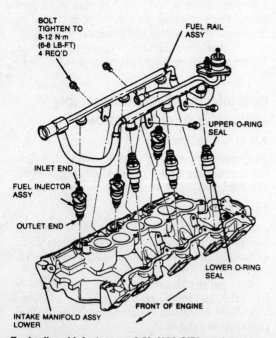

Fuel rail and injectors on 3.0L (182 CID) engine

Fuel Pressure Regulator
REMOVAL AND INSTALLATION
All Engines

1. Depressurize the fuel system as described earlier.

2. Remove the vacuum line at the pressure regulator.

3. Remove the three allen retaining screws from the regulator housing.

4. Remove the pressure regulator assembly, gasket and O-ring. Discard the gasket and check the O-ring for signs of cracks or deterioration.

5. Clean the gasket mating surfaces. If scraping is necessary, be careful not to damage the fuel pressure regulator or supply line gasket mating surfaces.

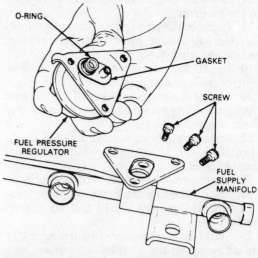

Typical fuel pressure regulator assembly mounting

6. Lubricate the pressure regulator O-ring with with light engine oil. Do not use silicone grease; it will clog the injectors.

7. Install the O-ring and a new gasket on the pressure regulator.

8. Install the pressure regulator on the fuel manifold and tighten the retaining screws to 27–40 in.lb. (3–4 Nm).

9. Install the vacuum line at the pressure regulator. Build up fuel pressure by turning the ignition switch on and off at least six times, leaving the ignition on for at least five seconds each time. Check for fuel leaks.

Throttle Position Sensor (TPS)
REMOVAL AND INSTALLATION
All Engines

1. Disconnect the throttle position sensor electrical connector.

2. On the 2.3L engine, remove the screw re-

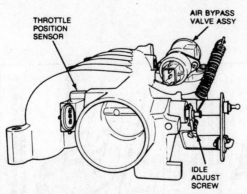

Location of throttle position sensor on 3.0L (182 CID) engine

taining the TPS electrical connector to the air throttle body.

3. Scribe alignment marks on the air throttle body and TPS sensor to indicate proper alignment during installation.

4. Remove the two TPS retaining screws, then remove the TPS and gasket from the throttle body.

5. To install, place the TPS and gasket on the throttle body, making sure the rotary tangs on the sensor are aligned with the throttle shaft blade. Slide the rotary tangs into posi-

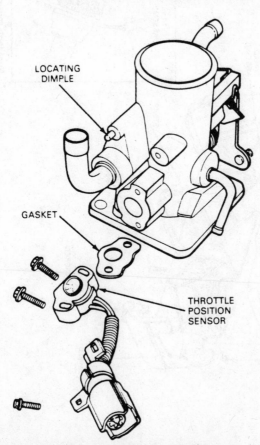

Throttle position sensor on 2.3L (140 CID) engine

tion over the throttle shaft blade, then rotate the throttle position sensor CLOCKWISE ONLY to its installed position (align the scribe marks made earlier).

CAUTION: *Failure to install the TPS in this manner may result in excessive idle speeds.*

6. Once the scribe marks are aligned, install the TPS retaining screws and tighten them to 14–16 in.lb. (1–2 Nm).

7. On the 2.3L engine, position the electrical connector over the locating dimple, then secure to the throttle body with the retaining screw.

8. Reconnect the TPS electrical connector, start the engine and check the idle speed.

NOTE: *Adjustment of the throttle position sensor requires the use of expensive test equipment that is not available to the do-it-yourself market. If adjustment is required, it should be performed by a qualified technician with the proper training and equipment to diagnose and repair the EEC-IV engine control system.*

Fuel Tank

REMOVAL AND INSTALLATION

1. Depressurize the fuel system and drain the fuel tank. Drain the gasoline into a suitable safety container and take precautions to avoid the risk of fire.

2. Loosen the filler pipe clamp.

3. Remove the bolt from the front strap and remove the front strap.

4. Remove the bolt from the rear strap and remove the rear strap.

5. Remove the fuel feed hose at the fuel gauge sender push connector.

6. Remove the fuel hose from the sender unit push connector.

7. Remove the fuel vapor hose from the vapor valve.

8. Lower the fuel tank from the chassis.

9. Remove the shield from the fuel tank.

10. To install the tank, first attach the fuel vapor hose to the vapor valve.

11. Install the front mounting bolt to the vehicle.

12. Attach the rear strap to the vehicle.

13. Install the shield on the fuel tank.

14. Position the tank to the vehicle and attach the front strap.

15. Install the fuel lines to the feed and return hoses at the fuel gauge sender push connector.

16. Install the filler pipe in position and tighten the filler pipe clamp.

17. Install the nut to the front mounting bolt and tighten it to 18–20 ft.lb. (25–30 Nm).

18. Install the bolt to the rear strap and tighten.

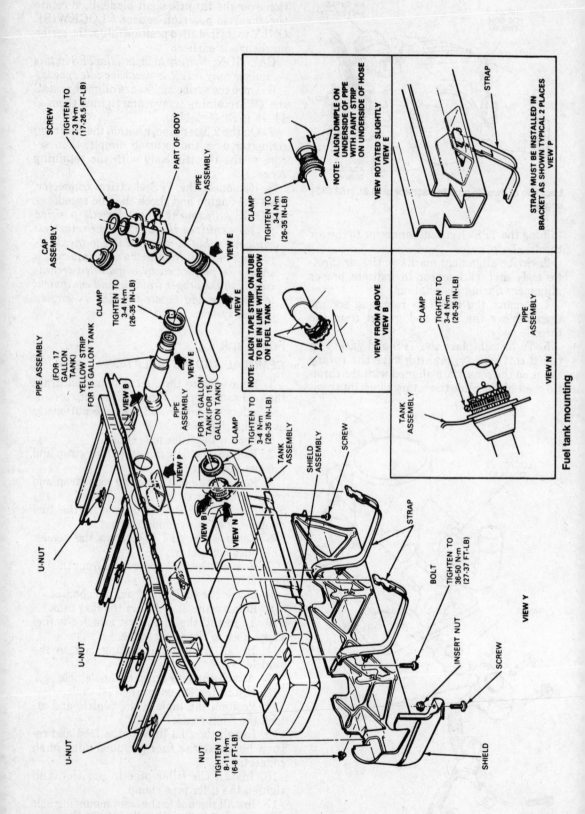

SCREW

TIGHTEN TO
2-3 N·m
(17-26.5 FT-LB)

PART OF BODY

PIPE
ASSEMBLY

VIEW E

CAP
ASSEMBLY

CLAMP

TIGHTEN TO
3-4 N·m
(26-35 IN-LB)

VIEW E

PIPE ASSEMBLY

(FOR 17
GALLON
TANK)

YELLOW STRIP
FOR 15 GALLON TANK

VIEW E

VIEW B

PIPE
ASSEMBLY
FOR 17 GALLON
TANK (FOR 15
GALLON TANK)

CLAMP

TIGHTEN TO
3-4 N·m
(26-35 IN-LB)

VIEW P

VIEW B

VIEW N

U-NUT

U-NUT

U-NUT

NUT

TIGHTEN TO
8-11 N·m
(6-8 FT-LB)

TANK
ASSEMBLY

SHIELD
ASSEMBLY

SCREW

STRAP

BOLT

TIGHTEN TO
36-50 N·m
(27-37 FT-LB)

INSERT NUT

SCREW

SHIELD

VIEW Y

NOTE: ALIGN DIMPLE ON
UNDERSIDE OF PIPE
WITH PAINT STRIP
ON UNDERSIDE OF HOSE

CLAMP

TIGHTEN TO
3-4 N·m
(26-35 IN-LB)

VIEW ROTATED SLIGHTLY
VIEW E

NOTE: ALIGN TAPE STRIP ON TUBE
TO BE IN LINE WITH ARROW
ON FUEL TANK

VIEW FROM ABOVE
VIEW B

CLAMP

TIGHTEN TO
3-4 N·m
(26-35 IN-LB)

PIPE
ASSEMBLY

TANK
ASSEMBLY

VIEW N

STRAP

STRAP MUST BE INSTALLED IN
BRACKET AS SHOWN TYPICAL 2 PLACES
VIEW P

Fuel tank mounting

Troubleshooting Basic Fuel System Problems

Problem	Cause	Solution
Engine cranks, but won't start (or is hard to start) when cold	• Empty fuel tank • Incorrect starting procedure • Defective fuel pump • No fuel in carburetor • Clogged fuel filter • Engine flooded • Defective choke	• Check for fuel in tank • Follow correct procedure • Check pump output • Check for fuel in the carburetor • Replace fuel filter • Wait 15 minutes; try again • Check choke plate
Engine cranks, but is hard to start (or does not start) when hot— (presence of fuel is assumed)	• Defective choke	• Check choke plate
Rough idle or engine runs rough	• Dirt or moisture in fuel • Clogged air filter • Faulty fuel pump	• Replace fuel filter • Replace air filter • Check fuel pump output
Engine stalls or hesitates on acceleration	• Dirt or moisture in the fuel • Dirty carburetor • Defective fuel pump • Incorrect float level, defective accelerator pump	• Replace fuel filter • Clean the carburetor • Check fuel pump output • Check carburetor
Poor gas mileage	• Clogged air filter • Dirty carburetor • Defective choke, faulty carburetor adjustment	• Replace air filter • Clean carburetor • Check carburetor
Engine is flooded (won't start accompanied by smell of raw fuel)	• Improperly adjusted choke or carburetor	• Wait 15 minutes and try again, without pumping gas pedal • If it won't start, check carburetor

Fuel System Calibration

Year	Engine Displacement Liters (cu. in.)	Emission Sticker Code	Calibration Number	Fuel Delivery System	Engine Control System
1986	2.3 (140)	AFZ	5-49J-R10	EFI	EEC IV
		AGB	5-49R-R10	EFI	EEC IV
	2.8 (173)	AAC ③	5-61H-R00	FBC	EEC IV
		AAA ③	5-61T-R00	FBC	EEC IV
		AAC ④	5-62F-R00	FBC	EEC IV
		AAB	5-62T-R00	FBC	EEC IV
	3.0 (182)	AME	6-55J-R02	EFI	EEC IV
		AMF	6-56J-R02	EFI	EEC IV
		AME ①	6-56J-R02	EFI	EEC IV
		AME ②	6-56J-R02	EFI	EEC IV
		AME ②	6-56J-R03	EFI	EEC IV
		AMF ①	6-56J-R04	EFI	EEC IV
		AME ②	6-56J-R04	EFI	EEC IV
1987	NOT AVAILABLE AT TIME OF PUBLICATION				

Note: Calibration numbers are necessary when ordering replacement fuel or engine control system components. See text for EEC IV operation.
EFI   Electronic Fuel Injection—Port type
FBC   Feedback carburetor—Motorcraft model 2150A
① with 3.73 rear axle
② with 3.45 or 4.10 rear axles
③ with manual transmission
④ with automatic transmission

Motorcraft 2150A Specifications

Year	Carburetor Identification	Dry Float Level (in.)	Wet Float Level (in.)	Pump Setting Hole No.	Choke Plate Pulldown (in.)	Fast Idle (rpm)	Dechoke (in.)	Choke Setting
1986–87	E69E-CA	$\frac{1}{16}$	.810	4	.136	3000	.250	V-Notch
	E69E-DA	$\frac{1}{16}$	.810	4	.136	3000	.250	V-Notch
	E69E-AA	$\frac{1}{16}$	.810	4	.136	3000	.250	V-Notch
	E69E-BA	$\frac{1}{16}$	.810	4	.136	3000	.250	V-Notch

Chassis Electrical

5

UNDERSTANDING AND TROUBLESHOOTING ELECTRICAL SYSTEMS

At the rate which both import and domestic manufacturers are incorporating electronic control systems into their production lines, it won't be long before every new vehicle is equipped with one or more on-board computer, like the EEC IV unit installed on the Aerostar. These electronic components (with no moving parts) should theoretically last the life of the vehicle, provided nothing external happens to damage the circuits or memory chips.

While it is true that electronic components should never wear out, in the real world malfunctions do occur. It is also true that any computer-based system is extremely sensitive to electrical voltages and cannot tolerate careless or haphazard testing or service procedures. An inexperienced individual can literally do major damage looking for a minor problem by using the wrong kind of test equipment or connecting test leads or connectors with the ignition switch ON. When selecting test equipment, make sure the manufacturers instructions state that the tester is compatible with whatever type of electronic control system is being serviced. Read all instructions carefully and double check all test points before installing probes or making any test connections.

The following section outlines basic diagnosis techniques for dealing with computerized automotive control systems. Along with a general explanation of the various types of test equipment available to aid in servicing modern electronic automotive systems, basic repair techniques for wiring harnesses and connectors is given. Read the basic information before attempting any repairs or testing on any computerized system, to provide the background of information necessary to avoid the most common and obvious mistakes that can cost both time and money. Although the replacement and testing procedures are simple in themselves, the systems are not, and unless one has a thorough understanding of all components and their function within a particular computerized control system, the logical test sequence these systems demand cannot be followed. Minor malfunctions can make a big difference, so it is important to know how each component affects the operation of the overall electronic system to find the ultimate cause of a problem without replacing good components unnecessarily. It is not enough to use the correct test equipment; the test equipment must be used correctly.

Safety Precautions

CAUTION: *Whenever working on or around any computer based microprocessor control system, always observe these general precautions to prevent the possibility of personal injury or damage to electronic components*

• Never install or remove battery cables with the key ON or the engine running. Jumper cables should be connected with the key OFF to avoid power surges that can damage electronic control units. Engines equipped with computer controlled systems should avoid both giving and getting jump starts due to the possibility of serious damage to components from arcing in the engine compartment when connections are made with the ignition ON.

• Always remove the battery cables before charging the battery. Never use a high output charger on an installed battery or attempt to use any type of "hot shot" (24 volt) starting aid.

• Exercise care when inserting test probes into connectors to insure good connections without damaging the connector or spreading the pins. Always probe connectors from the rear (wire) side, NOT the pin side, to avoid accidental shorting of terminals during test procedures.

• Never remove or attach wiring harness connectors with the ignition switch ON, especially to an electronic control unit.

• Do not drop any components during service procedures and never apply 12 volts directly to any component (like a solenoid or relay) unless instructed specifically to do so. Some component electrical windings are designed to safely handle only 4 or 5 volts and can be destroyed in seconds if 12 volts are applied directly to the connector.

• Remove the electronic control unit if the vehicle is to be placed in an environment where temperatures exceed approximately 176°F (80°C), such as a paint spray booth or when arc or gas welding near the control unit location in the car.

ORGANIZED TROUBLESHOOTING

When diagnosing a specific problem, organized troubleshooting is a must. The complexity of a modern automobile demands that you approach any problem in a logical, organized manner. There are certain troubleshooting techniques that are standard:

1. Establish when the problem occurs. Does the problem appear only under certain conditions? Were there any noises, odors, or other unusual symptoms?

2. Isolate the problem area. To do this, make some simple tests and observations; then eliminate the systems that are working properly. Check for obvious problems such as broken wires, dirty connections or split or disconnected vacuum hoses. Always check the obvious before assuming something complicated is the cause.

3. Test for problems systematically to determine the cause once the problem area is isolated. Are all the components functioning properly? Is there power going to electrical switches and motors? Is there vacuum at vacuum switches and/or actuators? Is there a mechanical problem such as bent linkage or loose mounting screws? Doing careful, systematic checks will often turn up most causes on the first inspection without wasting time checking components that have little or no relationship to the problem.

4. Test all repairs after the work is done to make sure that the problem is fixed. Some causes can be traced to more than one component, so a careful verification of repair work is important to pick up additional malfunctions that may cause a problem to reappear or a different problem to arise. A blown fuse, for example, is a simple problem that may require

more than another fuse to repair. If you don't look for a problem that caused a fuse to blow, for example, a shorted wire may go undetected. Experience has shown that most problems tend to be the result of a fairly simple and obvious cause, such as loose or corroded connectors or air leaks in the intake system; making careful inspection of components during testing essential to quick and accurate troubleshooting. Special, hand held computerized testers designed specifically for diagnosing the EEC-IV system are available from a variety of aftermarket sources, as well as from the vehicle manufacturer, but care should be taken that any test equipment being used is designed to diagnose that particular computer controlled system accurately without damaging the control unit (ECU) or components being tested.

NOTE: *Pinpointing the exact cause of trouble in an electrical system can sometimes only be accomplished by the use of special test equipment. The following describes commonly used test equipment and explains how to put it to best use in diagnosis. In addition to the information covered below, the manufacturer's instructions booklet provided with the tester should be read and clearly understood before attempting any test procedures.*

TEST EQUIPMENT

Jumper Wires

Jumper wires are simple, yet extremely valuable, pieces of test equipment. Jumper wires are merely wires that are used to bypass sections of a circuit. The simplest type of jumper wire is merely a length of multistrand wire with an alligator clip at each end. Jumper wires are usually fabricated from lengths of standard automotive wire and whatever type of connector (alligator clip, spade connector or pin connector) that is required for the particular vehicle being tested. The well equipped tool box will have several different styles of jumper wires in several different lengths. Some

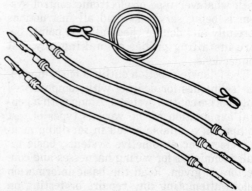

Typical jumper wires with various terminal ends

jumper wires are made with three or more terminals coming from a common splice for special purpose testing. In cramped, hard-to-reach areas it is advisable to have insulated boots over the jumper wire terminals in order to prevent accidental grounding, sparks, and possible fire, especially when testing fuel system components.

Jumper wires are used primarily to locate open electrical circuits, on either the ground (−) side of the circuit or on the hot (+) side. If an electrical component fails to operate, connect the jumper wire between the component and a good ground. If the component operates only with the jumper installed, the ground circuit is open. If the ground circuit is good, but the component does not operate, the circuit between the power feed and component is open. You can sometimes connect the jumper wire directly from the battery to the hot terminal of the component, but first make sure the component uses 12 volts in operation. Some electrical components, such as fuel injectors, are designed to operate on about 4 volts and running 12 volts directly to the injector terminals can burn out the wiring. By inserting an inline fuseholder between a set of test leads, a fused jumper wire can be used for bypassing open circuits. Use a 5 amp fuse to provide protection against voltage spikes. When in doubt, use a voltmeter to check the voltage input to the component and measure how much voltage is being applied normally. By moving the jumper wire successively back from the lamp toward the power source, you can isolate the area of the circuit where the open is located. When the component stops functioning, or the power is cut off, the open is in the segment of wire between the jumper and the point previously tested.

CAUTION: *Never use jumpers made from wire that is of lighter gauge than used in the circuit under test. If the jumper wire is of too small gauge, it may overheat and possibly*

melt. *Never use jumpers to bypass high resistance loads (such as motors) in a circuit. Bypassing resistances, in effect, creates a short circuit which may, in turn, cause damage and fire. Never use a jumper for anything other than temporary bypassing of components in a circuit.*

12 Volt Test Light

The 12 volt test light is used to check circuits and components while electrical current is flowing through them. It is used for voltage and ground tests. Twelve volt test lights come in different styles but all have three main parts; a ground clip, a probe, and a light. The most commonly used 12 volt test lights have pick-type probes. To use a 12 volt test light, connect the ground clip to a good ground and probe wherever necessary with the pick. The pick should be sharp so that it can penetrate wire insulation to make contact with the wire, without making a large hole in the insulation. The wrap-around light is handy in hard to reach areas or where it is difficult to support a wire to push a probe pick into it. To use the wrap around light, hook the wire to probed with the hook and pull the trigger. A small pick will be forced through the wire insulation into the wire core.

CAUTION: *Do not use a test light to probe electronic ignition spark plug or coil wires. Never use a pick-type test light to probe wiring on computer controlled systems unless specifically instructed to do so. Any wire insulation that is pierced by the test light probe should be taped and sealed with silicone after testing.*

Like the jumper wire, the 12 volt test light is used to isolate opens in circuits. But, whereas the jumper wire is used to bypass the open to operate the load, the 12 volt test light is used to locate the presence of voltage in a circuit. If the test light glows, you know that there is power

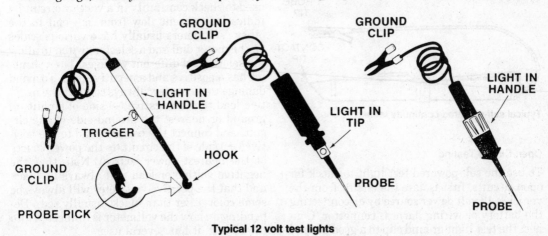

Typical 12 volt test lights

up to that point; if the 12 volt test light does not glow when its probe is inserted into the wire or connector, you know that there is an open circuit (no power). Move the test light in successive steps back toward the power source until the light in the handle does glow. When it does glow, the open is between the probe and point previously probed.

NOTE: *The test light does not detect that 12 volts (or any particular amount of voltage) is present; it only detects that some voltage is present. It is advisable before using the test light to touch its terminals across the battery posts to make sure the light is operating properly.*

Self-Powered Test Light

The self-powered test light usually contains a 1.5 volt penlight battery. One type of self-powered test light is similar in design to the 12 volt test light. This type has both the battery and the light in the handle and pick-type probe tip. The second type has the light toward the open tip, so that the light illuminates the contact point. The self-powered test light is dual purpose piece of test equipment. It can be used to test for either open or short circuits when power is isolated from the circuit (continuity test). A powered test light should not be used on any computer controlled system or component unless specifically instructed to do so. Many engine sensors can be destroyed by even this small amount of voltage applied directly to the terminals.

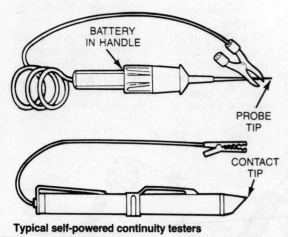

BATTERY IN HANDLE

PROBE TIP

CONTACT TIP

Typical self-powered continuity testers

Open Circuit Testing

To use the self-powered test light to check for open circuits, first isolate the circuit from the vehicle's 12 volt power source by disconnecting the battery or wiring harness connector. Connect the test light ground clip to a good ground

and probe sections of the circuit sequentially with the test light. (start from either end of the circuit). If the light is out, the open is between the probe and the circuit ground. If the light is on, the open is between the probe and end of the circuit toward the power source.

Short Circuit Testing

By isolating the circuit both from power and from ground, and using a self-powered test light, you can check for shorts to ground in the circuit. Isolate the circuit from power and ground. Connect the test light ground clip to a good ground and probe any easy-to-reach test point in the circuit. If the light comes on, there is a short somewhere in the circuit. To isolate the short, probe a test point at either end of the isolated circuit (the light should be on). Leave the test light probe connected and open connectors, switches, remove parts, etc., sequentially, until the light goes out. When the light goes out, the short is between the last circuit component opened and the previous circuit opened.

NOTE: *The 1.5 volt battery in the test light does not provide much current. A weak battery may not provide enough power to illuminate the test light even when a complete circuit is made (especially if there are high resistances in the circuit). Always make sure that the test battery is strong. To check the battery, briefly touch the ground clip to the probe; if the light glows brightly the battery is strong enough for testing. Never use a self-powered test light to perform checks for opens or shorts when power is applied to the electrical system under test. The 12 volt vehicle power will quickly burn out the 1.5 volt light bulb in the test light.*

Voltmeter

A voltmeter is used to measure voltage at any point in a circuit, or to measure the voltage drop across any part of a circuit. It can also be used to check continuity in a wire or circuit by indicating current flow from one end to the other. Voltmeters usually have various scales on the meter dial and a selector switch to allow the selection of different voltages. The voltmeter has a positive and a negative lead. To avoid damage to the meter, always connect the negative lead to the negative (–) side of circuit (to ground or nearest the ground side of the circuit) and connect the positive lead to the positive (+) side of the circuit (to the power source or the nearest power source). Note that the negative voltmeter lead will always be black and that the positive voltmeter will always be some color other than black (usually red). Depending on how the voltmeter is connected into the circuit, it has several uses.

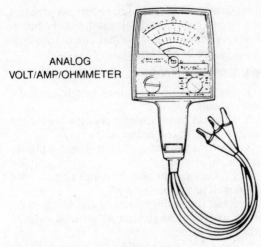

ANALOG
VOLT/AMP/OHMMETER

Typical analog volt/amp/ohmmeter

A voltmeter can be connected either in parallel or in series with a circuit and it has a very high resistance to current flow. When connected in parallel, only a small amount of current will flow through the voltmeter current path; the rest will flow through the normal circuit current path and the circuit will work normally. When the voltmeter is connected in series with a circuit, only a small amount of current can flow through the circuit. The circuit will not work properly, but the voltmeter reading will show if the circuit is complete or not.

Available Voltage Measurement

Set the voltmeter selector switch to the 20V position and connect the meter negative lead to the negative post of the battery. Connect the positive meter lead to the positive post of the battery and turn the ignition switch ON to provide a load. Read the voltage on the meter or digital display. A well charged battery should register over 12 volts. If the meter reads below 11.5 volts, the battery power may be insufficient to operate the electrical system properly. This test determines voltage available from

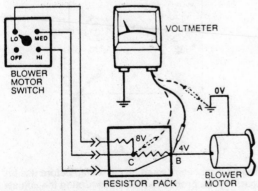

Measuring available voltage in a blower circuit

the battery and should be the first step in any electrical trouble diagnosis procedure. Many electrical problems, especially on computer controlled systems, can be caused by a low state of charge in the battery. Excessive corrosion at the battery cable terminals can cause a poor contact that will prevent proper charging and full battery current flow.

Normal battery voltage is 12 volts when fully charged. When the battery is supplying current to one or more circuits it is said to be "under load". When everything is off the electrical system is under a "no-load" condition. A fully charged battery may show about 12.5 volts at no load; will drop to 12 volts under medium load; and will drop even lower under heavy load. If the battery is partially discharged the voltage decrease under heavy load may be excessive, even though the battery shows 12 volts or more at no load. When allowed to discharge further, the battery's available voltage under load will decrease more severely. For this reason, it is important that the battery be fully charged during all testing procedures to avoid errors in diagnosis and incorrect test results.

Voltage Drop

When current flows through a resistance, the voltage beyond the resistance is reduced (the larger the current, the greater the reduction in voltage). When no current is flowing, there is no voltage drop because there is no current flow. All points in the circuit which are connected to the power source are at the same voltage as the power source. The total voltage drop always equals the total source voltage. In a long circuit with many connectors, a series of small, unwanted voltage drops due to corrosion at the connectors can add up to a total loss of voltage which impairs the operation of the normal loads in the circuit.

INDIRECT COMPUTATION OF VOLTAGE DROPS

1. Set the voltmeter selector switch to the 20 volt position.
2. Connect the meter negative lead to a good ground.
3. Probe all resistances in the circuit with the positive meter lead.
4. Operate the circuit in all modes and observe the voltage readings.

DIRECT MEASUREMENT OF VOLTAGE DROPS

1. Set the voltmeter switch to the 20 volt position.
2. Connect the voltmeter negative lead to the ground side of the resistance load to be measured.
3. Connect the positive lead to the positive side of the resistance or load to be measured.

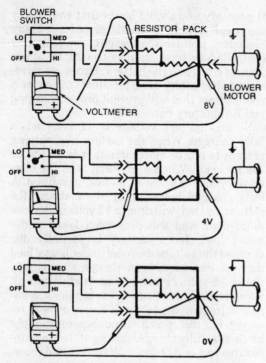

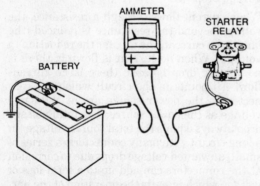

Direct measurement of voltage drops in a circuit

Battery current drain test. Use this test to determine if there is a constant current draw on the electrical system due to a short circuit

4. Read the voltage drop directly on the 20 volt scale.

Too high a voltage indicates too high a resistance. If, for example, a blower motor runs too slowly, you can determine if there is too high a resistance in the resistor pack. By taking voltage drop readings in all parts of the circuit, you can isolate the problem. Too low a voltage drop indicates too low a resistance. If, for example, a blower motor runs too fast in the MED and/or LOW position, the problem can be isolated in the resistor pack by taking voltage drop readings in all parts of the circuit to locate a possibly shorted resistor. The maximum allowable voltage drop under load is critical, especially if

there is more than one high resistance problem in a circuit because all voltage drops are cumulative. A small drop is normal due to the resistance of the conductors.

HIGH RESISTANCE TESTING

1. Set the voltmeter selector switch to the 4 volt position.
2. Connect the voltmeter positive lead to the positive post of the battery.
3. Turn on the headlights and heater blower to provide a load.
4. Probe various points in the circuit with the negative voltmeter lead.
5. Read the voltage drop on the 4 volt scale. Some average maximum allowable voltage drops are:

FUSE PANEL – 7 volts
IGNITION SWITCH – 5 volts
HEADLIGHT SWITCH – 7 volts
IGNITION COIL (+) – 5 volts
ANY OTHER LOAD – 1.3 volts
NOTE: *Voltage drops are all measured while a load is operating; without current flow, there will be no voltage drop.*

Ohmmeter

The ohmmeter is designed to read resistance (ohms) in a circuit or component. Although there are several different styles of ohmmeters, all will usually have a selector switch which permits the measurement of different ranges of resistance (usually the selector switch allows the multiplication of the meter reading by 10, 100, 1000, and 10,000). A calibration knob allows the meter to be set at zero for accurate measurement. Since all ohmmeters are powered by an internal battery (usual-

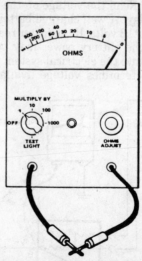

Analog ohmmeters must be calibrated before use by touching the probes together and turning the adjustment knob

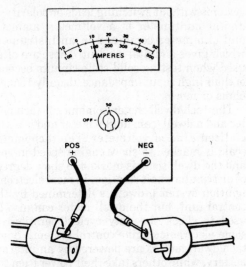

An ammeter must be connected in series with the circuit being tested

ly 9 volts), the ohmmeter can be used as a self-powered test light. When the ohmmeter is connected, current from the ohmmeter flows through the circuit or component being tested. Since the ohmmeter's internal resistance and voltage are known values, the amount of current flow through the meter depends on the resistance of the circuit or component being tested.

The ohmmeter can be used to perform continuity test for opens or shorts (either by observation of the meter needle or as a self-powered test light), and to read actual resistance in a circuit. It should be noted that the ohmmeter is used to check the resistance of a component or wire while there is no voltage applied to the circuit. Current flow from an outside voltage source (such as the vehicle battery) can damage the ohmmeter, so the circuit or component should be isolated from the vehicle electrical system before any testing is done. Since the ohmmeter uses its own voltage source, either lead can be connected to any test point.

NOTE: *When checking diodes or other solid state components, the ohmmeter leads can only be connected one way in order to measure current flow in a single direction. Make sure the positive (+) and negative (–) terminal connections are as described in the test procedures to verify the one-way diode operation.*

In using the meter for making continuity checks, do not be concerned with the actual resistance readings. Zero resistance, or any resistance readings, indicate continuity in the circuit. Infinite resistance indicates an open in the circuit. A high resistance reading where there should be none indicates a problem in

the circuit. Checks for short circuits are made in the same manner as checks for open circuits except that the circuit must be isolated from both power and normal ground. Infinite resistance indicates no continuity to ground, while zero resistance indicates a dead short to ground.

RESISTANCE MEASUREMENT

The batteries in an ohmmeter will weaken with age and temperature, so the ohmmeter must be calibrated or "zeroed" before taking measurements. To zero the meter, place the selector switch in its lowest range and touch the two ohmmeter leads together. Turn the calibration knob until the meter needle is exactly on zero.

NOTE: *All analog (needle) type ohmmeters must be zeroed before use, but some digital ohmmeter models are automatically calibrated when the switch is turned on. Self-calibrating digital ohmmeters do not have an adjusting knob, but its a good idea to check for a zero readout before use by touching the leads together. All computer controlled systems require the use of a digital ohmmeter with at least 10 meagohms impedance for testing. Before any test procedures are attempted, make sure the ohmmeter used is compatible with the electrical system or damage to the onboard computer could result.*

To measure resistance, first isolate the circuit from the vehicle power source by disconnecting the battery cables or the harness connector. Make sure the key is OFF when disconnecting any components or the battery. Where necessary, also isolate at least one side of the circuit to be checked to avoid reading parallel resistances. Parallel circuit resistances will always give a lower reading than the actual resistance of either of the branches. When measuring the resistance of parallel circuits, the total resistance will always be lower than the smallest resistance in the circuit. Connect the meter leads to both sides of the circuit (wire or component) and read the actual measured ohms on the meter scale. Make sure the selector switch is set to the proper ohm scale for the circuit being tested to avoid misreading the ohmmeter test value.

CAUTION: *Never use an ohmmeter with power applied to the circuit. Like the self-powered test light, the ohmmeter is designed to operate on its own power supply. The normal 12 volt automotive electrical system current could damage the meter.*

Ammeters

An ammeter measures the amount of current flowing through a circuit in units called amperes or amps. Amperes are units of electron flow which indicate how fast the electrons are flowing through the circuit. Since Ohms Law dictates that current flow in a circuit is equal to the circuit voltage divided by the total circuit resistance, increasing voltage also increases the current level (amps). Likewise, any decrease in resistance will increase the amount of amps in a circuit. At normal operating voltage, most circuits have a characteristic amount of amperes, called "current draw" which can be measured using an ammeter. By referring to a specified current draw rating, measuring the amperes, and comparing the two values, one can determine what is happening within the circuit to aid in diagnosis. An open circuit, for example, will not allow any current to flow so the ammeter reading will be zero. More current flows through a heavily loaded circuit or when the charging system is operating.

An ammeter is always connected in series with the circuit being tested. All of the current that normally flows through the circuit must also flow through the ammeter; if there is any other path for the current to follow, the ammeter reading will not be accurate. The ammeter itself has very little resistance to current flow and therefore will not affect the circuit, but it will measure current draw only when the circuit is closed and electricity is flowing. Excessive current draw can blow fuses and drain the battery, while a reduced current draw can cause motors to run slowly, lights to dim and other components to not operate properly. The ammeter can help diagnose these conditions by locating the cause of the high or low reading.

Multimeters

Different combinations of test meters can be built into a single unit designed for specific tests. Some of the more common combination test devices are known as Volt/Amp testers, Tach/Dwell meters, or Digital Multimeters. The Volt/Amp tester is used for charging system, starting system or battery tests and consists of a voltmeter, an ammeter and a variable resistance carbon pile. The voltmeter will usually have at least two ranges for use with 6, 12 and 24 volt systems. The ammeter also has more than one range for testing various levels of battery loads and starter current draw and the carbon pile can be adjusted to offer different amounts of resistance. The Volt/Amp tester has heavy leads to carry large amounts of current and many later models have an inductive ammeter pickup that clamps around the wire to simplify test connections. On some models, the ammeter also has a zero-center scale to allow testing of charging and starting

systems without switching leads or polarity. A digital multimeter is a voltmeter, ammeter and ohmmeter combined in an instrument which gives a digital readout. These are often used when testing solid state circuits because of their high input impedance (usually 10 megohms or more).

The tach/dwell meter combines a tachometer and a dwell (cam angle) meter and is a specialized kind of voltmeter. The tachometer scale is marked to show engine speed in rpm and the dwell scale is marked to show degrees of distributor shaft rotation. In most electronic ignition systems, dwell is determined by the control unit, but the dwell meter can also be used to check the duty cycle (operation) of some electronic engine control systems. Some tach/dwell meters are powered by an internal battery, while others take their power from the car battery in use. The battery powered testers usually require calibration much like an ohmmeter before testing.

Special Test Equipment

A variety of diagnostic tools are available to help troubleshoot and repair computerized engine control systems. The most sophisticated of these devices are the console type engine analyzers that usually occupy a garage service bay, but there are several types of aftermarket electronic testers available that will allow quick circuit tests of the engine control system by plugging directly into a special connector located in the engine compartment or under the dashboard. Several tool and equipment manufacturers offer simple, hand held testers that measure various circuit voltage levels on command to check all system components for proper operation. Although these testers usually cost about $300–500, consider that the average computer control unit (or ECM) can cost just as much and the money saved by not replacing perfectly good sensors or components in an attempt to correct a problem could justify the purchase price of a special diagnostic tester the first time it's used.

These computerized testers can allow quick and easy test measurements while the engine is operating or while the car is being driven. In addition, the on-board computer memory can be read to access any stored trouble codes; in effect allowing the computer to tell you where it hurts and aid trouble diagnosis by pinpointing exactly which circuit or component is malfunctioning. In the same manner, repairs can be tested to make sure the problem has been corrected. The biggest advantage these special testers have is their relatively easy hookups that minimize or eliminate the chances of making the wrong connections and getting false voltage readings or damaging the computer accidentally.

NOTE: *It should be remembered that these testers check voltage levels in circuits; they don't detect mechanical problems or failed components if the circuit voltage falls within the preprogrammed limits stored in the tester PROM unit. Also, most of the hand held testes are designed to work only on one or two systems made by a specific manufacturer.*

A variety of aftermarket testers are available to help diagnose different computerized control systems. Owatonna Tool Company (OTC), for example, markets a device called the OTC Monitor which plugs directly into the assembly line diagnostic link (ALDL). The OTC tester makes diagnosis a simple matter of pressing the correct buttons and, by changing the internal PROM or inserting a different diagnosis cartridge, it will work on any model from full size to subcompact, over a wide range of years. An adapter is supplied with the tester to allow connection to all types of ALDL links, regardless of the number of pin terminals used. By inserting an updated PROM into the OTC tester, it can be easily updated to diagnose any new modifications of computerized control systems.

Wiring Harnesses

The average automobile contains about ½ mile of wiring, with hundreds of individual connections. To protect the many wires from damage and to keep them from becoming a confusing tangle, they are organized into bundles, enclosed in plastic or taped together and called wire harnesses. Different wiring harnesses serve different parts of the vehicle. Individual wires are color coded to help trace them through a harness where sections are hidden from view.

A loose or corroded connection or a replacement wire that is too small for the circuit will add extra resistance and an additional voltage drop to the circuit. A ten percent voltage drop can result in slow or erratic motor operation, for example, even though the circuit is complete. Automotive wiring or circuit conductors can be in any one of three forms:

1. Single strand wire
2. Multistrand wire
3. Printed circuitry

Single strand wire has a solid metal core and is usually used inside such components as alternators, motors, relays and other devices. Multistrand wire has a core made of many small strands of wire twisted together into a single conductor. Most of the wiring in an automotive electrical system is made up of multistrand wire, either as a single conductor or grouped together in a harness. All wiring is color coded on the insulator, either as a solid color or as a colored wire with an identification stripe. A printed circuit is a thin film of copper or other conductor that is printed on an insulator backing. Occasionally, a printed circuit is sandwiched between two sheets of plastic for more protection and flexibility. A complete printed circuit, consisting of conductors, insulating material and connectors for lamps or other components is called a printed circuit board. Printed circuitry is used in place of individual wires or harnesses in places where space is limited, such as behind instrument panels.

Wire Gauge

Since computer controlled automotive electrical systems are very sensitive to changes in resistance, the selection of properly sized wires is critical when systems are repaired. The wire gauge number is an expression of the cross section area of the conductor. The most common system for expressing wire size is the American Wire Gauge (AWG) system.

Wire cross section area is measured in circular mils. A mil is $\frac{1}{1000}''$ (0.001); a circular mil is the area of a circle one mil in diameter. For example, a conductor ¼″ in diameter is 0.250 in. or 250 mils. The circular mil cross section area of the wire is 250 squared (250^2)or 62,500 circular mils. Imported car models usually use metric wire gauge designations, which is simply the cross section area of the conductor in square millimeters (mm^2).

Gauge numbers are assigned to conductors of various cross section areas. As gauge number increases, area decreases and the conductor becomes smaller. A 5 gauge conductor is smaller than a 1 gauge conductor and a 10 gauge is smaller than a 5 gauge. As the cross section area of a conductor decreases, resistance increases and so does the gauge number. A conductor with a higher gauge number will carry less current than a conductor with a lower gauge number.

NOTE: *Gauge wire size refers to the size of the conductor, not the size of the complete wire. It is possible to have two wires of the same gauge with different diameters because one may have thicker insulation than the other.*

12 volt automotive electrical systems generally use 10, 12, 14, 16 and 18 gauge wire. Main power distribution circuits and larger accessories usually use 10 and 12 gauge wire. Battery cables are usually 4 or 6 gauge, although 1 and 2 gauge wires are occasionally used. Wire length must also be considered when making

repairs to a circuit. As conductor length increases, so does resistance. An 18 gauge wire, for example, can carry a 10 amp load for 10 feet without excessive voltage drop; however if a 15 foot wire is required for the same 10 amp load, it must be a 16 gauge wire.

An electrical schematic shows the electrical current paths when a circuit is operating properly. It is essential to understand how a circuit works before trying to figure out why it doesn't. Schematics break the entire electrical system down into individual circuits and show only one particular circuit. In a schematic, no attempt is made to represent wiring and components as they physically appear on the vehicle; switches and other components are shown as simply as possible. Face views of harness connectors show the cavity or terminal locations in all multi-pin connectors to help locate test points.

If you need to backprobe a connector while it is on the component, the order of the terminals must be mentally reversed. The wire color code can help in this situation, as well as a keyway, lock tab or other reference mark.

NOTE: *Wiring diagrams are not included in this book. As trucks have become more complex and available with longer option lists,* *wiring diagrams have grown in size and complexity. It has become almost impossible to provide a readable reproduction of a wiring diagram in a book this size. Information on ordering wiring diagrams from the vehicle manufacturer can be found in the owner's manual.*

WIRING REPAIR

Soldering is a quick, efficient method of joining metals permanently. Everyone who has the occasion to make wiring repairs should know how to solder. Electrical connections that are soldered are far less likely to come apart and will conduct electricity much better than connections that are only "pig-tailed" together. The most popular (and preferred) method of soldering is with an electrical soldering gun. Soldering irons are available in many sizes and wattage ratings. Irons with higher wattage ratings deliver higher temperatures and recover lost heat faster. A small soldering iron rated for no more than 50 watts is recommended, especially on electrical systems where excess heat can damage the components being soldered.

There are three ingredients necessary for successful soldering; proper flux, good solder

WIRE HARNESS REPAIR PROCEDURES

Condition	Location	Correction
Non-continuity	Using the electric wiring diagram and the wiring harness diagram as a guideline, check the continuity of the circuit in question by using a tester, and check for breaks, loose connector couplings, or loose terminal crimp contacts.	**Breaks**—Reconnect the point of the break by using solder. If the wire is too short and the connection is impossible, extend it by using a wire of the same or larger size. Be careful concerning the size of wire used for the extension
		Loose couplings—Hold the connector securely, and insert it until there is a definite joining of the coupling. If the connector is equipped with a locking mechanism, insert the connector until it is locked securely.
	Crimp by using pliers / Solder	**Loose terminal crimp contacts**—Remove approximately 2 in. (5mm) of the insulation covering from the end of the wire, crimp the terminal contact by using a pair of pliers, and then, in addition, complete the repair by soldering.
Short-circuit	Using the electric wiring diagram and the wiring harness diagram as a guideline, check the entire circuit for pinched wires.	Remove the pinched portion, and then repair any breaks in the insulation covering with tape. Repair breaks of the wire by soldering.
Loose terminal	Pull the wiring lightly from the connector. A special terminal removal tool may be necessary for complete removal.	Raise the terminal catch pin, and then insert it until a definite clicking sound is heard. Catch pin

Note: There is the chance of short circuits being caused by insulation damage at soldered points. To avoid this possibility, wrap all splices with electrical tape and use a layer of silicone to seal the connection against moisture. Incorrect repairs can cause malfunctions by creating excessive resistance in a circuit.

and sufficient heat. A soldering flux is necessary to clean the metal of tarnish, prepare it for soldering and to enable the solder to spread into tiny crevices. When soldering, always use a resin flux or resin core solder which is non-corrosive and will not attract moisture once the job is finished. Other types of flux (acid core) will leave a residue that will attract moisture and cause the wires to corrode. Tin is a unique metal with a low melting point. In a molten state, it dissolves and alloys easily with many metals. Solder is made by mixing tin with lead. The most common proportions are 40/60, 50/50 and 60/40, with the percentage of tin listed first. Low priced solders usually contain less tin, making them very difficult for a beginner to use because more heat is required to melt the solder. A common solder is 40/60 which is well suited for all-around general use, but 60/40 melts easier, has more tin for a better joint and is preferred for electrical work.

Soldering Techniques

Successful soldering requires that the metals to be joined be heated to a temperature that will melt the solder—usually 360–460°F (182–238°C). Contrary to popular belief, the purpose of the soldering iron is not to melt the solder itself, but to heat the parts being soldered to a temperature high enough to melt the solder when it is touched to the work. Melting flux-cored solder on the soldering iron will usually destroy the effectiveness of the flux.

NOTE: *Soldering tips are made of copper for good heat conductivity, but must be "tinned" regularly for quick transference of heat to the project and to prevent the solder from sticking to the iron. To "tin" the iron, simply heat it and touch the flux-cored solder to the tip; the solder will flow over the hot tip. Wipe the excess off with a clean rag, but be careful as the iron will be hot.*

After some use, the tip may become pitted. If so, simply dress the tip smooth with a smooth file and "tin" the tip again. An old saying holds that "metals well cleaned are half soldered." Flux-cored solder will remove oxides but rust, bits of insulation and oil or grease must be removed with a wire brush or emery cloth. For maximum strength in soldered parts, the joint must start off clean and tight. Weak joints will result in gaps too wide for the solder to bridge.

If a separate soldering flux is used, it should be brushed or swabbed on only those areas that are to be soldered. Most solders contain a core of flux and separate fluxing is unnecessary. Hold the work to be soldered firmly. It is best to solder on a wooden board, because a metal vise will only rob the piece to be soldered of heat and make it difficult to melt the solder.

Hold the soldering tip with the broadest face against the work to be soldered. Apply solder under the tip close to the work, using enough solder to give a heavy film between the iron and the piece being soldered, while moving slowly and making sure the solder melts properly. Keep the work level or the solder will run to the lowest part and favor the thicker parts, because these require more heat to melt the solder. If the soldering tip overheats (the solder coating on the face of the tip burns up), it should be retinned. Once the soldering is completed, let the soldered joint stand until cool. Tape and seal all soldered wire splices after the repair has cooled.

Wire Harness and Connectors

The on-board computer (ECM) wire harness electrically connects the control unit to the various solenoids, switches and sensors used by the control system. Most connectors in the engine compartment or otherwise exposed to the elements are protected against moisture and dirt which could create oxidation and deposits on the terminals. This protection is important because of the very low voltage and current levels used by the computer and sensors. All connectors have a lock which secures the male and female terminals together, with a secondary lock holding the seal and terminal into the connector. Both terminal locks must be released when disconnecting ECM connectors.

These special connectors are weather-proof and all repairs require the use of a special terminal and the tool required to service it. This tool is used to remove the pin and sleeve terminals. If removal is attempted with an ordinary pick, there is a good chance that the terminal will be bent or deformed. Unlike standard blade type terminals, these terminals cannot be straightened once they are bent. Make certain that the connectors are properly seated and all of the sealing rings in place when connecting leads. On some models, a hinge-type flap provides a backup or secondary locking feature for the terminals. Most secondary locks are used to improve the connector reliability by retaining the terminals if the small terminal lock tangs are not positioned properly.

Molded-on connectors require complete replacement of the connection. This means splicing a new connector assembly into the harness. All splices in on-board computer systems should be soldered to insure proper contact. Use care when probing the connections or replacing terminals in them as it is possible to short between opposite terminals. If this happens to the wrong terminal pair, it is possible to damage certain components. Always use

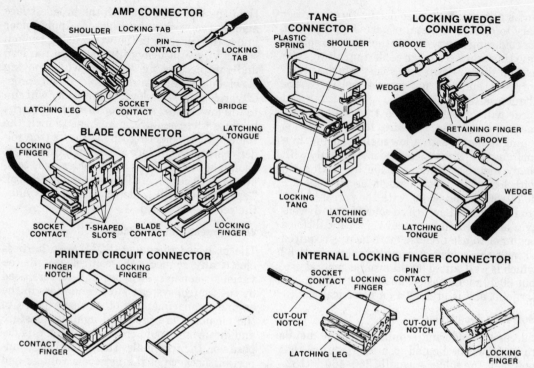

Various types of wire harness connectors used on Ford vehicles

jumper wires between connectors for circuit checking and never probe through weatherproof seals.

Open circuits are often difficult to locate by sight because corrosion or terminal misalignment are hidden by the connectors. Merely wiggling a connector on a sensor or in the wiring harness may correct the open circuit condition. This should always be considered when an open circuit or a failed sensor is indicated.

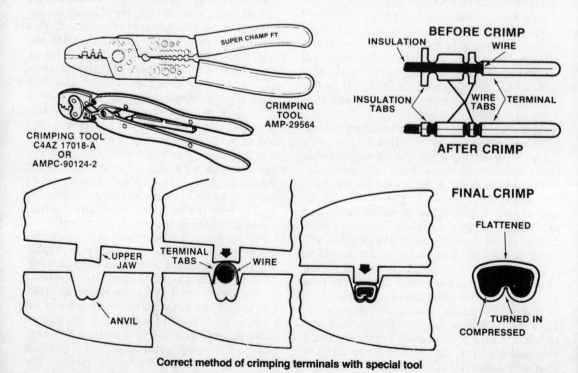

Correct method of crimping terminals with special tool

Intermittent problems may also be caused by oxidized or loose connections. When using a circuit tester for diagnosis, always probe connections from the wire side. Be careful not to damage sealed connectors with test probes.

All wiring harnesses should be replaced with identical parts, using the same gauge wire and connectors. When signal wires are spliced into a harness, use wire with high temperature insulation only. With the low voltage and current levels found in the system, it is important that the best possible connection at all wire splices be made by soldering the splices together. It is seldom necessary to replace a complete harness. If replacement is necessary, pay close attention to insure proper harness routing. Secure the harness with suitable plastic wire clamps to prevent vibrations from causing the harness to wear in spots or contact any hot components.

NOTE: *Weatherproof connectors cannot be replaced with standard connectors. Instructions are provided with replacement connector and terminal packages. Some wire harnesses have mounting indicators (usually pieces of colored tape) to mark where the harness is to be secured.*

In making wiring repairs, it's important that you always replace damaged wires with wires that are the same gauge as the wire being replaced. The heavier the wire, the smaller the gauge number. Wires are color-coded to aid in identification and whenever possible the same color coded wire should be used for replacement. A wire stripping and crimping tool is necessary to install solderless terminal connectors. Test all crimps by pulling on the wires; it should not be possible to pull the wires out of a good crimp.

Wires which are open, exposed or otherwise damaged are repaired by simple splicing. Where possible, if the wiring harness is accessible and the damaged place in the wire can be located, it is best to open the harness and check for all possible damage. In an inaccessible harness, the wire must be bypassed with a new insert, usually taped to the outside of the old harness.

When replacing fusible links, be sure to use fusible link wire, NOT ordinary automotive wire. Make sure the fusible segment is of the same gauge and construction as the one being replaced and double the stripped end when crimping the terminal connector for a good contact. The melted (open) fusible link segment of the wiring harness should be cut off as close to the harness as possible, then a new segment spliced in as described. In the case of a damaged fusible link that feeds two harness wires, the harness connections should be replaced with two fusible link wires so that each circuit will have its own separate protection.

NOTE: *Most of the problems caused in the wiring harness are due to bad ground connections. Always check all vehicle ground connections for corrosion or looseness before performing any power feed checks to eliminate the chance of a bad ground affecting the circuit.*

Repairing Hard Shell Connectors

Unlike molded connectors, the terminal contacts in hard shell connectors can be replaced. Weatherproof hard-shell connectors with the leads molded into the shell have non-replaceable terminal ends. Replacement usually involves the use of a special terminal removal tool that depress the locking tangs (barbs) on the connector terminal and allow the connector to be removed from the rear of the shell. The connector shell should be replaced if it shows any evidence of burning, melting, cracks, or breaks. Replace individual terminals that are burnt, corroded, distorted or loose.

NOTE: *The insulation crimp must be tight to prevent the insulation from sliding back on the wire when the wire is pulled. The insulation must be visibly compressed under the crimp tabs, and the ends of the crimp should be turned in for a firm grip on the insulation.*

The wire crimp must be made with all wire strands inside the crimp. The terminal must be fully compressed on the wire strands with the ends of the crimp tabs turned in to make a firm grip on the wire. Check all connections with an ohmmeter to insure a good contact. There should be no measurable resistance between the wire and the terminal when connected.

Mechanical Test Equipment

Vacuum Gauge

Most gauges are graduated in inches of mercury (in.Hg), although a device called a manometer reads vacuum in inches of water (in. H_2O). The normal vacuum reading usually varies between 18 and 22 in.Hg at sea level. To test engine vacuum, the vacuum gauge must be connected to a source of manifold vacuum. Many engines have a plug in the intake manifold which can be removed and replaced with an adapter fitting. Connect the vacuum gauge to the fitting with a suitable rubber hose or, if no manifold plug is available, connect the vacuum gauge to any device using manifold vacuum, such as EGR valves, etc. The vacuum gauge can be used to determine if enough vacuum is reaching a component to allow its actuation.

Hand Vacuum Pump

Small, hand-held vacuum pumps come in a variety of designs. Most have a built-in vacuum gauge and allow the component to be tested without removing it from the vehicle. Operate the pump lever or plunger to apply the correct amount of vacuum required for the test specified in the diagnosis routines. The level of vacuum in inches of Mercury (in.Hg) is indicated on the pump gauge. For some testing, an additional vacuum gauge may be necessary.

Intake manifold vacuum is used to operate various systems and devices on late model vehicles. To correctly diagnose and solve problems in vacuum control systems, a vacuum source is necessary for testing. In some cases, vacuum can be taken from the intake manifold when the engine is running, but vacuum is normally provided by a hand vacuum pump.

These hand vacuum pumps have a built-in vacuum gauge that allow testing while the device is still attached to the component. For some tests, an additional vacuum gauge may be necessary.

HEATING AND AIR CONDITIONING

Blower Motor

REMOVAL AND INSTALLATION

1. Disconnect the battery ground cable.
2. Remove the air cleaner or air inlet duct as necessary.
3. Remove the two screws attaching the vacuum reservoir to the blower assembly and remove the reservoir.
4. Disconnect the wire harness connector from the blower motor by pushing down on the

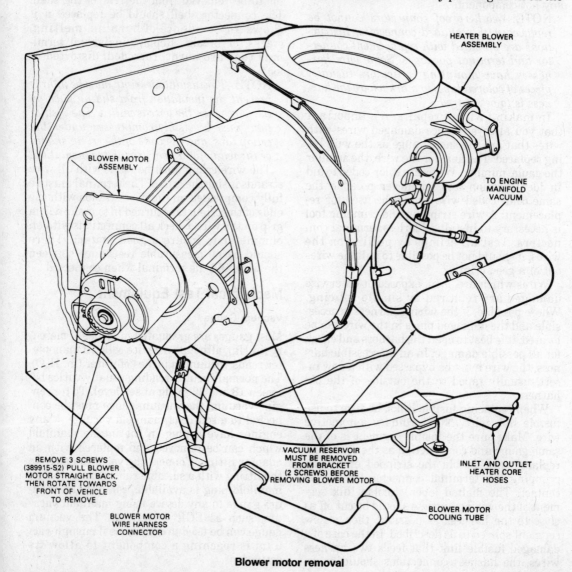

HEATER BLOWER ASSEMBLY

BLOWER MOTOR ASSEMBLY

TO ENGINE MANIFOLD VACUUM

REMOVE 3 SCREWS (389915-S2) PULL BLOWER MOTOR STRAIGHT BACK, THEN ROTATE TOWARDS FRONT OF VEHICLE TO REMOVE

VACUUM RESERVOIR MUST BE REMOVED FROM BRACKET (2 SCREWS) BEFORE REMOVING BLOWER MOTOR

INLET AND OUTLET HEATER CORE HOSES

BLOWER MOTOR WIRE HARNESS CONNECTOR

BLOWER MOTOR COOLING TUBE

Blower motor removal

connector tabs and pulling the connector off the motor.

5. Disconnect the blower motor cooling tube at the blower motor.

6. Remove the three screws attaching the blower motor and wheel to the heater blower assembly.

7. While holding the cooling tube aside, pull the blower motor and wheel from the heater blower assembly.

8. Remove the blower wheel hub clamp from the motor shaft, then pull the blower wheel from the motor shaft.

9. If the motor is being replaced, install the wheel on the new blower motor shaft and lock it in place with the hub clamp.

10. Glue a new motor housing gasket to the blower motor.

11. While holding the cooling tube aside, position the blower and wheel to the heater blower assembly. Install the three mounting screws.

12. Connect the blower motor cooling tube at the blower motor.

13. Connect the wire harness connector at the blower motor.

14. Install the vacuum reservoir on the bracket with two screws.

15. Install the air cleaner or air inlet duct assembly.

Heater Core

REMOVAL AND INSTALLATION

1. Allow the engine to cool completely. Using a thick cloth for protection, carefully open the radiator cap to its first stop and allow any residual cooling system pressure to vent. Once the pressure is released, tighten the radiator cap on the radiator.

2. Disconnect the heater hoses from the heater core tubes using tool T85T-18539-AH or equivalent, as illustrated. Plug the heater hoses to prevent coolant loss during the procedure.

3. Working in the passenger compartment, remove the six screws attaching the heater core access cover to the plenum assembly. Remove the access cover.

4. Depress the retainer bracket at the top of the heater core and pull the heater core rearward and down, removing it from the plenum assembly.

CAUTION: *Some coolant will remain in the heater core. Exercise caution when removing and lay a protective cloth down to protect the interior of the van during heater core removal.*

5. To install, first position the heater core and seal in the plenum assembly, snapping it into the retainer bracket at the top of the core.

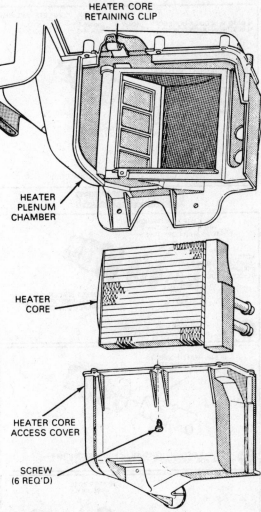

Typical heater core installation

6. Install the heater core access cover to the plenum assembly and secure it with the six screws.

7. Install the quick-connect heater hoses to the heater core tubes at the dash panel in the engine compartment as illustrated.

8. Check the coolant level and top off as necessary.

9. Start the engine, move the heater controls to the MAX HEAT position and check for leaks.

Heater Control Assembly

REMOVAL AND INSTALLATION

1. Disconnect the battery ground cable.

2. Remove the instrument cluster housing cover as described under "Instrument Panel Removal and Installation."

3. Remove the three screws attaching the control assembly to the instrument panel.

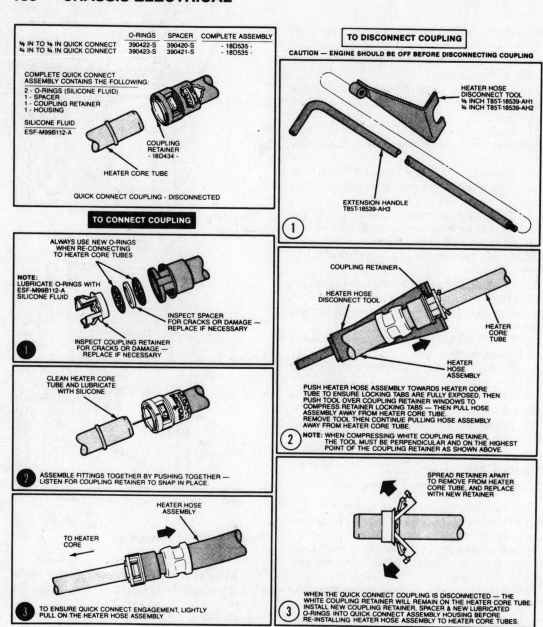

Disconnecting heater hose quick connect couplings

4. Pull the control assembly far enough rearward to allow removal of electrical connectors and remove the connectors.

5. Using a small pair of pliers, carefully release the function control cable (black) snap-in flag from the control bracket.

6. Pull enough cable through the instrument panel opening until the function control cable (black) can be held perpendicular to the control, then remove the control cable from the function control lever.

7. Repeat the process for the temperature control cable (blue).

8. To install, first pull temperature control cable (blue) through the opening in the instrument panel.

9. Attach the temperature cable wire (blue) to the temperature control lever and snap the cable flag into the control bracket.

10. Repeat the process for the function control cable (black).

11. Install the wire harness electrical connectors to the control assembly.

12. Position the control assembly to the instrument panel and install three attaching screws.

13. Install the instrument cluster housing cover.

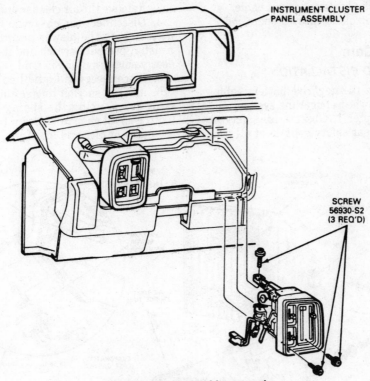

Heater control assembly removal

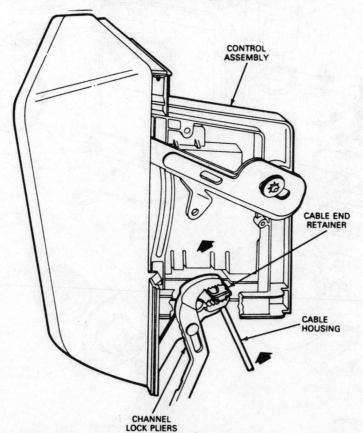

Control cable removal. Compress the cable end retainer, then pull the cable housing in direction of arrow

14. Connect the battery ground cable.
15. Check controls for proper operation.

Evaporator Core

REMOVAL AND INSTALLATION

1. Disconnect the negative battery cable.
2. Discharge the refrigerant system as described in Chapter 1. Observe all safety precautions and wear safety goggles at all times.

3. Remove the air cleaner and air inlet duct.
4. Disconnect the electrical hard shell connectors from the blower motor, blower motor resistor, pressure switch and the recirculation door vacuum motor solenoid.
5. Disconnect the liquid line from the inlet tube and the suction line(s) from the accumulator drier, using the spring lock coupling tools. Cap all open refrigerant lines to prevent the entry of dirt and moisture.

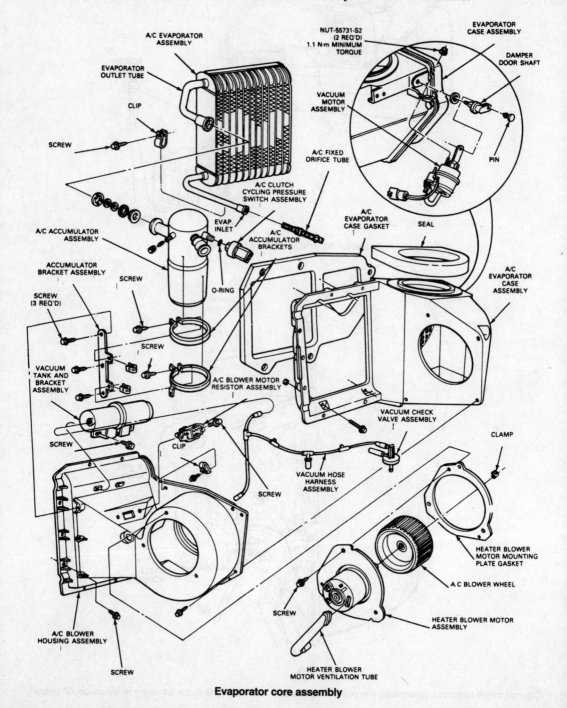

Evaporator core assembly

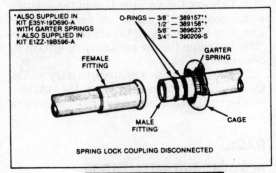

*ALSO SUPPLIED IN
KIT E35Y-19D690-A
WITH GARTER SPRINGS
† ALSO SUPPLIED IN
KIT E1ZZ-19B596-A

O-RINGS — 3/8" — 389157"†
1/2" — 389158"†
5/8" — 389623"
3/4" — 390209-S

FEMALE FITTING

GARTER SPRING

MALE FITTING

CAGE

SPRING LOCK COUPLING DISCONNECTED

TO CONNECT COUPLING

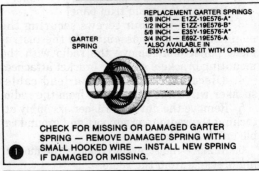

GARTER SPRING

REPLACEMENT GARTER SPRINGS
3/8 INCH — E1ZZ-19E576-A*
1/2 INCH — E1ZZ-19E576-B*
5/8 INCH — E35Y-19E576-A*
3/4 INCH — E69Z-19E576-A
*ALSO AVAILABLE IN
E35Y-19D690-A KIT WITH O-RINGS

(1) CHECK FOR MISSING OR DAMAGED GARTER SPRING — REMOVE DAMAGED SPRING WITH SMALL HOOKED WIRE — INSTALL NEW SPRING IF DAMAGED OR MISSING.

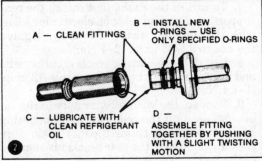

A — CLEAN FITTINGS

B — INSTALL NEW O-RINGS — USE ONLY SPECIFIED O-RINGS

C — LUBRICATE WITH CLEAN REFRIGERANT OIL

D — ASSEMBLE FITTING TOGETHER BY PUSHING WITH A SLIGHT TWISTING MOTION

(2)

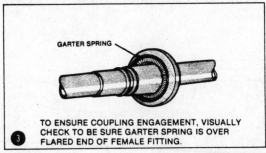

GARTER SPRING

(3) TO ENSURE COUPLING ENGAGEMENT, VISUALLY CHECK TO BE SURE GARTER SPRING IS OVER FLARED END OF FEMALE FITTING.

TO DISCONNECT COUPLING

CAUTION — DISCHARGE SYSTEM BEFORE DISCONNECTING COUPLING

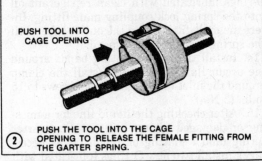

NOTE:
EACH END OF TOOL T81P-19623-Q IS A DIFFERENT SIZE TO FIT 3/8 and 1/2 INCH COUPLINGS

TOOL
T81P-19623-G - 3/8 & 1/2 INCH
T81P-19623-G1 - 3/8 INCH
T81P-19623-G2 - 1/2 INCH
T83P-19623-C - 5/8 INCH
T85L-19623-A - 3/4 INCH

CAGE OPENING

(1) FIT TOOL TO COUPLING SO THAT TOOL CAN ENTER CAGE OPENING TO RELEASE THE GARTER SPRING.

PUSH TOOL INTO CAGE OPENING

(2) PUSH THE TOOL INTO THE CAGE OPENING TO RELEASE THE FEMALE FITTING FROM THE GARTER SPRING.

(3) PULL THE COUPLING MALE AND FEMALE FITTINGS APART.

(4) REMOVE THE TOOL FROM THE DISCONNECTED SPRING LOCK COUPLING.

Removing and installing spring lock couplings

6. Remove the water valve and disconnect the vacuum line.

7. Disconnect the vacuum harness check valve from the engine source line and disconnect the vacuum line from the vacuum motor solenoid.

8. Remove the two mounting bands holding the accumulator drier to the evaporator core

and the clamp from around the evaporator inlet tube. Using the spring lock coupling tool, disconnect the accumulator drier from the evaporator core outlet tube and remove the accumulator drier. Cap all open refrigerant connections to prevent the entry of dirt and moisture.

9. Remove the eleven screws holding the

evaporator case blower housing to the evaporator case assembly. Remove the evaporator case blower housing from the vehicle.

10. Remove the evaporator core from the vehicle.

11. To install, first position the evaporator core into the installed evaporator case half.

12. Position the evaporator case blower housing to the evaporator case and install with eleven screws.

13. After checking the male fitting on the accumulator drier for a missing or damaged spring lock coupling garter spring (and replacing or repairing as necessary), install two new O-rings lubricated with clean refrigerant oil into the spring lock coupling male fitting. Insert the male fitting into the outlet tube until the spring lock is fully engaged.

14. Install the two mounting bands around the accumulator drier and install the clamp around the inlet line. Tighten the screws to 15 in.lb. (2 Nm).

15. After checking the liquid line for a missing or damaged spring lock coupling garter spring (and replacing or repairing as necessary), install two new O-rings lubricated with clean refrigerant oil into the spring lock coupling male fitting. Insert the male fitting into the inlet tube until the spring lock is fully engaged.

16. Install the suction line(s) to the accumulator drier, using the same procedure as for the liquid line above.

17. Connect the vacuum line to the water valve and install the water valve.

18. Connect the electrical hard shell connectors to the blower motor resistor and the vacuum motor.

19. Connect the vacuum line to the vacuum motor solenoid. Connect the vacuum source line from the engine to the check valve.

20. Recharge the air conditioning system as described in Chapter 1.

21. Reconnect the negative battery cable, then start the engine and check the A/C system for refrigerant leaks and proper operation.

RADIO

REMOVAL AND INSTALLATION

1. Disconnect the negative battery cable.

2. Remove the radio trim panel.

3. Remove the four screws securing the mounting brackets assembly to the instrument panel and remove the radio with the mounting brackets and rear bracket attached.

4. Disconnect the antenna lead cable, speaker wires and power wire from the radio.

5. Remove the nut and washer assembly attaching the radio rear support and ground cable on electronic radios.

6. Remove the screws to remove the mounting brackets from the radio.

7. To install the radio, first attach the rear support (and ground cable on electronic radios) with the nut and washer assembly. Tighten the nut to 22–35 in.lb. (2–4 Nm).

8. Install the mounting brackets to the radio and tighten the mounting screws to 9–12 in.lb. (1–1.4 Nm).

9. Connect the wiring connectors to the radio and position the radio with the mounting brackets to the instrument panel. Make sure the hairpin area of the rear bracket is engaged to the instrument panel support.

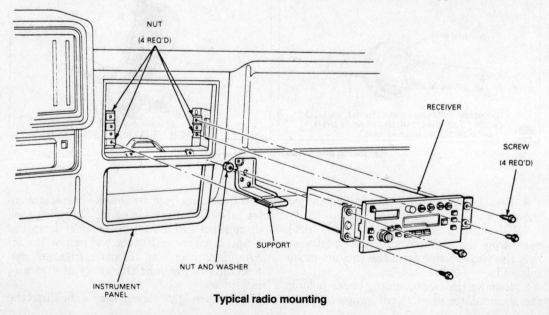

Typical radio mounting

10. Secure the radio and mounting brackets to the instrument panel with four screws. Make sure the mounting brackets are fully seated on the instrument panel.

11. Install the radio trim panel over the radio assembly.

12. Reconnect the battery ground cable.

WINDSHIELD WIPERS

Blade and Arm Assembly

Remove the blade and arm assemblies from the pivot shafts as illustrated. Turn on the wiper switch to allow the motor to move the pivot shafts three or four cycles, then turn off

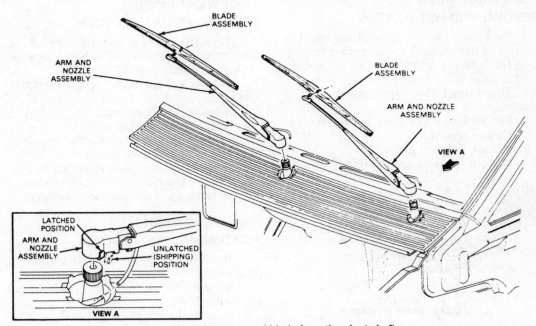

Removing wiper arm and blade from the pivot shaft

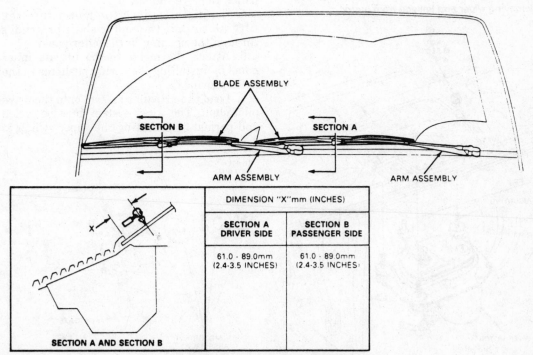

DIMENSION "X" mm (INCHES)	
SECTION A DRIVER SIDE	SECTION B PASSENGER SIDE
61.0 - 89.0mm (2.4-3.5 INCHES)	61.0 - 89.0mm (2.4-3.5 INCHES)

Installing the arm and blade assemblies

the wiper switch. This will place the pivot shafts in the PARK position. Install the arm and blade assemblies on the pivot shafts to dimension **X** as illustrated. This dimension is the distance between the centerline of the blade saddle and the top edge of the cowl top grille.

Front Wiper Motor
REMOVAL AND INSTALLATION

1. Turn the wiper switch on, then turn the ignition switch on until the blades are in mid-pattern. Turn the ignition switch off to keep the blades in mid-pattern.
2. Disconnect the wiper motor wiring connector.
3. Remove both wiper arms, noting their position before removal.
4. Remove the cowl grille.
5. Remove the linkage retaining clip and

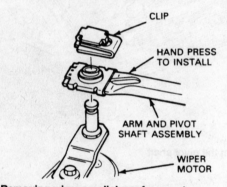

Removing wiper arm linkage from motor

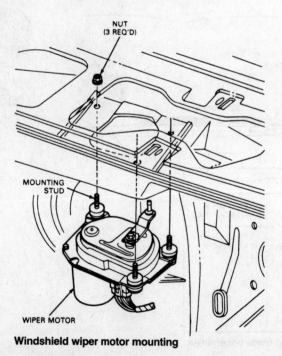

Windshield wiper motor mounting

disassemble the linkage from the motor crank arm.

6. Remove the wiper motor retaining nuts while holding the motor on its underside to prevent it from falling and possible damage.
7. Installation is the reverse of removal procedures.

Front Wiper Linkage
REMOVAL AND INSTALLATION

1. Turn the ignition and wiper switch on, then turn the ignition off when the wiper blades are in mid-pattern.
2. Disconnect the wiper motor electrical connector.
3. Remove the wiper arms.
4. Remove the cowl top grille.
5. Remove the clip retaining the linkage to the crank arm of the wiper motor.
6. Remove the four pivot retaining screws.
7. Remove the linkage from the vehicle.
8. Installation is the reverse of removal.

Rear Wiper Motor
REMOVAL AND INSTALLATION

1. Remove the wiper arm and blade as illustrated.
2. Remove the motor shaft attaching nut and wedge block.
3. Remove the liftgate trim panel.
4. Disconnect the electrical connector and remove the motor wiring pins from the inner panel. Remove the motor.
5. To install, place the motor into the liftgate so that the motor shaft protrudes through the opening in the outer panel.
6. Attach the motor to the liftgate inner panel by installing the wiring pushpins in the holes provided.
7. Load the articulating arm onto the drive pilot shaft. The wiper system must be cycled and parked by operating the wiper switch to

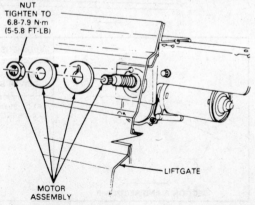

Rear wiper motor mounting

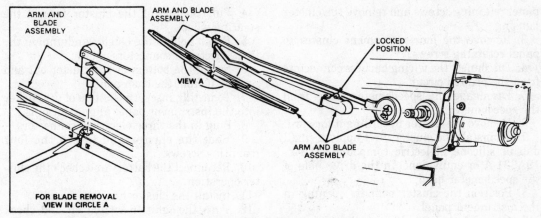

Removing rear wiper blade and arm

insure that the system linkage is in the PARK position before the arm and blade is installed.

8. Locate the blade to the specified installation position.

9. Install the arm onto the pivot shaft after the articulating arm is in place with the slide latch in the unlocked position.

10. While applying a downward pressure on the arm head to insure full seating, raise the other end of the arm sufficiently to allow the latch to slide under the pivot shaft to the locked position. Use finger pressure only to

slide the latch, then release the arm and blade against the rear window.

INSTRUMENTS AND SWITCHES

Instrument Cluster

REMOVAL AND INSTALLATION

Standard Cluster

1. Disconnect the negative battery cable.
2. Remove the seven cluster housing-to-

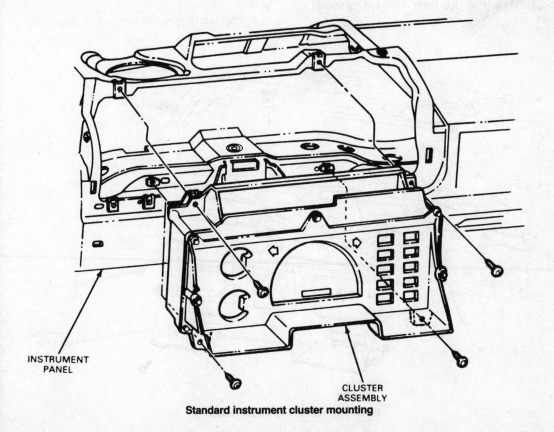

Standard instrument cluster mounting

panel retaining screws and remove the cluster housing.

3. Remove the four instrument cluster to panel retaining screws.

4. Disconnect the wiring harness connectors from the printed circuit.

5. Disengage the speedometer cable from the speedometer.

6. Remove the cluster by pulling it forward.

7. To install the cluster, first apply a small dab of silicone dielectric compound (D7AZ-19A331-A or equivalent) in the drive hole of the speedometer head.

8. Position the cluster near its opening in the instrument panel.

9. Connect the speedometer cable to the speedometer head.

10. Connect the wiring harness connectors to the printed circuit.

11. Position the cluster to the instrument panel and install the four cluster-to-panel retaining screws.

12. Install the cluster housing to the panel.

13. Connect the battery ground cable.

14. Turn the ignition switch on and check the operation of all gauges, lamps and signals.

Electronic Cluster

1. Disconnect the battery ground cable.

2. Remove the cluster housing.

3. Remove the four cluster mounting screws.

4. Pull the top of the cluster toward the steering wheel.

5. Reach behind the cluster and unplug the three electrical connectors.

6. Swing the bottom of the cluster out and remove it from the dash panel.

7. To install, insert the bottom of the cluster into the instrument panel alignment pins.

8. Plug in the three electrical connectors.

9. Seat the cluster and fasten the four mounting screws.

10. Reconnect the battery and check the cluster operation.

11. Install the cluster housing.

12. Turn the ignition switch on and check cluster operation.

Front Wiper Switch
REMOVAL AND INSTALLATION

1. Disconnect the negative battery cable.

2. Remove the cluster finish panel assembly five retaining screws.

3. Remove the three left control pod assembly retaining screws.

4. Remove the wiring connector from the switch.

5. Remove the two lamp switch-to-control pod retaining screws and remove the switch pod.

6. Installation is the reverse of removal.

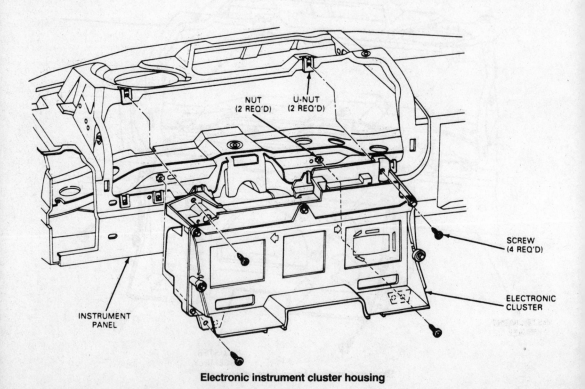

NUT (2 REQ'D)
U-NUT (2 REQ'D)
SCREW (4 REQ'D)
ELECTRONIC CLUSTER
INSTRUMENT PANEL

Electronic instrument cluster housing

Rear Wiper Switch
REMOVAL AND INSTALLATION

1. Disconnect the negative battery cable.
2. Remove the upper and lower trim shrouds.
3. Disconnect the quick connect electrical connector.
4. Peel back the foam sight shield, remove the two cross-recessed screws holding the switch and remove the wash/wipe switch.
5. Installation is the reverse of removal.

Headlight Switch
REMOVAL AND INSTALLATION

1. Disconnect the negative battery cable.
2. Remove the cluster finish panel assembly five retaining screws.
3. Remove the three left control pod assembly retaining screws.
4. Disconnect the wiring connector from the switch.
5. Remove the two lamp switch-to-control pod retaining screws and remove the switch.
6. Installation is the reverse of removal.

Speedometer Cable
REMOVAL AND INSTALLATION

1. Raise the van and support it safely.
2. Disengage the cable assembly from the transmission and remove it.

NOTE: *On vehicles equipped with a transmission mounted speed sensor, remove the speedometer cable by pulling it out of the speed sensor. Do not attempt to remove the spring retainer clip with the speedometer in the sensor. To install the speedometer cable, align the core with the sensor and snap the cable assembly into the speed sensor.*

3. Disengage all remaining cable clips.
4. Push the grommet out of the floor pan and the cable through the floor pan opening into the cab.

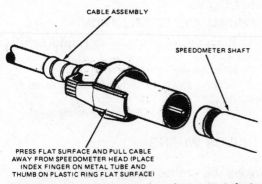

PRESS FLAT SURFACE AND PULL CABLE AWAY FROM SPEEDOMETER HEAD (PLACE INDEX FINGER ON METAL TUBE AND THUMB ON PLASTIC RING FLAT SURFACE)

Disconnecting speedometer from instrument cluster

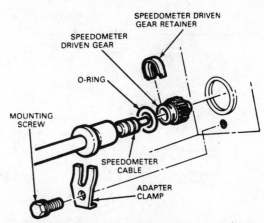

Speedometer cable mounting at the transmission

5. Remove the screw holding the cable clip to the steering column bracket.
6. Disconnect the speedometer cable from the speedometer and remove the cable.
7. To install, connect the speedometer cable to the speedometer head.
8. Route the cable through the floor pan opening and attach the clip to the steering column bracket.
9. Lubricate the cable core exposed at the transmission ferrule with silicone grease. Apply a coating of polyethylene grease to the O-ring on the ferrule.
10. Lubricate the inside diameter and the teeth of the driven gear with speedometer cable lubricant (DZAZ-19581-A or equivalent) and install the driven gear on the ferrule.
11. Assemble the driven gear retainer to the driven gear with the retainer tabs toward the gear teeth.
12. Insert the driven gear and cable into the transmission and retain with the clamp by tightening the retaining screw to 20–25 in.lb. (2–3 Nm).
13. Secure the cable with the clips and clamps at the locations indicated by the tape on the cable, then lower the vehicle.

NOTE: *The speedometer cable routing should avoid sharp bends and the cable should be straight for approximately 8 inches from the speedometer.*

LIGHTING

Headlights
REMOVAL AND INSTALLATION

1. Remove the headlight door attaching screws and remove the headlight door.
2. Remove the headlight retaining ring screws and remove the retaining ring. Do not disturb the adjusting screw settings.

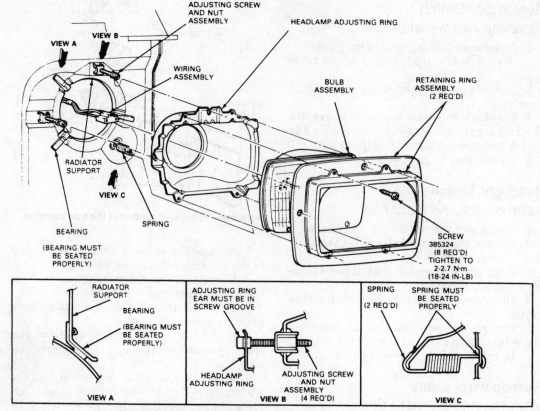

Headlight assembly showing mounting and adjustment screws

3. Pull the headlight door forward and disconnect the wiring connector from the bulb, then remove the headlight from the vehicle.

4. Connect the wiring connector to the new headlight and place the light in position, making sure the locating tabs are fitted in the positioning slots.

5. Install the headlamp retaining ring.

6. Place the headlight door in position and install the retaining screws.

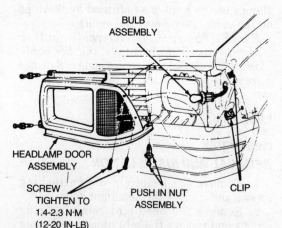

Front parking, turn and marker light assembly

Parking, Turn and Front Side Marker Lights

REMOVAL AND INSTALLATION

1. Remove the four screws securing the bezel and lamp assembly.

2. Remove the lamp assembly by removing the three screws retaining the lamp to the bezel.

3. Remove the socket from the lamp assembly.

4. Pull the bulb directly out from the socket.

5. Installation is the reverse of removal.

Rear Lights

REMOVAL AND INSTALLATION

1. Remove the four screws retaining the lamp assembly to the van.

2. Remove the lamp assembly.

3. Remove the bulb socket from the lamp assembly, then remove the bulb.

4. Installation is the reverse of removal.

TRAILER WIRING

Wiring the van for towing is fairly easy. The manufacturer provides a wiring kit as part of

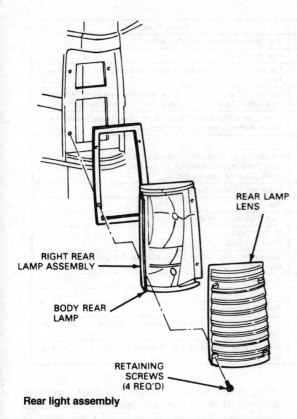

REAR LAMP
LENS

RIGHT REAR
LAMP ASSEMBLY

BODY REAR
LAMP

RETAINING
SCREWS
(4 REQ'D)

Rear light assembly

separate turn signals, you can purchase an isolation unit so that the brake lights won't blink whenever the turn signals are operated, or you can go to your local electronics supply house and buy four diodes to wire in series with the brake and turn signal bulbs. Diodes will isolate the brake and turn signals. The choice is yours. The isolation units are simple and quick to install, but far more expensive than the diodes. The diodes, however, require more work to install properly, since they require the cutting of each bulb's wire and soldering in place of the diode.

One final point; the best kits are those with a spring loaded cover on the vehicle mounted socket. This cover prevent dirt and moisture from corroding the terminals. Never let the vehicle socket hang loosely; always mount it securely to the bumper or hitch.

CIRCUIT PROTECTION

Fuse Panel

Most of the replaceable fuses for the electrical system are located on the fuse panel under the instrument panel to the left of the steering column. For access to the fuse panel, remove the fasteners from the lower edge of the cover, then pull the cover downward until the spring clips disengage from the instrument panel. On the base models, the cover simply snaps on and off. The fuses are replaced by simply pulling them out. A blown or open fuse can be seen as a break in the metal filament that runs between the blades. The fuse is made with a plastic body so the break can be clearly seen.

The locations of various fuses are illustrated. Fuses that open (blow) may by replaced, but will continue to open until the cause of the overload condition is corrected. If a fuse needs to be replaced, use only a new fuse rated ac-

the trailer towing option, but if the Aerostar was originally purchased without the trailer option, there are a number of good wiring kits available and these should be used, rather than trying to design your own. All trailers will need brake lights and turn signals as well as tail lights and side marker lights. Most states require extra marker lights for overwide trailers. Also, most states have recently required back-up lights for trailers, and most trailer manufacturers have been building trailers with back-up lights for several years.

Additionally, some Class I, most Class II and just about all Class III trailers will have electric brakes. Add to this number an accessories wire, to operate trailer internal equipment or to charge the trailer's battery, and you can have as many as seven wires in the harness.

Determine the equipment on your trailer and buy the wiring kit necessary. The kit will contain all the wires needed, plus a plug adapter set which included the female plug, mounted on the bumper or hitch, and the male plug, wired into, or plugged into the trailer harness. When installing the kit, follow the manufacturer's instructions. The color coding of the wires is standard throughout the industry.

One point to note: on most domestic vehicles, the brake lights and rear turn signals operate with the same bulb. For those vehicles with

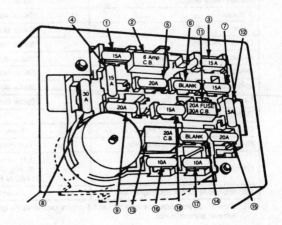

Typical fuse box assembly

Position	Description	Color	Circuit Protected
1	15 Amp Fuse	Light Blue	Stop Lamps, Emergency Warning Flasher
2	6 Amp C.B.		Front Wiper/Washer
3	15 Amp Fuse	Light Blue	Rear Lamps, Park Lamps, Marker Lamps, License Lamps, Trailer Lamps Relay
4	15 Amp Fuse	Light Blue	Turn Signal Flasher, Back-Up Lamps, Illuminated Visor Vanity, Illuminated Entry Module, Trailer Tow Turn Signal Relay, Electronic Day/Night Mirror
5	20 Amp Fuse	Yellow	Speed Control, Rear Wiper/Washer/Defrost, Clock Display, Washer Fluid Sensor, Warning Chime, Door Ajar, Heated Window
6	Not Used		
7	15 Amp Fuse	Light Blue	Courtesy Lamps, Dome Lamp, Glove Box Lamp, Radio Memory, Cargo Lamp, Trip Computer, Headlamps On Indicator, Footwell Lamp, Reading Lamps, Clock, Key Warning Buzzer
8	30 Amp Fuse	Light Green	Heater and A/C Motor Blower, A/C Clutch
9	20 Amp Fuse	Yellow	Flash to Pass
10	15 Amp Fuse	Light Blue	Radio/Tape Player, Amplifier
11	20 Amp Fuse 30 Amp C.B.	Yellow	RR Cigar Lighter Power Door Locks
12	5 Amp Fuse	Tan	Instrument Panel Illumination Lamps, Automatic Transmission Floor Shift Illumination
13	20 Amp C.B.		Power Windows
14	Not Used		
15	20 Amp Fuse	Yellow	Front Cigar Lighter, Horns
16	10 Amp Fuse	Red	Tachometer Cluster, Fuel Computer, Speedometer Cluster, Electronic Day Illumination
17	10 Amp Fuse	Red	Warning Lamps, Seat Belt Buzzer, Carburetor Circuits, Low Fuel Warning, Door Ajar

cording to the specifications and of the same amperage number as the one removed. Five spare fuses are located inside the fuse panel cover.

CAUTION: *Always replace a blown fuse or fuse link with the same rating as specified. Never replace a fuse with a higher amperage rating than the one removed, or severly wiring damage and a possible fire can result.*

Selected circuits, such as headlights and windshield wipers, are protected with circuit breakers. A circuit breaker is designed to stop current flow in case of a short-circuit or overload. It will automatically restore current flow after a few seconds, but will again interrupt current flow if the overload or short-circuit continues. This on/off cycle will continue as long as the overload or short-circuit exists, except for the circuit breakers protecting the power door lock and power window circuits will not restore current flow until the overload is removed.

Fusible Links

A fusible link is a short length of Hypalon (high temperature) insulated wire, integral with the wiring harness and should not be con-

Circuit Protected	Location	Size
Auxiliary Heater or A/C	Starter Motor Relay	16 GA. Fuse Link (Orange)
Alternator	Starter Motor Relay	16 GA. Fuse Link (Orange)
Trailer	Starter Motor Relay	16 GA. Fuse Link (Orange)
Engine Compartment Light	Starter Motor Relay	20 GA. Fuse Link (Blue)
Heated Backlite/Power Lumbar	Starter Motor Relay	16 GA. Fuse Link (Orange)
Headlight Switch Feed	Starter Motor Relay	16 GA. Fuse Link (Orange)
Ignition Switch Feed	Starter Motor Relay	16 GA. Fuse Link (Orange)
Electronic Engine Control Power Relay	Starter Motor Relay	20 GA. Fuse Link (Blue)
Electronic Engine		
Electronic Engine Control 2.3L Engine Only	Power Relay	20 GA. Fuse Link (Blue)
Electronic Fuel Pump 2.3L Engine Only	Fuel Pump Relay	20 GA. Fuse Link (Blue)
Electronic Engine Control 2.8L Engine Only	L.H. Fender near 60 Way Connector to EEC-IV Processor	20 GA. Fuse Link (Blue)
Electronic Engine Control 3.0L Engine Only	Power Relay	20 GA. Fuse Link (Blue)

NOTE: Under NO circumstances, use more than an 8.5 ampere load across the ignition switch terminals for the rear light circuit on ANY truck or bus which uses the hydraulic stoplamp switch.

Fusible link locations

fused with standard wire. The fusible link is several wire gauges smaller than the circuit it protects and is designed to melt and break the circuit should an overload occur. Under no circumstances should a fusible link be replaced with a standard length of wire.

The higher melting temperature properties and additional thickness of the Hypalon insu-

REMOVE EXISTING VINYL TUBE SHIELDING
REINSTALL OVER FUSE LINK BEFORE CRIMPING
FUSE LINK TO WIRE ENDS

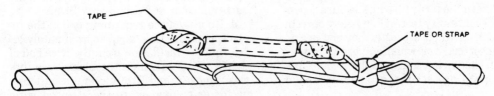

TAPE

TAPE OR STRAP

TYPICAL REPAIR USING THE SPECIAL #17 GA. (9.00" LONG-YELLOW) FUSE LINK REQUIRED FOR THE AIR/COND.
CIRCUITS (2) #687E and #261A LOCATED IN THE ENGINE COMPARTMENT

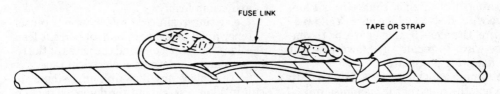

FUSE LINK

TAPE OR STRAP

TYPICAL REPAIR FOR ANY IN-LINE FUSE LINK USING THE SPECIFIED GAUGE FUSE LINK FOR THE SPECIFIC CIRCUIT

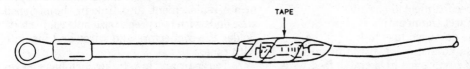

TAPE

TYPICAL REPAIR USING THE EYELET TERMINAL FUSE LINK OF THE SPECIFIED GAUGE FOR ATTACHMENT TO A CIRCUIT WIRE END

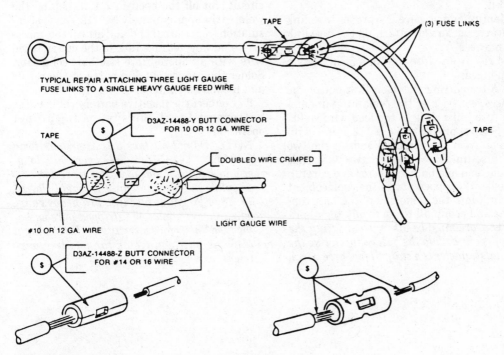

TAPE

(3) FUSE LINKS

TYPICAL REPAIR ATTACHING THREE LIGHT GAUGE
FUSE LINKS TO A SINGLE HEAVY GAUGE FEED WIRE

TAPE

D3AZ-14488-Y BUTT CONNECTOR
FOR 10 OR 12 GA. WIRE

DOUBLED WIRE CRIMPED

TAPE

#10 OR 12 GA. WIRE

LIGHT GAUGE WIRE

D3AZ-14488-Z BUTT CONNECTOR
FOR #14 OR 16 WIRE

FUSIBLE LINK REPAIR PROCEDURE

General fuse link repair procedure

lation will usually allow the undersized internal fuse wire to melt and disintegrate within the Hypalon casing with little damage to the high temperature insulation other than discoloration and/or bubbling of the insulation surface. In extreme cases of excessive circuit current, the insulation may separate after the fuse wire has disintegrated, however, the bare wire will seldom be exposed. If it becomes difficult to determine if the fuse link is burnt open, perform a continuity test. When heavy current flows, such as when a booster battery is connected incorrectly or when a short to ground occurs in the wiring harness, the fusible link burns out to protect the alternator and/or wiring.

Production fuse links have a flag moulded on the wire or on the terminal insulator. Color identification of the flag or connector is Blue–20 gauge wire, Red–18 gauge wire, Yellow–17 gauge wire, Orange–16 gauge wire, or Green–14 gauge wire. To repair any blown fuse link use the following procedure:

1. Determine which circuit is damaged, its location and the cause of the open fuse link. If the damaged fuse link is one of three fed by a common No. 10 or 12 gauge feed wire, determine the specific affected circuit.

2. Disconnect the negative battery cable.

3. Cut the damaged fuse link from the wiring harness and discard it. If the fuse link is one of three circuits fed by a single feed wire, cut it out of the harness at each splice end and discard it.

4. Identify and procure the proper fuse link and butt connectors for attaching the fuse link in the harness.

5. To repair any fuse link in a 3-link group with one feed:

   a. After cutting the open link out of the harness, cut each of the remaining undamaged fuse links close to the feed wire weld.

   b. Strip approximately ½" (12.7mm) of insulation from the detached ends of the two good fuse links. Then insert two wire ends into one end of a butt connector and carefully push one stripped end of the replacement fuse link into the same end of the butt connector and crimp all three firmly together. NOTE: *Care must be taken when fitting the three fuse links into the butt connector as the internal diameter is a snug fit for three wires.*

Make sure to use a proper crimping tool. Pliers, side cutters, etc. will not apply the proper crimp to retain the wires and withstand a pull test.

   c. After crimping the butt connector to the three fuse links, cut the weld portion from the feed wire and strip approximately ½" (12.7mm) of insulation from the cut end. Insert the stripped end into the open end of the butt connector and crimp very firmly.

   d. To attach the remaining end of the replacement fuse link, strip approximately ½" (12.7mm) of insulation from the wire end of the circuit from which the blown fuse link was removed, and firmly crimp a butt connector or equivalent to the stripped wire. Then, insert the end of the replacement link into the other end of the butter connector and crimp firmly.

   e. Using rosin core solder with a consistency of 60 percent tin and 40 percent lead, solder the connectors and the wires at the repairs and insulate with electrical tape.

6. To replace any fuse link on a single circuit in a harness, cut out the damaged portion, strip approximately ½" (12.7mm) of insulation from the two wire ends and attach the appropriate replacement fuse link to the stripped wire ends with two proper size butt connectors. Solder the connectors and wires and insulate with tape.

7. To repair any fuse link which has an eyelet terminal on one end such as the charging circuit, cut off the open fuse link behind the weld, strip approximately ½" (12.7mm) of insulation from the cut end and attach the appropriate new eyelet fuse link to the cut stripped wire with an appropriate size butt connector. Solder the connectors and wires at the repair and insulate with tape.

8. Connect the negative battery cable to the battery and test the system for proper operation.

NOTE: *Do not mistake a resistor wire for a fuse link. The resistor wire is generally longer and has print stating, "Resistor: don't cut or splice." When attaching a single No. 16, 17, 18 or 20 gauge fuse link to a heavy gauge wire, always double the stripped wire end of the fuse link before inserting and crimping it into the butt connector for positive wire retention.*

Troubleshooting Basic Turn Signal and Flasher Problems

Most problems in the turn signals or flasher system, can be reduced to defective flashers or bulbs, which are easily replaced. Occasionally, problems in the turn signals are traced to the switch in the steering column, which will require professional service.

F = Front   R = Rear   ● = Lights off   o = Lights on

Problem		Solution
Turn signals light, but do not flash		• Replace the flasher
No turn signals light on either side		• Check the fuse. Replace if defective. • Check the flasher by substitution • Check for open circuit, short circuit or poor ground
Both turn signals on one side don't work		• Check for bad bulbs • Check for bad ground in both housings
One turn signal light on one side doesn't work		• Check and/or replace bulb • Check for corrosion in socket. Clean contacts. • Check for poor ground at socket
Turn signal flashes too fast or too slow		• Check any bulb on the side flashing too fast. A heavy-duty bulb is probably installed in place of a regular bulb. • Check the bulb flashing too slow. A standard bulb was probably installed in place of a heavy-duty bulb. • Check for loose connections or corrosion at the bulb socket
Indicator lights don't work in either direction		• Check if the turn signals are working • Check the dash indicator lights • Check the flasher by substitution
One indicator light doesn't light		• On systems with 1 dash indicator: See if the lights work on the same side. Often the filaments have been reversed in systems combining stoplights with taillights and turn signals. Check the flasher by substitution • On systems with 2 indicators: Check the bulbs on the same side Check the indicator light bulb Check the flasher by substitution

Troubleshooting Basic Lighting Problems

Problem	Cause	Solution
Lights		
One or more lights don't work, but others do	• Defective bulb(s) • Blown fuse(s) • Dirty fuse clips or light sockets • Poor ground circuit	• Replace bulb(s) • Replace fuse(s) • Clean connections • Run ground wire from light socket housing to car frame
Lights burn out quickly	• Incorrect voltage regulator setting or defective regulator • Poor battery/alternator connections	• Replace voltage regulator • Check battery/alternator connections
Lights go dim	• Low/discharged battery • Alternator not charging • Corroded sockets or connections • Low voltage output	• Check battery • Check drive belt tension; repair or replace alternator • Clean bulb and socket contacts and connections • Replace voltage regulator
Lights flicker	• Loose connection • Poor ground • Circuit breaker operating (short circuit)	• Tighten all connections • Run ground wire from light housing to car frame • Check connections and look for bare wires
Lights "flare"—Some flare is normal on acceleration—if excessive, see "Lights Burn Out Quickly"	• High voltage setting	• Replace voltage regulator
Lights glare—approaching drivers are blinded	• Lights adjusted too high • Rear springs or shocks sagging • Rear tires soft	• Have headlights aimed • Check rear springs/shocks • Check/correct rear tire pressure
Turn Signals		
Turn signals don't work in either direction	• Blown fuse • Defective flasher • Loose connection	• Replace fuse • Replace flasher • Check/tighten all connections
Right (or left) turn signal only won't work	• Bulb burned out • Right (or left) indicator bulb burned out • Short circuit	• Replace bulb • Check/replace indicator bulb • Check/repair wiring
Flasher rate too slow or too fast	• Incorrect wattage bulb • Incorrect flasher	• Flasher bulb • Replace flasher (use a variable load flasher if you pull a trailer)
Indicator lights do not flash (burn steadily)	• Burned out bulb • Defective flasher	• Replace bulb • Replace flasher
Indicator lights do not light at all	• Burned out indicator bulb • Defective flasher	• Replace indicator bulb • Replace flasher

Troubleshooting Basic Dash Gauge Problems

Problem	Cause	Solution
Coolant Temperature Gauge		
Gauge reads erratically or not at all	• Loose or dirty connections • Defective sending unit	• Clean/tighten connections • Bi-metal gauge: remove the wire from the sending unit. Ground the wire for an instant. If the gauge registers, replace the sending unit.
	• Defective gauge	• Magnetic gauge: disconnect the wire at the sending unit. With ignition ON gauge should register COLD. Ground the wire; gauge should register HOT.
Ammeter Gauge—Turn Headlights ON (do not start engine). Note reaction		
Ammeter shows charge Ammeter shows discharge Ammeter does not move	• Connections reversed on gauge • Ammeter is OK • Loose connections or faulty wiring • Defective gauge	• Reinstall connections • Nothing • Check/correct wiring • Replace gauge
Oil Pressure Gauge		
Gauge does not register or is inaccurate	• On mechanical gauge, Bourdon tube may be bent or kinked	• Check tube for kinks or bends preventing oil from reaching the gauge
	• Low oil pressure	• Remove sending unit. Idle the engine briefly. If no oil flows from sending unit hole, problem is in engine.
	• Defective gauge	• Remove the wire from the sending unit and ground it for an instant with the ignition ON. A good gauge will go to the top of the scale.
	• Defective wiring	• Check the wiring to the gauge. If it's OK and the gauge doesn't register when grounded, replace the gauge.
	• Defective sending unit	• If the wiring is OK and the gauge functions when grounded, replace the sending unit
All Gauges		
All gauges do not operate	• Blown fuse • Defective instrument regulator	• Replace fuse • Replace instrument voltage regulator
All gauges read low or erratically	• Defective or dirty instrument voltage regulator	• Clean contacts or replace
All gauges pegged	• Loss of ground between instrument voltage regulator and car • Defective instrument regulator	• Check ground • Replace regulator
Warning Lights		
Light(s) do not come on when ignition is ON, but engine is not started	• Defective bulb • Defective wire	• Replace bulb • Check wire from light to sending unit
	• Defective sending unit	• Disconnect the wire from the sending unit and ground it. Replace the sending unit if the light comes on with the ignition ON.
Light comes on with engine running	• Problem in individual system • Defective sending unit	• Check system • Check sending unit (see above)

Troubleshooting the Heater

Problem	Cause	Solution
Blower motor will not turn at any speed	• Blown fuse • Loose connection • Defective ground • Faulty switch • Faulty motor • Faulty resistor	• Replace fuse • Inspect and tighten • Clean and tighten • Replace switch • Replace motor • Replace resistor
Blower motor turns at one speed only	• Faulty switch • Faulty resistor	• Replace switch • Replace resistor
Blower motor turns but does not circulate air	• Intake blocked • Fan not secured to the motor shaft	• Clean intake • Tighten security
Heater will not heat	• Coolant does not reach proper temperature • Heater core blocked internally • Heater core air-bound • Blend-air door not in proper position	• Check and replace thermostat if necessary • Flush or replace core if necessary • Purge air from core • Adjust cable
Heater will not defrost	• Control cable adjustment incorrect • Defroster hose damaged	• Adjust control cable • Replace defroster hose

Troubleshooting Basic Windshield Wiper Problems

Problem	Cause	Solution
Electric Wipers		
Wipers do not operate— Wiper motor heats up or hums	• Internal motor defect • Bent or damaged linkage • Arms improperly installed on linking pivots	• Replace motor • Repair or replace linkage • Position linkage in park and reinstall wiper arms
Wipers do not operate— No current to motor	• Fuse or circuit breaker blown • Loose, open or broken wiring • Defective switch • Defective or corroded terminals • No ground circuit for motor or switch	• Replace fuse or circuit breaker • Repair wiring and connections • Replace switch • Replace or clean terminals • Repair ground circuits
Wipers do not operate— Motor runs	• Linkage disconnected or broken	• Connect wiper linkage or replace broken linkage
Vacuum Wipers		
Wipers do not operate	• Control switch or cable inoperative • Loss of engine vacuum to wiper motor (broken hoses, low engine vacuum, defective vacuum/fuel pump) • Linkage broken or disconnected • Defective wiper motor	• Repair or replace switch or cable • Check vacuum lines, engine vacuum and fuel pump • Repair linkage • Replace wiper motor
Wipers stop on engine acceleration	• Leaking vacuum hoses • Dry windshield • Oversize wiper blades • Defective vacuum/fuel pump	• Repair or replace hoses • Wet windshield with washers • Replace with proper size wiper blades • Replace pump

MANUAL TRANSMISSION

Identification

All Aerostar models with manual transmission are equipped with a Mazda 5-speed overdrive unit, identified as a Code 5 on the Safety Standard Certification Label. In addition, all manual transmissions have service identification tags to identify the unit for service purposes. The tag is found at the side of the main case.

The 5-speed manual overdrive transmission is fully synchronized in all gears except Reverse, which is in constant mesh. The gearshift mechanism is a direct control with a floor shifter. The shifter mechanism has a remote shift adapter to transfer shift lever movement to the control lever in the extension housing. No shifter adjustments are necessary or possible.

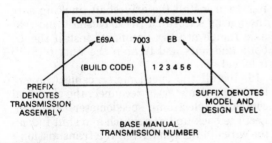

Transmission identification tag

REMOVAL AND INSTALLATION

1. Disconnect the negative battery terminal.
2. Shift the transmission into Neutral.
3. Remove the four bolts retaining the boot assembly to the floor, then raise the boot up the lever to allow working clearance.
4. Remove the four bolts retaining the shift lever assembly to the transmission remote shift rail adaptor. Remove the lever, knob and boot assembly.
5. Raise the vehicle and support it safely on jackstands.
6. Disconnect the starter cable and wires. Remove the starter retaining bolts and remove the starter.
7. Remove the clip retaining the tube to the hydraulic clutch slave cylinder. Remove the tube and fitting from the slave cylinder, then cap the end of the tube and slave cylinder to prevent the entry of dirt, moisture or other contaminants into the hydraulic clutch system.
8. Disconnect the back-up lamp switch and shift indicator and neutral position wires from the senders on the transmission. Remove the speedometer cable (conventional speedometer), or the electrical connector (electronic speedometer) from the fitting.
9. Scribe a mark on the driveshaft and rear axle flange to index the driveline position for installation and balance purposes. Remove the U-bolts and nuts from the rear axle flange,

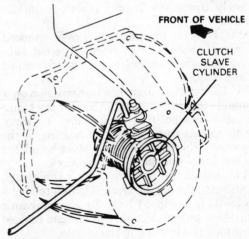

Location of clutch slave cylinder

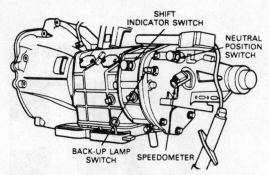

Electrical connections on the manual transmission

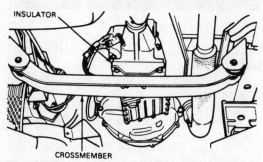

Front insulator and crossmember assembly

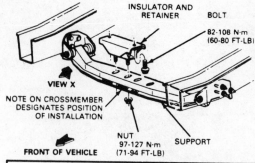

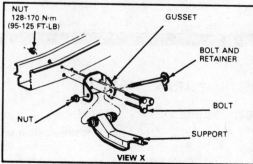

Front insulator and crossmember installation

then remove the driveshaft. Cap the transmission extension housing to prevent lubricant leakage.

10. Remove the nuts retaining the insulator to the crossmember. Loosen the nut and washer assemblies attaching the front insulators to the crossmember brackets.

11. Position a transmission jack under the transmission and slightly raise the transmission.

12. Remove the bolts retaining the clutch housing to the engine. Bring the transmission rearward to separate the clutch housing from the sowel pins in the rear of the engine block. Slowly lower the transmission from the vehicle.

NOTE: *If the transmission is to be removed from the vehicle for an extended period, support the rear of the engine with a safety stand and wood block.*

13. To install, position the transmission on a suitable transmission jack, then lift the transmission into position. Make sure the input shaft splines engage the pilot bearing in the flywheel. The clutch housing must be piloted in the dowel pins in the engine block.

14. Install the bolts retaining the clutch housing to the engine block. Tighten the bolts to 28–33 ft.lb. (38–51 Nm). To avoid galvanic corrosion, only aluminum washers can be used to attach the housing to the engine.

15. If removed, position the insulator on the transmission, then install and tighten the bolts to 60–80 ft.lb. (82–108 Nm).

16. Position the crossmember in the frame brackets, install the nuts and bolts and partially tighten.

17. Lower the transmission so the insulator studs are piloted in the proper holes in the crossmember. Install and tighten the nuts to 71–94 ft.lb. (97–127 Nm). Tighten the nut and washer assemblies attaching the front insulators to the frame brackets to the specified torque.

18. Remove the cap from the extension housing, then install the driveshaft, making sure the marks scribed on the driveshaft and rear axle flange are in alignment. Install the U-bolts and nuts and tighten the nuts to 8–15 ft.lb. (11–20 Nm).

19. Install the speedometer cable (conventional speedometer) or reconnect the electrical connector (electronic speedometer) and connect the back-up lamp switch and shift indicator wires to the senders on the transmission.

20. Remove the cap from the hydraulic clutch tube. Install the tube and fitting in the slave cylinder, then install the clip retaining the tube and fitting to the slave cylinder.

21. Position the starter on the housing, install the ground cable and start the bolts. Tighten the bolts to 15–20 ft.lb. (21–27 Nm). Connect the relay-to-starter cable and tighten the nut and washer, then lower the vehicle.

22. Install the shift lever in the shifter adaptor and tighten the bolts to 15–20 ft.lb. (20–27 Nm).

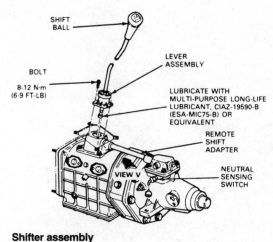

Shifter assembly

23. Position the rubber shift boot on the floor and install the bolts.
24. Connect the negative battery cable.
25. Bleed the hydraulic clutch system as described later in this chapter.

CLUTCH

Clutch Disc and Pressure Plate
REMOVAL AND INSTALLATION

CAUTION: *The clutch driven disc contains asbestos, which has been determined to be a cancer causing agent. Never clean clutch surfaces with compressed air and avoid inhaling any dust from any clutch surface. When cleaning clutch surfaces, use a commercially available brake cleaning fluid.*

1. Disconnect the clutch hydraulic system master cylinder from the clutch pedal and dash panel.
2. Raise the van and support it safely on jackstands.
3. Remove the starter.
4. Remove the hydraulic tube retainer clip at the slave cylinder. Remove the tube from the slave cylinder.
5. Remove the transmission and clutch housing.
6. Mark the assembled position of the pressure plate and cover to the flywheel for reassembly.
7. Loosen the pressure plate and cover attaching bolts evenly until the pressure plate springs are expanded and remove the bolts.
8. Remove the pressure plate, cover assembly and clutch disc from the flywheel.
9. Clean the pressure plate and flywheel surfaces with a suitable commercial alcohol base solvent to be sure that surfaces are free from any oil film. Do not use cleaners with a petroleum base and do not immerse the pressure plate in the solvent.
10. To install, position the clutch disc on the flywheel so that the clutch alignment tool (T74P-7137-K or equivalent) can enter the clutch pilot bearing and align the disc.
11. When installing the original pressure plate and cover assembly, align the assembly and flywheel according to the marks made during the removal procedure. Position the pressure plate and cover assembly on the flywheel, align the pressure plate and disc and install the retaining bolts that fasten the assembly to the flywheel. Tighten the bolts in the sequence

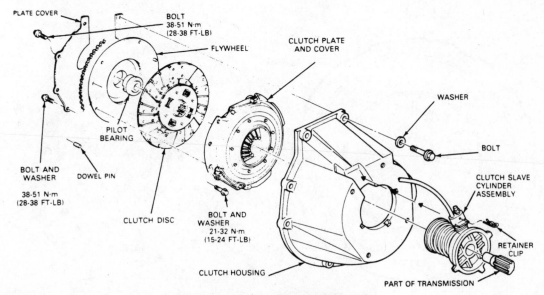

Clutch assembly on 2.3L (140 CID) engine

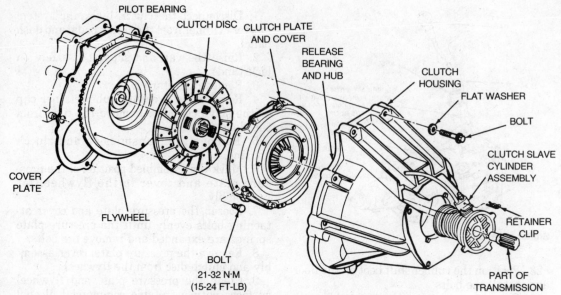

Clutch assembly on 2.8L (171 CID) and 3.0L (182 CID) engines

illustrated to 15–25 ft.lb. (21–32 Nm), then remove the clutch pilot tool.

12. Install the transmission and clutch housing as previously described. Reuse the aluminum washers under the retaining bolt to prevent galvanic corrosion.

13. Install the clutch hydraulic tube to the slave cylinder, being careful not to damage the O-ring seal. Install the retainer clip.

14. Connect the hydraulic clutch master cylinder to the clutch pedal and to the dash panel.

15. Bleed the clutch system as described later in this section.

CLutch Pilot Bearing
REMOVAL AND INSTALLATION

NOTE: *A needle roller bearing assembly is used as a clutch pilot bearing. It is inserted directly into the engine flywheel. The needle bearing clutch pilot can only be installed with the seal end of the bearing facing the transmission. The bearing and seal are pregreased and do not require additional lubrication. A new bearing must be installed whenever a bearing is removed.*

1. Remove the transmission, clutch pressure plate and disc as previously described.

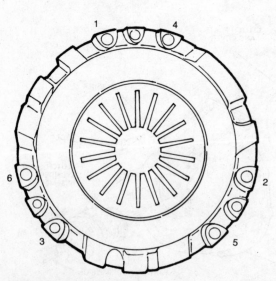

Clutch pressure plate torque sequence

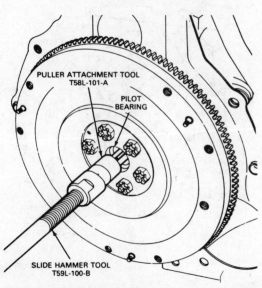

Removing clutch pilot bearing

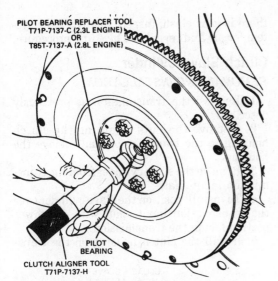

PILOT BEARING REPLACER TOOL
T71P-7137-C (2.3L ENGINE)
OR
T85T-7137-A (2.8L ENGINE)

PILOT
BEARING

CLUTCH ALIGNER TOOL
T71P-7137-H

Installing clutch pilot bearing with driver tool

2. Remove the pilot bearing using a slide hammer and adapter T58L-101-A or equivalent.

3. To install a new bearing, first coat the pilot bore in the crankshaft with a small quantity of multipurpose, long-life lubricant such as part number C1AZ-19590-A. Avoid using too much lubricant as it may be thrown on the clutch disc when the clutch revolves.

4. Using the proper driver tool, carefully install the pilot bearing with the seal facing the transmission.

5. Install the clutch pressure plate, disc and

transmission as previously described. Be careful not to damage the bearing during transmission installation while the transmission input shaft is being inserted into the bearing.

Clutch Master Cylinder and Reservoir

REMOVAL AND INSTALLATION

NOTE: *Do not separate the clutch master cylinder from the reservoir unless individual component replacement is required.*

1. Disconnect the clutch master cylinder pushrod from the clutch pedal by prying the retainer bushing and pushrod off the shaft.

2. Slide the clutch reservoir out of the slots located in the electrical cover box.

3. On the clutch housing, remove the clip retaining the tube to the slave cylinder. Remove the tube and fitting, then plug both lines to prevent the entry of dirt, moisture or other contaminants into the hydraulic system.

4. Disconnect the tube from the clips on the underbody siderail.

5. Remove the bolts retaining the clutch master cylinder to the engine compartment. Remove the clutch master cylinder, reservoir and tube as an assembly.

6. To install the master cylinder, first install the pushrod through the hole in the engine compartment. Make sure it is located on the correct side of the clutch pedal. Place the master cylinder assembly in position, install the bolts and tighten them to 15–20 ft.lb. (21–27 Nm).

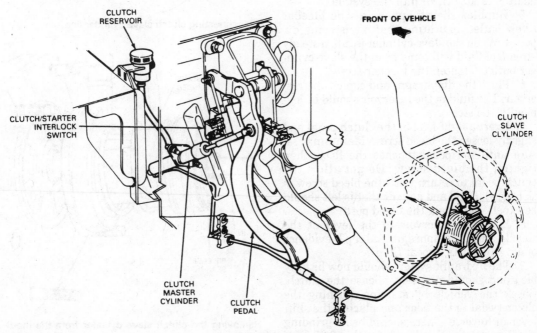

CLUTCH
RESERVOIR

FRONT OF VEHICLE

CLUTCH/STARTER
INTERLOCK
SWITCH

CLUTCH
SLAVE
CLYLINDER

CLUTCH
MASTER
CYLINDER

CLUTCH
PEDAL

Hydraulic clutch assembly

7. Insert the tube in the routing clips on the underbody siderail.

8. Insert the tube and fitting in the clutch slave cylinder and install the clip.

9. Position the clutch reservoir in the engine compartment electrical cover box slots.

10. Install the retainer bushing in the clutch master cylinder pushrod, then install the retainer and pushrod on the clutch pedal shaft.

11. Bleed the clutch hydraulic system as described below.

BLEEDING THE HYDRAULIC CLUTCH SYSTEM

After a clutch hydraulic system has been removed from the vehicle, or if air is trapped in the line, the system must be bled. The following procedure is used with the hydraulic system installed on the vehicle. The largest portion of the filling is carried out by gravity.

1. Clean all dirt and grease from around the reservoir cap.

2. Remove the cap and diaphragm and fill the reservoir to the top with approved DOT 3 brake fluid.

3. To keep brake fluid from entering the clutch housing, place a suitable rubber tube of appropriate inside diameter from the bleed screw to a clear container. Loosen the bleeder screw (located at the slave cylinder body) next to the inlet connection.

4. Fluid should now begin to flow from the master cylinder, down the red tube and into the slave cylinder. The reservoir must be kept full at all times to insure that there will be no additional air drawn into the system.

5. Bubbles should appear at the bleeder screw outlet, indicating that air is being expelled. When the slave cylinder is full, a steady stream of fluid will come from the slave cylinder outlet. Tighten the bleeder screw.

6. Place the diaphragm and cap on the reservoir. The fluid in the reservoir should be level with the step.

7. Exert a light load to the clutch pedal and slightly loosen the bleed screw. Maintain pressure until the pedal touches the floor, then tighten the bleed screw. Do not allow the clutch pedal to return until the bleed screw is tightened. Fluid and any air that is left should be expelled through the bleed port.

8. Refill the reservoir to the level at the step. Install the diaphragm and cap If evidence of air still exists, repeat Step 7.

9. The hydraulic system should now be fully bled and should properly release the clutch. Check the vehicle by starting, pushing the clutch pedal to the floor and placing the shift lever in Reverse. There should be no grinding of gears with the clutch pedal within 0.50 in. If there is gear clash, inspect the hydraulic system for air and repeat the bleeding procedure.

Clutch Slave Cylinder
REMOVAL AND INSTALLATION

1. Remove the transmission as previously described.

2. Remove the nuts retaining the clutch housing to the transmission and remove the housing.

3. Remove the slave cylinder from the transmission input shaft.

4. To install, position the slave cylinder over the transmission input shaft with the tower portion facing the transmission.

5. Install the clutch housing on the trans-

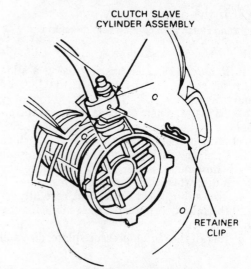

Disconnecting clutch slave cylinder line

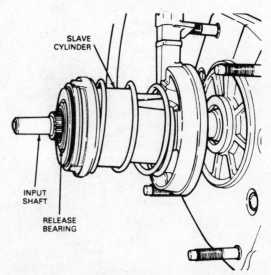

Removing the clutch slave cylinder from the input shaft

mission. Make sure the slave cylinder is properly located in the notches of the clutch housing.

6. Install the transmission as previously described.

7. Install the hydraulic clutch line retaining clip.

8. Bleed the clutch hydraulic system as previously described.

Clutch Release Bearing
REMOVAL AND INSTALLATION

1. Remove the clutch slave cylinder as described above.

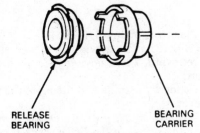

RELEASE BEARING   BEARING CARRIER

Clutch release bearing assembly

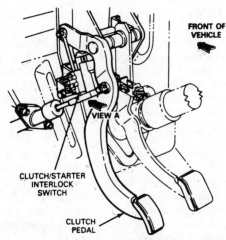

FRONT OF VEHICLE

VIEW A

CLUTCH/STARTER INTERLOCK SWITCH

CLUTCH PEDAL

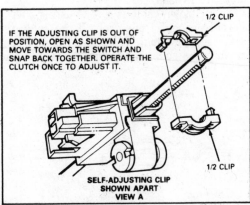

1/2 CLIP

IF THE ADJUSTING CLIP IS OUT OF POSITION, OPEN AS SHOWN AND MOVE TOWARDS THE SWITCH AND SNAP BACK TOGETHER. OPERATE THE CLUTCH ONCE TO ADJUST IT.

1/2 CLIP

SELF-ADJUSTING CLIP SHOWN APART VIEW A

Clutch/starter interlock switch adjustment

2. Remove the release bearing from the clutch slave cylinder by carefully bending back slightly the four symmetrical plastic retainers of the bearing carrier.

3. Prior to installation, lubricate the release bearing with multipurpose, long-life lubricant (such as part number C1AZ-19590-B). Fill the annular groove of the release bearing and apply a thin coat on the inside diameter of the release bearing.

4. Assemble the release bearing to the clutch slave cylinder by pushing the bearing into place while aligning the four symmetrical plastic retainers of the bearing carrier.

5. Install the clutch slave cylinder as previously described.

Clutch/Starter Interlock Switch
ADJUSTMENT

If the adjusting clip is out of position on the rod, remove both halves of the clip. Position both halves of the clip closer to the switch and snap the clips together on the rod. Depress the clutch pedal to the floor to adjust the switch.

AUTOMATIC TRANSMISSION

Identification

All vehicles are equipped with a Safety Standard Certification Label mounted on the left (driver) door frame. Refer to the stamped code in the space marked "Trans" for proper transmission identification. In addition, there is a transmission identification tag mounted on the transmission body. All Aerostar models are equipped with an automatic A4LD four speed overdrive transmission.

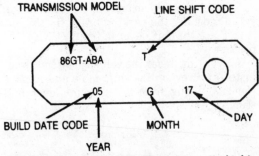

TRANSMISSION MODEL   LINE SHIFT CODE

86GT-ABA   T

05   G   17

BUILD DATE CODE   MONTH   DAY

YEAR

Automatic transmission identification tag attached to the lower left extension attaching bolt

TRANSMISSION FLUID DRAIN AND REFILL

Normal maintenance and lubrication requirements do not necessitate periodic automatic transmission fluid changes. If major service, such as a clutch band, bearing, etc. is required in the transmission, it will have to be removed for service. At this time, the converter, transmission cooler and cooler lines must be thoroughly flushed to remove any dirt.

When used under continuous or severe conditions, the transmission and torque converter should be drained and refilled with fluid as specified. Before adding fluid, make sure it meets or exceeds the manufacturer's specifications. The A4LD automatic transmission uses Dexron® II transmission fluid. The use of incorrect type transmission fluid can result in transmission malfunction and/or failure. Refer to the Capacities Specification Chart for transmission refill recommendations with and without the torque coverter. Drain the fluid as follows:

1. Raise the vehicle and support it safely on jackstands.

2. Place a suitable drain pan beneath the transmission.

3. Loosen the pan attaching bolts slowly, allowing one side to tip down and drain the fluid. This removes all fluid from the pan, but not from the torque converter.

4. When all fluid has drained from the transmission, remove and thoroughly clean the pan and screen. Discard the pan gasket and clean all gasket mating surfaces. Install the pan and screen with a new gasket.

5. Add 3 qts. of fluid to the transmission through the filler tube, then start the engine and shift the transmission through all gears, pausing briefly as each gear engages.

6. Place the transmission in Park and check the fluid level with the engine idling. Set the parking brake firmly.

Adjustments

SHIFT LINKAGE

1. Raise the vehicle and support it safely on jackstands. Set the parking brake firmly.

2. Place the shift lever in the OVERDRIVE position.

3. Working under the vehicle, loosen the adjustment screw on the shift cable and remove the end fitting from the manual lever ball stud.

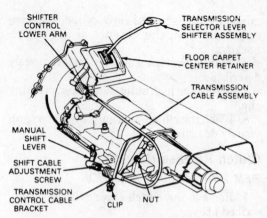

Automatic transmission shifter linkage

4. Place the manual lever in the OVERDRIVE position by moving the lever all the way rearward, then moving it three detents forward.

5. Connect the cable end fitting to the manual lever.

NOTE: *Too much pressure on the arm can move the shifter to the Drive position. Apply pressure only until the resistance of the detent nib is felt.*

6. Tighten the adjustment screw to 45-60 in.lb. (5-7 Nm). After adjustment, check for proper Park engagement. The control lever must move to the right when engaged in Park. Check the transmission control lever in all detent positions with the engine running to insure correct detent/transmission action and readjust if required.

KICKDOWN CABLE

The self-adjusting kickdown cable is attached to the accelerator pedal near the accelerator cable. The kickdown cable is routed from the transmission through the dash to the accelerator pedal. A self-adjuster mechanism is located in the engine compartment at the inlet for the cable on the dash.

The kickdown cable is self-adjusting over a tolerence range of one inch. If the cable requires readjustment, reset the cable by depressing the semi-circular metal tab on the

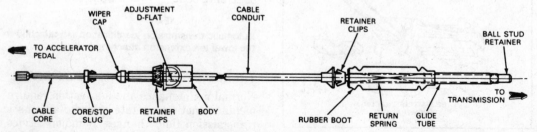

Typical kickdown cable

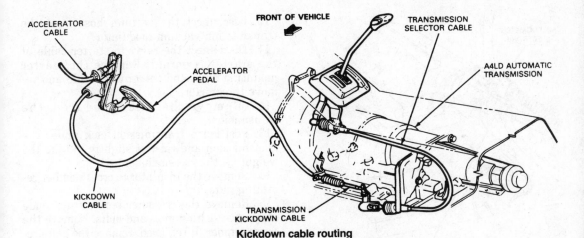

Kickdown cable routing

self-adjuster mechanism and pulling the cable forward (toward the front of the van) to the "zero" position setting. The cable will then automatically readjust to the proper length when kicked down.

Neutral Start Switch

REMOVAL AND INSTALLATION

1. Disconnect the negative battery cable.
2. Disconnect the neutral start switch electrical harness from the neutral start switch.
3. Remove the neutral start switch and O-ring using the neutral start switch socket tool T74P-77247-A, or equivalent.

CAUTION: *Other tools could crush or puncture the walls of the switch.*

4. Installation is the reverse of removal. Tighten the switch to 7–10 ft.lb. (10–14 Nm) and use a new O-ring. Check the operation of the switch with the parking brake engaged. The engine should only start with the transmission in Park or Neutral.

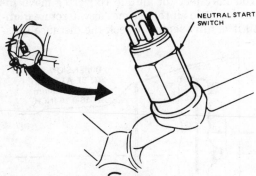

Neutral start switch installation

Transmission

REMOVAL AND INSTALLATION

1. Disconnect the negative battery cable.
2. Raise the vehicle and support it safely.

3. Place a drain pan under the transmission. Starting at the rear and working toward the front, loosen the transmission pan attaching bolts and allow the fluid to drain. After the fluid is drained, install four bolts at each corner to temporarily retain the pan.
4. Remove the converter access cover and adapter plate bolts from the lower end of the converter housing.
5. Remove the four flywheel to converter attaching nuts by placing a 22mm socket and breaker bar on the crankshaft pulley attaching bolt. Rotate the pulley clockwise (as viewed from the front) to gain access to each of the nuts.

CAUTION: *On belt driven overhead cam en-*

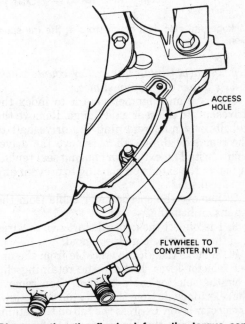

Disconnecting the flywheel from the torque converter

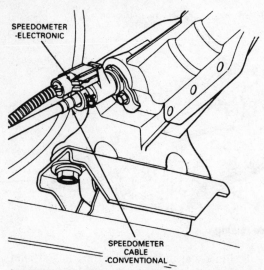

SPEEDOMETER
-ELECTRONIC

SPEEDOMETER
CABLE
-CONVENTIONAL

Speedometer cable attachment at the extension housing

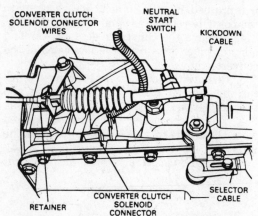

CONVERTER CLUTCH
SOLENOID CONNECTOR
WIRES

NEUTRAL
START
SWITCH

KICKDOWN
CABLE

RETAINER

CONVERTER CLUTCH
SOLENOID
CONNECTOR

SELECTOR
CABLE

Linkage and electrical connectors at the transmission

gines, never rotate the pulley counterclockwise under any circumstances.

6. Scribe an alignment mark to index the driveshaft to the rear axle flange. Remove the U-bolts and nuts retaining the driveshaft to the rear axle flange, then remove the driveshaft. Install an extension housing seal replacer tool in the extension housing to prevent any fluid leakage.

7. Remove the speedometer cable from the extension housing.

8. Disconnect the neutral start switch wires and the converter clutch solenoid.

9. Remove the kickdown cable from the upper selector lever. Remove the retaining clip from the selector cable bracket, then remove the selector cable from the ball stud on the lower selector lever. Depress the tab on the retainer and remove the kickdown cable from the bracket.

10. Disconnect the vacuum hose from the transmission vacuum modulator.

11. Disconnect the relay to starter cable at the starter terminal. Remove the starter mounting bolts and the ground cable and remove the starter.

12. Remove the filler tube from the transmision.

13. Position a transmission jack under the transmission and raise it slightly to take the weight off the crossmember.

14. Remove the insulator to crossmember retaining nuts.

15. Remove the crossmember to frame side support attaching nuts and bolts. Remove the crossmember. If required, remove the bolts retaining the insulator to the transmission and remove the insulator.

16. Remove the converter housing-to-engine fasteners.

17. Slightly lower the transmission jack to gain access to the oil cooler lines, then disconnect the oil cooler lines at the transmission. Plug all openings to prevent contamination by dirt or grease.

18. Move the transmission to the rear so it disengages from the dowel pins and the converter is disengaged from the flywheel. Carefully lower the transmission and remove it from the vehicle. Remove the torque converter by pulling it straight out from the transmission.

NOTE: *If the transmission is to be removed for an extended period of time, support the engine with a safety stand and wood block.*

19. To install the transmission, first position the torque converter to the transmission, making sure the converter hub is fully engaged in the pump gear. Slowly rotate the torque converter while pressing inward until it seats. You may feel the torque converter move inward a little bit three times as you rotate it until it is fully seated. Check the distance illus-

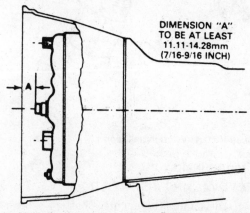

DIMENSION "A"
TO BE AT LEAST
11.11-14.28mm
(7/16-9/16 INCH)

A

Checking torque converter installation

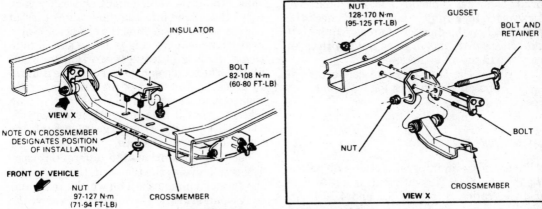

NUT
128-170 N·m
(95-125 FT-LB)

GUSSET

BOLT AND
RETAINER

INSULATOR

BOLT
82-108 N·m
(60-80 FT-LB)

VIEW X

NOTE ON CROSSMEMBER
DESIGNATES POSITION
OF INSTALLATION

FRONT OF VEHICLE

NUT
97-127 N·m
(71-94 FT-LB)

CROSSMEMBER

BOLT

NUT

CROSSMEMBER

VIEW X

Crossmember and insulator mounting

trated to make sure the torque converter is seated or it will bind when the transmission is tightened to the engine. Make sure the torque converter rotates freely and is not bound up.

20. With the converter properly installed, place the transmission on a transmission jack and secure it with a safety chain.

21. Rotate the converter so that the drive studs are in alignment with the holes in the flywheel.

22. Lift the transmission into position for installation enough to connect the oil cooler lines to the case.

23. Move the converter and transmission assembly forward into position, being careful not to damage the flywheel and converter pilot. THe converter housing is piloted into position by the dowels in the rear of the engine block.

NOTE: *Do not allow the transmission to get into a nose-down position during installation as this may cause the converter to move forward and disengage from the pump gear. The converter must rest squarely against the flywheel. This indicates that the converter pilot is not binding in the engine crankshaft.*

24. Install the converter housing-to-engine attaching fasteners and tighten to 28–38 ft.lb. (38–51 Nm).

25. If removed, position the insulator on the transmission, then install and tighten the retaining bolts to 60–80 ft.lb. (82–108 Nm).

26. Position the crossmember in the brackets in the frame. The markings on the crossmember indicate the direction of installation. Install the nuts and bolts and tighten.

27. Slowly lower the transmission so the insulator studs are installed in the proper slots in the crossmember. Install the nuts and tighten them to 71–94 ft.lb. (97–127 Nm). Disconnect the safety chain and remove the transmission jack.

28. Install the filler tube in the transmission.

29. Position the starter assembly on the converter housing. Install the ground cable and start and tighten the mounting bolts to 15–20 ft.lb. (21–27 Nm). Connect the relay-to-starter cable and tighten the nut and washer.

30. Connect the vacuum hose to the modulator on the right side of the transmission.

31. Position the selector cable in the bracket on the transmission case. Press the end of the cable on the ball stud on the lower portion of the selector lever, then install the retainer in the bracket.

32. Position the kickdown cable on the upper selector lever, then install the retainer in the bracket.

33. Connect the neutral start switch plug to the switch. Install the converter clutch solenoid connector.

34. Install the speedometer cable.

35. Position a 22mm socket and breaker bar on the crankshaft pulley bolt, then rotate the pulley clockwise (as viewed from the front) to gain access to the converter-to-flywheel studs. Install the nut on each stud and tighten to 20–34 ft.lb. (27–46 Nm).

CAUTION: *On belt driven overhead camshaft engines, never rotate the pulley in a counterclockwise direction as viewed from the front.*

36. Position the converter access cover and adapter plate on the converter housing, then install and tighten the attaching bolts to 12–16 ft.lb. (16–22 Nm).

37. Remove the plug from the extension housing and install the driveshaft so that the index marks made earlier are in alignment. Install the U-bolts and tighten the nuts to 8–15 ft.lb. (11–20 Nm).

38. Adjust the manual linkage as previously described.

39. Lower the van and fill the transmission to the proper level. If the converter was

drained during removal, add five quarts of Dexron®II, then run the engine and check the fluid level on the dipstick. Add as required. If the converter was not drained, start with three quarts and top off as necessary.

40. Check the transmission, converter assembly and oil cooler lines for leaks and correct as necessary.

REAR AXLE

All models use an integral carrier axle with a 7.5 in. ring gear. This differential is available in three ratios: 3.45:1, 3.73:1 and 4.10:1. An identification tag with the axle ratio stamped on is affixed to one bolt of the differential cover assembly.

Understanding Rear Axles

The rear axle is a special type of transmission that reduces the speed of the drive from the engine and transmission and divides the power to the rear wheels. Power enters the rear axle from the driveshaft via the companion flange. The flange is mounted on the drive pinion

shaft. The drive pinion shaft and gear which carry the power into the differential turn at engine speed. The gear on the end of the pinion shaft drives a large ring gear the axis of rotation of which is 90 degrees away from the of the pinion. The pinion and gear reduce the gear ratio of the axle, and change the direction of rotation to turn the axle shafts which drive both wheels. The rear axle gear ratio is found by dividing the number of pinion gear teeth into the number of ring gear teeth.

The ring gear drives the differential case. The case provides the two mounting points for the ends of a pinion shaft on which are mounted two pinion gears. The pinion gears drive the two side gears, one of which is located on the inner end of each axle shaft. By driving the axle shafts through the arrangement, the differential allows the outer drive wheel to turn faster than the inner drive wheel in a turn. The main drive pinion and the side bearings, which bear the weight of the differential case, are shimmed to provide proper bearing preload, and to position the pinion and ring gears properly.

NOTE: *The proper adjustment of the rela-*

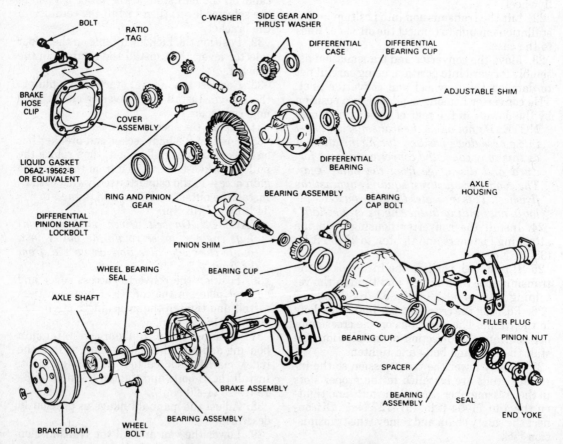

Exploded view of the rear axle assembly

tionship of the ring and pinion gears is critical. It should be attempted only by those with extensive equipment and/or experience.

Limited-slip differentials include clutches which tend to link each axle shaft to the differential case. Clutches may be engaged either by spring action or by pressure produced by the torque on the axles during a turn. During turning on a dry pavement, the effects of the clutches are overcome, and each wheel turns at the required speed. When slippage occurs at either wheel, however, the clutches will transmit some of the power to the wheel which has the greater amount of traction. Because of the presence of clutches, limited-slip units require a special lubricant.

Determining Axle Ratio

The drive axle of a vehicle is said to have a certain axle ratio. This number (usually a whole number and a decimal fraction) is actually a comparison of the number of gear teeth on the ring gear and the pinion gear. For example, a 4.11 rear means that theoretically, there are 4.11 teeth on the ring gear and one tooth on the pinion gear or, put another way, the driveshaft must turn 4.11 times to turn the wheels once. Actually, on a 4.11 rear, there might be 37 teeth on the ring gear and 9 teeth on the pinion gear. By dividing the number of teeth on the pinion gear into the number of teeth on the ring gear, the numerical axle ratio (4.11) is obtained. This also provides a good method of ascertaining exactly what axle ratio one is dealing with.

Another method of determining gear ratio is to jack up and support the car so that both rear wheels are off the ground. Make a chalk mark on the rear wheel and the driveshaft. Put the transmission in Neutral. Turn the rear wheel one complete turn and count the number of turns that the driveshaft makes. The number of turns that the driveshaft makes in one complete revolution of the rear wheel is an approximation of the rear axle ratio.

Axle Shaft

REMOVAL AND INSTALLATION

1. Raise the van and support it safely on jackstands.
2. Remove the rear brake drums.

CAUTION: *Brake shoes contain asbestos, which has been determined to be a cancer causing agent. Never clean the brake surfaces with compressed air and avoid inhaling any dust from any brake surface. When cleaning brake surfaces, use a commercially available brake cleaning fluid.*

3. Clean all dirt and grease from the area of the carrier cover with a wire brush and/or cloth.
4. Drain the rear axle lubricant into a suitable container by removing the housing cover.

NOTE: *For 3.45:1 ratio axles, perform Steps 5, 6 and 7. For 3.73:1 and 4.10:1 axles, perform Steps 8–11.*

5. Remove the differential pinion shaft lock bolt and differential pinion shaft. The pinion gears may be left in place. Once the axle shafts are removed, reinstall the pinion shaft and lock bolt.
6. Push the flanged end of the axle shafts toward the center of the vehicle and remove the C-lockwasher from the button end of the axle shaft.
7. Remove the axle shaft from the housing, being careful not to damage the oil seal.
8. For 3.73:1 and 4.10:1 ratio axles, remove the pinion shaft lock bolt.
9. Place your hand behind the differential case and push out the pinion shaft until the step on the shaft contacts the ring gear.

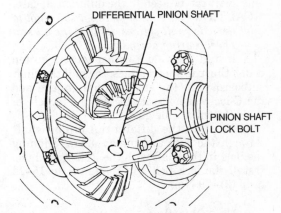

DIFFERENTIAL PINION SHAFT

PINION SHAFT LOCK BOLT

Removing differential pinion shaft on 3.45:1 ratio axles

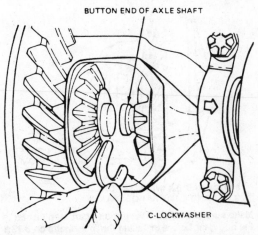

BUTTON END OF AXLE SHAFT

C-LOCKWASHER

Removing the C-lockwasher on 3.45:1 ratio axles

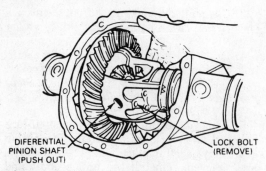

Removing the pinion shaft on 3.73:1 and 4.10:1 ratio axles

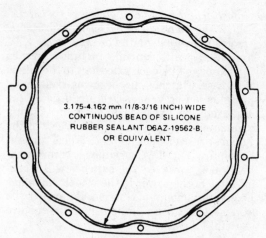

Apply sealer as shown on differential cover before installing

10. Remove the C-lockwasher from the axle shafts.

11. Remove the axle shafts from the housing, being careful not to damage the oil seal.

12. To permit axle shaft installation on 3.73:1 and 4.10:1 ratio axles, make sure the differential pinion shaft step contacts the ring gear before sliding the axle shaft into the axle housing. Start the splines into the side gear and push firmly until the button end of the axle shaft can be seen in the differential case.

CAUTION: *Care must be taken so as not to let the axle shaft splines damage the oil seal or wheel bearing assembly.*

13. Install the C-lockwasher on the button end of the axle shaft splines, the pull the shaft outboard until the shaft splines engage and the C-lockwasher seats in the counterbore of the differential side gear.

14. Position the differential pinion shaft through the case and pinion gears, aligning the hole in the shaft with the lock screw hole. Install the lock bolt and tighten it to 15–22 ft.lb. (21–29 Nm).

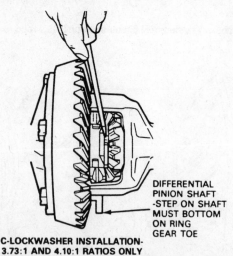

C-LOCKWASHER INSTALLATION- 3.73:1 AND 4.10:1 RATIOS ONLY

Make sure the differential pinion shaft step contacts the ring gear before installing the axle shafts on 3.73:1 and 4.10:1 ratio axles

15. Clean the gasket mounting surface on the rear axle housing and cover. Apply a continuous bead of silicone rubber sealant to the carrier casting face. Make sure the machined surface on both cover and carrier are clean before applying sealer.

16. Install the cover and tighten the cover bolts to 15–20 ft.lb. (21–27 Nm), except the ratio tag bolt, which is tightened to 15–25 ft.lb. (30–34 Nm). The cover assembly must be installed within 15 minutes of application of the sealer or new sealer must be applied.

17. Add lubricant until it is about $\frac{1}{2}$ in. below the bottom of the filler hole in the running position. Install the filler plug and tighten it to 15–30 ft.lb. (20–41 Nm).

Axle Shaft Oil Seal and Wheel Bearing

REMOVAL AND INSTALLATION

1. Remove the axle shaft as previously described.

2. Insert an axle bearing remover tool T85L-1225-AH attached to a slide hammer into the bore as illustrated and position it behind the bearing to the tangs on the tool engage the bearing outer race. Remove the bearing ans seal as a unit with the slide hammer.

3. Lubricate the new bearing with rear axle lubricant and install the bearing into the housing bore using bearing replacer tool T78P-1225-A, or equivalent.

4. Apply multipurpose, long-life grease between the lips of the axle shaft seal.

5. Install a new axle shaft seal using seal replacer tool T78P-1177-A, or equivalent.

CAUTION: *Installation of the bearing or seal assembly without the proper tool may result in an early bearing or seal failure. If the*

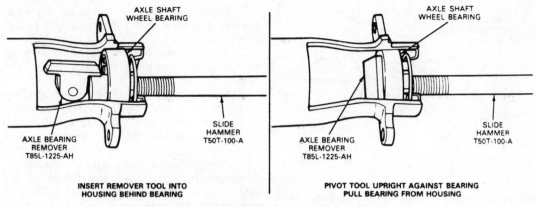

INSERT REMOVER TOOL INTO
HOUSING BEHIND BEARING

PIVOT TOOL UPRIGHT AGAINST BEARING
PULL BEARING FROM HOUSING

Removing axle shaft bearing and seal with remover tool

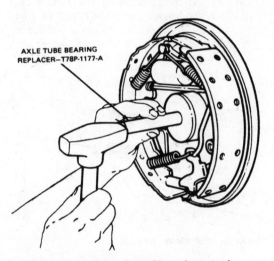

Installing axle shaft bearing with replacer tool

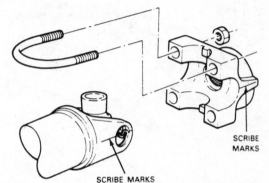

Scribe alignment marks as shown on the driveshaft and axle end yoke

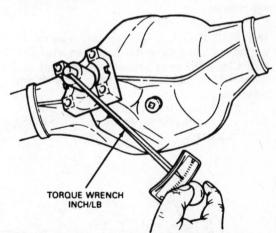

Checking rotational torque of the differential

seal becomes cocked in the bore during installation, remove it and install a new one.

6. Install the axle shaft as previously described.

Drive Pinion Oil Seal

REMOVAL AND INSTALLATION

NOTE: *Replacement of the pinion oil seal involves removal and installation of only the pinion nut and the axle end yoke. However, this operation disturbs the pinion bearing preload, and this preload must be carefully reset when assembling.*

1. Raise the van and support it safely on jackstands.

2. Remove the rear wheels.

3. Scribe marks on the driveshaft end and the axle end yoke to insure proper positioning of the driveshaft upon assembly.

4. Disconnect the driveshaft from the rear axle end yoke and remove the driveshaft from the transmission extension housing. Install an

oil seal replacer tool in the transmission extension housing to prevent oil leakage during the service procedures.

5. Install an inch pound torque wrench on the pinion nut, then record the torque required to maintain rotation of the pinion gear through several revolutions.

6. While holding the end yoke with holding

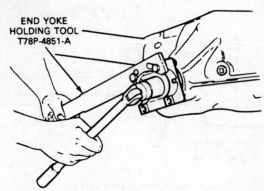

Hold the end yoke as shown to remove the pinion nut

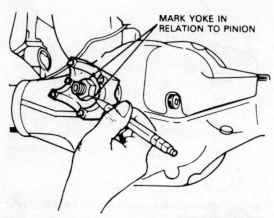

MARK YOKE IN RELATION TO PINION

Mark axle end yoke and pinion shaft as shown before removal

tool T78P-4851-A, or equivalent, remove the pinion nut using a suitable socket on a breaker bar. Clean the area around the oil seal and place a drain pan under the yoke to catch any fluid leakage.

7. Mark the axle yoke in relation to the pinion shaft so the flange can be installed in the same position.

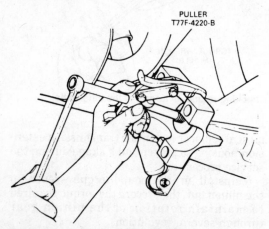

PULLER T77F-4220-B

Removing end yoke with puller tool

8. Use a suitable puller tool as illustrated to remove the axle end yoke from the pinion shaft.

9. Remove the pinion seal with a small prybar or other suitable tool and discard the seal.

10. Check the splines on the pinion shaft to make sure they are free from burrs or any other damage. If burrs are noted, remove them by using a fine crocus cloth, working in a rotational pattern.

11. Apply mulitpurpose, long-life grease between the lips of the pinion seal, the install the seal using seal replacer tool T79P-4676-A or equivalent. Place the seal on the tool, then drive it into position on the pinion.

CAUTION: *Installation of the pinion seal without the proper tool may result in early seal failure. If the seal becomes cocked during installation, remove it and install a new seal. Never hammer on a seal metal casing.*

DRIVE PINION OIL SEAL REPLACER—T79P-4676-A

Installing drive pinion oil seal

12. Check the seal surface of the yoke for scratches, nicks or a groove around the diameter. If any of these conditions exist, replace the yoke. Apply a small amount of lubricant to the end yoke splines, then align the mark on the end yoke with the mark on the pinion shaft and install the yoke. The companion shaft must never be hammered on or installed with power tools.

13. Wipe the pinion clean.

14. Install a new nut and spacer on the pinion shaft, then hold the end yoke as before and tighten the nut while rotating the pinion occasionally to insure proper bearing seating. In addition, take frequent pinion bearing torque preload readings with the inch pound torque wrench until the original recorded rotational torque reading is obtained or to 8–14 in.lb. (1–1.6 Nm).

NOTE: *Under no circumstances should the pinion nut be backed off to reduce preload. If reduced preload is required, a new collapsible pinion spacer and pinion nut must be installed.*

15. Remove the oil seal replacer tool from the

transmission extension housing and install the front of the driveshaft on the transmission output shaft. Connect the rear end of the drive-shaft to the axle end yoke, aligning the scribe marks made earlier. Apply Loctite® or equivalent to the threads of the attaching bolts and tighten the four U-bolt nuts to 70–95 ft.lb. (95–128 Nm).

16. Remove the filler plug and add hypoid gear lubricant until it is about $\frac{1}{2}$ in. below the bottom of the filler hole in the running position. Install the filler plug and tighten it to 15–30 ft.lb. (20–41 Nm).

Axle Housing
REMOVAL AND INSTALLATION

1. Raise the van and support it safely with jackstands. Place the jackstands on the frame, not on the rear axle housing.
2. Release the parking brake cable tension by pulling the front cable approximately two inches rearward. Clamp the cable behind the crossmember, being careful not to damage the plastic cable coating.
3. Remove the parking brake cables from the equalizer. Compress the tabs on the retainers and pull the cables through the rear crossmember.
4. Place a hydraulic jack under the differential housing and support the weight of the axle housing assembly.
5. Scribe marks on the driveshaft end and the axle end yoke to insure proper positioning of the driveshaft upon assembly, then remove the driveshaft.

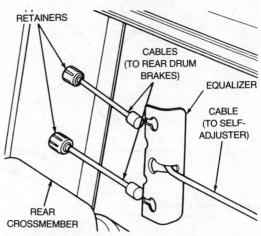

Disconnecting the parking brake cable assembly

6. Install an oil seal replacer tool in the transmission extension housing to prevent oil leakage during the service procedures.
7. Remove the rear wheels.
8. Disconnect the brake lines by disconnecting the brake jounce hose from the master cylinder rear tube. Plug the brake tube to prevent contamination of the hydraulic brake system. Remove the jounce hose and bracket from the frame.
9. Disconnect the axle vent tube from the clip on the frame.
10. Disconnect the shock absorbers from the lower control arms.
11. Carefully lower the axle assembly on the hydraulic jack until the springs are no longer under compression. Lower the axle slowly.

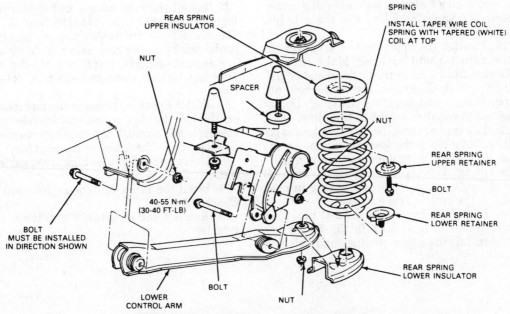

Exploded view of the rear suspension assembly

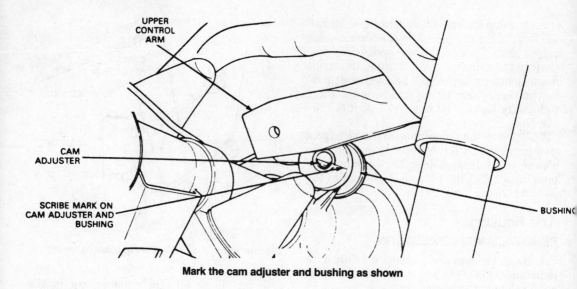

UPPER
CONTROL
ARM

CAM
ADJUSTER

SCRIBE MARK ON
CAM ADJUSTER AND
BUSHING

BUSHING

Mark the cam adjuster and bushing as shown

12. Remove the lower spring retainer, then the upper spring retainer and remove the coil spring.

13. Raise the axle to the normal load position with the hydraulic jack, then disconnect the control arms at the axle. Make sure adequate clearance exists to remove the bolts retaining the lower control arm to the axle.

14. Remove the bolt and nut retaining the upper control arm to the rear axle. Remove the upper control arm from the axle after scribing a mark aligning the position of the cam adjuster in the axle bushing.

15. Carefully lower the axle and remove it from underneath the vehicle.

16. To install the axle housing, first place the assembly on a hydraulic jack and roll it underneath the van. Carefully raise the axle into position.

17. Position the upper control arm over the cam adjuster and bushing. Make sure the matchmarks made on the bushing and adjuster are still in alignment. Install the bolt, nut and retainer and tighten until snug. Do not tighten to specified torque at this time.

18. Lower the axle to the spring unloaded position, then place the lower insulator on the control arm. Place the upper insulator on top of the spring. The tapered coil (white colored) must face upward. Install the spring in position on the control arm and axle.

19. Install the lower retainer and nut, then tighten the nut to 41–64 ft.lb. (55–88 Nm).

20. Install the upper retainer and bolt and

tighten the bolt to 30–40 ft.lb. (40–55 Nm).

21. Raise the axle to the normal load position and tighten the bolt and nut retaining the lower control arm to the axle to 100–129 ft.lb. (133–176 Nm).

22. Connect the shock absorber to the lower control arm. Install the shock bolt nut on the inside of the lower control arm bracket and tighten it to 41–64 ft.lb. (55–88 Nm).

23. Connect the axle vent hose to the clip on the frame. Route the hose in the far left hand hole in the crossmember and secure the clip in the second hole from the left.

24. Attach the brake jounce hose and bracket to the frame. Connect the hose to the line from the master cylinder.

25. Install the rear wheels and tighten the lugnuts to 85–115 ft.lb. (115–156 Nm).

26. Install the driveshaft, making sure the scribe marks on the rear axle and driveshaft are aligned properly. Install the U-bolts and nuts and tighten them to 8–15 ft.lb. (11–20 Nm).

27. Pull the parking brake cables and retainers through the clips on the vehicle underbody side rails and through the rear crossmember. Connect the brake cables to the equalizer.

28. Unclamp the front parking brake cable to restore cable tension.

29. Bleed the brake system as described in Chapter 8.

30. Remove the jackstands and lower the vehicle.

Troubleshooting the Manual Transmission

Problem	Cause	Solution
Transmission shifts hard	• Clutch adjustment incorrect • Clutch linkage or cable binding • Shift rail binding	• Adjust clutch • Lubricate or repair as necessary • Check for mispositioned selector arm roll pin, loose cover bolts, worn shift rail bores, worn shift rail, distorted oil seal, or extension housing not aligned with case. Repair as necessary.
	• Internal bind in transmission caused by shift forks, selector plates, or synchronizer assemblies • Clutch housing misalignment • Incorrect lubricant • Block rings and/or cone seats worn	• Remove, disassemble and inspect transmission. Replace worn or damaged components as necessary. • Check runout at rear face of clutch housing • Drain and refill transmission • Blocking ring to gear clutch tooth face clearance must be 0.030 inch or greater. If clearance is correct it may still be necessary to inspect blocking rings and cone seats for excessive wear. Repair as necessary.
Gear clash when shifting from one gear to another	• Clutch adjustment incorrect • Clutch linkage or cable binding • Clutch housing misalignment • Lubricant level low or incorrect lubricant • Gearshift components, or synchronizer assemblies worn or damaged	• Adjust clutch • Lubricate or repair as necessary • Check runout at rear of clutch housing • Drain and refill transmission and check for lubricant leaks if level was low. Repair as necessary. • Remove, disassemble and inspect transmission. Replace worn or damaged components as necessary.
Transmission noisy	• Lubricant level low or incorrect lubricant • Clutch housing-to-engine, or transmission-to-clutch housing bolts loose • Dirt, chips, foreign material in transmission • Gearshift mechanism, transmission gears, or bearing components worn or damaged • Clutch housing misalignment	• Drain and refill transmission. If lubricant level was low, check for leaks and repair as necessary. • Check and correct bolt torque as necessary • Drain, flush, and refill transmission • Remove, disassemble and inspect transmission. Replace worn or damaged components as necessary. • Check runout at rear face of clutch housing
Jumps out of gear	• Clutch housing misalignment • Gearshift lever loose • Offset lever nylon insert worn or lever attaching nut loose • Gearshift mechanism, shift forks, selector plates, interlock plate, selector arm, shift rail, detent plugs, springs or shift cover worn or damaged • Clutch shaft or roller bearings worn or damaged	• Check runout at rear face of clutch housing • Check lever for worn fork. Tighten loose attaching bolts. • Remove gearshift lever and check for loose offset lever nut or worn insert. Repair or replace as necessary. • Remove, disassemble and inspect transmission cover assembly. Replace worn or damaged components as necessary. • Replace clutch shaft or roller bearings as necessary

Troubleshooting the Manual Transmission (cont.)

Problem	Cause	Solution
Jumps out of gear (cont.)	• Gear teeth worn or tapered, synchronizer assemblies worn or damaged, excessive end play caused by worn thrust washers or output shaft gears • Pilot bushing worn	• Remove, disassemble, and inspect transmission. Replace worn or damaged components as necessary. • Replace pilot bushing
Will not shift into one gear	• Gearshift selector plates, interlock plate, or selector arm, worn, damaged, or incorrectly assembled • Shift rail detent plunger worn, spring broken, or plug loose • Gearshift lever worn or damaged • Synchronizer sleeves or hubs, damaged or worn	• Remove, disassemble, and inspect transmission cover assembly. Repair or replace components as necessary. • Tighten plug or replace worn or damaged components as necessary • Replace gearshift lever • Remove, disassemble and inspect transmission. Replace worn or damaged components.
Locked in one gear—cannot be shifted out	• Shift rail(s) worn or broken, shifter fork bent, setscrew loose, center detent plug missing or worn • Broken gear teeth on countershaft gear, clutch shaft, or reverse idler gear • Gearshift lever broken or worn, shift mechanism in cover incorrectly assembled or broken, worn damaged gear train components	• Inspect and replace worn or damaged parts • Inspect and replace damaged part • Disassemble transmission. Replace damaged parts or assemble correctly.

Troubleshooting Basic Clutch Problems

Problem	Cause
Excessive clutch noise	Throwout bearing noises are more audible at the lower end of pedal travel. The usual causes are: • Riding the clutch • Too little pedal free-play • Lack of bearing lubrication A bad clutch shaft pilot bearing will make a high pitched squeal, when the clutch is disengaged and the transmission is in gear or within the first 2″ of pedal travel. The bearing must be replaced. Noise from the clutch linkage is a clicking or snapping that can be heard or felt as the pedal is moved completely up or down. This usually requires lubrication. Transmitted engine noises are amplified by the clutch housing and heard in the passenger compartment. They are usually the result of insufficient pedal free-play and can be changed by manipulating the clutch pedal.
Clutch slips (the car does not move as it should when the clutch is engaged)	This is usually most noticeable when pulling away from a standing start. A severe test is to start the engine, apply the brakes, shift into high gear and SLOWLY release the clutch pedal. A healthy clutch will stall the engine. If it slips it may be due to: • A worn pressure plate or clutch plate • Oil soaked clutch plate • Insufficient pedal free-play
Clutch drags or fails to release	The clutch disc and some transmission gears spin briefly after clutch disengagement. Under normal conditions in average temperatures, 3 seconds is maximum spin-time. Failure to release properly can be caused by: • Too light transmission lubricant or low lubricant level • Improperly adjusted clutch linkage
Low clutch life	Low clutch life is usually a result of poor driving habits or heavy duty use. Riding the clutch, pulling heavy loads, holding the car on a grade with the clutch instead of the brakes and rapid clutch engagement all contribute to low clutch life.

Troubleshooting Basic Automatic Transmission Problems

Problem	Cause	Solution
Fluid leakage	• Defective pan gasket	• Replace gasket or tighten pan bolts
	• Loose filler tube	• Tighten tube nut
	• Loose extension housing to transmission case	• Tighten bolts
	• Converter housing area leakage	• Have transmission checked professionally
Fluid flows out the oil filler tube	• High fluid level	• Check and correct fluid level
	• Breather vent clogged	• Open breather vent
	• Clogged oil filter or screen	• Replace filter or clean screen (change fluid also)
	• Internal fluid leakage	• Have transmission checked professionally
Transmission overheats (this is usually accompanied by a strong burned odor to the fluid)	• Low fluid level	• Check and correct fluid level
	• Fluid cooler lines clogged	• Drain and refill transmission. If this doesn't cure the problem, have cooler lines cleared or replaced.
	• Heavy pulling or hauling with insufficient cooling	• Install a transmission oil cooler
	• Faulty oil pump, internal slippage	• Have transmission checked professionally
Buzzing or whining noise	• Low fluid level	• Check and correct fluid level
	• Defective torque converter, scored gears	• Have transmission checked professionally
No forward or reverse gears or slippage in one or more gears	• Low fluid level	• Check and correct fluid level
	• Defective vacuum or linkage controls, internal clutch or band failure	• Have unit checked professionally
Delayed or erratic shift	• Low fluid level	• Check and correct fluid level
	• Broken vacuum lines	• Repair or replace lines
	• Internal malfunction	• Have transmission checked professionally

Lockup Torque Converter Service Diagnosis

Problem	Cause	Solution
No lockup	• Faulty oil pump	• Replace oil pump
	• Sticking governor valve	• Repair or replace as necessary
	• Valve body malfunction	• Repair or replace valve body or its internal components as necessary
	(a) Stuck switch valve	
	(b) Stuck lockup valve	
	(c) Stuck fail-safe valve	
	• Failed locking clutch	• Replace torque converter
	• Leaking turbine hub seal	• Replace torque converter
	• Faulty input shaft or seal ring	• Repair or replace as necessary
Will not unlock	• Sticking governor valve	• Repair or replace as necessary
	• Valve body malfunction	• Repair or replace valve body or its internal components as necessary
	(a) Stuck switch valve	
	(b) Stuck lockup valve	
	(c) Stuck fail-safe valve	
Stays locked up at too low a speed in direct	• Sticking governor valve	• Repair or replace as necessary
	• Valve body malfunction	• Repair or replace valve body or its internal components as necessary
	(a) Stuck switch valve	
	(b) Stuck lockup valve	
	(c) Stuck fail-safe valve	
Locks up or drags in low or second	• Faulty oil pump	• Replace oil pump
	• Valve body malfunction	• Repair or replace valve body or its internal components as necessary
	(a) Stuck switch valve	
	(b) Stuck fail-safe valve	

Lockup Torque Converter Service Diagnosis (cont.)

Problem	Cause	Solution

Sluggish or stalls in reverse	• Faulty oil pump
	• Plugged cooler, cooler lines or fittings
	• Valve body malfunction
	  (a) Stuck switch valve
	  (b) Faulty input shaft or seal ring
		• Replace oil pump as necessary
		• Flush or replace cooler and flush lines and fittings
		• Repair or replace valve body or its internal components as necessary

Loud chatter during lockup engagement (cold)	• Faulty torque converter • Failed locking clutch • Leaking turbine hub seal	• Replace torque converter • Replace torque converter • Replace torque converter
Vibration or shudder during lockup engagement	• Faulty oil pump • Valve body malfunction • Faulty torque converter • Engine needs tune-up	• Repair or replace oil pump as necessary • Repair or replace valve body or its internal components as necessary • Replace torque converter • Tune engine
Vibration after lockup engagement	• Faulty torque converter • Exhaust system strikes underbody • Engine needs tune-up • Throttle linkage misadjusted	• Replace torque converter • Align exhaust system • Tune engine • Adjust throttle linkage
Vibration when revved in neutral Overheating: oil blows out of dip stick tube or pump seal	• Torque converter out of balance • Plugged cooler, cooler lines or fittings • Stuck switch valve	• Replace torque converter • Flush or replace cooler and flush lines and fittings • Repair switch valve in valve body or replace valve body
Shudder after lockup engagement	• Faulty oil pump • Plugged cooler, cooler lines or fittings • Valve body malfunction • Faulty torque converter • Fail locking clutch • Exhaust system strikes underbody • Engine needs tune-up • Throttle linkage misadjusted	• Replace oil pump • Flush or replace cooler and flush lines and fittings • Repair or replace valve body or its internal components as necessary • Replace torque converter • Replace torque converter • Align exhaust system • Tune engine • Adjust throttle linkage

Transmission Fluid Indications

The appearance and odor of the transmission fluid can give valuable clues to the overall condition of the transmission. Always note the appearance of the fluid when you check the fluid level or change the fluid. Rub a small amount of fluid between your fingers to feel for grit and smell the fluid on the dipstick.

If the fluid appears:	It indicates:
Clear and red colored	• Normal operation
Discolored (extremely dark red or brownish) or smells burned	• Band or clutch pack failure, usually caused by an overheated transmission. Hauling very heavy loads with insufficient power or failure to change the fluid, often result in overheating. Do not confuse this appearance with newer fluids that have a darker red color and a strong odor (though not a burned odor).
Foamy or aerated (light in color and full of bubbles)	• The level is too high (gear train is churning oil) • An internal air leak (air is mixing with the fluid). Have the transmission checked professionally.
Solid residue in the fluid	• Defective bands, clutch pack or bearings. Bits of band material or metal abrasives are clinging to the dipstick. Have the transmission checked professionally.
Varnish coating on the dipstick	• The transmission fluid is overheating

Troubleshooting Basic Driveshaft and Rear Axle Problems

When abnormal vibrations or noises are detected in the driveshaft area, this chart can be used to help diagnose possible causes. Remember that other components such as wheels, tires, rear axle and suspension can also produce similar conditions.

BASIC DRIVESHAFT PROBLEMS

Problem	Cause	Solution
Shudder as car accelerates from stop or low speed	• Loose U-joint • Defective center bearing	• Replace U-joint • Replace center bearing
Loud clunk in driveshaft when shifting gears	• Worn U-joints	• Replace U-joints
Roughness or vibration at any speed	• Out-of-balance, bent or dented driveshaft • Worn U-joints • U-joint clamp bolts loose	• Balance or replace driveshaft • Replace U-joints • Tighten U-joint clamp bolts
Squeaking noise at low speeds	• Lack of U-joint lubrication	• Lubricate U-joint; if problem persists, replace U-joint
Knock or clicking noise	• U-joint or driveshaft hitting frame tunnel • Worn CV joint	• Correct overloaded condition • Replace CV joint

BASIC REAR AXLE PROBLEMS

First, determine when the noise is most noticeable.

Drive Noise: Produced under vehicle acceleration.

Coast Noise: Produced while the car coasts with a closed throttle.

Float Noise: Occurs while maintaining constant car speed (just enough to keep speed constant) on a level road.

Road Noise

Brick or rough surfaced concrete roads produce noises that seem to come from the rear axle. Road noise is usually identical in Drive or Coast and driving on a different type of road will tell whether the road is the problem.

Tire Noise

Tire noises are often mistaken for rear axle problems. Snow treads or unevenly worn tires produce vibrations seeming to originate elsewhere. **Temporarily** inflating the tires to 40 lbs will significantly alter tire noise, but will have no effect on rear axle noises (which normally cease below about 30 mph).

Engine/Transmission Noise

Determine at what speed the noise is most pronounced, then stop the car in a quiet place. With the transmission in Neutral, run the engine through speeds corresponding to road speeds where the noise was noticed. Noises produced with the car standing still are coming from the engine or transmission.

Front Wheel Bearings

While holding the car speed steady, lightly apply the footbrake; this will often decease bearing noise, as some of the load is taken from the bearing.

Rear Axle Noises

Eliminating other possible sources can narrow the cause to the rear axle, which normally produces noise from worn gears or bearings. Gear noises tend to peak in a narrow speed range, while bearing noises will usually vary in pitch with engine speeds.

Suspension and Steering

7

FRONT SUSPENSION

Coil Springs

REMOVAL AND INSTALLATION

1. Place the steering wheel and steering in the centered (straight ahead) position. Any time the steering linkage is disconnected from the spindle, the steering system must be centered prior to beginning any work.

2. Raise the van and support it safely on jackstands. Place the jackstands on the frame at the jacking pads.

3. Disconnect the stabilizer bar link bolt from the lower control arm.

4. Remove the two bolts attaching the shock absorber to the lower arm assembly.

5. Remove the upper nut and washer retaining the shock absorber and remove the shock.

6. Remove the steering center link from the pitman arm.

7. Using spring compressor tool D78P-5310-A or equivalent, install one plate with the pivot ball seat facing downward into the coils of the spring. Rotate the plate so that it is flush with the upper surface of the lower arm.

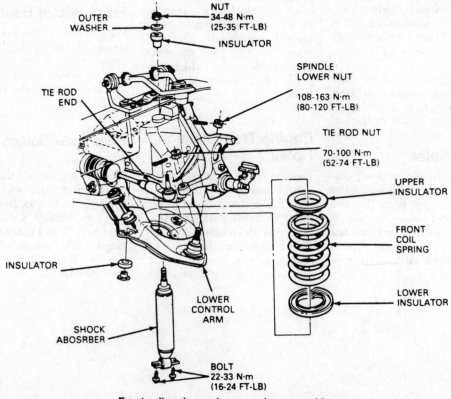

OUTER WASHER

NUT
34-48 N·m
(25-35 FT-LB)

INSULATOR

TIE ROD END

SPINDLE LOWER NUT

108-163 N·m
(80-120 FT-LB)

TIE ROD NUT

70-100 N·m
(52-74 FT-LB)

INSULATOR

UPPER INSULATOR

FRONT COIL SPRING

LOWER INSULATOR

LOWER CONTROL ARM

SHOCK ABOSRBER

BOLT
22-33 N·m
(16-24 FT-LB)

Front coil spring and suspension assembly

8. Install the other plate with the pivot ball seat facing upward into the coils of the spring, so that the nut rests in the upper plate.

9. Insert the compression rod into the opening in the lower arm, through the upper and lower plate and upper ball nut. Insert the securing pin through the upper ball nut and compression rod. This pin can only be inserted one way into the upper ball nut because of a stepped hole design.

10. With the upper ball nut secured, turn the upper plate so that it walks up the coil until it contacts the upper spring seat, then back it off ½ turn.

11. Install the lower ball nut and thrust washer on the compression rod, then screw on the forcing nut. Tighten the forcing nut until the spring is compressed enough so that it is free in its seat.

12. Loosen the two lower arm pivot bolts. Remove the cotter pin and loosen, but not not remove the nut attaching the lower ball joint to the spindle. Using pitman arm puller T64P-3590-F, or equivalent, loosen the lower ball joint.

13. Remove the puller tool.

14. Support the lower control arm with a hydraulic jack, then remove the ball joint nut. Slowly lower the control arm and remove the coil spring.

CAUTION: *Handle the coil spring with care. A compressed coil spring has enough stored energy to be dangerous if suddenly released. Mount the spring securely in a vise and slow-*

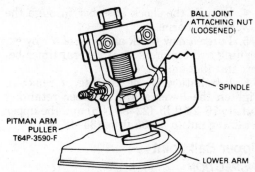

Disconnecting the ball joint with separator tool

ly loosen the spring compressor if the spring is being replaced.

15. If the coil spring is being replaced, measure the compressed length of the old spring and mark the position of the compressor plates on the old spring with chalk. Remove the spring compressor from the old spring carefully.

16. Install the spring compressor on the new spring, placing the compressor plates in the same position as marked on the old spring. Make sure the upper ball nut securing pin is installed properly, then compress the new spring to the compressed length of the old spring.

17. Position the coil spring assembly into the lower control arm.

18. Place a hydraulic jack under the lower control arm and slowly raise it into position. Reconnect the ball joint and install the nut. Tighten the ball joint castle nut to 80–120 ft.lb. (108–163 Nm) and install a new cotter pin. The nut may be tightened slightly to align the cotter pin hole, but not loosened.

19. Slowly release the spring compressor and remove it from the coil spring.

20. Reconnect the steering center link to the pitman arm.

21. Install the shock absorber.

22. Reconnect the stabilizer bar link bolt to the lower control arm.

23. Lower the vehicle. Although this procedure should not disturb any alignment settings, any time the front end is disassembled for service, the alignment should be checked.

Shock Absorber

REMOVAL AND INSTALLATION

1. Raise the vehicle and support it safely on jackstands.

2. Remove the nut and washer retaining the shock absorber to the coil spring upper bracket.

3. Remove the two bolts retaining the shock absorber to the bottom of the lower control arm.

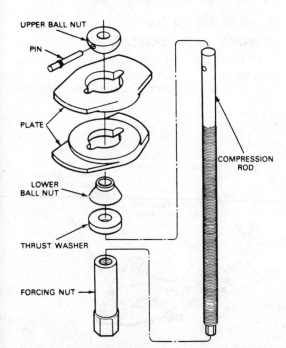

Typical spring compressor

4. Remove the shock absorber through the lower control arm.

5. Purge a new shock absorber of air by extending and compressing it several times before installation.

6. Installation is the reverse of removal. Tighten the lower shock absorber retaining nuts to 16–24 ft.lb. (22–33 Nm) and the upper retaining nut to 25–35 ft.lb. (34–48 Nm).

Upper Ball Joint

INSPECTION

1. Raise the vehicle by placing a hydraulic floor jack under the lower control arm.

2. Have an assistant grasp the top and bottom of the tire and move the wheel in and out.

3. As the wheel is being moved, observe the upper control arm where the spindle attaches to it. Any movement between the upper part of the spindle and the upper ball joint indicates a worn ball joint which must be replaced.

NOTE: *During this check, the lower ball joint will be unloaded and may move; this is normal and not an indication of a worn ball joint. Also, do not mistake a loose wheel bearing for a defective ball joint.*

REPLACEMENT

NOTE: *Ford Motor Company recommends replacement of the upper control arm and ball joint as an assembly, rather than replacement of the ball joint alone. However, aftermarket ball joints are available. The following procedure is for replacement of the ball joint only. See the procedure under Upper Control Arm Removal and Installation for complete assembly replacement.*

1. Raise the van and support it safely with jackstands placed under the frame lifting pads. Allow the front wheels to fall to their full down position.

2. Place a hydraulic floor jack under the lower control arm and raise the jack until it just contacts the arm.

3. Drill a ⅛″ (3mm) hole completely through each ball joint attaching rivet.

4. Use a chisel to cut the head off of each rivet, then drive them from the upper control arm with a suitable small drift or blunt punch.

5. Raise the lower control arm about 6″ (153mm) with the hydraulic jack.

6. Remove the pinch nut and bolt holding the ball joint stud from the spindle.

7. Using a suitable tool, loosen the ball joint stud from the spindle and remove the ball joint from the upper arm.

8. Clean all metal burrs from the upper arm and install a new ball joint, using the service part nuts and bolts to attach the ball joint to the upper arm. Do not attempt to rivet the ball joint again once it has been removed.

9. Attach the ball joint stud to the spindle, then install the pinch bolt and nut and tighten.

10. Remove the hydraulic jack and lower the van. Check the front end alignment.

Lower Ball Joint

REPLACEMENT

The lower ball joint is pressed into the lower control arm. Replacement involves removing the lower control arm, pressing the old ball joint out and pressing a new one in. See the procedures under Lower Control Arm Removal and Installation and remove the lower control arm to service the lower ball joints.

Front Stabilizer Bar

REMOVAL AND INSTALLATION

1. Raise the van and support it safely on jackstands.

2. Loosen and remove the nuts retaining the

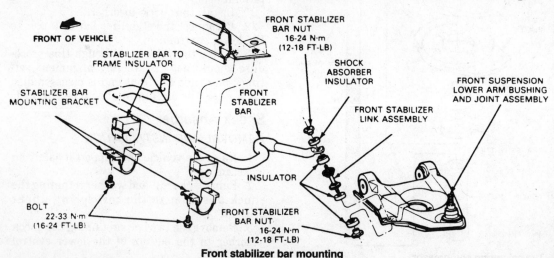

Front stabilizer bar mounting

stabilizer bar to the lower control arm link on each side, then remove the insulators and disconnect the bar from the links.

3. If required, remove the nuts retaining the links to the lower control arm, then remove the insulators and links.

4. Remove the bolts retaining the bar mounting bracket to the frame and remove the stabilizer bar. If required, remove the insulators from the stabilizer bar.

5. If the stabilizer bar insulators are being replaced, install them on the stabilizer bar. Place the bar, insulators and mounting bracket in position on the frame and install the retaining bolts. Tighten the retaining bolts to 16–24 ft.lb. (22–33 Nm).

6. If removed, connect the link and insulators to the lower control arm. Install and tighten the nut to 12–18 ft.lb. (16–24 Nm).

7. Connect the links and insulators to the

stabilizer bar, then install and tighten the nuts to 12–18 ft.lb. (16–24 Nm).

8. Lower the vehicle.

Lower Control Arm
REMOVAL AND INSTALLATION

1. Place the steering wheel and front wheels in the centered (straight ahead) position.

NOTE: *Any time the steering linkage is disconnected from the spindle, the steering system must be centered before beginning the service procedure.*

2. Raise the van and support it safely with jackstands placed under the frame lifting pads. A hydraulic floor jack should be placed under the control arm to raise and lower the arm during coil spring removal. Make sure the van is supported securely on the jackstands and only work on one side at a time.

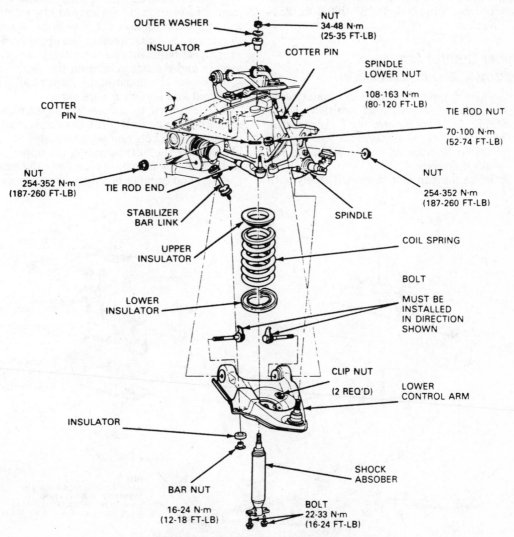

Exploded view of the lower control arm assembly

3. Remove the coil spring as previously described.

4. Remove the bolts and nuts retaining the lower control arm to the crossmember and remove the lower control arm from the frame.

5. If control arm bushings or ball joints are necessary, replace the entire lower control arm assembly.

6. Position the new lower control arm assembly to the frame crossmember and install the retaining bolts in the direction illustrated. Temporarily snug the bolts, but do not tighten to specifications.

7. If the old crossmember is being installed, inspect the lower ball joint boot and replace it if necessary.

8. Install the coil spring as previously described.

9. Lower the van so it rests in the normal ride position on a level surface.

10. Tighten the lower control arm-to-crossmember mounting bolts to 187–260 ft.lb. (254–352 Nm).

Upper Control Arm

REMOVAL AND INSTALLATION

1. Place the steering wheel and front tires in the centered (straight ahead) position.

NOTE: *Any time the steering linkage is disconnected from the spindle, the steering system must be centered before beginning the service procedure.*

2. Raise the van and support it safely with jackstands placed under the frame lifting pads. A hydraulic floor jack should be placed under the control arm to raise and lower the arm during coil spring removal. Make sure the van is supported securely on the jackstands and only work on one side at a time. Never service both front suspension assemblies at the same time.

3. Remove the spindle as described later in this chapter.

4. Remove the bolt retaining the cowl drain bracket and bolt retainer plate and remove the bracket and plate.

5. Matchmark the position of the control arm mounting brackets on the flat plate.

6. Remove the bolt and washer retaining the front mounting bracket to the flat plate.

7. From beneath the rail, remove the three nuts from the bolts retaining the two upper control arm mounting brackets to the body rail.

8. Remove the three long bolts retaining the mounting brackets to the body rail by rotating the upper control arm out of position in order to remove the bolts. Remove the upper control arm, upper ball joint and mounting bracket assembly and the flat plate from the van.

9. Inspect the upper and/or lower ball joint boot seal and replace if necessary.

10. If required to service the upper control arm and upper ball joint assembly or the mounting brackets and adjusting arm assembly, remove the nuts retaining the upper control arm to the adjusting arm. Note the **exact** position and number of shims on each control

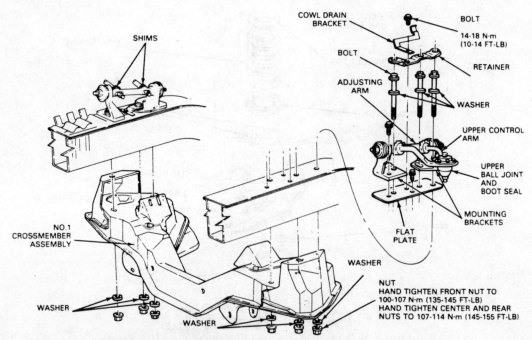

Exploded view of the upper control arm assembly and crossmember

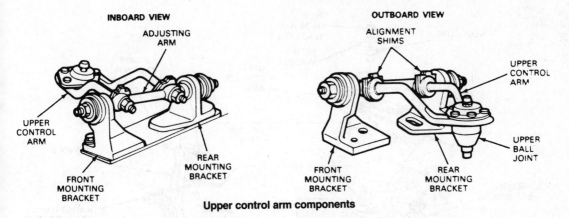

INBOARD VIEW

ADJUSTING ARM

UPPER CONTROL ARM

FRONT MOUNTING BRACKET

REAR MOUNTING BRACKET

OUTBOARD VIEW

ALIGNMENT SHIMS

UPPER CONTROL ARM

UPPER BALL JOINT

FRONT MOUNTING BRACKET

REAR MOUNTING BRACKET

Upper control arm components

arm stud. These shims control caster and camber. Remove the upper control arm from the adjusting arm.

NOTE: *The adjusting arm and mounting brackets are serviced as an assembly. Ford recommends that the upper control arm and upper ball joint also be serviced as an assembly, however aftermarket ball joint kits are available.*

11. If removed, install the upper control arm in the adjusting arm. Install the shims on the control arm studs with the same number of shims in the exact position as marked during removal. Install and tighten the nuts retaining the shims to the control arm.

12. Place the flat plate for the mounting brackets in position on the body rail, then install and tighten the bolts to 10–14 ft.lb. (14–18 Nm).

13. Place the mounting brackets and upper control arm assembly in position on the flat plate.

14. Install the three long bolts and washers retaining the mounting brackets to the body rail. Rotate or rock the upper control arm and mounting bracket assembly until the bolt heads rest against the mounting bracket and the studs extend through the body rail.

15. Move the mounting brackets into the position marked on the flat plate during removal. Install and tighten the nuts and washers retaining the mounting bracket bolts to the body rail to 135–145 ft.lb. (100–107 Nm) for the front bolt, and 145–155 ft.lb. (107–114 Nm) for the center and rear bolts. Make sure the mounting brackets do not move from the marked position on the flat plate to minimize corrections.

CAUTION: *The torque required for the mounting bracket-to-body rail nuts and bolts is critical. Be precise when tightening to the specified torque and use an accurate torque wrench. Torque with one, smooth motion rather than short jerks.*

16. Install and tighten the bolt retaining the front mounting bracket to the flat plate.

17. Place the bolt retainer plate and cowl drain bracket in position on the mounting bracket and flat plate assembly, then install and tighten the bolt to 10–14 ft.lb. (14–18 Nm).

18. Install the spindle as described later in this chapter.

19. Align the front end. Caster and camber are adjusted by adding or removing shims.

Spindle

REMOVAL AND INSTALLATION

1. Place the steering wheel and front tires in the centered (straight ahead) position.

NOTE: *Any time the steering linkage is disconnected from the spindle, the steering system must be centered before beginning the service procedure.*

2. Raise the van and support it safely with jackstands placed under the frame lifting pads. A hydraulic floor jack should be placed under the control arm to raise and lower the arm during coil spring removal. Make sure the van is supported securely on the jackstands and only work on one side at a time. Never service both front suspension assemblies at the same time.

3. Remove the front tire(s).

4. Remove the caliper, rotor and dust shield from the spindle as described in Chapter 8.

5. Remove the cotter pin and nut retaining the tie rod end to the spindle lower arm. Disconnect the tie rod end with a suitable pitman arm puller such as tool T64P-3590-F or equivalent.

6. Support the lower control arm with a hydraulic floor jack. Make sure the jack pad securely contacts the control arm. Remove the cotter pin, then loosen the nut retaining the spindle to the lower control arm ball joint. Disconnect the lower ball joint from the spindle using the same pitman arm puller used in Step

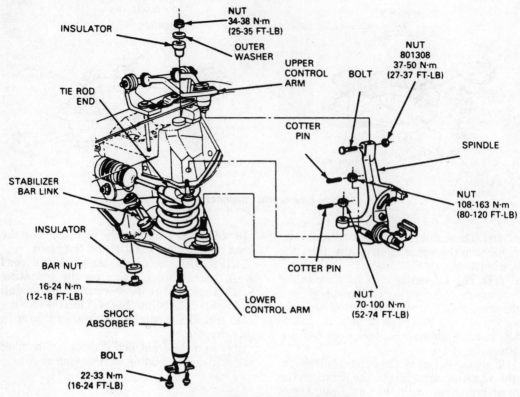

Exploded view of the spindle assembly

5, then remove the tool and ball joint retaining nut.

7. *Slowly* lower the jack under the control arm until the ball joint is disengaged from the spindle.

CAUTION: *Use extreme caution when lowering the lower control arm. The coil spring may quickly expand with dangerous force. Never lower the control arm quickly.*

8. Remove the bolt and nut retaining the spindle to the upper control arm ball joint, then remove the spindle from the van.

9. To install, first position the spindle upper arm on the upper ball joint. Install the nut and bolt an tighten to 27–37 ft.lb. (37–50 Nm). In-

spect the upper and lower ball joint boot seals for damage and replace if necessary.

10. Position the spindle lower arm over the ball joint stud, then **slowly** raise the lower control arm with the hydraulic jack until the ball joint stud extends through the spindle arm and is seated in the spindle. Install the ball joint castle nut and tighten it to 80–120 ft.lb.

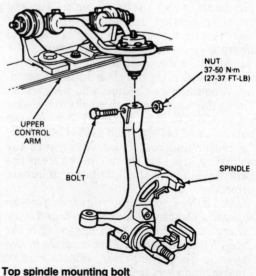

Top spindle mounting bolt

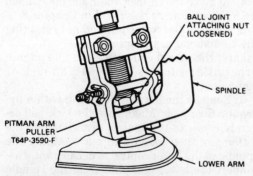

Disconnecting the lower ball joint from the spindle

(108–163 Nm), then install a new cotter pin. The castle nut may be tightened slightly to align the castellations with the cotter pin hole, but under no circumstances loosen the nut to align.

11. Connect the tie rod end to the spindle arm. Firmly seat the tie rod end stud into the tapered hole to prevent rotation while tightening the castellated nut. Torque the tie rod nut to 52–74 ft.lb. (70–100 Nm), then install a new cotter pin. The castle nut may be tightened slightly to align the castellations with the cotter pin hole, but under no circumstances loosen the nut to align.

12. Install the dust shield, rotor and caliper as described in Chapter 8.

13. Install the front tire(s) and tighten the lugnuts to 85–115 ft.lb. (116–155 Nm).

14. Lower the vehicle.

Front Wheel Bearings

ADJUSTMENT

1. Raise the van until the front tire clears the ground.

2. Remove the wheel cover and the grease cap from the hub.

3. Wipe any excess grease from the end of the spindle, then remove the cotter pin and retainer. Discard the cotter pin.

4. Loosen the adjusting nut three turns. Obtain running clearance between the brake rotor surface and the brake pads by rocking the entire wheel assembly in and out several times to push the caliper and brake pads away from the rotor. An alternate method is to lightly tap

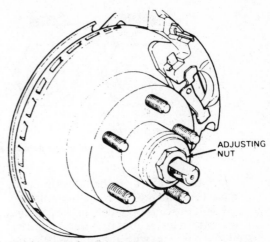

Front wheel bearing adjustment

on the caliper housing, but be sure not to tap on any other area that may damage the rotor or brake lining surfaces. Do not pry on the phenolic caliper piston.

NOTE: *This running clearance must be maintained throughout the bearing adjustment procedure. If proper clearance cannot be maintained, the caliper must be removed as described in Chapter 8.*

5. Rotate the wheel assembly while tightening the adjusting nut to 17–25 ft.lb. (23–34 Nm) to seat the bearings.

6. Loosen the adjusting nut ½ turn, then retighten to 18–20 in.lb. (2–3 Nm) using and inch pound torque wrench. Note that the final adjustment is in inch pounds, **not** foot pounds.

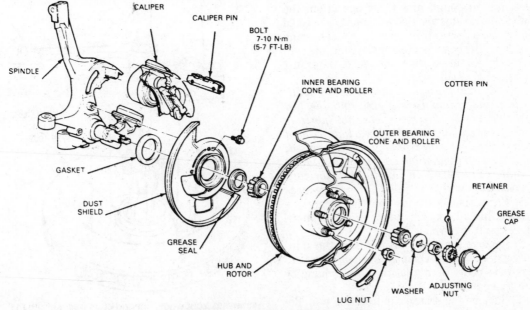

Exploded view of the front wheel assembly

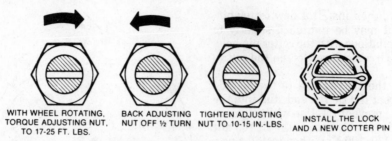

WITH WHEEL ROTATING,
TORQUE ADJUSTING NUT,
TO 17-25 FT. LBS.

BACK ADJUSTING
NUT OFF ½ TURN

TIGHTEN ADJUSTING
NUT TO 10-15 IN.-LBS.

INSTALL THE LOCK
AND A NEW COTTER PIN

Front wheel bearing adjustment procedure

7. Place the retainer on the adjusting nut. The castellations on the retainer must be aligned with the cotter pin hole in the spindle. Do not turn the adjusting nut to make castellations line up with the spindle hole, remove the retainer and turn it one flat to re-index and try to fit the cotter pin again. Repeat this procedure until the castellations line up with the spindle hole correctly.

8. Insert a new cotter pin to lock the retainer in place and bend the ends around the castellated flange of the retainer to secure the cotter pin in place.

9. Check the front wheel rotation. If the wheel rotates properly, install the grease cap and wheel cover. If rotation is noisy or rough, remove, inspect and lubricate the bearing cones and cups as described in the Removal and Installation procedure that follows.

10. Before moving the van, pump the brake pedal several times to restore normal brake travel.

REMOVAL AND INSTALLATION

If wheel bearing adjustment will not eliminate looseness or rough and noisy operation, the hub and bearings should be cleaned, inspected and repacked with lithium base wheel bearing grease. If the bearing cups or the cone and roller assemblies are worn or damaged, they must be replaced as follows:

NOTE: *Sodium base grease is not compatible with lithium base grease and the two should not be intermixed. Do not lubricate the front and/or rear wheel bearings without first identifying the type of grease being used. Usage of incompatible wheel bearing lubricant could result in premature lubricant breakdown and subsequent bearing damage.*

1. Raise the van until the tire clears the ground. Install a jackstand for safety, then remove the front tire(s).

2. Remove the brake caliper from the spindle as described in Chapter 8, then wire it to the underbody. Do not let the caliper hang by the brake hose.

3. Remove the grease cup from the hub. Remove the cotter pin, castellated retainer, ad-

justing nut and flat washer from the spindle. Remove the outer bearing cone and roller assembly.

4. Pull the hub and rotor assembly off the spindle.

5. Place the hub and rotor on a clean workbench, with the back side facing up, and remove the grease seal using a suitable seal remover or small prybar. Discard the grease seal.

6. Remove the inner bearing cone and roller assembly from the hub.

7. Clean the inner and outer bearing cups with solvent. Inspect the cups for scratches, pits, excessive wear and other damage. If the cups are worn or damaged, remove them with a bearing cup puller (T77F-1102-A or equivalent) as illustrated.

8. Wipe all old lubricant from the spindle

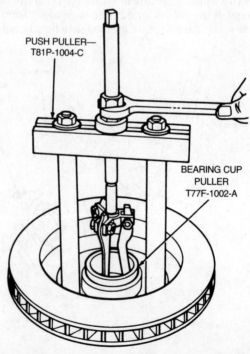

PUSH PULLER—
T81P-1004-C

BEARING CUP
PULLER
T77F-1002-A

Removing front wheel bearing cups (races) from the hub

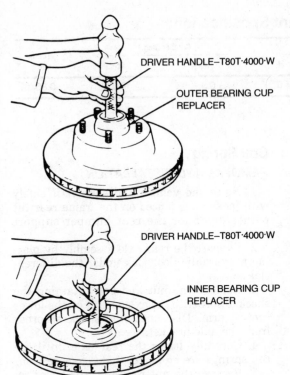

DRIVER HANDLE—T80T·4000·W

OUTER BEARING CUP REPLACER

DRIVER HANDLE—T80T·4000·W

INNER BEARING CUP REPLACER

Installing bearing cups in the hub assembly

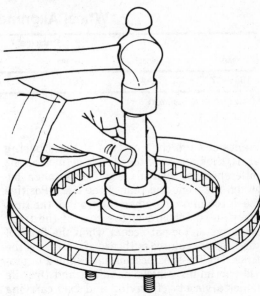

Installing grease seal in the hub assembly

and the inside of the hub with a clean rag. Cover the spindle and brush all loose dirt and dust from the dust shield. Remove the cover cloth carefully to prevent dirt from falling on it.

9. If the inner or outer bearing cups were removed, install replacement cups using a suitable driver tool (T80T-4000-W or equivalent) and bearing cup replacer. Make sure the cups are seated properly in the hub and not cocked in the bore.

10. Thoroughly clean all old grease from the surrounding surfaces.

11. Pack the bearing and cone assemblies with suitable wheel bearing grease using a bearing packer tool. If a packer tool is not available, work as much grease as possible between the rollers and cages, then grease the cone surfaces.

12. Place the inner bearing cone and roller assembly in the inner cup. Apply a light film of grease to the lips of a new grease seal and install the seal with an appropriate driver tool as illustrated. Make sure the grease seal is properly seated and not cocked in the bore.

13. Install the hub and rotor assembly on the spindle. Keep the hub centered on the spindle to prevent damage to the retainer and the spindle threads.

14. Install the outer bearing cone and roller assembly and the flatwasher on the spindle,

then install the adjusting nut finger tight. Adjust the wheel bearing(s) as described above.

15. Install the caliper to the spindle as described in Chapter 8.

16. Install the front tire(s), then lower the van and tighten the lugnuts to 85–115 ft.lb. (115–155 Nm). Install the wheel cover.

17. Before moving the van, pump the brake pedal several times to restore normal brake travel.

Front End Alignment

Caster and camber adjustment is provided by shims on the upper control arm. The two different shims initially provided from the assembly plant include one 0.078″ (2mm) thickness and one 0.236″ (6mm) thickness for a total shim stack thickness of 0.315″ (8mm) at each leg of the upper control arm. These shims are added, removed, or switched from the front and rear legs of the upper control arms as required to adjust the front end alignment.

Camber adjustment is obtained by removing or adding an equal number of shims to the front and rear leg of the wire arm. Caster adjustment is obtained by removing shims from the front leg and installing them on the rear leg, and vice-versa. If the same amount is switched from one leg to the other, caster will be changed but camber will not be affected. If unequal amounts are removed and added to the front and rear legs, both caster and camber will be changed.

Toe-in should only be checked and adjusted after the caster and camber have been adjusted to specifications. Caster and camber adjust-

Wheel Alignment Specifications

Years	Model	Caster (deg.)		Camber (deg.)		Toe-in (in.)
		Range	Pref.	Range	Pref.	
1986–87	All	3.0–5.0	4.0	−0.3 + .07	+0.2	0.80 ①

① ³⁄₃₂ in. Out to ⁵⁄₃₂ in. In

ments change the position of the steering arms, thus affecting toe. Toe is defined as the difference between measurements taken between the front and rear of the tires. Positive toe or toe-in occurs when the front of the tires are pointed inboard of the rear of the tires. Negative or toe-out occurs when the front of the tires are pointed outboard of the rear of the tires. The toe specification is designed to provide optimum vehicle handling and tire life under a variety of driving and load carrying conditions.

NOTE: *All wheel alignment adjustments and readings must be performed on an alignment rack level to within ¹⁄₁₆" (1.6mm) side-to-side and front-to-rear. Refer all alignment checks and adjustments to a qualified repair shop.*

REAR SUSPENSION

The Aerostar rear suspension is a coil spring type system. It supports and links the rear axle to the frame with one upper control arm and two lower control arms. The rear suspension uses low pressure gas shock absorbers, telescopic double acting type.

Coil Spring

REMOVAL AND INSTALLATION

1. Raise the vehicle and support it safely with jackstands placed on the frame rear lift points or under the rear bumper support brackets.
2. Support the rear axle assembly by placing a hydraulic floor jack under the differential housing.
3. Remove the nut and bolt retaining the shock absorber to the axle mount on the lower control arm. Disconnect the shock absorber from the axle bracket.
4. Carefully lower the rear axle until the coil springs are no longer under compression.
5. Remove the nut retaining the lower retainer and spring to the control arm.
6. Remove the bolt retaining the upper retainer and spring to the frame.
7. Remove the spring and retainers, then remove the upper and lower insulators.
8. Before installing the spring, first make sure the axle is in the lowered (spring unloaded) position. Place the lower insulator on the control arm and the upper insulator at the top of the spring.
9. Install the coil spring in position between the control arm and frame. The small diame-

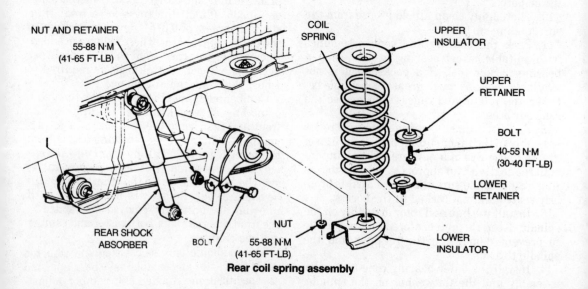

NUT AND RETAINER
55-88 N·M
(41-65 FT-LB)

COIL SPRING

UPPER INSULATOR

UPPER RETAINER

BOLT
40-55 N·M
(30-40 FT-LB)

LOWER RETAINER

REAR SHOCK ABSORBER

BOLT

NUT
55-88 N·M
(41-65 FT-LB)

LOWER INSULATOR

Rear coil spring assembly

ter, tapered coils (white colored) must face upward.

10. Install the upper retainer and bolt, then tighten the bolt to 30–40 ft.lb. (40–55 Nm).

11. Install the lower retainer and nut and tighten the nut to 41–65 ft.lb. (55–88 Nm).

12. Raise the axle to the normal ride position with the hydraulic jack.

13. Position the shock absorber in the axle bracket, then install the bolt so the head is positioned outboard of the bracket. Install the nut and tighten it to 41–65 ft.lb. (55–88 Nm).

14. Remove the jackstands and lower the vehicle.

Shock Absorber

REMOVAL AND INSTALLATION

CAUTION: *The low pressure gas shock absorbers are charged with 135 psi of Nitrogen gas. Do not attempt to open the shock absorbers.*

1. Raise the van and support it safely on jackstands. Place the jackstands under the axle to take the load off of the shock absorbers.

2. Remove the shock absorber lower attaching bolt and nut, then swing the lower end free of the mounting bracket on the axle housing.

3. Remove the attaching bolt and washer from the upper mounting bracket, then remove the shock absorber.

4. Installation is the reverse of removal. Tighten the lower mounting nut to 41–65 ft.lb. (55–88 Nm), and the upper mounting bracket bolt and washer to 25–35 ft.lb. (38–48 Nm).

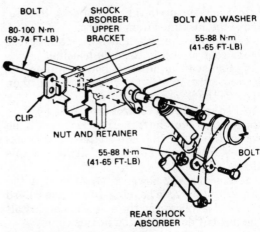

Rear shock absorber mounting

Lower Control Arm

REMOVAL AND INSTALLATION

1. Raise the vehicle and support it safely with jackstands placed on the frame rear lift points or under the rear bumper support brackets.

2. Support the rear axle assembly by placing a hydraulic floor jack under the differential housing.

3. Remove the nut and bolt retaining the shock absorber to the axle mount on the lower control arm. Disconnect the shock absorber from the axle bracket.

4. Carefully lower the rear axle until the coil springs are no longer under compression.

5. Remove the nut retaining the lower re-

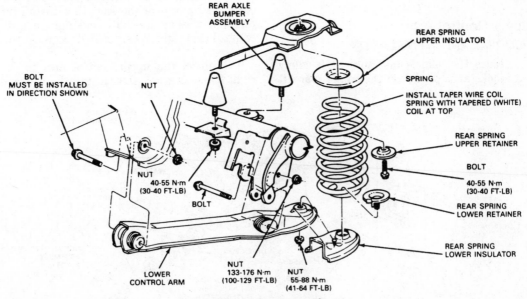

Lower control arm mounting

tainer and spring to the control arm, then remove the insulator from the arm.

6. Remove the bolt and nut retaining the lower control arm to the axle housing.

7. Remove the nut and bolt retaining the lower control arm to the frame bracket, then remove the lower control arm.

8. To install the control arm, first position the lower arm in the frame bracket. Install the bolt so the head is inboard on the frame bracket. Install the nut but do not tighten at this time.

9. Position the lower control arm in the bracket on the axle housing. Install the bolt so the head is inboard on the axle bracket. Install the nut but do not tighten at this time.

10. Install the insulator on the lower control arm.

11. With the axle in the lowered (spring unloaded) position, install the coil spring and lower retainer on the lower control arm.

12. Install the nut attaching the retainer and spring to the lower control arm. Tighten the nut to 41–65 ft.lb. (55–88 Nm).

13. Raise the axle to the normal load position, then tighten the nut and bolt retaining the lower control arm to the axle housing to 100–145 ft.lb. (135–197 Nm). Tighten the nut and bolt retaining the lower control arm to the frame bracket to 100–145 ft.lb. (135–197 Nm).

14. Position the shock absorber in the lower axle mounting bracket, then install the bolt so the head is outboard of the axle bracket. Install the nut and tighten it to 41–65 ft.lb. (55–88 Nm).

15. Remove the jackstands and lower the vehicle.

Upper Control Arm

REMOVAL AND INSTALLATION

1. Raise the vehicle and support it safely with jackstands placed on the frame rear lift points or under the rear bumper support brackets.

2. Support the rear axle assembly by placing a hydraulic floor jack under the differential housing.

3. Remove the nut and bolt retaining the shock absorber to the axle mount on the lower control arm. Disconnect the shock absorber from the axle bracket.

4. Carefully lower the rear axle until the coil springs are no longer under compression.

5. Remove the bolt and nut retaining the upper control arm to the rear axle. Disconnect the upper control arm from the axle. Scribe a mark aligning the position of the cam adjuster in the axle bushing. The cam adjuster controls the rear axle pinion angle for driveline angularity.

6. Remove the bolt and nut retaining the upper control arm to the right frame bracket. Rotate the arm to disengage it from the body bracket.

7. Remove the nut and washer retaining the upper control arm to the left frame bracket. Remove the outer insulator and spacer, then remove the control arm from the bracket. Remove the inner insulator and washer from the control arm stud.

NOTE: *If the left bracket attachments are loosened prior to disengaging the arm from the right bracket, the uncompressed left bushing will force the arm against the right hand bracket and make removal difficult.*

8. To install, first position the washer and inner insulator on the control arm stud. Install the control arm so the stud extends through the left frame bracket. Install the spacer and outer insulator over the stud, then install the nut and washer assembly and tighten until snug. Do not tighten to specified torque at this time.

9. Position the upper control arm in the right frame bracket, then install the bolt and

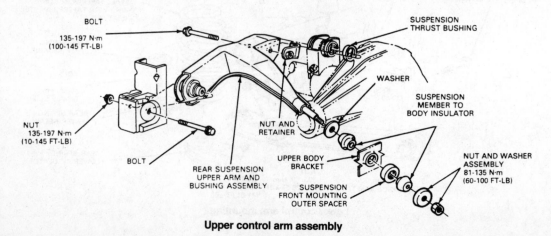

Upper control arm assembly

nut and tighten until snug. Do not tighten to specified torque at this time.

10. Making sure the scribe marks on the cam adjuster and axle bushing are in alignment, connect the upper control arm to the axle. Install the nut and bolt and tighten until snug. Do not tighten to specified torque at this time.

11. Raise the axle to the normal ride position.

12. Position the shock absorber in the lower mounting bracket, then install the bolt so the head is outboard of the axle bracket. Install the nut and tighten to 41–65 ft.lb. (55–88 Nm).

13. With the axle in the normal ride position, tighten all upper control arm fasteners to the specified torque. Tighten the nut and washer assembly retaining the control arm to the left frame bracket to 60–100 ft.lb. (81–135 Nm). Tighten the nut and bolt retaining the control arm to the right frame bracket to 100–145 ft.lb. (135–197 Nm). Tighten the nut and bolt retaining the control arm to the axle to 100–145 ft.lb. (135–197 Nm).

14. Remove the jackstands and lower the vehicle.

Rear Wheel Hub and Bearing
REMOVAL AND INSTALLATION

The rear wheel bearing is pressed into the outer axle tube housing. A grease seal is pressed into the tube over the bearing. The axle shaft is retained in the carrier assembly by a C-clip in the differential case. When the C-clip is removed, the axle shaft can be removed from the axle tube. See the procedure under Rear Axle Removal and Installation for details.

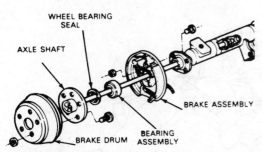

Rear wheel hub and bearing assembly

STEERING

Steering Wheel
REMOVAL AND INSTALLATION

1. Disconnect the negative battery cable.

2. Remove the steering wheel horn cover by removing the screws from the spokes and lifting the steering wheel horn cover.

3. Disconnect the horn switch/speed control

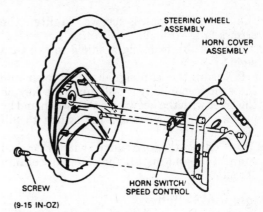

Removing steering wheel pad

wires by pulling the connectors apart, then remove the horn cover assembly.

4. Remove the steering wheel attaching bolt.

5. Using a suitable steering wheel puller, such as tool T67L-3600-A or equivalent, remove the steering wheel from the upper steering shaft. Do not strike the end of the steering column upper shaft with a hammer or steering shaft bearing damage will occur.

6. Installation is the reverse of removal. Align the mark and the flats on the steering wheel with the mark and the flats on the shaft. Tighten the retaining bolt to 23–33 ft.lb. (31–45 Nm).

Turn Signal/Hazard Flasher Switch
REMOVAL AND INSTALLATION

1. Remove the steering wheel as previously described. If equipped with tilt column, remove the upper extension shroud by squeezing it at the six and twelve o'clock positions and popping it free of the retaining plate at the three o'clock position.

2. Remove the two trim shroud halves from the steering column by removing the two attaching screws.

3. Remove the turn signal switch lever by grasping the lever and by suing a pulling and twisting motion of the hand while pulling the lever straight out from the switch.

4. Peel back the foam sight shield from the turn signal switch.

5. Disconnect the two turn signal switch electrical connectors.

6. Remove the two self-tapping screws attaching the turn signal switch to the lock cylinder housing, then disengage the switch from the housing.

7. To install, first align the turn signal switch mounting holes with the corresponding holes in the lock cylinder housing and install

the two self-tapping screws. Tighten the screws to 18–26 in.lb. (2–3 Nm).

8. Stick the foam sight shield to the turn signal switch.

9. Install the turn signal switch lever into the switch manually by aligning the key on the lever with the keyway in the switch and by pushing the lever toward the switch to full engagement.

10. Connect the turn signal switch electrical connectors and install the steering column shrouds.

Ignition Switch

REMOVAL AND INSTALLATION

1. Rotate the lock cylinder key to the LOCK position and disconnect the negative battery cable.

2. If equipped with a tilt column, remove the upper extension shroud by squeezing it at the six and twelve o'clock positions and popping it free of the retaining plate at the three o'clock position.

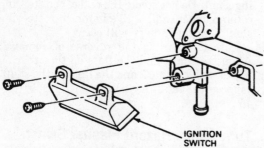

IGNITION
SWITCH

Typical ignition switch mounting inside steering column

3. Remove the two trim shroud halves by removing the two attaching screws.

4. Disconnect the ignition switch electrical connector.

5. Drill out the break-off head bolts connecting the switch to the lock cylinder housing with a ⅛" (3mm) drill, then remove the two bolts using an EX-3 screw extractor tool or equivalent screw extractor.

6. Disengage the ignition switch from the actuator pin and remove the switch.

7. To install, first rotate the ignition key to the RUN position (approximately 90° clockwise from LOCK).

8. Install the replacement switch by aligning the holes on the switch casting base with the holes in the lock cylinder housing. Note that the replacement switch is provided in the RUN position. Minor movement of the lock cylinder to align the actuator pin with the U-shaped slot in the switch carrier may be necessary.

9. Install new break-off head bolts and tighten until the heads shear off.

10. Connect the electrical connector to the ignition switch.

11. Connect the negative battery terminal, then check the ignition switch for proper operation in all modes. If correct, install the steering column shrouds.

Ignition Lock Cylinder

REMOVAL AND INSTALLATION

NOTE: *The following procedure pertains to vehicles that have functional lock cylinders, with ignition keys that are available or igni-*

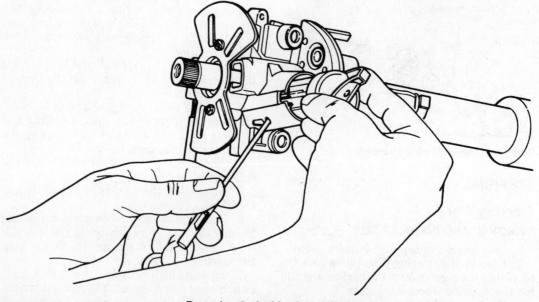

Removing the ignition lock cylinder

tion key numbers are known and the proper key can be made at a dealer.

1. Disconnect the negative battery cable.

2. Remove the trim shroud, then remove the electrical connector from the key warning switch.

3. Turn the lock cylinder to the RUN position.

4. Place a ⅛″ (3mm) diameter pin or small drift punch in the hole located at 4 o'clock and 1¼″ (32mm) from the outer edge of the lock cylinder housing. Depress the retaining pin and pull out the lock cylinder.

5. Prior to installing the lock cylinder, lubricate the cylinder cavity, including the drive gear with lock lubricant D8AZ-19587-A or equivalent.

6. To install the lock cylinder, turn the lock cylinder to the RUN position, depress the retaining pin, and insert it into the lock cylinder housing. Make sure the cylinder is fully seated and aligned into the interlocking washer before turning the key to the OFF position. This action will permit the cylinder retaining pin to extend into the hole in the lock cylinder housing.

7. Using the ignition key, rotate the lock cylinder to insure correct mechanical operation in all positions. Install the electrical connector onto the key warning switch.

8. Connect the negative battery cable, then check for proper ignition functions and verify that the column is locked in the LOCK position. Install the trim shrouds.

NOTE: *The following procedure applies to vehicles where the ignition lock is inoperative and the lock cylinder cannot be rotated due to a lost or broken ignition key.*

1. Disconnect the negative battery cable.

2. Remove the horn cover and the steering wheel.

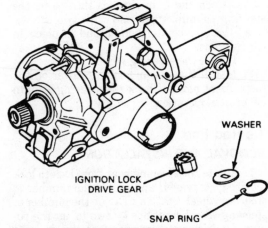

IGNITION LOCK DRIVE GEAR

WASHER

SNAP RING

Removing ignition lock drive gear

3. Remove the trim shrouds and the connector from the key warning switch.

4. Use a ⅛″ (3mm) diameter drill to drill out the retaining pin, being careful not to drill any deeper than ½″ (12.7mm).

5. Place a chisel at the base of the ignition lock cylinder cap, then use a hammer to strike the chisel with sharp blows to break the cap away from the lock cylinder.

6. Using a ⅜″ (9.5mm) diameter drill, drill down the middle of the ignition lock key slot approximately 1¾″ (45mm) until the lock cylinder breaks loose from the breakaway base of the cylinder. Remove the lock cylinder and drill shavings from the lock cylinder housing.

7. Remove the snapring, washer and ignition lock drive gear. Thoroughly clean all drill shavings and other foreign materials from the casting.

8. Carefully inspect the lock cylinder housing for damage from the removal operation. If any damage is apparent, the housing must be replaced.

9. Position the lock drive gear in the base of the lock cylinder housing in the same position as noted during the removal procedure. The position of the lock drive gear is correct if the last tooth on the drive gear meshes with the last tooth on the rack. Verify correct gear to rack alignment by inserting a flat bladed screwdriver in the recess of the gear and rotating it to the full counterclockwise position. After verification, rotate the drive gear back to the original removal position. Install the washer and snapring. Note that the flats in the recess of the drive gear align with the flats in the washer.

10. Install the ignition lock cylinder as described in the previous procedure.

11. Connect the key warning switch wire, then install the shroud.

12. Install the steering wheel and horn cover.

13. Connect the negative battery cable.

14. Check for proper ignition and accessory operation and verify that the column locks in the LOCK position.

Steering Column

REMOVAL AND INSTALLATION

CAUTION: *The outer tube steering column upper bracket affects the energy absorption on impact. It is absolutely necessary to handle related components with care when performing any service operation. Avoid hammering, jarring, dropping or leaning any portion of the column. When reassembling column components, use only the specified screws, nuts and bolts and tighten to specified torque.*

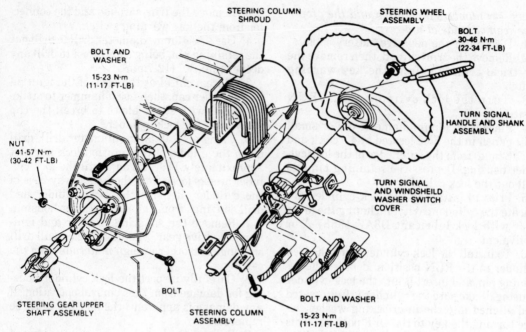

Removing steering column assembly

1. Disconnect the negative battery cable.

2. Remove the bolt attaching the column steering shaft to the intermediate shaft assembly.

3. Remove the steering wheel.

4. Remove the steering column trim shrouds by loosening the two screws. On tilt columns, remove the upper extension shroud by squeezing it at the six and twelve o'clock positions and popping it free of the retaining plate at the three o'clock position.

5. Remove the steering column cover directly under the column on the instrument panel.

6. Disconnect all electrical connections to the steering column switches.

7. Loosen the two bolts retaining the steering column to the lower instrument panel bracket. Do not remove the bolts.

8. Remove the three screws retaining the steering column toeplate/lower seal to the dash.

9. Remove the two bolts retaining the steering column to the instrument panel.

10. Lower the steering column and pull it out from the vehicle.

NOTE: *Clamping is not permitted on the outer tube overlap joint. Care must be taken not to permanently deform the tube wall. Damage to the tube may affect column energy absorption performance.*

11. Install the steering column by inserting the lower end of the steering column through the opening in the dash panel. Use care not to damage the column during installation.

12. Align the steering column support bracket to the lower instrument panel bracket. Attach the bolts loosely, so that the column hangs with clearance between the column and the instrument panel.

13. Align the steering column toe plate three mounting holes to the dash weld nuts, then install the three bolts and tighten them to 11–17 ft.lb. (15–23 Nm).

14. Tighten the column support brackets two bolts to 11–17 ft.lb. (15–23 Nm).

15. Connect the column switch connectors.

16. Slide the upper steering intermediate shaft assembly onto the steering column lower shaft. Attach with the bolt and nut previously removed and tighten to 30–42 ft.lb. (41–57 Nm).

17. Attach the trim shrouds that cover the steering column upper end with two screws. Snap the upper extension shroud in place on tilt columns.

18. Install the steering wheel.

19. Install the steering column cover on the instrument panel. Check the steering column for proper operation.

Tie Rod End

REMOVAL AND INSTALLATION

1. Rotate the steering gear from lock to lock (entire gear travel) and record the number of steering wheel rotations. Divide the number of steering wheel rotations by two to get the required number of turns to place the steering

wheel in the centered (straight ahead) position. From one lock position, rotate the steering wheel the required number of turns to center the steering rack.

2. Mark the tie rod end jam nut in relation to the inner ball joint assembly threads for installation purposes.

3. Remove and discard the cotter pin from the tie rod end ball stud and remove the nut.

4. Separate the tie rod ends from the spindle arms using remover tool T64P-3590-F, or equivalent.

5. Hold the tie rod end with a wrench and loosen the tie rod jam nut.

6. Grip the tie rod with locking pliers and remove the tie rod end from the inner ball joint assembly. Note and record the number of turns required to remove the tie rod end.

7. Thread the new tie rod onto the inner ball joint assembly the same number of turns recorded during removal. Tighten the jam nut against the tie rod end in the position marked prior to removal, then tighten the nut to 35–60 ft.lb. (48–68 Nm).

8. With the steering gear, steering wheel and front wheels in the centered position, attach the tie rod ends to the spindle arms. Install the nuts and tighten them to 52–73 ft.lb. (70–100 Nm). If required, advance the castle nuts to the next castellation and install new cotter pins. Do not loosen the nuts to line up the cotter pin hole.

NOTE: *Make sure the tie rod ball studs are seated in the spindle tapers to prevent rotation while tightening the nut.*

9. Have the toe-in and front end alignment checked at a qualified service shop.

Manual Steering Gear

REMOVAL AND INSTALLATION

1. Rotate the steering gear from lock to lock (entire gear travel) and record the number of steering wheel rotations. Divide the number of steering wheel rotations by two to get the required number of turns to place the steering wheel in the centered (straight ahead) position. From one lock position, rotate the steering wheel the required number of turns to center the steering rack.

2. Raise the vehicle and support it safely, then remove the bolt retaining the intermediate steering column shaft to the steering gear pinion. Separate the shaft from the pinion.

3. Remove and discard the cotter pin retaining the nut to the tie rod ends. Remove the nut, then separate the tie rod ends from the spindle arms using remover tool T64P-3590-F, or equivalent.

4. Support the steering gear and remove the

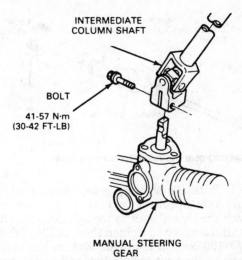

Separating the intermediate steering shaft from the pinion

two nuts, bolts and washers retaining the gear to the crossmember. Remove the gear and, if required, remove the front and rear insulators from the gear housing.

5. To install, first install the front and rear insulators in the gear housing, if removed.

6. Position the steering gear on the crossmember, then install the nuts, bolts and washers. Tighten the nuts to 65–90 ft.lb. (88–122 Nm).

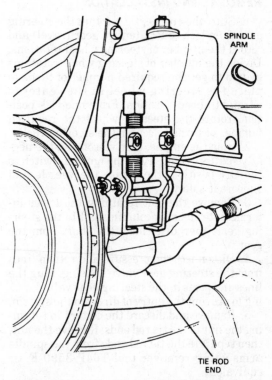

Separating the tie rod end from the spindle arm with remover tool

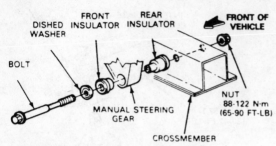

Steering gear mounting to crossmember

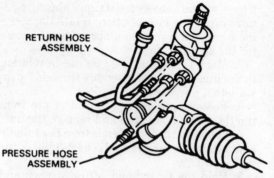

Disconnecting the power steering lines from the rack

7. With the steering gear, steering wheel and front wheels in the centered position, attach the tie rod ends to the spindle arms. Install the nuts and tighten them to 52–73 ft.lb. (70–100 Nm). If required, advance the castle nuts to the next castellation and install new cotter pins. Do not loosen the nuts to line up the cotter pin hole.

NOTE: *Make sure the tie rod ball studs are seated in the spindle tapers to prevent rotation while tightening the nut.*

8. Connect the steering column intermediate shaft to the gear pinion, then install the bolt and tighten it to 30–42 ft.lb. (41–57 Nm).

9. Have the toe-in and front end alignment checked at a qualified service shop.

Power Steering Gear

REMOVAL AND INSTALLATION

1. Start the engine, then rotate the steering gear from lock to lock (entire gear travel) and record the number of steering wheel rotations. Divide the number of steering wheel rotations by two to get the required number of turns to place the steering wheel in the centered (straight ahead) position. From one lock position, rotate the steering wheel the required number of turns to center the steering rack.

2. Stop the engine, then disconnect the negative battery cable. Turn the ignition switch to the ON position, then raise the vehicle and support it safely.

3. Remove the bolt retaining the lower intermediate steering column shaft to the steering gear, then disconnect the shaft from the gear.

4. Disconnect the pressure and return lines from the steering gear valve housing. Plug the lines and ports in the steering gear valve housing to prevent the entry of dirt into the system.

5. Remove and discard the cotter pin retaining the nut to the tie rod ends. Remove the nut, then separate the tie rod ends from the spindle arms using remover tool T64P-3590-F, or equivalent.

6. Support the steering gear and remove the two nuts, bolts and washers retaining the gear

to the crossmember. Remove the gear and, if required, remove the front and rear insulators from the gear housing.

7. To install the steering rack, first install the insulators in the gear housing, if removed. The rubber insulators must be pushed completely inside the gear housing before the gear is installed against the crossmember. No gap is allowed between the insulator and the face of the rear boss. Use rubber lubricant or soapy water to facilitate installation of the insulators in the gear housing.

8. Position the steering gear on the crossmember, then install the nuts, bolts and washers. Tighten the nuts to 65–90 ft.lb. (88–122 Nm).

9. Connect the pressure and return lines to the appropriate ports on the steering gear valve housing, then tighten the fittings to 10–15 ft.lb. (15–20 Nm). The fitting design allows the hoses to swivel when properly tightened. Do not attempt to eliminate this looseness by overtightening or damage to the fittings will occur.

10. With the steering gear, steering wheel and front wheels in the centered position, attach the tie rod ends to the spindle arms. Install the nuts and tighten them to 52–73 ft.lb. (70–100 Nm). If required, advance the castle nuts to the next castellation and install new cotter pins. Do not loosen the nuts to line up the cotter pin hole.

NOTE: *Make sure the tie rod ball studs are seated in the spindle tapers to prevent rotation while tightening the nut.*

11. Connect the steering column intermediate shaft to the gear pinion, then install the bolt and tighten it to 30–42 ft.lb. (41–57 Nm).

12. Lower the vehicle and turn the ignition key to the OFF position, then connect the negative battery cable.

13. Check the power steering fluid level in the pump and top off as required.

14. Have the toe-in and front end alignment checked at a qualified service shop.

Power Steering Pump
REMOVAL AND INSTALLATION

NOTE: *An identification tag is attached to the power steering pump reservoir. The top line of this tag indicates the basic model number (HBC) and the suffix. Always use these tags when requesting service parts as there may be slight differences in internal components.*

2.3L (140 CID) Engine

1. Drain the power steering fluid from the pump by disconnecting the fluid return hose at the reservoir and draining the fluid into a suitable container.

2. Remove the pressure hose from the pump. If required, disconnect and remove the power steering pressure switch from the fitting on the gear assembly. Disconnect the electrical connector from the switch and unscrew the switch from the fitting.

3. Loosen the pivot bolt and adjusting bolt on the alternator bracket to release belt tension, then remove the drive belt from the power steering pump pulley.

4. Install a steering pump pulley remover tool (T69L-10300-B or equivalent) on the pul-

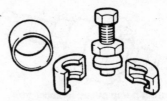

Power steering pump pulley remover tool

ley. Hold the pump and rotate the tool nut counterclockwise to remove the pulley. Do not apply in-and-out pressure on the pump shaft or the internal thrust areas will be damaged.

5. Remove the bolts attaching the pump to the bracket and remove the pump.

6. To install, first position the pump on the bracket, then install and tighten the bolts to 30–45 ft.lb. (41–61 Nm).

7. Install a power steering pump pulley replacer tool (T65P-3A733-C or equivalent) and press the pulley onto the pump shaft. The pull-off groove must face the front of the vehicle and the pulley must be pressed on the shaft until flush with a tolerance of 0.010″ (0.254mm).

8. Position the belt on the pulley, then place a 1″ wrench on the alternator boss and lift up on the alternator until the specified belt tension is read on a suitable belt tension gauge.

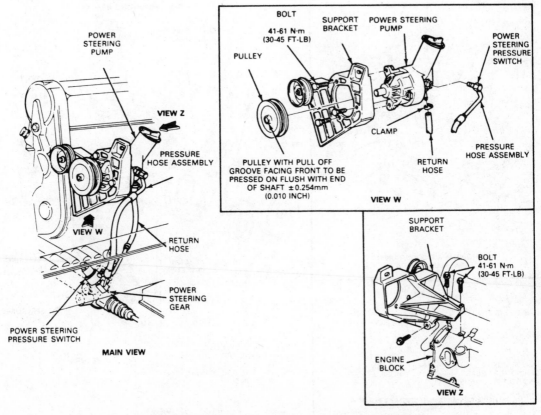

Power steering pump installation on 2.3L (140 CID) engine

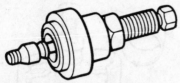

Power steering pump pulley replacer tool

Tighten the adjustment bolt to 24–40 ft.lb. (33–54 Nm) and the pivot bolt to 45–57 ft.lb. (61–78 Nm).

9. Install the pressure hose to the pump fitting. If removed, install the power steering pressure switch on the gear assembly and connect the wires.

10. Connect the return hose to the pump and tighten the clamp.

11. Fill the reservoir with specified power steering fluid, then start the engine and turn the steering wheel from stop to stop to remove any air from the system.

12. Check the system for leaks.

2.8L (171 CID) and 3.0L (182 CID) Engines

1. Drain the power steering fluid from the pump by disconnecting the fluid return hose at the reservoir and draining the fluid into a suitable container.

2. Remove the pressure hose from the pump fitting by unscrewing the hose swivel nut.

3. Slacken belt tension by loosening the pivot bolt and adjustment bolt on the idler pulley assembly, then remove the drive belt from the power steering pump pulley.

4. Install a steering pump pulley remover tool (T69L-10300-B or equivalent) on the pulley. Hold the pump and rotate the tool nut counterclockwise to remove the pulley. Do not apply in-and-out pressure on the pump shaft or the internal thrust areas will be damaged.

5. Remove the support and the bolts attaching the pump to the bracket, then remove the pump.

6. Position the new pump on the bracket, then install and tighten the bolts to 35–47 ft.lb. (47–64 Nm). Position the support on the bracket and install and tighten the mounting bolts to 35–47 ft.lb. (47–64 Nm).

7. Install a power steering pump pulley replacer tool (T65P-3A733-C or equivalent) and press the pulley onto the pump shaft. The pull-off groove must face the front of the vehicle and

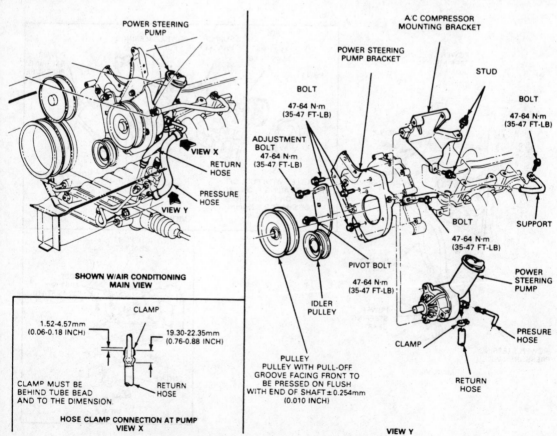

Power steering pump installation on V6 engines

the pulley must be pressed on the shaft until flush with a tolerance of 0.010″ (0.254mm).

8. Position the drive belt on the pulley, then insert a ½″ drive breaker bar in the slot in the idler pulley assembly. Rotate the pulley assembly until the specified belt tension is obtained, then tighten the adjustment bolt and pivot bolt to 35–47 ft.lb. (47–64 Nm).

9. Connect the pressure hose to the pump fitting. Connect the return hose to the pump and tighten the clamp.

10. Refill the power steering reservoir with the specified fluid, then start the engine and check for leaks. Turn the steering wheel from lock to lock several times to remove any trapped air from the system.

Noise Diagnosis

The Noise Is	Most Probably Produced By
· Identical under Drive or Coast	· Road surface, tires or front wheel bearings
· Different depending on road surface	· Road surface or tires
· Lower as the car speed is lowered	· Tires
· Similar with car standing or moving	· Engine or transmission
· A vibration	· Unbalanced tires, rear wheel bearing, unbalanced driveshaft or worn U-joint
· A knock or click about every 2 tire revolutions	· Rear wheel bearing
· Most pronounced on turns	· Damaged differential gears
· A steady low-pitched whirring or scraping, starting at low speeds	· Damaged or worn pinion bearing
· A chattering vibration on turns	· Wrong differential lubricant or worn clutch plates (limited slip rear axle)
· Noticed only in Drive, Coast or Float conditions	· Worn ring gear and/or pinion gear

Troubleshooting Basic Steering and Suspension Problems

Problem	Cause	Solution
Hard steering (steering wheel is hard to turn)	· Low or uneven tire pressure	· Inflate tires to correct pressure
	· Loose power steering pump drive belt	· Adjust belt
	· Low or incorrect power steering fluid	· Add fluid as necessary
	· Incorrect front end alignment	· Have front end alignment checked/adjusted
	· Defective power steering pump	· Check pump
	· Bent or poorly lubricated front end parts	· Lubricate and/or replace defective parts
Loose steering (too much play in the steering wheel)	· Loose wheel bearings	· Adjust wheel bearings
	· Loose or worn steering linkage	· Replace worn parts
	· Faulty shocks	· Replace shocks
	· Worn ball joints	· Replace ball joints
Car veers or wanders (car pulls to one side with hands off the steering wheel)	· Incorrect tire pressure	· Inflate tires to correct pressure
	· Improper front end alignment	· Have front end alignment checked/adjusted
	· Loose wheel bearings	· Adjust wheel bearings
	· Loose or bent front end components	· Replace worn components
	· Faulty shocks	· Replace shocks
Wheel oscillation or vibration transmitted through steering wheel	· Improper tire pressures	· Inflate tires to correct pressure
	· Tires out of balance	· Have tires balanced
	· Loose wheel bearings	· Adjust wheel bearings
	· Improper front end alignment	· Have front end alignment checked/adjusted
	· Worn or bent front end components	· Replace worn parts
Uneven tire wear	· Incorrect tire pressure	· Inflate tires to correct pressure
	· Front end out of alignment	· Have front end alignment checked/adjusted
	· Tires out of balance	· Have tires balanced

Troubleshooting the Steering Column

Problem	Cause	Solution
Will not lock	· Lockbolt spring broken or defective	· Replace lock bolt spring
High effort (required to turn ignition key and lock cylinder)	· Lock cylinder defective · Ignition switch defective · Rack preload spring broken or deformed · Burr on lock sector, lock rack, housing, support or remote rod coupling · Bent sector shaft · Defective lock rack · Remote rod bent, deformed · Ignition switch mounting bracket bent · Distorted coupling slot in lock rack (tilt column)	· Replace lock cylinder · Replace ignition switch · Replace preload spring · Remove burr · Replace shaft · Replace lock rack · Replace rod · Straighten or replace · Replace lock rack
Will stick in "start"	· Remote rod deformed · Ignition switch mounting bracket bent	· Straighten or replace · Straighten or replace
Key cannot be removed in "off-lock"	· Ignition switch is not adjusted correctly · Defective lock cylinder	· Adjust switch · Replace lock cylinder
Lock cylinder can be removed without depressing retainer	· Lock cylinder with defective retainer · Burr over retainer slot in housing cover or on cylinder retainer	· Replace lock cylinder · Remove burr
High effort on lock cylinder between "off" and "off-lock"	· Distorted lock rack · Burr on tang of shift gate (automatic column) · Gearshift linkage not adjusted	· Replace lock rack · Remove burr · Adjust linkage
Noise in column	· One click when in "off-lock" position and the steering wheel is moved (all except automatic column) · Coupling bolts not tightened · Lack of grease on bearings or bearing surfaces · Upper shaft bearing worn or broken · Lower shaft bearing worn or broken · Column not correctly aligned · Coupling pulled apart · Broken coupling lower joint · Steering shaft snap ring not seated · Shroud loose on shift bowl. Housing loose on jacket—will be noticed with ignition in "off-lock" and when torque is applied to steering wheel.	· Normal—lock bolt is seating · Tighten pinch bolts · Lubricate with chassis grease · Replace bearing assembly · Replace bearing. Check shaft and replace if scored. · Align column · Replace coupling · Repair or replace joint and align column · Replace ring. Check for proper seating in groove. · Position shroud over lugs on shift bowl. Tighten mounting screws.
High steering shaft effort	· Column misaligned · Defective upper or lower bearing · Tight steering shaft universal joint · Flash on I.D. of shift tube at plastic joint (tilt column only) · Upper or lower bearing seized	· Align column · Replace as required · Repair or replace · Replace shift tube · Replace bearings
Lash in mounted column assembly	· Column mounting bracket bolts loose · Broken weld nuts on column jacket · Column capsule bracket sheared	· Tighten bolts · Replace column jacket · Replace bracket assembly

Troubleshooting the Steering Column (cont.)

Problem	Cause	Solution
Lash in mounted column assembly (cont.)	• Column bracket to column jacket mounting bolts loose	• Tighten to specified torque
	• Loose lock shoes in housing (tilt column only)	• Replace shoes
	• Loose pivot pins (tilt column only)	• Replace pivot pins and support
	• Loose lock shoe pin (tilt column only)	• Replace pin and housing
	• Loose support screws (tilt column only)	• Tighten screws
Housing loose (tilt column only)	• Excessive clearance between holes in support or housing and pivot pin diameters	• Replace pivot pins and support
	• Housing support-screws loose	• Tighten screws
Steering wheel loose—every other tilt position (tilt column only)	• Loose fit between lock shoe and lock shoe pivot pin	• Replace lock shoes and pivot pin
Steering column not locking in any tilt position (tilt column only)	• Lock shoe seized on pivot pin	• Replace lock shoes and pin
	• Lock shoe grooves have burrs or are filled with foreign material	• Clean or replace lock shoes
	• Lock shoe springs weak or broken	• Replace springs
Noise when tilting column (tilt column only)	• Upper tilt bumpers worn	• Replace tilt bumper
	• Tilt spring rubbing in housing	• Lubricate with chassis grease
One click when in "off-lock" position and the steering wheel is moved	• Seating of lock bolt	• None. Click is normal characteristic sound produced by lock bolt as it seats.
High shift effort (automatic and tilt column only)	• Column not correctly aligned	• Align column
	• Lower bearing not aligned correctly	• Assemble correctly
	• Lack of grease on seal or lower bearing areas	• Lubricate with chassis grease
Improper transmission shifting—automatic and tilt column only	• Sheared shift tube joint	• Replace shift tube
	• Improper transmission gearshift linkage adjustment	• Adjust linkage
	• Loose lower shift lever	• Replace shift tube

Troubleshooting the Ignition Switch

Problem	Cause	Solution
Ignition switch electrically inoperative	• Loose or defective switch connector	• Tighten or replace connector
	• Feed wire open (fusible link)	• Repair or replace
	• Defective ignition switch	• Replace ignition switch
Engine will not crank	• Ignition switch not adjusted properly	• Adjust switch
Ignition switch wil not actuate mechanically	• Defective ignition switch	• Replace switch
	• Defective lock sector	• Replace lock sector
	• Defective remote rod	• Replace remote rod
Ignition switch cannot be adjusted correctly	• Remote rod deformed	• Repair, straighten or replace

Troubleshooting the Turn Signal Switch

Problem	Cause	Solution
Turn signal will not cancel	• Loose switch mounting screws • Switch or anchor bosses broken • Broken, missing or out of position detent, or cancelling spring	• Tighten screws • Replace switch • Reposition springs or replace switch as required
Turn signal difficult to operate	• Turn signal lever loose • Switch yoke broken or distorted • Loose or misplaced springs • Foreign parts and/or materials in switch • Switch mounted loosely	• Tighten mounting screws • Replace switch • Reposition springs or replace switch • Remove foreign parts and/or material • Tighten mounting screws
Turn signal will not indicate lane change	• Broken lane change pressure pad or spring hanger • Broken, missing or misplaced lane change spring • Jammed wires	• Replace switch • Replace or reposition as required • Loosen mounting screws, reposition wires and retighten screws
Turn signal will not stay in turn position	• Foreign material or loose parts impeding movement of switch yoke • Defective switch	• Remove material and/or parts • Replace switch
Hazard switch cannot be pulled out	• Foreign material between hazard support cancelling leg and yoke	• Remove foreign material. No foreign material impeding function of hazard switch—replace turn signal switch.
No turn signal lights	• Inoperative turn signal flasher • Defective or blown fuse • Loose chassis to column harness connector • Disconnect column to chassis connector. Connect new switch to chassis and operate switch by hand. If vehicle lights now operate normally, signal switch is inoperative • If vehicle lights do not operate, check chassis wiring for opens, grounds, etc.	• Replace turn signal flasher • Replace fuse • Connect securely • Replace signal switch • Repair chassis wiring as required
Instrument panel turn indicator lights on but not flashing	• Burned out or damaged front or rear turn signal bulb • If vehicle lights do not operate, check light sockets for high resistance connections, the chassis wiring for opens, grounds, etc. • Inoperative flasher • Loose chassis to column harness connection • Inoperative turn signal switch • To determine if turn signal switch is defective, substitute new switch into circuit and operate switch by hand. If the vehicle's lights operate normally, signal switch is inoperative.	• Replace bulb • Repair chassis wiring as required • Replace flasher • Connect securely • Replace turn signal switch • Replace turn signal switch
Stop light not on when turn indicated	• Loose column to chassis connection • Disconnect column to chassis connector. Connect new switch into system without removing old.	• Connect securely • Replace signal switch

Troubleshooting the Turn Signal Switch (cont.)

Problem	Cause	Solution
Stop light not on when turn indicated (cont.)	Operate switch by hand. If brake lights work with switch in the turn position, signal switch is defective.	
	• If brake lights do not work, check connector to stop light sockets for grounds, opens, etc.	• Repair connector to stop light circuits using service manual as guide
Turn indicator panel lights not flashing	• Burned out bulbs • High resistance to ground at bulb socket • Opens, ground in wiring harness from front turn signal bulb socket to indicator lights	• Replace bulbs • Replace socket • Locate and repair as required
Turn signal lights flash very slowly	• High resistance ground at light sockets • Incorrect capacity turn signal flasher or bulb • If flashing rate is still extremely slow, check chassis wiring harness from the connector to light sockets for high resistance • Loose chassis to column harness connection • Disconnect column to chassis connector. Connect new switch into system without removing old. Operate switch by hand. If flashing occurs at normal rate, the signal switch is defective.	• Repair high resistance grounds at light sockets • Replace turn signal flasher or bulb • Locate and repair as required • Connect securely • Replace turn signal switch
Hazard signal lights will not flash— turn signal functions normally	• Blow fuse • Inoperative hazard warning flasher • Loose chassis-to-column harness connection • Disconnect column to chassis connector. Connect new switch into system without removing old. Depress the hazard warning lights. If they now work normally, turn signal switch is defective. • If lights do not flash, check wiring harness "K" lead for open between hazard flasher and connector. If open, fuse block is defective	• Replace fuse • Replace hazard warning flasher in fuse panel • Conect securely • Replace turn signal switch • Repair or replace brown wire or connector as required

Troubleshooting the Manual Steering Gear

Problem	Cause	Solution
Hard or erratic steering	• Incorrect tire pressure • Insufficient or incorrect lubrication • Suspension, or steering linkage parts damaged or misaligned • Improper front wheel alignment • Incorrect steering gear adjustment • Sagging springs	• Inflate tires to recommended pressures • Lubricate as required (refer to Maintenance Section) • Repair or replace parts as necessary • Adjust incorrect wheel alignment angles • Adjust steering gear • Replace springs

Troubleshooting the Manual Steering Gear (cont.)

Problem	Cause	Solution
Play or looseness in steering	• Steering wheel loose	• Inspect shaft spines and repair as necessary. Tighten attaching nut and stake in place.
	• Steering linkage or attaching parts loose or worn	• Tighten, adjust, or replace faulty components
	• Pitman arm loose	• Inspect shaft splines and repair as necessary. Tighten attaching nut and stake in place
	• Steering gear attaching bolts loose	• Tighten bolts
	• Loose or worn wheel bearings	• Adjust or replace bearings
	• Steering gear adjustment incorrect or parts badly worn	• Adjust gear or replace defective parts
Wheel shimmy or tramp	• Improper tire pressure	• Inflate tires to recommended pressures
	• Wheels, tires, or brake rotors out-of-balance or out-of-round	• Inspect and replace or balance parts
	• Inoperative, worn, or loose shock absorbers or mounting parts	• Repair or replace shocks or mountings
	• Loose or worn steering or suspension parts	• Tighten or replace as necessary
	• Loose or worn wheel bearings	• Adjust or replace bearings
	• Incorrect steering gear adjustments	• Adjust steering gear
	• Incorrect front wheel alignment	• Correct front wheel alignment
Tire wear	• Improper tire pressure	• Inflate tires to recommended pressures
	• Failure to rotate tires	• Rotate tires
	• Brakes grabbing	• Adjust or repair brakes
	• Incorrect front wheel alignment	• Align incorrect angles
	• Broken or damaged steering and suspension parts	• Repair or replace defective parts
	• Wheel runout	• Replace faulty wheel
	• Excessive speed on turns	• Make driver aware of conditions
Vehicle leads to one side	• Improper tire pressures	• Inflate tires to recommended pressures
	• Front tires with uneven tread depth, wear pattern, or different cord design (i.e., one bias ply and one belted or radial tire on front wheels)	• Install tires of same cord construction and reasonably even tread depth, design, and wear pattern
	• Incorrect front wheel alignment	• Align incorrect angles
	• Brakes dragging	• Adjust or repair brakes
	• Pulling due to uneven tire construction	• Replace faulty tire

Troubleshooting the Power Steering Gear

Problem	Cause	Solution
Hissing noise in steering gear	• There is some noise in all power steering systems. One of the most common is a hissing sound most evident at standstill parking. There is no relationship between this noise and performance of the steering. Hiss may be expected when steering wheel is at end of travel or when slowly turning at standstill.	• Slight hiss is normal and in no way affects steering. Do not replace valve unless hiss is extremely objectionable. A replacement valve will also exhibit slight noise and is not always a cure. Investigate clearance around flexible coupling rivets. Be sure steering shaft and gear are aligned so flexible coupling rotates in a flat plane and is not distorted as shaft rotates. Any metal-to-metal contacts through flexible coupling will transmit valve hiss into passenger compartment through the steering column.

Troubleshooting the Power Steering Gear (cont.)

Problem	Cause	Solution
Rattle or chuckle noise in steering gear	• Gear loose on frame	• Check gear-to-frame mounting screws. Tighten screws to 88 N·m (65 foot pounds) torque.
	• Steering linkage looseness	• Check linkage pivot points for wear. Replace if necessary.
	• Pressure hose touching other parts of car	• Adjust hose position. Do not bend tubing by hand.
	• Loose pitman shaft over center adjustment	• Adjust to specifications
	NOTE: A slight rattle may occur on turns because of increased clearance off the "high point." This is normal and clearance must not be reduced below specified limits to eliminate this slight rattle.	
	• Loose pitman arm	• Tighten pitman arm nut to specifications
Squawk noise in steering gear when turning or recovering from a turn	• Damper O-ring on valve spool cut	• Replace damper O-ring
Poor return of steering wheel to center	• Tires not properly inflated	• Inflate to specified pressure
	• Lack of lubrication in linkage and ball joints	• Lube linkage and ball joints
	• Lower coupling flange rubbing against steering gear adjuster plug	• Loosen pinch bolt and assemble properly
	• Steering gear to column misalignment	• Align steering column
	• Improper front wheel alignment	• Check and adjust as necessary
	• Steering linkage binding	• Replace pivots
	• Ball joints binding	• Replace ball joints
	• Steering wheel rubbing against housing	• Align housing
	• Tight or frozen steering shaft bearings	• Replace bearings
	• Sticking or plugged valve spool	• Remove and clean or replace valve
	• Steering gear adjustments over specifications	• Check adjustment with gear out of car. Adjust as required.
	• Kink in return hose	• Replace hose
Car leads to one side or the other (keep in mind road condition and wind. Test car in both directions on flat road)	• Front end misaligned	• Adjust to specifications
	• Unbalanced steering gear valve	• Replace valve
	NOTE: If this is cause, steering effort will be very light in direction of lead and normal or heavier in opposite direction	
Momentary increase in effort when turning wheel fast to right or left	• Low oil level	• Add power steering fluid as required
	• Pump belt slipping	• Tighten or replace belt
	• High internal leakage	• Check pump pressure. (See pressure test)
Steering wheel surges or jerks when turning with engine running especially during parking	• Low oil level	• Fill as required
	• Loose pump belt	• Adjust tension to specification
	• Steering linkage hitting engine oil pan at full turn	• Correct clearance
	• Insufficient pump pressure	• Check pump pressure. (See pressure test). Replace relief valve if defective.
	• Pump flow control valve sticking	• Inspect for varnish or damage, replace if necessary
Excessive wheel kickback or loose steering	• Air in system	• Add oil to pump reservoir and bleed by operating steering. Check hose connectors for proper torque and adjust as required.

Troubleshooting the Power Steering Gear (cont.)

Problem	Cause	Solution
Excessive wheel kickback or loose steering (cont.)	• Steering gear loose on frame	• Tighten attaching screws to specified torque
	• Steering linkage joints worn enough to be loose	• Replace loose pivots
	• Worn poppet valve	• Replace poppet valve
	• Loose thrust bearing preload adjustment	• Adjust to specification with gear out of vehicle
	• Excessive overcenter lash	• Adjust to specification with gear out of car
Hard steering or lack of assist	• Loose pump belt	• Adjust belt tension to specification
	• Low oil level **NOTE:** Low oil level will also result in excessive pump noise	• Fill to proper level. If excessively low, check all lines and joints for evidence of external leakage. Tighten loose connectors.
	• Steering gear to column misalignment	• Align steering column
	• Lower coupling flange rubbing against steering gear adjuster plug	• Loosen pinch bolt and assemble properly
	• Tires not properly inflated	• Inflate to recommended pressure
Foamy milky power steering fluid, low fluid level and possible low pressure	• Air in the fluid, and loss of fluid due to internal pump leakage causing overflow	• Check for leak and correct. Bleed system. Extremely cold temperatures will cause system aeriation should the oil level be low. If oil level is correct and pump still foams, remove pump from vehicle and separate reservoir from housing. Check welsh plug and housing for cracks. If plug is loose or housing is cracked, replace housing.
Low pressure due to steering pump	• Flow control valve stuck or inoperative	• Remove burrs or dirt or replace. Flush system.
	• Pressure plate not flat against cam ring	• Correct
Low pressure due to steering gear	• Pressure loss in cylinder due to worn piston ring or badly worn housing bore	• Remove gear from car for disassembly and inspection of ring and housing bore
	• Leakage at valve rings, valve body-to-worm seal	• Remove gear from car for disassembly and replace seals

Troubleshooting the Power Steering Pump

Problem	Cause	Solution
Chirp noise in steering pump	• Loose belt	• Adjust belt tension to specification
Belt squeal (particularly noticeable at full wheel travel and stand still parking)	• Loose belt	• Adjust belt tension to specification
Growl noise in steering pump	• Excessive back pressure in hoses or steering gear caused by restriction	• Locate restriction and correct. Replace part if necessary.
Growl noise in steering pump (particularly noticeable at stand still parking)	• Scored pressure plates, thrust plate or rotor	• Replace parts and flush system
	• Extreme wear of cam ring	• Replace parts
Groan noise in steering pump	• Low oil level	• Fill reservoir to proper level
	• Air in the oil. Poor pressure hose connection.	• Tighten connector to specified torque. Bleed system by operating steering from right to left—full turn.

Troubleshooting the Power Steering Pump (cont.)

Problem	Cause	Solution
Rattle noise in steering pump	• Vanes not installed properly • Vanes sticking in rotor slots	• Install properly • Free up by removing burrs, varnish, or dirt
Swish noise in steering pump	• Defective flow control valve	• Replace part
Whine noise in steering pump	• Pump shaft bearing scored	• Replace housing and shaft. Flush system.
Hard steering or lack of assist	• Loose pump belt • Low oil level in reservoir **NOTE:** Low oil level will also result in excessive pump noise • Steering gear to column misalignment • Lower coupling flange rubbing against steering gear adjuster plug • Tires not properly inflated	• Adjust belt tension to specification • Fill to proper level. If excessively low, check all lines and joints for evidence of external leakage. Tighten loose connectors. • Align steering column • Loosen pinch bolt and assemble properly • Inflate to recommended pressure
Foaming milky power steering fluid, low fluid level and possible low pressure	• Air in the fluid, and loss of fluid due to internal pump leakage causing overflow	• Check for leaks and correct. Bleed system. Extremely cold temperatures will cause system aeriation should the oil level be low. If oil level is correct and pump still foams, remove pump from vehicle and separate reservoir from body. Check welsh plug and body for cracks. If plug is loose or body is cracked, replace body.
Low pump pressure	• Flow control valve stuck or inoperative • Pressure plate not flat against cam ring	• Remove burrs or dirt or replace. Flush system. • Correct
Momentary increase in effort when turning wheel fast to right or left	• Low oil level in pump • Pump belt slipping • High internal leakage	• Add power steering fluid as required • Tighten or replace belt • Check pump pressure. (See pressure test)
Steering wheel surges or jerks when turning with engine running especially during parking	• Low oil level • Loose pump belt • Steering linkage hitting engine oil pan at full turn • Insufficient pump pressure	• Fill as required • Adjust tension to specification • Correct clearance • Check pump pressure. (See pressure test). Replace flow control valve if defective.
Steering wheel surges or jerks when turning with engine running especially during parking (cont.)	• Sticking flow control valve	• Inspect for varnish or damage, replace if necessary
Excessive wheel kickback or loose steering	• Air in system	• Add oil to pump reservoir and bleed by operating steering. Check hose connectors for proper torque and adjust as required.
Low pump pressure	• Extreme wear of cam ring • Scored pressure plate, thrust plate, or rotor • Vanes not installed properly • Vanes sticking in rotor slots • Cracked or broken thrust or pressure plate	• Replace parts. Flush system. • Replace parts. Flush system. • Install properly • Freeup by removing burrs, varnish, or dirt • Replace part

Brakes

8

BRAKE SYSTEM

Adjustments

DRUM BRAKES

Rear drum brakes are adjusted automatically by alternately driving the vehicle forward and reverse , and sharply applying the brakes when the vehicle is driven forward and reverse. Brake adjustment occurs during reverse stops only.

BRAKE PEDAL

Push Rod

The push rod has an adjustment screw to maintain the correct relationship between the booster control valve plunger and the master cylinder piston.

To check the adjustment of the screw, fabricate a gauge and place it against the master cylinder mounting surface of the booster body. Adjust the push rod screw by turning it until the end of the screw just touches the inner edge of the slot in the gauge.

Master Cylinder

REMOVAL

1. Disconnect the brake warning lamp connector.

2. Disconnect the hydraulic lines from the brake master cylinder.

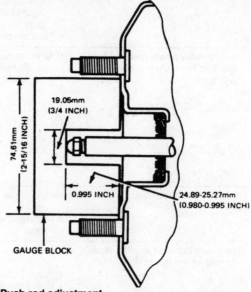

Push rod adjustment

3. Remove the nuts retaining the master cylinder to the brake booster and remove the master cylinder.

INSTALLATION

1. Before installing the master cylinder, adjust the booster assembly push rod as outlined earlier.

2. Position the master cylinder assembly over the booster push rod and unto the two

Brake Specifications

All Specifications in inches

| Years | Model | Master Cyl. Bore | Brake Disc | | | Brake Drum | | | Wheel Cyl. or Caliper Bore | |
			Original Thickness	Minimum Thickness	Maximum Run-out	Orig. Inside Dia.	Max. Wear Limit	Maximum Machine O/S	Front	Rear
1986–87	All	NA	1.180	0.81	0.010	NA	0.090	0.060	NA	NA

NA   Not available at time of publication

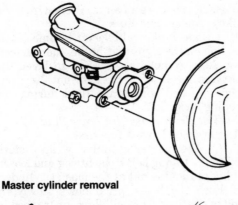

Master cylinder removal

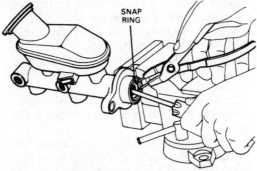

SNAP
RING

Depressing the primary piston and removing the snap ring

studs on the booster assembly. Install and tighten the attaching nuts.

3. Reconnect the brake warning light.

4. Loosely connect the hydraulic brake system lines to the master cylinder. Fill the master cylinder reservoir with DOT 3 brake fluid to the fill line on the side of the master cylinder. Bleed the air from the master cylinder and the entire hydraulic system as outlined in Hydraulic System Bleeding, Then tighten all hydraulic lines.

5. Make sure the master cylinder reservoir is filled to the proper level and install the cap diaphragm.

OVERHAUL

1. Clean the outside of the master cylinder and remove the filler cap and diaphragm. Drain and discard the any brake fluid that remains in the cylinder.

2. Depress the primary piston and remove the snapring from the retaining groove at the rear of the master cylinder bore.

3. Remove the primary piston assembly from the master cylinder bore and inspect for seal damage or twisting. Discard the assembly.

4. Remove the secondary piston assembly by directing compressed air into the outlet port at the blind end of the bore while plugging the other outlet port. Inspect the seal for damage or twisting and discard the assembly.

5. Inspect the master cylinder bore for pitting or scoring. If the bore is damaged replace with a new master cylinder assembly.

6. If the bore is not damaged obtain a repair kit to rebuild the master cylinder.

7. Clean the master cylinder body with clean isopropyl alcohol to remove any contamination.

8. Dip the repair kit piston assemblies in clean brake fluid to lubricate the seals.

9. Carefully insert the complete secondary piston assembly in the master cylinder bore.

10. Carefully insert the primary piston assembly in the master cylinder bore.

11. Depress the primary piston and install the snapring in the cylinder bore groove.

12. Install the cap and diaphragm on the master cylinder reservoir.

13. Bleed the master cylinder as follows:

a. Support the master cylinder body in a vise (clamp by the flange only) and fill the reservoir with brake fluid.

b. Install plugs in the front and rear brake outlet ports. Bleed the rear brake system first.

c. Loosen the plug in the rear brake outlet port. Depress the primary piston slowly to force the air out of the master cylinder. Tighten the plug while the piston is depressed or air will enter the master cylinder.

d. Repeat this procedure until air ceases to exit at the outlet port.

e. Repeat Steps c and d for the front brake outlet port with the rear brake outlet plugged.

f. Tighten the plugs and try to depress the piston. Depressing the piston should be harder after all air is expelled.

g. Install the cap and diaphragm assembly making sure the cap is tightened securely. Remove the plugs.

Power Brake Booster

REMOVAL

1. Disconnect the brake warning lamp connector.

2. Support the master cylinder from underneath with a prop.

3. Remove the nuts retaining the master cylinder to the brake booster.

4. Loosen the clamp that secures the manifold vacuum hose to the booster check valve, and remove the hose. Remove the booster check valve.

5. From inside the cab on vehicles equipped with a pushrod mounted stop lamp switch, remove the hairpin retainer and slide the stop lamp switch, push rod, spacers and bushing off the brake pedal arm.

6. From the engine compartment remove

the bolts that attach the booster to the dash panel.

INSTALLATION

1. Mount the booster assembly on the engine side of the dash panel by sliding the bracket mounting bolts and valve operating rod in through the holes in the dash panel.

2. From inside the van, install the booster retaining bolts.

3. Position the master cylinder on the booster assembly, install the retaining nuts, and remove the prop from underneath the master cylinder.

4. Install the booster check valve. Connect the manifold vacuum hose to the booster check valve and secure with a clamp.

5. From inside the cab on vehicles equipped with the push rod mounted stop lamp switch, install the bushing and position the switch on the end of the push rod. Then install the switch and rod on the pedal arm, along with the spacers on each side, and secure with the hairpin retainer.

6. Connect the stop lamp switch wiring.

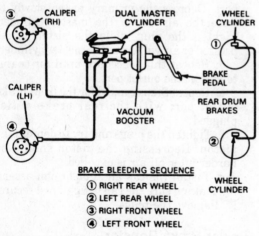

BRAKE BLEEDING SEQUENCE
① RIGHT REAR WHEEL
② LEFT REAR WHEEL
③ RIGHT FRONT WHEEL
④ LEFT FRONT WHEEL

Brake bleeding sequence

7. Start the engine and check the brake operation.

NOTE: *Make sure that the booster rubber reaction disc is properly installed. A dislodged disc may cause excessive pedal travel and extreme pedal sensitivity.*

Hydraulic System Bleeding

When any part of the hydraulic system has been disconnected for repair or replacement, air may get into the lines and cause a spongy pedal action. This requires the bleeding of the hydraulic system after it has been properly connected to be sure all air is expelled from the brake cylinders and lines.

Bleed one brake cylinder at a time. Start bleeding on the right rear brake, then the left rear. After completing, proceed to bleed the right front brake, then the left front. Keep the reservoir filled with brake fluid during the bleeding operation.

NOTE: *Never reuse bled brake fluid.*

1. Bleed the longest line first.

2. On the master cylinder, wrap a cloth around the tubing below the fitting and loosen the hydraulic line nut at the master cylinder.

3. Push the brake pedal down slowly by hand to the floor. This will force air trapped in the master cylinder to escape at the fitting.

4. Hold the pedal down and tighten the fitting. Release the brake pedal.

NOTE: *Do not release the brake pedal until the fitting is tightened or air will reenter the master cylinder.*

5. Repeat this procedure until air ceases to escape at the fitting and the brake pedal is firm.

6. Place a box wrench on the bleeder fitting on the brake wheel cylinder. Attach a rubber drain tube to the bleeder fitting.

NOTE: *Make sure the end of the tube fits snugly around the bleeder fitting.*

7. Submerge the free end of the tube in a container partially filled with clean brake fluid. Loosen the bleeder fitting approximately ¾ of a turn.

8. Slowly push the brake pedal all the way down. Close the bleeder fitting, and return the brake pedal to the fully released position. Repeat this procedure until air bubbles no longer appear at the submerged end of the bleeder tube.

9. When the fluid is completely free of air bubbles, close the bleeder fitting and remove the bleeder tube.

10. Repeat this procedure at the brake wheel cylinder on the opposite side. Refill the master cylinder reservoir after each wheel cylinder is bled.

11. When the bleeding operation is complete, fill the master cylinder to the maximum level line on the reservoir.

FRONT DISC BRAKES

CAUTION: *Brake shoes contain asbestos, which has been determined to be a cancer causing agent. Never clean the brake surfaces with compressed air! Avoid inhaling any dust from any brake surface! When cleaning brake surfaces, use a commercially available brake cleaning fluid.*

Brake Pads
INSPECTION

Replace the front pads when the pad thickness is at the minimum thickness recommended by Ford Motor Co., which is $^1/_{16}''$ (1.5mm), or at the minimum allowed by the applicable state or local motor vehicle inspection code. Pad thickness may be checked by removing the wheel and looking through the inspection port in the caliper assembly.

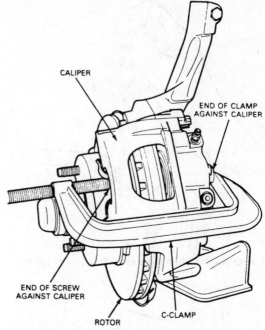

Use a C-clamp to bottom the piston in the bore

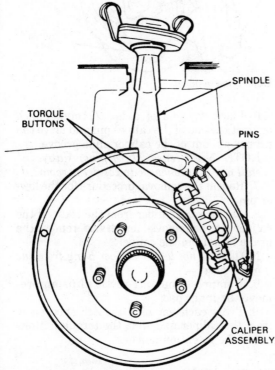

Assembled view of the caliper and rotor

Front Caliper and Disc Brake Pads
REMOVAL AND INSTALLATION

NOTE: *Always replace all disc pad assemblies on an axle. Never service one wheel only.*

1. To avoid fluid overflow when the caliper piston is pressured into the caliper cylinder bores, siphon or dip part of the brake fluid out of the larger master cylinder reservoir (connected to the front disc brakes). Discard the removed fluid.

2. Raise the vehicle and install jackstands. Remove a front wheel and tire assembly.

3. Place an 8″ (203mm) C-clamp on the caliper and tighten the clamp to bottom the caliper piston in the cylinder bore. Remove the clamp.

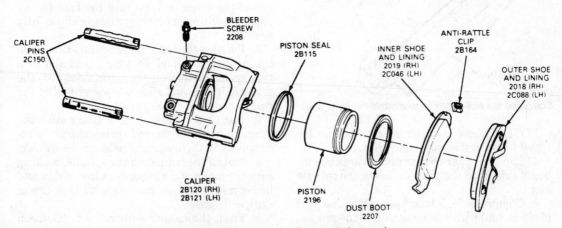

Disassembled view of caliper and shoe pads

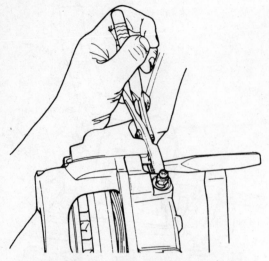

Compress the inboard pin tab with a pair of pliers

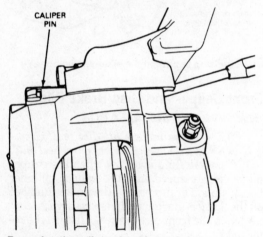

Removing the caliper pin with a punch

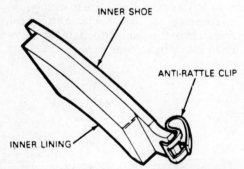

Compress the anti-rattle clip to remove the inner shoe

NOTE: *Do not use a screwdriver or similar tool to pry piston away from the rotor.*

4. Tap the upper caliper pin towards the inboard side until the pin tabs touch the spindle face.

5. Compress the inboard pin tab with a pair of pliers, and with a hammer, drive the pin until the tab slips into the spindle groove.

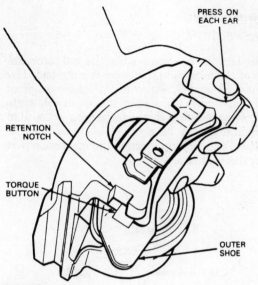

Outer shoe removal

6. Place one end of a $\frac{7}{16}$" (11mm) punch against the end of the caliper pin and drive the caliper pin out of the caliper slide groove.

NOTE: *Never reuse caliper pins. Always install new pins whenever a caliper is removed.*

7. Repeat the removal procedure for the lower pin.

8. Remove the caliper from the rotor. If the caliper is to be removed for service, remove the brake hose from the caliper.

NOTE: *Do not let the caliper hang from the brake hose.*

9. Compress the anti-rattle clips and remove the inner pad.

10. Press each ear of the outer shoe away from the caliper and slide the torque buttons out of the retention notches.

INSTALLATION

1. Place a new anti-rattle clip on the lower end of the inner pad. Be sure the tabs on the clip are positioned properly and the clip is fully seated.

2. Position the inner pad and anti-rattle clip tab against the pad abutment and the loop type spring away from the rotor. Compress the anti-rattle clip and slide the upper end of the pad in position.

3. Install the outer pad, making sure the torque buttons on the pad spring clip are seated solidly in the matching holes in the caliper.

4. Install the caliper on the spindle, making sure the mounting surfaces are free of dirt and lubricate the caliper grooves with Disc Brake Caliper Grease.

5. From the caliper outboard side, position the pin between the caliper and spindle

grooves. The pin must be positioned so the tabs will be installed against the spindle outer face.

NOTE: *Never reuse caliper pins. Always install new pins whenever a caliper is removed.*

6. Tap the pin on the outboard end with a hammer. Continue tapping the pin inward until the retention tabs on the sides of the pin contact the spindle face. Repeat this procedure for the lower pin.

NOTE: *During the installation procedure do not allow the tabs of the caliper pin to be tapped too far into the spindle groove. If this happens it will be necessary to tap the other end of the caliper pin until the tabs snap into place. The tabs on each end of the caliper pin must be free to catch on the spindle face.*

7. If removed, install the brake hose to the caliper.

8. Bleed the brakes as described earlier in this chapter.

9. Install the wheel and tire assembly. Torque the lug nuts to 85–115 ft.lb.

10. Remove the jackstands and lower the ve-

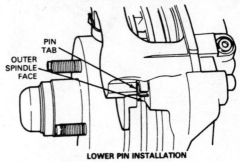

Correct pin installation

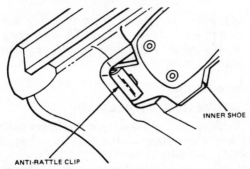

Correct inner shoe installation

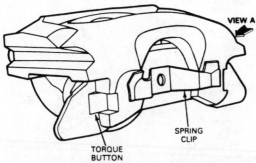

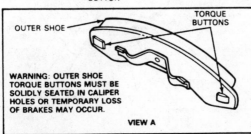

Correct outer shoe installation

hicle. Check the brake fluid level and fill as necessary. Check the brakes for proper operation.

CALIPER OVERHAUL

1. For caliper removal, see the above procedure. Disconnect the brake hose.

2. Clean the exterior of the caliper with denatured alcohol.

3. Remove the plug from the caliper inlet port and drain the fluid.

4. Air pressure is necessary to remove the piston. When a source of compressed air is found, such as a shop or gas station, apply air to the inlet port slowly and carefully until the piston pops out of its bore.

CAUTION: *If high pressure air is applied the piston will pop out with considerable force and cause damage or injury.*

5. If the piston jams, release the air pressure and tap sharply on the piston end with a soft hammer. Reapply air pressure.

6. When the piston is out, Remove the boot from the piston and the seal from the bore.

7. Clean the housing and piston with denatured alcohol. Dry with compressed air.

8. Lubricate the new piston seal, boot and piston with clean brake fluid, and assemble them in the caliper.

9. The dust boot can be worked in with the fingers and the piston should be pressed straight in until it bottoms. Be careful to avoid cocking the piston in the bore.

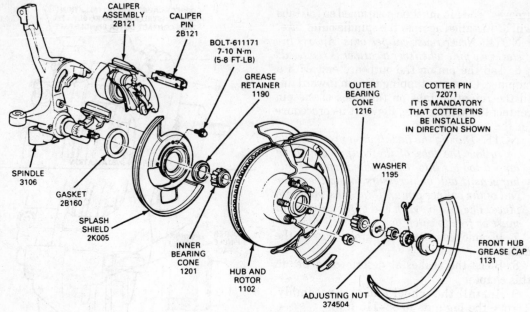

Hub, rotor and splash shield

10. A C-clamp may be necessary to bottom the piston.

11. Install the caliper using the procedure given in the pad and caliper replacement procedure above.

Rotor (Disc)
REMOVAL AND INSTALLATION

1. Jack up the front of the vehicle and support on jackstands.

2. Remove the wheel and tire.

3. Remove the caliper assembly as described earlier in this chapter.

4. Follow the procedure given under hub and wheel bearing removal in Chapter 7 for models with manual and automatic locking hubs.

NOTE: *New rotor assemblies come protected with an anti-rust coating which should be removed with denatured alcohol or degreaser. New hubs must be packed with EP wheel bearing grease. If the old rotors are to be reused, check them for cracks, grooves or waviness. Rotors that aren't too badly scored or grooved can be resurfaced by most automotive shops. Minimum rotor thickness should be stamped on the rotor. If refinishing exceeds that, the rotor will have to be replaced.*

REAR DRUM BRAKES

CAUTION: *Brake shoes contain asbestos, which has been determined to be a cancer causing agent. Never clean the brake surfaces*

with compressed air! Avoid inhaling any dust from any brake surface! When cleaning brake surfaces, use a commercially available brake cleaning fluid.

Brake Drums
REMOVAL AND INSTALLATION

1. Raise the vehicle so that the wheel to be worked on is clear of the floor and install jackstands under the vehicle.

2. Remove the wheel. Remove the 3 retain-

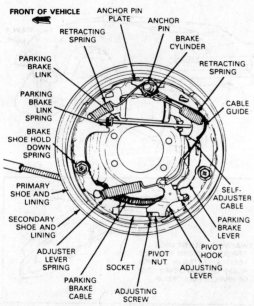

9.0 inch rear brake assembly (left side)

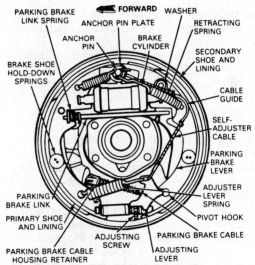

PARKING BRAKE LINK SPRING — FORWARD — WASHER — ANCHOR PIN PLATE — RETRACTING SPRING — ANCHOR PIN — BRAKE CYLINDER — SECONDARY SHOE AND LINING — BRAKE SHOE HOLD-DOWN SPRINGS — CABLE GUIDE — SELF-ADJUSTER CABLE — PARKING BRAKE LEVER — ADJUSTER LEVER SPRING — PARKING BRAKE LINK — PRIMARY SHOE AND LINING — PIVOT HOOK — ADJUSTING SCREW — PARKING BRAKE CABLE — PARKING BRAKE CABLE HOUSING RETAINER — ADJUSTING LEVER

10.0 inch rear brake assembly (left side)

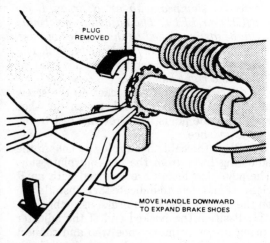

PLUG REMOVED

MOVE HANDLE DOWNWARD TO EXPAND BRAKE SHOES

Brake shoe adjuster

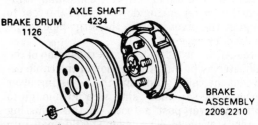

AXLE SHAFT 4234

BRAKE DRUM 1126

BRAKE ASSEMBLY 2209 2210

Drum and brake assembly

ing nuts and remove the brake drum. It may be necessary to back off the brake shoe adjustment in order to remove the brake drum. This is because the drum might be grooved or worn from being in service for an extended period of time.

3. Before installing a new brake drum, be sure and remove any protective coating with carburetor degreaser.

4. Install the brake drum in the reverse order of removal and adjust the brakes.

INSPECTION

After the brake drum has been removed from the vehicle, it should be inspected for runout, severe scoring, cracks, and the proper inside diameter.

Minor scores on a brake drum can be removed with fine emery cloth, provided that all grit is removed from the drum before it is installed on the vehicle.

A badly scored, rough, or out-of-round (runout) drum can be ground or turned on a brake drum lathe. Do not remove any more material from the drum than is necessary to provide a smooth surface for the brake shoe to contact. The maximum diameter of the braking surface is shown on the inside of each brake drum. Brake drums that exceed the maximum braking surface diameter shown on the brake drum, either through wear or refinishing, must be replaced. this is because after the outside wall of the brake drum reaches a certain thickness (thinner than the original thickness) the drum loses its ability to dissipate the heat created by the friction between the brake drum and the brake shoes, when the brakes are applied. Also the brake drum will have more tendency to warp and/or crack.

The maximum braking surface diameter specification, which is shown on each drum, allows for a 0.060" (1.5mm) machining or cut over the original nominal drum diameter plus 0.030" (0.76mm) additional wear before reaching the diameter where the drum must be discarded. Use a brake drum micrometer to measure the inside diameter of the brake drums.

Brake Shoes
REMOVAL AND INSTALLATION

1. Raise and support the vehicle and remove the wheel and brake drum from the wheel to be worked on.

   NOTE: *If you have never replaced the brakes on a car before and you are not too familiar with the procedures involved, only disassemble and assemble one side at a time, leaving the other side intact as a reference during reassembly.*

2. Install a clamp over the ends of the wheel cylinder to prevent the pistons of the wheel cylinder from coming out, causing loss of fluid and much grief.

3. Contract the brake shoes by pulling the self-adjusting lever away from the starwheel adjustment screw and turn the starwheel up and back until the pivot nut is drawn onto the starwheel as far as it will come.

4. Pull the adjusting lever, cable and automatic adjuster spring down and toward the rear to unhook the pivot hook from the large hole in the secondary shoe web. Do not attempt to pry the pivot hook from the hole.

5. Remove the automatic adjuster spring and the adjuster lever.

6. Remove the secondary shoe-to-anchor spring with a brake tool. (Brake tools are very common implements and are available at auto parts stores.) Remove the primary shoe-to-anchor spring and unhook the cable anchor. Remove the anchor pin plate, if so equipped.

7. Remove the cable guide from the secondary shoe.

8. Remove the shoe holddown springs, shoes, adjusting screw, pivot nut, and socket. Note the color and position of each holddown spring for assembly. To remove the holddown springs, reach behind the brake backing plate and place one finger on the end of one of the brake holddown spring mounting pins. Using a pair of pliers, grasp the washer type retainer on top of the holddown spring that corresponds to the pin that you are holding. Push down on the pliers and turn them 90° to align the slot in the washer with the head on the spring mounting pin. Remove the spring and washer retainer and repeat this operating on the holddown spring on the other shoe.

9. Remove the parking brake link and spring. Disconnect the parking brake cable from the parking brake lever.

10. After removing the rear brake secondary shoe. On 9″ (229mm) brakes remove the parking brake lever from the shoe. On 10″ (254mm) brakes disassemble the parking brake lever from the shoe by removing the retaining clip and spring washer.

INSTALLATION

1. Assemble the parking brake lever to the secondary shoe, and on 10″ (254mm) brakes secure it with the spring washer and retaining clip.

2. Apply a light coating of Lubriplate® at the points where the brake shoes contact the backing plate.

3. Position the brake shoes on the backing plate, and install the holddown spring pins, springs, and spring washer type retainers. Install the parking brake link, spring and washer. Connect the parking brake cable to the parking brake lever.

4. Install the anchor pin plate, and place the cable anchor over the anchor pin with the crimped side toward the backing plate.

5. Install the primary shoe-to-anchor spring with the brake tool.

6. Install the cable guide on the secondary shoe web with the flanged holes fitted into the hole in the secondary shoe web. Thread the cable around the cable guide groove.

7. Install the secondary shoe-to-anchor (long) spring. Be sure that the cable end is not cocked or binding on the anchor pin when installed. All of the parts should be flat on the anchor pin. Remove the wheel cylinder piston clamp.

8. Apply Lubriplate® to the threads and the socket end of the adjusting starwheel screw. Turn the adjusting screw into the adjusting pivot nut to the limit of the threads and then back off ½ turn.

NOTE: *Interchanging the brake shoe adjusting screw assembles from one side of the vehicle to the other would cause the brake shoes to retract rather than expand each time the automatic adjusting mechanism operated. To prevent this, the socket end of the adjusting screw is stamped with an R or an L for RIGHT or LEFT. The adjusting pivot nuts can be distinguished by the number of lines machined around the body of the nut; one line indicates left hand nut and two lines indicates a right hand nut.*

9. Place the adjusting socket on the screw and install this assembly between the shoe ends with the adjusting screw nearest to the secondary shoe.

10. Place the cable hook into the hole in the adjusting lever from the backing plate side. The adjusting levers are stamped with an **R** right, or an **L** left, to indicate their installation on the right or left hand brake assembly.

11. Position the hooked end of the adjuster spring in the primary shoe web and connect the loop end of the spring to the adjuster lever hole.

12. Pull the adjuster lever, cable and automatic adjuster spring down toward the rear to engage the pivot hook in the large hole in the secondary shoe web.

13. After installation, check the action of the adjuster by pulling the section of the cable between the cable guide and the adjusting lever toward the secondary shoe web far enough to lift the lever past a tooth on the adjusting screw starwheel. The lever should snap into position behind the next tooth, and release of the cable should cause the adjuster spring to return the lever to its original position. This return action of the lever will turn the adjusting screw starwheel one tooth. The lever should contact the adjusting screw starwheel one tooth above the center line of the adjusting screw.

If the automatic adjusting mechanism does not perform properly, check the following:

a. Check the cable end fittings. The cable

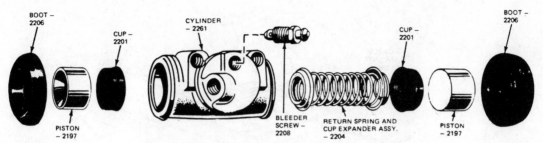

Exploded view of the wheel cylinder

ends should fill or extend slightly beyond the crimped section of the fittings. If this is not the case, replace the cable.

b. Check the cable guide for damage. The cable groove should be parallel to the shoe web, and the body of the guide should lie flat against the web. Replace the cable guide if this is not so.

c. Check the pivot hook on the lever. The hook surfaces should be square with the body on the lever for proper pivoting. Repair or replace the hook as necessary.

d. Make sure that the adjusting screw starwheel is properly seated in the notch in the shoe web.

Wheel Cylinders
REMOVAL AND INSTALLATION

1. To remove the wheel cylinder, jack up the vehicle and remove the wheel, hub, and drum.

2. Disconnect the brake line at the fitting on the brake backing plate.

3. Remove the brake assemblies.

4. Remove the screws that hold the wheel cylinder to the backing plate and remove the wheel cylinder from the vehicle.

5. Installation is the reverse of the above removal procedure. After installation adjust the brakes as described earlier in this chapter.

OVERHAUL

Wheel cylinder rebuilding kits are available for reconditioning wheel cylinders. The kits usually contain new cup springs, cylinder cups, and in some, new boots. The most important factor to keep in mind when rebuilding wheel cylinders is cleanliness. Keep all dirt away from the wheel cylinders when you are reassembling them.

1. Remove the wheel cylinder as described earlier.

2. Remove the rubber dust covers on the ends of the cylinder. Remove the pistons and piston cups and the spring. Remove the bleeder screw and make sure that it is not plugged.

3. Discard all of the parts that the rebuilding kit will replace.

4. Examine the inside of the cylinder. If it is severely rusted, pitted or scratched, then the cylinder must be replaced as the piston cups won't be able to seal against the walls of the cylinder.

5. Using a wheel cylinder hone or emery cloth and crocus cloth, polish the inside of the cylinder. The purpose of this is to put a new surface on the inside of the cylinder. Keep the inside of the cylinder coated with brake fluid while honing.

6. Wash out the cylinder with clean brake fluid after honing.

7. When reassembling the cylinder, dip all of the parts in clean brake fluid. Assemble the wheel cylinder in the reverse order of removal and disassembly.

PARKING BRAKE

The parking brake system is self adjusting and requires no adjustment, however if any component in the parking brake system requires servicing (or removing the rear axle), the cable tension must be released. After servicing is completed, the cables are connected to the equalizer and tension is reset.

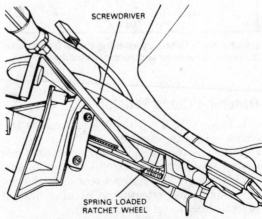

Rotating the spring loaded ratchet wheel

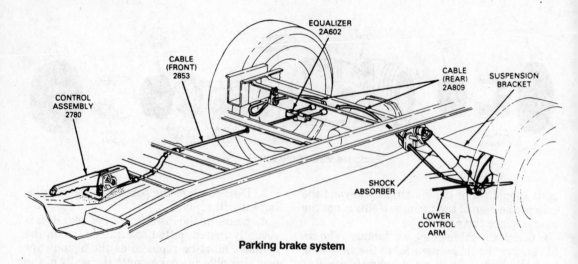

Parking brake system

Cable Tension Release

1. Remove the boot cover from the parking brake control assembly and place the control in the released position.

2. With a suitable tool , rotate the spring loaded ratchet wheel (in the self adjuster mechanism) back as far as possible to release the cable tension.

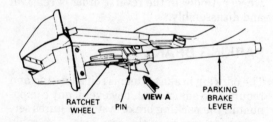

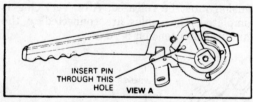

Lock the ratchet wheel by inserting a steel pin through the holes in the lever and control assembly

Resetting Cable Tension

1. Make sure the parking brake cables are connected to the equalizer.

2. Remove the steel pin from the holes in the control assembly being careful to keep fingers out of the way. This restores tension to the cables. Apply and release the parking brakes several times to set cable tension.

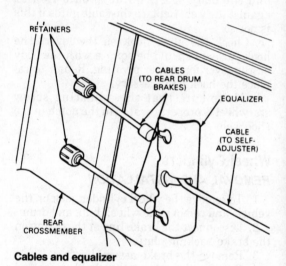

Cables and equalizer

Front Cable
REMOVAL

1. Place the control in the released position and insert the lock pin in the control assembly. Refer to Tension Release procedure.

2. Disconnect the rear parking brake cables from the equalizer. Remove the equalizer from the front cable.

3. Remove the bolts retaining the cover from the underbody reinforcement bracket. Remove the cover.

NOTE: *It may be necessary to loosen the fuel tank straps and partially lower the fuel tank to gain access to the cover.*

4. Remove the cable anchor pin from the pivot hole in the control assembly ratchet plate. Guide the front cable from the control assembly.

5. Insert a ½″ (12.7mm) box end twelve point wrench over the front fitting of the front

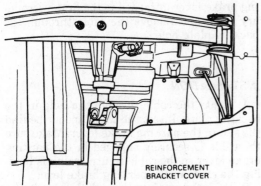

Location of reinforcement bracket cover

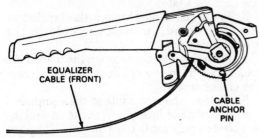

Anchor pin location

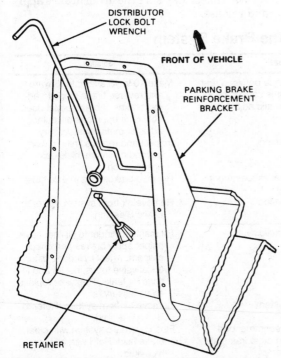

Using a distributor lock bolt wrench to remove the front cable

cable. Push the wrench onto the cable retainer fitting in the crossmember. Compress the retainer fingers and push the retainer rearward through the hole.

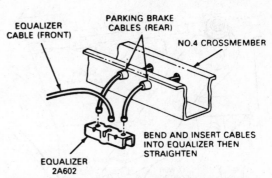

Feed the cables through the holes in the crossmember

NOTE: *Ford recommends using a distributor lock bolt wrench for the above step.*

6. Compress the retainer fingers on the rear crossmember and remove the retainer from the crossmember. Pull the cable ends through the crossmembers and remove the cable.

INSTALLATION

1. Feed the cables through both the holes in both crossmembers. Push the retainers through the holes so the fingers expand over each hole.

2. Route the cable around the control assembly pulley and insert the cable anchor pin in the pivot hole in the ratchet plate.

3. Connect the equalizer to the front and rear cables.

4. Remove the lock pin from the control assembly to apply cable tension.

5. Position the cover on the reinforcement bracket. Install and tighten the bolts after visually checking to be sure the front cable is attached to the control.

6. Position the boot over the control. Install and tighten the screws.

7. Apply and release the control. Make sure the rear brakes are applied and released.

Rear Cables (Equalizer To Drum)
REMOVAL

1. Place the control in the released position and insert the lock pin in the control assembly. Refer to Tension Release procedure.

2. Raise the vehicle and remove the hub cap, wheel and tire, and brake drum.

3. Disconnect the rear parking brake cables from the equalizer.

4. Compress the retainer fingers on the rear crossmember and remove the cable retainer from the rear crossmember. Remove the cable from the crossmember and from the bracket on the frame.

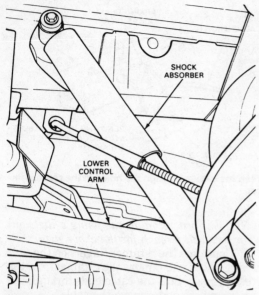

SHOCK ABSORBER

LOWER CONTROL ARM

Route the rear cable through the hole in the cross-member

ing brake lever (attached to the brake secondary shoe) and remove the cable through the backing plate hole.

INSTALLATION

1. Route the cable through the hole in the backing plate. Insert the cable anchor behind the slot in the parking brake lever. Make sure the cable is securely engaged in the parking brake lever so the cable return spring is holding the cable in the parking brake lever.

2. Push the retainer through the hole in the backing plate so the retainer fingers engage the backing plate.

3. Route the cable through the bracket on the frame and through the hole in the crossmember.

4. Push the retainer through the hole in the crossmember so the retainer fingers engage the crossmember.

5. Connect the rear cable to the equalizer.

6. Remove the lock pin from the control assembly to apply cable tension.

7. Apply and release the control assembly several times. May sure the drum brakes apply and release.

5. On the wheel side of the backing plate, compress the retainer fingers so the retainer passes through the hole in the backing plate.

6. Lift the cable out of the slot in the park-

Troubleshooting the Brake System

Problem	Cause	Solution
Low brake pedal (excessive pedal travel required for braking action.)	• Excessive clearance between rear linings and drums caused by inoperative automatic adjusters	• Make 10 to 15 alternate forward and reverse brake stops to adjust brakes. If brake pedal does not come up, repair or replace adjuster parts as necessary.
	• Worn rear brakelining	• Inspect and replace lining if worn beyond minimum thickness specification
	• Bent, distorted brakeshoes, front or rear	• Replace brakeshoes in axle sets
	• Air in hydraulic system	• Remove air from system. Refer to Brake Bleeding.
Low brake pedal (pedal may go to floor with steady pressure applied.)	• Fluid leak in hydraulic system	• Fill master cylinder to fill line; have helper apply brakes and check calipers, wheel cylinders, differential valve tubes, hoses and fittings for leaks. Repair or replace as necessary.
	• Air in hydraulic system	• Remove air from system. Refer to Brake Bleeding.
	• Incorrect or non-recommended brake fluid (fluid evaporates at below normal temp).	• Flush hydraulic system with clean brake fluid. Refill with correct-type fluid.
	• Master cylinder piston seals worn, or master cylinder bore is scored, worn or corroded	• Repair or replace master cylinder
Low brake pedal (pedal goes to floor on first application—o.k. on subsequent applications.)	• Disc brake pads sticking on abutment surfaces of anchor plate. Caused by a build-up of dirt, rust, or corrosion on abutment surfaces	• Clean abutment surfaces

Troubleshooting the Brake System (cont.)

Problem	Cause	Solution
Fading brake pedal (pedal height decreases with steady pressure applied.)	• Fluid leak in hydraulic system	• Fill master cylinder reservoirs to fill mark, have helper apply brakes, check calipers, wheel cylinders, differential valve, tubes, hoses, and fittings for fluid leaks. Repair or replace parts as necessary.
	• Master cylinder piston seals worn, or master cylinder bore is scored, worn or corroded	• Repair or replace master cylinder
Decreasing brake pedal travel (pedal travel required for braking action decreases and may be accompanied by a hard pedal.)	• Caliper or wheel cylinder pistons sticking or seized	• Repair or replace the calipers, or wheel cylinders
	• Master cylinder compensator ports blocked (preventing fluid return to reservoirs) or pistons sticking or seized in master cylinder bore	• Repair or replace the master cylinder
	• Power brake unit binding internally	• Test unit according to the following procedure: (a) Shift transmission into neutral and start engine (b) Increase engine speed to 1500 rpm, close throttle and fully depress brake pedal (c) Slow release brake pedal and stop engine (d) Have helper remove vacuum check valve and hose from power unit. Observe for backward movement of brake pedal. (e) If the pedal moves backward, the power unit has an internal bind—replace power unit
Spongy brake pedal (pedal has abnormally soft, springy, spongy feel when depressed.)	• Air in hydraulic system	• Remove air from system. Refer to Brake Bleeding.
	• Brakeshoes bent or distorted	• Replace brakeshoes
	• Brakelining not yet seated with drums and rotors	• Burnish brakes
	• Rear drum brakes not properly adjusted	• Adjust brakes
Hard brake pedal (excessive pedal pressure required to stop vehicle. May be accompanied by brake fade.)	• Loose or leaking power brake unit vacuum hose	• Tighten connections or replace leaking hose
	• Incorrect or poor quality brakelining	• Replace with lining in axle sets
	• Bent, broken, distorted brakeshoes	• Replace brakeshoes
	• Calipers binding or dragging on mounting pins. Rear brakeshoes dragging on support plate.	• Replace mounting pins and bushings. Clean rust or burrs from rear brake support plate ledges and lubricate ledges with molydisulfide grease. **NOTE:** If ledges are deeply grooved or scored, do not attempt to sand or grind them smooth—replace support plate.
	• Caliper, wheel cylinder, or master cylinder pistons sticking or seized	• Repair or replace parts as necessary
	• Power brake unit vacuum check valve malfunction	• Test valve according to the following procedure: (a) Start engine, increase engine speed to 1500 rpm, close throttle and immediately stop engine (b) Wait at least 90 seconds then depress brake pedal

Troubleshooting the Brake System (cont.)

Problem	Cause	Solution
Hard brake pedal (excessive pedal pressure required to stop vehicle. May be accompanied by brake fade.) (cont.)	• Power brake unit has internal bind	(c) If brakes are not vacuum assisted for 2 or more applications, check valve is faulty • Test unit according to the following procedure: (a) With engine stopped, apply brakes several times to exhaust all vacuum in system (b) Shift transmission into neutral, depress brake pedal and start engine (c) If pedal height decreases with foot pressure and less pressure is required to hold pedal in applied position, power unit vacuum system is operating normally. Test power unit. If power unit exhibits a bind condition, replace the power unit.
	• Master cylinder compensator ports (at bottom of reservoirs) blocked by dirt, scale, rust, or have small burrs (blocked ports prevent fluid return to reservoirs). • Brake hoses, tubes, fittings clogged or restricted	• Repair or replace master cylinder **CAUTION:** Do not attempt to clean blocked ports with wire, pencils, or similar implements. Use compressed air only. • Use compressed air to check or unclog parts. Replace any damaged parts.
	• Brake fluid contaminated with improper fluids (motor oil, transmission fluid, causing rubber components to swell and stick in bores • Low engine vacuum	• Replace all rubber components, combination valve and hoses. Flush entire brake system with DOT 3 brake fluid or equivalent. • Adjust or repair engine
Grabbing brakes (severe reaction to brake pedal pressure.)	• Brakelining(s) contaminated by grease or brake fluid	• Determine and correct cause of contamination and replace brakeshoes in axle sets
	• Parking brake cables incorrectly adjusted or seized	• Adjust cables. Replace seized cables.
	• Incorrect brakelining or lining loose on brakeshoes	• Replace brakeshoes in axle sets
	• Caliper anchor plate bolts loose • Rear brakeshoes binding on support plate ledges	• Tighten bolts • Clean and lubricate ledges. Replace support plate(s) if ledges are deeply grooved. Do not attempt to smooth ledges by grinding.
	• Incorrect or missing power brake reaction disc • Rear brake support plates loose	• Install correct disc • Tighten mounting bolts
Dragging brakes (slow or incomplete release of brakes)	• Brake pedal binding at pivot • Power brake unit has internal bind	• Loosen and lubricate • Inspect for internal bind. Replace unit if internal bind exists.
	• Parking brake cables incorrrectly adjusted or seized	• Adjust cables. Replace seized cables.
	• Rear brakeshoe return springs weak or broken	• Replace return springs. Replace brakeshoe if necessary in axle sets.
	• Automatic adjusters malfunctioning	• Repair or replace adjuster parts as required
	• Caliper, wheel cylinder or master cylinder pistons sticking or seized	• Repair or replace parts as necessary
	• Master cylinder compensating ports blocked (fluid does not return to reservoirs).	• Use compressed air to clear ports. Do not use wire, pencils, or similar objects to open blocked ports.

Troubleshooting the Brake System (cont.)

Problem	Cause	Solution
Vehicle moves to one side when brakes are applied	• Incorrect front tire pressure	• Inflate to recommended cold (reduced load) inflation pressure
	• Worn or damaged wheel bearings	• Replace worn or damaged bearings
	• Brakelining on one side contaminated	• Determine and correct cause of contamination and replace brakelining in axle sets
	• Brakeshoes on one side bent, distorted, or lining loose on shoe	• Replace brakeshoes in axle sets
	• Support plate bent or loose on one side	• Tighten or replace support plate
	• Brakelining not yet seated with drums or rotors	• Burnish brakelining
	• Caliper anchor plate loose on one side	• Tighten anchor plate bolts
	• Caliper piston sticking or seized	• Repair or replace caliper
	• Brakelinings water soaked	• Drive vehicle with brakes lightly applied to dry linings
	• Loose suspension component attaching or mounting bolts	• Tighten suspension bolts. Replace worn suspension components.
	• Brake combination valve failure	• Replace combination valve
Chatter or shudder when brakes are applied (pedal pulsation and roughness may also occur.)	• Brakeshoes distorted, bent, contaminated, or worn	• Replace brakeshoes in axle sets
	• Caliper anchor plate or support plate loose	• Tighten mounting bolts
	• Excessive thickness variation of rotor(s)	• Refinish or replace rotors in axle sets
Noisy brakes (squealing, clicking, scraping sound when brakes are applied.)	• Bent, broken, distorted brakeshoes	• Replace brakeshoes in axle sets
	• Excessive rust on outer edge of rotor braking surface	• Remove rust
Noisy brakes (squealing, clicking, scraping sound when brakes are applied.) (cont.)	• Brakelining worn out—shoes contacting drum of rotor	• Replace brakeshoes and lining in axle sets. Refinish or replace drums or rotors.
	• Broken or loose holdown or return springs	• Replace parts as necessary
	• Rough or dry drum brake support plate ledges	• Lubricate support plate ledges
	• Cracked, grooved, or scored rotor(s) or drum(s)	• Replace rotor(s) or drum(s). Replace brakeshoes and lining in axle sets if necessary.
	• Incorrect brakelining and/or shoes (front or rear).	• Install specified shoe and lining assemblies
Pulsating brake pedal	• Out of round drums or excessive lateral runout in disc brake rotor(s)	• Refinish or replace drums, re-index rotors or replace

Body and Trim

9

EXTERIOR

Doors

REMOVAL AND INSTALLATION

1. Remove the upper and lower hinge access hole cover plates, if so equipped, and mark the location of the hinge and body.

2. Remove the door to lower hinge retaining bolts.

3. Place a jack or jackstand under the door to support it, and remove the the door to upper hinge retaining bolts. Slide the door off the hinges.

4. When installing the door, position the door on the hinges, install the retaining bolts snug.

5. Adjust the door, and tighten all the retaining bolts securely.

NOTE: *To provide a good weatherstrip seal, the upper front edge of the door must be $^3/_{16}$" (5mm) inboard of the upper part of the pillar*

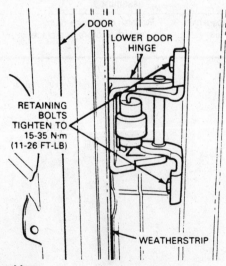

Door hinge

from the belt line to a point near the top of the door. This adjustment is made by adjusting the upper striker of the right hand door inboard.

ADJUSTMENT

Front

1. Determine which hinge bolts must be loosened to move the door in the desired direction.

2. Loosen the bolts just enough to permit movement to the door with a padded pry bar.

3. Move the door as necessary for the proper fit and tighten the hinge bolts securely.

4. Check the striker plate alignment for proper door closing.

Sliding Door

The sliding door latch is located at the rear of the door and when the door is pushed forward to close, the latch engages the striker which will position the rera of the sliding door flush to the body. There are two wedges located on the front of the sliding door which fit into two slots located on the B pillar. These wedges must enter the two slots to assure proper fit and closed position for the front of the sliding door.

NOTE: *For proper sliding door operation it is critical that the two wedges on the front face of the sliding door fit smoothly into the two wedge pockets located in the B pillar. If any of the following adjustments, re-alignment of the to wedge-to-wedge pockets may be necessary.*

IN OR OUT

Support the sliding door so that no up or down movement is made to the door during this adjustment.

CHILTON'S
AUTO BODY
REPAIR TIPS

Tools and Materials • Step-by-Step Illustrated Procedures
How To Repair Dents, Scratches and Rust Holes
Spray Painting and Refinishing Tips

With a little practice, basic body repair procedures can be mastered by any do-it-yourself mechanic. The step-by-step repairs shown here can be applied to almost any type of auto body repair.

TOOLS & MATERIALS

You may already have basic tools, such as hammers and electric drills. Other tools unique to body repair — body hammers, grinding attachments, sanding blocks, dent puller, half-round plastic file and plastic spreaders — are relatively inexpensive and can be obtained wherever auto parts or auto body repair parts are sold. Portable air compressors and paint spray guns can be purchased or rented.

Auto Body Repair Kits

The best and most often used products are available to the do-it-yourselfer in kit form, from major manufacturers of auto body repair products. The same manufacturers also merchandise the individual products for use by pros.

Kits are available to make a wide variety of repairs, including holes, dents and scratches and fiberglass, and offer the advantage of buying the materials you'll need for the job. There is little waste or chance of materials going bad from not being used. Many kits may also contain basic body-working tools such as body files, sanding blocks and spreaders. Check the contents of the kit before buying your tools.

BODY REPAIR TIPS

Safety

Many of the products associated with auto body repair and refinishing contain toxic chemicals. Read all labels before opening containers and store them in a safe place and manner.

• Wear eye protection (safety goggles) when using power tools or when performing any operation that involves the removal of any type of material.

• Wear lung protection (disposable mask or respirator) when grinding, sanding or painting.

Sanding

1 Sand off paint before using a dent puller. When using a non-adhesive sanding disc, cover the back of the disc with an overlapping layer or two of masking tape and trim the edges. The disc will last considerably longer.

2 Use the circular motion of the sanding disc to grind *into* the edge of the repair. Grinding or sanding away from the jagged edge will only tear the sandpaper.

3 Use the palm of your hand flat on the panel to detect high and low spots. Do not use your fingertips. Slide your hand slowly back and forth.

WORKING WITH BODY FILLER

Mixing The Filler

Cleanliness and proper mixing and application are extremely important. Use a clean piece of plastic or glass or a disposable artist's palette to mix body filler.

1 Allow plenty of time and follow directions. No useful purpose will be served by adding more hardener to make it cure (set-up) faster. Less hardener means more curing time, but the mixture dries harder; more hardener means less curing time but a softer mixture.

2 Both the hardener and the filler should be thoroughly kneaded or stirred before mixing. Hardener should be a solid paste and dispense like thin toothpaste. Body filler should be smooth, and free of lumps or thick spots.

Getting the proper amount of hardener in the filler is the trickiest part of preparing the filler. Use the same amount of hardener in cold or warm weather. For contour filler (thick coats), a bead of hardener twice the diameter of the filler is about right. There's about a 15% margin on either side, but, if in doubt use less hardener.

3 Mix the body filler and hardener by wiping across the mixing surface, picking the mixture up and wiping it again. Colder weather requires longer mixing times. Do not mix in a circular motion; this will trap air bubbles which will become holes in the cured filler.

Applying The Filler

1 For best results, filler should not be applied over ¼" thick.

Apply the filler in several coats. Build it up to above the level of the repair surface so that it can be sanded or grated down.

The first coat of filler must be pressed on with a firm wiping motion.

Apply the filler in one direction only. Working the filler back and forth will either pull it off the metal or trap air bubbles.

REPAIRING DENTS

Before you start, take a few minutes to study the damaged area. Try to visualize the shape of the panel before it was damaged. If the damage is on the left fender, look at the right fender and use it as a guide. If there is access to the panel from behind, you can reshape it with a body hammer. If not, you'll have to use a dent puller. Go slowly and work the metal a little at a time. Get the panel as straight as possible before applying filler.

1 This dent is typical of one that can be pulled out or hammered out from behind. Remove the headlight cover, headlight assembly and turn signal housing.

2 Drill a series of holes ½ the size of the end of the dent puller along the stress line. Make some trial pulls and assess the results. If necessary, drill more holes and try again. Do not hurry.

3 If possible, use a body hammer and block to shape the metal back to its original contours. Get the metal back as close to its original shape as possible. Don't depend on body filler to fill dents.

4 Using an 80-grit grinding disc on an electric drill, grind the paint from the surrounding area down to bare metal. Use a new grinding pad to prevent heat buildup that will warp metal.

5 The area should look like this when you're finished grinding. Knock the drill holes in and tape over small openings to keep plastic filler out.

6 Mix the body filler (see Body Repair Tips). Spread the body filler evenly over the entire area (see Body Repair Tips). Be sure to cover the area completely.

7 Let the body filler dry until the surface can just be scratched with your fingernail. Knock the high spots from the body filler with a body file ("Cheesegrater"). Check frequently with the palm of your hand for high and low spots.

8 Check to be sure that trim pieces that will be installed later will fit exactly. Sand the area with 40-grit paper.

9 If you wind up with low spots, you may have to apply another layer of filler.

10 Knock the high spots off with 40-grit paper. When you are satisfied with the contours of the repair, apply a thin coat of filler to cover pin holes and scratches.

11 Block sand the area with 40-grit paper to a smooth finish. Pay particular attention to body lines and ridges that must be well-defined.

12 Sand the area with 400 paper and then finish with a scuff pad. The finished repair is ready for priming and painting (see Painting Tips).

Materials and photos courtesy of Ritt Jones Auto Body, Prospect Park, PA.

REPAIRING RUST HOLES

There are many ways to repair rust holes. The fiberglass cloth kit shown here is one of the most cost efficient for the owner because it provides a strong repair that resists cracking and moisture and is relatively easy to use. It can be used on large and small holes (with or without backing) and can be applied over contoured areas. Remember, however, that short of replacing an entire panel, no repair is a guarantee that the rust will not return.

1 Remove any trim that will be in the way. Clean away all loose debris. Cut away all the rusted metal. But be sure to leave enough metal to retain the contour or body shape.

2 Grind away all traces of rust with a 24-grit grinding disc. Be sure to grind back 3-4 inches from the edge of the hole down to bare metal and be sure all traces of paint, primer and rust are removed.

3 Block sand the area with 80 or 100 grit sandpaper to get a clear, shiny surface and feathered paint edge. Tap the edges of the hole inward with a ball peen hammer.

4 If you are going to use release film, cut a piece about 2-3″ larger than the area you have sanded. Place the film over the repair and mark the sanded area on the film. Avoid any unnecessary wrinkling of the film.

5 Cut 2 pieces of fiberglass matte to match the shape of the repair. One piece should be about 1″ smaller than the sanded area and the second piece should be 1″ smaller than the first. Mix enough filler and hardener to saturate the fiberglass material (see Body Repair Tips).

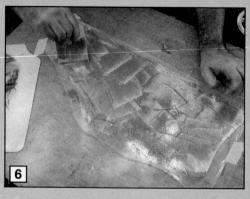

6 Lay the release sheet on a flat surface and spread an even layer of filler, large enough to cover the repair. Lay the smaller piece of fiberglass cloth in the center of the sheet and spread another layer of filler over the fiberglass cloth. Repeat the operation for the larger piece of cloth.

7 Place the repair material over the repair area, with the release film facing outward. Use a spreader and work from the center outward to smooth the material, following the body contours. Be sure to remove all air bubbles.

8 Wait until the repair has dried tack-free and peel off the release sheet. The ideal working temperature is 60°-90° F. Cooler or warmer temperatures or high humidity may require additional curing time. Wait longer, if in doubt.

9

9 Sand and feather-edge the entire area. The initial sanding can be done with a sanding disc on an electric drill if care is used. Finish the sanding with a block sander. Low spots can be filled with body filler; this may require several applications.

10

10 When the filler can just be scratched with a fingernail, knock the high spots down with a body file and smooth the entire area with 80-grit. Feather the filled areas into the surrounding areas.

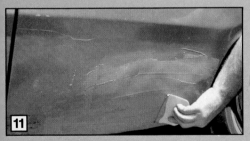

11

11 When the area is sanded smooth, mix some topcoat and hardener and apply it directly with a spreader. This will give a smooth finish and prevent the glass matte from showing through the paint.

12

12 Block sand the topcoat smooth with finishing sandpaper (200 grit), and 400 grit. The repair is ready for masking, priming and painting (see Painting Tips).

Materials and photos courtesy Marson Corporation, Chelsea, Massachusetts

PAINTING TIPS

Preparation

1 SANDING — Use a 400 or 600 grit wet or dry sandpaper. Wet-sand the area with a 1/4 sheet of sandpaper soaked in clean water. Keep the paper wet while sanding. Sand the area until the repaired area tapers into the original finish.

2 CLEANING — Wash the area to be painted thoroughly with water and a clean rag. Rinse it thoroughly and wipe the surface dry until you're sure it's completely free of dirt, dust, fingerprints, wax, detergent or other foreign matter.

3 MASKING — Protect any areas you don't want to overspray by covering them with masking tape and newspaper. Be careful not get fingerprints on the area to be painted.

4 PRIMING — All exposed metal should be primed before painting. Primer protects the metal and provides an excellent surface for paint adhesion. When the primer is dry, wet-sand the area again with 600 grit wet-sandpaper. Clean the area again after sanding.

4

Painting Techniques

P aint applied from either a spray gun or a spray can (for small areas) will provide good results. Experiment on an old piece of metal to get the right combination before you begin painting.

SPRAYING VISCOSITY (SPRAY GUN ONLY) — Paint should be thinned to spraying viscosity according to the directions on the can. Use only the recommended thinner or reducer and the same amount of reduction regardless of temperature.

AIR PRESSURE (SPRAY GUN ONLY) — This is extremely important. Be sure you are using the proper recommended pressure.

TEMPERATURE — The surface to be painted should be approximately the same temperature as the surrounding air. Applying warm paint to a cold surface, or vice versa, will completely upset the paint characteristics.

THICKNESS — Spray with smooth strokes. In general, the thicker the coat of paint, the longer the drying time. Apply several thin coats about 30 seconds apart. The paint should remain wet long enough to flow out and no longer; heavier coats will only produce sags or wrinkles. Spray a light (fog) coat, followed by heavier color coats.

DISTANCE — The ideal spraying distance is 8″-12″ from the gun or can to the surface. Shorter distances will produce ripples, while greater distances will result in orange peel, dry film and poor color match and loss of material due to overspray.

OVERLAPPING — The gun or can should be kept at right angles to the surface at all times. Work to a wet edge at an even speed, using a 50% overlap and direct the center of the spray at the lower or nearest edge of the previous stroke.

RUBBING OUT (BLENDING) FRESH PAINT — Let the paint dry thoroughly. Runs or imperfections can be sanded out, primed and repainted.

Don't be in too big a hurry to remove the masking. This only produces paint ridges. When the finish has dried for at least a week, apply a small amount of fine grade rubbing compound with a clean, wet cloth. Use lots of water and blend the new paint with the surrounding area.

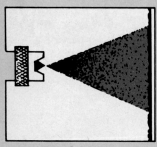

WRONG

CORRECT

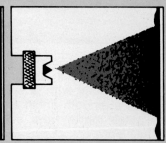

WRONG

Thin coat. Stroke too fast, not enough overlap, gun too far away.

Medium coat. Proper distance, good stroke, proper overlap.

Heavy coat. Stroke too slow, too much overlap, gun too close.

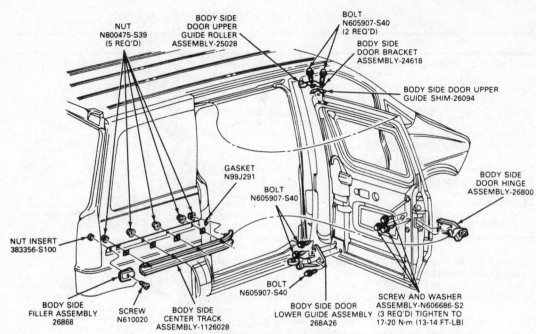

NUT
N800475-S39
(5 REQ'D)

BODY SIDE
DOOR UPPER
GUIDE ROLLER
ASSEMBLY-25028

BOLT
N605907-S40
(2 REQ'D)

BODY SIDE
DOOR BRACKET
ASSEMBLY-24618

BODY SIDE DOOR UPPER
GUIDE SHIM-26094

GASKET
N99J291

BOLT
N605907-S40

BODY SIDE
DOOR HINGE
ASSEMBLY-26800

NUT INSERT
383356-S100

BODY SIDE
FILLER ASSEMBLY
26868

SCREW
N610020

BODY SIDE
CENTER TRACK
ASSEMBLY-1126028

BOLT
N605907-S40

BODY SIDE DOOR
LOWER GUIDE ASSEMBLY
268A26

SCREW AND WASHER
ASSEMBLY-N606686-S2
(3 REQ'D) TIGHTEN TO
17-20 N·m (13-14 FT-LB)

Sliding door adjustment locations

FRONT UPPER

To adjust the front upper edge of the sliding door, loosen the two nuts retaining the body side door bracket assembly to the upper guide roller assembly in or out as required to obtain a flush fit of the door to the body. The upper guide roller assembly rides freely within the upper track on the body. The bracket assembly and upper guide do not support the sliding door.

FRONT LOWER

The lower edge of the sliding door is adjusted by loosening the adjusting nut on the lower guide assembly and moving the door in or out as required to obtain a flush fit. The lower guide vertical roller is a load bearing roller and should roll easily within the lower track as the sliding door is opened or closed.

STRIKER REAR LATCH

Adjusting the striker in or out will position the rear edge of the sliding door as required to obtain the proper fit to the body.

NOTE: *The striker adjusts in or out only. Up and down adjustment is obtained with the rear hinge and lower front guide.*

HINGE ASSEMBLY

To adjust the sliding door for and aft, the three bolts retaining the center door hinge to the door may be loosened and the hinge adjusted for and aft as required.

NOTE: *Some up and down adjustments may be obtained from the center hinge by moving*

the center hinge strap up or down as desired prior to securing the retainer bolts. The vertical hinge rollers within the body center track assembly must be parallel to the top of the track and maintain a minimum clearance of 0.040″ (1mm) from the top of the track run for smooth operation

Door Locks

REMOVAL AND INSTALLATION

All Front

1. Remove the trim panel and water shield from the door.
2. Remove the remote control assembly and disconnect the rod.
3. Disconnect the push button rod and handle rod from the latch.
4. Remove the lock assembly attaching screws and remove the lock from the door.
5. Install the rod retaining clips in the new lock assembly. The remote control rod, lock cylinder rod, and the anti-theft shield should be attached should be attached to the lock before installation.
6. Position the lock in the door and install and tighten securely the lock retaining screws.
7. Connect the rods to the handle, lock cylinder and the remote control.
8. Connect the handle rod and push button rod to the lock and check the operation of the lock.
9. Install the watershield and trim panel to the door.

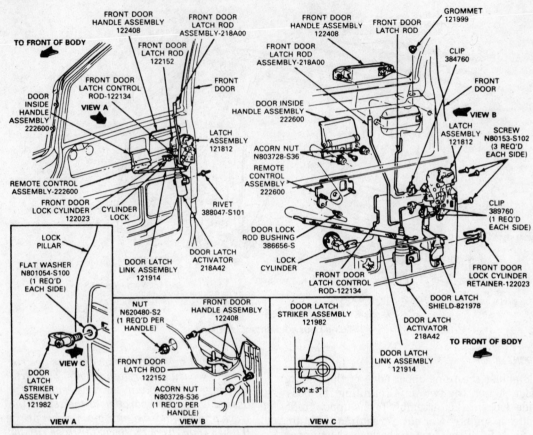

Front door lock (latch) assembly

Sliding Door Rear

1. Remove the sliding door panels, water shield and access hole cover plates.

2. Unlatch the sliding door.

3. Remove the actuator rod retainer from the center door retainer hole.

4. Disconnect the rear door lock actuator rod from the remote control assembly.

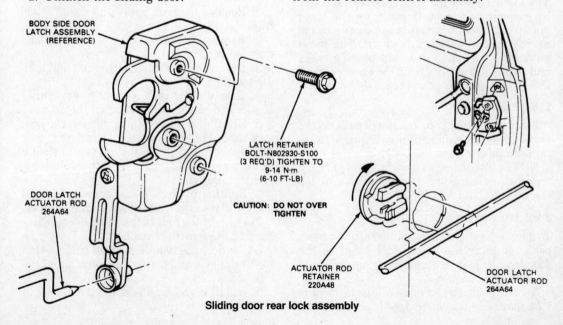

Sliding door rear lock assembly

5. Open the door enough to gain access to the three lock retainer bolts attaching the rear lock to the sliding door and remove the bolts.

6. Remove the sliding door rear lock with the remote control actuator rod attached to the lock.

7. Installation is the reverse of removal. Do not tighten the three lock retainer bolts more than 6–10 ft.lb.

Hood

REMOVAL AND INSTALLATION

1. Open the hood and prop in the open position.

2. Cover the cowl area to prevent damage to the paint.

3. With the aid of a helper to hold the hood, remove the hinge bolts to the hood and remove the hood from the vehicle.

4. Installation is the reverse of removal. Torque the hinge-to-hood bolts to 12–19 ft.lb. Close the hood, check the alignment and adjust as necessary.

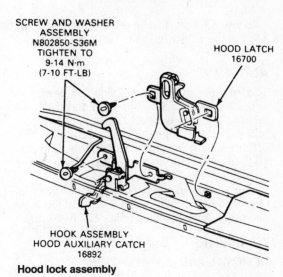

Hood lock assembly

hood fit by loosening the lock attaching screws and moving as necessary.

Liftgate

REMOVAL AND INSTALLATION

1. Open the liftgate door.

2. Remove the upper rear center garnish moulding by removing the three retaining screws.

3. Support the door in the open position and disconnect the liftgate gas cylinder assist rod assemblies by using a suitable tool to push the locking wedge or locking spring out of the ball socket on both sides of the assist rod.

4. Move the headliner out of position and remove the hinge-to-header panel attaching nuts and remove the liftgate with the hinge attached.

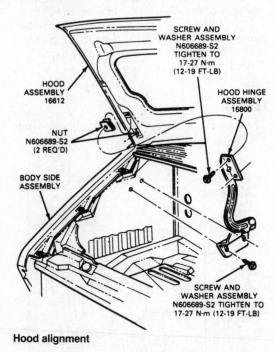

Hood alignment

ALIGNMENT

The hood can be adjusted for and aft and side to side by loosening the hood-to-hinge attaching bolts and reposition the hood. To raise or lower the hood, loosen the hinge hood on body attaching bolts and raise or lower the hinge as necessary.

The hood lock can be moved from side-to-side and up and down and laterally to obtain a snug

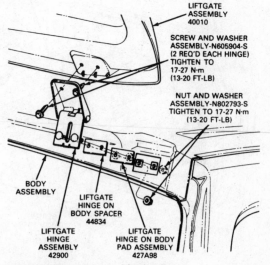

Liftgate hinge and attaching parts

5. Installation is the reverse of removal. Torque the attaching nuts to 13–20 ft.lb.

ALIGNMENT

The liftgate can be adjusted side-to-side and up and down by loosening the hinge-to-header attaching nut and washer. Adding spacers permits in or out adjustments as required. The liftgate should be adjusted for an even and parallel fit with the door opening. Tighten the nuts to 13–20 ft.lb.

The striker assembly can be moved $1/6''$ (4mm) radially (side-to-side/back and forth) as necessary. Tighten the striker to 30–40 ft.lb.

Windshield

REMOVAL AND INSTALLATION

The Aerostar uses a Urethane type sealed windshield which requires the use of special tools for removal and installation. It is advised that if the windshield needs replacement the vehicle be taken to a professional glass shop.

INTERIOR

Front Door Panels

REMOVAL AND INSTALLATION

Hi Series

1. Remove the screw retaining the front door trim finish panel to the door inner panel.
2. Remove the screws retaining the front

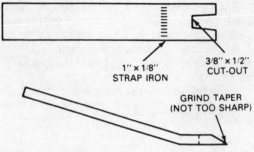

Push pin removal tool

door trim panel moulding assembly to the door inner panel.

3. Remove the screw retaining the door window regulator handle and remove the handle and washer.

4. At each plastic clip location, carefully pry the trim panel away from the door inner panel (upward to clear the door release handle, and door lock control), then remove the trim panel.

NOTE: *The manufacturer recommends making a special push pin removal tool, shown in the illustration to complete Step 4.*

5. Installation is the reverse of removal. Replace bent or broken trim clips as necessary.

NOTE: *Do not use the trim panel to pull the clips from the inner panel holes.*

Lo Series

The door panel is removed by simply removing the seven retaining screws.

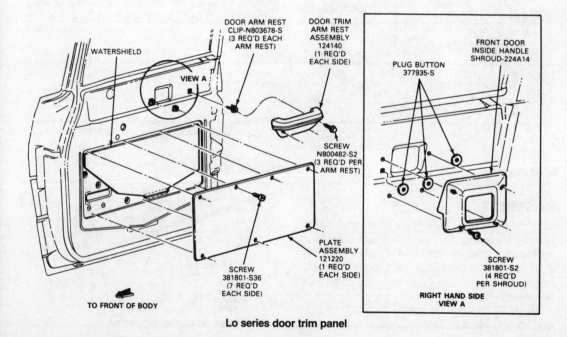

Lo series door trim panel

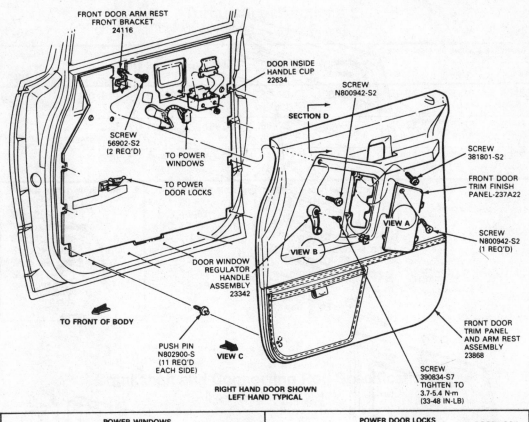

Hi series door trim panel

Sliding Door Trim Panel

REMOVAL AND INSTALLATION

Mid And Hi Series

1. Remove the screws retaining the sliding door garnish moulding to the sliding door inner panel, then remove the garnish panel.

2. Remove the screws retaining the sliding door trim panel to the sliding door inner panel then remove the trim panel. Remove the screw at the ash tray bezel.

3. Installation is the reverse of removal.

Front Door Glass

REMOVAL

1. Remove the door trim panel and watershield.

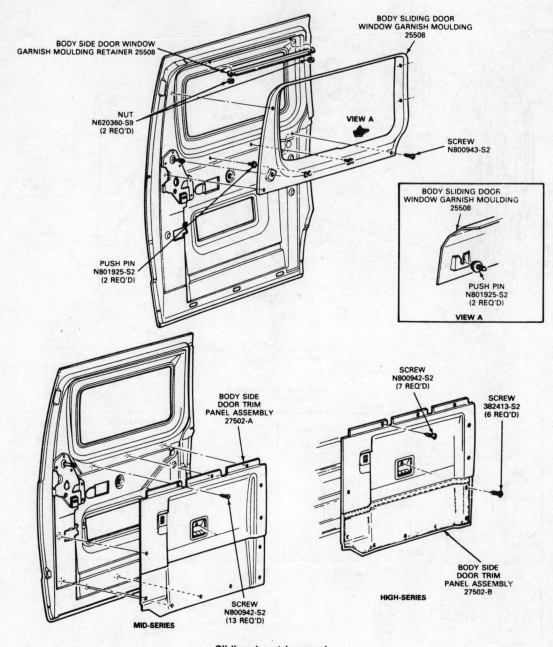

BODY SLIDING DOOR
WINDOW GARNISH MOULDING
25508

BODY SIDE DOOR WINDOW
GARNISH MOULDING RETAINER 25508

VIEW A

NUT
N620360-S9
(2 REQ'D)

SCREW
N800943-S2

PUSH PIN
N801925-S2
(2 REQ'D)

BODY SLIDING DOOR
WINDOW GARNISH MOULDING
25508

PUSH PIN
N801925-S2
(2 REQ'D)

VIEW A

SCREW
N800942-S2
(7 REQ'D)

SCREW
382413-S2
(6 REQ'D)

BODY SIDE
DOOR TRIM
PANEL ASSEMBLY
27502-A

BODY SIDE
DOOR TRIM
PANEL ASSEMBLY
27502-B

HIGH-SERIES

SCREW
N800942-S2
(13 REQ'D)

MID-SERIES

Sliding door trim panels

2. Raise the glass to the full UP position.

3. Remove the rear glass run retainer from the door.

4. Lower the glass to gain access to the glass bracket and glass retention rivets.

5. Remove the center pin from the glass retention rivets using a drift punch. Then use a ¼″ (4mm) diameter drill carefully drill out each rivet.

6. Remove the glass through the door belt opening.

INSTALLATION

1. Install the glass spacer and retainer into the glass retention holes.

2. Install the glass into the door through the door belt opening.

3. Position the door glass to the door glass bracket and align the glass and glass bracket retaining holes

4. Install the retaining rivets.

5. Raise the glass to the full UP position.

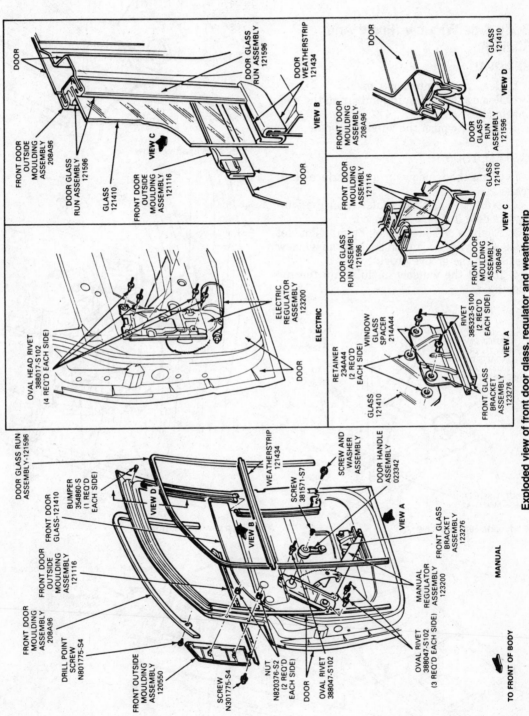

Exploded view of front door glass, regulator and weatherstrip

DOOR

DOOR

DOOR GLASS RUN ASSEMBLY 121596

DOOR WEATHERSTRIP 121434

FRONT DOOR OUTSIDE MOULDING ASSEMBLY 208A96

DOOR GLASS RUN ASSEMBLY 121596

GLASS 121410

FRONT DOOR OUTSIDE MOULDING ASSEMBLY 121116

VIEW C

DOOR

VIEW B

DOOR

GLASS 121410

VIEW D

FRONT DOOR MOULDING ASSEMBLY 208A96

DOOR GLASS RUN ASSEMBLY 121596

FRONT DOOR MOULDING ASSEMBLY 121116

DOOR GLASS RUN ASSEMBLY 121596

GLASS 121410

FRONT DOOR MOULDING ASSEMBLY 208A96

VIEW C

OVAL HEAD RIVET 388017-S102 (4 REQ'D EACH SIDE)

ELECTRIC REGULATOR ASSEMBLY 123200

DOOR

ELECTRIC

RETAINER 234A44 (2 REQ'D EACH SIDE)

WINDOW GLASS SPACER 214A44

RIVET 385323-S100 (2 REQ'D EACH SIDE)

GLASS 121410

FRONT GLASS BRACKET ASSEMBLY 123276

VIEW A

DOOR GLASS RUN ASSEMBLY-121596

FRONT DOOR OUTSIDE MOULDING ASSEMBLY 121116

FRONT DOOR GLASS-121410

BUMPER 354860-S (1 REQ'D EACH SIDE)

WEATHERSTRIP 121434

SCREW 381571-S7

SCREW AND WASHER ASSEMBLY

DOOR HANDLE ASSEMBLY 02342

VIEW D

VIEW B

VIEW A

FRONT GLASS BRACKET ASSEMBLY 123276

FRONT DOOR MOULDING ASSEMBLY 208A96

DRILL POINT SCREW N801775-S4

FRONT OUTSIDE MOULDING ASSEMBLY 120550

SCREW N301775-S4

NUT N820376-S2 (2 REQ'D EACH SIDE)

DOOR

OVAL RIVET 388047-S102

OVAL RIVET 388047-S102 (3 REQ'D EACH SIDE)

MANUAL REGULATOR ASSEMBLY 123200

MANUAL

TO FRONT OF BODY

6. Install the rear glass run retainer and rear glass run.

7. Check the operation of the window.

8. Install the trim panel and watershield.

Body Side Window (Fixed And Sliding)

REMOVAL

1. Remove the interior trim.

2. Remove the retaining nuts from the window module.

3. Carefully push the window module out.

INSTALLATION

1. Clean the window opening surface of all sealer.

2. Clean the existing sealer from the window module if it is to be reused.

3. Apply a ¼" to $^5/_{16}$" (4–8mm) diameter bead of butyl sealer to the back of the window module on the groove provided.

4. Install the window module into the the opening.

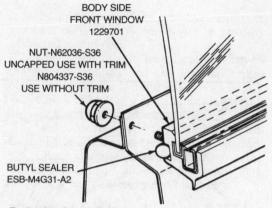

Body side fixed window

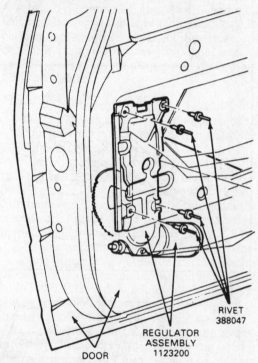

Electric window motor

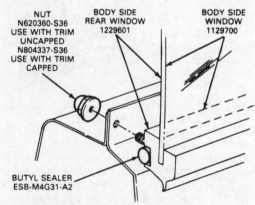

Body side rear window

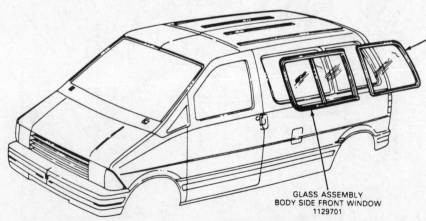

Body side windows

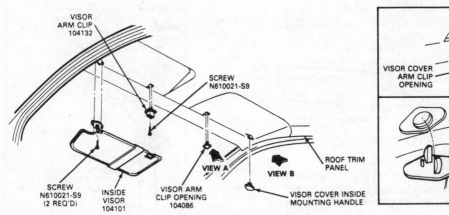

Sun visor removal

Electric Window Motor
REMOVAL AND INSTALLATION

1. Disconnect the battery ground cable.
2. Remove the door trim panel.
3. Disconnect the electric window motor wire from the wire harness connector.
4. Using a ½″ diameter drill bit, drill two holes in the door inner panel at the drill dimples located opposite the two unexposed motor drive retainer screws.

NOTE: *Check inside the door to make sure that electrical wires are not in line with the holes to be drilled in the door inner panel.*

5. Remove the three motor mount retainer screws using the two drilled holes and larger hole access to the screw heads.
6. Push the motor toward the outside sheet metal to disengage the motor and drive from the regulator gear. Prop the window in the full up position, after the motor and drive are disengaged.

7. Remove the motor and drive from inside of the door.
8. Installation is the reverse of removal.

Headliner
REMOVAL AND INSTALLATION
Roof Trim Panel Front

1. Remove the front seats.
2. Remove the sun visors.
3. Remove the screws retaining the sun visor arm clips to the roof front trim panel and remove the clips. Disconnect the feed wire for illuminated sun visors.
4. Remove the roof console cover, and then

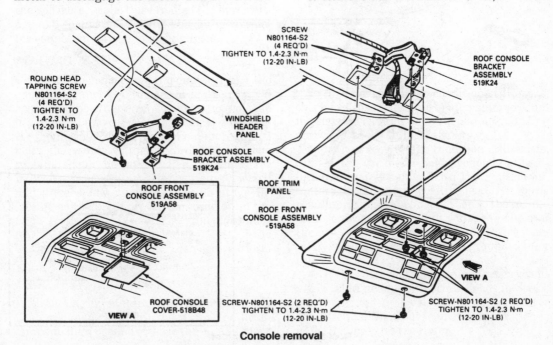

Console removal

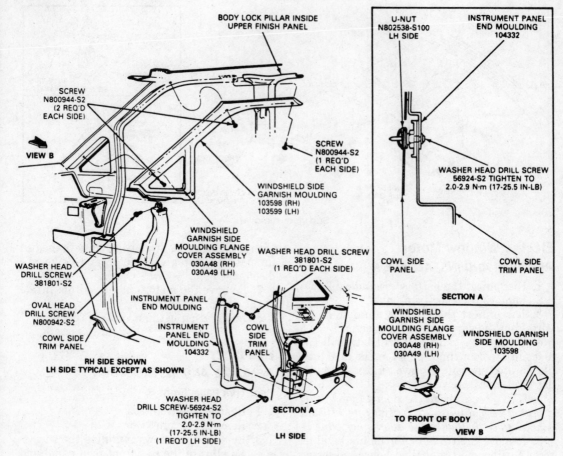

BODY LOCK PILLAR INSIDE
UPPER FINISH PANEL

U-NUT
N802538-S100
LH SIDE

INSTRUMENT PANEL
END MOULDING
104332

SCREW
N800944-S2
(2 REQ'D
EACH SIDE)

VIEW B

SCREW
N800944-S2
(1 REQ'D
EACH SIDE)

WINDSHIELD SIDE
GARNISH MOULDING
103598 (RH)
103599 (LH)

WASHER HEAD DRILL SCREW
56924-S2 TIGHTEN TO
2.0-2.9 N·m (17-25.5 IN-LB)

WINDSHIELD
GARNISH SIDE
MOULDING FLANGE
COVER ASSEMBLY
030A48 (RH)
030A49 (LH)

WASHER HEAD DRILL SCREW
381801-S2
(1 REQ'D EACH SIDE)

COWL SIDE
PANEL

COWL SIDE
TRIM PANEL

WASHER HEAD
DRILL SCREW
381801-S2

SECTION A

OVAL HEAD
DRILL SCREW
N800942-S2

INSTRUMENT PANEL
END MOULDING

COWL SIDE
TRIM PANEL

INSTRUMENT
PANEL END
MOULDING
104332

COWL SIDE
TRIM
PANEL

WINDSHIELD
GARNISH SIDE
MOULDING FLANGE
COVER ASSEMBLY
030A48 (RH)
030A49 (LH)

WINDSHIELD GARNISH
SIDE MOULDING
103598

**RH SIDE SHOWN
LH SIDE TYPICAL EXCEPT AS SHOWN**

WASHER HEAD
DRILL SCREW-56924-S2
TIGHTEN TO
2.0-2.9 N·m
(17-25.5 IN-LB)
(1 REQ'D LH SIDE)

SECTION A

TO FRONT OF BODY

VIEW B

LH SIDE

Inside trim panel and mouldings

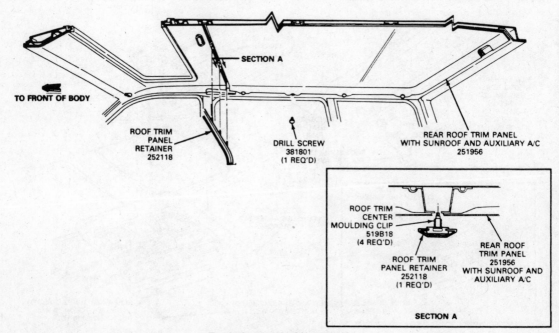

SECTION A

TO FRONT OF BODY

ROOF TRIM
PANEL
RETAINER
252118

DRILL SCREW
381801
(1 REQ'D)

REAR ROOF TRIM PANEL
WITH SUNROOF AND AUXILIARY A/C
251956

ROOF TRIM
CENTER
MOULDING CLIP
519B18
(4 REQ'D)

ROOF TRIM
PANEL RETAINER
252118
(1 REQ'D)

REAR ROOF
TRIM PANEL
251956
WITH SUNROOF AND
AUXILIARY A/C

SECTION A

Roof trim panel with sunroof

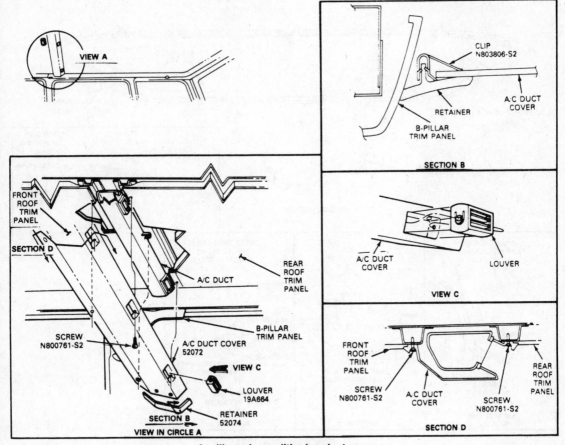

Auxiliary air conditioning duct cover

remove the screws retaining the roof front console assembly to the roof trim panel and remove the console.

5. Remove the front dome lamp assembly.

6. Raise the manual sunroof glass panel assembly to facilitate removal of the color-keyed headliner retainer, if so equipped.

7. Remove the screws retaining the windshield garnish side mouldings to roof trim front panel and remove the mouldings.

8. Remove the body side door header rail garnish moulding retaining screws and then remove the moulding.

9. Remove the screws retaining the body lock pillar inside finish upper panels (RH and LH) to body, then remove the panels.

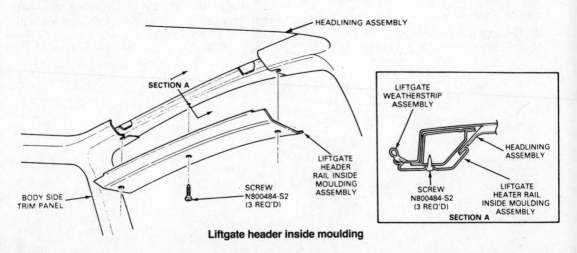

Liftgate header inside moulding

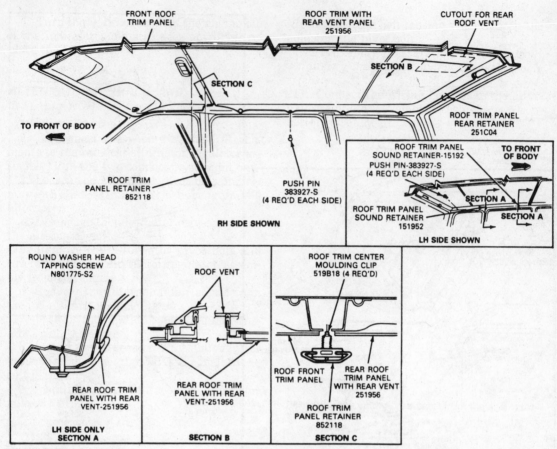

FRONT ROOF TRIM PANEL

ROOF TRIM WITH REAR VENT PANEL 251956

CUTOUT FOR REAR ROOF VENT

SECTION B

SECTION C

TO FRONT OF BODY

ROOF TRIM PANEL REAR RETAINER 251C04

ROOF TRIM PANEL RETAINER 852118

PUSH PIN 383927-S (4 REQ'D EACH SIDE)

RH SIDE SHOWN

ROOF TRIM PANEL SOUND RETAINER-15192 PUSH PIN-383927-S (4 REQ'D EACH SIDE)

TO FRONT OF BODY

ROOF TRIM PANEL SOUND RETAINER 151952

SECTION A

SECTION A

LH SIDE SHOWN

ROUND WASHER HEAD TAPPING SCREW N801775-S2

ROOF VENT

ROOF TRIM CENTER MOULDING CLIP 519B18 (4 REQ'D)

REAR ROOF TRIM PANEL WITH REAR VENT-251956

LH SIDE ONLY SECTION A

REAR ROOF TRIM PANEL WITH REAR VENT-251956

SECTION B

ROOF FRONT TRIM PANEL

REAR ROOF TRIM PANEL WITH REAR VENT 251956

ROOF TRIM PANEL RETAINER 852118

SECTION C

Roof trim panel rear

10. Remove the RH and LH body side trim panel.

11. On base vans, remove the screws along the rear edge of the headliner at the roof reinforcement.

12. Using an appropriate tool, carefully pry the four roof trim panel retainer clips from the roof trim front panel.

13. Installation is the reverse of removal.

Roof Trim Panel Rear

1. Remove the rear seats.
2. Remove the rear cargo lamp.

3. Remove the screws retaining the roof A/C duct cover to body and remove the cover.

4. Remove the screws retaining the liftgate header rail inside moulding.

5. Using an appropriate tool, carefully pry the four roof trim panel retainer clips from the roof trim rear panel.

6. Remove the RH and LH body side trim panel assemblies.

7. Raise the liftgate and remove the rear roof trim panel-to-body retaining screws, and remove the trim panel.

8. Installation is the reverse of removal.

How to Remove Stains from Fabric Interior

For rest results, spots and stains should be removed as soon as possible. Never use gasoline, lacquer thinner, acetone, nail polish remover or bleach. Use a 3' x 3" piece of cheesecloth. Squeeze most of the liquid from the fabric and wipe the stained fabric from the outside of the stain toward the center with a lifting motion. Turn the cheesecloth as soon as one side becomes soiled. When using water to remove a stain, be sure to wash the entire section after the spot has been removed to avoid water stains. Encrusted spots can be broken up with a dull knife and vacuumed before removing the stain.

Type of Stain	How to Remove It
Surface spots	Brush the spots out with a small hand brush or use a commercial preparation such as K2R to lift the stain.
Mildew	Clean around the mildew with warm suds. Rinse in cold water and soak the mildew area in a solution of 1 part table salt and 2 parts water. Wash with upholstery cleaner.
Water stains	Water stains in fabric materials can be removed with a solution made from 1 cup of table salt dissolved in 1 quart of water. Vigorously scrub the solution into the stain and rinse with clear water. Water stains in nylon or other synthetic fabrics should be removed with a commercial type spot remover.
Chewing gum, tar, crayons, shoe polish (greasy stains)	Do not use a cleaner that will soften gum or tar. Harden the deposit with an ice cube and scrape away as much as possible with a dull knife. Moisten the remainder with cleaning fluid and scrub clean.
Ice cream, candy	Most candy has a sugar base and can be removed with a cloth wrung out in warm water. Oily candy, after cleaning with warm water, should be cleaned with upholstery cleaner. Rinse with warm water and clean the remainder with cleaning fluid.
Wine, alcohol, egg, milk, soft drink (non-greasy stains)	Do not use soap. Scrub the stain with a cloth wrung out in warm water. Remove the remainder with cleaning fluid.
Grease, oil, lipstick, butter and related stains	Use a spot remover to avoid leaving a ring. Work from the outisde of the stain to the center and dry with a clean cloth when the spot is gone.
Headliners (cloth)	Mix a solution of warm water and foam upholstery cleaner to give thick suds. Use only foam—liquid may streak or spot. Clean the entire headliner in one operation using a circular motion with a natural sponge.
Headliner (vinyl)	Use a vinyl cleaner with a sponge and wipe clean with a dry cloth.
Seats and door panels	Mix 1 pint upholstery cleaner in 1 gallon of water. Do not soak the fabric around the buttons.
Leather or vinyl fabric	Use a multi-purpose cleaner full strength and a stiff brush. Let stand 2 minutes and scrub thoroughly. Wipe with a clean, soft rag.
Nylon or synthetic fabrics	For normal stains, use the same procedures you would for washing cloth upholstery. If the fabric is extremely dirty, use a multi-purpose cleaner full strength with a stiff scrub brush. Scrub thoroughly in all directions and wipe with a cotton towel or soft rag.

Mechanic's Data

General Conversion Table

Multiply By	To Convert	To	
LENGTH			
2.54	Inches	Centimeters	.3937
25.4	Inches	Millimeters	.03937
30.48	Feet	Centimeters	.0328
.304	Feet	Meters	3.28
.914	Yards	Meters	1.094
1.609	Miles	Kilometers	.621
VOLUME			
.473	Pints	Liters	2.11
.946	Quarts	Liters	1.06
3.785	Gallons	Liters	.264
.016	Cubic inches	Liters	61.02
16.39	Cubic inches	Cubic cms.	.061
28.3	Cubic feet	Liters	.0353
MASS (Weight)			
28.35	Ounces	Grams	.035
.4536	Pounds	Kilograms	2.20
—	To obtain	From	Multiply by

Multiply By	To Convert	To	
AREA			
.645	Square inches	Square cms.	.155
.836	Square yds.	Square meters	1.196
FORCE			
4.448	Pounds	Newtons	.225
.138	Ft./lbs.	Kilogram/meters	7.23
1.36	Ft./lbs.	Newton-meters	.737
.112	In./lbs.	Newton-meters	8.844
PRESSURE			
.068	Psi	Atmospheres	14.7
6.89	Psi	Kilopascals	.145
OTHER			
1.104	Horsepower (DIN)	Horsepower (SAE)	.9861
.746	Horsepower (SAE)	Kilowatts (KW)	1.34
1.60	Mph	Km/h	.625
.425	Mpg	Km/1	2.35
—	To obtain	From	Multiply by

Tap Drill Sizes

National Coarse or U.S.S.

Screw & Tap Size	Threads Per Inch	Use Drill Number
No. 5	40	39
No. 6	32	36
No. 8	32	29
No. 10	24	25
No. 12	24	17
$1/4$	20	8
$5/16$	18	F
$3/8$	16	$5/16$
$7/16$	14	U
$1/2$	13	$27/64$
$9/16$	12	$31/64$
$5/8$	11	$17/32$
$3/4$	10	$21/32$
$7/8$	9	$49/64$

National Coarse or U.S.S.

Screw & Tap Size	Threads Per Inch	Use Drill Number
1	8	$7/8$
$1\frac{1}{8}$	7	$63/64$
$1\frac{1}{4}$	7	$1^7/64$
$1\frac{1}{2}$	6	$1^{11}/32$

National Fine or S.A.E.

Screw & Tap Size	Threads Per Inch	Use Drill Number
No. 5	44	.37
No. 6	40	.33
No. 8	36	.29
No. 10	32	.21

National Fine or S.A.E.

Screw & Tap Size	Threads Per Inch	Use Drill Number
No. 12	28	15
$1/4$	28	3
$6/16$	24	1
$3/8$	24	Q
$7/16$	20	W
$1/2$	20	$29/64$
$9/16$	18	$33/64$
$5/8$	18	$37/64$
$3/4$	16	$11/16$
$7/8$	14	$13/16$
$1\frac{1}{8}$	12	$1^3/64$
$1\frac{1}{4}$	12	$1^{11}/64$
$1\frac{1}{2}$	12	$1^{27}/64$

Drill Sizes In Decimal Equivalents

Inch	Dec-imal	Wire	mm	Inch	Dec-imal	Wire	mm	Inch	Dec-imal	Wire & Letter	mm	Inch	Dec-imal	Let-ter	mm	Inch	Dec-imal	mm
1/64	.0156		.39		.0730	49			.1614		4.1		.2717		6.9		.4331	11.0
	.0157		.4		.0748		1.9		.1654		4.2		.2720	I		7/16	.4375	11.11
	.0160	78			.0760	48			.1660	19			.2756		7.0		.4528	11.5
	.0165		.42		.0768		1.95		.1673		4.25		.2770	J		29/64	.4531	11.51
	.0173		.44	5/64	.0781		1.98		.1693		4.3		.2795		7.1	15/32	.4688	11.90
	.0177		.45		.0785	47			.1695	18			.2810	K			.4724	12.0
	.0180	77			.0787		2.0	11/64	.1719		4.36	9/32	.2812		7.14	31/64	.4844	12.30
	.0181		.46		.0807		2.05		.1730	17			.2835		7.2		.4921	12.5
	.0189		.48		.0810	46			.1732		4.4		.2854		7.25	1/2	.5000	12.70
	.0197		.5		.0820	45			.1770	16			.2874		7.3		.5118	13.0
	.0200	76			.0827		2.1		.1772		4.5		.2900	L		33/64	.5156	13.09
	.0210	75			.0846		2.15		.1800	15			.2913		7.4	17/32	.5312	13.49
	.0217		.55		.0860	44			.1811		4.6		.2950	M			.5315	13.5
	.0225	74			.0866		2.2		.1820	14			.2953		7.5	35/64	.5469	13.89
	.0236		.6		.0886		2.25		.1850	13		19/64	.2969		7.54		.5512	14.0
	.0240	73			.0890	43			.1850		4.7		.2992		7.6	9/16	.5625	14.28
	.0250	72			.0906		2.3		.1870		4.75		.3020	N			.5709	14.5
	.0256		.65		.0925		2.35	3/16	.1875		4.76		.3031		7.7	37/64	.5781	14.68
	.0260	71			.0935	42			.1890		4.8		.3051		7.75		.5906	15.0
	.0276		.7	3/32	.0938		2.38		.1890	12			.3071		7.8	19/32	.5938	15.08
	.0280	70			.0945		2.4		.1910	11			.3110		7.9	39/64	.6094	15.47
	.0292	69			.0960	41			.1929		4.9	5/16	.3125		7.93		.6102	15.5
	.0295		.75		.0965		2.45		.1935	10			.3150		8.0	5/8	.6250	15.87
	.0310	68			.0980	40			.1960	9			.3160	O			.6299	16.0
1/32	.0312		.79		.0981		2.5		.1969		5.0		.3189		8.1	41/64	.6406	16.27
	.0315		.8		.0995	39			.1990	8			.3228		8.2		.6496	16.5
	.0320	67			.1015	38			.2008		5.1		.3230	P		21/32	.6562	16.66
	.0330	66			.1024		2.6		.2010	7			.3248		8.25		.6693	17.0
	.0335		.85		.1040	37		13/64	.2031		5.16		.3268		8.3	43/64	.6719	17.06
	.0350	65			.1063		2.7		.2040	6		21/64	.3281		8.33	11/16	.6875	17.46
	.0354		.9		.1065	36			.2047		5.2		.3307		8.4		.6890	17.5
	.0360	64			.1083		2.75		.2055	5			.3320	Q		45/64	.7031	17.85
	.0370	63		7/64	.1094		2.77		.2067		5.25		.3346		8.5		.7087	18.0
	.0374		.95		.1100	35			.2087		5.3		.3386		8.6	23/32	.7188	18.25
	.0380	62			.1102		2.8		.2090	4			.3390	R			.7283	18.5
	.0390	61			.1110	34			.2126		5.4		.3425		8.7	47/64	.7344	18.65
	.0394		1.0		.1130	33			.2130	3		11/32	.3438		8.73		.7480	19.0
	.0400	60			.1142		2.9		.2165		5.5		.3445		8.75	3/4	.7500	19.05
	.0410	59			.1160	32		7/32	2188		5.55		.3465		8.8	49/64	.7656	19.44
	.0413		1.05		.1181		3.0		.2205		5.6		.3480	S			.7677	19.5
	.0420	58			.1200	31			.2210	2			.3504		8.9	25/32	.7812	19.84
	.0430	57			.1220		3.1		.2244		5.7		.3543		9.0		.7874	20.0
	.0433		1.1	1/8	.1250		3.17		.2264		5.75		.3580	T		51/64	.7969	20.24
	.0453		1.15		.1260		3.2		.2280	1			.3583		9.1		.8071	20.5
	.0465	56			.1280		3.25		.2283		5.8	23/64	.3594		9.12	13/16	.8125	20.63
3/64	.0469		1.19		.1285	30			.2323		5.9		.3622		9.2		.8268	21.0
	.0472		1.2		.1299		3.3		.2340	A			.3642		9.25	53/64	.8281	21.03
	.0492		1.25		.1339		3.4	15/64	.2344		5.95		.3661		9.3	27/32	.8438	21.43
	.0512		1.3		.1360	29			.2362		6.0		.3680	U			.8465	21.5
	.0520	55			.1378		3.5		.2380	B			.3701		9.4	55/64	.8594	21.82
	.0531		1.35		.1405	28			.2402		6.1		.3740		9.5		.8661	22.0
	.0550	54		9/64	.1406		3.57		.2420	C		3/8	.3750		9.52	7/8	.8750	22.22
	.0551		1.4		.1417		3.6		.2441		6.2		.3770	V			.8858	22.5
	.0571		1.45		.1440	27			.2460	D			.3780		9.6	57/64	.8906	22.62
	.0591		1.5		.1457		3.7		.2461		6.25		.3819		9.7		.9055	23.0
	.0595	53			.1470	26			.2480		6.3		.3839		9.75	29/32	.9062	23.01
	.0610		1.55		.1476		3.75	1/4	.2500	E	6.35		.3858		9.8	59/64	.9219	23.41
1/16	.0625		1.59		.1495	25			.2520		6.		.3860	W			.9252	23.5
	.0630		1.6		.1496		3.8		.2559		6.5		.3898		9.9	15/16	.9375	23.81
	.0635	52			.1520	24			.2570	F		25/64	.3906		9.92		.9449	24.0
	.0650		1.65		.1535		3.9		.2598		6.6		.3937		10.0	61/64	.9531	24.2
	.0669		1.7		.1540	23			.2610	G			.3970	X			.9646	24.5
	.0670	51		5/32	.1562		3.96		.2638		6.7		.4040	Y		31/32	.9688	24.6
	.0689		1.75		.1570	22		17/64	.2656		6.74	13/32	.4062		10.31		.9843	25.0
	.0700	50			.1575		4.0		.2657		6.75		.4130	Z		63/64	.9844	25.0
	.0709		1.8		.1590	21			.2660	H			.4134		10.5	1	1.0000	25.4
	.0728		1.85		.1610	20			.2677		6.8	27/64	.4219		10.71			

AIR/FUEL RATIO: The ratio of air to gasoline by weight in the fuel mixture drawn into the engine.

AIR INJECTION: One method of reducing harmful exhaust emissions by injecting air into each of the exhaust ports of an engine. The fresh air entering the hot exhaust manifold causes any remaining fuel to be burned before it can exit the tailpipe.

ALTERNATOR: A device used for converting mechanical energy into electrical energy.

AMMETER: An instrument, calibrated in amperes, used to measure the flow of an electrical current in a circuit. Ammeters are always connected in series with the circuit being tested.

AMPERE: The rate of flow of electrical current present when one volt of electrical pressure is applied against one ohm of electrical resistance.

ANALOG COMPUTER: Any microprocessor that uses similar (analogous) electrical signals to make its calculations.

ARMATURE: A laminated, soft iron core wrapped by a wire that converts electrical energy to mechanical energy as in a motor or relay. When rotated in a magnetic field, it changes mechanical energy into electrical energy as in a generator.

ATMOSPHERIC PRESSURE: The pressure on the Earth's surface caused by the weight of the air in the atmosphere. At sea level, this pressure is 14.7 psi at 32°F (101 kPa at 0°C).

ATOMIZATION: The breaking down of a liquid into a fine mist that can be suspended in air.

AXIAL PLAY: Movement parallel to a shaft or bearing bore.

BACKFIRE: The sudden combustion of gases in the intake or exhaust system that results in a loud explosion.

BACKLASH: The clearance or play between two parts, such as meshed gears.

BACKPRESSURE: Restrictions in the exhaust system that slow the exit of exhaust gases from the combustion chamber.

BAKELITE: A heat resistant, plastic insulator material commonly used in printed circuit boards and transistorized components.

BALL BEARING: A bearing made up of hardened inner and outer races between which hardened steel ball roll.

BALLAST RESISTOR: A resistor in the primary ignition circuit that lowers voltage after the engine is started to reduce wear on ignition components.

BEARING: A friction reducing, supportive device usually located between a stationary part and a moving part.

BIMETAL TEMPERATURE SENSOR: Any sensor or switch made of two dissimilar types of metal that bend when heated or cooled due to the different expansion rates of the alloys. These types of sensors usually function as an on/off switch.

BLOWBY: Combustion gases, composed of water vapor and unburned fuel, that leak past the piston rings into the crankcase during normal engine operation. These gases are removed by the PCV system to prevent the build-up of harmful acids in the crankcase.

BRAKE PAD: A brake shoe and lining assembly used with disc brakes.

BRAKE SHOE: The backing for the brake lining. The term is, however, usually applied to the assembly of the brake backing and lining.

BUSHING: A liner, usually removable, for a bearing; an anti-friction liner used in place of a bearing.

BYPASS: System used to bypass ballast resistor during engine cranking to increase voltage supplied to the coil.

CALIPER: A hydraulically activated device in a disc brake system, which is mounted straddling the brake rotor (disc). The caliper contains at least one piston and two brake pads. Hydraulic pressure on the piston(s) forces the pads against the rotor.

CAMSHAFT: A shaft in the engine on which are the lobes (cams) which operate the valves. The camshaft is driven by the crankshaft, via a belt, chain or gears, at one half the crankshaft speed.

CAPACITOR: A device which stores an electrical charge.

CARBON MONOXIDE (CO): a colorless, odorless gas given off as a normal byproduct of combustion. It is poisonous and extremely dangerous in confined areas, building up slowly to toxic levels without warning if adequate ventilation is not available.

CARBURETOR: A device, usually mounted on the intake manifold of an engine, which mixes the air and fuel in the proper proportion to allow even combustion.

CATALYTIC CONVERTER: A device installed in the exhaust system, like a muffler, that converts harmful byproducts of combustion into carbon dioxide and water vapor by means of a heat-producing chemical reaction.

CENTRIFUGAL ADVANCE: A mechanical method of advancing the spark timing by using flyweights in the distributor that react to centrifugal force generated by the distributor shaft rotation.

CHECK VALVE: Any one-way valve installed to permit the flow of air, fuel or vacuum in one direction only.

CHOKE: A device, usually a moveable valve, placed in the intake path of a carburetor to restrict the flow of air.

CIRCUIT: Any unbroken path through which an electrical current can flow. Also used to describe fuel flow in some instances.

CIRCUIT BREAKER: A switch which protects an electrical circuit from overload by opening the circuit when the current flow exceeds a predetermined level. Some circuit breakers must be reset manually, while other reset automatically

COIL (IGNITION): A transformer in the ignition circuit which steps of the voltage provided to the spark plugs.

COMBINATION MANIFOLD: An assembly which includes both the intake and exhaust manifolds in one casting.

COMBINATION VALVE: A device used in some fuel systems that routes fuel vapors to a charcoal storage canister instead of venting them into the atmosphere. The valve relieves fuel tank pressure and allows fresh air into the tank as fuel level drops to prevent a vapor lock situation.

COMPRESSION RATIO: The comparison of the total volume of the cylinder and combustion chamber with the piston at BDC and the piston at TDC.

CONDENSER: 1. An electrical device which acts to store an electrical charge, preventing voltage surges.
2. A radiator-like device in the air conditioning system in which refrigerant gas condenses into a liquid, giving off heat.

CONDUCTOR: Any material through which an electrical current can be transmitted easily.

CONTINUITY: Continuous or complete circuit. Can be checked with an ohmmeter.

COUNTERSHAFT: An intermediate shaft which is rotated by a mainshaft and transmits, in turn, that rotation to a working part.

CRANKCASE: The lower part of an engine in which the crankshaft and related parts operate.

CRANKSHAFT: The main driving shaft of an engine which receives reciprocating motion from the pistons and converts it to rotary motion.

CYLINDER: In an engine, the round hole in the engine block in which the piston(s) ride.

CYLINDER BLOCK: The main structural member of an engine in which is found the cylinders, crankshaft and other principal parts.

CYLINDER HEAD: The detachable portion of the engine, fastened, usually, to the top of the cylinder block, containing all or most of the combustion chambers. On overhead valve engines, it contains the valves and their operating parts. On overhead cam engines, it contains the camshaft as well.

DEAD CENTER: The extreme top or bottom of the piston stroke.

DETONATION: An unwanted explosion of the air fuel mixture in the combustion chamber caused by excess heat and compression, advanced timing, or an overly lean mixture. Also referred to as "ping".

DIAPHRAGM: A thin, flexible wall separating two cavities, such as in a vacuum advance unit.

DIESELING: A condition in which hot spots in the combustion chamber cause the engine to run on after the key is turned off.

DIFFERENTIAL: A geared assembly which allows the transmission of motion between drive axles, giving one axle the ability to turn faster than the other.

DIODE: An electrical device that will allow current to flow in one direction only.

DISC BRAKE: A hydraulic braking assembly consisting of a brake disc, or rotor, mounted on an axle, and a caliper assembly containing, usually two brake pads which are activated by hydraulic pressure. The pads are forced against the sides of the disc, creating friction which slows the vehicle.

DISTRIBUTOR: A mechanically driven device on an engine which is responsible for electrically firing the spark plug at a predetermined point of the piston stroke.

DOWEL PIN: A pin, inserted in mating holes in two different parts allowing those parts to maintain a fixed relationship.

DRUM BRAKE: A braking system which consists of two brake shoes and one or two wheel cylinders, mounted on a fixed backing plate, and a brake drum, mounted on an axle, which revolves around the assembly. Hydraulic action applied to the wheel cylinders forces the shoes outward against the drum, creating friction and slowing the vehicle.

DWELL: The rate, measured in degrees of shaft rotation, at which an electrical circuit cycles on and off.

ELECTRONIC CONTROL UNIT (ECU): Ignition module, module, amplifier or igniter. See Module for definition.

ELECTRONIC IGNITION: A system in which the timing and firing of the spark plugs is controlled by an electronic control unit, usually called a module. These systems have not points or condenser.

ENDPLAY: The measured amount of axial movement in a shaft.

ENGINE: A device that converts heat into mechanical energy.

EXHAUST MANIFOLD: A set of cast passages or pipes which conduct exhaust gases from the engine.

FEELER GAUGE: A blade, usually metal, of precisely predetermined thickness, used to measure the clearance between two parts. These blades usually are available in sets of assorted thicknesses.

F-Head: An engine configuration in which the intake valves are in the cylinder head, while the camshaft and exhaust valves are located in the cylinder block. The camshaft operates the intake valves via lifters and pushrods, while it operates the exhaust valves directly.

FIRING ORDER: The order in which combustion occurs in the cylinders of an engine. Also the order in which spark is distributed to the plugs by the distributor.

FLATHEAD: An engine configuration in which the camshaft and all the valves are located in the cylinder block.

FLOODING: The presence of too much fuel in the intake manifold and combustion chamber which prevents the air/fuel mixture from firing, thereby causing a no-start situation.

FLYWHEEL: A disc shaped part bolted to the rear end of the crankshaft. Around the outer perimeter is affixed the ring gear. The starter drive engages the ring gear, turning the flywheel, which rotates the crankshaft, imparting the initial starting motion to the engine.

FOOT POUND (ft.lb. or sometimes, ft. lbs.): The amount of energy or work needed to raise an item weighing one pound, a distance of one foot.

FUSE: A protective device in a circuit which prevents circuit overload by breaking the circuit when a specific amperage is present. The device is constructed around a strip or wire of a lower amperage rating than the circuit it is designed to protect. When an amperage higher than that stamped on the fuse is present in the circuit, the strip or wire melts, opening the circuit.

GEAR RATIO: The ratio between the number of teeth on meshing gears.

GENERATOR: A device which converts mechanical energy into electrical energy.

HEAT RANGE: The measure of a spark plug's ability to dissipate heat from its firing end. The higher the heat range, the hotter the plug fires.

HUB: The center part of a wheel or gear.

HYDROCARBON (HC): Any chemical compound made up of hydrogen and carbon. A major pollutant formed by the engine as a byproduct of combustion.

HYDROMETER: An instrument used to measure the specific gravity of a solution.

INCH POUND (in.lb. or sometimes, in. lbs.): One twelfth of a foot pound.

INDUCTION: A means of transferring electrical energy in the form of a magnetic field. Principle used in the ignition coil to increase voltage.

INJECTION PUMP: A device, usually mechanically operated, which meters and delivers fuel under pressure to the fuel injector.

INJECTOR: A device which receives metered fuel under relatively low pressure and is activated to inject the fuel into the engine under relatively high pressure at a predetermined time.

INPUT SHAFT: The shaft to which torque is applied, usually carrying the driving gear or gears.

INTAKE MANIFOLD: A casting of passages or pipes used to conduct air or a fuel/air mixture to the cylinders.

JOURNAL: The bearing surface within which a shaft operates.

KEY: A small block usually fitted in a notch between a shaft and a hub to prevent slippage of the two parts.

MANIFOLD: A casting of passages or set of pipes which connect the cylinders to an inlet or outlet source.

MANIFOLD VACUUM: Low pressure in an engine intake manifold formed just below the throttle plates. Manifold vacuum is highest at idle and drops under acceleration.

MASTER CYLINDER: The primary fluid pressurizing device in a hydraulic system. In automotive use, it is found in brake and hydraulic clutch systems and is pedal activated, either directly or, in a power brake system, through the power booster.

MODULE: Electronic control unit, amplifier or igniter of solid state or integrated design which controls the current flow in the ignition primary circuit based on input from the pickup coil. When the module opens the primary circuit, the high secondary voltage is induced in the coil.

NEEDLE BEARING: A bearing which consists of a number (usually a large number) of long, thin rollers.

OHM: (Ω) The unit used to measure the resistance of conductor to electrical flow. One ohm is the amount of resistance that limits current flow to one ampere in a circuit with one volt of pressure.

OHMMETER: An instrument used for measuring the resistance, in ohms, in an electrical circuit.

OUTPUT SHAFT: The shaft which transmits torque from a device, such as a transmission.

OVERDRIVE: A gear assembly which produces more shaft revolutions than that transmitted to it.

OVERHEAD CAMSHAFT (OHC): An engine configuration in which the camshaft is mounted on top of the cylinder head and operates the valve either directly or by means of rocker arms.

OVERHEAD VALVE (OHV): An engine configuration in which all of the valves are located in the cylinder head and the camshaft is located in the cylinder block. The camshaft operates the valves via lifters and pushrods.

OXIDES OF NITROGEN (NOx): Chemical compounds of nitrogen produced as a byproduct of combustion. They combine with hydrocarbons to produce smog.

OXYGEN SENSOR: Used with the feedback system to sense the presence of oxygen in the exhaust gas and signal the computer which can reference the voltage signal to an air/fuel ratio.

PINION: The smaller of two meshing gears.

PISTON RING: An open ended ring which fits into a groove on the outer diameter of the piston. Its chief function is to form a seal between the piston and cylinder wall. Most automotive pistons have three rings: two for compression sealing; one for oil sealing.

PRELOAD: A predetermined load placed on a bearing during assembly or by adjustment.

PRIMARY CIRCUIT: Is the low voltage side of the ignition system which consists of the ignition switch, ballast resistor or resistance wire, bypass, coil, electronic control unit and pick-up coil as well as the connecting wires and harnesses.

PRESS FIT: The mating of two parts under pressure, due to the inner diameter of one being smaller than the outer diameter of the other, or vice versa; an interference fit.

RACE: The surface on the inner or outer ring of a bearing on which the balls, needles or rollers move.

REGULATOR: A device which maintains the amperage and/or voltage levels of a circuit at predetermined values.

RELAY: A switch which automatically opens and/or closes a circuit.

RESISTANCE: The opposition to the flow of current through a circuit or electrical device, and is measured in ohms. Resistance is equal to the voltage divided by the amperage.

RESISTOR: A device, usually made of wire, which offers a preset amount of resistance in an electrical circuit.

RING GEAR: The name given to a ring-shaped gear attached to a differential case, or affixed to a flywheel or as part a planetary gear set.

ROLLER BEARING: A bearing made up of hardened inner and outer races between which hardened steel rollers move.

ROTOR: 1. The disc-shaped part of a disc brake assembly, upon which the brake pads bear; also called, brake disc.
2. The device mounted atop the distributor shaft, which passes current to the distributor cap tower contacts.

SECONDARY CIRCUIT: The high voltage side of the ignition system, usually above 20,000 volts. The secondary includes the ignition coil, coil wire, distributor cap and rotor, spark plug wires and spark plugs.

SENDING UNIT: A mechanical, electrical, hydraulic or electromagnetic device which transmits information to a gauge.

SENSOR: Any device designed to measure engine operating conditions or ambient pressures and temperatures. Usually electronic in nature and designed to send a voltage signal to an on-board computer, some sensors may operate as a simple on/off switch or they may provide a variable voltage signal (like a potentiometer) as conditions or measured parameters change.

SHIM: Spacers of precise, predetermined thickness used between parts to establish a proper working relationship.

SLAVE CYLINDER: In automotive use, a device in the hydraulic clutch system which is activated by hydraulic force, disengaging the clutch.

SOLENOID: A coil used to produce a magnetic field, the effect of which is produce work.

SPARK PLUG: A device screwed into the combustion chamber of a spark ignition engine. The basic construction is a conductive core inside of a ceramic insulator, mounted in an outer conductive base. An electrical charge from the spark plug wire travels along the conductive core and jumps a preset air gap to a grounding point or points at the end of the conductive base. The resultant spark ignites the fuel/air mixture in the combustion chamber.

SPLINES: Ridges machined or cast onto the outer diameter of a shaft or inner diameter of a bore to enable parts to mate without rotation.

TACHOMETER: A device used to measure the rotary speed of an engine, shaft, gear, etc., usually in rotations per minute.

THERMOSTAT: A valve, located in the cooling system of an engine, which is closed when cold and opens gradually in response to engine heating, controlling the temperature of the coolant and rate of coolant flow.

TOP DEAD CENTER (TDC): The point at which the piston reaches the top of its travel on the compression stroke.

TORQUE: The twisting force applied to an object.

TORQUE CONVERTER: A turbine used to transmit power from a driving member to a driven member via hydraulic action, providing changes in drive ratio and torque. In automotive use, it links the driveplate at the rear of the engine to the automatic transmission.

TRANSDUCER: A device used to change a force into an electrical signal.

TRANSISTOR: A semi-conductor component which can be actuated by a small voltage to perform an electrical switching function.

TUNE-UP: A regular maintenance function, usually associated with the replacement and adjustment of parts and components in the electrical and fuel systems of a vehicle for the purpose of attaining optimum performance.

TURBOCHARGER: An exhaust driven pump which compresses intake air and forces it into the combustion chambers at higher than atmospheric pressures. The increased air pressure allows more fuel to be burned and results in increased horsepower being produced.

VACUUM ADVANCE: A device which advances the ignition timing in response to increased engine vacuum.

VACUUM GAUGE: An instrument used to measure the presence of vacuum in a chamber.

VALVE: A device which control the pressure, direction of flow or rate of flow of a liquid or gas.

VALVE CLEARANCE: The measured gap between the end of the valve stem and the rocker arm, cam lobe or follower that activates the valve.

VISCOSITY: The rating of a liquid's internal resistance to flow.

VOLTMETER: An instrument used for measuring electrical force in units called volts. Voltmeters are always connected parallel with the circuit being tested.

WHEEL CYLINDER: Found in the automotive drum brake assembly, it is a device, actuated by hydraulic pressure, which, through internal pistons, pushes the brake shoes outward against the drums.

ABBREVIATIONS AND SYMBOLS

A: Ampere

AC: Alternating current

A/C: Air conditioning

A-h: Ampere hour

AT: Automatic transmission

ATDC: After top dead center

μA: Microampere

bbl: Barrel

BDC: Bottom dead center

bhp: Brake horsepower

BTDC: Before top dead center

BTU: British thermal unit

C: Celsius (Centigrade)

CCA: Cold cranking amps

cd: Candela

cm^2: Square centimeter

cm^3, cc: Cubic centimeter

CO: Carbon monoxide

CO_2: Carbon dioxide

cu.in., in^3: Cubic inch

CV: Constant velocity

Cyl.: Cylinder

DC: Direct current

ECM: Electronic control module

EFE: Early fuel evaporation

EFI: Electronic fuel injection

EGR: Exhaust gas recirculation

Exh.: Exhaust

F: Fahrenheit

F: Farad

pF: Picofarad

μF: Microfarad

FI: Fuel injection

ft.lb., ft. lb., ft. lbs.: foot pound(s)

gal: Gallon

g: Gram

HC: Hydrocarbon

HEI: High energy ignition

HO: High output

hp: Horsepower

Hyd.: Hydraulic

Hz: Hertz

ID: Inside diameter

in.lb.; in. lb.; in. lbs: inch pound(s)

Int.: Intake

K: Kelvin

kg: Kilogram

kHz: Kilohertz

km: Kilometer

km/h: Kilometers per hour

kΩ: Kilohm

kPa: Kilopascal

kV: Kilovolt

kW: Kilowatt

l: Liter

l/s: Liters per second

m: Meter

mA: Milliampere

mg: Milligram

mHz: Megahertz

mm: Millimeter

mm^2: Square millimeter

m^3: Cubic meter

MΩ: Megohm

m/s: Meters per second

MT: Manual transmission

mV: Millivolt

μm: Micrometer

N: Newton

N-m: Newton meter

NOx: Nitrous oxide

OD: Outside diameter

OHC: Over head camshaft

OHV: Over head valve

Ω: Ohm

PCV: Positive crankcase ventilation

psi: Pounds per square inch

pts: Pints

qts: Quarts

rpm: Rotations per minute

rps: Rotations per second

R-12: A refrigerant gas (Freon)

SAE: Society of Automotive Engineers

SO$_2$: Sulfur dioxide

T: Ton

t: Megagram

TBI: Throttle Body Injection

TPS: Throttle Position Sensor

V: 1. Volt; 2. Venturi

μV: Microvolt

W: Watt

∞: Infinity

<: Less than

>: Greater than

Index

Chilton's Repair & Tune-Up Guides

The Complete line covers domestic cars, imports, trucks, vans, RV's and 4-wheel drive vehicles.

RTUG Title	Part No.
AMC 1975-82	7199
Covers all U.S. and Canadian models	
Aspen/Volare 1976-80	6637
Covers all U.S. and Canadian models	
Audi 1970-73	5902
Covers all U.S. and Canadian models.	
Audi 4000/5000 1978-81	7028
Covers all U.S. and Canadian models including turbocharged and diesel engines	
Barracuda/Challenger 1965-72	5807
Covers all U.S. and Canadian models	
Blazer/Jimmy 1969-82	6931
Covers all U.S. and Canadian 2- and 4-wheel drive models, including diesel engines	
BMW 1970-82	6844
Covers all U.S. and Canadian models	
Buick/Olds/Pontiac 1975-85	7308
Covers all U.S. and Canadian full size rear wheel drive models	
Cadillac 1967-84	7462
Covers all U.S. and Canadian rear wheel drive models	
Camaro 1967-81	6735
Covers all U.S. and Canadian models	
Camaro 1982-85	7317
Covers all U.S. and Canadian models	
Capri 1970-77	6695
Covers all U.S. and Canadian models	
Caravan/Voyager 1984-85	7482
Covers all U.S. and Canadian models	
Century/Regal 1975-85	7307
Covers all U.S. and Canadian rear wheel drive models, including turbocharged engines	
Champ/Arrow/Sapporo 1978-83	7041
Covers all U.S. and Canadian models	
Chevette/1000 1976-86	6836
Covers all U.S. and Canadian models	
Chevrolet 1968-85	7135
Covers all U.S. and Canadian models	
Chevrolet 1968-79 Spanish	7082
Chevrolet/GMC Pick-Ups 1970-82 Spanish	7468
Chevrolet/GMC Pick-Ups and Suburban 1970-86	6936
Covers all U.S. and Canadian $1/2$, $3/4$ and 1 ton models, including 4-wheel drive and diesel engines	
Chevrolet LUV 1972-81	6815
Covers all U.S. and Canadian models	
Chevrolet Mid-Size 1964-86	6840
Covers all U.S. and Canadian models of 1964-77 Chevelle, Malibu and Malibu SS; 1974-77 Laguna; 1978-85 Malibu; 1970-86 Monte Carlo; 1964-84 El Camino, including diesel engines	
Chevrolet Nova 1986	7658
Covers all U.S. and Canadian models	
Chevy/GMC Vans 1967-84	6930
Covers all U.S. and Canadian models of $1/2$, $3/4$, and 1 ton vans, cutaways, and motor home chassis, including diesel engines	
Chevy S-10 Blazer/GMC S-15 Jimmy 1982-85	7383
Covers all U.S. and Canadian models	
Chevy S-10/GMC S-15 Pick-Ups 1982-85	7310
Covers all U.S. and Canadian models	
Chevy II/Nova 1962-79	6841
Covers all U.S. and Canadian models	
Chrysler K- and E-Car 1981-85	7163
Covers all U.S. and Canadian front wheel drive models	
Colt/Challenger/Vista/Conquest 1971-85	7037
Covers all U.S. and Canadian models	
Corolla/Carina/Tercel/Starlet 1970-85	7036
Covers all U.S. and Canadian models	
Corona/Cressida/Crown/Mk.II/Camry/Van 1970-84	7044
Covers all U.S. and Canadian models	

RTUG Title	Part No.
Corvair 1960-69	6691
Covers all U.S. and Canadian models	
Corvette 1953-62	6576
Covers all U.S. and Canadian models	
Corvette 1963-84	6843
Covers all U.S. and Canadian models	
Cutlass 1970-85	6933
Covers all U.S. and Canadian models	
Dart/Demon 1968-76	6324
Covers all U.S. and Canadian models	
Datsun 1961-72	5790
Covers all U.S. and Canadian models of Nissan Patrol; 1500, 1600 and 2000 sports cars; Pick-Ups; 410, 411, 510, 1200 and 240Z	
Datsun 1973-80 Spanish	7083
Datsun/Nissan F-10, 310, Stanza, Pulsar 1977-86	7196
Covers all U.S. and Canadian models	
Datsun/Nissan Pick-Ups 1970-84	6816
Covers all U.S and Canadian models	
Datsun/Nissan Z & ZX 1970-86	6932
Covers all U.S. and Canadian models	
Datsun/Nissan 1200, 210, Sentra 1973-86	7197
Covers all U.S. and Canadian models	
Datsun/Nissan 200SX, 510, 610, 710, 810, Maxima 1973-84	7170
Covers all U.S. and Canadian models	
Dodge 1968-77	6554
Covers all U.S. and Canadian models	
Dodge Charger 1967-70	6486
Covers all U.S. and Canadian models	
Dodge/Plymouth Trucks 1967-84	7459
Covers all $1/2$, $3/4$, and 1 ton 2- and 4-wheel drive U.S. and Canadian models, including diesel engines	
Dodge/Plymouth Vans 1967-84	6934
Covers all $1/2$, $3/4$, and 1 ton U.S. and Canadian models of vans, cutaways and motor home chassis	
D-50/Arrow Pick-Up 1979-81	7032
Covers all U.S. and Canadian models	
Fairlane/Torino 1962-75	6320
Covers all U.S. and Canadian models	
Fairmont/Zephyr 1978-83	6965
Covers all U.S. and Canadian models	
Fiat 1969-81	7042
Covers all U.S. and Canadian models	
Fiesta 1978-80	6846
Covers all U.S. and Canadian models	
Firebird 1967-81	5996
Covers all U.S. and Canadian models	
Firebird 1982-85	7345
Covers all U.S. and Canadian models	
Ford 1968-79 Spanish	7084
Ford Bronco 1966-83	7140
Covers all U.S. and Canadian models	
Ford Bronco II 1984	7408
Covers all U.S. and Canadian models	
Ford Courier 1972-82	6983
Covers all U.S. and Canadian models	
Ford/Mercury Front Wheel Drive 1981-85	7055
Covers all U.S. and Canadian models Escort, EXP, Tempo, Lynx, LN-7 and Topaz	
Ford/Mercury/Lincoln 1968-85	6842
Covers all U.S. and Canadian models of FORD Country Sedan, Country Squire, Crown Victoria, Custom, Custom 500, Galaxie 500, LTD through 1982, Ranch Wagon, and XL; MERCURY Colony Park, Commuter, Marquis through 1982, Gran Marquis, Monterey and Park Lane; LINCOLN Continental and Towne Car	
Ford/Mercury/Lincoln Mid-Size 1971-85	669
Covers all U.S. and Canadian models of FORD Elite, 1983-85 LTD, 1977-79 LTD II, Ranchero, Torino, Gran Torino, 1977-85 Thunderbird; MERCURY 1972-85 Cougar,	

continued on ne

RTUG Title	Part No.	RTUG Title	Part No.
1983-85 Marquis, Montego, 1980-85 XR-7; LINCOLN 1982-85 Continental, 1984-85 Mark VII, 1978-80 Versailles		Mercedes-Benz 1974-84 Covers all U.S. and Canadian models	6809
Ford Pick-Ups 1965-86 Covers all $^1/_2$, $^3/_4$ and 1 ton, 2- and 4-wheel drive U.S. and Canadian pick-up, chassis cab and camper models, including diesel engines	6913	**Mitsubishi, Cordia, Tredia, Starion, Galant 1983-85** Covers all U.S. and Canadian models	7583
Ford Pick-Ups 1965-82 Spanish	7469	**MG 1961-81** Covers all U.S. and Canadian models	6780
Ford Ranger 1983-84 Covers all U.S. and Canadian models	7338	**Mustang/Capri/Merkur 1979-85** Covers all U.S. and Canadian models	6963
Ford Vans 1961-86 Covers all U.S. and Canadian $^1/_2$, $^3/_4$ and 1 ton van and cutaway chassis models, including diesel engines	6849	**Mustang/Cougar 1965-73** Covers all U.S. and Canadian models	6542
		Mustang II 1974-78 Covers all U.S. and Canadian models	6812
GM A-Body 1982-85 Covers all front wheel drive U.S. and Canadian models of BUICK Century, CHEVROLET Celebrity, OLDSMOBILE Cutlass Ciera and PONTIAC 6000	7309	**Omni/Horizon/Rampage 1978-84** Covers all U.S. and Canadian models of DODGE omni, Miser, 024, Charger 2.2; PLYMOUTH Horizon, Miser, TC3, TC3 Tourismo; Rampage	6845
GM C-Body 1985 Covers all front wheel drive U.S. and Canadian models of BUICK Electra Park Avenue and Electra T-Type, CADILLAC Fleetwood and deVille, OLDSMOBILE 98 Regency and Regency Brougham	7587	**Opel 1971-75** Covers all U.S. and Canadian models	6575
		Peugeot 1970-74 Covers all U.S. and Canadian models	5982
GM J-Car 1982-85 Covers all U.S. and Canadian models of BUICK Skyhawk, CHEVROLET Cavalier, CADILLAC Cimarron, OLDSMOBILE Firenza and PONTIAC 2000 and Sunbird	7059	**Pinto/Bobcat 1971-80** Covers all U.S. and Canadian models	7027
		Plymouth 1968-76 Covers all U.S. and Canadian models	6552
GM N-Body 1985-86 Covers all U.S. and Canadian models of front wheel drive BUICK Somerset and Skylark, OLDSMOBILE Calais, and PONTIAC Grand Am	7657	**Pontiac Fiero 1984-85** Covers all U.S. and Canadian models	7571
		Pontiac Mid-Size 1974-83 Covers all U.S. and Canadian models of Ventura, Grand Am, LeMans, Grand LeMans, GTO, Phoenix, and Grand Prix	7346
GM X-Body 1980-85 Covers all U.S. and Canadian models of BUICK Skylark, CHEVROLET Citation, OLDSMOBILE Omega and PONTIAC Phoenix	7049	**Porsche 924/928 1976-81** Covers all U.S. and Canadian models	7048
		Renault 1975-85 Covers all U.S. and Canadian models	7165
GM Subcompact 1971-80 Covers all U.S. and Canadian models of BUICK Skyhawk (1975-80), CHEVROLET Vega and Monza, OLDSMOBILE Starfire, and PONTIAC Astre and 1975-80 Sunbird	6935	**Roadrunner/Satellite/Belvedere/GTX 1968-73** Covers all U.S. and Canadian models	5821
		RX-7 1979-81 Covers all U.S. and Canadian models	7031
...ranada/Monarch 1975-82 ...overs all U.S. and Canadian models	6937	**SAAB 99 1969-75** Covers all U.S. and Canadian models	5988
...nda 1973-84 ...ers all U.S. and Canadian models	6980	**SAAB 900 1979-85** Covers all U.S. and Canadian models	7572
...rnational Scout 1967-73 ...rs all U.S. and Canadian models	5912	**Snowmobiles 1976-80** Covers Arctic Cat, John Deere, Kawasaki, Polaris, Ski-Doo and Yamaha	6978
...1945-87 ...s all U.S. and Canadian CJ-2A, CJ-3A, ...CJ-5, CJ-6, CJ-7, Scrambler and ...er models	6817	**Subaru 1970-84** Covers all U.S. and Canadian models	6982
		Tempest/GTO/LeMans 1968-73 Covers all U.S. and Canadian models	5905
...agoneer, Commando, Cherokee, ...957-86 ...ll U.S. and Canadian models of ..., Cherokee, Grand Wagoneer, ...Jeepster Commando, J-100, J-...J-10, J20, FC-150 and FC-170	6739	**Toyota 1966-70** Covers all U.S. and Canadian models of Corona, MkII, Corolla, Crown, Land Cruiser, Stout and Hi-Lux	5795
		Toyota 1970-79 Spanish	7467
...ona 1984-85 ...S. and Canadian models	7563	**Toyota Celica/Supra 1971-85** Covers all U.S. and Canadian models	7043
...met 1970-77 ...S. and Canadian models	6634	**Toyota Trucks 1970-85** Covers all U.S. and Canadian models of pick-ups, Land Cruiser and 4Runner	7035
...84 ...and Canadian models of RX-...808, 1300, 1600, Cosmo,	6981	**Valiant/Duster 1968-76** Covers all U.S. and Canadian models	6326
		Volvo 1956-69 Covers all U.S. and Canadian models	6529
...s 1972-86 ...nd Canadian models	7659	**Volvo 1970-83** Covers all U.S. and Canadian models	7040
...1959-70 ...d Canadian models	6065	**VW Front Wheel Drive 1974-85** Covers all U.S. and Canadian models	6962
...968-73 ...Canadian models	5907	**VW 1949-71** Covers all U.S. and Canadian models	5796
		VW 1970-79 Spanish	7081
		VW 1970-81 Covers all U.S. and Canadian Beetles, Karmann Ghia, Fastback, Squareback, Vans, 411 and 412	6837

Tune-Up Guides are available at your local retailer or by mailing a check or money ...us **$3.25** to cover postage and handling to:

Chilton Book Company
Dept. DM
Radnor, PA 19089

...lering be sure to include your name & address, book part No. & title.